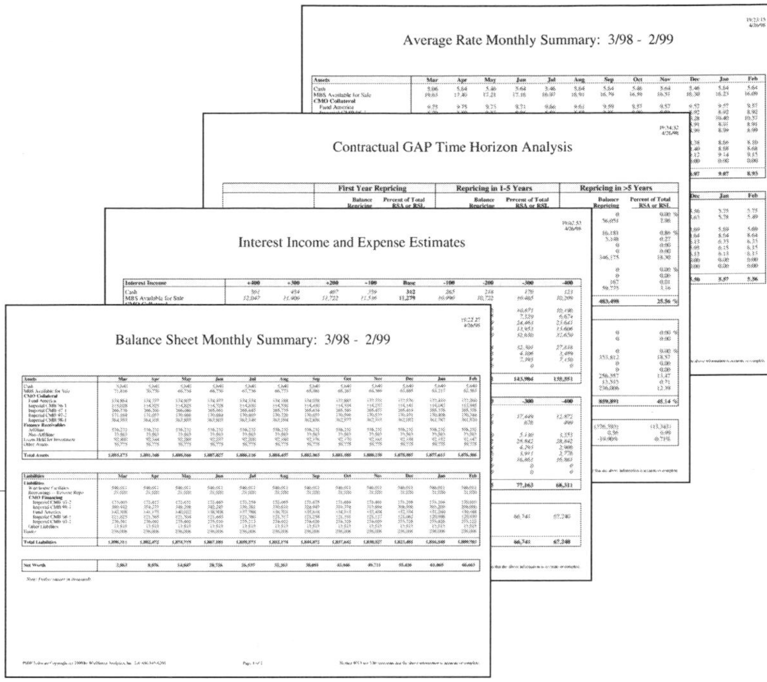

Solutions for Portfolio Management

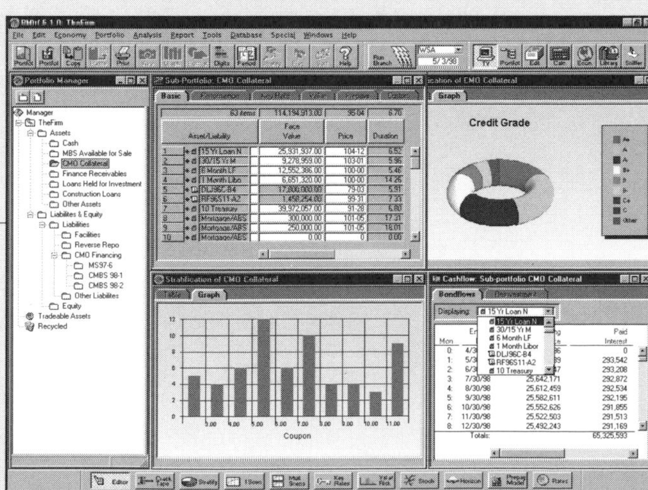

Wall Street Analytics, Inc. • 2370 Watson Court, Suite 200 • Palo Alto, CA 94304 • Phone: (650) 845-6260 • Fax: (650) 845-6280 • www.wsainc.com

Michael H. Trenk

Handbook of Structured Financial Products

Edited by

Frank J. Fabozzi, CFA
Adjunct Professor of Finance
School of Management
Yale University

Published by Frank J. Fabozzi Associates

ISBN: 1-883249-43-0

Printed in the United States of America

Table of Contents

Contributing Authors

Steven Abrahams	Morgan Stanley
William J. Adams	Massachusetts Finance Services
James S. Anderson	First Union Capital Markets
Ryan Asato	Merrill Lynch & Co.
Len Blum	Prudential Securities Incorporated
Elen Callahan	Credit Suisse First Boston
Da Cheng	Wall Street Analytics, Inc.
Steven A. Columbaro	First Union Capital Markets
Karen Cook	Bankers Trust Company
Adrian R. Cooper	Wall Street Analytics, Inc.
F. Jim Della Sala	Bankers Trust Company
Joseph F. DeMichele	Conseco Capital Management, Inc.
Martin DeVito	TCM Asset Management
Ralph DiSerio	Merrill Lynch & Co.
John N. Dunlevy	Beacon Hill Capital Advisers, LLC
Howard Esaki	Morgan Stanley
Frank J. Fabozzi	Yale University
Mark Feldman	Bear, Stearns & Co., Inc.
Jeff Fisher	Indiana University
Chris Flanagan	Merrill Lynch & Co.
Sunita Ganapati	Lehman Brothers
Jason Huang	Wall Street Analytics, Inc.
Michael A. Mattera	Prudential Securities Incorporated
John N. McElravey	First Chicago Capital Markets, Inc.
James E. Myers	Lewtan Technologies, Inc.
George J. Pappadopoulos	Property & Portfolio Research, Inc.
Paul Puleo	Lehman Brothers
Jennifer O. Quisenberry	Structured Finance Advisors, Inc.
Robert Restrick	
Mark Retik	Lehman Brothers
Kevin Roach	Morgan Stanley
W. Alexander Roever	First Chicago Capital Markets, Inc.
Michael J. P. Selby	Imperial College of Science, Technology and Medicine
Charles N. Schorin	Morgan Stanley
Glenn M. Schultz	First Chicago Capital Markets, Inc.
Scott H. Shannon	First Union Capital Markets
Joseph D. Smallman	Vining-Sparks IBG
Beth Starr	Lehman Brothers
Craig S. Stein	Schulte Roth & Zabel LLP
Anthony V. Thompson	Goldman, Sachs & Co.

Ronald E. Thompson Jr.	Citicorp Securities, Inc.
Shlomo C. Twerski	Schulte Roth & Zabel LLP
Patrick Van den Eynde	BACOB Bank s.c., Brussels, Belgium
Frederic P. Vigneron	Securities Valuation Office
Karen Wagner	Credit Suisse First Boston
Paul N. Watterson Jr.	Schulte Roth & Zabel LLP
Steven Weinreich	Morgan Stanley
Dale Westhoff	Bear, Stearns & Co., Inc.
Lisa N. Wilhelm	First Chicago Capital Markets, Inc.
Michael D. Youngblood	Chase Securities Inc.
Eva F. J. Yun	Citicorp Securities, Inc.

Index of Advertisers

Bankers Trust

BARRA

Capital Access International

Charter Research

Chase

Derivative Solutions

Duff & Phelps Credit Rating Co.

Ernst & Young

First Chicago Capital Markets

GMAC-RFC

Interactive Data

Intex Solutions

Lewtan Technologies

Norwest

Price Waterhouse

Prudential Securities

Residential Funding Securities Corporation

Schulte Roth & Zabel

Union Planters Bank

Vining Sparks Europe

Wall Street Analytics

Chapter 1

Overview

Frank J. Fabozzi, Ph.D., CFA
Adjunct Professor of Finance
School of Management
Yale University

INTRODUCTION

The high interest rates in the early 1980s and the significant volatility of rates that had not been seen prior to that time were the driving force in the development of new corporate bond structures. Two simple structures, commonplace today, are the zero-coupon bond and the putable bond. The purpose of these simple structures was to provide investors with protection against one or more risks introduced by high and volatile rates. Zero-coupon structures provided protection against reinvestment risk; put structures provided protection against a rise in interest rates above the issue's coupon rate. By providing structures that gave investor's protection against certain risks, the issuer benefited in the form of a lower funding cost.

By the mid-1980s, the corporate bond market saw the introduction of structures in which the credit quality of an issue was not based on the credit quality of the issuer, or more precisely, the "sponsor" of the issue. Specifically, securities were structured in which the underlying collateral was a pool of loans or receivables and their cash flow characteristics mirrored those of the underlying collateral. The securities created are called *asset-backed securities*.

While there is no standard industry definition of an asset-backed security, market participants generally agree that these securities have the following characteristics:

1. The rating is derived primarily from the quality of an underlying pool of loans or receivables (that is, there is more than one obligor).

2. There is credit enhancement of the underlying pool of loans or receivables.

I thank Ronald Thompson (Citicorp), Anthony Thompson (Goldman Sachs), Chip Shorin (Morgan Stanley), and Alex Roever (First Chicago Capital Markets) for their insightful comments on an earlier version of this chapter.

3. There is a "true sale" of the assets to a bankruptcy remote legal structure which insulates investors from a deterioration in the seller/servicer credit quality.

While virtually any loan or receivable could qualify as collateral for an asset-backed security, the definition in the U.S. market generally excludes those securities where the underlying collateral is first mortgage loans. Also, single obligor transactions are generally not considered asset-backed securities.[1]

The process of pooling loans or receivables and the issuance of securities backed by the pool is called *securitization*. The securitization of loans did not begin in the corporate market. In the late 1960s, securities were issued by government agencies that were backed by residential first mortgage loans. The resulting product is called a *mortgage-backed security*. When these securities are issued by either the Government National Mortgage Association ("Ginnie Mae"), the Federal National Mortgage Association ("Fannie Mae"), or the Federal Home Loan Mortgage Corporation ("Freddie Mac"), they are referred to as *agency mortgage-backed securities*. In the case of Ginnie Mae mortgage-backed securities, there is no credit risk since the securities are backed by the full faith and credit of the U.S. government. Since Fannie Mae and Freddie Mac are government sponsored enterprises, their guarantee does not carry the full faith and credit of the U.S. government. There is some credit risk but market participants typically view this credit risk as minimal.

From agency mortgage-backed securities, investment bankers learned first how to securitize loans. This was the basic mortgage passthrough security where cash flows are distributed to certificate holders on a pro rata basis. However, despite the absence of credit risk, all mortgage-backed securities had prepayment risk. This is the uncertainty of the timing of principal repayments because the borrower has the right to prepay all or a portion of the mortgage loan before the scheduled due date. The second major lesson that investment bankers learned from agency mortgage-backed securities was how to redistribute prepayment risk to different classes of bonds, called *tranches*. This was done by creating a multiple class passthrough security called a *collateralized mortgage obligation*. By redistributing prepayment risk, bond classes with different average lives and prepayment risk exposure were created.

As investment bankers were learning how to slice and dice prepayment risk, they were also asked to get involved in the creation of mortgage-backed securities that were not issued by a government agency or government sponsored enterprise and therefore exposed investors to credit risk, as well as prepayment risk. These securities are called *nonagency mortgage-backed securities*. Investment bankers worked with the commercial rating companies to structure securities with credit enhancements to achieve a targeted credit rating. One such mechanism involved redistribution of credit risk to different bond classes — senior classes and

[1] For example, a sale-and-leaseback arrangement is not considered an asset-backed security.

different levels of subordinated classes. Within the senior class or any subordinated class, prepayment risk could be redistributed. Thus, with nonagency mortgage-backed securities, investment bankers developed the tools to carve up credit risk.

These skills were carried over to the creation of asset-backed securities. In fact, a good number of investment bankers in the asset-backed securities area are those who migrated from mortgage-backed securities and from the derivatives market. It wasn't a painful transition for these professionals since they were familiar with the issues associated with structuring cash flows and redistributing prepayment risk and credit risk. The only skill set that had to be developed was an understanding of the characteristics of the loans or receivables that were being securitized.

In the United States, because of the historical development of securitization, a distinction is made between mortgage-backed securities and asset-backed securities.[2] Asset-backed securities are viewed as securities in which the underlying is anything other than first mortgage loans on residential on-site built homes. Thus, while home equity loans and manufactured housing loans may be backed by residential properties, they are typically viewed as asset-backed securities, not mortgage-backed securities. The distinction continues in most investment banking organizations because the mortgage-backed group is separate and distinct from the asset-backed group. Other than historical reasons, a distinction between asset-backed securities and mortgage-backed securities exists because of the corporate financing issues involved. In the mortgage-backed area, mortgages are originated and then sold. For other asset types, an asset-backed security is one of several possible funding vehicles for the corporate issuer.

Regardless of the distinction made between mortgage-backed securities and asset-backed securities, both are classified as *structured financial products*. That is, the securities are structured from the cash flows of the underlying pool of assets. The purpose of this book is to describe the wide range of structured financial products. In this book, the product description is classified based on whether the underlying collateral is a non-mortgage-related loan/receivable or a mortgage-related loan.

While securitization began in the mortgage market in 1970, the first offering of an asset-backed security was in March 1985 when Sperry Lease Finance Corporation issued a note backed by computer leases. Two months later, General Motors Acceptance Corporation issued securities backed by automobile loans. Since then, there has been a wide range of loans and receivables that have been used as collateral for an asset-backed security. Securities backed by credit card receivables were first issued in January 1987.

Structured financial products offer investors the opportunity to invest in products that were unthinkable at one time as an investment vehicle because of

---

[2] Outside the United States no distinction is made between asset-backed securities and mortgage-backed securities. The mortgage-backed securities market is viewed as a sector within the asset-backed securities market. This is because outside the United States, the development of the market for securities backed by mortgage and non-mortgage assets is occurring simultaneously.

lack of liquidity, difficulty of achieving diversification, the problems of servicing loans, and the difficulties of credit monitoring. At one time, a money manager approaching a client about allocating funds to claims on delinquent real estate taxes of a municipality or the future royalties of a rock star would have been asked to seek psychiatric help as a condition for retention. Today, that same request would be considered by enlightened clients as a potential credit spread product.

Over time, structured financial products have evolved to take the same or new cash flows and transform the cash flows into targeting new investors. For example, investors tend to prefer bullet-type maturities. To meet that demand, structurers created credit card receivable backed securities with a soft bullet.

OVERVIEW OF BOOK

There are 31 chapters that follow. The chapters are divided into three sections.

In Section I, background information is provided. Chapter 2 provides an overview and recent developments of securitization in Europe. Chapter 3 discusses how investor's should view securities backed by non-traditional asset types and provides a spectrum of life stages for various asset types. Chapter 4 discusses the issues associated with structuring nontraditional U.S. assets for European investors. An important factor in the rating of an asset-backed security is the quality of the servicer. In Chapter 5, the technology requirements associated with a securitization from the issuer's perspective are discussed — from the conceptualization of a deal and deal formation, through the ongoing needs for servicing, accounting, and surveillance. The due diligence role of the investment banker is the subject of Chapter 6 and the role of the trustee is explained in Chapter 7. In Chapter 8, relative value analysis of fixed-rate and floating-rate asset-backed securities is explained. Chapter 9, the last chapter in Section I, focuses on insurance companies' investment in asset-backed securities. Specifically, it discusses the role of the NAIC's Security Valuation Office's structured securities department.

In Sections II and III, we look at securities backed by different asset types. In Section II the focus is on non-mortgage related asset types and in Section III on mortgage-related asset types. The following products are included in Section II: auto loans and leases (Chapters 10 and 11), credit card receivables (Chapters 12 and 13), equipment financings (Chapter 14), student loans (Chapter 15), collateralized bond and loan obligations (Chapters 16, 17, and 18), utility stranded costs (Chapter 19), catastrophe-linked securities (Chapter 20), and index amortizing asset-backed securities (Chapter 21).

The 11 chapters in Section III cover securities backed by residential and commercial mortgage loans. Chapter 22 provides an overview of residential mortgage-backed securities products. For those readers not familiar with the structuring of prepayment and credit risks, this chapter might be worthwhile reviewing before reading about some of the other structured products discussed in the book.

Home equity loan backed securities are the subject of Chapters 23 through 26. Manufactured housing backed securities are covered in Chapters 27 and 28. The last five chapters of the book focus on commercial mortgage-backed securities — the securities (Chapter 29), their prepayment characteristics (Chapter 30), and their valuation (Chapter 31 and 32).

Section I:

Background Information

Chapter 2

Securitization in Europe: Overview and Recent Developments

Patrick Van den Eynde
Director of the Securitization Department
BACOB Bank s.c., Brussels, Belgium

INTRODUCTION

Securitization has taken off in Europe since 1996. Compared with the U.S. securitization market, the European market is small. However, it is now the second-largest market in the world after the United States.[1] Exact definitions of what constitutes an international asset-backed security may differ but, according to figures from Moody's Investors Service,[2] the volume of public offerings in Europe reached \$33.7 billion in 1996, up sharply from the 1995 figure of \$9.2 billion and \$15.9 billion in 1994.[3]

HISTORICAL PERSPECTIVE

The European securitization market has developed dramatically since it began. The securitization market is developing at different paces in each country. In terms of volume and variety of assets in Europe, the United Kingdom is the most advanced securitization market, surpassed globally only by the United States. Thereafter, France constitutes the second-largest securitization market in Europe. Markets in Spain, Germany, Italy, and the Scandinavian countries are much smaller. Belgium and the Netherlands, which began securitization in 1996, are rapidly catching up and going forward. (See Exhibit 1.) A more balanced development can be expected in Europe. (See Exhibit 2.)

---

[1] Helena Morrissey, *International Securitisation Report No 19* (August 1996).

[2] Moody's Investors Service, "International Structured Finance," Fabozzi/IMN Global Asset Securitisation conference, Cork, Ireland (June 22-25, 1997).

[3] Dollar equivalents for nondollar-denominated securitizations are based on Federal Reserve Bank exchange rates for September 15, 1997.

Exhibit 1: 1996 New Issuance Volume in Europe

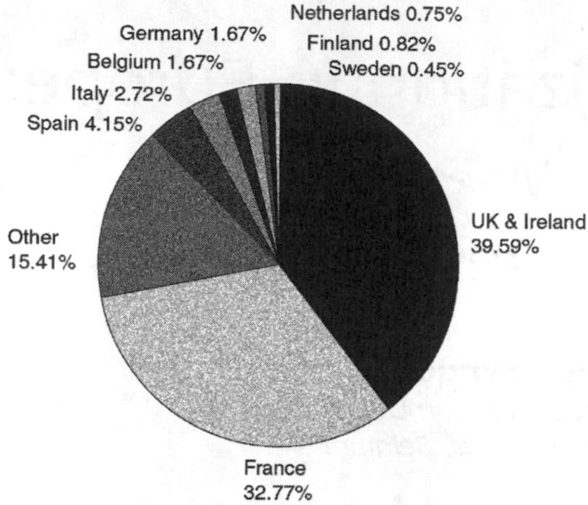

Source: Moody's

Exhibit 2: Market Participation

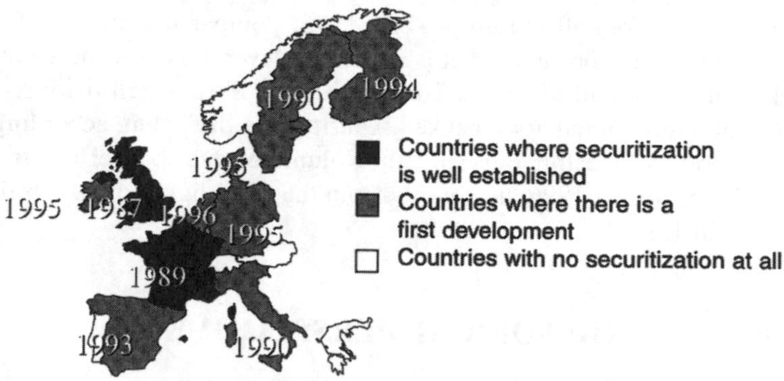

Source: BACOB Bank

In 1995, new rating agencies entered the European structured-finance market. With the arrival of Duff & Phelps and Fitch Investors Service, Moody's and Standard & Poor's were no longer alone in the European structured-finance credit rating business.

BACKGROUND AND TENDENCIES

While recent developments are encouraging, and even if a few one-off jumbo transactions[4] distorted the 1996 growth picture, the actual move to a single currency — the EURO — may significantly boost the securitization markets in Europe.

[4] Details on jumbo transactions will appear later in this chapter, country by country.

However, the European asset-backed market lags the U.S. markets. Lack of homogeneity of assets and differing regulatory, legal, and fiscal frameworks across many jurisdictions have slowed down the development of the market overall. This also makes it more difficult to generalize transaction structures. The European markets, therefore, tend to work more on a case-by-case basis involving high up-front costs and risks. Another obstacle may have been the existence of relatively well developed markets for domestic mortgage bonds in several countries, with the German *Pfandbriefe* as prime example. Mortgage bonds account for approximately 30% of mortgage funding in Europe.[5]

The involvement of government-sponsored entities was key to the early development of the markets in the United States. In Europe, the first deals were mostly private-sector initiatives. The development of a government-related, asset-backed market in Europe over the past year augurs well for the sector, accounting for almost one-third of the 1996 deals. The EMU entry goal has clearly focused European government attention on the off-balance-sheet attractions of securitization. A need to keep budget deficits in check, as European countries strive to meet the Maastricht criteria, has been the prime motivation for this trend. Governments are tapping the ABS market to finance major public infrastructure projects, privatizations, or the reorganization of state-owned institutions. Recently, the United Kingdom, Spain, France, and Italy have become major users of these techniques, and several national governments have securitized portfolios of social housing loans.

In 1997 there were 17 rated, asset-backed multiseller conduits active in the European Market.[6] Three types of vehicle have emerged in Europe as an echo of the developments in the United States: (1) client-based units, tailored to individual corporates, (2) arbitrage vehicles, and (3) standard conduits that do securitization. The focus is on trade receivables, but also on equipment leases, mortgage-backed assets, and insurance premiums, as well as rated bonds. Europe is following the history of the U.S. market, which was first dominated by the trade-receivables business. Trade receivables in conduits now account for 60% of outstanding assets in Europe and, according to S&P, are losing ground.

In 1996, U.S. banks offered asset-backed securities in various European markets through public offerings on six different occasions, to diversify their investor base. According to Compagnie Bancaire, this push to reach European investors is likely to continue and will add debt, volume, and liquidity to the European securitization market.[7]

THE COMMON-LAW COUNTRIES

United Kingdom

The securitization market opened in the United Kingdom in 1987. It wasn't difficult for the U.K. to transpose to common law the securitization structures and

---

[5] "Mortgage Banks and the Mortgage Bond in Europe," Baden-Baden: Nomos Verlags gesellschaft.
[6] Helena Morrissey, *International Securitisation Report No 24* (July 1997), pp. 26-28.
[7] "Why Invest in a French FCC?" Compagnie Bancaire (1996).

techniques developed in the United States. Generally, there are few legal obstacles to complete securitization in the U.K. The Bank of England has taken a neutral stance on securitization, neither encouraging nor discouraging this form of finance. The United Kingdom securitization market is the largest outside of the United States, despite a number of setbacks, particularly in 1995 due to lower economic growth. A major recent innovation has been the use in some structures of a "secured loan" approach rather than the traditional "true sale" approach (for example, the Natwest Rose funding transaction).

In terms of both volume and variety of assets, the United Kingdom is the most advanced securitization market outside of the United States. By the end of 1995, approximately £21 billion ($34 billion) of asset-backed securities had been issued in more than 100 transactions since the first was launched by National Home Loans in February 1987. Approximately £9 billion ($14.6 billion) of this total was in outstanding sterling public term asset-backed securities. The centralized lenders — National Home Loans, the Mortgage Corporation, and Household Mortgage Company — represented 50% of the market up to 1991.

Almost all issues have been structured as floating-rate securities, even if the underlying assets generate a fixed-income stream, based on investor demand for floating paper. The credit enhancement shifted from third-party insurance policies to overcollateralization, as over recent years a number of transactions have suffered a rating downgrade as result of downgrades of credit-enhancement providers. Virtually all transactions between 1993 and 1996 have included a subordinated tranche of securities and a first-loss fund (typically in the form of a spread account). No rated asset-backed security has defaulted in the U.K. market as of year-end 1997.

The U.K. can continue to be the largest securitization market in Europe. Conditions are favorable for continued and accelerated growth over time. A new development that will increase the level of issuance is the U.K. government's private finance initiative (PFI) projects, designed to channel private capital into projects that would previously have tended to be financed via the public sector. The PFI has made available a stream of large-scale asset pools. Many of these have covered at least partial government guarantees, and so provided ideal raw material for the U.K. securitization markets.[8] There also are hopes for the growth of new consumer markets in the U.K., particularly for credit cards. There is a growing policy for some banks to take assets on their balance sheet with a view to issuing securitization as an exit route.

Ireland

The Irish common-law system is similar to that of the U.K. In 1992, the Central Bank of Ireland established its rules on securitization. These rules are very similar to those published by the Bank of England. The statutory framework at this point, however, does not facilitate securitization of domestic assets other than mortgages.

[8] "Structured Finance," *Euroweek* (June 1997), pp. 10-12.

Prior to 1995, the only securitizations undertaken by Irish companies were the aircraft lease portfolio (ALPs) transactions in 1992 and 1994 arranged by GPA as a true, international securitization. However, toward the end of 1995, two Irish transactions were denominated in the punt, or Irish pounds sterling. Irish Life Home Loans issued I£100 million ($150 million) floating-rate notes. Ulysses was a I£140 million ($210 million) securitization of a portfolio of housing loans from local authorities set up by Ireland's National Treasury Management Agency. The Irish government used the Ulysses securitization vehicle for another I£150 million ($225 million) in August 1996. The Aaa credit rating of Ulysses was dependent on the explicit support provided by the Republic of Ireland. The securitization of Irish domestic assets is unlikely to be more than a few securitizations a year, because the asset base is small.

The introduction of the 1996 Finance Act confirmed the tax treatment for securitization vehicles in the International Financial Services Center (IFSC). These provisions are designed for the cross-border securitization of non-Irish assets. A number of securitization SPVs have already been located in the IFSC, including Fennica and St. Eric Securities.[9] In late March 1996, GPA securitized aircraft leases in the amount of $4.048 million. Within the IFSC, an increasing number of banks are investing in asset-backed securities.

The importance of this location to the European securitization market is expected to continue to grow as an offshore center for European assets.

France

France, like the United Kingdom, has seen a steady flow of new issues over recent years as well as progress on legal and regulatory issues. The facilitation — or *titrisation* — legislation passed in December 1988 and modifications to the basic framework have encouraged a wide range of applications of securitization in this market. In France, it is important to note that the law on securitization is prescriptive; that is, if the law does not specifically permit a structure, it cannot be used.

French securitization law provides for a *Fonds Commun de Créances* (FCC) as issuing vehicle. An FCC is a pool of assets co-owned by investors, has no legal personality, and, therefore, cannot become insolvent or bankrupt. French securitization law requires mandatory involvement of a management company (société de gestion). This company represents investors' interests and is in charge of management and administration of the FCC. Assets are transferred to an FCC in the form of a true sale. The FCC becomes the real owner of the receivables at the sale date.

The French securitization market has seen a steady development since the first asset-backed deal in January 1990, a personal loan transaction by Crédit Lyonnais[10] and the first mortgage-backed transaction in December 1991 by Crédit Foncier.[11] In 1996, the total-issuance volume increased sharply to more than 50 billion

[9] See section on Scandinavia.
[10] CL-FCC-90-1.
[11] Foncier-FCC-1991.

French francs (about $8.4 billion), even though the number of public transactions issued in 1996 remained comparable to the level of 1995. This was mainly due to the launch of the biggest securitization ever realized: the FCC Cyber Val created by Crédit Lyonnais for an amount of FRF40 billion ($6.7 billion) in June 1996. This transaction forms part of the restructuring of the French state-owned bank, Crédit Lyonnais, of which much of the risk taken by investors is French government risk.[12] A new Cybenol transaction in the amount of 40 billion French francs was issued in September 1997.

At the end of 1996, the French securitization market totaled FRF85 billion ($14.3 billion) in terms of outstanding balance of public transactions, and 10 management companies administered 166 FCCs. Since 1995, investor demand has dictated a number of structural innovations. To satisfy a demand for more predictable cash flow, more revolving structures were issued.[13]

In most French transactions, credit enhancement is provided by the combination of excess spread and subordinated units. Subordinated units may be protected by a reserve account.

According to Moody's, the majority of assets securitized so far under French law have been loans to individuals. Moody's expects to see growing emergence of new types of assets such as commercial real estate, trade receivables, and CBO/CLOs in the French market. Banks are using securitization both as a balance-sheet management instrument and as a funding tool.

Overall, the assessment of the French asset-backed market is positive. However, some off-shore transactions backed by French assets have also taken place. Furthermore, a French law adopted in July 1996 will favor the FCCs to continue issuing securities past their initial established date.

Spain

After the United Kingdom and France, Spain has been an important user of the securitization technique. The Spanish market opened in July 1993, after a specific legal structure was adopted for mortgage securitization in 1992. The market recently has been boosted by permission to securitize rights to receive payments related to the moratorium on nuclear power.

The 1992 legislation created an issuing vehicle for mortgage-backed transactions. The legislation allowed for the creation of Fondos de Titulización Hipotecaria (Fondos). A Fondo is a closed-end mutual fund with a single purpose. The sociedades Gestoras de Fondos de Titulización Hipotecaria (Gestoras) are management companies with broad powers that represent the Fondos. At the beginning of 1996, a reported total of 13 securitization transactions were launched for an amount of 230 billion pesetas (about $1.54 billion). The total amount of MBS in circulation amounted to 198 billion pesetas ($1.32 billion) at the end of 1996.

---

[12] The bonds are not directly government-backed but carry an implicit guarantee from the French government.

[13] Moody's Investors Service, "French Structured Finance," Fabozzi/IMN Global Asset Securitisation conference, Cork, Ireland (June 22-25, 1997).

In December 1995, new legislation enabled Spanish entities to securitize 725 billion pesetas ($4.85 billion) of debt to finance the nuclear assets under moratorium. This resulted in a bond issue for an amount of 215 billion pesetas ($1.44 billion), making it one of the larger securitization transactions in Europe for 1996. The 1996 securitization of tariffs related to the nuclear power moratorium in Spain was a prominent example of the opening of the public sponsored securitization sector in Europe. The transaction was collateralized by future cash flows in the form of surcharges on electricity bills paid by Spanish households.

In accordance with the legislation of 1995, the Spanish government guaranteed minimum annual payments allowing the bonds an AAA rating in local currency. A key selling point for these bonds was their unique status as the only available state-guaranteed, floating-rate, peseta bonds.

In the years to follow, the Spanish market is likely to set new benchmarks as the legislation will allow for the securitization of any asset types.[14] According to knowledgeable observers, investors will prefer high credit quality on new instruments — ranging from Aa to Aaa in a market that is not yet mature.

Italy

In Italy, there is no specific legislation on securitization and there still exist legal and fiscal hurdles.[15] For the moment in Italy, securitization is only possible by using two vehicles, one of which needs to be offshore. The first vehicle is used to buy the assets in Italy. This can be done without notification for certain asset types. The second vehicle is usually domiciled outside Italy and is the bond issuer, in order to avoid heavy tax burden on the Italian vehicle. Up to 1996, 10 public securitization transactions have been launched for an amount of 2.400 billion lire (about $1.39 billion). In 1996, only three transactions were launched; however, the total issuance volume increased. Italy's government securitization of nuclear moratorium debt — Orchid — was issued for $355 million in 1996. The market is becoming more mature, according to Moody's,[16] as deals, for the first time, are involving a rated mezzanine class.

If no specific law is adopted, the market will continue to grow slowly but regularly as securitization is accepted as a viable funding tool for Italian entities.

NORDIC COUNTRIES

In the Scandinavian countries — Sweden, Denmark, and Finland — there is no specific legal framework on securitization.

---

[14] New legislation and implementing decree is expected to pass before year-end 1997.

[15] Problems of withholding tax, *tax hypothecaire* of 3%.

[16] Moody's, Special Report, "Italian Structured Finance Market," Fabozzi/IMN Global Asset Securitisation conference, Cork, Ireland (June 22-25, 1997).

Sweden

Sweden was one of the first European countries to issue a securitization with Osprey 1 in 1990. Until 1995, the market was dominated by one originator (SE-Banken), which was responsible for eight Osprey and one Fulmar mortgage-backed transactions.

The St. Eric transaction, completed in June 1995, was the first securitization of social housing loans at local authority level by the city of Stockholm. Most recently, there was a 1.2 billion krona ($157 million) securitization transaction for Sweden's largest municipal housing company, AB Svenska Bostadar.

All securitization transactions went offshore to avoid domestic legal and regulatory issues.

Denmark

In Denmark, as in Sweden, there is an active market of mortgage bond instruments that resemble pfandbriefe. Only two operations of mortgages have been launched since 1995 by Unicredit in Denmark.

Finland

The first securitization of mortgages in Finland took place in 1994. In November 1995, the Finnish government securitized $360 million of social housing loans — the first sponsored government deal. Fennica-1 used an SPV incorporated in the Irish Financial Services Centre (IFSC). Fennica's triple-A rating relied on the high quality of the underlying loan portfolio and the Republic of Finland involvement was limited to the provision of a currency swap.

The Finnish government is involved in other levels of the Fennica structures. For example, the servicer is Valtiokommari, Finland's State Treasury. Fennica-1 was followed by Fennica-2 for an amount of 1.45 million Finnish marka (about $273,000) in 1996. A third offering was announced in 1997.

GERMANY

There is no specific legislation in Germany on securitization. However, in the actual legal framework it is possible to do securitization operations.

In Germany, the main finance source is the Pfandbriefe market, an efficient housing financing system involving mortgage-backed bonds. This well developed market, which has been in existence for 200 years, represents 35% of the German bond market. However, mortgage loans guaranteeing the Pfandbriefe must have an loan-to-value ratio of less than 60%. Pfandbriefe are on-balance-sheet instruments and cannot be prepaid. The issuing of mortgage bonds has nothing to do with balance-sheet management.

Only a few securitization transactions have emerged in the German market. In 1990, we have seen a 230 million German mark (about $130 million) securitization of personal loans by KKB Bank (Citibank).

As recently as April 1995, GEMS — the first securitization transaction of mortgage loans for an amount of DEM 522 million ($295 million) — emerged from Rheinhyp, the mortgage subsidiary of Commerzbank.

In January 1996, Volkswagen AG launched a DEM 500 million ($282 million) lease-backed bond, the first public securitization from the German corporate sector. The credit enhancement was done by an indemnity insurance policy. Volkswagen launched a repeat issue of another DEM 500 million in November 1996, for the first time using a senior/subordinated structure[17] in the German ABS market.

Recent regulatory changes in Germany may pave the way for greatly improved volumes of DEM asset securitization. The resulting guidelines[18] from the BAK (Bundesaufsichtambt für das Kreditwesen) appear more restrictive than in other jurisdictions, according to Merrill Lynch.[19] However, there is now a framework. Germany, as the largest European economy, could potentially support the biggest securitization market in Europe in the medium term. There is also significant investor interest in high-quality German asset-backed paper.

THE BENELUX COUNTRIES

Belgium

The Belgian securitization market took off in 1996. The law of Belgium allows for creation of either a SIC (*Sociétés d'Investissement en Créances*) or an FPC (*Fonds de Placement en Créances*) as the securitization vehicle.

An SIC is a corporate entity with a minimum capital of 2.5 million Belgian francs ($68,000). An FPC, which has no legal personality, is a pool of assets co-owned by the investors. Both type of vehicles must be managed by a management company. All transactions in Belgium are managed by Titrisation Belge-Belgische Effectisering (TBE), the only management company (société de gestion) currently operating in the Belgian market.[20]

Belgian securitization by product type as of 1996-1997 was as follows: 18% mortgage-backed securities, 57% consumer loans, and 25% government related. The market took off with BACOB's launch of Atrium-1, a securitization of social housing loans guaranteed by the Flemish government in May 1996. The Atrium-1 bonds are not prepayable and pay a fixed interest rate. Shortly afterward, BBL launched B-Cars 1, an auto-loan-backed issuance of floating-rate notes. BACOB followed up in January 1997 with the first securitization of residential mortgages. The total outstanding volume in 1996 and the first nine months of 1997 reached BEF 52 billion ($1.4 billion) in five transactions. In most Belgian transactions, credit enhancement is provided by excess spread and subordinated notes.

---

[17] Deutsche Morgan Grenfell, internal information.

[18] BAK circular May 20, 1997.

[19] Merrill Lynch, *European ABS*, June 1997.

[20] Shareholders TBE: BACOB, BBL Bear Stearns, and Generale de Banque.

In the meantime, the regulators keep improving the regulatory framework in order to allow conduit structures and private transactions.[21] According to Moody's, the legal framework for the Belgian securitization market is more mature and sophisticated than the framework that applied in France and Spain at their early stages.[22] This legislation will lead to the entrance of new sellers and new asset classes in the Belgian securitization market.

The Netherlands

To date, only one issue has emerged from the Dutch securitization market. VSB group — a subsidiary of Fortis — issued 500 million Netherlands guilders ($251 million) through FIMS in July 1996. The underlying assets were housing loans guaranteed by Nationale Hypotheken Guarantee, a government-owned agency. The deal's Aaa rating from Moody's was based in large part on the guarantee of the principal and interest on the mortgages by a combination of Dutch local authorities and state-affiliated National Hypotheken Guarantee. Although there is no specific legal framework on securitization in the Netherlands, FIMS is bankruptcy-remote.

The Central Bank issued a regulatory framework in March 1997 and, in September 1997, ABN finalized its 2 billion Dutch guilder EMS1 securitization backed by residential mortgages.

CONCLUSION

The benefits gained by originators and investors involved in securitization provides good reason to expect the logic of securitization to continue to prevail in the European markets, overcoming obstacles that no doubt still will arise.

Originators increasingly understand the benefits of this form of financing. Although in summary, the economic environment for securitization is looking much brighter than it has for several years we should not forget the strong capital position of many of the larger European banks and their general hunger for assets. However this is starting to change, particularly with acquisition-related activities. Asset hungry policies have driven down bank lending margins and created significant price competition in the capital markets.

We believe that the emergence of a single currency in Europe is likely to lead to a significant boast in securitization activity and that the recent development of a public sponsored ABS market will lead to a more balanced development of securitization in Europe.

Few European investors have so far developed the expertise to closely monitor opportunities in the European ABS market. The advent of the simple currency is expected to change all this. Parallels are drawn with the U.S. bond mar-

[21] Law, December 1996.

[22] Moody's Investors Service, "The Belgian Structured Finance Market," Fabozzi/IMN Global Asset Securitisation conference, Cork, Ireland (June 22-25, 1997).

ket. The reason is that investors in individual countries will increasingly become European investors, considering opportunities across the continent and trading between deals. The actual move to a single European currency will be a significant leap forward to a more homogeneous Euro ABS market.

Chapter 3

Securitization of Non-Traditional Asset Types: An Investor's Perspective

Jennifer O. Quisenberry, CFA
Vice President
Structured Finance Advisors, Inc.

INTRODUCTION

The first asset-backed securities (ABS) appeared in the late 1970s as an offshoot of the mortgage-backed securities market. The concept was the same: the pooling of cash flowing assets in a bankruptcy remote structure against which various classes of securities with targeted credit risk and average life parameters were issued. The ABS market expanded dramatically in the early 1990s with the securitization of billions of dollars of credit card and automobile loan assets. Up to and through the early 1990s, investors could capture excess yield attributable to "structural complexity," despite the fact that the securities were largely triple-A quality. As investor participation in the segment grew, bringing greater liquidity and market depth, yields on these commodity assets diminished. Investors then began looking to the next frontier: securities backed by non-traditional or emerging asset types.

Participants in the ABS arena attach different meanings to "nontraditional" or "emerging" assets. Some view the category to encompass all assets except for mainstream assets such as credit cards, auto loans, manufactured housing, and equipment leasing. For more sophisticated participants, emerging assets are limited to assets being securitized for the first time or for which the attendant asset or servicer risks translate into the opportunity for significant absolute return. This chapter discusses the market and marketing of transactions backed by emerging asset types and presents a life cycle theory to describe their development. An outline of the critical due diligence and monitoring steps required of an educated and effective investor is also presented. This chapter does not address cross border transactions which, although a significant and growing area of the asset-backed market, lend themselves to a different analytical approach and credit analysis.

MARKETS AND MARKET MAKING FOR STRUCTURED SECURITIES

Asset-backed bonds, broadly defined as fixed income securities backed by a stream of cash flows, have historically enjoyed a yield premium to their corporate bond counterparts due to the complexity of structured transactions, average life variability (prepayment or extension risk), and liquidity. As the volume of outstanding U.S. domestic transactions has grown, with greater participation by U.S. and foreign investors, the liquidity premium for the most mature asset classes has shrunk. Nonetheless, marginal spread or yield premiums for even the most "bullet-proof" structures continue to exist. With respect to the more "off-the-run" asset types, there has been a corresponding tightening of spreads due to a larger number of previously uninvolved investors venturing into nontraditional asset types in search of yield. Another factor contributing to yield compression relates to the marketing and distribution capabilities of intermediaries. ABS securities are executed through three primary channels: private/direct placement, Rule 144A, or public.

Private/Direct Placement

In a private or direct transaction, investors have the opportunity to perform extensive due diligence, including in-depth review of the transaction documents by legal counsel, resulting in an ability to exert influence on the transaction structure and pricing. Transactions executed in this manner are structurally complex or involve unique asset or servicer risks. Due to the time, effort, and due diligence required to reach an investment decision, they may be solicited only to a select number of experienced structured finance buyers for review. The security may be highly illiquid, depending on the number of investors involved in the transaction and market acceptance of the asset type.

Rule 144A Transactions

Rule 144A provides an exemption from the registration requirements of the Securities Act of 1933 for resales of privately placed securities to qualified institutional buyers or "QIBs." Since QIBs are presumed to be established and experienced institutions (a QIB is defined as an investor with at least $100 million of assets under management on a discretionary basis), the SEC does not regulate or approve disclosure requirements. Rule 144A placements represent a grey and potentially dangerous area between private and public markets. Securities issued under Rule 144A are typically transactions of meaningful size ($50 million and above), and are broadly marketed to potential investors.

While Rule 144A transactions are presented under the guise of a private transaction, they are more commonly executed under a "take it or leave it" arrangement with respect to pricing and terms. Aside from a review of the offering memorandum, investors may or may not be given an opportunity to review the underlying transaction documents and to perform their own due diligence on the issuer. This trend is particularly troubling to the seasoned private placement buyers. There appears to be a false sense of security derived from the size of the transaction (implying liquidity) or the assumption among investors that "many eyes have looked at the deal." Investors should be aware that the Rule 144A designation does not relieve the investor from the need to perform a level of independent due diligence appropriate for the asset type and servicer risk.

Public Placement

The public market is usually reserved for commodity type assets. Investor due diligence is minimal; an offering memorandum may or may not have been received and reviewed by the investor prior to a commitment to purchase by an investor, and liquidity is very high.

In marketing a transaction, intermediaries choose the most efficient channel to distribute the bonds which in most cases will be the path of least resistance. This motivation is at odds with that of the investors' need to spend the required amount of time to perform analysis and gain a thorough understanding of the assets and servicer. The onus is on the investor to determine the appropriate level of due diligence required and to insist of intermediaries that these requirements are met.

THE LIFE CYCLE OF SECURITIZABLE ASSETS

Exhibit 1 presents a spectrum of life stages for various asset types. Emerging asset types are typically introduced into the private placement market where the transaction structure is vetted and assets are examined in depth by a single or small number of sophisticated investors. Transaction size is generally small (less than $50 million of issuance), making them suitable and appropriate for a private placement execution. Investors in this early stage can earn a significant yield premium reflecting their time, effort and due diligence in completing the first transaction. As multiple issues are completed by an issuer or within an asset type, together with increased transaction size, the issuer or asset matures to the 144A and eventually, the public market.

Five broad categories are presented to describe the development of an asset type: nascent, early/developing, transitional, developed/mature, and commodity. Normally, an asset type will proceed chronologically from one end of the spectrum to the other. One exception was the recent securitization of stranded utility assets. The first securitization of the asset class by a California utility totaled $5 billion in a widely distributed public offering priced at public market spreads. A description of each of these categories is provided below.

Nascent Category

Assets in the nascent stage have been securitized by a very limited number of issuers. These assets may have difficulty emerging from this category because of structural impediments or external factors. For example, securitizations involving lottery payments have been hindered by difficulties in obtaining a legal assignment in certain state jurisdictions. Another example involves the securitization of viatical settlements which are life insurance benefits purchased at a discount from terminally ill patients. Fortunately for terminally ill AIDS patients (and unfortunately for bondholders), medical advancements involving the combination of medications has had the effect of extending the lives of patients. This has had the effect of decreasing cash flows on the underlying assets, thus significantly extending the average life of the security.

Early/Developing Category

Similar to the nascent stage, assets in the early/developing stage have been securitized in limited number. At the early/developing stage, however, a certain legitimacy for the asset type is being developed by some, but not all, investors in the market. The securitization of 12b-1 fees is one example. 12b-1 fees represent the ongoing fee paid to distributors of mutual funds and are based on the value of the fund over a fixed period of time. It is unlikely that transactions backed by 12b-1 fees will gain widespread market acceptance, as some investors continue to view the assets as a derivative of the equity and bond markets. The securitization of distressed assets carries a different stigma. Despite the satisfactory performance of the distressed asset securitizations outstanding, certain investors will only be convinced of the asset's value through sustained, long term portfolio performance.

Exhibit 1: Life Cycle Stage of Various Asset Types

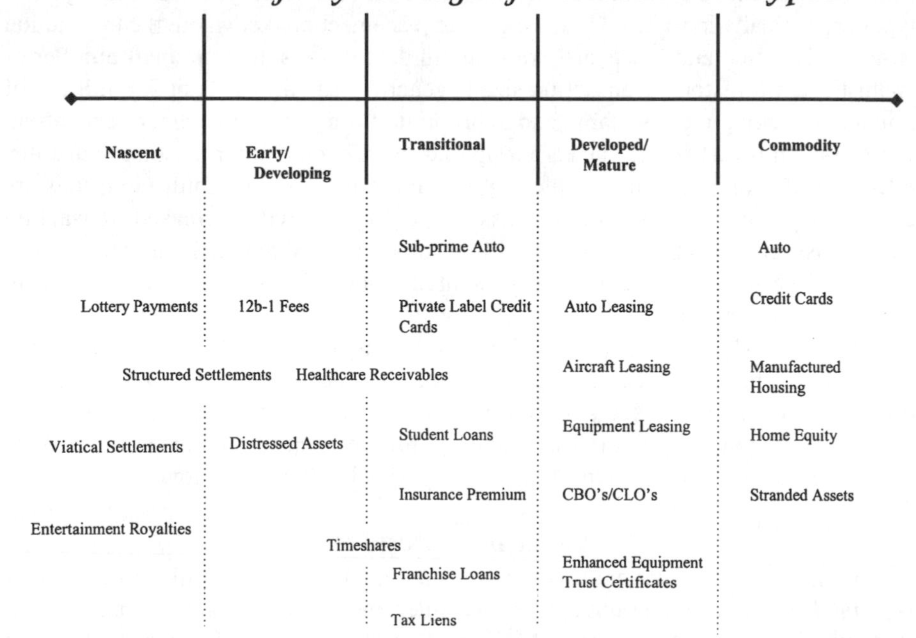

Transitional Category

The transitional category is categorized by issuers with varying degrees of experience and track record, such that the assets "transition" within the lifecycle spectrum. Private label credit card issuers, for example, range from the first time issuer with limited servicing capabitilies to the major national retail chain with multiple transactions outstanding in the market. Obviously, yields for a single asset within the transitional category can vary widely.

Developed/Mature Category

The developed/mature category includes assets whose risks are well understood by investors, for which an established structure exists, and for which a sizeable amount of issuance has created substantial market liquidity. Within this stage and the commodity stage, "credit tiering" develops, referring to differential spreads attributable to different issuers of the same asset class. Within the CBO (Collateralized Bond Obligations) and CLO (Collateralized Loan Obligations) segment, the pooling and securitization of high yield debt and bank loans to take advantage of spread arbitrage, issues trade according to the quality and reputation of the investment manager.

Commodity Category

Securities backed by commodity assets are highly liquid and there is limited pricing differentiation (just a few basis points) among different issuers of the same asset type. Within both the developed/mature and commodity segments, there exists an opportunity for investors to pick up additional yield by participating in the subordinated classes of these securities. The risk profile of the subordinated class needs to be examined in comparison to the senior class, including a thorough understanding of all subordination provisions.

INVESTOR DUE DILIGENCE AND MONITORING

Investors venturing into the truly emerging assets through privately negotiated transactions should be prepared to devote extensive time and effort to complete the transaction. Exhibit 2 presents an outline of certain basic due diligence steps when analyzing non-traditional asset types. This list is by no means all inclusive, and should be tailored to fit the requirements of a particular asset type. A complete due diligence process for an emerging asset type can take anywhere from three months to one year. For the first time securitization, the analysis begins at a very fundamental level to assure that the legal and performance risks of the assets are understood or that structural or legal protections are in place to mitigate them. Each of the rating agency, intermediary, and investor thus plays a critical role in the analysis and the identification of potential risks. The most effective investor is an active participant in the process.

Exhibit 2: Due Diligence Procedures

I. Screening
  A. Audited financial statements (3 years preferred)
  B. Management biographies
  C. Static pool data
  D. Portfolio aging
  E. Credit Policy and Procedure manual

II. Pre-Circle Due Diligence and Analysis
  A. Company background and history
  B. Financial condition of issuer with a focus on liquidity
  C. Origination process
  D. Underwriting criteria and comparison of assets to underwriting criteria
  E. Assessment of obligor quality (credit grading)
  F. Analysis of historical asset performance (static pool and default pools)
  G. Model transaction cash flows including stress test scenarios
  H. Industry considerations and competition
  I. Third party resources
    1. Nexus/Lexus search
    2. Outside consultants and auditors
    3. Third party investigator
  J. Pre-circle on site due diligence
  K. Analysis of transaction economics (cost to generate, acquire asset, retained equity interest)
  L. Flow of cash, lockbox arrangements

III. Post-Circle Due Diligence
  A. On site due diligence
  B. Legal Review
  C. Establish reporting requirements
  D. Third party audit of collateral pool

The due diligence process begins with an in depth analysis of the asset performance. The analysis begins with a static pool analysis of a seasoned portfolio originated by the issuer. A static pool presents the historical performance of discrete pools of assets originated during specific time increments. The data shows the performance of the pool over time, providing a benchmark for the rate and timing of defaults and prepayments. More important than the absolute level of defaults is the consistency of asset performance. A sufficient level of enhancement can be designed around high and predictable defaults; such is not the case with volatile asset performance. One limitation of using static pool data as a barometer of future performance is that the underwriting parameters may have changed over time. This was the case with certain of the sub-prime auto loan securitizers. Investors based their investment decision on static pool data for historical performance at a time when, in response to competitive pressure in the subprime auto loan market, issuers were granting new loans to obligors of lower and lower credit quality. Investors found that actual default rates were well above the static pool indicators. A file review comparing current originations to the underwriting criteria can identify this problem up-front.

For first time issuers or start-up operations, producing a sufficient amount of historical portfolio data may be impossible. In these cases, it is possible to use market data or the performance measures of comparable issuers as a proxy for the securitization portfolio. The other aspect of the asset review involves an assessment of any pertinent legal issues of the asset. Can a security interest in the assets be perfected? Is it necessary to retitle the assets for the benefit of the securities issued? Can the issuer be truly separated from the assets in the event of a bankruptcy? These and other questions must be satisfactorily answered to qualify as a securitization.

The other major area of due diligence focus is the servicer responsible for collecting on the assets throughout the term of the deal. Overriding concerns are servicer viability and fraud risk. In order to complete a securitization, it is not necessary for the servicer to be a highly creditworthy entity. Indeed in most cases, the issuing entity is of a below investment grade quality looking to securitization as an alternative funding source to traditional lending sources. In cases where the servicer is small, inexperienced, or financially weak, a back-up servicer is required. Fraud risk presents a particularly difficult challenge for investors, since it is very difficult to anticipate the likelihood of fraud. Investors can take a few steps to help to mitigate this risk. Background checks of key management will reveal past litigation, business affiliations, and financial position. Steps need to be taken to segregate the cash of the issuer from that of the transaction. A lockbox mechanism is typically established whereby cash collected on the assets flows directly into an account for the benefit of the securities, with no ability for the servicer to access the cash. The servicer needs to demonstrate a sufficient amount of liquidity and capital resources as a liquidity shortfall could drive an issuer to take desperate steps to save his or her company. A direct relationship with the issuer should be established and maintained after the deal closes in order to gain a comfort level with the people involved in the transaction. Finally, the investor should also pay attention to his or her intuition; the "gut feeling" is often times the best judge of character.

The importance of closely monitoring transactions backed by emerging assets after the deal closes cannot be overestimated. The key to an effective monitoring program is to identify negative trends immediately and to address issues, discrepancies, and inconsistencies promptly. Asset performance must be tracked in order to identify negative trends and to compare asset performance levels to established requirements within the deal. It is important to verify that each of the reporting requirements is being met. A missed monthly report or failure to provide audits may be an indicator of more serious problems at the servicer level. Finally, experienced investors have learned the importance of a direct dialogue with both the issuer and trustee so that any potential problems can be swiftly addressed. Constant communication with the issuer serves as an important reminder that the investor is a concerned party, and may help to mitigate the risk of fraud.

ROLE OF AN ADVISOR

The substantial resources and expertise required to be an effective and successful investor in the emerging assets prevents some investors from participating in the sector. Another option for investors is to contract with a reputable and experienced advisor to source, analyze, and negotiate transactions on their behalf. In addition to gaining the experience and market knowledge of the advisor without the delay of developing the expertise internally, the relationship presents an opportunity for the investor to tap into a source of deals that are typically reserved for the larger, more sophisticated players. The monitoring function of an advisor provides a necessary value added service that is critical to maintaining the quality of a portfolio of truly emerging assets.

Chapter 4

Securitizing Nontraditional U.S. Assets for European Markets

Joseph D. Smallman
Managing Director
London Branch
Vining-Sparks IBG

Michael J. P. Selby, Ph.D.
Centre for Quantitative Finance
Imperial College of Science, Technology and Medicine

INTRODUCTION

Twenty-five years ago the markets for Eurodollar and securitized instruments were in their infancy. Both of these markets have shown phenomenal growth through financial innovation. In particular, a key element contributing to the growth of the securitization market has been the demand by European investors for floating-rate instruments. As these products evolved, their spreads have tightened, thus creating an opportunity for nontraditional securitized instruments.

Traditionally, mortgages, credit card receivables, and automobile loans, for example, are securitized in the United States for global distribution. These securities are issued in both fixed- and floating-rate form. When originally issued, the spread for both mortgage-backed and asset-backed securities was relatively large. The pricing reflected the innovative nature of the products. Today, these are seasoned products in a well-developed liquid market, trading at tight spreads.

To satisfy the demand for wider spreads, nontraditional asset classes are making their way to the market. In 1996 Standard & Poor's published a review and discussed the new criteria used for rating several of these nontraditional assets, such as tax liens, nonperforming consumer loans, 12-b(1) fees (a fee some mutual funds receive), franchise loans, rental car fleets, and small business loans.[1]

At first, the methods discussed in this chapter used to securitize nontraditional U.S. dollar assets for European markets may seem odd. However, we hope that the rationale will take form as we explain the reasons why we use these methods to overcome international obstacles.

[1] "Structured Finance Ratings — Asset-Backed Securities Beyond the Traditional Asset Classes: New Assets '96," Standard & Poor's (October 1996).

THE EURODOLLAR MARKET VERSUS THE U.S. DOMESTIC MARKET

The European U.S. dollar market provides a unique opportunity for placing many of these nontraditional U.S. assets via securitization. Before we discuss the methods used to securitize these assets for European investors, it is important to compare and contrast the U.S. market with the European market.

The European U.S. dollar market, more commonly called the Eurodollar market, refers to all U.S. dollars invested outside of the United States. The evolution of this market began during the Cold War between the Soviet Union and the United States. The Soviets feared that the U.S. authorities would freeze or hold the deposits that they had with the Federal Reserve Bank. To eliminate this problem, the Soviets lent these dollars to Commercial de l'Europe du Nord located in Paris and the Moscow Narody Bank in London. This practice of moving U.S. dollars offshore, away from U.S. domestic regulations — such as Regulation Q, which capped lending rates — was quickly adopted by other European merchant banks and U.S. banks, resulting in the birth of the Eurodollar market. It is amazing how communist ideology blended with U.S. paranoia gave birth to a new capital market.

According to the International Securities Market Association,[2] the dollar remains the largest denomination in the Euromarkets. Issuance increased from $50 billion in 1991 to $270 billion in 1996. In 1996 the market increased the previous year's issues by over $100 billion to a total of $270 billion. (Total market size at year-end 1996 was $1.457 trillion.) Much of this growth came from the increased issuance of asset-backed securities, with more than $80 billion being issued in 1996.

One may very well ask: Why are so many U.S. assets finding a home in Europe? The European market is made up of various countries with different currencies, languages, and cultures. The European Economic Community is working on eliminating this first difference by introducing the Euro, formerly called the European Currency Unit (ECU). This is not to be confused with the Eurodollar. The ECU is a basket currency. From January 1, 1999, one "ECU-basket" will equal one Euro. The Euro will eventually replace all the European Community countries' currencies.[3] This situation will resemble circumstances in the United States before the Federal Reserve System was introduced, when each state issued its own currency.

The U.S. dollar remains the currency of choice for the European banks. It is easy to convert into a home currency and to be the base currency for a variety of structured products — which simplifies lending, swapping, or hedging. If one looks to all the various markets, the U.S. dollar-based market is always the most liquid.

---

[2] Clive Horwood, *Quarterly Comment* 28 (January 1997): p. 6.

[3] Graham Bishop, Jose Perez, and Sammy van Tuyll, "The User Guide to the Euro," *Federal Trust* (1996): pp. 29-31.

Given this large, efficient financial market for Eurodollars, it may be thought surprising that there does not exist a natural, underlying base for U.S. dollar-denominated assets. Why not? Although many sovereign states and corporate entities will borrow from banks and issue debt in U.S. dollars, most — if not all — consumer debt is in the home currency. Therefore, there does not exist a naturally matched asset base such as there is in the United States for mortgages, credit cards, auto loans, etc.

The European and U.S. banks also differ in the way they run their treasury operations. Most European banks match funds. That is to say, they fund their assets to match their liabilities. For example, if they plan to lend a corporation $100 million, they will give an adjustable loan indexed to the 3-month London Interbank Offer Rate (LIBOR). They may offer the corporation a fixed loan but they will swap it into a floating-rate one.

To fund this loan, banks will borrow at the 3-month LIBOR rate. The spread between funding cost and lending rate will be their profit. They are indifferent to changes in interest rates because their funding cost moves lockstep to their receivable. Just as they lend, so they invest. The floating-rate note (FRN) market is very active in Europe and has shown remarkable recent growth, more than doubling in size in 1996, with new issuance exceeding $1.4 billion compared with only $600 million in 1995.[4]

These features explain why the U.S. dollar asset-backed and mortgage-backed floating-rate securities are so actively traded in the Eurodollar market. They easily fit into a European bank's balance sheet.

In contrast, most U.S. banks lend and invest at fixed rates. If one asked U.S. bankers what they think of the FRN market they would probably be ignorant as to what one was asking. Also, a vast number of them would not know the meaning of LIBOR.

The common question a U.S. bond broker will ask a banker is: Where is your bogey? Translation: What maturity and spread over the U.S government's borrowing rate do you want? A common response may be "20 over the 10 year," meaning that the banker is looking for a fixed investment that will return 20 basis points over the current U.S. 10-year bond rate.

The main traditional U.S. assets traded in the European markets are floating-rate instruments such as corporate bonds, asset-backed credit cards, floating-rate CMO tranches, and floating-rate U.S. agency paper.

As the Eurodollar market evolves, it is natural for nontraditional U.S. assets to find a home in Europe. One asset class we found to be attractive to European investors is based on the U.S. Small Business Administration (SBA) Guaranteed Loan Pools Certificates (GLPC).[5] To illustrate how a nontraditional U.S. asset is placed in Europe, we are going to review how we securitized GLPC for Europe.

---

[4] Bank for International Settlements, 67th Annual Report: 129.

[5] When we refer to pools we are referring to the SBA GLPC.

Since the U.S. government guarantees the GLPC and issues the currency, there is no higher level of credit. If the U.S. government fails, so does the currency. The extremely high credit rating of the U.S. government, combined with the fact that most loans and GLPC have high coupons, normally causes them to trade at a premium to face value. As a result, we are able to construct, via securitization, an instrument that is issued at par with the underlying collateral priced at a premium. This creates an undercollateralized instrument. By securitizing a large portfolio of premium-priced pools via an offshore trust, called SBA International, we transform GLPC into an investment suitable for European investors.

So far as we can determine, this product is one of the first securitizations that is undercollateralized; most asset-backed securities are overcollateralized. The special-purpose vehicle that holds the assets and issues the security normally has a face value smaller than the aggregate principal value of the collateral. The reason for this is that in most — if not all — cases, the credit quality of the collateral is lower than the credit rating of the ABS. The overcollateralization serves to absorb any delays and defaults.

To understand this unique approach of using undercollateralization, we will first describe the GLPC collateral. Next, we will focus on the SBA International's key element of risk, the premium risk due to prepayment.

U.S. SBA GUARANTEED LOAN POOLS CERTIFICATES

SBA GLPC are securitized SBA 7(a) guaranteed loans that are backed by the full faith and credit of the U.S. government. These floating-rate bonds pay monthly and amortize to stated final maturities ranging from five to 25 years. The coupons are indexed to the U.S. prime rate of interest and reset either monthly or quarterly. The SBA pools can offer a very attractive yield spread compared with other U.S. government credits. Before we describe the security, we shall explain the SBA's origins and economic function.

The SBA Origins and Economic Function

According to its own vision statement, "The U.S. Small Business Administration (SBA) was created in 1953 as an independent agency of the Federal government to aid, counsel, assist and protect the interests of small business concerns, to preserve free competitive enterprise, and to maintain and strengthen the overall economy of our Nation. Small business is critical to our economic recovery, to building America's future and to helping the United States compete in today's global marketplace."

One method this agency uses to achieve its mission is through the U.S. government's 7(a) loan guarantee scheme. The purpose of this program is to provide long-term capital (five to 25 years) to the small businesses of America (such as day care, doctors' offices, plumbing, and other grass-roots, community-based companies). U.S. banks are set up to provide short-term financing. In practice, most traditional small business loans have a 5-year final maturity or call feature. The SBA 7(a) program fills the need for providing long-term funding for U.S. small businesses.

Prior to 1985, SBA 7(a) loan guarantees could be sold only on an individual basis by the lender and purchased individually by the investor. These guarantees, made on loans with a variable rate of interest for a term of five to 25 years, ranged in size from $10,000 to the SBA guaranteed maximum of $750,000. Based on the loan's coupon and maturity, the loans will normally trade in a range from par to a 10% premium. An investor who purchases a variable-rate SBA guaranteed loan, with a coupon higher than that of the U.S. government's borrowing rate, would expect to pay some premium above par value, commensurate with the rate on the loan purchased.

In purchasing a variable-rate loan guarantee the investor receives the following:

- A margin above or below the U.S. prime rate of interest that will adjust periodically (monthly or quarterly).
- Principal and interest payments that are guaranteed by the full faith and credit of the U.S. government.
- Monthly principal and interest payments.
- An investment product that can be held on a U.S. bank's loan portfolio.
- An investment which, in most cases, is pledgeable at the Federal Reserve or as collateral for public funds.

Despite all of these significant benefits, individual loan guarantees have had several disadvantages:

- Premiums paid are lost if the loan defaults or prepays prior to maturity. In the event of default, the SBA repays the loan.
- In order to satisfy an investment requirement involving several millions of dollars, many individual loans must be purchased.
- An investor's payment stream is interrupted if the borrower or lender does not remit payments.

To eliminate these problems and to enhance market efficiency, the U.S. Congress passed the Small Business Secondary Market Improvements Act of 1984. This legislation established the mechanism, regulation, and standards for GLPC and the SBA pool assemblers.

From this foundation, securitization of SBA loans — that is, SBA GLPC — has promoted market efficiency by allowing investors to diversify by taking a fractional interest in many loans versus a total interest in only one loan. To demonstrate, assume an individual $100,000 loan guarantee is purchased at a price of, say, 106; the purchaser is exposed immediately to a potential loss of the $6,000 premium in the event of prepayment or default. In the event of default, the U.S. government repays the loan. However, if one invested $106,000 in a GLPC from a $5,000,000 pool with 50 similar loans at the same price of 106, this would greatly diminish the possibility of total premium loss. All 50 loans in the pool would have to prepay concurrently in order to produce the same total loss of premium, which is highly unlikely. This probability shall be reviewed in detail later in this chapter.

As is clearly evident, all premium value is lost in the case of prepayment of an individual loan, since 100% of the principal is prepaid. However, if one invested the $106,000 in the pool we described above, only 2% of the principal of the pool is paid down.[6] The resulting effect is only a $2,120 paydown of the investment in the GLPC. The premium loss of this prepayment is therefore only $120 in premium (2% of the $6,000 premium).

Guaranteed Timely Payment Feature

The holder of an individual loan is sent a monthly principal and interest (P&I) payment by Colson, currently the U.S. government-appointed fiscal transfer agent (FTA), only if the payment is received by the FTA. In contrast, the holder of a GLPC is guaranteed a timely remittance of P&I on the 25th of each month, whether or not payment is received by the FTA. This timely payment guarantee protects the GLPC holder against nonpayment or late payment.

Features of SBA GLPC

SBA GLPC have the following features:

- A U.S. government full-faith-and-credit guarantee.
- Guaranteed timely payment.
- Minimal price volatility and liquid market.
- 0% capital risk weighting
- Easily monitored via the Bloomberg system.

The credit risk on GLPC is the same as that of the U.S. government. However, the reason one is able to earn a spread above LIBOR lies in the fact that there are two risks — prime/LIBOR basis risk and premium risk due to prepayment.

The prime rate is the consumer lending rate in the United States — credit cards, auto loans, and other consumer financing. It is estimated that over 80% of all U.S. floating-rate loans under $1 million are indexed to prime. Therefore, since these prime-indexed investments are booked on the asset side of the balance sheet, prime is considered an asset index. Financial institutions do not fund themselves at the prime rate. Most developed countries use a consumer lending rate much like the prime rate in the United States or base rate in the United Kingdom. Therefore, since the prime rate of interest is fixed solely by U.S. banks, there is a strong commercial reason for this spread to stay wide. The historical spread between U.S. prime rate of interest and U.S. dollar LIBOR interest rate has been consistently wide. Furthermore, an active prime/LIBOR swap market out to 10 years shows that this relationship is expected to continue.

---

[6] One pool divided by 50 pools is 2%. Therefore only 2 of premium would be lost.

Exhibit 1: CPR Speed Relative to Age
For All Uncapped SBA Pools with a Maximum of 240 Months Original Maturity

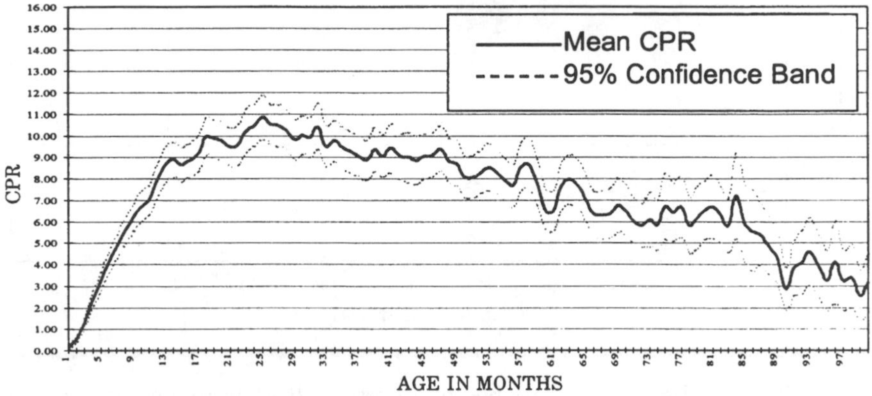

The key area of risk on premium-priced GLPC is prepayment. The U.S. government guarantees only the par value of the pools. Any premium paid for the bond is subject to early prepayment and, if a large number of the loans prepay, it could greatly reduce the yield. In order to quantify this risk, one must look to the historical evidence.

The Behavior of SBA CPRs

In order to quantify the prepayment risk, we carried out a detailed empirical analysis. Empirical evidence shows that prepayments on uncapped SBA pools are not affected by changes in interest rates. However, we have identified age as the primary independent variable that affects the CPR, or constant prepayment rate. CPR is the annual percentage of additional principal repayment above the scheduled amortization of principal.

We investigated how CPR speeds change relative to age. We examined the monthly CPR speeds of all uncapped GLPC with original month to maturity from 0 to 240 months from Colson. The Colson tape provided us with the GLPC's number, issue date, maturity date, original face value, coupon relative to prime, identified capped versus uncapped, number of loans, and the monthly CPR speed. We emphasize that the tape contains the total SBA pool population.

Next, we weighted the monthly CPR speeds relative to the pool's original dollar value. This was to provide "a level view of the data."

Using the weighted data, the mean and standard deviation of the CPR for each month were calculated. From this we are able to determine that 95% of the CPRs were found to be within approximately ±2% of the average CPR. As shown in Exhibit 1, we can draw a 95% confidence band about the mean CPR speed. This establishes, with an extremely high degree of statistical confidence, a precise range of anticipated CPR speeds for the GLPC.

Exhibit 2: Confidence Bands versus Number of Pools

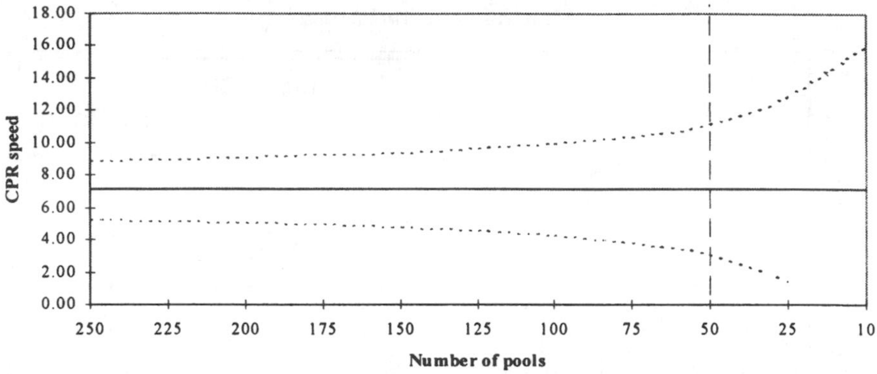

It is obviously not possible to purchase the entire universe of SBA GLPC. How does one create a portfolio that will track the GLPC universe or, equivalently, how many pools should an investor purchase to emulate the universe?

As depicted in Exhibit 2, if we started with the whole universe there would be no deviations from the mean or average CPR speed. However, as we own fewer and fewer pools our prepayment expectations become less certain and our confidence band starts to widen. Starting from the far left, we begin decreasing the number of pools to see what effect this has on our confidence band. Evidently, the confidence bands start to expand rapidly or become unstable at less than 50 pools. Therefore, we conclude through empirical analysis that an investor should purchase at least 50 pools in order to mimic the historical prepayment speeds of all SBA with an original maturity of 240 months or less.

SBA International

Many European institutional investors have purchased portfolios of SBA GLPC and are able to benefit from the positive spread they receive over their LIBOR funding rate. However, many European investors are unable to participate in this market because of limited resources or investment mandates prohibiting them from taking a prime/LIBOR basis risk. As we discussed earlier, one must purchase many pools to diversify away the prepayment risk. Additionally, if investors are required by mandate to hedge the prime/LIBOR risk, they will need to structure and monitor a swap program. It takes time to review each pool, to monitor the portfolio, and to structure a swap. Also, because SBA pools pay with a 55-day delay, it is difficult to match-fund the portfolio.

To compensate for these drawbacks and restrictions, SBA International was developed. This structure emulates a conventional amortizing FRN. The principal benefits this product offers are:

- Substantial yield over LIBOR
- Pays a monthly coupon indexed to 1-month LIBOR
- Eliminates delay days
- Issued at par
- Simplistic
- Retains a low capital risk weighting.

SBA International uses a grantor trust structure that issues triple-A-rated A trust certificates. The proceeds from the A trust certificates are used to purchase premium-priced GLPC. As we explained earlier, this creates an undercollaterized structure. SBA International purchases SBA pools with a coupon of approximately prime plus 1%, which, based on historical SBA CPR speeds, produces a substantial yield over LIBOR. This yield is passed though the trust to the A trust certificate holders. This structure is robust in that the trust has a subordinated tranche that serves to absorb the majority of any deterioration in the yield from the GLPC caused by increased CPR speeds. This provides the A-trust certificate holders with a great deal of comfort because the CPR speeds on the GLPC would have to substantially surpass the 95% confidence band in our study before the A-certificate coupon would become impaired.

Through our structuring techniques, we are able to provide to the A-trust certificate holders a substantial spread over LIBOR, say 30 basis points plus an optional prime/LIBOR swap. Those investors who do not hedge are able to receive an additional yield, being the difference between the spot prime/LIBOR spread and swap strike price. Those who do not hedge are exposed to basis compression; conversely, they will benefit from any expansion in the prime/LIBOR spread as well as the stated A-certificate LIBOR spread.

Furthermore, we eliminate the delay days though warehousing the collateral. This allows us to pass through the principal and interest payments immediately to the A-certificate holders. This is a feature greatly appreciated by many European investors who prefer to perfectly match fund.

The A Trust certificates are issued at par and appear in the investor's management accounts as a single line item with a single monthly principal and interest payment. This simplifies the investment for the investor versus, say, accounting for 200 GLPC with 200 different principal and interest payments every month.

Finally, we use the grantor trust structure to preserve the low capital risk weighting of the SBA pools. GLPC are considered 0% risk weighted by most European central banks. European conventional securitizations form a corporation as the SPV that owns and controls the assets. These structures require a 100% risk weighting in most cases. In most securitizations, the collateral is already 100% risk-weighted; therefore the trust structure provides no benefit over the corporate structure. However, since a grantor trust is transparent in form, most regulators will look through to the trust's collateral for the appropriate risk weighting.

SUMMARY AND CONCLUSIONS

A key feature of our work has been the ability to demonstrate that securitization procedures can bring nontraditional assets to new markets. However, we have shown that nontraditional methods may be required when dealing with nontraditional asset classes. In our example of SBA International we used a combination of undercollateralization within a grantor trust structure to create a synthetic Eurodollar FRN.

In this chapter we have described how a nontraditional asset class is entering the Eurodollar market via securitization. This is only one example of many that are bound to follow. We foresee structures that will include not only nontraditional U.S.-originated asset classes, but also other Eurodollar asset classes. These could include asset classes such as European time-share receivables, Russia-based U.S. dollar leases, and royalties.

Chapter 5

Technology Issues in Asset-Backed Securitization

James E. Myers
Marketing Manager
Lewtan Technologies, Inc.

INTRODUCTION

Why is technology an important part of the securitization process? Many of the reasons are no different from those in other financial service applications — large volumes of data processed in an environment where accuracy, auditability, and automation are of paramount importance. Asset securitization is a highly data-intensive endeavor with a set of diverse information and reporting needs.

However, other technological requirements are still unique to the securitization process. The very nature of establishing a special-purpose vehicle (SPV), which requires a new set of books to account for the sold receivables, is a financial innovation that encourages technology. With ever-changing structures, the permutations for investors are nearly boundless. To satisfy investor appetite for variety and maximum yields, any asset with an anticipated cash flow is a target for securitization. (For proof, just look at viatical settlements, future flows, and stranded utility costs.) Consequently, systems must be flexible, expandable, and continuously updated.

Compounding the difficulties surrounding ABS systems is the relative scarcity of systems knowledge among ABS professionals. Consider how many activities in an organization require interaction of participants from legal, accounting, operations, finance, and systems areas.

Typically, people who understand the structured-finance aspects of securitizations lack in-depth understanding of how a receivables accounting system accrues interest, allocates payments, or handles bounced checks. There is ample occasion for miscommunication, and all participants follow a learning curve as they gain understanding of other departmental functions and attempt to put systems in place.

Furthermore, with the considerable number of internal and external participants involved in a single ABS transaction, the hand-off of deal documents and actual data is extensive. Information passes through underwriters, lawyers, credit enhancers, rating agencies, investors, and issuers, among others. Many of these players have sophisticated systems requirements to analyze, structure, and monitor the transaction from preclosing through cleanup call.

This chapter offers a primer for a subset of ABS systems and technology issues. It covers the following:

- Requirements of securitization participants over the transaction's life cycle.
- Some calculations of a securitized transaction that require servicing and accounting unrelated to an issuer's normal processing of the underlying assets.
- Details to cover when developing or selecting the appropriate securitiziation technology.
- Technical innovations available for modeling new ABS transactions or reverse-engineering existing deals.
- A prediction for the future of securitization technology.

TECHNOLOGY REQUIREMENTS OVER THE DEAL LIFE CYCLE

To understand fully the technology requirements for an ABS system, the needs of participants at each phase of a deal must be considered. This chapter considers the roles of issuer/servicer, underwriter, rating agency, credit enhancer, and investor.

Not considered here are other systems used in the originator's organization for credit scoring, primary servicing of the underlying asset, collections tracking for chargeoffs, and general ledger reporting, since each of those systems exists in the absence of securitization.

Similarly, the systems employed by the trustee for handling collections and tracking bondholder information are not considered here as they are the same as those used for other fixed-income products. Although asset-backed commercial paper conduits bring a unique set of systems requirements to bear, only the systems employed for term asset-backed deals will be discussed herein for the sake of clarity.

The technology requirements for securitization begin with the conceptualization of a deal, continue through the analysis and deal formation, and end with the ongoing servicing, accounting, and surveillance.

Exhibit 1 provides a bird's eye view of some technology requirements of major players in an asset-backed transaction.

Pool Selection

The process begins when the decision is made to examine ABS as a financing alternative. First, the assets under consideration are dissected and analyzed. Second, historical loss and prepayment experience are sought to provide a prediction for future cash-flow experience. Third, assets that will not pass rating agency and investor scrutiny are filtered out of the eligible asset pool. The remaining assets form the basis for the securitized pools.

Exhibit 1: Technology Checklist

	Conduit Sponsor	Issuer Servicer	Underwriter	Rating Agency	Credit Enhancer	Investor
Collateral Analysis	X	X	X		X	
Pool Selection	X	X	X			
Cash Flow Projections	X	X	X	X	X	X
Deal Structuring	X	X	X	X	X	
Receivables Purchase	X					
Point of Sale Reporting		X				
Collection Tracking	X	X				
Static Pool Analysis	X	X	X			
Average Daily Balance Calc.		X				
Asset/Liability Management	X					
Gain in Sale Computation		X				
Investor Reporting	X	X				
Surveillance	X	X	X	X	X	X
Investment Analysis						X
Cash Management	X					
Accounting	X	X				

Systems are required in this phase to provide the segregation of assets and to sort through the multifarious permutations of deal criteria. Geographic concentration limits, desired coupon rates to ensure sufficient excess spread, and minimum and maximum acceptable balances are all considered. Systems will assist in identifying the assets eligible for securitization.

When proceeding with a transaction, the analysis of the deal becomes more extensive. The issuer or underwriter continues to require systems for the analysis of the underlying collateral and for pool selection. Once the proposed pool of assets is selected, systems are required to create the stratifications and cross-tabulations of data that comprise the prospectus and rating agency reports. Point-of-sale reports detail the assets that have been selected. It is often important to have a procedure in place to tag the selected assets for removal from an issuer's balance sheet as well as to untag them — to return them to the books should the deal unwind before coming to market.

Static Pool Analysis

It is becoming more and more common to provide "static pool" or "vintage" reporting in addition to basic asset summary reports to the rating agencies when presenting a pool of assets for securitization. Static pool or vintage analysis involves unique requirements that are not met by most operational reports and systems.

A static-pool analysis helps reveal how delinquencies, losses, and prepayments develop over time. A critical question that the rating agencies and guarantors ask is: How will the fixed pool of assets being securitized perform over the life of the securitization? Looking at the performance of the entire portfolio (dynamic pool) does not help. The overall growth in total assets over time can easily mask trends in the older receivables. Looking at different static pools (vintages) helps show how the assets have performed over long periods of time.

Components

The components of a static-pool analysis illustrate why traditional "snapshot" reporting is insufficient to satisfy the rating agencies' requirements. The following steps create a typical static-pool analysis:

1. Break portfolio into vintages, typically quarterly (all originations during a particular quarter).
2. Prepare tables illustrating how each vintage performed month by month or quarter by quarter, from the point of the origination.
3. For each quarter, determine:
   - Beginning/ending number of loans in vintage still active.
   - Beginning/ending principal balance.
   - Amortization during period.
   - Prepayments during period.
   - Delinquencies in each category as of end of period.
   - Gross/net losses during period.

While these steps are easy to understand, there are many technological hurdles to clear.

Historical Data

The first hurdle in preparing a static pool analysis often arises in the availability and accessibility of historical data. Backup procedures can change over time along with specific hardware and software used to store data. Some companies may not maintain historical data for a period of time sufficient to develop significant reports (typically at least five years of historical data are requested). Additionally, the operational procedures in some institutions may create a situation in which accounts are eliminated from record after a year or so of inactivity, or the same account numbers may be reassigned after a given period of time. Such occurrences make the technological challenges of static-pool reporting as much an art as a science.

Interpretation

Interpreting and analyzing the data from historical backup present the second difficulty in developing static pool reports. Provided that the data can be accessed successfully, there can be multiple systems involved and consequently multiple data retrievals for even the same historical point in time. Operational methods may have changed over time. Even the underlying receivable accounting system may have been converted, added to, or otherwise modified over the historical period in question.

Deal Modeling

Intricate modeling systems are required by various parties before a deal goes to market. Stress tests are performed for a variety of bond structures to identify which circumstances will produce shortfalls to the various classes of investors.

Essential deal-structuring functions include the ability to size tranches, generate price/yield tables, model complex trigger events that could alter the payout sequence of the bonds, and manipulate credit enhancement and other deal features. The capacity to modify quickly and easily the prepayment, default, delinquency, and recovery assumptions for the underlying collateral is also important.

Servicing

Once the securitization has closed, the servicer's reporting to the trust becomes the ongoing systems concern. Servicing for a securitization requires the translation of asset-related information into investor-related information. For most asset classes, recording the appropriate values on the servicer's certificate or settlement statement will dictate calculations to be made at the asset level. A system that reconciles every output that the investor views back to the account level will provide assurance for auditors, rating agencies, and investors.

Flexibility

A securitization tracking system should also be flexible. As many issuers intend to come to market more than once, the ability to create different calculations and bond payout hierarchies is critical. A securitization system will ideally support all accrual and asset types in an issuer's portfolio to ensure that the system's capabilities do not limit an organization's financing objectives.

Independence

Because a securitization system is independent of a receivable accounting system, the ability to track all issuances on a single system simplifies the ongoing reporting task. Independence of an issuer's primary receivable accounting system is important to ensure that securitization reports can be generated in a timely manner. Moreover, there are many securitization-specific calculations that mandate the maintenance of separate fields in the system to house securitization values that do not exist on most receivable accounting systems.

Interface with General Ledger

A securitization system should have the ability to interface with the issuer's general ledger. While many organizations are able to tag and segregate accounts through a subledger balance, other issuers prefer to tag the accounts through a separate securitization system and employ contra-accounts to remove the assets and associated income from their books. In the most sophisticated systems, a user has the automatic ability to repurchase receivables that violate the representations and warranties of the deal rather than requiring separate "exception" checks and ad hoc reports. Regardless of the accounting methods chosen, securitization requires the maintenance of a new set of books for the SPV.

Surveillance

After the deal closes, the same parties must keep an eye on the performance of the deal via systems. An increase in delinquencies has heightened market sensitivity to the investigation of default scenarios. As delinquencies increase, so does the need for surveillance. Any threat of an economic downturn on the horizon increases this need. Today's market offers a prevalence of lower-quality asset securitizations (B and C auto paper was the largest asset class by dollar volume in second-quarter 1996). This tendency brings an ever-present need to monitor new asset types to justify better pricing in subsequent deals. All of these factors signal the importance of systemic, regular surveillance.

The systems that exist to monitor an ABS deal begin with the originator's own internal portfolio management reporting and continue through the investor's portfolio management systems. Issuers demand a streamlined, intuitive surveillance software that performs functions the issuers are hard-pressed to perform on their own. Some examples are:

- Sophisticated trend analysis.
- Automated tracking and re-valuation of the gain on sale.
- Early-warning tools or ticklers that would automate deal triggers and identify actions the issuer could take to salvage a deal from a negative trend in collateral performance.

Investors that actively monitor their ABS deals require:

- Accurate, timely security pricing to evaluate performance.
- Standard interfaces to their portfolio management systems.
- The ability to track senior and subordinated pieces.
- The ability to mark their portfolios to market.
- Reprojection capability to reevaluate the underlying deal from time to time.

Rating agencies rely on the quality of data, speed, access of data for their analysts, flexibility to adapt to future market changes, and an automated, systematic approach to surveillance to minimize costs. Credit enhancers benefit from surveillance in many of the same ways as rating agencies but also require a system that can project fees, forecast revenues, and determine whether reserve balances should be adjusted. An underwriter's trading and sales support functions require a high-performance processing server for instantaneous response time. An underwriter relies on systems for the pricing it provides to investors on a regular basis and for reengineering cash flows. Thus, ABS systems impact all parties in a securitized transaction.

SECURITIZATION SYSTEMS VERSUS RECEIVABLE ACCOUNTING SYSTEMS

Asset-backed securitization introduces calculations, reporting requirements, and operational processes for the servicer that do not otherwise exist. In the nonsecuritized world, a receivable accounting system is used to track asset information such as payment history, balances, special statuses (such as nonaccruals, foreclosures, or bankruptcies), rate information, and other variables that detail the terms and performance of the assets. When a securitization is issued, the same asset servicing requirements exist, but a whole new set of variables must be tracked as well. A securitization system must calculate and store values at two levels:

- Asset level, to produce the calculations that are required for securitization of certain asset types. When aggregated, these asset-level variables typically comprise trust-level values.
- Trust level, to track all of the balances, statistics, and other information created by the securitization such as reserve fund balances, certificate balances for the different investor tranches, coupon rates, and scheduled interest for the bond classes.

As it is usually the servicer's goal to keep the obligor unaware that his or her particular receivable has been securitized, the underlying receivable accounting system must continue processing as in the absence of securitization and the securitization system must provide the rest of the information needed for the deal.

Asset-Level Calculations

To best illustrate the types of asset-level calculations that are required of an ABS servicing system, consider a bank that has performed a securitization of auto loans. Suppose the bank has originated assets in several states and has a variety of accrual types including simple interest, actuarial, and Rule of 78s. Imagine the bank has force-placed insurance on some of these loans. Also, the bank may have set up a variety of dealer plans and is tracking the dealer reserve amounts, as well. For simplicity, our example has the bank issuing into a grantor trust.

This situation introduces some accounting and regulatory reporting challenges that the bank's securitization systems must address. If the bank achieves true sale treatment, the assets must be removed from the bank's balance sheet. Contra-accounting can be performed when the assets are segregated. On an ongoing basis, new force-placed insurance must be split from the sold loan amount, introducing split-balance accounting; a grantor trust does not allow for the addition of assets subsequent to closing. If the issuer offers a payment extension to one of the obligors to a date that extends beyond the securitization's stated legal maturity date, that loan must be repurchased and added back on to the seller's books. Of course, the securitization-specific accounting for the excess servicing income, servicer advance balances, and related items must also be established and maintained in a system. The average daily balance reported to the Office of the Comptroller of the Currency must reflect a mean that does not include the sold loans.

Meaningful Differences

Some calculations have meaning only when a loan has been securitized. For a public auto securitization, the balances carried on a servicer's books are different from that loan's pool balance to the securitization. Even in the case of a simple interest loan, events such as small credit balances, force-placed insurance additions, or defaults through delinquency (where the securitization may have a defined number of days before a loan must be defaulted to the investor even though the loan may not have been charged off on the seller's books) can leave that loan's contribution to the total securitized balance far different from the balance it would carry if not securitized. Even the actuarial and Rule of 78s accrual types, which are typically sold on a scheduled basis, will have far different book versus securitization balances.

Additionally, a servicer must track how much has been advanced on a particular delinquent loan, because if that loan defaults, the servicer is entitled to recoup any prior advances. Rule of 78s or actuarial loans that have paid in advance of schedule may be put into the trust's payahead account. Compensating interest, yield supplement amounts, pre-cutoff accrued interest, and other accruals are all based on a balance that does not exist on the underlying loan accounting system.

Benefits of Independent Processing

Even asset classes that do not require new calculations at the asset level for securitization (such as trade receivables or credit cards) benefit from the independent processing of a securitization servicing system. Static pool reporting dictates tracking receivable-level information. Home equity lines of credit require tracking new draws separately from sold portions. Leases can have a variety of payment schedules, residual treatments, and other nuances. Commercial mortgages have such unique contracts that reviewing each account's performance is mandatory. The list goes on and on.

Aggregation

Statistics and other information must be aggregated for the investor reports, for example: delinquencies, repossessions, bankruptcies, chargeoffs, weighted average coupons, weighted average remaining terms, and the number of active loans in the pool.

Trust-Level Calculations

We must next consider the servicing of trust-level information. The pooling of assets into a security introduces the need for systems to track the liability side as well as the assets that support them. Maintaining the balances for the credit enhancement, calculating the amounts due to investors and other parties, and rolling that information forward from month to month are major functions of the securitization system.

The most sophisticated securitization system will automate the entire process. From automatically repurchasing receivables that violate the representations and warranties of the deal to rebooking any remaining assets for the cleanup call, the securitization system performs functions unique to the ABS world.

BACK-OFFICE TECHNOLOGY: BUY VERSUS BUILD

A key strategic decision is whether to purchase software that is readily available on the market or to build software in-house. For repeat issuers or conduit sponsors, the cost of building and maintaining a system may be far greater than the cost of outsourcing that responsibility. The deal parameters are often changing up to the last minute, and the systems development time schedule is independent of market conditions that may impact when to bring the deal to market. Combined with the dissimilar agendas of various internal departments, building a system is a difficult task.

Project Team Competition

When making a buy-versus-build decision, consider the organization's ability to adapt to changing requirements. Have members of the project team already worked on similar projects? Have they ever worked together? Is there a strong project manager with securitization experience? Change must be managed both at the beginning of the project and through the life of the deal. The underwriter and rating agencies call for changes in pool composition and format for investor reports. The deal could be postponed if the market conditions are not right. Does the issuer have the ability to tag the sold receivables and then untag them should the deal unwind? What other projects are competing for the time of the securitization team members?

Ongoing Operating Costs

Ongoing costs of operating a system should also be considered when weighing the decision of a software purchase. Software providers typically invest tens of thousands of hours per year in updating their products to remain current with the industry and available technology. In-house systems can quickly become obsolete if the market changes. Moreover, they are often rendered useless if an issuer wishes to expand into a new asset class. Supporting variations from deal to deal, maintaining the ability to securitize a large portion of a portfolio, adapting to regulatory changes, and keeping pace with modifications to the underlying receivable accounting system are all considerations that must be assessed in line with a potential software purchaser's anticipated securitization plans.

The bottom line is that vendor-supported systems must provide the necessary reduction in operating expenses to mandate purchase. In addition to rewriting or scrapping old systems, there are many questions to be answered even if plans call for issuing only a single deal. How much staff time is required to produce the necessary reports? How much staff time is required to generate the accounting entries? How much incremental staff time does it take to support additional deals? Does the issuer's securitization servicing system preclude launching a new deal fast enough to take advantage of opportune market conditions?

Quality of Output

There is no room for compromise on quality of the system's output. Does the system provide a strictly controlled environment with comprehensive audit trails? Can the entries on investor reports be reconciled with detailed asset level information? How much re-keying of information is required, and what risks does that create? Will the annual audit fare well? If the staff that developed this system moves to other departments, can the system still be supported and/or modified?

The output of the securitization servicing system reflects the competence of an organization to the outside world. Therefore, there should be no compromise when investing in the back-office operations that will make the overall securitization as profitable as anticipated.

FRONT-OFFICE: FINDING THE RIGHT MODELING ENVIRONMENT

For underwriters, investors, rating agencies, credit enhancers, issuers, and any other party wishing to analyze a deal, the ability to model complicated ABS deal structures is important. The only party that may not employ a structuring model to analyze a deal is an investor purchasing senior tranches for which the underlying credit enhancement has decreased the need for sophisticated analytics. In that case, purchases are made based solely on triple-A ratings. But for all other parties, structuring tools are used from a deal's inception through its entire life cycle.

Scenario Analysis

Structuring systems feature the ability to analyze cash flows in a variety of deal structures. The ability to run multiple cash-flow scenario analyses is essential for stress-testing the structure of the deal, sizing the tranches, and pricing. At the most basic level, a user should have the ability to use the standard industry prepayment models (CPR, ABS, SMM, etc.), vary the prepayment speeds, loss and recovery amounts and timing, and delinquency assumptions, among other variables.

More sophisticated systems will allow for modeling sophisticated cash-flow "waterfalls" to multiple tranches, credit enhancement types, and fees. Standard system reports depicting the amortization of each tranche and general statistics such as duration, yield to maturity, convexity, and a price/yield table will significantly reduce an analyst's time in reviewing the output.

Reusability

The reusability of the model is also important. The servicer will require a model for analyzing the anticipated excess servicing fee and for the reprojection of the deal in midlife for the purposes of repricing or adjusting the gain on sale.

Selecting Options

The market for vendor-supported systems for securitization structuring is filled with many participants, unlike the market for any other type of securitization software. In addition to off-the-shelf products, many underwriters have developed in-house, proprietary models. For those who do not use securitization-specific software, spreadsheets are most often the tool of choice. With many options to choose from, how does someone wishing to structure or reverse-engineer an existing deal know what to use? This section discusses the pros and cons of each approach while delineating the basic environments of the vendor-supported systems.

Collateral Capability

Prior to modeling the features of the bond, there are systems requirements surrounding the selection of eligible receivables. Securitization functionality at this stage must allow for assets to be filtered out that do not meet restrictive covenants of a deal. Occasionally, purchasing additional assets that would otherwise make the eligible pool is disallowed due to the increased concentration risk introduced by selecting too many assets with similar characteristics. A robust system has the ability to segregate eligible assets, analyze the performance of those assets both historically and on a forecasted basis, and produce the necessary stratification and cross-tabular reports as needed for a prospectus.

Spreadsheets Versus Vendor-Supported Software

There are many advantages to using a spreadsheet to model an ABS transaction. Spreadsheets are flexible and easy to use. They are relatively inexpensive in terms of upfront, hard-dollar costs compared with the cost of a system designed specifically for securitization. Most people in the financial arena are familiar with spreadsheets and have them readily accessible. Moreover, the output from a spreadsheet model can be used to create attractive reports, graphs, and exhibits.

The disadvantages of a spreadsheet environment may not be as apparent. Spreadsheets offer limited functionality. They were designed for multiple purposes — from maintaining accounting reports to creating graphs to acting as a database application. Securitization-specific software can provide better avenues to communicate the structure of an asset-backed deal once it is modeled. Moreover, a spreadsheet lacks the conveniences of off-the-shelf software. Spreadsheets are not auditable. A stand-alone system, on the other hand, will offer the ability to "freeze" a model once a user decides the model is stable (that is, when the deal has closed). Spreadsheet models are unwieldy with complexity. Often, the person who originally modeled the deal must be present to explain what a spreadsheet is doing. When that person moves on to another deal, he or she may not be able to recall how the old model performed. Finally, a spreadsheet will typically perform much more slowly for a sophisticated deal structure, making it prohibitive in environments that demand a broad scenario analysis. The sum of these all-in costs makes spreadsheets a more expensive alternative for many.

Vendor Software

Up to this point, we have not differentiated the many types of vendor software available. These variations can result in more or less end-user functionality but, in most cases, the biggest difference is in the philosophical approach to deal modeling. The structuring software on the market today has one or more of three basic characteristics: table-driven tools, script-based languages, and object-based environments. The pros and cons of each are discussed below.

Table Driven When a structuring tool houses a data base of tranches, prepayment models, and other variables, it can often model simple deals with ease. One problem with a table-driven system for the securitization market, however, is that deal nuances and new deal structures are constantly emerging. Consequently, the data base of user options may not contain the right deal feature until after that feature has been introduced to the market and incorporated into the software. Alternatively, a new deal structure may result in a change to the fundamental relationship between the elements in multiple tables, rendering the system obsolete for cutting-edge transactions or as structural innovations emerge.

Script-Based These products offer a greater range of flexibility than table-driven modeling tools. However, what they make up for in flexibility they typically lose in ease of use. Often a program is designed in C++ or an equivalent programming language that requires a programmer to construct the deal's payout waterfall. As discussed earlier in this chapter, it is rare to find many individuals who possess both a thorough understanding of ABS and an accomplished programming skill set.

Object-Based Structuring tools that are object-based offer the best of both worlds. While a pallette of standard objects can be found to provide all of the deal features that could otherwise be stored in a data base, this type of product utilizes an open environment to allow for users to create new deal elements as they model. As seen in Exhibit 2, the object-based product has an additional advantage: the flow of funds through the deal is depicted visually, allowing for better communication among parties on how the deal is constructed. The disadvantage to this modeling tool is its newness. While the other types of software have a user base that has made progress up the learning curve, object-based software is not typical in other financial service applications.

Exhibit 2: An Object-Based Structuring Tool

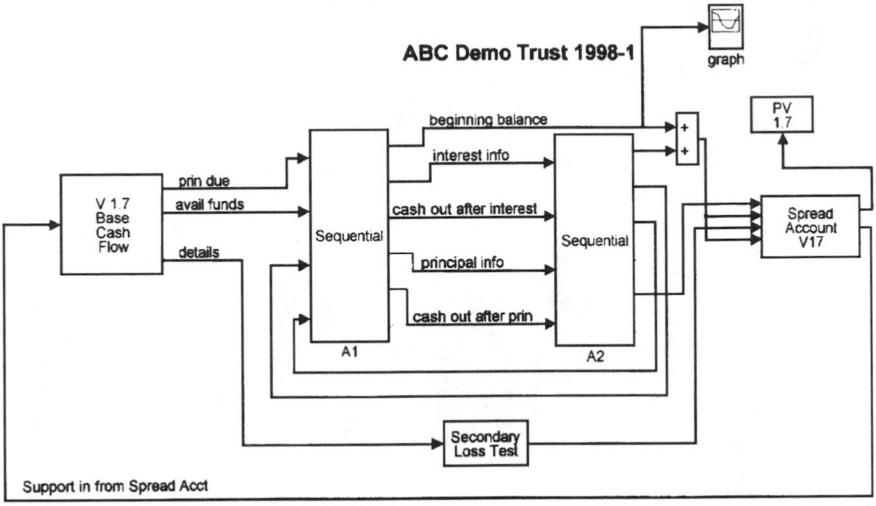

FUTURE TECHNOLOGY DIRECTION IN ABS

What does the future hold for securitization technology? As stated earlier in this chapter, securitization is a highly data-intensive industry. It employs complex, innovative, financial structures. Today's hot new software can rapidly become tomorrow's legacy system. As securitization continues to expand into new asset classes and into international arenas, collateral-tracking, bond-tracking, and deal-structuring software will follow.

For ABS deals backed by commodity-type assets, market efficiency will demand a standardization of data elements describing each deal. Systems that house these asset classes will undergo a process of data normalization as the industry begins to adopt the data standard. The systems currently in place will undergo revisions to simplify the exchange of data among deal participants.

In the end, technology makes the exchange of data and information more efficient and automated.

Chapter 6

Finance Company Transactional Due Diligence

Len Blum
Managing Director
Asset-Backed Finance
Prudential Securities Incorporated

Michael A. Mattera
Associate
Investment Banking
Prudential Securities Incorporated

INTRODUCTION

Due diligence is the process of discovering and analyzing risks, as well as ascertaining that disclosure is adequate. Numerous parties are involved; their respective goals and concerns often are unique. Such parties include investment bankers, lawyers, credit enhancers, investors, rating agencies, accountants, and others. This chapter provides a brief overview of the process. It is not complete or a checklist; it is an overview. Furthermore, issues will vary based on the originator, the servicer, the asset type, the transaction, the parties involved, and the perceived potential risks.

DESCRIPTIVE AND NORMATIVE DUE DILIGENCE

There are two types of due diligence: descriptive and normative. *Descriptive* due diligence is the process through which transaction parties ascertain that disclosure is accurate and complete. *Normative* due diligence focuses on ascertaining that risks are understood and potentially quantified.

Descriptive Due Diligence

The securities laws address descriptive due diligence in Section 17 (a) of the Securities Act of 1933, as amended (the "33 Act"), which states that "it shall be

The authors would like to thank Norman Chaleff of Prudential Securities and Rick Fried of Stroock & Stroock & Lavan for their input and guidance.

unlawful for any person in the offer or sale of any securities...to obtain money or property by means of any untrue statement of a material fact or any omission to state a material fact necessary in order to make the statements made, in the light of the circumstances under which they were made, not misleading."[1] Note that the Securities Act addresses disclosure only, not investment merit. Simply stated, for purposes of the 33 Act, material risk can exist if it is disclosed.

If a security is sold with an untrue statement or an omission of a material fact in its disclosure documentation, "any person acquiring a security registered under the Registration Statement may, pursuant to Section 11 (a) of the 33 Act, sue the issuer, its directors, its principal executive and financial officers, certain experts who participate in preparation of the Registration Statement, and each underwriter."[2] Moreover, liability is absolute: "In connection with a Section 11 cause of action, it is not necessary to prove 'intention' or 'knowledge' with respect to the misstatement or omission..."[3] This means that, for an officer or director of the registrant, even if the statements were made in good faith, if they are untrue, those parties still will be liable.[4]

Non-issuer parties also should ascertain that disclosure is adequate. First, this is good business practice. Second, due diligence may provide a defense against disclosure liability for defendants other than the issuer. For example, an underwriter may avoid disclosure liability if "... a reasonable investigation is conducted, resulting in reasonable grounds to believe, and actual belief by the underwriter, that the registration statement is accurate and valid."[5] "In determining... what constitutes reasonable investigation and reasonable grounds for belief, the standard of reasonableness shall be that required of a prudent man in the management of his own property."[6]

Normative Due Diligence

Normative diligence addresses three issues: risk dynamics, investment appropriateness, and return adequacy. Descriptive diligence is a task for issuers, lawyers, "experts," and underwriters; normative diligence involves additional parties:

- Rating agencies ascertain that ratings adequately describe risk.
- Bankers and investors[7] verify that risks are understood, fairly priced, and appropriate.

---

[1] *SEC Handbook, Volume 1: Securities Act of 1933*, Section 17(a), RR Donnelley Financial International Printing Services, 1996.

[2] *Outline of Due Diligence Investigation Procedures*. Segment of section 11(a) of the Securities Act of 1933.

[3] "Due Diligence: Some Basic Considerations," Stroock & Stroock & Lavan, October 1996.

[4] For purposes of the 33 Act liability, the sponsor of the trust has absolute liability, even though a trust (or other issuance vehicle) may be the literal issuer.

[5] *SEC Handbook, Volume 1: Securities Act of 1933*, Section 11(c).

[6] Ibid.

[7] As used hereinafter, the term "investors" applies to both purchasers of securities and credit enhancers.

Normative diligence fundamentally means constructing the logic chain that leads to the conclusion that, based on facts known at the offering, the investment should perform appropriately to its risk-adjusted pricing, and verifying appropriate chain links. Descriptive diligence is affected by normative diligence; the construction of the chain clarifies what issues should be covered by disclosure. The standard of descriptive due diligence is whether the information would materially affect an investor's decision to participate.

ARCHITECTURE AND DUE DILIGENCE

The transaction's architects must understand the potential risks involved. Structuring is often the optimal response to a risk, especially when structure can mitigate risks to an investor without imposing burdensome costs to an issuer. In other words, structure sometimes can maximize aggregate (for all parties), risk-adjusted present value.

One example of a structural element that addresses specific risk is the "trigger" event. Triggers require that certain procedures occur if prespecified "events" happen. These events are early-warning signs that risk may be increasing. For example, servicing triggers often specify that if a significant deterioration in asset quality, servicing performance, or servicer financial strength occurs, the servicer may be replaced. The documents may further require the backup servicer to be ready to act quickly (a so-called "hot backup"). Accordingly, the hot backup may receive tape updates, and other procedures may occur. If participants believe that servicing risk is manageable, a "cold backup" could be used. A cold backup would take longer to act than a hot backup; therefore, this provision addresses a lower-risk situation.

Collateral triggers can be useful, especially when parties disagree about the risk of pool deterioration. Such triggers can require increased enhancement when it is most needed (for example, by increasing the then-current reserve requirements) or take the form of an early-amortization event.

Outside-event triggers can address specific risks. In a Prudential Securities airline-ticket securitization, for example, an early-amortization event addressed labor-stoppage risk. In the event of a strike, significant pool dilution could occur. Because the Railway Labor Act requires a cooling-off period before a labor stoppage, we addressed this risk by making the inception of a cooling-off period an early-amortization event. This provided a safety net to investors if and when the likelihood of a strike increased.

Concentration limits often are established during due diligence. For example, in a timeshare transaction, the risk of foreign obligors may be identified. Foreign obligors may be risky because of sovereign considerations; and because the receivables are denominated in United States dollars, currency fluctuations could result in increased foreclosure frequency. To address this risk, limits on the aggregate amount of foreign borrowers or borrowers from any one foreign country or specific countries may be used.

INVESTIGATIVE SCOPE

Prior to on-site diligence, gather and analyze general information, list potential risks, and construct a list of contact parties (based on the identified risks). As parties are interviewed and information is gathered, more questions are likely to arise, or new risks may surface. Due to these considerations (and because each transaction is unique), it is inadvisable to have an all inclusive "due diligence list". Instead, questions often arise due to prior inquiry. Careful, active listening skills, experience, and, most of all, common sense are the keys to successful diligence.

Any material risk should be identified and analyzed. This analysis occurs on numerous levels. For example, the selection of credit enhancers, servicers, trustees, and other parties affects the risk profile. The legal, regulatory, economic, and demographic environment also should be considered. The collateral pool also may possess unique risks; it should be stratified and analyzed. Furthermore, a variety of parties may conduct analysis. It is not unusual to rely on "experts." As discussed later in this chapter, accountants, lawyers, appraisers, contract underwriters, and other specialists often are utilized.

TRADE-OFFS: DILIGENCE VERSUS REPRESENTATIONS AND WARRANTIES

If a creditworthy party gives representations and warranties about specific aspects of a transaction, it alleviates concern about those issues. Representations and warranties also can accelerate and/or lower the cost of diligence. Note that issuers often give representations which they are not 100% sure are factual. Why would a party do this? Because representations shift liability; often the only remedy for a breached representation is the repurchase of the affected receivable. So, in planning due diligence, examine representations, warranties, and the sponsor's creditworthiness. Obviously, any risk factors not covered by a creditworthy entity should be diligenced more carefully.

Representations and warranties often are negotiated during structuring. Negotiations regarding specific representations (as well as, in more limited cases, certain affirmative and negative covenants) can occur for a variety of reasons. As discussed, creditworthy risk assumption can significantly accelerate diligence, reduce costs, and shift liability. To transact quickly, a sponsor may grant fairly comprehensive representations. On a more subtle level, the sponsor may grant specific representations (or potentially limited guarantees[8]) to lower cost. Because more risk is retained, less is assumed by investors. And pricing is affected by the risk/reward relationship.

---

[8] Guarantees often are limited to enhance bankruptcy remoteness.

OFFSET DYNAMICS

After an asset is sold in a securitization, events can occur that may reduce the amounts that can be collected. This situation can occur when an obligor has an offsetting claim against the creditor arising from returns, contractual provisions (such as prompt-pay discounts or price-protection agreements), defective merchandise, or other liabilities. Furthermore, risks of legislative and case-law change should be understood. Practical offset often relates to debtor satisfaction. Note that channel dynamics affect risk; for example, if auto loans are purchased from an inadequate dealer, offsets may be significant. Concentrations (both obligor and channel) also affect offset. For example, private-label credit cards with significant retailer concentration(s) have greater risk than bank cards.

THE FALLACY OF BANKRUPTCY REMOTENESS

In securitizations, the "issuer" is, in a sense, the single purpose entity that holds the asset pool. Asset-backed transactions are expected to be bankruptcy remote. Generally, counsel issues an opinion that, in the event of a bankruptcy of the sponsor, the assets neither would or should be considered part of the sponsor's estate, nor would or should the issuer be substantively consolidated with the sponsor. This opinion is not considered law (as in a judicial opinion). Rather, it is the opinion of presumably reputable counsel. It also shifts some liability to the writer of the opinion (or their insurer).

Bankruptcy opinions do not address business risk. They are legal in nature. In reality, risk can increase if the sponsor or servicer (or other important party) becomes bankrupt and/or its credit deteriorates, even if the structure is legally bankruptcy-remote. For example, there may not be a creditworthy party from which to pursue remedies if representations are breached. Servicing may deteriorate or be expected to deteriorate; yet the bankruptcy court may be unwilling to allow servicer replacement. And transferring servicing in such an event could cause pool performance to deteriorate.

A bankruptcy of the seller/servicer can affect practical and legal offset risk. For example, bankruptcy can increase merchandise returns dramatically. If the credit of a sponsor's manufacturing affiliate deteriorates, the value of the underlying collateral and the willingness of obligors to pay may suffer.

Some parties conduct due diligence almost as if the transaction was an issuance of secured debt, not a bankruptcy-remote securitization. While this view may, in many instances, be extreme, it is logical: do not rely blindly on a legal opinion; instead, consider practical consequences of credit deterioration, and construct diligence accordingly.

MARKET DYNAMICS

Consider the market in which the company operates; business practices vary in different competitive environments. For example, subprime lenders currently operate in a market where speed of execution, amount of credit extended, loan tenor, and price often drive high-volume origination. Increasing execution speed beyond capacity, setting credit lines beyond a debtor's means or that which the collateral justifies, or reducing risk-adjusted pricing can spell disaster.

Channel dynamics can impact competitive factors. Wholesale or indirect channels can introduce risk or reduce profitability; originators/sellers[9] "shop" more than consumers do. Such originators/sellers often have an incentive to get the highest possible advance and/or the lowest effective yield. When many competitive buyers for paper exist, price-adjusted risk can increase.

Evaluate the potential for increased competition, and analyze the company appropriately. Barriers to entry and their sustainability can indicate how difficult it is for competition to increase. Expected market size also is important; competition can increase as growth slows. The entrance of securitization into an industry can attract competition.

These questions address market conditions and competition:

- What are the target markets and typical borrower profile(s)?
- What are the issuer's relevant market shares? Are they stable, growing or declining?
- What trends could affect the market (for example, marketing approach, products or services, litigation, government regulations, consolidations)?
- What are the seasonality/cyclicality/periodicity considerations?
- Where are the company's main geographical markets? Does management plan to expand or contract geographically? Why? Is competition geographically fragmented?
- Who are the major competitors for each product line, service or geographic region? How does the company compare?
- What sustainable (and temporary) advantages does the company have and what advantages do its competitors enjoy (for example, costs (for example, scale economies), methods of marketing (for example, cross-selling), expertise/experience, services, quality, and speed)?
- Are competitors expanding? Are competitors having difficulties?
- Is the business obligated by, or does it hold, any non-competition agreements? Have any recently expired or will soon expire?

---

[9] Examples of originators/sellers are dealers (manufactured housing and auto), mortgage brokers (home equity), contractors (home improvement), and developers (timeshares).

MANAGEMENT

It is impossible to overstate the importance of strong management. Management should have direct and relevant experience, preferably with the specific asset type and credit-grade being originated. All key departments — origination, finance, marketing, and servicing — should have experience and depth. Consider performing background investigations on and/or checking references for key personnel. Obtain organizational charts.

Strong incentives — tied to appropriate goals — are important. Inside ownership can provide an economic incentive and decrease the probability of management departures. Incentives should be tied to appropriate goals.

STRATEGY

Business strategy addresses the company's strengths, weaknesses, opportunities, and threats, as well as sources of sustainable competitive advantage (of both the company and its competitors). Business strategy must be understood to address cogently its implementation in functional areas (for example, marketing, underwriting, and servicing).

Channel and product diversification is an important part of strategy. But it can be a double-edged sword. Companies that "stick to their knitting" often are rewarded. Yet diversified originators sometimes enjoy more stable revenues and/or possess enhanced ability to change. Geographic diversification can reduce risk by limiting exposure to regional trends.

FINANCIAL ANALYSIS

Much has been written about financial statement analysis; we will not belabor the point here. However, it is important to note that it is dangerous to apply standard formulas. For example, if the subject has lower capital ratios than the industry average, it does not mean that the company is undercapitalized. Such an analysis must consider the potential risks that the company faces, its potential growth, and its access to funds. Capital is a cushion for mistakes and risk. Therefore, riskier companies (or those with liberal accounting practices) need more capital. Capital also is a base for growth, and should be analyzed in light of the company's plans and opportunities. Ready access to capital and diversification of financing sources mitigates the effects of capital needs, as do other factors. Pay close attention to liquidity; liquidity crises are the single largest cause of finance company failures. Also examine asset and earnings quality (including assumptions used in capitalizing excess servicing and reserve adequacy).

Consider structural subordination. If separate corporate affiliates have varying access to capital, pay careful attention to each entity's responsibilities, including provisions of guarantees, representations, warranties, and indemnifications.

ORIGINATION

Origination areas include marketing, underwriting, collateral valuation (where applicable), and quality control. Determine whether marketing is effective, underwriting is logical and appropriately consistent, appraisals are reasonable, and quality is monitored. Loan quality cannot be analyzed in a vacuum. Risky loans are not bad, per se, if risks are understood, controllable, priced accordingly, and the originator can bear or lay off the risk.

Marketing

The following attributes are positive:

- Marketing procedures are consistent with the company's strategy.
- The company understands its borrowers; its marketing is targeted.
- The company maintains logical, current pricing guidelines.
- Borrower screening is efficient and thorough.
- Marketing is efficient and can adapt to change.

Focused marketing results from cogent strategy. The type of loan and borrower that the company's internal policies, processes, and systems accommodate also should be compatible with strategy.

Determine the current marketing activities and analyze changes. For example, if a company changes focus to lower-credit borrowers or reduces price, focus on the need for increased servicing efforts and effects on profitability.

Marketing should be flexible. Companies alter strategies, create new products, and attempt to meet changing customer needs. If the industry is changing and the company is not, asset quality and/or effective portfolio yield could be impacted.

The following questions assess marketing strategy:

- Who are the company's customers?
- What are their needs?
- How is each product sold and/or distributed (i.e., direct sales, third parties, direct mail, telemarketing)?
- How has this changed over time?
- Why do customers borrow from the company?

Other key aspects of market-strategy assessment include:

- Price/rebates/incentives.
- User-friendliness.
- Post-purchase service.
- Product offering.
- Advertising/effect of sales effort/market presence.
- Existing relationships/cross-selling.

UNDERWRITING

Understand the company's underwriting philosophy. What factors does it consider important? Does it use credit scoring, objective criteria and/or subjective criteria? It can be helpful to ask an underwriter to explain the analysis for a given group of loans.

Personnel and departmental organization are important. Analyze the background and experience of underwriters. In growing markets, experienced personnel are scarce, and experienced underwriters (and servicers) can be critical to quality. Effective approval authority should exist, and training should be adequate. If guideline exceptions are made, the process (including approval authority) should be reviewed.

Approval analysis should be crisp. Processing that is too rapid can cause portfolio deterioration. Conversely, if the issuer is slow or disorganized, frustrated, qualified borrowers may shop elsewhere, which may leave the issuer with customers that cannot otherwise borrow. Speed should be consistent with industry standards in light of the originator's efficiency.

Many companies purchase loans from other originators on bulk, minibulk or flow bases. Loans can be closed in the name of the originator or a third party. Each procedure creates its own particular risks.

Examine purchase procedures. Some originators re-underwrite all loans, while others use statistical samples. Both procedures can be appropriate. Also evaluate the procedures used to re-underwrite.

Compare purchase standards with retail criteria. If standards vary significantly, the company may be buying loans that it does not understand or cannot service appropriately.

Understand third-party procedures and standards for approving correspondents. A third party's experience, reputation, and financial viability can be reliable indicators of loan quality. Third-party actions also can affect performance. For example, home-improvement loans originated through contractors that stand behind their high-quality work perform. If quality is shoddy, borrowers may become frustrated and refuse to pay. Examine the following:

- Underwriting guidelines (which usually are published).
- Internal approval procedures.
- Consistency of underwriting standards.
- Procedures for overriding guidelines.
- Procedures for reviewing the appropriateness of underwriting criteria
- Process for valuing underlying collateral (if applicable).
- Internal quality control mechanisms in place (such as loan reunderwriting and verification of borrower information).

Approval rates address the conservatism of the underwriting process (as well as marketing focus). A relatively high approval rate may signal that a company has reduced underwriting standards to originate more loans.

The following questions address underwriting:

- Does the company underwrite subjectively or strictly to specified criteria? Is credit scoring used?
- What is the general philosophy and approach to pricing? What is documented? Does price compensate for risk?
- What are the normal terms given on loans? Are amortization periods, advance rates and documentation criteria rigid or only a starting point?
- Who is ultimately responsible for decisions?
- What is the background of a typical underwriter?
- Is there a training program?

COLLATERAL VALUATION

For certain products, particularly those enjoying liens on real properties, appraisal quality can be critical. Generally, the more the lender's underwriting policies rely on collateral, the more important it is to value that collateral correctly. Collateral reliance often increases (decreases) as borrower creditworthiness decreases (increases).

In home-equity lending, lenders generally use independent appraisers. This is appropriate. Regional expertise is required, and high loan volume is necessary to justify staff appraisers in many locations.

A formal process should exist to review each appraisers' experience, credentials, and reputation. All appraisers should be properly licensed and monitored. Appraisers should have knowledge of the property types with which and the areas in which they are working.

The company should maintain an "approved" appraiser list with requirements for remaining on that list. It should be clear what type of appraisal errors or other issues cause removal from the list.

Understand how appraisers are selected for particular loans. The individual or broker originating the loan should not exert control. During the quality control process, a random sampling of properties should be reappraised. Reappraisals should occur regularly, be analyzed by appraiser, and affect eligibility for the approved appraiser list.

QUALITY CONTROL

The quality control department is important; it monitors underwriting and appraisal quality. Additionally, the quality control department establishes policies for reviewing the conformity of new employees and third-party originators and monitors with industry standards and company guidelines. The quality control department should be staffed by experienced personnel and have a separate reporting function to avoid conflicts of interest. Internal quality control reports should be generated on a monthly basis, at minimum, and reviewed by senior management.

INTERNAL SYSTEMS

Systems diligence focuses on the accuracy, integration, and effectiveness of the system. A quality data processing system has the following attributes:

- Utilizes current technology.
- Is expandable to accommodate higher loan volume.
- Has adaptability.
- Meets servicing needs of the specific collateral.
- Is compatible with the origination arm and the servicing arm.
- Has appropriate backup and disaster recovery procedures.

An issuer with old technology is not necessarily in trouble, but it could be delaying purchases. Future changes could create a servicing interruption, which may negatively impact delinquencies.

SERVICING AND COLLECTIONS

Good servicers are oriented to their borrower types. In sub-prime lending, servicing is often the most crucial aspect of collateral performance. Sub-prime borrowers need proactive servicing, including frequent customer calls, follow-up, late notices and notification of intent to foreclose. A prime servicer may have difficulty adjusting to the focused approach required for sub-prime borrowers.

Servicers often are tested by the performance and loss mitigation of their serviced portfolio. The servicer should have experience servicing each particular type of product. A servicer incorporating a new product into its portfolio should be scrutinized closely due to lack of experience and potential systems shortfalls. A servicer proficient in one product type may not have immediate proficiency with another.

Increased sub-prime volume has created the need for large servicing platforms and increased staffing. Determine if the ratio of servicers and collectors to borrowers is within industry standards; however, note that a servicer can operate competently at a lower ratio if it is efficient.

Generally, tools and procedures that organize servicing and/or enhance information flow increase efficiency dramatically. One example is the automated, predictive dialing system. Another example is the tracking of borrower calls and servicing effectiveness.

Pay attention to the workout and collection effort. This group determines if borrowers are suitable for payment restructurings, or if foreclosures will maximize recovery. For example, with mortgage loans, payment restructurings may make more sense for loans with high loan-to-value ratios. Assistance should be provided to borrowers that are experiencing financial distress but are expected to ultimately recover. For example, in a small business loan the borrower may have suffered from an illness but the underlying business remains strong. Borrowers that seem unlikely to cure should be encouraged to sell the properties prior to foreclosure. Review statistics on the number of borrowers that adhere to restructurings.

Foreclosure and bankruptcy units should be experienced and have access to attorney networks. Examine the duration of the foreclosure process by state relative to industry standards. With mortgage loans, the effectiveness of the real estate owned group will affect loss severity. Properties should be sold in the shortest amount of time for the highest possible price. With auto loans, assess the disposition process. Time to sale and recovery rates should be reviewed and compared with industry standards.

The servicer may also have a responsibility in investor accounting and reporting. The servicer should understand the accounting group's responsibilities. If a master servicing arrangement exists, reporting must be crisp to allow the master servicer to review documents and remit appropriate funds to the trustee and, ultimately, the investor.

DATA ANALYSIS

Analyze the issuer/servicer's historical performance data, both on loan performance and prepayment levels. In particular, static pool analysis can offer tremendous insights. In such an analysis, specific loans, originated during a certain time period are isolated, and their performance is tracked. These pools isolate loan performance; growth and change in a dynamic pool can mask performance. For example, in a growing portfolio, if losses are lower early in a loan's life, losses will be understated.

Calculate expected loss and prepayment curves during static pool analysis. These can be used as vectors to estimate performance in stress scenarios.

Compare static pool data with industry standards. Also, understand a pool's behavior over time. For example, increased losses in certain months may be due to collateral deterioration. Decreased losses may be due to lower than expected loan-to-value ratios caused by collateral appreciation. Static pools from different time periods should be compared. If performance has changed from period to period, analyze the cause of the changes. It could be the result of changed underwriting guidelines, external factors, and/or servicing effects.

Understand definitions of delinquency and chargeoff. Not all companies apply the same definitions to these terms. Delinquencies can be on contractual or recency bases. Due dates relative to delinquency-measurement dates and definitions of delinquency tenor can affect performance data. Charge off policies (for example, a specified aging, foreclosure, or subjective judgment) can increase (decrease) delinquencies, thereby decreasing (increasing) periodic losses.

POOL ANALYSIS

Perform a data integrity check to ensure that loan-level information is accurate.[10] Pick a random sample of loan files and compare the data on the loan tape to the individual files. For certain assets or data fields, data will be tied to internal management reports (i.e., not the loan files). Check that these reports are credible. Consider verifying with borrowers that loans exist. For illustrative purposes, we have listed some of the data that should be checked in a typical home equity pool:

- Customer name.
- State in which the home collateral is located.
- Original loan amount.
- Interest rate (APR).
- Original number of payments.
- Amount of periodic payment.
- Original loan-to-value ratio.
- First payment date.

Aggregate values also are verified and comforted. The following is a general list of data in a home-equity transaction:

- The number and aggregate unpaid principal balance of loans in the pool.
- The number and aggregate unpaid principal balance of loans that were (a) originated by the issuer and (b) originated by third parties and purchased by the issuer.
- The number of states represented in the pool.
- The weighted-average term to scheduled maturity of the loans.
- The final scheduled payment date of the loan(s) with the latest maturity.
- The earliest and latest dates of origination.
- The lowest and highest term to scheduled maturity.
- The average outstanding principal balance.
- The weighted-average loan-to-value ratio at origination.
- The number of loans, the aggregate principal balance outstanding, and the percentage of the total pool by outstanding principal balance for each of the following tables:
  Geographical distribution of collateral.
  Years of origination.
  Distribution of original principal amount.
  Distribution of original loan-to-value ratios.
  Coupon rates.
  Remaining months to maturity.

---

[10] This can be done by a number of parties. If a surety is used, the bond insurer, as well as the accountants, will do the required verification. If a surety is not used, an outside accounting firm will perform the analysis alone.

- The greatest original loan amount and percentage it represents of the aggregate principal balance of the loans at origination.
- Comparison of the number of loans, dollar amounts, and percentages as listed under the following tables in the disclosure document to the corresponding information contained in or summarized from the general accounting records of the issuer:
  Loan origination.
  Loan servicing portfolio.
  Delinquency experience.
  Loan loss experience.

Accountants write "agreed-upon procedures" letters that compare the tape data with the information presented in the prospectus. Compare the transaction's statistics to previous pools originated by the issuer, the pools from which static performance curves were derived, and industry standards.

Lawyers are hired to give various opinions. To do this, lawyers conduct a legal review of official documents of the issuer such as the certificate of incorporation, by-laws, indentures, loan agreements, and other debt agreements. These agreements often contain negative covenants that can conflict with the securitization. In such event, appropriate consents or waivers may have to be obtained. In addition, legal counsel should examine thoroughly any past or pending litigation involving the issuing company. The importance of that litigation for disclosure should be decided by both counsel and the underwriter. All original-document information must agree with the information provided in the prospectus.

In addition, counsel should also opine that the proper corporate formalities have been addressed and that entering into the transaction does not conflict with any other agreement to which they are a party. The lawyers should also provide a 10b-5 opinion that the prospectus does not contain any untrue statement or an omission of a material fact.

Chapter 7

The Role of the Trustee in Asset-Backed Securitization

Karen Cook
Assistant Vice President
Bankers Trust Company

F. Jim Della Sala
Principal
Bankers Trust Company

INTRODUCTION

The role of the trustee originated during the early years of the mortgage loan industry's development and evolved out of the need for an individual to represent the collective interests of investors who held direct interests in defaulted or foreclosed mortgages. A bank was appointed as trustee for a bond issued under a trust indenture for the first time in 1839. Although the duties of the trustee were minimal, the benefits to naming an institution, rather than an individual, as trustee was a significant step in the development and expansion of the functions of the trustee.

As transactions became more complex and more first-time issuers entered the marketplace, the number of defaulted bonds in the industry increased. The role of the trustee adapted to these changes by assuming additional responsibilities under the trust indenture. This empowered the trustee to better protect the interests of bondholders in default scenarios. Institutions offering corporate trust services found it necessary to create separate corporate trust departments within their organization and to more carefully evaluate their responsibilities as a trustee. As a result, standard policies and business practices were developed to protect their own interests as well. The SEC passed the Trust Indenture Act of 1939, which defines the eligibility requirements for a trustee and guidelines on the standard conduct of a trustee.[1]

Many different types of trustees exist in the asset-backed industry. They can be broadly categorized as indenture, owner, off-shore, and successor. The role of trustees are basically the same for all trustee types. The main responsibility of the trustee is to represent the interest of the securityholders, particularly during an

[1] Robert I. Landau, *Corporate Trust Administration and Management, 4th Ed.* (New York: Columbia University Press, 1992), pp. 51-54.

event of default. Other responsibilities of the trustee include monitoring covenant compliance, authentication of the asset-backed securities, and enforcement of remedies during an event of default as defined in the governing documents.

"TYPES" OF TRUSTEES

Indenture Trustee

Some of the administrative functions of the indenture trustee include monitoring the cash flow, account reconciliation, investment of funds held in trust accounts, custody of securities for the benefit of securityholders, holding security interest in the assets, and payment of principal, interest and trust expenses on the distribution date.

The trustee should monitor the transaction proactively throughout the life of the transaction. The trustee receives periodic reports from the servicer which detail principal paydown, collections, defaults, and delinquencies of the receivables pool. By reviewing these reports, the trustee can identify potential trigger events or servicer defaults. The trustee evaluates whether the form of the reports and opinions required to be delivered by the other parties to the transaction conform to the requirements of the governing documents. These governing documents also specify how a trustee should proceed after being notified of any triggers or events of default.

Owner Trustee

An owner trustee holds legal title to the owner trust estate which includes funds on deposit in trust accounts and all other property of the trust. The owner trustee represents the interest of certificateholders who own trust certificates evidencing their beneficial interest to the trust estate. In an owner trust structure, the indenture trustee represents the beneficial interests of the noteholders and retains the typical duties of an indenture trustee pursuant to the trust indenture.

Off-Shore Trustee

The appointment of an off-shore trustee is most common in cross border securitizations originated by issuers located in countries within Latin America, Europe or Asia. A special purpose entity, which purchases the assets for the receivables pool and issues the asset-backed securities, is established in an off-shore location such as the Cayman or Jersey Islands. The transaction documents are generally governed under the local trust law (where the trust is established). Collections generated from the receivables are deposited in off-shore trust accounts which are held by the off-shore trustee much like an indenture trustee. The off-shore trustee receives and invests funds and makes periodic disbursements as directed by the servicer.

An institution must meet specific qualifications in order to become an off-shore trustee. The requirements varies for each off-shore location; however, a corporate trust office must be established within the country's jurisdiction in order to receive local corporate trust powers.

Successor Trustee

A successor trustee is appointed if the original trustee either resigns or is removed from a transaction. The successor trustee inherits the same duties and responsibilities as the original trustee named in the documents. The successor trustee must coordinate with the departing trustee to transfer trust accounts, notify the securityholders, and coordinate with the servicer and depository of any revisions to instructions pertaining to collections and distributions.

AGENCY APPOINTMENTS

The appointment as trustee is typically packaged with related agency appointments of registrar, paying agent, and successor servicer. In addition, because of the sophisticated nature of asset-backed securities, the trustee is often asked to perform "non-traditional" roles in order to increase the marketability of the securities. These enhanced agency roles include calculation agent, document custodian, tax reporting agent, and back-up servicer.

Registrar

The primary responsibility of the registrar is to maintain a current record of registered securityholders and to process exchanges and registrations of transfers. Unlike the expanding role of the trustee in asset-backed transactions, the day-to-day responsibilities of the registrar have decreased over time. This is a result of the increased issuance of (fully registered) book-entry certificates instead of physical certificates. For book-entry issues, the securities are registered as a global certificate in the nominee name of the depository (i.e., Cede & Co. for The Depository Trust Company), and the registrar treats the nominee as the sole registered holder. The depository maintains the records of the participants and their corresponding holdings of the asset-backed securities. The depository is also responsible for sending notices and copies of servicer reports to investors and for effecting certificate or position transfers.

Paying Agent

A few days prior to the distribution date, the paying agent receives a servicer report from the servicer specifying the payment instructions for the distribution date. Either on or prior to the distribution date, the paying agent receives the full distribution amount from the servicer. On the distribution date, principal and interest payments to securityholders and other disbursements are made by the paying agent.

As with the role of the registrar, the role of the paying agent has narrowed in scope with the widespread issuance of (fully registered) book-entry certificates. On each distribution date, the entire principal and interest distribution amount is sent (via fedwire) by the paying agent to the depository for further distribution to the ultimate beneficial holders of the asset-backed securities.

Successor or Back-Up Servicer

A primary duty of the trustee is to assume the role of successor servicer in the event that the original servicer is removed or terminated.[2] The trustee is most likely to be required to step in as the successor servicer if there is an event of servicer default and subsequent termination and removal of the servicer. The successor servicer ensures that collections and other cash flows remain uninterrupted and that distributions continue to be paid to securityholders.

Some asset-backed transactions designate a separate entity in the governing documents, usually the trustee, as the back-up servicer. These types of situations generally arise for asset-backed transactions in which the issuer or servicer has a low credit rating or for transactions securitizing new or unique asset types. An additional level of monitoring of the servicer may be required in order for the transaction to obtain an investment grade rating.

Usually, the back-up servicer assumes the responsibility of reviewing and reverifying calculations on the servicer report. Prior to a servicer termination event, the back-up servicer may also run parallel reporting along with the existing servicer. The back-up servicer may also receive tapes from the servicer on a monthly basis and recalculate specific data contained in the servicer reports. The back-up servicer must be ready to immediately assume the role of the servicer should it become necessary.

The essential requirements for a back-up servicer include sophisticated systems, collection expertise, and an analytical staff to fulfill the servicing duties. The back-up servicer should examine the servicer's collection and reporting system for compatibility with its own internal asset servicing system. The back-up servicer should develop a plan for the migration of the receivable information onto its asset servicing system as well as determining how to monitor and manage ongoing contractual trigger events. The back-up servicer should schedule periodic on-site reviews of servicing facilities. It also must review the cash management procedures in regard to the asset collection and lockbox processing.

The trustee should identify any servicer advancing responsibilities for delinquent payments on the receivables or for the repurchase of non-conforming receivables and should evaluate any credit issues or conflicts which might arise with these advancing responsibilities. In some instances, where advancing is a requirement under the pooling and servicing agreement, the servicer or issuer is required to establish a reserve account with the trustee on the closing date and maintain a specified reserve balance for the duration of the transaction.

In certain situations, where the successor or back-up servicer is unable to fulfill all or part of the administrative and/or operational requirements internally, it may engage the services of a third-party vendor. The appointment of a third-party vendor does not replace the successor or back-up servicer's liability or contractual obligations on the transaction; however, through the engagement of a third-party vendor, some or all of the relevant administrative duties can be outsourced.

---

[2] The successor servicer is also known as "servicer of last resort".

Oftentimes, for a revolving asset type, an event of servicer termination will trigger the liquidation of the assets in the receivables pool and the final distribution payment to securityholders. Although this may not preclude the trustee from having to step in as successor servicer, it may eliminate some of the servicing, collection, and advancing responsibilities.

The appointment of a successor or back-up servicer on an asset-backed transaction adds value to the transaction by providing assurances to the rating agencies and investors that the collections and application of funds will continue uninterrupted regardless of economic distress of the servicer. Obviously, every attempt is made by the original servicer to avoid its removal from the transaction. The repercussions to the servicer of being terminated would include, but certainly not be limited to, a rating downgrade and a negative implication on the issuer's reputation in the asset-backed industry.

Document Custodian

A document custodian holds custody documents which typically represent the ownership interest in the underlying assets. These documents may be tangible assets such as notes, mortgages, and/or titles relating to the sale of assets to the trust or intangible assets such as collateral held in trust accounts (i.e., a letter of credit) which may be part of the credit enhancement for the transaction.

The custodian is often required to perform an initial review of the files to verify that certain documents are located in the files and to certify that information on the documents correspond to a master list description. The custodian, however, will not attest to the authenticity of the documents within the files. The custodian will also add trailing documents to files to cure exceptions, release files upon request, and provide periodic reports relating to the assets held in custody.

For warehouse lines, the role of the custodian may be enhanced to include cash management (account maintenance, wire transfers, and investments) for fundings and/or settlements, borrowing base calculation, and additional online reporting services.

Calculation Agent

The calculation agent receives collateral data from the servicer in a computer readable format. The data is validated by applying either basic or enhanced duc diligence criteria, and is aggregated according to the specific transaction's requirements. Structured cash flow projection models are then used to periodically calculate and produce reports that describe distribution amounts to the various classes of securities issued within the transaction.

Tax Reporting Agent

The tax reporting agent ensures that annual tax returns are prepared and filed for the special purpose entity or trust issuing the asset-backed securities. Additionally, the tax reporting agent calculates any reportable original issue discount or premium on the asset pool in accordance with provisions of the Internal Revenue Code, as well as prepare, sign, and file the federal and state tax returns and all related schedules.

TRUSTEE'S ROLE IN THE LIFE OF AN ABS TRANSACTION

Pre-Closing

Upon appointment as trustee on an asset-backed transaction, the trustee receives (usually from the issuer's counsel) draft copies of the governing documents with related exhibits and the term sheet. The trustee's primary focus is to determine its specific duties and responsibilities for the asset-backed transaction. The trustee engages the services of either external or in-house counsel to review the legal aspects and risks associated with the trustee appointment.

When reviewing the governing documents, the trustee focuses on sections of the documents relating to the mechanics of the transaction, its duties, language relating to the perfection of security interest in the collateral, representations and warranties, incumbency language, indemnification and gross negligence (exculpatory) clauses, and event of default triggers and remedies. The trustee will review the events that would trigger the removal of the servicer, how the securityholders are notified, and the timing and procedures to step in as successor servicer. The trustee will also evaluate the servicing fee to ensure that it would be appropriately compensated for its services, should it become the successor servicer.

Numerous trust accounts need to be set-up by the trustee prior to closing. At the very least, collection and distribution accounts are required. All trust accounts for the transaction are registered in the name of the trustee for the benefit of the securityholders. Depending upon the transaction structure, a reserve account and/or collateral account may also be established and maintained by the trustee.

The servicer will open one or more lockbox accounts for the daily or periodic receipt of collections generated from the receivables. Although these accounts are maintained and operated by the servicer, these accounts are also registered in the name of the trustee and the trustee has the right, upon a servicer termination event, to direct the lockbox account provider to terminate the servicer's access to these accounts.

As part of its internal approval process, the trustee may conduct an internal credit review of the issuer and servicer before accepting an appointment as trustee. The review process typically includes reviewing financials of the servicer and issuer, their operating and management structure, company history, and operational capability.

If successor or back-up servicing is required, the trustee determines its ability to service assets in-house or its need to outsource the servicing to a third-party vendor. Also, as part of the servicing review, the trustee evaluates its own systems compatibility with the servicer's systems. The trustee may request an on-site due diligence tour of the servicing operations.

Closing

At closing, the trustee authenticates and delivers securities, executes the governing documents, and delivers the Trustee Certificate. The trustee also receives the initial funding into the trust accounts, which represents proceeds from the sale of the asset-backed securities to investors. An incumbency certificate from the issuer identifies the officers of the company who are authorized to direct the trustee to make investments and transfer funds held in trust accounts.

Post-Closing

The trustee is responsible for the periodic receipt of funds from the servicer which represent collections generated from the receivables. The servicer notifies the trustee of the amount which is to be deposited into each trust account and provides the trustee with investment instructions for the trust account balances. The eligible investments section of the governing documents defines the permitted investments for the trust funds.

Prior to each distribution date, the servicer sends the trustee a servicing report instructing the trustee of the disbursements to be made on the distribution date. The trustee may be responsible for providing copies of the servicing report to the securityholders, rating agencies, and credit enhancement providers. On each payment date, the trustee makes principal and interest payments to securityholders and pays servicing and other miscellaneous fees related to the transaction as specified in the servicer report.

Deal Defaults

If the trustee is notified of or obtains actual knowledge of a trigger event or an event of default, the governing documents specify the required steps to be taken. The bankruptcy or insolvency of the issuer or servicer are typical events which may result in an event of default. Furthermore, this may trigger a downgrading of the asset-backed security.

A possible repercussion from an event of default is the removal of the servicer. The trustee must be prepared to take over the servicing responsibilities which would include taking over the collection process. A trigger event may trigger the liquidation of assets and/or the amortization of notes. Should there be bankruptcy proceedings, the trustee's primary responsibility is to represent the beneficial interests of the securityholders and protect the "true sale" nature of the receivables.

Deal Termination

Generally, a provision in the governing documents allows for a "clean-up" call on the remaining principal balance of securities when the principal amount outstanding falls below a specified threshold of the original issuance amount.[3] The issuer will notify the trustee of the details regarding the final distribution date, including the

---

[3] Usually this is 10% of the original principal balance.

final distribution amount, the payment of fees and expenses and the transfer of interest on remaining assets, receivables, investments, and cash. The trustee will notify the securityholders of the final distribution date and the final distribution amount.

TRUSTEE RISKS

Inherent to any business arrangement is the risk to the parties involved in the transaction. Other than the investor, the trustee on an asset-backed securitization is subject to the most amount of risk. There are three different types of risks for the trustee: servicer non-performance, faulty transaction structure, and operational errors.

Servicer Non-Performance

After an asset-backed securitization closes, the trustee and the servicer of the assets are normally the only entities that retain any ongoing contractual duties. The trustee's day-to-day duties are dependent on getting timely and accurate information from the servicer. Additionally, the trustee may ultimately become the successor servicer if the existing servicer defaults on its contractual responsibilities.

Timely and Accurate Reporting of the Servicer

The trustee on an asset-backed securitization is responsible for taking direction from authorized individuals of the servicer for the investments and distributions made by the trustee. The operational timeframes in the transactions are structured very tightly to minimize the time between payments on the underlying assets and the principal and interest distributions to the securityholders. The trustee is reliant on the servicer for providing underlying asset payment information and determining distribution amounts to be paid on the next succeeding distribution date. If the servicer does not get the distribution information to the trustee in the designated timeframe, the trustee may not be able to make payments to the securityholders on the expected distribution date. Since the securityholders generally associate late payments as a "trustee problem," potential for future business for the trustee could be affected.

With asset-backed securitizations that are structured with a revolving period, the servicer is continuously[4] authorizing the trustee to transfer funds from the collection account to the asset funding account. Even in amortizing transactions, the trustee receives payment directions at least monthly. If the trustee receives erroneous directions, funds may be disbursed incorrectly. The trustee, after receiving notification of an incorrect payment direction by the servicer, is responsible for correcting the mistake. A servicer that continuously makes mistakes in its payment directions to the trustee will create additional work for the trustee which may cause the transaction to become unprofitable.

---

[4] In credit card transactions it is common for there to be daily funding, which are directed by the servicer.

Successor Servicing

A major risk to which the trustee is exposed is the risk that a servicer termination event occurs. This may require the trustee to assume the role of primary servicer. Asset-backed securitizations typically prohibit resignation by the servicer. When the role of servicing the assets is transferred to the trustee or a successor servicer, the portfolio is typically underperforming, servicing records are incomplete, and significant operational remediation is required.

The trustee may confront a situation which the original servicing fees no longer cover the expenses incurred for servicing the portfolio adequately.[5] Unless cash reserves or additional servicing fees exist in the transaction, the trustee may be required to cover the servicing fee shortfall in the transaction. If advancing on delinquent accounts is required of the servicer, the successor servicer, may lack the appetite for exposing its own capital for the benefit of the securityholders. The trustee may choose to delay the transfer of servicing until the remaining transaction participants (securityholders, bond insurer, and possibly the issuer/servicer) agree to cover all servicing fee shortfalls and servicer advances.

If the trustee does not have the internal expertise or infrastructure to service the assets in the transaction, it may hire a third-party servicer to service the assets. A third-party servicer may also be hired because the trustee does not have the proper legal or regulatory authorization in the location (state, county or city) of the obligor to service the assets. Thorough due diligence of the third-party servicer is very important in selecting the successor servicer by the trustee. The trustee's responsibility and liability, as named successor or back-up servicer, is normally not subrogated if a third-party entity is hired.

Faulty Transaction Structure

The transaction structure of an asset-backed securitization must be legally sound and must adequately distinguish the duties and responsibilities of each of the transaction parties in a clear and logical manner. If the legality of the transaction is challenged by any individual or governing authority, such as a Bankruptcy Court, the trustee must defend the true sale aspect of the transaction on behalf of the securityholders. A major concern of the securityholders is that the trust maintains a security interest in the underlying assets and that the entity status of the trust remains intact. The trustee is additionally concerned that the governing documents do not unnecessarily burden the transaction parties in performing their duties and responsibilities.

Operational Errors

Because of the complexities of an asset-backed securitization, the trustee is at greater risk of an operational error than on a typical capital markets transaction.

[5] This can be further exasperated when, as is the case in the majority of transactions, the servicing fees are calculated as percentage of the declining balance of the assets over time. Unfortunately, the costs for servicing the assets are not declining over time.

Operational errors may include an incorrect or missed distribution, misapplication of funds between transaction participants, incorrect investment of funds, lost collateral documentation, and the untimely or missed notification of a significant event.

On most asset-backed securitizations, the trustee receives distribution information from the servicer as part of the servicer's monthly report. An incorrect distribution may cause negative arbitrage causing shortages in funds to cover debt service for the expected life of the security. Unless the distributions are carefully calculated by the servicer, a mistake may not be identified immediately which could result in a significant claim against the trust.

If the income earned on invested cash is used to support the transaction's flow of funds, it becomes critical that the trustee invest the funds correctly. If the funds are not invested in a timely manner by the trustee, the payments to the underlying securityholders may be affected. Furthermore, if the trustee invests funds outside the acceptable investment criteria of the transaction, the trustee could expose the trust to investment losses.

To maintain the security interest in many asset-backed securitizations, the servicer is required to file UCC continuation statements and safekeep evidence of security title (notes, mortgages, titles, etc.). If there is a lapse in a UCC continuation filing, it is conceivable that the lien priority of the security may be lost or reduced. If the documented evidence of title or security interest is lost or misplaced, the obligor could petition a court to eliminate the indebtedness.

The trustee disseminates, as required under the governing documents, all pertinent information that it may acquire regarding the underlying assets, servicer[6] or other matters having a material effect on the investors. If the trustee does not forward beneficial information to the investors, that gives the investors notice to take action which may benefit them, then the trustee may be held accountable.

Many of the risks the trustee must address on an asset-backed securitization could cause severe economical hardship for the trustee.

TRUSTEE QUALIFICATIONS

Trustee qualifications are very stringent in the asset-backed market and contribute to the relative small number of market participants. Trustees must meet certain regulatory qualifications and minimum capitalization requirements. Qualified trustees must also have a well-seasoned and trained staff with securitization experience and knowledge of a variety of asset types and transaction structures. Additionally, trustees must invest significantly in operations processes and systems technology to process these complicated transactions. Successful trustees must also be able to demonstrate a commitment to the trust business that can be measured by the management resources and control infrastructure dedicated to asset-backed securitizations.

---

[6] The trustee is normally required to receive quarterly financials and annual audit reports from the servicer.

Regulatory and Capitalization Requirements

Depending on the bank charter and state domicile of the trustee, the trustee may be regulated by a number of agencies including, but not limited to, the appropriate state banking authority, FDIC, Federal Reserve, and The Office of the Controller of the Currency. Additionally, the Trust Indenture Act of 1939 ("TIA"), as amended, establishes requirements for trustees of most public offerings in excess of $10,000,000. These requirements cover minimum net worth of trustees, standard of care limits, conflict of interest rules, and regulatory reporting requirements. Since most asset-backed securitizations are structured such that the investor is holding certificates of interests in the underlying assets, as opposed to debt, they are generally exempt from the TIA. Although it may not be a legal requirement, trustees may still be required to meet the TIA requirements.

The combined capital and surplus requirements of the trustee by the TIA are set at a very minimal amount of $150,000. Many transaction structures of an asset-backed securitizations have a much more restrictive capital requirement of $50,000,000 or greater. Additionally, many transaction structures require the trustee to maintain a principal office location in New York City.[7]

Staffing Requirements

Because of the high degree of specialization and complexity associated with the asset-backed securitization industry, proper staffing by the trustee is a critical success factor for ongoing administration of the transaction. Qualified trustees should have experienced account managers with a proven record of administering similar structured transactions and a familiarity of the specific asset type. Additionally, the ongoing administration of the transaction should be performed by trust officers who have received significant training in trust administration, trust banking systems, ethical business practices and customer service.

If the trustee is performing additional functions (tax reporting agent, bond calculation agent, backup servicer, etc.) it is also important that the trustee staff demonstrate an appropriate amount of expertise in each of those areas.

Operations and Technology

Providing trust services to the asset-backed securitization market is a demanding operational and technological proposition. Large scale trustee participants have an immense operational staff to handle the intricate securities processing requirements of asset-backed transactions. This includes providing registrar and bond recordkeeping services, funds disbursements, and document custodian services.

Sophisticated computer systems are required to support the trustee in providing services to asset-backed marketplace. The funds disbursement systems must be able to process thousands of simultaneous transactions for the proper distribution of funds on the bond distribution date. The trustee must have links to all major

---

[7] Some asset-backed securitizations have required the trustee to maintain offices in California.

clearing organizations (CEDEL, Euroclear, DTC, PTC, etc.) to ensure the swift movement of moneys to the correct corresponding entities. Additionally, significant technological resources are needed to support the tickler system that computerizes many of the administrative follow-up items required of the trustee. Advanced technology, including imaging, is required to support the evolving document custody process, while a flexible technology architecture is needed to handle the complexities associated with the tax reporting and bond payment calculation agent functions. Since many of these services and products are now required to be offered online or via the Internet, trustees need to maintain up-to-date technologies.

Commitment to Trust Business

Because of the staffing, operational, and technological commitments, coupled with a steady declining pricing environment, many trustees have decided to exit the corporate trust business. The remaining trust entities must continue to invest in superior technology and a knowledgeable staff to remain viable market participants. Additionally, to minimize risk to themselves and ensure appropriate service to clients, the trustee must have a significant control and management oversight infrastructure. This includes appropriate transaction acceptance procedures and ongoing self assessment and deal review procedures. Trustees who are committed to the asset-backed securitization sector will continue to invest significant resources and examine ways to institute best practices across all trust business functions.

Chapter 8

Identifying Relative Value in the ABS Market

Lisa N. Wilhelm
Managing Director
Head of Fixed-Income Research
First Chicago Capital Markets, Inc.

W. Alexander Roever, CFA
Director
ABS Research
First Chicago Capital Markets, Inc.

INTRODUCTION

For bond investors, relative value is a beautiful thing. Indeed, finding a bond that offers an above-average rate of return in exchange for a given level of risk is the holy grail of most portfolio managers. But, because investors have individual preferences and risk tolerances, value — like beauty — can be in the eye of the beholder. Just as philosophers may disagree over what constitutes beauty, investors often differ over what constitutes relative value. After all, every bond trade requires both a buyer and a seller, each of whom has simultaneously evaluated the same security and concluded, respectively, that the bond is cheap or rich.

This apparent paradox demonstrates that relative value is not a market-wide phenomenon but, instead, a concept unique to each investor. Relative-value analysis should be viewed as an investor-specific process for identifying those securities that are most likely to provide a superior return over a given horizon for a given level of risk. But, with respect to measuring both return and risk, ABS can provide some unique challenges relative to other fixed-income securities. Most of these challenges are by-products of securitization, the process that transforms cash flows received from relatively risky forms of collateral into less risky securities. Securitization shapes and transfers risk through the use of financial and legal structuring techniques. In doing so it can create opportunities and pose problems that investors inexperienced with ABS may have trouble spotting. The purpose of this chapter is to provide investors with a usable set of tools for identifying relative value in the asset-backed securities market.

The ABS market contains a rich array of security types supported by many diverse kinds of collateral. There are numerous ways to stratify this market. The most meaningful cut, from a relative-value perspective, is by coupon type. Although there are often opportunities between the fixed- and floating-rate market that can be exploited through the use of derivatives, the vast majority of comparisons are made between assets of similar coupon type. As a reflection of this concentration on coupon type, the chapter is organized into two parts focused on identifying relative value in fixed- and floating-rate ABS.

RELATIVE VALUE IN FIXED-RATE ABS

Embedded in the price of every bond are views about the timing and certainty of its expected cash flows, as well as an expectation of its future performance versus similar instruments. All else being equal, bonds that are more creditworthy, bonds with known payment timing, and bonds with better total-return characteristics will command higher prices than otherwise similar bonds lacking these attributes.

These same principles hold in the ABS market. But, the diversity of collateral types securitized, the wide range of collateral maturities, the delinquency and loss profiles of the collateral, the variety of structures employed, the sensitivity of the structures to changes in collateral payment rates, and a host of other factors can complicate relative-value analysis. This analysis can be simplified for fixed-rate ABS by evaluating three attributes of each security: cash-flow profile, volatility of collateral cash flows, and underlying credit profile.

Cash-Flow Profiles

In the bond market, the trading price of a security is determined by adding a spread to the yield of a benchmark security, then discounting the future cash flows at the combined yield. By convention, the benchmark security is usually the U.S. Treasury note or bond with a maturity that most closely matches the average life of the bond being priced. This pricing convention can cause problems in the ABS market, where, for almost any given average life, there are many bonds and many different cash-flow profiles.

Cash-flow profiles common in ABS include bullets, passthrough securities, and sequential-pay bonds. These profiles are largely reflective of the term of the underlying assets and the structures employed in securitization. Most short-lived collateral types such as credit card or trade receivables usually rely on revolving structures and produce ABS with bullet profiles. Longer-dated collateral, such as auto or mortgage loans, are securitized using structures that pass through cash flows as they are collected. Depending on the structure employed, either pure passthrough or time-tranched ABS can be based on these types of collateral.

Because bonds with different profiles behave differently and are exposed to different levels of market risk over time, investors will usually express their preference for a given profile in the price of the bond. All else being equal, and given a positively sloped yield curve, investors will usually pay more for bonds with bullet profiles and less for bonds with amortizing profiles. Since bullets and amortizing bonds with identical average lives price off the same benchmark, the investor's preference is reflected as wider spreads for bonds with more widely dispersed payments.

Exhibit 1 illustrates how different cash-flow profiles behave over time, and how this affects the relative value of the securities. The exhibit presents three bonds which initially have identical average lives. Bond A is a bullet. Bond B is a sequential-pay bond that receives no principal until the end of the second year. Bond C is a passthrough structure that begins receiving principal the first year. All three bonds pay a 5% coupon annually and sell for par.

Exhibit 1: Behavior of Cash-Flow Profiles over Time

	Term	Expected Cash Flows		
Period	Structure (%)	Bond A	Bond B	Bond C
1	4.00	$5.00	$5.00	$25.00
2	4.50	5.00	38.33	24.00
3	5.00	105.00	36.66	23.00
4	5.25		35.01	22.00
5	5.50			21.00

Changes in Average Life

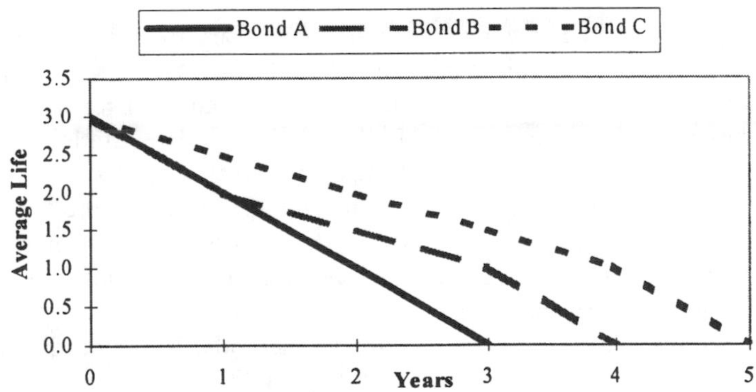

Roll Down Prices

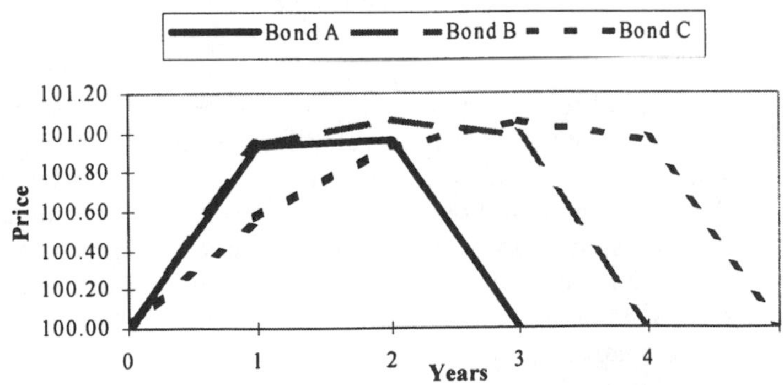

As time passes, each structure will age differently, and these differences have implications for the returns investors can earn on the bonds. After one year has passed, bonds A and B have a remaining average life of two years, but bond C has a remaining average life of 2.5 years. If the curve is upward sloping, bonds A and B will reprice off a lower-yielding benchmark than bond C, which should result in bonds A and B having a higher price than bond C. This upward change in price due to aging is known as "rolling down the yield curve." Bonds that age faster have better "roll" characteristics and, all else being equal, will earn greater total returns. Since amortizing bonds roll slower than bullet bonds, they tend to have lower returns than otherwise identical bullet bonds. Sequential-pay bonds that are locked out from principal payments for a period of time will roll like bullets during the lockout period and like amortizing bonds during their payout phase. Over a horizon that is longer than its lockout period, a sequential-pay bond will roll less than an otherwise identical bullet and, therefore, have a lower return.

To offset the disadvantage posed by wider principal payment windows, investors will usually require a higher yield. Since convention requires bonds, regardless of profile, to be spread off the yield of a benchmark with the same average life, wider yields translate into wider nominal spreads. As a rule, the wider the principal payment window, the wider the nominal spread must be to offset this disadvantage.

Determining just how much spread is necessary to compensate for differences in payment windows can be accomplished through use of static spread analysis. Unlike the conventional method of valuing a bond by discounting all of its cash flows by a single rate and summing the resultant values, static spread analysis requires that each of a bond's cash flows be discounted using the spot rate method. Essentially, this method discounts using a unique rate for each of a bond's cash flows. The unique rate used is the sum of the benchmark spot rate corresponding to the timing of each cash flow, plus a single, uniform — or static — spread added to every benchmark spot rate.

Exhibit 2 contrasts the two valuation methods. In effect, the single-rate method provides an average valuation of the bonds' cash flows, while the spot method calculates a time-specific valuation for each cash flow. Relative to the spot-rate method, the single-rate method undervalues bond cash flows occurring prior to the average life, because the single rate is greater than the spot rates associated with these payments. Conversely, the single-rate method overvalues the flows after the average life because the single rate is less than the corresponding spot rates. By comparing these average valuations with the spot valuations, it becomes possible to judge whether the single-rate valuation has, on balance, overvalued or undervalued the cash flows. Since static spread is measured over the yield curve rather than off of a single point on the curve, differences between the static spreads and the nominal spreads can be used as an indicator of whether the investor is being adequately compensated for buying a nonbullet bond. If the static spread of an amortizing bond is equal to its nominal spread, then the overvalued and undervalued cash flows have offset one another and the bond is priced fairly. If the static spread is greater than the nominal spread, then the undervalued cash flows are on balance greater than the overvalued cash flows and, therefore, the bond's price understates its value. Conversely, if a static spread is less than the nominal spread, the bond is overvalued.

Static-spread analysis is a useful, albeit imperfect, tool for relative-value analysis. Since it assumes a fixed term structure, it essentially ignores the effects that changing interest rates will have on bond values. For this reason, it is useful to use static-spread analysis in conjunction with traditional risk measures such as duration and convexity. One way to make static-spread analysis more robust is to repeat the calculations using several different term structures. This approach can help investors to quantify the effects that yield-curve reshaping (such as flattening, steepening, or inversion) will have on bonds with differing cash-flow profiles.

Cash-Flow Volatility

Another drawback to static-spread analysis is that it assumes cash flows are fixed. This assumption can be problematic for passthrough ABS with collateral that is subject to early repayment. For these bonds, changes in the rate of repayment can significantly alter a security's cash flow profile and, therefore, its relative attractiveness. All else being equal, bonds with relatively stable and predictable cash flows offer greater value than those with less predictable payments.

Exhibit 2: Single-Rate Versus Spot-Rate Valuation

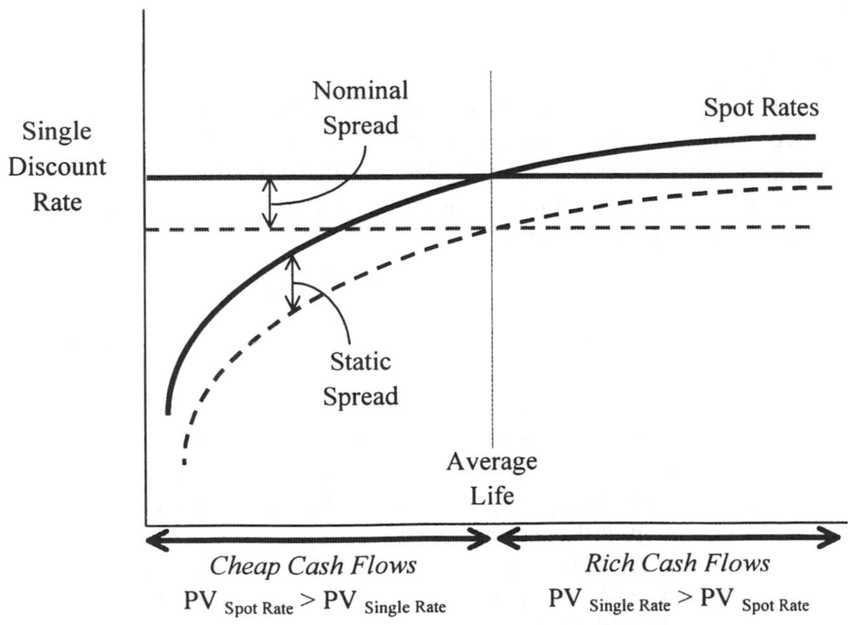

Prepayments are an important fact of life in the ABS market. They may indeed be the single most important determinant of a fixed-rate bond's relative value. Assumptions about collateral repayment determine the average lives and benchmarks used to price most ABS. Variations in collateral prepayment rates from their expected levels can negatively impact investors. If actual prepayment rates prove slower than expected prepayment rates, too short an average life will have been used in pricing the bond and returns earned will be less than expected. If the actual speed of prepayments exceeds expectations, it is possible that investors may have to reinvest bond proceeds at interest rates lower than on the bonds they purchased. This is particularly a risk for ABS supported by interest rate-sensitive collateral such as various kinds of mortgage products. Many factors can affect ABS prepayment rates as explained in the following sections.

Normal Turnover

Normal economic activity causes some level of prepayment for nearly every type of financial asset securitized. Examples of this include equipment lease contracts that are terminated because the lessee upgrades equipment or auto loans that are repaid by insurance proceeds following an accident or theft.

Curtailments

These partial prepayments occur when borrowers pay more than their scheduled monthly payment. They are common in some consumer asset types like mortgages and auto loans, but usually contribute only a small amount to overall prepayments.

Defaults

With most ABS collateral types, borrower defaults will result in the value of the defaulted contract being paid out to investors as principal (assuming sufficient credit enhancement is available). The effect of prepayment-driven defaults varies widely by asset and obligor quality. For some asset types, defaults can be the most significant source of prepayments.

Refinancing

As is the case with the MBS market, decreases in interest rates can incentivize people to refinance loans. But for several reasons, a given change in rates will affect ABS prepayments less than MBS prepayments. In general, people refinance only when they can save money, or reduce their debt-service payment. The savings are greatest on large, long-lived collateral and least on small, short-lived collateral. For instance, auto loans are rarely refinanced because the potential savings are small. Mortgages offer potentially greater savings and, therefore, are refinanced more readily. Besides interest rates, other factors including borrower creditworthiness and refinancing costs will affect the speed of repayment. Less creditworthy obligors and other individuals facing high refinancing costs will be less prone to refinance.

Exhibit 3: Projected Loss Multiples

Rating	Minimum Loss Multiple
AAA	4 – 5 × Base-Case Losses
AA	3 – 4 ×
A	2 – 3 ×
BBB	1.75 – 2 ×
BB	1.5 – 1.75 ×

Source: Standard & Poor's, by permission.

Credit Profile

The third piece of the ABS relative-value puzzle is the credit profile. The credit profile serves as an indicator of the certainty of ultimate principal repayment and goes beyond the concept of credit ratings. At least four dimensions of credit have implications for the relative risk of any ABS: structural enhancement, collateral seasoning, servicer quality, and liquidity considerations.

Structural Enhancement

The credit rating of every ABS is a function of the structure of the securitization from which it was issued. When assembling transactions, investment bankers — on behalf of the sponsor — work with the rating agencies to design the most efficient and cost-effective securitization structure. Such a structure is usually achieved by maximizing the number of bonds issued and minimizing the overall interest cost and levels of credit enhancement. One of the primary tasks of the rating agency is to determine the appropriate level of credit enhancement necessary for the ABS sold to achieve the desired credit rating. The enhancement can come from either external or internal sources. External enhancement typically takes the form of a specialized insurance policy or letter of credit. Common types of internal enhancement include reserve accounts, overcollateralization, and subordination.

For ABS that rely on internal enhancement, the rating agencies calculate or "size" the amount of credit enhancement needed for each class of bonds to achieve the rating by scaling the enhancement to a multiple of projected losses, as shown in Exhibit 3. The goal of the sizing process is to provide every rated ABS with a cushion of credit enhancement and liquidity capable of absorbing losses and promoting timely coupon payments. Higher ratings require higher enhancement multiples.

When evaluating two or more bonds with otherwise identical features, those bonds which feature greater credit enhancement will have less credit risk and, therefore, offer greater value. If the rating agencies are consistent in the way they rate new securities, bonds with similar loss profiles should initially have similar levels of credit enhancement. However, investors should be cognizant that the level of actual losses sustained by the collateral may differ from the loss assumptions embedded in the credit enhancement. If the actual collateral performance proves substantially better or worse than projected performance for a sustained period, then the ABS might, respectively, become a candidate for a rating upgrade or downgrade.

Exhibit 4: Stress-Testing Alternative

Issue	Issue Date	Weighted Average Seasoning at Issue	Current Weighted Average Seasoning*	Cumulative Losses*	Credit Enhancement for Seniors*	Enhancement as a Multiple of Losses
Chase Manhattan Grantor Trust Series 1995-B	11/15/95	11 months	34 months	0.32%	6.25%	19.5×
Ford Credit Grantor Trust Series 1995-B	11/15/95	4 months	27 months	1.80%	8.53%	4.7×

* As of 10/31/97

Rather than waiting for a rating agency to initiate a ratings review, investors may want to take a more proactive approach to structural analysis. After all, they ultimately bear the risks and stand to reap the rewards created by disparities between expected and actual collateral performance. Among the structural analysis tools available to investors are *stress testing* and *loss-multiple analysis*.

Stress testing requires modeling every aspect of a securitization from its collateral to its capital structure and cash-flow allocation mechanisms, then stressing the collateral's performance until the ABS suffers a loss. Structures that can suffer higher levels of stress are superior. While stress testing can provide a very accurate indication of how well protected ABS are from collateral losses, they can be difficult and time-consuming to construct properly; meanwhile, the bonds in question may be sold away before a conclusion can be reached.

A simpler and quicker alternative to stress testing evaluates credit enhancement levels as a multiple of actual or expected losses. Exhibit 4 illustrates two very similar bonds, Chase Manhattan Grantor Trust 1995-B, Class A and Ford Credit Grantor Trust 1995-B, Class A. Based on their loss-coverage multiples, the Chase bonds appear to offer a greater margin of safety.

Even though the use of loss multiples can be an extremely helpful tool, investors should exercise caution to ensure they are making a fair comparison. Differences in the structure of credit enhancement need to be taken into account when comparing coverage multiples from different bonds. For example, while some ABS have credit enhancement levels that remain relatively constant over the life of the bonds, other structures feature enhancement levels that may change during the life of the bond. For instance, many bonds are protected by mechanisms that cause changes in the level of enhancement relative to the remaining bonds. Structural devices like spread accounts (reserve accounts that are funded with excess spread), minimum reserve-account requirements, and subordinate bonds with principal-lockout features will all change the levels of enhancement over the life of an ABS. Other mechanisms such as loss and delinquency triggers can, if invoked, also increase enhancement levels. Investors should take care to incorporate the effects of these structural devices into their analysis.

Exhibit 5: Behavior of Pool Loss Rates over Time

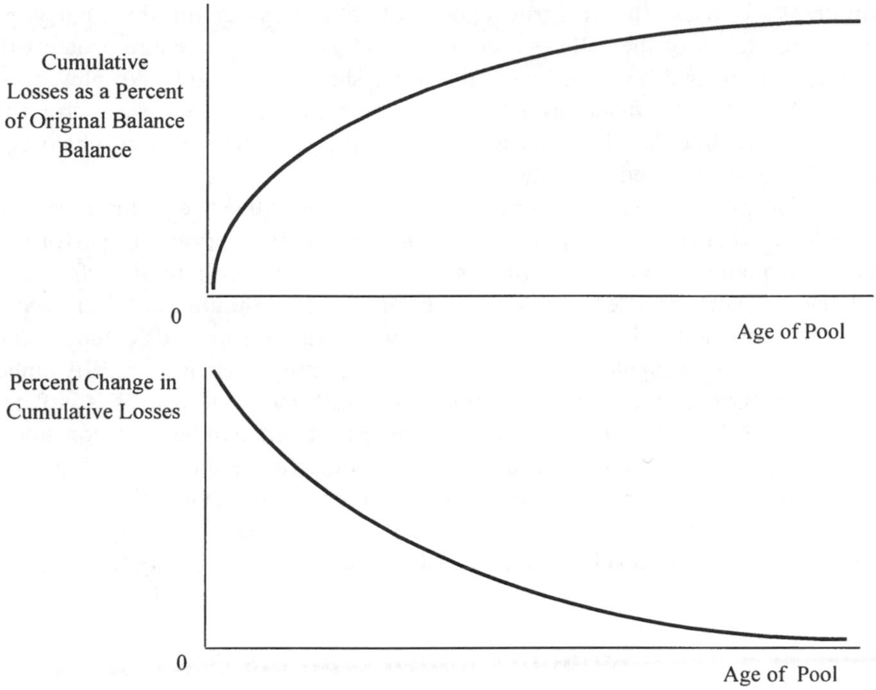

Collateral Seasoning

It is exceptionally rare for loan defaults and losses to be spread evenly over the life of a collateral pool. Instead, many collateral types when pooled tend to exhibit a loss life cycle in which the rate of loss is greatest in the early months, then slows as the bonds age. This relationship can be seen in static-loss curves, which depict the relationship between the age of a collateral pool and the cumulative losses it has sustained. The two graphs in Exhibit 5 illustrate a typical static loss curve and the behavior of a pool's loss rates over time.

Analysis of a pool's static losses can aid in relative-value decisions. For instance, by helping to identify where a collateral pool stands in its loss cycle, pool analysis can provide an indication of future collateral performance, which investors can then use in determining the adequacy of credit enhancement. Also, static-pool analysis can be useful over time for monitoring the performance of firms that originate and service ABS collateral. Increases in static losses from series to series can signal important changes in credit and collection procedures and other business practices at an originator/servicer. Unless credit enhancement levels change in step, newer series will be less creditworthy than vintage series, even though ABS from the different series continue to carry the same rating.

Servicer Quality

One of the main benefits of securitization is that the financial assets serving as collateral are, by virtue of a true sale to a bankruptcy-remote third party, put beyond the reach of the seller's creditors. This true-sale procedure protects the collateral securing ABS in the event the seller should fall into bankruptcy. However, if the seller also functions as the servicer on a transaction it is important for investors to realize that their investment is not fully insulated against changes in the seller/servicer's credit quality.

Despite its bankruptcy-remote status, securitized collateral remains exposed to its servicer's ability to perform. Failure of a servicer to perform its duties adequately can often result in significantly worse collateral performance and, thereby, compromise the credit quality of the ABS. Should a servicer become financially strained, it is quite possible that its operating standards could become compromised. To mitigate against this possibility, rating agencies typically embed servicer performance tests into ABS transactions. If one of these tests is violated, a servicer can be replaced. However, servicing transfers can be time-consuming and collateral performance could continue to deteriorate during the transition period. Ultimately, the best protection against this type of servicer risk is to invest in transactions for which the seller/servicer is in a financially secure position. All things considered, ABS subject to greater levels of servicer risk should reflect that risk in their pricing.

Liquidity Considerations

A long time truism of the bond market is that liquidity is always available until it is needed. This quip hints at the fickle and credit-sensitive nature of bond liquidity. In the bond market, liquidity is reflected in pricing and, therefore, has implications for relative value. Bonds with greater liquidity command tighter spreads to their benchmark than relatively illiquid securities.

Among the many factors affecting liquidity in the ABS market are collateral type, issue size, and issuer reputation. Bonds supported by mature and widely understood collateral types will almost always price better than similar bonds backed by less closely followed assets. Similarly, ABS issued from large securitizations will tend to have greater liquidity because the large issues are more widely held and therefore more investors are generally aware of the bonds and their performance. Along the same lines, securities originated by frequent or well known issuers tend to have a wider following and command better pricing.

On the negative side, ABS liquidity is very occasionally subject to "headline" risk, in which negative news regarding an originator, a collateral type, or some other aspect of a securitization causes a dramatic and sudden drop in demand. An excellent example of this occurred in early 1997 when several bankruptcies rocked the subprime auto finance industry. Reacting to the news, spreads on all subprime auto ABS, not just those of the firms affected, widened significantly.

In spite of its potentially negative effects, illiquidity is not always a bad thing. Investors who are by nature buy-and-hold or who have the ability to allocate some portion of their portfolios in illiquid instruments, may be able to enhance their long-term returns by systematically purchasing illiquid ABS at relatively cheap prices.

RELATIVE VALUE IN FLOATING-RATE ABS

In the previous section, we discussed variables important to measuring relative value in fixed-rate ABS. Credit quality assessment, cash-flow profiles, and cash-flow volatility are also key inputs to accessing relative value in floating-rate ABS. Factors unique to floaters include some characteristics of basis risk, the need to recalibrate deals to a common benchmark, and the calculation of spread duration.

Floating-rate ABS structures are common in those sectors where the finance charges or interest payments earned on the underlying receivables are also floating. These finance charges and interest payments float at a fixed spread over a predetermined market index. Examples of ABS sectors with floating-rate collateral include credit cards, adjustable-rate home equity loans, home equity lines of credit, trade receivables, and student loans. Floating-rate tranches have also been carved out of the short-term cash flows off fixed-rate collateral. In 1996, for example, Chrysler's four auto loan deals included a floating-rate sequential tranche collateralized with fixed-rate auto loans. Floating-rate tranches off fixed-rate home equity loans are another example. For the purposes of this chapter, references to home equity floaters will apply to structures collateralized with adjustable-rate home equity loans and not floaters structured off of fixed-rate loans.

Yield spreads for floating-rate ABS are quoted in terms of a discount margin to the underlying reset index. A floating-rate bond's discount margin is the difference between the yield on the reset index and the yield on the security. The term of the reset index typically matches the coupon reset and payment frequency. For example, most credit card floaters are quoted at a discount margin to one-month LIBOR, corresponding to a monthly coupon reset and a monthly coupon payment to bondholders. The coupon rate and amount adjusts monthly based upon the value of the underlying reset index. The coupon formula is stated as a fixed spread to the underlying reset index.

Basis Risk

Basis risk refers to a possible mismatch between adjustments to the ABS coupon rate paid to the investor and the yield on the underlying portfolio of collateral. Before paying a coupon to the investor, the yield on a portfolio of collateral must pay fees for servicing, surety, and other functions, and cover principal losses. The amount of yield remaining after fees, principal losses, and the bond coupon are paid is referred to as excess spread for most asset types, and the available funds margin[1] for home equity floaters. Losses, delinquencies, and non-interest rate related fees on underlying collateral cause much of the variation in excess spreads and the available funds margin. Basis risk refers to that portion of the mismatch unrelated to collateral performance.

Basis risk is driven by factors that are uncertain at the time of purchase, such as the frequency and magnitude of changes in the level of rates and the shape of the Treasury and Eurodollar yield curves. A few sources of basis risk are common over most collateral asset types, such as index risk and reset risk. Collateral containing "teaser" rates or interest rate caps can also introduce basis risk.

Index Risk

Index risk represents the yield curve risk between the coupon rate paid to bondholders and the portfolio yield generated by the underlying receivables. Many fixed-rate and most floating-rate ABS structures have exposure to index risk. In credit card ABS structures, finance charges on outstanding credit card balances reset at a fixed spread over the prime rate while the coupon on the ABS securities collateralized with those balances resets at a spread to 1-month LIBOR. The mortgages collateralizing home equity floaters may be indexed off 6-month LIBOR or a constant-maturity Treasury index and support a coupon on the ABS indexed to 1-month LIBOR.

In both examples, a mismatch exists between the coupon rate paid to investors and the index which sets the portfolio yield. Coupons paid reset off the front of the Eurodollar curve. Yet the interest income supporting those coupons is driven by a constant-maturity Treasury (CMT) index or the prime rate, which both move with the Treasury yield curve. The positive yield curve slope usually protects investors from index risk. Investor coupons typically float over an index with a shorter term than the index associated with the collateral. Conversely, an inverted yield curve could increase the effects of index risk.

Reset Risk

Most floating-rate ABS structures are also exposed to reset risk, defined as the mismatch between the frequency of investor coupon resets and the frequency of the resets on the underlying collateral. Finance charges on seasoned credit card balances reset daily over the prime rate versus monthly coupon resets on ABS collateralized with credit card receivables. Interest rates on adjustable-rate home equity loans reset annually or twice per year, versus monthly coupon resets on home equity floaters. Since home equity floaters are collateralized with new production loans, reset dates on the underlying mortgages can be lumped together rather than equally distributed across the calendar.

Reset risk is mitigated for most asset classes by the wide margins between the coupons paid to investors and interest earned on the underlying col-

---

[1] The available funds margin (AFM) is the amount available to pay the bondholder's coupon, the servicing fees, and other fees:

AFM = Gross Coupon – Servicing – Other Fees – Surety Spread – (Coupon Index – Margin)

lateral. The wide margins reflect the difference in credit quality between the security, which is often rated triple-A, and the underlying consumer or commercial borrower. For instance, home equity floaters collateralized with B and C loans run little reset risk due to very wide margins. Mortgage rates on collateral typically reset at 500-700 basis points above either 6-month LIBOR or 1-year CMT versus a coupon rate indexed to 1-month LIBOR plus 50 to 100 basis points.

An illustration of the sizable available funds margin on home equity floaters can be found in the Exhibit 6 description of the Aames 97-1 Class A bond. The Aames 97-1 bond is indexed to 1-month LIBOR + 20 basis points, whereas the underlying mortgage collateral is indexed to both 6-month LIBOR (79%) and 1-year CMT (21%). If 1-month LIBOR increases while both 6-month LIBOR and 1-year CMT remain constant, the amount available to pay the coupon, the available funds cap,[2] has decreased. All other things equal, an investor would require a wider discount margin on a bond for which the underlying collateral exhibits an unevenly distributed reset schedule.

Teaser Risk

Teaser risk refers to the impairment on the portfolio yield from below-market rates earned on underlying receivables. Some credit card issuers offer "teaser" rates to attract new cardholders. The issuer guarantees a below-market rate of interest on credit card balances for six months or one year. When credit card receivables with teaser rates are added to a revolving master trust by the issuer, ABS bondholders are at risk of falling portfolio yields. As the proportion of receivables with teaser rates increases in a revolving master trust, portfolio yields and excess spreads fall and investors usually require wider spreads to hold the securities.

Exhibit 6: ABS Floater Characteristics

Issue	FUSAM 1997-4	AAMES 1997-1
Class	A	A
Coupon	1-month LIBOR + 21 basis points	1-month LIBOR + 20 basis points
Average Life	10-year soft bullet	3.12 years at 25 CPR
Collateral Description Revolving structure of credit card receivables		Type: Adjustable Rate
Portfolio Yield: 17.42% (3-month average)		Gross Weighted Average Coupon 10.38%
Base Rate: 7.93% (3-month average)		Weighted Average Gross Margin 6.71%
Excess spread: 2.93% (3-month average)		Net Weighted Average Coupon: 9.88% Weighted Average Life Cap: 17% Servicing Fee: 0.5%
Index 1 month LIBOR: 5.65% Prime Rate: 8.50%		6 month LIBOR: 5.90 (79%) 1 Year CMT: 0.49% (21%) Blended Rate: 5.81%

[2] The available funds cap (AFC) is the maximum amount available to pay the coupon:
AFC = Gross Coupon – Servicing – Other Fees – Surety Spread

Teaser risk is defined differently for adjustable-rate mortgage collateral. ARM issuers also entice borrowers with a below-market — teaser — interest rate for an initial period ranging from six months to three years. When the teaser period expires, interest on the underlying mortgage resets to market levels. Teaser risk represents the reduction in the available funds margin from which coupons and fees for surety, servicing, and other functions get paid. Yield enhancements in the form of overcollateralization and acceleration features mitigate the risk that the available funds margin will not cover expenses associated with the transactions. The excess interest generated by overcollateralization is used to pay down principal on the structures.

Cap Risk

Cap risk measures the impact of periodic and lifetime caps on floating-rate collateral. Most floating-rate collateral is subject to some form of cap on interest rates charged the borrower. For example, state usury laws usually place a cap on rates that finance companies can charge consumer borrowers. Home equity floaters have periodic and lifetime caps that limit the amount that mortgage rates can increase at each reset and over the life of the mortgage. Some ABS structures have caps on coupons paid to investors. For example, some credit card issues have embedded coupon caps ranging from 11% to 14%. Many cap options embedded in ABS deals are out of the money and have little impact on relative value and bond pricing. That said, investors need to be aware of how cap options are valued in the market.

Home equity floater structures usually include multiple periodic cap options and a lifetime cap option. Most 6-month LIBOR ARMs have 100 basis point periodic caps, which equate to a 200 bp annual cap. Caps on 1-year CMT ARMs average 200 bp annually. Lifetime caps limit rate adjustments over the life of the mortgage and typically range from 15% to 18%. Home equity floaters collateralized with B and C loans run little risk of hitting the available fund cap due to the high yields on the underlying mortgages relative to the coupon on the ABS. For example, the weighted average life cap of the Aames 97-1 (Exhibit 7) collateral is 17%, which translates into a life cap for the Class A bond of 16.5%. By subtracting the indexed coupon on Class A from the life cap, we calculated a life cap margin[3] of 1,061 basis points. This means that 1-month LIBOR would have to increase 1,061 basis points or reach 16.3% before the class-A bond would hit the life cap. The Aames example is not uncommon for most home equity floaters in the ABS sector. Life caps are so far out of the money that cap option values are only one to two basis points.

The average life of a security also affects the valuation of the embedded short-cap options. The longer the length of the cap, the higher the probability that

---

[3] The life cap margin is the difference between the life cap and the indexed investor coupon, where the life cap is defined as the difference between the weighted average life cap (WALC) and all the fees:

Life Cap = Weighted Average Life Cap (WALC) – Servicing – Other Fees – Surety Spread

Life Cap Margin (LCM) = Life Cap – (Index – Margin)

the cap will be hit at some point and the higher the time value of the cap option. Therefore the term structure of spreads on home equity floaters should be steeper than the term structure of floaters with no embedded options.

Evaluating ABS Floaters Relative to Common Benchmarks

Bond investors are accustomed to comparing two or more securities on the basis of a spread to the underlying Treasury yield curve. Because spreads on floating-rate securities are referencing dissimilar indices, yields should be restated as an effective money-market yield. The three most common references for floating-rate ABS are 1-month LIBOR, 3-month LIBOR, and 91-day Treasury bills. The most common reference index for floating-rate instruments is 1-month LIBOR because it corresponds to monthly coupon payments to investors and on the underlying collateral. The effective money-market yield allows the investor to compare the relative value of floating-rate ABS products indexed with more than one benchmark.

Exhibit 7 illustrates the steps to convert nominal yield spreads off different indices into an effective money-market yield. The first step is to restate the discount margin as an effective nominal yield by adding the discount margin to the index yield. Next, convert the effective nominal yield to an effective money market yield by restating the yield on an actual/360 discounting basis. Yields on floating-rate structures priced and reset off the Eurodollar curve are typically stated using actual/360 discounting. Therefore, when comparing yields on securities indexed off more than one LIBOR rate, this final calculation is unnecessary.

The floating-rate investor can also look at the different reset indexes as a means of making a directional interest rate or curve play. Investors with a bullish outlook should, all else being equal, prefer longer reset periods. As interest rates fall, the investor's coupon resets down less frequently and the return on the instrument should exceed that of a security with a shorter reset period.

Exhibit 7: Restating Yields on Floating-Rate ABS

Prices as of September 30, 1997

		Reset Margin	Index Yield	DM	Effective Nominal Yield	Effective Money Market Yield
SLMA 97-3 A2 7.2 year average life	Weekly reset quarterly pay Interest paid actual/actual	+ 64 > 3-month T-bill Available funds cap	5.03%	+64	5.68%	5.60% Conversion formula: 5.68% × 360/365 = 5.60%
MBNAM 97-JA 7.0 year average life	Monthly reset, monthly pay Interest paid actual/360	+12 > 1 month LIBOR no cap	5.66%	+12	5.78%	5.78% LIBOR floaters are usually actual/360; therefore, no restatement required

Bearish investors would pursue the opposite strategy, preferring securities, again all things being equal, with more frequent reset periods. As interest rates increase, the more frequent reset provides the investor with a higher yield and a higher return. Investors expecting the yield curve to flatten might use floating-rate instruments with frequent reset periods as the short end of a barbell strategy.

The preceding discussion is simplistic in that it does not account for the term structure of nominal yields corresponding to the frequency of the reset. The Eurodollar curve off which LIBOR is based is usually positively sloped. Therefore, the investor accepts a smaller nominal yield in exchange for more frequent resets. In order to assess accurately the possible outcomes associated with the strategies discussed earlier, the investor should perform horizon analysis to determine whether the nominal yield differences are offset by expected rate moves.

The availability of floating-rate ABS product indexed off both the Treasury curve and the Eurodollar curve provides investors with tools to take a position on the TED spread. The TED spread is the price spread between the 3-month Treasury bill futures contract and the 3-month Eurodollar futures contract. An increase in market volatility accompanied by a widening in the TED spread will cause a floater indexed off Treasury bills to underperform the LIBOR floater. The discount margin on the Treasury bill floater will widen to keep effective nominal yields in line with LIBOR floaters.

The opposite also holds true. A decrease in market volatility accompanied by a falling TED spread allows the spreads on Treasury bill floaters to decline as nominal yields decline on LIBOR floaters. Clearly, spread volatility on Treasury bill floaters exceeds that of LIBOR floaters. Unfortunately, opportunities for investors to trade volatility in the floaters market through the TED spread are limited. At this time, Sallie Mae is the only sizable ABS issuer with Treasury-indexed floating-rate coupons.

Term Structure of Discount Margins

Similar to yield spreads on fixed-rate ABS, there is a term structure to spreads for floating-rate ABS. Investors are compensated for a longer period of credit exposure and structure risk with a wider spread over the benchmark index. Exhibit 8 illustrates the term structure of spreads on floating-rate credit cards and home equity floaters as of September 30, 1997.

Spread Duration

One reason why the term structure of discount margins is typically upward sloping is that floating-rate investors — like their fixed-rate counterparts — want to be compensated for bearing the greater price risk inherent in longer-lived bonds. Although floaters are, by virtue of their periodic coupon resets, largely insulated from interest rate risk, discount margins can be affected by changes in credit quality and average life. The impact of changes in discount margin on the price of a bond can be estimated through the use of spread duration. Because spread is a component of a fixed-rate bond's aggregate yield, a fixed-rate bond's spread duration is no different than its modified or effective duration. Therefore, the expected change in price from a given change in the yield is a product of the duration times the change in yield.

Exhibit 8: Term Structure of Spreads on Floating-Rate Credit Card ABS and Home Equity Floater ABS: September 30, 1997

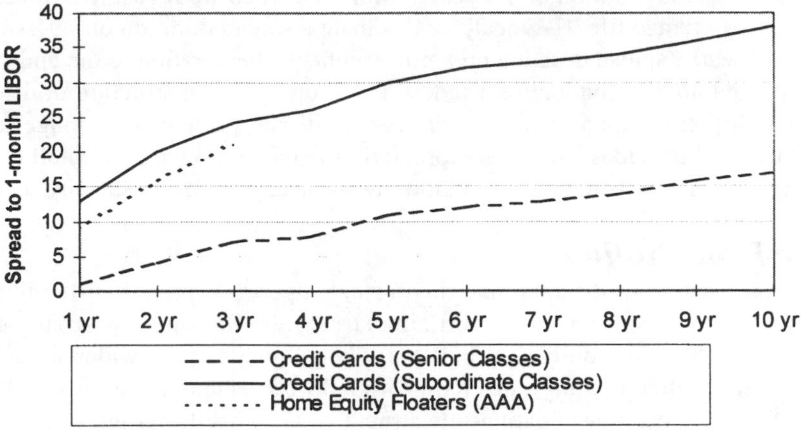

Exhibit 9: Spread Durations on Floating-Rate ABS

Issue:	MBNMA 97-J		MBNAM 97-E	
Class:	Class A		Class A	
Reference Index:	1-mo LIBOR		3-mo LIBOR	
Average Life:	6.8 yr		4.4 yr	
Index Duration:	0.08 years		0.25 years	
Pricing Spread less 10 basis points:	2 DM	100-18	–2 BM	100-12+
Pricing Spread:	*12 DM*	*100-00*	*8 DM*	*100-00*
Pricing Spread plus 10 basis points:	22 DM	99-14	18 DM	99-19+
Price change from 10 bp move (32nd)	18/32nds		12.5/32nds	
Price change from 10 bp move (%):	0.563%		0.391%	
Implied Spread Duration	5.63 years		3.91 years	

Analysis as of 10/16/97

For fixed-rate securities:

$$\text{Price Change} = \text{Effective Duration} \times \text{Change in Yield Spread} \quad (1)$$

Therefore,

$$\text{Price Change/Change in Yield Spread} = \text{Spread Duration} \quad (2)$$

Equation (1) does not hold true for floating-rate securities when the maturity of the security exceeds the term of the reset index. If we applied the same concept to floating-rate ABS, the price change from a change in the yield spread would be negligible since the duration of the floating-rate ABS reflects the duration of the reset index on the coupon. Exhibit 9 illustrates that the impact on price from a change in spread results in a spread duration very close to that of a fixed-rate bond with the same maturity. When we adjust the spread on the MBNAM 97-J Class A by 10 basis points, and plug the price change into equation (2) above, we calculate a spread duration of 5.6 years. Similarly, when we repeat the process for the 4.4 year average life 97-E deal, we calculate a spread duration of 3.91 years.

Clearly, spread duration on a floater reflects the duration to the underlying maturity and not the coupon reset index. Therefore the term structure of discount margins further compensates investors for additional price risk on longer-dated structures and provides for price appreciation from rolldown. Said another way, floating-rate ABS do benefit from rolldown as the average life of a security shortens.

Cash-Flow Profiles

The term structure of discount margins further supports a pricing differential for bullet ABS floaters relative to amortizing structures. Because amortizing structures do not shorten as quickly as bullet structures, they require wider spreads.

Soft-bullet, floating-rate credit card ABS issues tend to be the benchmark against which most other floating-rate structures are priced. Earlier, in Exhibit 8, we illustrated spread curves for home equity floaters and credit card floaters. The spread differential associated with bullet versus amortizing structures is not directly comparable for these two sectors due to the embedded prepayment options and cap options in securities collateralized with residential home mortgages. Better comparisons include the Class A2 floating-rate tranches in the Chrysler (PRAT) 96-1, 96-2, 96-3, and 96-4 auto loan ABS, and the AT&T Capital Equipment (CAPRT) 97-1 Class A-5.

The Class A2 notes in each of the PRAT 96 issues had an original average life of one year with a 12-month payment window. PRAT 96-1 Class A2 and its three sisters priced two to three basis points wider than comparable spreads on floating-rate credit card soft bullets. The CAPRT 97-1 equipment lease ABS included a 1.6-year average life floating-rate note (Class A5) with a 4-year window that priced five basis points wider than cards.

To ascertain the breakeven spread between soft bullet and amortizing floaters, investors can compare horizon returns. If the return on the bullet exceeds the return on the amortizer, then the investor is not adequately compensated for the loss of rolldown and should prefer the soft bullet. Conversely, when the horizon return on the amortizing note exceeds the return on the bullet, the investor is adequately compensated for the lack of rolldown. The investor is indifferent between the two structures when horizon returns are equal.

CONCLUSION

Characteristics such as cash-flow profile, the volatility of collateral cash flows, and servicer creditworthiness can all significantly impact the relative attractiveness of both floating- and fixed-rate ABS. As with any fixed income investment, investors should demand higher yields as compensation for any factor that negatively affects the timing or certainty of future cash flows. In this chapter we have described relative value tools intended to help investors quantify whether the prospective returns offered by an ABS are adequate compensation for the risks embedded in the security. Although such tools are helpful, they can, at their best, only provide a consistent framework with which to evaluate ABS. Only once an insurer considers such an evaluation in the context of their own risk biases and constraints can a determination of value be made.

Chapter 9

The NAIC Securities Valuation Office's Analysis of Asset-Backed Securities

Frederic P. Vigneron
Senior Securities Analyst
National Association of Insurance Commissioners
Securities Valuation Office

INTRODUCTION

The National Association of Insurance Commissioners (NAIC) is an unincorporated association of the chief state insurance officials, formed in 1871 to provide coordination of insurance regulation and policy formation among the various states. Current membership includes insurance regulators from all 50 states, the District of Columbia, and the four U.S. territories. Although the NAIC itself is not a regulatory body, its members are the chief regulatory officials of the various states.

OBJECTIVES OF THE NAIC

The NAIC's objectives, as specified in its constitution, include preservation to the several states of the regulation of the business of insurance and assistance to state insurance regulators, individually and collectively, in serving the public interest. The NAIC is committed to achieving the following fundamental insurance regulatory goals:

- Protecting the public interest; encouraging competitive markets; and facilitating the fair, just, and equitable treatment of insurance consumers.
- Promoting the reliability, solvency, and financial solidity of insurance institutions.
- Supporting and improving state regulation of insurance in a responsive, efficient, and cost-effective manner consistent with the wishes of its members.

Sections of this chapter concerning the organizational structure of the NAIC/SVO and related regulatory matters greatly benefitted from suggestions and contributions provided by SVO counsel Robert Carcano.

Pursuant to these goals, the NAIC or its staff, on behalf of its members, conducts the following activities:

- Organizing the national, interim, and zone meetings.
- Drafting of model laws, legal staff research, analysis, and coordination as well as the editing and maintenance of model laws, regulations, and guidelines.
- Drafting of insurance consumer guides.
- Development and maintenance of market information systems.
- Development of health plan accountability standards.
- Production of standard and custom statistical reports through the Services and Support Office (SSO) research division.
- Continuing education for regulators through the SSO education and training department.
- The production and distribution of NAIC publications and database products.
- Management of the regulator accreditation program; baseline standards for solvency regulation.
- Technical support in financial reporting, accounting, examinations, reinsurance, investments and internal insurance issues to the regulators.
- Solvency surveillance and financial analysis through the financial analysis division.
- Quality assessment of and assignment of NAIC designations to bonds and the tracking of stock values by the SVO.
- Federal government, international, and media relations.
- Tracking of non-U.S. insurers seeking to do business in the United States through the international insurers department.
- Development and maintenance of the U.S. insurance industry annual statement database.[1]

Subdivisions of the Association

As used in this chapter, NAIC refers to the collective membership of the association. The NAIC is supported by a staff, collectively referred to as the Services and Support Office. The SSO, headquartered in Kansas City, also maintains offices in New York and Washington, D.C. SSO officers coordinate policy issues with the members and handle executive and administrative functions. Kansas City staff members provide direct support to a variety of member initiatives. Staff of the New York City office (referred to as the Securities Valuation Office or SVO) is engaged in the credit assessment of insurer-owned and reported bond investments and the valuation of preferred and common stock. The Financial Analysis Office, located in Washington, performs financial analysis of nationally significant insurers. The

---

[1] For a detailed explanation of these activities, readers should refer to *A Tradition of Consumer Protection* (1993, 1995), which is available from the NAIC publications department.

Government Relations Office provides legal support and handles relationships between the NAIC and Congress and between the NAIC and international entities.

FUNCTION AND AUTHORITY OF THE SVO

As the credit quality and value of insurance company investments are important indicators for the purpose of financial solvency regulation, the NAIC has developed credit assessment and valuation policies for insurer-owned investments. Those investments take the form of bonds, preferred stock, common stock, and similar instruments. They are reported by the insurer to state insurance departments on Schedule D of the insurers' quarterly and annual statements through the completion of NAIC-developed special forms known as the financial statement blanks.

The NAIC has established and maintains a credit assessment and valuation policy that is administered through the NAIC's Valuation of Securities Task Force (VOS/TF). That policy is published in the Purposes and Procedures Manual of the NAIC Securities Valuation Office (P&P). The P&P describes instructions, credit assessment methodologies, and valuation policies of the NAIC's VOS/TF. As such, the P&P is binding on the SVO. The P&P identifies the SVO as the professional staff of the VOS/TF responsible for performing the day-to-day credit quality assessment and valuation of securities owned by state-regulated insurance companies.

The NAIC created the SVO to provide members with uniform investment-quality and valuation opinions for those insurer-owned investments eligible for Schedule D reporting. In fulfillment of this charge, the SVO conducts credit analysis to determine the credit quality of an investment owned and reported by an insurer. The SVO's opinion of credit quality is expressed through the assignment of an NAIC designation. The SVO also provides NAIC members with information on the value (unit price) of securities. Together, NAIC designations and unit prices for securities are called association values. Under the regulatory reporting framework developed by the NAIC and adopted by the various states, insurers are required to report SVO-assigned association values on Schedule D of their quarterly and annual NAIC financial statement blanks. Regulators use association values as an aid in making a variety of regulatory decisions related to the financial solvency of the insurance companies falling under their jurisdiction.

The NAIC/SVO committee structure flow chart is shown in Exhibit 1. The SVO is organized into four analytical departments:

- Corporate securities, subdivided into industry specialty groups, including project finance.
- Government, and municipal securities.
- Structured securities, covering both commercial real estate-related asset-backed- and residential mortgage-backed securities. In addition, the structured securities department is responsible for counterparty ratings and credit-linked securities.

Exhibit 1: NAIC/SVO Committee Structure Flow Chart

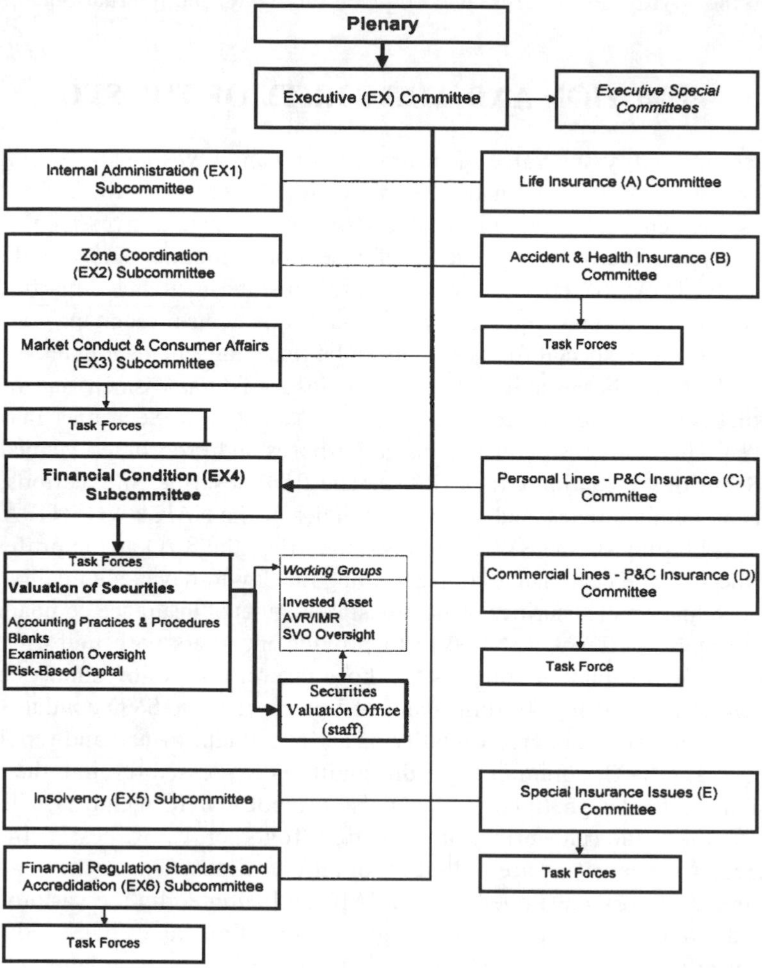

- Subsidiaries, which assesses the value of U.S. insurance company subsidiaries. Analyst responsibility for specific types of securities is determined by the assignment of standard industrial codes (SIC). These can be found in the appendix of the P&P.

Measured in terms of NAIC designation assignments in a single year, the SVO either added or updated 224,498 security issues through December 31, 1996. These issues make up over $2.2 trillion in assets (measured in terms of the par value of these securities as reported by the nation's insurance companies as of year-end 1996). This figure does not take into account the additional assets held by insurance companies in the form of subsidiaries, which the SVO also values annually.

- Schedule A: Real estate owned.
- Schedule B: Long-term mortgage loans.
- Schedule BA: Other long-term invested assets.
- Schedule C: Long-term loans.
- Schedule DA: Short-term investments.

SCHEDULE D

Schedule D is a series in the NAIC financial statement blanks through which insurance companies are required to list their debt and equity security investments. With some exceptions, the SVO analyzes only insurance companies' assets that fall within this schedule. Other asset schedules include:

The NAIC's annual statement instructions provide filers with guidance for the categorization of insurance company investments within any of these schedules.

Schedule D is divided between equity and debt securities. Debt securities are subdivided between direct corporate debt (defined as issuer obligations) and securities generally issued by special-purpose entities and backed by pools of financial assets (collectively referred to as loan-backed). All asset-backed and mortgage-backed securities fall within this loan-backed category of Schedule D. Loan-backed securities are currently organized between two reporting subgroups:

- Pass-through certificates, defined as single-class securitizations in which the payment of interest and/or principal of the security is directly proportional to interest and/or principal received from the loans supporting the security.
- Structured securities, defined as loan-backed securities, in which the payment of interest and/or principal of the security has been allocated in a manner not directly proportional to interest and/or principal received from the loans supporting the security.

As the markets have developed new instruments which have challenged the traditional definitions of debt and equity, the Valuation of Securities Task Force recognized the need to provide investors with formal guidelines for the proper categorization of these investments for financial reporting purposes. Exhibit 2 summarizes these guidelines.

All securities are assigned codes by the SVO which classify the type of issuer (group codes) and issue (group code extensions). Effective January 1, 1998, the group code extensions for Schedule D bonds were modified to allow for a more detailed breakdown of the increasingly complex category generically known as structured securities. Exhibit 3 compares these codes at year-end 1997 with the changes as of 1998. Exhibit 4 shows the new group code extension flow chart.

Exhibit 2: New Instrument Debt or Equity Status

	Equity	Debt
Rights	Right of Ownership — Voting rights in the management of the company	Creditor rights
Periodic Payments	Dividends as declared	Stated schedule of repayment of both principal and interest. Failure to perform as contractually stated would be an act of default.
Priority at Liquidation	After all creditors are satisfied	Creditor status
Taxation	Dividends are paid after tax of the issuer and are not deductible	Payments are pre-tax and deductible by the issuer. Security holders receive IRS 1099-INT or 1099-OID.
Principal	No principal protection	Principal protection, except for credit risk
Rights on Liquidation	Residual value based on percentage of ownership	Par value maximum

Source: Purposes and Procedures Manual of the NAIC Securities Valuation Office

THE STRUCTURED SECURITIES DEPARTMENT

Assignment of NAIC Designations

Analytical Method and Prioritization

The SVO's role, as defined, is limited to providing NAIC members and the regulatory community they represent, with independent quality assessment and valuation for a specific population of insurer-owned investments. Insurance companies are obligated by investment and other applicable state laws and by fiduciary obligations to policyholders to perform their own due diligence on the investments they purchase. Insurers are also tasked by their state regulators to provide the SVO with appropriate and necessary information to permit the SVO to assess and value those investments.

With the exception of the advance rating service (ARS), discussed later in this chapter, the P&P manual contemplates that an insurer will have already purchased an investment prior to the time it is reported to the SVO. The structured securities department is not charged with the detailed analysis of all the tranches of every securitization filed with the office. Similarly, on-sight due diligence of financial asset pool originators and servicers is not performed.

For collection and processing of transaction data, the department relies on reports from insurers that own the security, along with information from knowledgeable third parties connected with the transaction. With respect to structured securities that fall within a category which is informally defined as "well tested," the SVO relies primarily upon the analysis of the nationally recognized statistical rating organizations (NRSROs). For new and innovative structures and collateral classes, however, the structured securities department will perform a more detailed analysis of the NRSRO rating methodologies.

Exhibit 3: January 1, 1988 Schedule D Bonds — Group Code Extension Revision

Group Code Extension	OLD		NEW		Change/Comments
	Name	*Definition*	*Name*	*Definition*	
10	**Non-Loan Backed**	IOU payable by a business entity or a bond guaranteed by a third party and/or where collateral is not a loan or pool of loans, *and* is not a securitization.	**Issuer Obligations**	IOU payable by a business entity or a bond guaranteed by a third party and/or where collateral is not a loan or pool of loans, *and* is not a securitization.	No change.
20	**Pass-Through Certificates**	Single-class mortgage or asset-backed securities where investors have pro-rata payments of principal & interest.	**Single Class Mortgage-Backed/Asset-Backed Securities**	Single-class mortgage or asset-backed securities where investors have pro-rata payments of principal & interest.	No change.
30	**Collateralized Mortgage Obligations**	GSE and private label multi-class; NRSRO rated >=AA-; 100% 1st lien 1-4 family residential; (NAIC modified SMMEA definition).	**Defined Multi-Class Residential Mortgage-Backed Securities**	GSE and private label multi-class; NRSRO rated AA-; 100% 1st lien 1-4 family residential; (SMMEA definition).	No change.
40	**Other Structured Securities**	Non-NAIC-modified SMMEA CMOs & all non-1st lien residential mortgage related securitizations including ABS and CMBS.	**Other Multi-Class Residential Mortgage-Backed Securities**	Private label 1st lien CMOs; NRSRO rated <AA- & other mortgage-related securizations backed by liens of any seniority of any rating.	Stripped down version of the former 40 only including non-SMMEA conforming private label multi-class residential mortgage related securitizations (e.g., sub. AA- CMOs, home equity and home improvement loans, etc.).
50	N/A	N/A	**Defined Multi-Class Commercial Mortgage-Backed Securities**	SMMEA conforming CMO, not 100% 1-4 family residential.	*New* Extension, formally a sub-set of 40.
60	N/A	N/A	**Other Multi-Class Commercial Mortgage-Backed/Asset-Backed Securities**	Non-SMMEA conforming CMBS + all multi-class non-mortgage-related asset-backed securities.	*New* Extension, formally a sub-set of 40.

Exhibit 4: Schedule D Bonds Group Code Extension Flow Chart

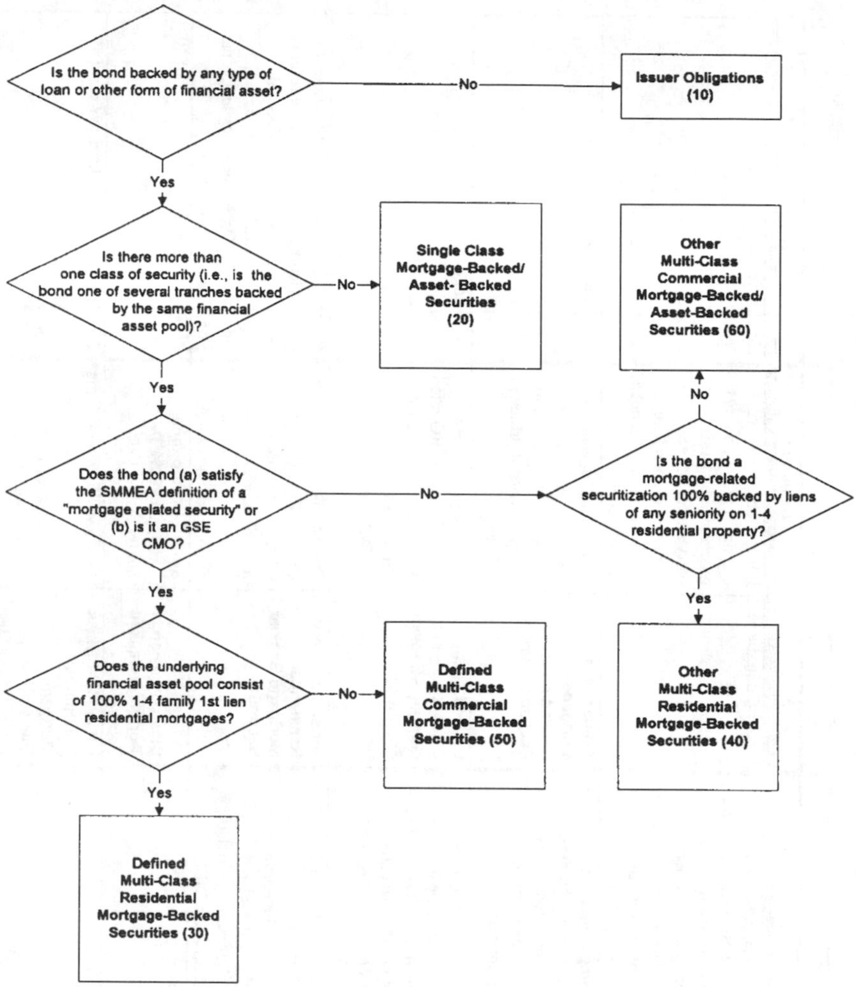

SVO Database Maintenance Philosophy

On a day-to-day basis, the primary responsibility of the SVO structured securities analyst is the assignment of new designations or the update of existing NAIC designations on the VOS database. In furtherance of this mission, the structured securities department applies what it defines as the three A's of NAIC designation database entry and documentation: accuracy, adequacy, and accountability.

By authorizing the SVO to incorporate NRSRO analysis into its decision-making process, the Valuation of Securities Task Force has made it possible for structured securities analysts to devote more time to value-added priorities such as split-rated securities; new or controversial financial asset classes or structures;

special research projects for the benefit of the Invested Asset Working Group or other working groups of the VOS/TF; and the development of improved and up-to-date credit policies, administrative procedures, operational systems, problem credits, and advance rating service applications.

Treatment of New Transaction Types

As the SVO authority to assign NAIC designations is governed by the text of the P&P, the SVO cannot assess or value a new transaction type unless it can confirm that policies providing sufficient analytical and/or regulatory guidance are contained within the manual. If appropriate guidance is not specified in the P&P, the SVO staff is required to present the VOS/TF with a description and analysis of the new form of security, along with a list of key questions and issues related to the instrument. The task force will then review such information, usually within the context of a series of public hearings involving industry and other interested parties (for example, investment banks or NRSROs). Such discussions are expected to yield instructions from the VOS/TF to the Securities Valuation Office.

Should developments in the securities markets or the evolution of credit analysis technology and standards require an adaptation to the NAIC financial conditions framework, the same procedure is followed. (The NAIC financial conditions framework is defined in the P&P as, "the instructions, formulas, regulatory treatment, devices, or mechanisms set forth in the NAIC Accounting Practices and Procedures Manual, annual statement instructions, and Financial Condition Examiners Handbook as adopted by the states.") While the SVO may not be able to proceed with the assignment of NAIC designations for securities that fall under these regulatory review categories, insurance companies are still required to proceed with the normal filing of security acquisition or annual update reports with the office unless specifically instructed otherwise.

In some cases, the VOS/TF may instruct insurance companies to suspend normal filing procedures with the SVO pending the satisfactory resolution of outstanding issues. In other cases, the task force may instruct the SVO to apply an interim policy while new or modified analytical procedures are developed and refined.

Required Information

The level of analytical detail required for the assignment of NAIC designations for structured securities may vary considerably. For most of the well tested asset classes and structures (such as credit card, A-credit automobile loan, or home equity loan securitizations) basic information on the structure, financial asset class, and type of credit enhancement, as well as appropriate forms of NRSRO confirmations, are sufficient. For many new asset classes and structures, however, a relatively detailed analysis, often incorporating most if not all of the information required for advance rating service applications is performed.

The type and detail of information required for SVO structured securities filings may also depend upon the type of application being filed. These are discussed later in this chapter, in the section on NAIC Designation Reports and Applications.

Structured Securities Research

Structured Securities Market Surveillance

It is the responsibility of structured securities analysts to monitor the asset- and mortgage-backed markets for information that may affect the performance of securities in the Valuation of Securities (VOS) database. This task is performed through the review of specialized structured securities periodicals, newsletters, and NRSRO reports. Reports and releases from other regulatory or quasi-regulatory bodies are also reviewed. It should be noted, however, that it is the ultimate responsibility of filers to notify the SVO of material changes in the creditworthiness of securities, either through the annual update or appeal and material change E-Forms.

Special Projects

When not analyzing specific securities for NAIC designation assignments and database entry, structured securities analysts perform research and analysis for special projects. These can include the analysis of new types of structured securities and financial asset pools for the development and approval of analytical methodologies, technical support of other NAIC department projects that require structured securities expertise, and administrative projects required for the management and modernization of a large and complex securities database.

The structured securities department has recently either led or participated in projects involving filing requirements for annual update reports, cross-border securitizations and the sovereign rating ceiling, and statutory accounting codification.

Interdepartmental Support

Other SVO Departments

As the public and private issuance volume of asset securitization continues to grow and diversify, the need for interdepartmental cooperation and communication also grows and is essential to the proper management of a comprehensive credit analysis and monitoring function. This is because securitization has evolved from a specialized and experimental capital markets instrument to a core funding and balance-sheet management technique for an increasingly broad range of financial services, commercial, and industrial corporations. The development of increasingly complex or hybrid structures also often requires analysts to ask: Is this an asset-backed security? Consequently, the structured securities department cooperates with the corporate and municipal/government departments in analyzing the mechanics of new structures and assessing the nature of the credit risks associated with securities, irrespective of their final departmental assignment.

Other NAIC Departments

The SVO staff is always available to provide support to other NAIC departments in matters it is qualified to address. Some inquiries, such as those addressing specialized securities statutory accounting issues, are usually handled in coordination with the NAIC's financial reporting department in Kansas City. As with SVO interdepartmental questions, the issue of what defines the various forms of structured securities, debt versus equity, or even a security may require an analysis of the transaction's cash flow and legal structure as well as the underlying financial assets or other form of collateral, if any. Considerable care is taken in this process, as the improper categorization of a security could produce inaccurate risk-based capital calculations.

The Role of Nationally Recognized Statistical Rating Organizations

The ability of the SVO to convert NRSRO alpha ratings to NAIC designations is essential to its productivity. Currently, the SVO can only assign NAIC designations to asset-backed (and other structured securities) that have been rated by at least one NRSRO. As discussed earlier in this chapter, this policy is a function of several operational and regulatory factors. While the department may have the technical skills to analyze a limited number of structures and asset classes in detail, covering the growing universe of structured securities simultaneously in a manner comparable to that of the NRSROs is not part of its mission.

For example, the SVO does not perform on-site due diligence of issuer/originator operations. NRSRO ratings conversions are only permitted, however, if the SVO analyst can demonstrate a thorough understanding of the NRSRO's rating rationale for the applicable financial asset pool class and structure. Furthermore, should an SVO analyst disagree with an NRSRO's methodology and conclusions, the analyst may assign an NAIC Designation that is lower than what would normally be applied through the use of the equivalency table shown in Exhibit 5. SVO analysts may not, however, assign NAIC designations that would be higher than the equivalent of the highest NRSRO rating issued for that security. In cases of split NRSRO ratings, which translate to split NAIC designations, the VOS database will default to the lower NAIC designation. Should this occur, filers may appeal for the recognition of the higher NRSRO rating by the SVO. If the analyst agrees with the methodology and conclusion of the NRSRO assigning the higher rating, he may override the database default and assign the higher NAIC designation.

NAIC DESIGNATION REPORTS AND APPLICATIONS

Post-Acquisition Applications

Only an insurance company subject to the jurisdiction of a state or territory of the United States and obligated by its regulator to file Schedule D assets with the Securities Valuation Office may request a credit assessment or valuation from the SVO.

Exhibit 5: NAIC Designation and Corresponding NRSRO Ratings

NAIC Designation	NRSRO Ratings DCR	Fitch IBCA	Moody's	S&P	NAIC Meaning
1	AAA	AAA	Aaa	AAA	Highest Quality
1	AA+	AA+	Aa1	AA+	Highest Quality
1	AA	AA	Aa2	AA	Highest Quality
1	AA-	AA-	Aa3	AA-	Highest Quality
1	A+	A+	A1	A+	Highest Quality
1	A	A	A2	A	Highest Quality
1	A-	A-	A3	A-	Highest Quality
2	BBB+	BBB+	Baa1	BBB+	High Quality
2	BBB	BBB	Baa2	BBB	High Quality
2	BBB-	BBB-	Baa3	BBB-	High Quality
3	BB+	BB+	Ba1	BB+	Medium Quality
3	BB	BB	Ba2	BB	Medium Quality
3	BB-	BB-	Ba3	BB-	Medium Quality
4	B+	B+	B1	B+	Low Quality
4	B	B	B2	B	Low Quality
4	B-	B-	B3	B-	Low Quality
5	CCC	CCC	—	CCC+	Lower Quality
5	—	—	Caa	CCC	Lower Quality
5	—	—		CCC-	Lower Quality
5	—	CC	Ca	CC	Lower Quality
5	—	—	C	C	Lower Quality
5		—	—	D	Lower Quality
6	DD	C, DDD, DD, or D	In or Near Default	In or Near Default	In or Near Default

Security Acquisition Reports

Security acquisition reports (SARs) are filed by reporting insurance companies through the use of the NAIC's complimentary E-Form software. These reports must be completed by insurance companies or their designated filers (together generally known as the filers) and submitted to the SVO along with the appropriate documentation as specified in the P&P.

Rated Security Acquisition Reports

SVO filing requirements for the following types of NRSRO rated structured securities are relatively simple:

- Asset-backed securities.
- Common or preferred stock issued by a real estate investment trust (REIT).
- Commercial mortgage-backed securities.
- Residential mortgage-backed securities.
- Collateralized mortgage obligations (CMOs).
- Collateralized bond obligations (CBOs) and collateralized loan obligations(CLOs).
- Cross-border structured securities.

For securities falling within these categories, insurance companies are required to submit a completed SAR, evidence of a current rating from an NRSRO (issued or updated within the past 12 calendar months), and a prospectus or private-placement memorandum for the transaction.

While this information usually suffices for the assignment of an NAIC designation (especially for well tested financial asset classes and structures), the increasingly complex and diversified nature of asset securitizations often requires the SVO analyst to request additional information from the filer, the applicable NRSROs, or other parties related to the transaction.

Non-Rated Security Acquisition Reports

With the exception of credit tenant loans (CTLs), non-rated security acquisition reports (NRSARs) are currently not being accepted by the SVO for structured securities including asset-backed securities, residential mortgage-backed securities, commercial mortgage-backed securities, and REIT debt and preferred stock. As of first-quarter 1998, the Valuation of Securities Task Force, with the support of the SVO, was reviewing a proposal submitted by the interested parties for the formulation of an NAIC designation assignment policy for certain types of non-NRSRO-rated structured securities.

Annual Updates

Insurance companies are required to file annual update reports for all structured securities with the exception of agency CMOs, for which only SARs are required. In January 1996, the SVO was asked by the Invested Asset Working Group (IAWG) to coordinate with industry in developing a more sophisticated methodology for the annual update of asset- and residential mortgage-backed structured securities. The project was divided into three phases relating to the NRSRO status of the subject securities and the level of independent due diligence which the SVO is expected to apply.

Phase I

Phase I covers structured securities that were rated at closing and continue to be monitored by at least one NRSRO. For such securities, the reporting insurance companies are required to submit evidence of a current rating surveillance and action by the NRSRO. In cases where two or more NRSROs have assigned ratings that convert into different NAIC designations, the reporting companies are required to submit evidence of rating surveillance by all NRSROs that issued original ratings and that continue to monitor those ratings.

For example, suppose one NRSRO continues to assign an A rating (which converts to an NAIC 1) to the security and another NRSRO assigns a BBB rating (which converts to an NAIC 2) to the same security. That disparity would produce a split rating for NAIC conversion purposes, requiring confirmations for both ratings. Should one NRSRO assign an A while another has assigned an AA, however, only one of the rating confirmations would be required, as both ratings convert to an NAIC 1.

Phase II

Phase II structured securities were rated by at least one NRSRO at closing but are no longer monitored. Otherwise known as snapshot-rated, Phase II securities presented the SVO and regulators with a dilemma: How much information is required for a prudent credit decision? How can the SVO apply a single set of criteria for every possible type of securitized asset class and structure?

The solution prescribed by the VOS/TF was a two-tier information collection procedure that would allow the SVO to collect the core set of information required while allowing analysts to request additional information as deemed appropriate. In the first level of information collection reporting, insurance companies must submit certain core requirements to the Securities Valuation Office, namely, a copy of a current distribution/trustee report; and a description of the security's structural aspects providing protection from credit-related losses, such as the original and current credit enhancement levels.

If, after reviewing the security, the SVO analyst judges that the core requirements are insufficient to assess potential credit-related problems, additional information may be requested from the reporting insurance company. This might include data on the security's asset pool principal amortization, delinquencies, and cumulative loss experience.

Phase III

Phase III securities were never rated by an NRSRO. As of early 1998, the SVO did not accept new filings for such securities. Insurance companies that hold these securities may assign their own designations provided they add the Z and * suffixes. These suffixes inform the state regulators that the security has not been assigned an NAIC designation by the SVO because the type of investment is under regulatory review by the Valuation of Securities Task Force.

Appeal and Material Change

Appeal and material change forms are used by filers when they wish to appeal the assignment of a designation which they (usually) believe is too low, or provide the SVO with information on a security that has experienced a material change in its credit profile.

Exempt Securities

Many U.S. government and certain federal agencies securities need not be filed with the SVO unless a specific written request to do so is made by a state department of insurance. These include participation certificates in pass-through mortgage pools issued and guaranteed by Government National Mortgage Association (GNMA), Federal Home Loan Mortgage Corporation (FHLMC), and Federal

National Mortgage Association (FNMA) — with the exception of collateralized mortgage obligations issued by these agencies.

Also exempt from filing with the SVO are Treasury bills, notes and bonds. For a complete list of exempt securities, filers should consult the P&P or contact the SVO staff.

Advance Rating Service Applications

The advance rating service (ARS) offers filers the opportunity to secure a preliminary NAIC designation for a security prior to its purchase. While the volume of ARSs is relatively small in comparison to SARs, many filers find this service useful for determining the SVO's position, and, therefore, likely regulatory treatment under the NAIC financial conditions framework, for new structures or asset classes in which the nature of the transaction may present innovative structural elements or unique analytical issues. Insurance companies often rely on the proposed transaction's investment bankers to provide the SVO with the required information, and may designate such persons as information contacts.

While the Securities Valuation Office is authorized to assess a security on a pre-acquisition basis through the ARS, it is not required to do so. ARS requests are initiated by insurance companies through the filing of an advance rating service application/application and statement of terms and conditions form (the ARS application form) with the valuation office. For asset-backed and residential mortgage-backed securities, the structured securities department requires applicants to provide the SVO with the information outlined in a questionnaire specifically tailored for these transactions and to complete the associated forms.

Should the SVO issue a preliminary NAIC designation pursuant to an ARS application, the filer will still be required to submit an SAR if it chooses subsequently to purchase the security. It should be noted that the assignment of a preliminary NAIC designation is not published in the VOS publication or released on CD ROM, may not be used as a reporting mechanism for statutory accounting or state insurance regulatory purposes, and does not commit the SVO to assign an identical post-purchase designation. Preliminary NAIC designations are not binding and are valid only on the date of issuance, since these designations are a reflection of draft documents and assumed collateral asset pool data. Nevertheless, it is unlikely the SVO will assign a designation that differs from the preliminary NAIC designation if the final form and substance of the security issued and purchased by the applicant is not materially different from that reviewed during the ARS application process.

ARS Questionnaire

For asset-backed and residential mortgage-backed securities, the SVO structured securities department requires ARS applicants to submit a comprehensive analytical package for proposed transactions. While required information may vary depending upon the nature of the financial asset pool and the proposed structure, the following outline and attached questionnaires have been drafted to provide guidance to applicants.

Credit Package

The credit package should cover all the basic components of the transaction, including:

- The nature and history of the financial asset pool (and associated obligors) to be securitized.
- The cash flow priority of payments and transaction legal structure.
- The financial condition, operational characteristics, and industry position of the seller/servicer.
- An overview of the identity and role of all counter-parties and third-party credit enhancement, liquidity support, and all other transaction specific service providers.

Generally, a typical structured security private placement memorandum satisfies these and other information criteria.

NRSRO Package

All information provided to the nationally recognized statistical rating organizations (i.e., rating agencies) should be submitted to the Securities Valuation Office. The NRSRO's preliminary rating letter should also be included.

Cash Flow Model

A detailed cash flow model of the transaction should be provided. The model should include a key explaining the nature and purpose of all inputs and outputs and showing the formulae for all calculation fields as well as the interrelationship between fields. The model should be submitted in hard copy form for both base and stress scenarios. An input field justification memorandum should be included. Additionally, a diskette with the model (preferably written in Microsoft Excel) is requested.

Due Diligence Reports

Financial asset pool originator due diligence reports — preferably drafted by an independent accounting firm — should be included if available.

Transaction Diagrams

Transaction diagrams should be included, illustrating expected and contingent funds flows as well as identifying the roles of all transaction participants.

Form of Investor Report

A form-of-investor (i.e., trustee) report should be prepared with a key showing the calculations for the source and uses of the transaction cash flows. The report should include a section specifying all the trigger events, whether driven by cash flow or financial ratio event. It should be made available in a PC. spreadsheet form (preferably written in Microsoft Excel). The SVO structured securities department requires formulation and clear formatting of a specific methodology for tracking all key surveillance variables for the purpose of security annual updates.

Form of Legal Opinions

The form of bankruptcy-remote and true-sale legal opinions should be provided by appropriate counsel. For transactions involving non-U.S. legal risks, opinions should also be provided with respect to the risk of the local functional equivalent of the U.S. Bankruptcy Court's automatic stay procedures.

Proposed Transaction Information Tables

The following questionnaires (as shown in Exhibits 6, 7, 8, 9, and 10) should be completed. For portions of the questionnaires that are not applicable, the applicant may either draw a diagonal line in the space or insert N/A.

- Working Party List.
- Security Profile.
- Transaction Participant NRSRO Ratings.
- Top Obligor NRSRO Ratings.
- Originator/Issuer Borrowing History.

The SVO analyst retains complete discretion to extend the investigation to whatever extent deemed necessary in order to arrive at an appropriate NAIC designation.

CONCLUSION

The NAIC/SVO's structured securities department is a new entity formed in January 1995 along with several other product and industry specialty departments within the context of the office's last reorganization. The department has divided analytical responsibilities between analysts covering commercial mortgage-related securities and counterparty risks and analysts covering asset/residential mortgage-backed securities. A major project to review all structured securities on the database has been undertaken and numerous special projects have been completed addressing the characteristics of new and developing forms of financial asset securitizations.

In addition, the SVO is working with industry and the interested parties in developing analytical criteria for non-NRSRO rated securitizations. Given the increasing importance and the sheer magnitude of securitization as a financing instrument and investment vehicle on a national and, increasingly, on an international scale, the ability of the SVO to promptly and intelligently respond to inquiries from industry and NAIC member states is key to the satisfactory fulfillment of the department's mission.

Exhibit 6: Working Party List

TRANSACTION

SVO DEPARTMENT	SENIOR ANALYST(S)	TELEPHONE

COMPANY	CONTACT	TELEPHONE

Issuer/Originator[A]

A. Party may also be defined as "Seller", "Borrower" or "Transferor."

Investment Bank(s)

NRSROs

Duff & Phelps Credit Rating Co.		
Fitch Investors Service, L.P.		
Moody's Investors Service		
Standard & Poor's Ratings Group		

Issuer/Originator Counsel

Issuer/Originator Accountant

Trustee/Issuing & Paying Agent

Lead Investors

Lead Investor Counsel

Rating Agency Counsel

DCR			
Fitch			
Moody's			
S & P			

Exhibit 7: Security Profile

1. Financial Asset Pool

Type Financial Asset Pool (Asset/Obligors)					
$ Amount Financial Asset Pool ('000,000)		***Max.***	***Min.***	***Avg.***	***Median***
$ Amount Receivable/Mortgage					
Number of Obligors					
Weighted Average Original Life (WAOL)		**Weighted Average Coupon or**			
Weighted Average Remaining Life (WARL)		**Gross Portfolio Yield**			

2. Tranche Size and NRSRO Rating(s)

Tranche	**Amount** ($ '000,000)	**% Total**	**Preliminary NRSRO Ratings**			
			DCR	*Fitch*	*Moody's*	*S&P*
A						
Total						

3. Tranche Amortization and Maturity

Tranche	**Closing Date**	**Legal Maturity**	**Expected Maturity**	**Expected WAL**[A]	**Prepayment Speed**		**1st Pmt. Principal**	**Amort./ Bullet?**[C]
					Type[B]	*Speed*		
A								

A. Expected Weighted Average Life
B. Single Monthly Mortality (SMM); Constant Prepayment Rate (CPR); Public Securities Association (PSA) Convention, etc.
C. Amortizing or Bullet paydown?

4. Tranche Spread & Yield

Tranche	**Coupon**	**Price** (%)	**Index**	**Spread** (+/- %)	**Yield**	**1st Pmt. Interest**	**Pmts Yr.**[A]	**Basis**[B]	**U/W Fee** (%)
A									

A. Number of payments per year;
B. Basis (i.e. (30/365), etc.)

5. Tranche Investor Profile

Tranche	**Investor**	**Investor** State/Country	**Amount** ($ '000,000)	**% Total Tranche**	**% Total Transaction**
A					
Total					

Exhibit 8: Transaction Participant NRSRO Ratings

Type	Entity	Long-Term Senior Unsecured NRSRO Rating[1]						
		DCR	Fitch	IBCA[6]	Moody's	S&P	Thomson[7]	
Borrower/[2] Transferor								
Servicer								
B/T Country								
B/T Parent 1[3]								
B/T Parent 2[3]								
Credit Enhancer								
Surety[4]								
Counter-party[5]								
Lead Investor A								
Lead Investor B								

1. If a rating other than the long-term senior unsecured rating is available, include such rating and specify type debt or form of paying ability rated.
   If no rating is available mark "NR."
   If the rating is on a form of NRSRO credit watch, specify by noting "?-" for credit watch with *negative* implications or "?+" for credit watch with *positive* implications after the alpha rating.
2. If the transaction is a secured loan, the entity will be a "*borrower.*" If the transaction is a securitization of financial assets, the entity will be a "*transferor.*"
3. Always specify "parent" ownership % of borrower/transferor after name of company.
4. If the subject transaction includes a performance bond, specify issuer of the surety bond and ratings, if any. (Monoline financial guarantee companies should be listed under Credit Enhancer.)
5. If the transaction involves a material form of counterparty risk (i.e. a swap), specify ratings of the applicable counterparties.
6. IBCA: Limited to ratings of any Non-US Institution and any US Financial Institution.
7. Thomson Bank Watch: Limited to rating of issuers who are banking and financial institutions.

Exhibit 9: Top Obligor NRSRO Ratings

No.	Obligor & Parent[1]		G.?[2]	Long-Term Senior Unsecured NRSRO Rating[4]						
			%[3]	DCR	Fitch	IBCA[5]	Moody's	S&P	Thomson[6]	
1	O									
	P		%							
2	O									
	P		%							
3	O									
	P		%							
4	O									
	P		%							
5	O									
	P		%							
6	O									
	P		%							
7	O									
	P		%							
8	O									
	P		%							
9	O									
	P		%							
10	O									
	P		%							

1. Obligor ("O") & Parent ("P")
2. Does the parent guarantee its subsidiary's obligation? (Y/N)
3. Always specify "parent" ownership % of obligor after name of company.
4. If a rating other than the long-term senior unsecured rating is available, include such rating and specify type debt or form of paying ability rated
   If no rating is available mark "NR."
   If the rating is on a form of NRSRO credit watch, specify by noting "?-" for credit watch with *negative* implications or "?+" for credit watch with *positive* implications after the alpha rating.
5. IBCA: Limited to ratings of any Non-US Institution and any US Financial Institution.
6. Thomson Bank Watch: Limited to rating of issuers who are banking and financial institutions.

Exhibit 10: Originator/Issuer Borrowing History

	Borrowing			
	1	2	3	4
Security Name				
CUSIP/PPN/CINS:				
Type Borrowing/Facility				
Transaction Date				
Last Settlement Date				
Original Amount (US$ MM)				
Outstanding Amount (US$ MM)				
Description				
Status				

Section II:

Non-Mortgage Related ABS Products

Chapter 10

Auto Loan Asset-Backed Securities

W. Alexander Roever, CFA
Director Asset Backed Research
First Chicago Capital Markets, Inc.

John N. McElravey
Vice President Asset Backed Research
First Chicago Capital Markets, Inc.

Glenn M. Schultz
Vice President Asset Backed Research
First Chicago Capital Markets, Inc.

INTRODUCTION

Since the first transactions were completed in 1985, the securitization of auto loans has been a staple of the ABS market. Between 1985 and 1997, over $200 billion of publicly traded ABS backed by auto loans and leases were issued (Exhibit 1). The auto sector has consistently been one of the market's largest contributors, accounting for slightly more than 20% of all public ABS issuance since 1994.

The growth of the auto ABS market has coincided with, and has undoubtedly contributed to, the growth of the auto finance market. Between 1985 and 1996 annual issuance of auto ABS grew at an annualized rate in excess of 30%. Over the same period the amount of auto loans outstanding approximately doubled. According to the Federal Reserve, securitization was the ultimate funding source for more than one of every eight auto loans outstanding at the end of 1996 (Exhibit 2).

Compared to the traditional means of financing their operations, securitization has proven an attractive funding alternative for many auto lenders. Most auto lenders have historically been "balance sheet lenders," meaning they financed their operations using various forms of on-balance sheet debt such as bank loans, commercial paper, and corporate bonds. Relying on these kinds of financing alone, a lender's revenue, and ultimately its profitability, is constrained by its ability to leverage the assets on its balance sheet. This competitive paradigm favored larger, well capitalized lenders with strong credit profiles because they had access to large amounts of money at relatively low costs of funds. Smaller lenders, and others of lesser credit quality, were competitively disadvantaged in this scheme since their size and greater costs of funds restricted their ability to grow their businesses.

The advent of securitization transformed auto lending's competitive landscape by providing lenders with a new source of financing that was both off-balance sheet and relatively low cost. This new source of funding provided a steady source of liquidity which could be used to fuel asset creation. This liquidity eliminated the barriers to competition that had constrained many lenders. The off-balance sheet nature of securitization meant the size of a lender's portfolio no longer needed to be limited by its ability to leverage its assets. Better still, through the use of various structuring techniques and means of credit enhancement, a non-investment grade lender could use its loans to create a AAA rated security, with an all-in financing cost comparable to that of high grade corporate debt.

Exhibit 1: Issuance History
Publicly Traded Auto ABS

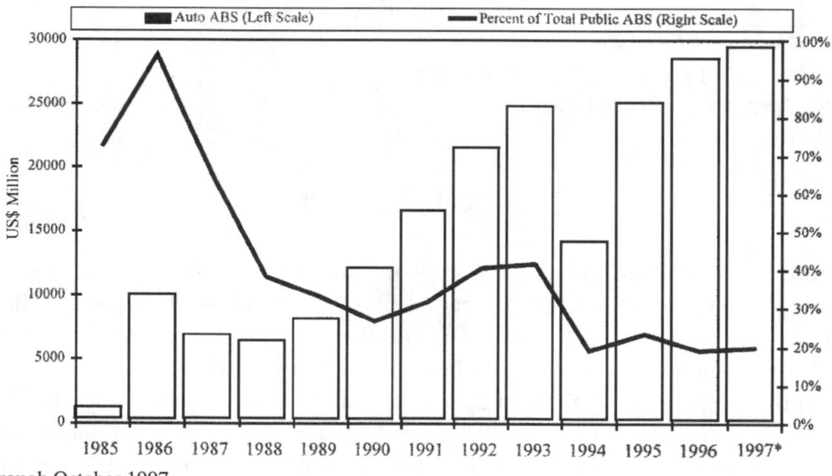

* Through October 1997

Exhibit 2: Auto Loan Securitization

	Year Ended December 31							
	1989	1990	1991	1992	1993	1994	1995	1996
Auto Loans Outstanding ($ Bil.)	$292	$285	$261	$258	$282	$329	$365	$393
Percent:								
Held by Banks	43	44	43	42	43	43	41	39
Held by Finance Companies	29	26	24	22	20	21	22	22
Held by Other Lenders*	22	21	21	22	23	24	25	25
Held in Securitized Pools**	6	9	11	13	14	11	12	13

* Other lenders are primarily credit unions.

** Includes assets supporting ABS, ABCP Conduits, and bulk sales of loans.

Source: Federal Reserve

Even so, the advantages of securitization for auto lenders go beyond increased liquidity and lower costs of funds. Securitization can also be a source of accounting profit, and a method of income management. Current U.S. accounting regulations, such as SFAS 125,[1] allow qualifying securitizers to realize the present value of expected excess servicing (the difference between interest earned and expenses paid in a securitization) as *a gain* at the time that a pool of loans is sold into a securitization. This can be a significant benefit to auto lenders since auto loans, depending on the credit quality of the obligor, may have anywhere from 3% to 10% or more excess servicing. By securitizing the loan and applying "gain-on-sale" accounting techniques, lenders have the ability to accelerate earnings by realizing excess servicing as current income, rather than waiting to book the income as payments are made over the life of the loan.

AUTO SECURITIZATION IS DRIVEN BY SEVERAL TYPES OF LENDERS

The auto finance industry is currently populated by several types of lenders, most of whom have relied on securitization to varying degrees. ABS investors should be aware that each type of lender presents a different risk profile with respect to the obligor quality of the loans they securitize and their stability as servicers.

Banks

Banks have historically originated more auto loans than any other type of lender, but have generated a proportionately lesser volume of ABS. From 1985 through late 1997, banks originated about 22% of public auto ABS issuance. From an investor's perspective, banks generally provide an attractive risk profile both in terms of the collateral they originate and their strength as servicers. Many banks, such as Chase Manhattan, originate and securitize high quality loan portfolios which tend to experience low levels of delinquencies and defaults. Other banks, like Chevy Chase, have instead focused on loans to individuals with poor credit histories. Although the credit performance of these loans tends to be poorer, the performance is usually more than offset by the higher coupons charged to borrowers.

Banks also have several attractive qualities compared with some other auto loan servicers. Chief among these traits is the continuity of servicing banks can offer. In the event a bank's auto lending operation begins to experience losses, banks generally have other sources of revenue which can be used to support their loan servicing operation.

Captive Finance Companies

Captive finance companies are the dedicated finance subsidiaries of auto manufacturers. Historically, captives have been responsible for the majority of auto

[1] SFAS 125, *Accounting for Transfers and Servicing of Financial Assets and Extinguishments of Liabilities.*

ABS origination. Since 1985, captives originated over half of all auto ABS, with the bulk of their issues supported by prime quality obligors. Like banks, the captives annual contributions have fluctuated. In recent years, some of the larger captives like GMAC and Ford Credit have shifted some of their securitization activities from the ABS market into the asset-backed commercial paper market, which can offer even lower cost funding. Offsetting this trend has been a growing use of the ABS market by foreign captives such as Toyota, Honda, and Nissan.

The captives' primary business purpose is to promote and support the sales of their parents' manufacturing operation. For this reason there may exist some incentive for captives to price loans aggressively in order to promote sales. As such, pools originated by captives may experience higher delinquencies and losses than otherwise identical pools originated by other types of lenders. On the positive side, in the event the captive were to experience financial difficulties, its manufacturing parent has a significant incentive (although not necessarily an obligation) to support the finance subsidiaries operations.

Monoline Lenders

Monoline lenders are independent finance companies that specialize in auto lending. These specialized firms have been perhaps the biggest beneficiaries of securitization, and are a growing presence in the ABS market. Between 1985 and late 1997, monolines accounted for 25% of auto ABS originations, but in both 1996 and 1997 monolines accounted for about one third of total volume.

Most monolines originate loans to credit impaired borrowers. The larger monolines like Arcadia Financial, Union Acceptance Corporation, and WFS Financial focus on marginally weaker obligors, while many smaller monolines concentrate their operations at the absolute bottom of the credit spectrum. While the majority of the securitization activities of sub-prime monolines has historically been in the private placement market, some of these firms, including AmeriCredit and National Auto Finance, have achieved sufficient scale to regularly securitize in the public market.

Because they are independent and typically non-investment grade companies, monolines can present greater servicing risks than other types of lenders. In the event a monoline servicer comes into financial difficulty, there are relatively few safeguards, short of employing a replacement servicer, available to ensure servicing continuity. Such continuity is particularly important in servicing non-prime and sub-prime obligors where any servicing disruption is likely to result in a significant increase in losses.

Multiline Lenders

Multiline lenders are independent financial institutions, where auto finance is one of several business lines. Recent growth in this small segment of the auto ABS market has been fueled by the entrance of lenders like The Money Store and Advanta into the sub-prime sector of the market. Drawn by the potential profitability of sub-prime lending and the opportunity to benefit from the consolidation of a fragmented industry, these lenders have quickly become leading originators of sub-prime auto ABS.

Although the multilines are relatively new to sub-prime auto lending, the financial strength created by their diversified business mix, as well as their demonstrated ability to service a wide variety of asset types, should provide investors with some margin of comfort versus competing monoline lenders.

AUTO ABS ARE OFTEN CATEGORIZED BY OBLIGOR TYPE

There is a tendency within the auto sector to segment the market by obligor quality. Descriptive labels such as "prime," "non-prime," and "sub-prime" and quality grades such as A, B, C, and D are commonly used in describing the credit quality of the underlying assets. Unfortunately for investors, these terms are very subjective, and their meaning often varies from one lender to another. As a result, there can be some disagreement among lenders over what constitutes a prime, non-prime, or sub-prime borrower. What one lender considers a prime quality loan, might be considered non-prime by another lender.

The absence of clear and consistent credit quality delineation makes the task of assessing collateral quality more challenging but not impossible. Exhibit 3 attempts to better define the most common collateral labels. In a perfect world, it might be possible to judge pool quality by comparing some objective quality measure such as average credit scores. Credit scoring models, like those produced by Fair, Isaac & Co. (FICO), evaluate several obligor specific factors including but not limited to delinquency and default history, prior bankruptcy, and number and usage of credit lines and assigns a score to each obligor. Although credit scores are widely used by auto lenders, data regarding scores are rarely made available to ABS investors.

In the absence of objective collateral quality measures, investors can use a pool's weighted average coupon (WAC), or alternatively its weighted average annualized percentage rate, as an indicator of average obligor quality. Assuming that lenders appropriately price the risk of loss into their loans, pools with higher WACs should be riskier than identical pools with lower WACs. While this assumption is generally a valid one, there are situations where it may not apply. One such situation could occur when a manufacturer's finance subsidiary originates loans at artificially low rates in order to promote vehicle sales. Another such situation could occur when a lender, new to a market, under prices loans either inadvertently or purposely, as a tactic to gain market share.

Using WACs as an indicator of collateral credit risk, it is possible to develop an issuance history by pool quality. Exhibit 4 shows this history and demonstrates that securitizations backed by non-prime obligors always accounted for a significant portion of auto ABS transaction volume.

Exhibit 3: Making Sense of Obligor Quality

Borrower Quality	Prime			Non-Prime		Sub-Prime
Borrower Grade	A+	A	A−	B	C	D
FICO Scale*	900 720	660	620	600	500	400
Credit History	Good credit, No Derogatories		Very minor, explainable problems	Moderate, perhaps recurring problems	Serious, recurring problems	Sever problems, demonstrated unwillingness to pay
Typical Weighted Average Collateral Coupon	8<12%			12<16%	16<20%	20% or greater (up to state usury limits)
Typical Pool Delinquency Rate	<2.5%			<5%	<10%	<20%
Typical Pool Cumulative Foreclosure Rate	<3%			<6%	<20%	<40%
Typical Pool Cumulative Losses	<2%			4%	10%	>10%

* FICO scores are a product of Fair, Issac and Company and are based on predictive data available in individual credit bureau reports. The scores shown are intended as a general indicator of obligor credit quality, and are based on research conducted by First Chicago Capital Markets. The scores presented are not endorsed by Fair, Issac and Company. Different lenders can have varying interpretations of credit scores.

Exhibit 4: Auto ABS Issuance by WAC

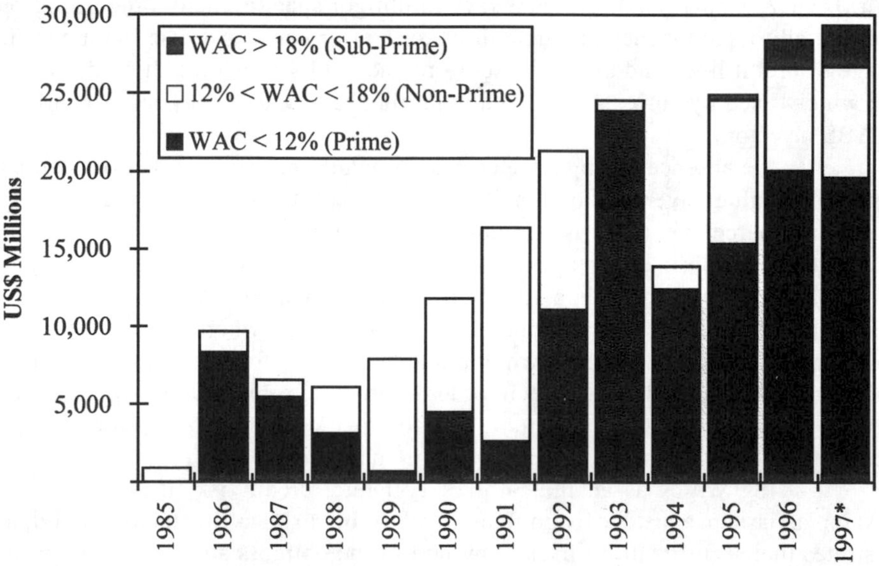

* Through October 1997

Exhibit 5: Market Segmentation
*Issuer Type: 1985-1997**

	Prime <12%	Non-Prime 12%<18%	Sub-Prime >18%	As % of Auto ABS Issuance
Banks	21%	26%	2%	22%
Captives	55%	49%	0%	52%
Monolines	23%	26%	74%	25%
Multilines	1%	0%	24%	1%
Total	100%	100%	100%	100%

Obligor Type

	Prime <12%	Non-Prime 12%<18%	Sub-Prime >18%	Total
Banks	60%	40%	0%	100%
Captives	68%	32%	0%	100%
Monolines	57%	36%	7%	100%
Multilines	54%	0%	46%	100%
As % of Auto ABS Issuance	63%	35%	2%	100%

* Analysis as of October 1997

It is also possible, using WACs as a guideline, to decompose the industry by originator and obligor type as in Exhibit 5. Between 1985 and October 1997, prime, non-prime, and sub-prime collateral accounted for 63%, 35%, and 2% of total issuance, respectively. Captive finance companies were responsible for over half of all issuance, and were the largest issuers of both prime and non-prime ABS. Monolines have accounted for approximately three-quarters of all public market sub-prime issuance.

RATING AGENCY EVALUATION OF AUTO ABS

As in any ABS transaction, rating agency analysis of an auto loan securitization includes key credit, structural, and legal issues. A rating agency will conduct a due diligence review of the servicer's collection capabilities, review the underwriting criteria of the originator of the loans, analyze the performance characteristics of the loan portfolio over time with regard to delinquencies and defaults, examine the transaction structure, stress test the cash flows, and review any pertinent legal issues. Each of these factors play a role in the calculation of the credit enhancement needed to maintain the desired rating on the securities issued.

Originator/Servicer

In general, the originator of the loans will also service the loan portfolio. The quality of the originator's underwriting criteria and its ability to service the portfolio are key elements in a transaction's rating. The rating agency's due diligence on a company will include a review of its history, management's experience in auto lending and its policies and procedures, the business plan and strategy for the firm's growth, and its capital structure and financial strength. Three to five years of operating history is preferred by the agencies; however, firms with less operating history, but more experienced management, may be able to pass muster. Some firms, particularly in the sub-prime lending arena, have been in business only a short time, but have senior managers who have been active in the field with another entity. A rating agency may take into account management's experience and track record at another firm when deciding whether to rate a transaction for a lender with less operating history.

The underwriting standards of the originator are one of the critical pieces of the rating agency review. The make-up and consistency of the credit extension process is closely scrutinized, including key underwriting criteria, the use of credit scoring models, whether loans are originated in a central location or at the branch level, and the terms and conditions of the loan. In addition, the servicing capabilities of the company are an important consideration because good servicing can improve a transaction, and poor servicing can harm an otherwise sound transaction. The elements of a servicer analyzed by the rating agencies include the firm's ratio of accounts to collectors, whether the firm utilizes monthly notices or a coupon book for obligors to make payments, its repossession criteria, and the ability and speed with which the firm liquidates repossessed inventory. These servicing skills become even more critical when the transaction involves sub-prime obligors because of the extra attention that those loans require.

Despite the emphasis on the ability of the originator/servicer in the due diligence process, the agencies will generally assume that the servicer will go bankrupt and not be available to service the portfolio during the life of the transaction. This is especially true for servicers whose own debt rating is below investment-grade or which is unrated. As a result, the provisions for transferring servicing to a back-up servicer will be reviewed closely. For some transactions, including those from relatively new issuers with shorter histories, an investment-grade back-up servicer may need to be named at the outset.

Portfolio Characteristics and Performance

To determine the level of credit enhancement needed to support the rating, the agencies will stress the actual performance of the portfolio with regard to delinquencies, defaults, and recoveries. The rating agencies stress test a transaction to achieve an investment-grade rating by using a multiple of the historical loss experience to simulate a transaction's performance in a stressful economic environment (see Exhibit 6). Higher loss multiples are used for higher rating categories.

To perform this analysis, static pool performance data are required and the delinquency and charge-off policies of the company are examined. As noted above, the agencies prefer to have at least three to five years of data in order to calculate a loss curve for the servicer because cumulative losses on auto loan portfolios tend to peak between 12 and 24 months. This relationship makes it difficult to accurately predict performance for startup companies that have little historical performance data or for companies that have high rates of growth. For these reasons, the static pool data is a necessary part of the rating process.

Exhibit 6: Loss Multiples Used to Rate Auto ABS

Rating	Minimum Loss Multiples
AAA	4-5× base-case loses
AA	3-4×
A	2-3×
BBB	1.75-2×
BB	1.5-1.75×

Source: Standard & Poor's

The credit risk analysis looks to the characteristics of the loan portfolio to determine the stress multiples applied to the historical performance data. Some of the key characteristics used to measure the risk profile of the portfolio include the proportion of used cars relative to new cars, the distribution of autos by model year, the level of recourse back to the dealer, the geographic concentration in any one city, state, or region of the country, the seasoning of the accounts, and the level of delinquencies that may impact the risk of liquidity shortfalls. Any risk added by these factors can be accounted for by adjusting the multiple applied to the historical loss data. For example, higher geographic concentrations or higher proportions of used cars, which can add to the risk in a transaction and can be accounted for by using a higher loss multiple.

Stress Tests, Transaction Structure, and Legal Issues

Once a stressed loss assumption is calculated it can be applied to the transaction structure to stress the cash flows and determine the level of credit enhancement required to maintain the rating on the securities, even in the event of severe economic events. The rating agency will compile the assumptions under a worst case scenario, and use that scenario as its basis for establishing credit enhancement levels.

As part of this analysis, the agency will review the structure of the transaction. One of the key elements of an auto transaction, and particularly a subprime auto transaction, is the amount of excess spread produced by the loan portfolio. Under normal conditions, excess spread would be available to flow back to the servicer after all other obligations have been satisfied. In the event of rising delinquencies or losses, that excess spread would flow through the cash flow waterfall and be available to absorb losses or provide liquidity. In addition, there may be trigger events in the transaction based on the level of delinquencies or losses. These triggers could be used as a signal to trap excess cash in a reserve account to provide additional credit enhancement in the case where delinquencies or losses are greater than expected. If triggers are a part of a transaction, the rating agency will look closely to see that the level at which the trigger is tripped is adequate to protect the note holders from a loss of principal or interest.

The priority of payments is also closely examined by the agency to make sure that there is proper protection for each class of note holders, and that the conditions of the rating accurately reflect the cash flow priority. In addition to these structural issues, the other parties to the transaction, such as the trustee or any external credit enhancement providers, would also be analyzed to ensure that they can fulfill their assigned role in the transaction. Finally, legal document review is undertaken to ensure that the requirements of the rating are accurately reflected in the indenture or pooling and servicing agreements, legal opinions, and other documents.

FACTORS TO CONSIDER IN RELATIVE VALUE ANALYSIS OF AUTO ABS

Several factors impact relative value in the auto ABS market. The first of these factors are issuer and collateral type. Over the life of an ABS, an originator/servicer with a strong credit profile is less likely than a weaker servicer to encounter problems that could interfere with its ability to effectively service loans. ABS supported by stronger servicers should garner higher prices because there is less risk of a servicing interruption, and therefore greater certainty that collateral collections will be made and applied in a timely fashion. Likewise, since collections from sub-prime collateral can be more unpredictable than those from prime collateral, and because this unpredictability translates into greater risk for the originator/servicer, ABS supported by sub-prime loans price at a discount to otherwise comparable bonds.

The greater servicer risk posed by the specialty finance companies is reflected in their respective ABS pricing. Exhibit 7 illustrates that these risks translate into spread tiering in the 2-year auto sector. Both banks and captive automobile ABS issuers enjoy pricing that is somewhat better than the market average, while the independent finance companies, both multiline and monoline, price at wider spreads.

Another factor affecting relative value is the structure of the securitization and its effect on the cash flow profile of the bond. Automobile ABS securities are structured as either a grantor trust or a owner trust. Although there are significant legal and tax differences between the two types of trusts, these differences are largely irrelevant from a relative value perspective. However, the profile of expected repayments implied by each trust type significantly affects relative value.

Exhibit 7: Pricing Differentials in the Auto Market

Issuer	Issuer Type	Collateral Type	Avg. Life (yr.)	Spread 11/21/1997
FORDO 1997-B A3	Captive	Prime	1.8	49
CMOAT1997-B A3	Bank	Prime	1.7	50
UAC 1996-D A2	Monoline	Non-Prime	1.9	60
TMSGT 1996-2 A3	Multiline	Sub-Prime	2.0	69

In a grantor trust principal and interest are passed through to the investors on a pro rata basis. While ABS issued from grantor trusts may be tranche into senior and subordinate bonds, no time tranching is allowed. Grantor trust ABS are repaid over the life of the securitization and as a result have wide payment windows. In contrast to the grantor trust, an owner trust structure provides for maturity tranching. The tranching of the owner trust allows the issuer to create bonds designed to satisfy investors' maturity preferences and alters the timing of the cash flows received by the bond holder. When assessing relative value, investors must determine the merits of wide window structures (grantor trusts) versus tighter window structures (owner trusts). Wide window auto ABS do not "roll down" the curve as fast as tight window auto ABS.[2] Consequently, investors require a higher spread for a wide window bond as compensation for the lack of price appreciation caused by the slower roll down. This spread differential between wide window and tight window ABS will increase as the yield curve steepens, and will decrease as it flattens.

Still another factor to consider is the effect of prepayments on the average life of the bond. The use of the appropriate prepayment assumption is critical when pricing auto ABS. Faster than expected prepayments result in a shorter than expected average life. Conversely, slower prepayments result in a longer average life.

Fortunately for investors, auto ABS demonstrate relatively stable prepayments as measured by the absolute prepayment speed (ABS) scale. The ABS scale is used because auto loans tend to demonstrate increasing prepayment speeds as they season when measured by Constant Payment Rate (CPR). The ABS scale is calculated using the actual number of loans in a pool. Next, the survivability factor is determined and the number of loans paid off is calculated and expressed as a percentage of the original number of loans in the pool. For purposes of yield and average life calculations, the original balance and contract rate of the individual loans is assumed to be equal to the average original balance and contract rate of the pool. Consequently, a ABS scale expresses prepayments as a percentage of the original balance. For example, a 1.5% ABS indicates that 1.5% of the original balance is prepaid each month.

The difference between the ABS and CPR measurement lies in the outstanding balance used to calculate monthly prepayment rates. ABS is calculated by comparing actual monthly prepayments to the original outstanding balance, whereas CPR is calculated by comparing the current outstanding balance to actual monthly prepayments as measured by the single monthly mortality rate (SMM). The ABS to CPR conversion is performed as follows:

1. Convert the ABS into a SMM using the following equation:[3]

---

[2] "Roll down" refers to the rate at which a bond's average life shortens as the bond ages. Assuming a static, positively sloping yield curve, a fixed-rate bond will appreciate in price as it ages because the benchmark used to reprice the bond will have a lower yield than its original benchmark. All else being equal, the greater a bond's rate of roll down, the greater its period total will be.

[3] Anand K. Bhattacharya, "Prepayment Nomenclature in the ABS Market," Chapter 22 in Anand K. Bhattacharya and Frank J Fabozzi (eds.), *Asset Backed Securities* (New Hope, PA: Frank J. Fabozzi and Associates 1996).

Exhibit 8: CPR Equivalent of 1.5 ABS

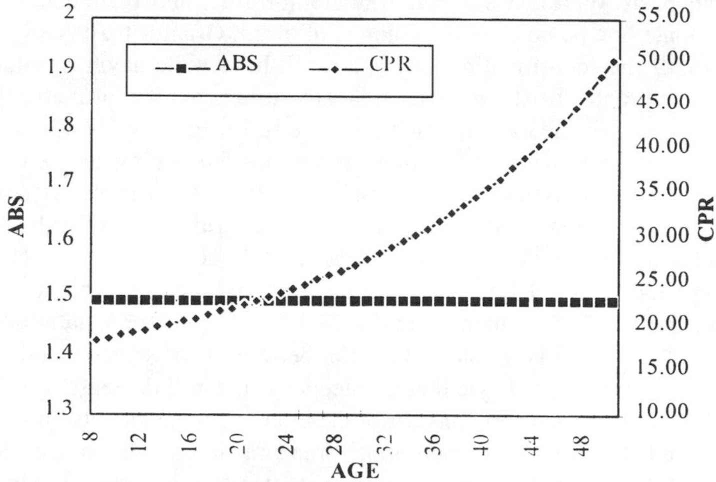

$$SMM = (100 \times ABS) \div [100 - ABS(M-1)] \tag{1}$$

where

SMM = percentage of the remaining balance at the beginning of the month after subtracting the scheduled principal payment that will prepay in the month.

M = months from origination.

2. Compute the annual CPR as follows:[4]

$$CPR = (1 - SMM)^{12} - 1 \tag{2}$$

Exhibit 8 provides an ABS to CPR conversion assuming a constant 1.5 ABS scale. The exhibit shows that a constant ABS scale pricing assumption implies a continuously rising CPR curve. This is the principal flaw of the constant ABS pricing assumption. Fortunately for the investor, there is only a small principal balance outstanding at the end of the pool's life. As a result, constant ABS pricing does not result in a significant error when calculating either the yield to maturity or average life of a pool.

Actual experience shows that auto prepayments, expressed as a CPR, do not continually rise as a pool seasons. Exhibit 9 provides an example of typical automobile prepayment rates in both ABS and CPR terms. The exhibit shows that prepayments measured in CPR terms tend to increase for about 36 months and then level off. As a result, prepayments in ABS terms do not remain constant over the life of the pool. Instead, ABS prepayments remain constant for about 36 months and then decline near the end of the pool's life

[4] Frank J. Fabozzi, *Fixed Income Mathematics* (Chicago, IL: Probus Publishing, 1993).

Exhibit 9: GMAC 1994 Prepayments

(a) GMAC 1994-A Actual versus Pricing ABS

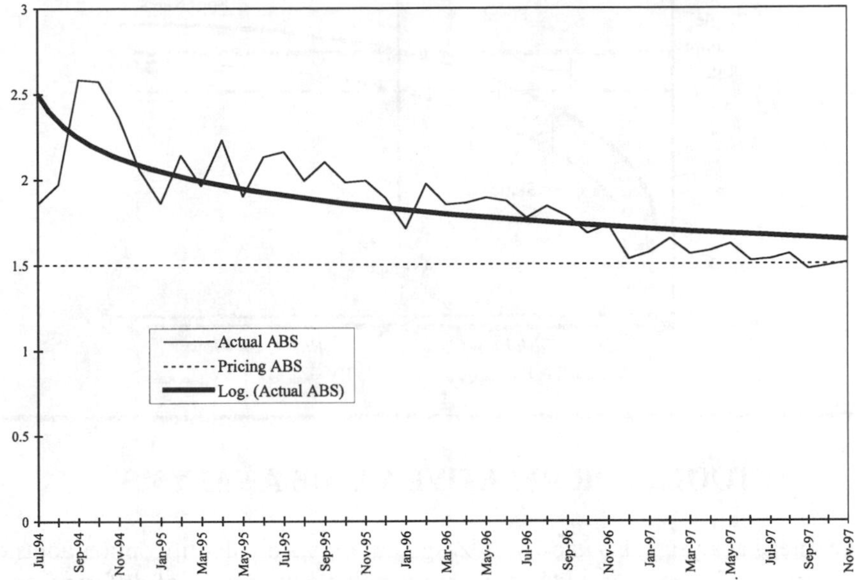

(b) GMAC 1994-A Actual versus Pricing CPR

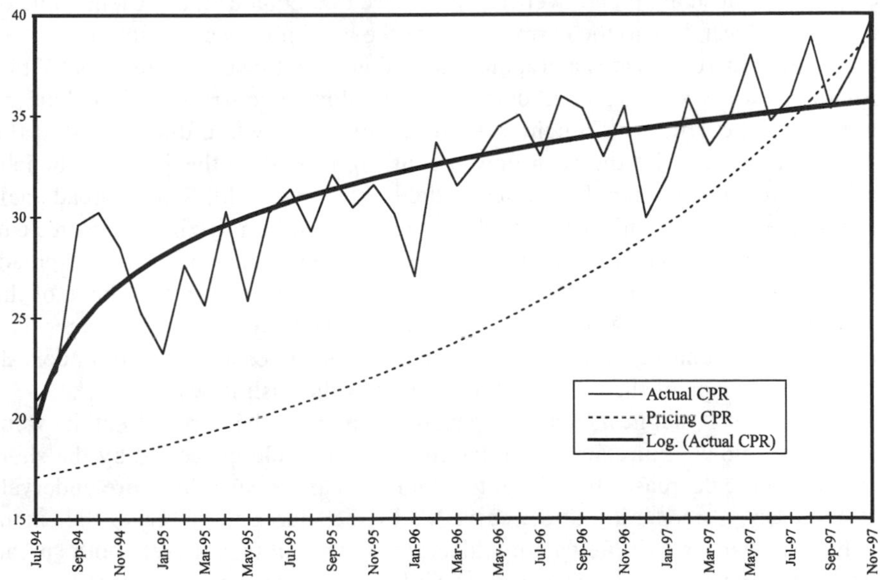

Exhibit 10: Static Spread Analysis

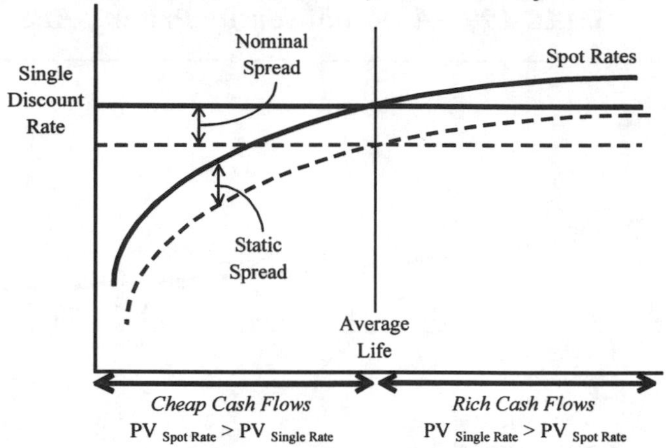

TOOLS FOR RELATIVE VALUE ANALYSIS

Static spread analysis (also known as "Z-spread" or "zero volatility option-adjusted spread analysis") can be used to compare the bullet equivalency of different structures. Static spread analysis views the cash flows of an amortizing structure as a series of zero-coupon cash flows. Using the basic bond pricing formula, the static spread is the constant spread over the spot curve that equates the present value of the projected cash flow to the current price of the bond plus accrued interest.

Exhibit 10 provides a graphic illustration of static spread analysis. With a normal, upwardly sloping yield curve the cash flows occurring earlier than the maturing of the Treasury benchmark are undervalued when discounted at the benchmark yield, while the cash flows occurring later than the Treasury benchmark are overvalued when discounted at the benchmark yield. Static spread analysis provides a framework through which the spread of amortizing securities can be normalized and compared. If the static spread is less than the nominal spread, then a greater proportion of the cash flows are overvalued given the shape of the curve and timing of the cash flows. Conversely, if the static spread is greater than the pricing benchmark, then a greater proportion of the cash flows are undervalued given the shape of the curve and the timing of the cash flows.

Exhibit 10 suggests that changes in the shape of the curve affect the valuation of cash flows. For example, a flattening of the yield curve led by the short end of the curve decreases the extent to which the earlier cash flows are undervalued. Similarly, a steepening of the curve led by the short end increases the extent to which the earlier cash flows are undervalued. This in turn affects both spread differentials and expected total return of wide window securities relative to securities with tighter payment windows.

Exhibit 11: Relative Value Comparisons

Description:	CMGT 1996-B	CMAOT 1996-C
Class:	A	A3
Type	Grantor Trust	Owner Trust
Collateral:	Auto WAC 9.23%; WAM 42; Cage 15	Auto WAC 9.427%; WAM 45, Cage 13
Coupon:	6.61%	5.95%
Pricing Speed:	1.5 ABS	1.5 ABS
Average Life:	1.28	1.22
Spread:	+77 over interpolated Treasury	+69 over interpolated Treasury
Price:	100-14+	99-24+

Static Spread Analysis

	Price	Yield	Average Life	Spread Over Interpolated Treasury	Static Spread
CMGT 1996-B, A	100-14+	6.31%	1.28	+77bp	+71bp
CMAOT 1996-C, A3	99-24+	6.10%	1.70	+69bp	+69bp
Difference		0.21%	0.39	+8bp	+3bp

Exhibit 11 compares two auto ABS with similar average lives issued by Chase Manhattan Bank. The first is CMGT 1996-B A, issued from a grantor trust; the second is CMAOT 1996-C A3, issued from an owner trust. The exhibit provides a comparative analysis of nominal versus static spreads. The exhibit shows that CMGT 1996-B is priced to a nominal spread of +77 bp and a static spread of +71 bp. Given that the static spread is less than the nominal spread we can conclude that the cost of the payment window is +6 bp and that the bond is priced rich relative to the benchmark Treasury. Similarly, CMAOT 1996-C A3 is priced to a nominal spread of +69 bp and a static spread of +69 bp. Since the spreads are identical we can conclude that the pricing benchmark is accurate, the cost of the window is zero, and the bond is fairly priced given the shape of the curve and timing of the cash flows.

Total Return Analysis

The two major components of total return are price appreciation and coupon income. In a positively sloped yield curve environment, the price appreciation associated with rolling down the yield curve contributes to the investor's expected horizon return. Total return analysis can be used to determine whether the higher yield of a wide window bond is sufficient to offset superior roll down related price appreciation that may be experienced by tighter window bonds. Exhibit 12 shows that CMGT 1996-B A does not roll down the curve as fast as CMAOT 1996-C A3. At the end of the 12-month horizon, the CMAOT 1996-C A3 fully rolls down the curve and the CMGT 1996-B only rolls down the curve 0.38 years. The inferior roll down the curve of the CMGT 1996-B A is due to its wide window. Despite an 8 bp yield advantage, the CMGT 1997-B A underperforms the CMAOT 1996-C A3 in the "no change" scenario.

Finally, investors should be aware that the expected shape of the yield curve at the end of the horizon also determines relative performance between wide window and tight window auto ABS. Exhibit 12 also illustrates this point. Under a yield curve steepening scenario from Fed Funds to the 1-year Treasury, the horizon total return of the CMGT 1996-B A remains unchanged because the bond does not roll into the steeper part of the curve. However, since the CMAOT 1996-C A3 does roll down the curve, the horizon total return increases as the yield curve steepens. Conversely, when the yield curve flattens from Fed Funds to the 1-year Treasury, the expected horizon total return of the CMAOT 1996-C A3 declines and the total return advantage is shifted to the wide window CMGT 1996-B A.

CONCLUSION

When evaluating auto ABS, investors must consider several qualitative and quantitative factors that we have outlined in this chapter. Qualitative factors which impact a transaction's relative attractiveness include the issuer/servicer's business type (bank, captive, etc.), its underwriting and servicing standards, its obligor mix (prime, non prime, or sub prime), its credit enhancement, and its structure. These factors contribute to a unique pricing structure in the auto ABS market depending upon investors' perception of the cost or value associated with each.

Quantitative factors such as differing cash flow profiles and the shape of the yield curve also influence perceptions of relative value. Quantitative tools for determining relative value include static spread and total return analysis. Static spread analysis allows investors to compute the bullet equivalent spread of an amortizing security by normalizing spreads and allowing for direct comparisons among securities with different cash flow profiles. Likewise, comparing the prospective total returns of different bonds over a given horizon, and across various interest rate scenarios, can reveal information about the value of the bonds relative to each other. All else being equal, bonds with the greatest prospective performance offer the greatest value.

By blending both qualitative and quantitative analysis investors can identify and profit from the opportunities that exist in one of the most dynamic and mature sectors of the ABS market.

Exhibit 12: 12-Month Horizon Total Return Analysis

	No Change	Steepen 20 bp	Flatten 20 bp
CMGT 1996-B, A			
Yield at Horizon	6.30%	6.30%	6.30%
Avg. Life at Horizon	0.90	0.90	0.90
Horizon Total Return	6.12%	6.12%	6.12%
CMAOT 1996-C, A3			
Yield at Horizon	6.22%	6.02%	6.42%
Avg. Life at Horizon	0.50	0.50	0.50
Horizon Total Return	6.16%	6.22%	6.11%
Return Difference	+0.04%	+0.10%	-0.01%

Chapter 11

Automobile Lease ABS

Charles N. Schorin
Principal
Director of ABS Research
Morgan Stanley

INTRODUCTION

Leasing has become a significant portion of the automobile finance market. Whereas leasing had previously been a means of financing primarily high-priced luxury cars, leasing has become a common finance tool for even less expensive automobiles.

Leasing's popularity stems from the rapid growth in new car prices in the late 1980s and early 1990s, as it allows consumers to drive automobiles that would be prohibitive to purchase. The growth in new car prices spurred demand for used cars, the prices of which have surged more recently. Leasing is now used to finance one-third of personal-use automobile transactions, compared to only 12% in the mid-1980s.

Despite the rapid growth of automobile leasing, the securitization of automobile leases has been relatively limited (Exhibit 1). The primary impediments to automobile lease securitization have been managing residual value risk, overcoming issues related to vehicle titling, and resolving the competing tax and accounting goals of potential issuers. The first two concepts are particular to leasing and are not present in automobile sales.

This chapter provides an introduction to automobile lease securitizations. It begins with a discussion of the mechanics of automobile leasing to familiarize investors with the relevant components of a lease transaction. The chapter then discusses residual value risk and explains how leasing has altered the traditional relationship between car manufacturers, dealers, and lenders. An important distinction is then made between finance and operating leases, which determines the relevant accounting guidelines. Securitization is introduced next, first with a discussion of the historical impediments to securitization, followed by an explanation of how these impediments have been overcome. A discussion of credit enhancement and lease-backed ABS cash flows concludes this chapter.

MECHANICS OF AUTOMOBILE LEASING

Before addressing lease securitization, we first step back and examine the features of an automobile lease transaction. Understanding the elements of the lease will help investors appreciate issues involved in lease securitization.

Exhibit 1: Automobile Lease ABS has been Relatively Limited

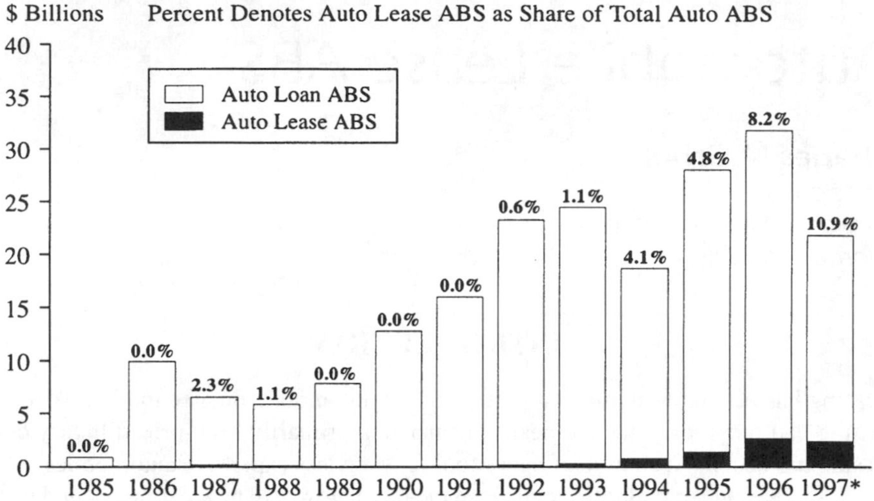

* Through October 1, 1997.

Source: Morgan Stanley

A consumer who decides to lease chooses a vehicle from an automobile dealer, who then sells the car to a third party (the *lessor*). The third party then leases the car to the consumer (the *lessee*). Upon taking possession of the car, the lessee usually must make a down payment, as well as pay an acquisition fee, security deposit, initial monthly payment, and any taxes, title and registration fees. Once the lessee takes possession of the car, he is responsible for its maintenance and insurance, just as if he were its legal owner. At the termination of the lease, the lessee has the option of purchasing the automobile at its residual value.

The lessee's monthly payment is derived from four components:

- the net capitalized cost of the automobile
- the automobile's residual value at the end of the lease
- the term of the lease
- the "money factor"

These elements are related to the monthly payment by the following equation:

$$\text{Monthly payment} = \frac{\text{Net cap cost} - \text{Residual}}{\text{Term}} + (\text{Net cap cost} + \text{Residual}) \times \text{Money factor}$$

The net capitalized cost (or net cap cost) of the automobile is the car's negotiated purchase price. The net cap cost is calculated by taking the manufacturer's suggested retail price, deducting the dealer discount and down payment, and adding back in the acquisition or initiation fee, as well as any taxes or other fees. Lessees typically must make a down payment — sometimes called a *capitalized cost reduction* — and pay an acquisition fee.

The residual value is the automobile's projected value at the end of the lease period. Estimates of residual values are provided in industry publications such as *Automotive Lease Guide* and the National Automobile Dealers Association (NADA) *Official Used Car Guide*. In addition, some dealers use statistically estimated residual value forecasting models, in conjunction with these industry publications, to determine residual values.

The "money factor" is essentially the leasing analog of the annual percentage rate (APR) of a sales contract, converted to a monthly number. To get an intuitive understanding of the money factor, consider the monthly payment equation above. The first expression on the right hand side of the equation is essentially the "principal" component of the monthly payment: the net cap cost minus the residual is the depreciation of the car, or the amount of principal "used" over the term of the lease; dividing by the lease term provides the depreciation charge, or principal usage, per month of the lease. The second expression in the monthly payment equation is the interest, or finance, component of the payment. A leasing approximation to an APR is given by the money factor times 2,400, or put differently, the money factor is approximately the "APR" divided by 2,400. Substituting this expression into the interest component of the monthly payment equation gives

$$(\text{Net cap cost} + \text{Residual}) \times \frac{\text{“APR”}}{2{,}400}$$

If we decompose the 2,400 in the denominator to factors of 2, 12, and 100, we can write the interest expression as

$$\frac{(\text{Net cap cost} + \text{Residual})}{2} \times \frac{\text{“APR”}}{12 \times 100}$$

This interest expression now has the interpretation of applying an annual percentage rate to the average of the value of the car at the beginning and the end of the lease, as given by the sum of the net cap cost and residual value of the car divided by 2. The 12 in the denominator scales the APR into a monthly number, while the 100 just converts a decimal reading into a percent. Note that we called this an *approximate* APR: it essentially is a linear approximation because we are applying it to an average, rather than an amortizing, balance. Since this is an approximate, rather than actual, APR, it should not be compared to true APRs from automobile purchase contracts. It can, however, be compared to other approximate APRs from other leases. A numerical example of an automobile lease transaction is provided in Exhibit 2.[1]

---

[1] The example in Exhibit 2 borrows heavily from *Automobile Buying and Leasing '97*, "More Car, Less Money: What Leasing Promises. What It Delivers," 1997.

Exhibit 2: Example of an Automobile Lease Transaction

Consider an automobile with a manufacturer's suggested retail price of $20,000 (Item 1 in the table below). The lessee is able to negotiate a reduction in "purchase" price to $18,000, resulting in a dealer discount of $2,000 (Item 2). Assume a down payment (or capitalized cost reduction) of $750 (Item 3), an acquisition (or initiation) fee of $500 (Item 4) and taxes and other fees of $300 (Item 5). The result is a net capitalized cost of $18,050 (Item 6).

Assuming a residual value that is 55% of the manufacturer's suggested retail price (Item 7), depreciation (Item 8) — given by the difference between the net cap cost and the residual value — is $7,050, the extent of the car that is "used up" over the term of the lease. The length of the lease (Item 10) and the money factor (Item 11) can be used with the above terms to determine the monthly payment (Item 12), from which the interest or finance component (Item 15) can be derived. The money factor (Item 11) also can be used to approximate an APR (Item 16).

1	Manufacturer's Suggested Retail Price	$20,000.00
2	Dealer Discount	2,000.00
3	Down Payment (or Capitalized Cost Reduction)	750.00
4	Acquisition (or Initiation) Fee	500.00
5	Taxes and Other Fees	$300.00
6	Net Capitalized Cost (Item #1 – #2 – #3 + #4 + #5)	18,050.00
7	Residual Value (Assumed 55% of Item #1)	11,000.00
8	Depreciation (Item #6 – #7)	7,050.00
9	Net Cap Cost Plus Residual (Item #6 + #7)	$29,050.00
10	Term	30 months
11	Money Factor	0.00116488
12	Monthly Payment ([Item #6 – #7]/#10 + [#6 + #7] × #11)	$268.84
13	Total Monthly Payments (Item #12 × #10)	$8,065.19
14	Total Finance Charges (Item #13 – #8)	1,015.19
15	Monthly Interest Charge (Item #14/#10)	33.84
16	Approximate APR (Item #11 × 2,400)	2.796%

Source: *Automobile Buying and Leasing '97*.

RESIDUAL VALUE RISK

The primary risk in an automobile leasing transaction is that of the residual value of the vehicle. The lessee has a call option on the car, with its contractually stated residual value as the strike price. If the true market value of the car exceeds its contractual residual value, the lessee is likely to exercise his option and purchase the car; otherwise, he will let the option expire.

If the lessee chooses not to exercise his option, the dealer from whom he leased the car has an option to purchase the car. If the dealer also elects not to exercise his option, the lessor — who actually purchased the car from the dealer — takes possession of the automobile. This means that the vehicles that come off lease and are returned to the lessor are almost by definition worth less than their originally projected residual values (although some consumers undoubtedly choose not to purchase cars that are worth more than their contractual residual values). This makes the estimation of the residual value the most important aspect of the automobile lease.

The true residual value of a vehicle that comes off lease is influenced by several factors, some of which are interrelated: demand for the particular vehicle model, demand for used cars, prices of new cars, demand for competitors' models and general economic conditions. As each of these factors changes in unforeseen ways between the beginning and end of an automobile lease, the contractual or projected residual value could be dramatically different from the actual residual value at the termination of the lease.

LEASING AND THE RELATIONSHIP OF MANUFACTURERS, DEALERS, AND AUTO LENDERS

Leasing has changed the relationship among manufacturers, dealers, and automobile lenders that previously existed.[2] Whereas previously, these parties acted independently, there is, through leasing arrangements, much more of an interrelation among them.

The consumer who purchases, rather than leases, a car may seek financing from either an independent third party, or from a captive finance subsidiary of the manufacturer. With leasing, however, the captive finance unit supplies the financing. This has resulted in loss-sharing arrangements between manufacturers and their captive finance units, to manage the residual value risk of the cars that come off lease.

In addition, when a consumer purchases an automobile, he bears the secondary market value risk. In contrast, a consumer who leases an automobile has transferred that risk to the dealer and/or lessor. In turn, because the dealer and lessor now bear that risk, they are more tightly related with leasing because either one may ultimately own the automobile when it comes off lease. As a result, the dealer is incented to service the car, and the manufacturer/lessor is incented to support the servicing, to help the vehicle retain as much value as possible at the termination of the lease.

FINANCE VERSUS OPERATING LEASES

Whether a lease is a finance or operating lease has implications for its accounting. FASB 13 provides criteria to distinguish whether the lease is a finance or operating lease for accounting purposes. FASB 125 governs the treatment of sales or securitizations of finance leases, while FASB 13 covers operating leases.[3]

---

[2] See Moody's Investors Service, *Automobile Leasing: Implications of this Alternative Retail Financing Technique for the Auto Manufacturers*, Special Comment, January 1995.

[3] See Financial Accounting Standards Board, *Accounting for Leases*, Statement of Financial Accounting No. 13, and Financial Accounting Standards Board, *Accounting for Transfer and Servicing of Financial Assets and Extinguishment of Liabilities*, Statement of Financial Accounting No. 125.

Operating leases are structured to cover less than 90% of the leased item's cost, and the item typically must be remarketed at the conclusion of the lease term to recoup the initial investment in it. Finance leases return virtually all of the cost of the leased item, plus a return on the investment, to the lessor. Automobile leases are almost exclusively operating leases.

For accounting purposes, a lease is considered a finance lease if the present value of the lease payments exceeds 90% of the leased item's fair market value, the lease term exceeds 75% of the item's useful life or the lease offers the lessee a discount purchase option. Conceptually, in these cases the lessor's residual interest in the item is sufficiently insignificant that it can be viewed as effectively sold to the lessee. [4]

AUTOMOBILE LEASE ABS

Historical Impediments to Securitization

Securitizing automobile leases has been impeded by three issues:

- vehicle ownership or titling
- residual value risk
- competing tax and accounting goals of potential issuers.

We address each of these issues in turn, then the manner in which they have been resolved and other issues that have arisen due to their resolution. In the past few years, the development of more flexible legal structures and new accounting rules have increased the viability of automobile lease ABS.

Vehicle Titling

The legal and administrative aspects of lease contracts create unique situations for lessors contemplating securitization. In the case of automobile *loans*, which are recognized as *financial* assets, transfer of the ownership of the loans is effected by selling them to the trust issuing the security. The trust has an ownership interest in the loans under the Uniform Commercial Code, which is recognized in every state.

In the case of automobile *leases*, however, the asset is the vehicle, in addition to the lease, and is not considered a financial asset. Indication of ownership of the vehicles is governed by each state's motor vehicle and titling laws, which vary considerably. Without formally indicating the legal transfer of ownership from the lessor to the issuing trust, there is a question whether a bankruptcy court would recognize the transfer, if clear and established procedures for titling were not followed.

---

[4] See Financial Accounting Standards Board, *Accounting for Leases*, Statement of Financial Accounting No. 13.

Actually attempting to amend the title for each automobile in a lease securitization is an extremely onerous task. Not only is there considerable paperwork, but transfer of ownership may trigger a sales tax or transfer fee, which could render a securitization inefficient. Means that have been developed to circumvent these titling problems are discussed below.

Residual Value Risk

Inherent to an automobile lease is the uncertainty of the vehicle's value at the termination of the lease. Estimates of the vehicle's ultimate residual value are made at the origination of the lease and are incorporated into the lease contract. To the extent that the true resale value of the automobile at lease termination is less than the originally estimated residual value, the lessor may suffer a loss. Related to residual value risk is the risk of loss in the event of lessee default.

Residual value risk can be compounded by dealer incentive programs that may include relatively high stated residual values — an example of what is referred to as a *subvented lease*. Setting a high residual value would result in less contractual asset depreciation and therefore lower monthly payments for the lessee. The problem is that at the lease termination, the lessor is more likely to face a loss on resale due to a larger difference between the contracted residual value and the true market price of the vehicle.

The uncertainty of vehicle residual value requires greater credit enhancement levels on lease securitizations than on automobile loan securitizations, or a residual value insurance policy or guarantee, because the issuing trust suffers a loss whenever the contractual residual value exceeds the actual market value of the automobile. The increased credit enhancement or necessity of an insurance policy or guarantee owing to residual value risk reduces the efficiency of the securitization.

Accounting and Tax Conflicts

As stated above, operating leases are not considered to be financial assets. The key to an automobile lease-backed securitization from an accounting standpoint is to achieve off-balance sheet sale treatment. This can be accomplished either by converting the operating leases into financial assets so that their transfer off-balance sheet will be subject to FASB 125, or by engaging in a sale/leaseback structure and getting accounting sale treatment via EITF 93-8.[5] The conflict arises by lease securitizations trying to achieve off-balance sheet sale treatment, while still maintaining enough ownership to retain the tax depreciation benefits of the assets. On-balance-sheet debt treatment for tax purposes is relatively straightforward to achieve.

One difficulty with achieving sale treatment for accounting purposes is that if a vehicle is sold from a manufacturer to a dealer, and then is subsequently repurchased subject to an operating lease, it has not really been sold. If the

---

[5] See Financial Accounting Standards Board, Emerging Issues Task Force Issue No. 93-8, *Accounting for the Sale and Leaseback of an Asset that is Leased to Another Party.*

accounting profession were to determine that the lease did not represent a true asset sale, then securitizations would be impacted dramatically. This issue has been resolved by EITF 95-4, however, which permits sale treatment subject to certain independence tests of the dealer.[6]

A separate issue concerns true sale and residual values. Whereas we would expect that vehicles with true market prices above their contracted residual values would be bought by the lessee and either kept or resold, there are in reality numerous cases in which the lessee declined to exercise his purchase option, despite its being in-the-money. These cases would represent a windfall to the lessor. If the lessor were to retain this windfall, however, it implies that the lessor has an economic interest in the sold assets; if so, the lessor has recourse and may be considered not to have engaged in a true sale for bankruptcy purposes.

A major tax issue in an automobile lease securitization is to avoid taxation at the issuing entity level by achieving debt treatment for tax purposes by having enough equity in the transaction. Debt-for-tax treatment would permit the issuer to avoid having to realize capital gains, as well as retain the benefit of depreciation deductions from the vehicles. Even though the depreciation benefits may represent a deferral, rather than a permanent reduction, in tax liability, it can be significant for a large lessor with a long history of leasing. Nonetheless, there may be situations where the deferral may provide minimal value to the originator, if it cannot be effectively employed, owing to an alternative minimum tax position, a net operating loss carry-forward or a multinational taxation structure that minimizes tax liability.

Other Issues in Automobile Lease Securitization

Bankruptcy Concerns

Automobile lease securitizations attempt to achieve the opposite goals of sale treatment for book accounting and debt treatment for tax purposes. Reaching a balance between these two goals creates stress on the true sale element for bankruptcy purposes that is part of AAA-rated ABS transactions.

In order to make the transaction bankruptcy remote, the assets may either be sold by the originator directly to investors in a legal true sale (rather than pledged to secure the asset backed securities), or the assets may first be sold in a legal true sale to a bankruptcy-remote entity that then issues the securities. In the latter case, the entity must avoid "substantive consolidation" in the event the parent declares bankruptcy.

In both methods of insulating a securitization, at least one true sale opinion is required. In the case of a securitization with a residual value guarantee provided by the transferor of the leases, the difficulty is that the protection comes from the original chain of ownership of the asset. Separating the guarantee provider from the chain of ownership of the vehicles and lease contracts reduces this

[6] See Financial Accounting Standards Board, Emerging Issues Task Force Issue No. 95-4, *Revenue Recognition on Equipment Sold and Subsequently Repurchased Subject to an Operating Lease.*

risk. If a bankruptcy court were to determine that the seller has retained a sufficient amount of the economic benefits or risks, the seller would be deemed to have recourse and the sale would be recharacterized as a pledge to secure debt.

Vicarious Tort Liability

In some states, a person suffering injury in an accident involving a leased vehicle may bring suit against the owner/lessor of the vehicle merely by virtue of that ownership. In a securitization, specific coverage of this risk has not been a factor in calculating credit enhancement levels. This risk may be covered directly by the creditworthiness of the issuer to the extent that it is a well-capitalized and highly rated company. Alternatively, the issuer can obtain a contingent and excess liability insurance policy naming the trust as beneficiary. The amount and deductible of such a policy would be subject to rating agency review.

ERISA Issues

The Pension Benefit Guaranty Corporation (PBGC) was chartered under the Employee Retirement Income Security Act of 1974 (ERISA) with broad powers to create "super" liens on the assets of any part of an "affiliated group" in order to satisfy unpaid obligations of any other member of the affiliated group. PBGC liens have priority over most other types of lien or security interest.

If any of the special purpose entities in a lease securitization were to be considered part of the affiliated group of the issuer, the PBGC could look to the vehicles and leases to fund the issuer's ERISA obligations in the event of a bankruptcy of the issuer. The lack of any lien on the vehicles noted on title documents in favor of the ABS transaction increases the possibility that the PBGC could impose a lien on the vehicles.

As a consequence of this, investors must consider the extent an issuer has an underfunded pension obligation. Rating agencies are unlikely to confer a AAA rating on lease securitizations that include this risk. Issuers will need to satisfy the unfunded pension liability or ensure that the leased assets are truly outside the affiliated group. The rating agencies might require periodic certifications of fully funded pension liabilities, as is done by both Ford Credit and World Omni.

Issuers with unfunded pension liabilities will need to create special structures to avoid the risk that the PBGC would be able to create a lien on the vehicles or leases backing a securitization. One method of achieving this could be to have a separate entity own the assets.

STRUCTURAL ASPECTS OF AUTOMOBILE LEASE ABS TRANSACTIONS

Titling Trust

A *titling trust* is a legal entity that is created for the purpose of owning the leased vehicles. It was first used by World Omni for its automobile lease securitization.

The titling trust removes most of the risks and costs of retitling, transferring the economic benefits of ownership to third parties, while still maintaining the separation of assets from the originator. Since the titling trust is a limited-purpose, bankruptcy-remote entity, it can own all of an issuer's vehicles and facilitate multiple securitizations without creating a separate titling trust for each transaction. Ownership of the vehicles is recorded on the certificate of title in the name of the titling trust or its trustee.

The titling trust itself is owned by holders of beneficial interests that transfer the *economic value* of specific assets in the trust. These *beneficial interests* themselves can be transferred without retitling the vehicles because legal title to the *automobiles* does not change.

In a lease securitization, the titling trust issues a certificate of beneficial interest in the vehicles to the seller. Rather than transfer the vehicles and related leases to the securitization trust, the seller transfers the certificate of beneficial interest to the securitization trust in a transaction intended to be a true sale. The securitization trust also obtains a perfected security interest in the certificate of beneficial interest and the proceeds of the leases. A titling trust of the type employed by Toyota in its inaugural lease securitization is displayed schematically in Exhibit 3.

A titling trust presents potential complications of its own. For example, the trust must be licensed to conduct business in most states where the vehicles are titled. In addition, trusts are not recognized in every state as legally legitimate owners of vehicles, while other states may treat the titling trust as a taxable entity.

To overcome the problem in states in which a trust cannot be the owner of the vehicles, the trustee of the titling trust could be the owner of record of the vehicles. The trustee may also need to be a licensed lessor in each state in which it owns the vehicles. For states in which the form of titling trust may be a taxable entity, another form, such as a limited liability company, may suffice as an entity.

Exhibit 3: Lease Securitization Employing a Titling Trust

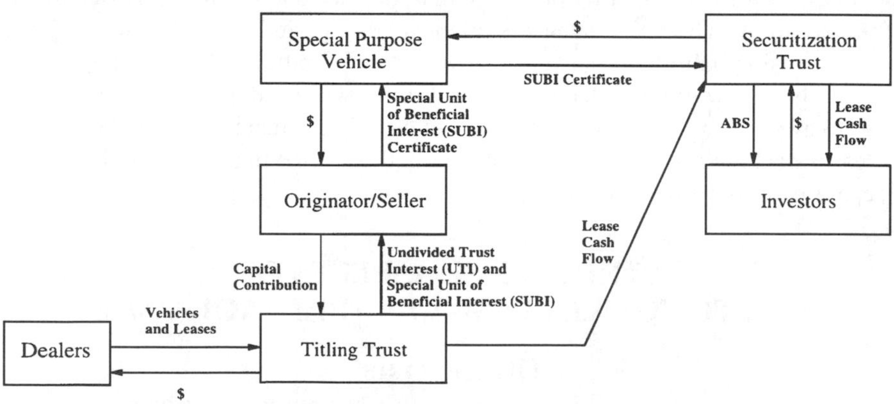

Source: Morgan Stanley

Exhibit 4: Lease Securitization Employing Sale/Leaseback Structure

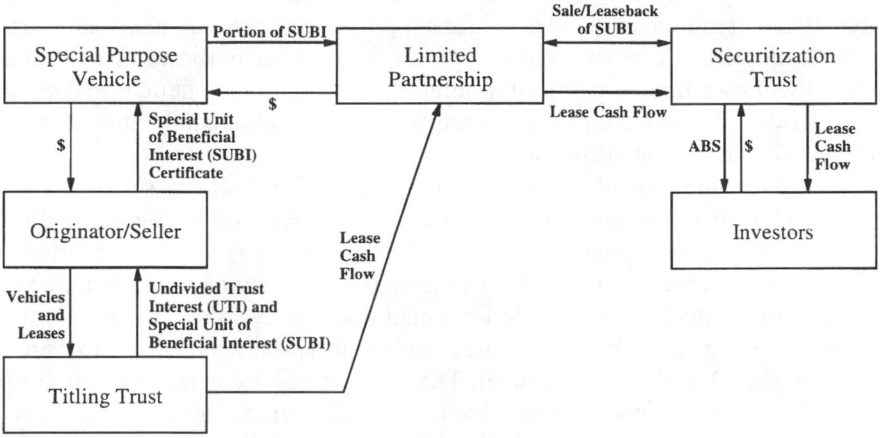

Source: Morgan Stanley

Sale/Leaseback Structure

A sale/leaseback structure was employed by Ford Credit in its automobile lease securitizations. This structure can achieve off-balance-sheet treatment for accounting purposes, while still retaining a significant portion of residual value risk. The originator of the leases causes the vehicles and lease contracts to be purchased in the name of a titling trust, with beneficial interests in the titling trust representing indirect ownership of the vehicles and lease contracts. The beneficial interest may be either initially owned by the lease originator and a bankruptcy-remote subsidiary, or the bankruptcy-remote entity may be the direct purchaser of the beneficial interests and provide it with capital and funding.

A portion of the beneficial interests in the titling trust would be transferred to an intermediate limited partnership formed by the originator and a wholly-owned, limited-purpose, bankruptcy-remote subsidiary. The remaining unallocated beneficial interest will remain with the bankruptcy-remote subsidiary, which may pledge such interest in any interim financing arrangement.

The limited partnership that owns the asset — the beneficial interest in the leases to be securitized — then enters into a sale/leaseback transaction with a third party by selling the beneficial interest to the securitization trust issuing the ABS, and leasing back the asset. The sale/leaseback arrangement allows the originator/seller to achieve accounting sale treatment through FASB 13. The sale/leaseback structure of the type employed by Ford Credit in its securitizations is depicted in Exhibit 4.

To achieve proper accounting treatment, the terms of the transaction must conform to the guidelines of EITF 93-8. Since the sale/leaseback will involve assets *indirectly* through allocated beneficial interests, rather than the assets themselves, the transaction must be structured to remove any accounting concerns regarding the sale/leaseback of a certificate versus the operating asset.

The vehicles and lease contracts represented by the allocated beneficial interest and credit enhancements would support a trust offering notes and certificates. If the trust is characterized as a partnership for tax purposes, the certificate holders will own limited partnership interests subject to the publicly traded partnership rules. The passive income exemption used in retail automobile loan ABS is not available in a sale/leaseback.

While the form of a sale/leaseback under EITF 93-8 may satisfy accounting considerations, the level of residual value risk retention by the originator, in the form of corporate guarantees, may cause concerns as to whether sufficient value has been received for the assets to have the transaction viewed as a true sale for bankruptcy purposes. The sale/leaseback form allows the originator to treat the transaction as debt for tax purposes and retain virtually all of the tax benefits in the original lease to the consumer. The calculation of capital accounts for tax purposes among the originator and holders of ABS certificates must reconcile to the allocation of tax benefits. At the issuer's discretion, all or a portion of tax benefits may be sold to third party equity participants.

Residual Value Insurance

Automobile leases are almost exclusively operating leases.[7] Residual value insurance, however, can be used to convert operating leases into finance leases for accounting purposes, as well as reduce residual value risk. The insurance effectively removes the residual value risk from the lessor's balance sheet, making the lease a finance lease in accounting terms. Once considered a finance lease, the accounting for its securitization is governed by FASB 125, since a finance lease is treated as a financial asset. This allows an originator to use standard existing ABS structures for *loan* securitizations to achieve accounting sale treatment for a *lease* securitization.

Even though residual value insurance converts operating leases into finance leases for accounting purposes, the bankruptcy considerations remain: the vehicles must be segregated from the bankruptcy estate of the originator to be available to support the transaction. Utilizing the titling trust discussed above and the transfer of beneficial interests, as part of the overall structure, can achieve the necessary separation.

The tax treatment of the securities will depend upon the form of the securitization structure chosen. Two possibilities are the *revolving structure* and the *owner trust structure*. The revolving structure would provide for full debt treatment for tax purposes, while the owner trust structure would involve the sale of an equity class. Any equity class would be structured to look like a bond for tax purposes, allowing the issuer to retain all of the tax benefits in the retained equity class. In either structure, all or a portion of tax benefits may be sold to third party equity participants.

---

[7] See the earlier section on finance versus operating leases.

CREDIT ENHANCEMENT FOR AUTOMOBILE LEASE ABS

Rating agencies may look toward the following factors in setting enhancement levels on automobile lease ABS transactions:

- residual value
- prepayments
- return rates
- loss severity

Residual value is expressed as a percentage of the original asset value remaining at maturity, while prepayments (or, more accurately, non-prepayments) are described as the percentage of leases that reach their full term. The return rate refers to the percentage of vehicles returned, rather than purchased, at the termination of the lease. Loss severity is the loss on returned vehicles as a percentage of the residual value.

Moody's, for example, attempts to model residual value risk by taking a lease-by-lease approach to each lease in a securitization. They apply a depreciation curve to the vehicle behind each lease, based upon the type and model of leased vehicle, to derive residual values on each of the leased vehicles. Return rates are then used to scale the derived aggregate residual value and estimate the actual amount of expected loss. Moody's then analyzes the sensitivity of this result, by stressing the depreciation curves and return rates and determining the sensitivity of the residual value risk to these stressed scenarios.

Credit enhancement has taken various forms in automobile lease ABS transactions, including overcollateralization, subordinated seller interest, subordinated class of securities, purchase price holdback and combinations of the above. Unlike automobile loan transactions, where most prime portfolios exhibit similar terms and characteristics due to the level of product standardization created by a competitive lending environment, there is little standardization of credit enhancement levels for automobile lease transactions.

World Omni achieved a total credit enhancement level of 11.5% in its 1994 securitizations, which reflected low return rates owing to an active returns management program and the high residual value of Toyotas, especially over shorter lease terms. Ford Credit had to endure a much higher enhancement level of 24% in its 1995 transaction due to the short lease term of 24 months or less and the state of the used car market for Fords.

Events Triggering Increased Enhancement

Lease securitizations typically have criteria that can trigger increases in credit support. These triggers provide extra protection for investors in the event that the lessees do not perform as well as expected or that the residual value of the vehicles is lower than initially anticipated. For example, in Toyota 97-A, the reserve fund will double from 2.5% to 5.0% of the original balance if any of the following occur:

- 3-month average of charge-offs exceeds 1.25%
- 3-month average of the sum of 60+ day delinquencies and repossessions exceeds 1.25%
- vehicle return rate exceeds 25% and the 3-month average of the vehicle residual value proceeds is less than 75% of the average residual values of vehicles liquidated during the period.

AUTOMOBILE LEASE ABS CASH FLOWS

The complications of automobile lease-backed securities primarily must be faced by the issuer of the securities. Although these securities present complications not found in loan-backed securities, once the transaction is structured, the investor faces a relatively straightforward series of cash flows. Issuers have employed both amortizing and revolving securitization structures.

Cash flows could be relatively fast if, for example, the issuer/lessor engages in active sales promotion prior to the termination of the lease. On the other hand, cash flow to the investor can be structured into bullet-pay bonds, as was the case with Toyota 97-A.

In general, the terms of automobile lease transactions are shorter than those of automobile loan ABS. Whereas most automobile loan contracts are four or five year terms, most lease transactions are on the order of two to three years.

CONCLUSION

Automobile leases represent both one of the oldest, yet least developed, sectors of the asset backed securities arena. Issues specific to leases arise that make these transactions complicated from the issuer's standpoint. Nonetheless, once these legal, accounting and structural issues are resolved, the investor in an automobile lease transaction is left with a straightforward series of cash flows.

Chapter 12

Credit Card Asset-Backed Securities

Charles N. Schorin
Principal
Director of ABS Research
Morgan Stanley

INTRODUCTION

Credit card asset-backed securities (ABS) were introduced into the public market in 1987. Since their introduction, credit cards have comprised the largest single sector in the ABS market. There have been approximately $240 billion in public U.S. dollar credit card ABS issued as of the first quarter of 1997, with more than $160 billion still outstanding.

Credit card ABS issuance has recently changed from being predominantly fixed-rate securities to being more heavily weighted toward floating-rate issuance. This reflects primarily issuers' desire to match fund their increasingly floating-rate assets with floating-rate securities.

The leading credit card ABS issuers have been Citibank, MBNA, and Chase.[1] The top issuers are reported in Exhibit 1. Credit card lenders with the largest amount of outstanding receivables, and the extent of their securitized product, are listed in Exhibit 2.

Credit card usage has grown dramatically over the past several years. Outstanding receivables grew from about $235 billion in 1990 to almost $350 billion by the end of 1996.[2] Some of the growth was due to increased convenience use of credit cards by consumers, as well as consumers taking advantage of co-branding and affinity programs. These programs enable the card holder to receive additional benefits, such as frequent flyer miles, from card usage.

Growth in credit card receivables has been spurred also by greater acceptance of credit cards as a means of payment. For example, many doctors and practically all supermarkets now routinely accept credit cards for payment. Most gasoline service stations and department stores also now accept bank credit cards, whereas most previously accepted only their own private label card.

---

[1] The Chase issuance includes that of the former Chemical Bank.

[2] Fitch Investors Service, *ABCs of Credit Card ABS*, Structured Finance Special Report, April 1, 1996, and *The Nilson Report*, Issue 640, March 1997.

Exhibit 1: Largest Issuers of Credit Card ABS Since 1995

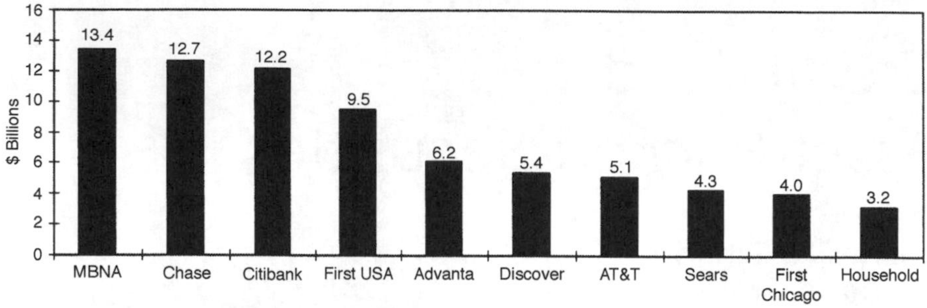

Note: Chase includes both the Chase Manhattan and former Chemical Bank trusts.

Source: Morgan Stanley

Exhibit 2: Credit Card Lenders with Largest Amount of Outstanding Receivables and their Outstanding Credit Card ABS (as of Year-End 1996)

Issuer	Receivables*	Credit Card ABS*
Citibank	$47.0 billion	$20.9 billion
MBNA America	35.3	20.8
Discover	34.4	11.5
American Express	28.5	4.7
Sears	26.7	5.8
Chase	25.2	12.2
First USA	22.2	14.0
Household	18.1	5.6
First Chicago NBD	18.1	8.4
AT&T Universal	13.5	5.1
Advanta	12.7	9.4
Capital One	12.5	5.3

* as of December 31, 1996

Source: *The Nilson Report*, Issue 636, January 1997, Fitch Investors Service, Morgan Stanley

TYPES OF CARDS

Credit cards can be divided into bank cards and private label (or, retail) cards. Bank cards are credit cards issued by commercial banks that can be used at any location worldwide that accepts MasterCard, VISA, or Discover. In contrast, private label credit cards may be used only at the respective store that issued the card.

Charge cards strictly are *not* credit cards, per se. Whereas credit card loans may revolve, payments for charge card purchases are due each month. Exhibit 3 is a summary of credit and charge card issuers. While the characteristics within each category may not fit for each issuer in the respective category, the exhibit nonetheless provides a generalization of the different types of issuers.

CREDIT CARD RECEIVABLES

Credit card receivables are unsecured revolving debt obligations. Underlying the receivables is a contractual agreement between the credit card holder and the card issuer that states the terms and conditions for repayment. Receivables consist of both principal receivables and finance charge receivables. Principal receivables comprise loans made to finance purchases of goods and services, as well as cash advances. Finance charge receivables consist of the annual percentage rate charged to the card holders who maintain balances (revolvers), annual fees, and often other fees related to card usage, such as interchange.[3] Account balances fluctuate each month as card holders make payments on their outstanding balances and use their card for new purchases.

Exhibit 3: Credit Card ABS Issuer Summary

	Bank Card	Private Label Card	Charge Card
Seller/ Servicer	Bank	Retailer	Bank or Financial Services Firm
Underlying Assets	Visa, MasterCard or Discover receivables (unsecured)	Store-credit card receivables (unsecured)	Travel, entertainment and business purchase receivables (unsecured)
Yield Components	Either fixed (16-18%) or variable (prime rate + spread) finance charge, annual and late fees, interchange	Fixed rate (18-20%) finance charge, but no additional fees	Annual fee and interchange, but no finance charge
AAA Credit Enhancement	Subordination, Cash Collateral Account, Collateral Invested Amount	Subordination, Cash Collateral Account, Collateral Invested Amount	Subordination, Discount factor
Credit Enhancement Level	MBNA: 15% on floating rate*	Sears: 11% on fixed rate*	American Express: 7.5% on floating rate*
Principal Pay Structure	Soft bullet, Controlled amortization	Soft bullet, Controlled amortization	Soft bullet
Maturity	3-, 5-, 7-, 10-, 12-, 15-year average life	3-, 5-, 7-year average life	4-, 5-, 7-, 10-year average life
Issue Size	$500 million – $1 billion	$500 million – $1 billion	$300-600 million
Acceptance	General	Store only	General

* Enhancement levels for floating rate transactions generally are 200-300 bp higher than for fixed rate transactions

Source: Morgan Stanley

[3] Interchange refers to fees received by the seller of the receivables from VISA and MasterCard as partial compensation for taking credit risk, absorbing fraud losses and funding receivables for a limited period prior to initial billing. Interchange is usually, but not always, incorporated as part of portfolio yield.

Credit card receivables often are pledged to a trust. Once accounts are in the trust, increases in receivables are automatically transferred to the trust. The seller interest (discussed more fully below) fluctuates to accommodate increases in trust receivables due to card usage and decreases owing to card holders paying their bills.

CREDIT CARD ABS

The transfer of credit card receivables from the originator to a trust is designed to isolate the receivables and the investors from the effects of a bankruptcy or insolvency of the seller of the receivables. The property of a credit card trust includes a portfolio of credit card receivables and the benefit of any additional credit enhancement to cover losses.

To accommodate the fluctuating nature of credit card account balances, a credit card master trust comprises two classes: an investor interest and a seller interest. Both classes have a *pari passu* ownership interest in the trust. Current balances plus all future receivables arising in the selected pool of accounts are transferred to the trust.

Increases in the amount of receivables, above the fixed investor interest, are collected in the seller interest. The seller interest is the residual interest in the trust and is designated to absorb fluctuations in the amount of receivables owned by the trust. In most credit card securitizations, the seller of the receivables continues to provide billing, collection, and customer service and is referred to as the servicer. The servicer in a credit card transaction is paid a fee, typically 2% of the balance of receivables serviced.

Most credit card issuers moved to a master trust structure in 1991. The basic master trust supports the issuance of multiple series of certificates. The structure and term of each series are defined by the series supplement within the general guidelines of the master trust. Each series issued out of the master trust shares a pro rata claim to the cash flow from the underlying pool of credit card receivables.

Master Trusts

Credit card securities are issued out of trusts. Prior to 1991, securities had been issued out of discrete trusts: one trust, one transaction. The asset-backed market evolved, however, in 1991 to issuing credit card transactions out of master trusts.

The master trust structure allows several separate transactions to be issued out of the same trust. As a credit card lender/issuer expands its lending and issues more receivables, and needs to fund those receivables, it may seek funding in the asset backed market. By pledging additional receivables to the master trust, it expands the trust. All securities issued out of a master trust are backed by the entire pool of receivables in the trust; there is no segregation of receivables to specific transactions.

There are several advantages to the master trust structure vis-a-vis the discrete trust. The master trust is more efficient from the issuer's standpoint, because fixed legal and administrative costs of setting up the trust are spread over potentially several transactions. The master trust also gives the issuer considerable structuring flexibility, allowing, for example, excess principal from one series to cover shortfalls in another, issued from the same master trust. From the investor's perspective, however, the primary benefit of the master trust is that each security issued from it is backed by the performance of *all* of the receivables in the trust. This means that any individual transaction is not subject to an issuer's solicitation over a relatively short period of time. The performance of a security issued out of a discrete trust that comprises only a few of an issuer's solicitations is subject to the quality of only those solicitations and lacks the diversification provided by a master trust. On the other hand, since a master trust issues securities backed by all of an issuer's solicitations, the impact of a particularly poor quality — or high quality, for that matter — solicitation on the securities issued from the trust is mitigated.

Analysis of a credit card security should focus on the quality of the seller/servicer, the underlying portfolio of receivables and the legal and structural characteristics of the transaction. Portfolio performance factors that directly affect investor cash flows are portfolio yield, charge-off rates and payment rates. Each of these variables is interrelated and subject to outside influences, such as competition, regulation and general economic conditions.

Master Trust Statistics

Portfolio Yield

Portfolio yield is calculated by dividing finance charges and fees billed by the amount of average receivables outstanding. When interchange is included in portfolio yield, the yield from interchange is added to the yield calculated from finance charges and fees. Portfolio yield generally is allocated to series issued from a master trust proportionally to the principal balance of the series. [4]

One factor affecting portfolio yield is the extent of convenience use of the credit cards. Convenience use refers to card holders who use credit cards as a cash or check substitute, benefiting from the interest free float and perhaps co-branding awards such as frequent flyer miles, but pay off their balances in full each month and avoid the finance charges. Convenience use varies by issuer and the profiles of its borrowers. For example, Citibank offers a credit card that is co-branded[5] with the American Airlines frequent flyer program. Citibank's portfolio has one of the highest payment rates in the industry, currently almost 20%, suggesting that relatively many of its borrowers take advantage of their cards for convenience use. The average payment rate over all credit card issuers, however, is in

[4] There are some cases, for example Advanta Credit Card Master Trust II, for which interchange is allocated differently among the series, so that portfolio yields for all series issued out of this trust are not identical.

the range of 12 to 15%, implying that about 85% of credit card balances revolve — and are subject to finance charges — each month.

Increases in convenience use will limit portfolio yield. On the other hand, convenience use increases the monthly payment rate on the portfolio. This increases cash flow to the trust and reduces investor exposure to losses in the event of an early amortization, because the faster payment rate will return principal to investors more quickly.

Charge-Offs

After an account has been delinquent for a specified number of days — usually 180, but for some lenders, 150 — the lender charges off the account and records the account balance as a loss. Charge-offs are allocated to series issued from the trust proportionally to the series' principal balances.

VISA and MasterCard do not require adherence to specific underwriting criteria. Diversity in account solicitation methods and strategies and underwriting guidelines among issuers have resulted in significant variations in portfolio loss experience.

Recently, rising charge-offs as a result of weakness in the consumer sector and rising bankruptcies have been features of the credit card asset backed market. The rising charge-offs came about from aggressive lender solicitation of accounts and resultant adverse selection of borrowers.

Most static pools of credit card receivables have historically experienced peak losses between months 18 and 24. Some portfolios have seen this seasoning pattern shortened considerably owing to balance transfers by borrowers who subsequently declare bankruptcy. The account may have defaulted after a relatively short tenure on its last card, even though the borrower may have transferred balances among several cards over the previous 18-24 months.

Base Rate

The base rate refers to expenses of the transaction, which are the securities' coupons and servicing fees. The base rate for series issued from the same trust would differ due to different coupons on the securities, which is especially likely if some securities carry fixed rates and others have floating rates.

Excess Spread

The excess spread on a security is the amount of the portfolio yield that remains after paying the certificates' coupons and servicing fees and charging off bad loans. An example is provided in Exhibit 4, for MBNA 1995-H as of March 1997.

---

[5] Co-branding refers to credit cards that are issued in conjunction with a program that appeals to the card holder. One of the most popular co-brandings is with airlines' frequent flyer programs, so that card holder use of the card is linked to receiving frequent flyer miles. In contrast to a co-branded card is the affinity card, for which borrower use may result in benefits to a particular organization, such as a university alumni club, to which the card holder belongs.

Exhibit 4: Excess Spread Calculation: MBNA 1995-H as of March 1997

Portfolio Yield	17.84 %
− Weighted Avg Coupon	5.37
− Servicing Fee	2.00
− Charge-offs	4.50
= Excess Spread	5.97 %

Source: Fitch Investors Service

Positive excess spread reverts to the seller of the receivables. This source of income, coupled with relatively inexpensive financing in the asset-backed market, has made the credit card business very profitable. The profitability in turn has spurred heavy competition among credit card lenders and aggressive solicitation of borrowers.

If the 3-month average of excess spread is negative, an early amortization event will be triggered.[6] Early amortization is a principal protection mechanism, essentially a "credit put" to the issuer of the securities. When early amortization is triggered, a security's revolving period ends and investors begin to receive principal payments. Since investors receive a share of the principal payments made by card holders in a given month, the rate at which bonds pay down in an early amortization depends upon the portfolio's monthly payment rate.

Monthly Payment Rate

The monthly payment rate is the principal, finance charges, and fees paid by card holders in a month, as a share of the portfolio's outstanding balance. This represents balances that borrowers pay off, rather than revolve, in a given month. Monthly payment rates vary by portfolio. Most credit card lenders require a minimum monthly payment that is the larger of a percentage of the outstanding account balance — typically 2-3% — or a minimum dollar payment (usually on the order of $10).

The payment rate directly affects the timing of cash flows to the trust issuing credit card securities. The higher the monthly payment rate, the faster that bondholders will be paid off in the event of early amortization. Rating agencies put considerable weight on the monthly payment rate (as well as on historical portfolio loss and delinquency performance) in setting enhancement levels and legal final maturities of credit card transactions. The higher the monthly payment rate on a portfolio, the greater the effective size of the credit enhancement in a transaction.[7]

---

[6] In some cases, such as with Spiegel Master Trust private label credit card, early amortization is triggered when excess spread is less than 1%. For Sears Credit Account Master Trust II, early amortization occurs when there are three draws on the credit enhancement before it is replenished.

[7] See the Morgan Stanley *Mortgage Research Weekly*, "Credit Card B Pieces: Analysis & Value," November 21, 1996.

Cash Flow Allocations in Master Trusts

Seller Interest

Master trusts have two components: the investor interest and the seller interest. The investor interest is represented by the credit card ABS issued by the trust. The seller interest is the difference between the aggregate trust balance and the investor interest, and represents the portion of the trust that is owned by the seller of the receivables. As such, it remains on the seller's balance sheet.

The major purpose of the seller interest is to provide a buffer between the naturally fluctuating balance of the receivables and the investor interest. Trust balances display a seasonal component, fluctuating over the year due to particularly heavy or light use of credit cards, and a random element.

The seller must maintain an interest in the trust that is a certain minimum percentage of the receivables balance. If the seller's interest falls below that percentage — usually 7% — then the seller must add receivables to the trust to increase the seller's interest to the minimum. If the seller is unable to do so, an early amortization event will be triggered, causing transactions issued from the trust to begin paying down principal.

Principal Allocations

Principal payments received by the trust are allocated to individual series based upon the size of the respective series. During their revolving periods, however, the individual series do not need the principal, since it is not being distributed. The principal that is not needed to pay down certificates for one series can be used to support other series in the master trust, if needed and if permitted by the trust.[8] Trusts differ in the manner in which this principal is reallocated among different series. If not needed to support other series, the principal is used to purchase new receivables for the trust.

Exhibit 5 illustrates how principal payments can be reallocated from series that do not need them to those that do. Series I in the example is in its revolving period, so it does not require the principal that is allocated to it. A portion of this principal gets reallocated to Series II, which is in its controlled amortization period, but is experiencing a shortfall in its principal allocation relative to the principal it is required to pay. The reallocation of principal allows Series II to pay its certificates on schedule without having a detrimental effect on Series I.

Finance Charge Allocations

Finance charges generally are allocated to series issued from the trust based upon the size of the respective series. Depending upon the trust, excess finance charges allocated to one series may be reallocable to another series, or they may be released from the trust to the servicer.

---

[8] Many of the older master trusts did not permit principal collections to be reallocated to other series within the trust, but most of the trusts created in the past few years have allowed reallocation.

Exhibit 5: Allocation of Master Trust Principal

Consider a master trust that has issued two series, I and II. Series I is in its revolving period, and so requires no principal; Series II is in its controlled amortization period.

Assume a monthly payment rate of 10% and a controlled amortization period of 6 months. Series I and Series II both have original principal balances of $500.

	Series I	Series II
Allocated Principal	$50.00	$50.00
− Required Principal	0.00	83.33
= Excess Principal	$50.00	($33.33)
Reallocated Principal	($33.33)	$33.33
+ Original Allocation	50.00	50.00
= Available Principal	$16.67	$83.33
− Required Principal	0.00	83.33
= Excess Principal	$16.67	$0.00

Source: Morgan Stanley

Another alternative is that finance charges may be allocated to series in the trust based upon the respective series expenses. Expenses differ among series in a trust to the extent that different series carry different coupons. This latter type of master trust, in which finance charges are allocated based upon each respective series' needs, are sometimes referred to as *socialized trusts*.

Groups

Some master trusts have subsets called *groups* to which some of the series issued from the master trust belong. Series that are part of a group may display certain allocations of finance charges only among those series in the group. For example, excess finance charges may be reallocated among series in a group to cover a particular series' shortfall, but perhaps not to another series in a different group. The result is that a series in another group may suffer a shortfall, even when there is sufficient cash to cover that shortfall in the master trust, albeit not in the same group.

Exhibit 6 provides examples of finance charge allocations within master trusts. These examples also are relevant for allocations within master trust groups. In Exhibit 6, Case I shows that without reallocating finance charges, it is possible to have some series with negative excess spreads and others with positive excess spreads. In this event, the series with the negative spread has a shortfall and requires a draw on credit enhancement, whereas the positive excess spread from the other series reverts from the trust to the servicer.

Case II in Exhibit 6 shows the situation when excess spread gets reallocated from series with positive, to those with negative, excess spreads. In this example, the reallocation prevents a series from having to post a negative excess spread. The final example, Case III, shows finance charges being allocated to series on an as-needed basis. Sometimes referred to as socialized trusts — since those in need are provided for — the series from these trusts generally have excess spreads that are very similar.

Exhibit 6: Allocation of Master Trust Finance Charges

Consider a master trust that has issued two series, I and II, with original principal balances of $500 and $600, respectively. The coupon for Series I is 8%, while that for Series II is 6%. The master trust has $1500 of receivables, with a seller interest of $400.

Assume a trust portfolio yield of 16%, charge-offs of 7%, servicing fee of 2% and monthly payment rate of 10%.

*Case I: Finance Charges Not Reallocated For Shortfalls**

	Series I	Series II
Allocated Finance Charges	$6.67	$8.00
– Coupon Expenses	3.33	3.00
– Charge-offs	2.92	3.50
– Servicing	0.83	1.00
= Excess Spread	–0.41	0.50

Without reallocating finance charges, Series I has a negative 41 bp excess spread and Series II has a positive 50 bp excess spread, which gets released from the trust to the servicer.

*Case II: Finance Charges Reallocated for Shortfalls**

	Series I	Series II
Allocated Finance Charges	$6.67	$8.00
– Coupon Expenses	3.33	3.00
– Charge-offs	2.92	3.50
– Servicing	0.83	1.00
= Excess Spread	–0.41	0.50
+Reallocated Excess Spread	0.41	–0.41
= Excess Spread	0.00	0.09

After reallocating excess finance charges, Series I has an excess spread of 0, whereas Series II has excess spread of 9 bp, which gets released from the trust to the servicer.

*Case III: Finance Charges Allocated Based Upon Series Expenses**

Total finance charges allocated to investor interest: $14.67

	Series I	Series II
Coupon Expenses	3.33	3.00
Coupon Expense Allocation	3.33	3.00
Finance charges after coupon allocation: $8.34		
Charge-offs	2.92	3.50
Charge-offs Allocation	2.92	3.50
Finance charges after coupon and charge-off allocation: $1.92		
Servicing Expense	0.83	1.00
Servicing Expense Allocation	0.83	1.00
Finance charges after coupon, charge-off and servicing fee allocation: $0.09		
Excess Spread	0.04	0.05

After reallocating excess finance charges, Series I has excess spread of 4 bp and Series II has excess spread of 5 bp. The excess spreads of both series are released from the trust to the servicer.

* Allocated Finance Charges = Portfolio Yield × Series Principal/12
Coupon Expenses = Series Coupon × Series Principal /12
Charge-offs = Charge-off Rate × Series Principal/12
Servicing = Series Principal × Servicing fee/12

Source: Morgan Stanley

Exhibit 7: Master Trusts that do not Reallocate Finance Charges

Advanta Credit Card Master Trust	JCP Master Credit Card Trust
American Express Master Trust	MBNA Master Credit Card Trust
Bridgestone/Firestone Master Trust	National City Credit Card Master Trust
First Consumers Master Trust	PB&T Master Credit Card Trust
First Omni Credit Card Master Trust	Private Label Credit Card Master Trust
First USA Credit Card Master Trust	SFA Master Trust

Source: Moody's Investors Service, "Credit Card Master Trusts: Assessing the Risks of Cash Flow Allocations," *Structured Finance Special Report*, May 26, 1995, and Standard & Poor's *Credit Card Criteria 1997*, Structured Finance Ratings, Asset Backed Securities, 1997.

Exhibit 8: Master Trusts that Reallocate Finance Charges

Advanta Credit Card Master Trust II	MBNA Master Credit Card Trust II
Banc One Credit Card Master Trust	Mellon Credit Card Master Trust I
BA Master Credit Card Trust	Mercantile Credit Card Master Trust
Capital One Master Trust	Metris Master Trust
Charming Shoppes Master Trust	NationsBank Credit Card Master Trust
Chase Manhattan Credit Card Master Trust	Neiman Marcus Group Credit Card Master Trust
Chase Master Trust (formerly Chemical)	PB&T Master Credit Card Trust II
Chevy Chase Master Credit Card Trust	People's Bank Credit Card Master Trust
Circuit City Master Trust	Prime Credit Card Master Trust
Dayton Hudson Credit Card Master Trust	Sears Credit Account Master Trust I
Discover Card Master Trust I	Sears Credit Account Master Trust II
Fingerhut Master Trust	Spiegel Master Trust
First Chicago Master Trust II	Tandy Master Trust
First Deposit Master Trust	Wachovia Credit Card Master Trust
First of America Credit Card Master Trust	World Financial Network Credit Card Master Trust
First Union Credit Card Master Trust	Younkers Master Trust

Source: Moody's Investors Service, "Credit Card Master Trusts: Assessing the Risks of Cash Flow Allocations," *Structured Finance Special Report*, May 26, 1995, and Standard & Poor's *Credit Card Criteria 1997*, Structured Finance Ratings, Asset Backed Securities, 1997.

Exhibit 9: Master Trusts that Allocate Finance Charges Based upon Series Expenses and Size

American Express Credit Account Master Trust	Household Affinity Credit Card Master Trust I
AT&T Universal Card Master Trust	Household Credit Card Master Trust I
CHOICE Master Trust I	Household Private Label Credit Card Master Trust II
Citibank Credit Card Master Trust I	

Source: Moody's Investors Service, "Credit Card Master Trusts: Assessing the Risks of Cash Flow Allocations," *Structured Finance Special Report*, May 26, 1995, and Standard & Poor's *Credit Card Criteria 1997*, Structured Finance Ratings, Asset Backed Securities, 1997.

Exhibits 7, 8, and 9 report Moody's and Standard & Poor's classifications of master trusts with regard to the manner in which the trusts allocate finance charges among their series.

ABS TRANSACTION STRUCTURES

Revolving Period

The expected life of credit card receivables generally is about 6 to 8 months. Issuers have converted these historically short-term credit card receivables into long-term securities by incorporating a revolving period.

During the revolving period, only interest is paid to investors, while the investors' share of monthly principal payments is used to purchase new receivables arising in the accounts. This continuing purchase mechanism works to maintain a constant investor interest during the revolving period. The revolving period has a scheduled term and may be prematurely discontinued by an early amortization event.

Principal Paydown

Principal in credit card transactions is paid either in a bullet payment on the expected final payment date or is amortized over a scheduled period of time.

Accumulation Period and Soft Bullet

A bullet structure repays principal on a scheduled payment date. This structure is designed to look and trade like a corporate bond. In bullet structures, the revolving period is followed by an accumulation period, during which principal is deposited into an account held by the trustee. This account is referred to as the *principal funding account*. The accumulation period is set such that a sufficient amount of principal will be accumulated by the scheduled payment date.

Two types of bullet payments have been used for credit card certificates. The most common form of credit card bullet has been referred to as a *soft bullet*. A soft bullet structure accumulates principal and pays it to investors in one scheduled bullet payment. Liquidity protection is provided by the portfolio's monthly payment rate and the sharing of principal collections among investor series. The structure does not include a third party liquidity enhancement to be available on the expected final maturity date if the receivables have not fully amortized the outstanding investor interest. This is the sense in which the structure is a soft, rather than a hard, bullet. A soft bullet structure with a 6-month accumulation period is depicted in Exhibit 10.

On the other hand is the hard bullet structure, which provides for an external liquidity enhancement or a longer accumulation period. This is sized to provide liquidity to guarantee investor maturity payment in the rating agency worst case. JC Penney Master Credit Card Trust 1990-C and Euro Credit Card Trust 1989-A are examples of credit card ABS transactions that employ hard bullet structures.

Issuers and investors have been sufficiently comfortable with portfolio payment histories and structural features designed to provide the soft bullet principal payment on the expected maturity date that the hard bullet structure has not been viewed as a necessary enhancement. In fact, only three transactions have missed paying down completely by their expected maturity date and each of these finished paying down one month after their respective expected maturity date. Moreover, all of these trusts were *discrete* trusts; no *master* trust has missed paying down by its expected maturity date. In master trusts, principal reallocation from series that do not require principal to those that do may enable series in their paydown phase to more likely meet their expected maturity dates.

Controlled Amortization

As an alternative to the accumulation period and soft bullet, the revolving period may be followed instead by a controlled amortization period. A controlled amortization repays investor principal in equal scheduled payments. The use of this structure has declined considerably over the past few years.

The most common controlled amortization period is 12 months in length, although 6-month controlled amortization periods are not uncommon. A credit card transaction with a 6-month controlled amortization is depicted in Exhibit 11.

Issuers structure amortization periods to take into account their particular portfolio performance characteristics, especially their portfolio's monthly payment rate. This is necessary in order to give investors comfort that the probability of meeting the payment schedule is very high. As an example, series issued out of Sears Credit Account Master Trust II have 24-month controlled amortization periods to address the portfolio's relatively low monthly payment rate.

Exhibit 10: Credit Card Transaction with Soft Bullet and 6-Month Accumulation Period

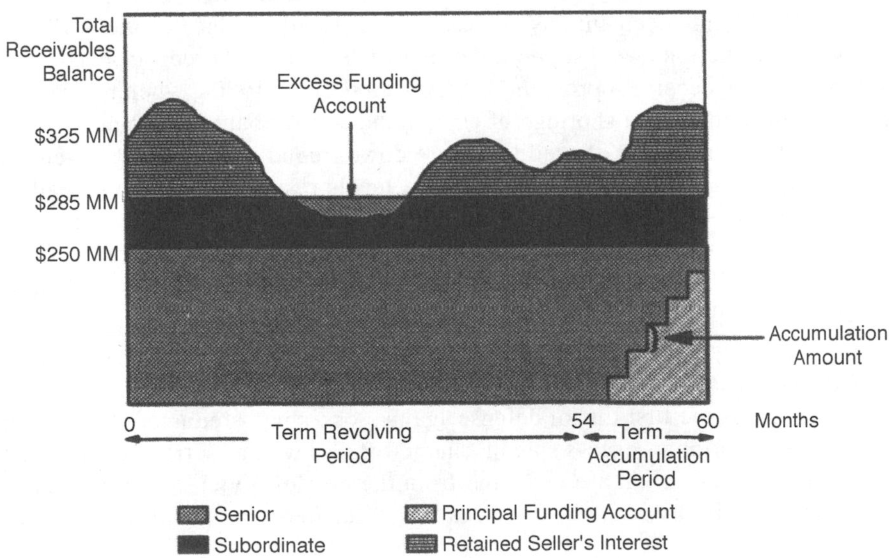

Source: Morgan Stanley

Exhibit 11: Credit Card Transaction with 6-Month Controlled Amortization

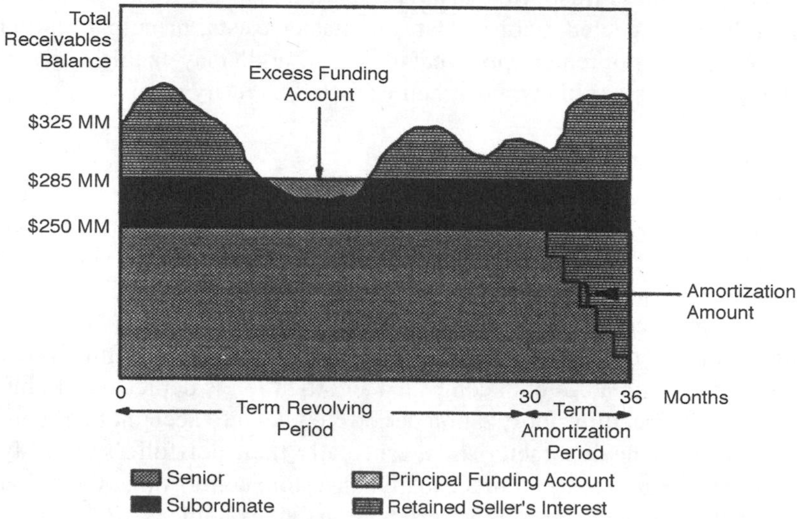

Source: Morgan Stanley

Credit Enhancement

The credit quality of a credit card ABS transaction is enhanced by early amortization events and structured credit enhancement. The structured credit enhancement protects investors from loss. Types of credit enhancement are discussed in this section.[9]

Credit enhancement has evolved from the earliest days of the ABS market, when transactions were supported primarily by letters of credit from commercial banks. This became a problem, however, in the late 1980s, when the banking industry suffered from a shortage of capital and several banks — some of which were providers of letters of credit — were downgraded by the ratings agencies. The downgrading of the banks to sub-AAA levels resulted in the downgrade of the ABS for which the banks were providing letters of credit. In fact, the only downgrades of AAA-rated ABS have been the result of the downgrade of their respective credit enhancer. No AAA-rated asset backed transaction to-date has suffered a ratings downgrade owing to collateral performance.

Excess Spread in First Loss Position

Excess spread is the first line of defense against losses in a credit card transaction. In the determination of excess spread, charge-offs, as well as series expenses such as coupon and servicing, are deducted from the portfolio yield generated by the receivables. It is this remaining spread — after netting out losses — that is

[9] For a more complete discussion, see the Morgan Stanley Asset Backed Securities Product Note, *Credit Enhancement in Credit Card ABS*, April 1996.

released from the trust to the servicer. If excess spread is insufficient to cover charge-offs — i.e., excess spread is negative after subtracting out losses — the transaction has to draw on its structured enhancement.

Early Amortization Events

In an early amortization event, the revolving period ends immediately and a pass-through period begins, regardless of original structure. Early amortization events can be viewed as principal protection mechanisms that allow a deal to pay down early if certain potentially adverse circumstances occur. While the market often attaches a black mark to early amortization, it is important to note that early amortization essentially is an automatic *credit put* back to the issuer of the securities.

The early amortization trigger on which the market most commonly focuses is the excess spread trigger, which almost always takes the form that an early amortization would occur if the 3-month average excess spread on a series is negative.[10] There are, however, other triggers for early amortization, such as:

- minimum seller interest
- seller default or bankruptcy
- available credit enhancement
- failure of seller to perform
- violation of reps and warranties.

To further protect the investor, master trusts employ a fixed allocation of principal between investor and seller interests in the case of an early amortization. The allocation is fixed based upon the proportion of investor-to-seller interests at the *start* of the early amortization. This means that as the investor interest pays down, the remaining investor interest is allocated an increasing proportion of principal relative to its declining balance.

After the Class A principal is paid down in an early amortization, the Class B principal pays down. If the payment rate is sufficient, Class B pays down in a single bullet payment.

Subordination

Senior/subordinate structures are issued as multiple tranches of securities in a single transaction. The senior certificates have a priority on the cash flow from the underlying receivables. The subordinated certificates provide enhancement by having principal cash flow available to cover losses on the senior piece that is not covered by the excess spread or by more subordinate enhancement.

Most credit card transactions have been structured with a AAA-rated senior class and a A-rated subordinate class. The subordinate class itself typically is supported by either a cash collateral account or collateral invested amount.

---

[10] In some cases, such as Spiegel Master Trust, the trigger is set off if the 3-month average excess spread falls below 100 bp.

Exhibit 12: Senior/Sub Structure with Shared Cash Collateral Account

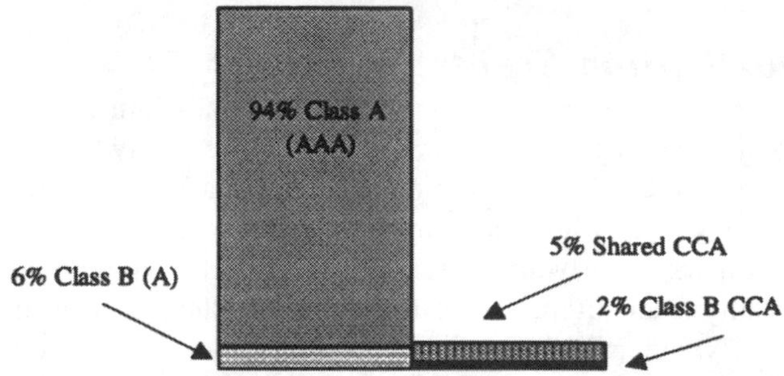

Source: Morgan Stanley

Cash Collateral Account

Credit card issuers turned to cash collateral accounts (CCA) to avoid the risk of a ratings downgrade of a letter of credit provider. A CCA essentially is a bank account that is in a loss position subordinate to any senior securities. Until the cash is actually needed to cover losses, it earns interest. The credit card's senior class can receive a AAA rating as long as the CCA invests in A1+/P1 rated instruments.

The CCA is funded by a loan from a third party credit enhancer. The enhancer — generally a bank — lends the CCA money at a reduced rate because the CCA guarantees to invest in commercial paper or other short-term debt of the lender.

Exhibit 12 shows a CCA used as enhancement for a senior/subordinate structure. It is assumed in this exhibit that 11% credit enhancement is required for Class A to receive a AAA rating and 7% support is necessary for Class B to get an A rating. The actual support necessary for any particular credit card portfolio would depend, of course, upon its specific characteristics.

In the senior/sub structure, the 11% protection for the AAA-rated Class A comes from two sources: 6% from an A-rated subordinate Class B and 5% from a CCA that is shared between Classes A and B. Credit enhancement for Class B is comprised of 5% from the shared CCA and a 2% CCA that is devoted exclusively to Class B.

Collateral Invested Amount

From the CCA, issuers moved to an even more efficient use of collateral — credit enhancement with a collateral invested amount (CIA). The CIA is similar to a CCA, except that it invests in credit card receivables within the structure, not the commercial paper of an outside source. Therefore, a CIA can effectively be considered a C class, subordinate to Classes A and B. The CIA is depicted in Exhibit 13.

Exhibit 13: Senior/Subordinate Structure with Collateral Invested Amount

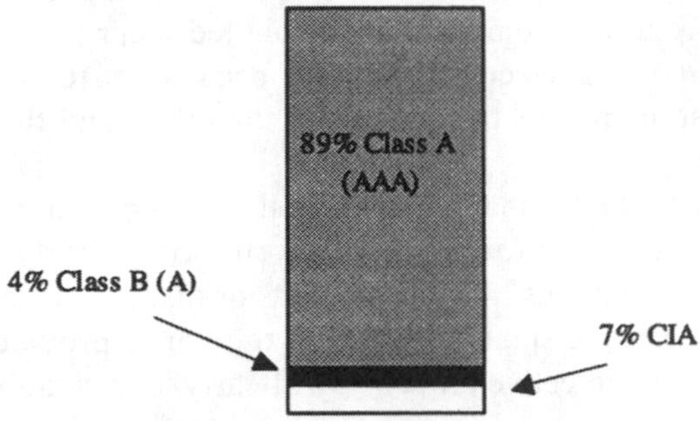

Source: Morgan Stanley

Like the example in Exhibit 12, the AAA-rated class in Exhibit 13 has 11% credit enhancement. Here 4% comes from the subordinate Class B, while 7% is provided by the CIA.

Generally, CIAs and CCAs are enhanced by reserve funds or spread accounts. These accounts are financed out of excess spread and/or may be in place upfront at the start of the deal. Funding a non-upfront reserve account involves certain portfolio performance triggers. When given levels of excess spread are breached, excess spread is diverted from the servicer to the reserve account.

Certificated C Pieces

There recently have been some credit card transactions in which the C piece was issued as a tradable security or certificate, rather than being placed with an enhancement provider. These so-called certificated C pieces are structured similar to CIAs, with delinquency triggers to provide extra protection for investors. When the delinquency triggers are tripped, excess spread gets diverted to reserve funds to provide additional enhancement. First USA, MBNA, Chevy Chase, and Providian have included certificated C pieces in some of their recent credit card transactions.

AVOIDING EARLY AMORTIZATION

Credit card ABS issuers have gone to lengths to stave off early amortization when excess spreads on their respective trusts reached relatively low levels. Issuers fear that an early amortization event would be perceived as a black mark and reduce their access to funding in the future, or at least increase their cost of funding.

Investors holding credit card securities that early amortize get their principal returned at par. When the bond market was rallying and ABS spreads tightened consistently, credit cards traded above par. Early amortization would have caused investors to lose the premium and reinvest at tighter spreads.

As the market has begun to trade lower, many fixed rate cards are trading below par and many floaters are close to par, whether above or below. For bonds purchased below par, early amortization can actually be a positive event: investors get their principal returned from a possibly troubled security, capture the discount and, if spreads widen in the sector generally because of the early amortization, may get to reinvest at spreads that are wider than the bond that experienced the early amortization.

For credit card ABS that are above par and displaying weak trust performance, investors should try to assess the likelihood of early amortization and what this means for the bonds' realized spreads or discount margins. The investor can determine whether the spread offered on the bonds provides sufficient compensation, given their subjective probability of early amortization.[11]

Discounting Receivables

Many credit card issuers have provisions in their pooling and servicing agreements that allow them to sell receivables to their trust at a discount, or use a yield discount factor effectively to treat a portion of principal collections as finance charge collections. This essentially generates additional portfolio yield. By selling receivables at a discount, the seller takes an upfront loss on the sale. Part of the discount is offset by the seller's recognition of the present value of excess spread at the time of the sale. The trust will capture the discount, which will be counted towards portfolio yield.

This mechanism of averting early amortization had always been viewed as a powerful weapon in the issuer's quiver. Last year, however, the Office of the Comptroller of the Currency (OCC) effectively removed the discounting option from bank issuers of credit cards as a means of saving a deal.[12] The OCC argued that discounting receivables — or taking any action to "save" a deal — implies that the issuer has an economic interest in the receivables; if so, then the trust has recourse to the issuer and the seller has not engaged in a "true sale."

The OCC stressed that this was not a new policy, but rather a clarification of existing policy. The issuer is not precluded from discounting receivables, but rather would have to put the receivables back on balance sheet and hold capital against them. This capital requirement effectively removes discounting as a means of averting early amortization. The OCC policy applies directly only to national banks, although it is likely that state chartered banks — which are regulated by the Federal Deposit Insurance Corporation — will be subject to a similar interpretation of recourse, given the move toward regulatory conformity over the past several years.

---

[11] For a methodology that relates realized spreads or discount margins to probabilities of early amortization, see the Morgan Stanley *Mortgage Research Weekly*, "Valuing Early Amortization Risk in Credit Card ABS," April 17, 1997.

[12] See the Morgan Stanley *Mortgage Research Weekly*, "Discounting Receivables Imposes Capital Charge for Credit Card Issuers", June 27, 1996, and "ABS Market Snapshot: Third Quarter Wrap-Up," October 10, 1996.

Automatic Additions

The current rating agency standard is to allow automatic account additions to the master trust up to a maximum of 15% per quarter or 20% per year. The First Chicago Master Trust II is the only outstanding trust to have unlimited automatic additions. The automatic additions allow the trust to perform more like an ongoing portfolio than a static pool of accounts.

In addition to adding accounts to facilitate future securitizations, some credit card issuers have used automatic additions as a means of diluting charge-off percentages in their trusts. Adding accounts lowers the reported charge-off percentages in a trust because the denominator (total receivables) increases more than the numerator (total charge-offs). The OCC specifically avoided in their formal statement addressing the issue of whether account additions constitute recourse.[13] As a practical matter, it is extremely difficult to distinguish between adding accounts to facilitate future securitizations and adding accounts to save a troubled deal.

Additions with Rating Agency Approval

Issuers can make additions larger than those permitted automatically if they obtain rating agency consent. The purpose of the rating agency approval is to be certain that the characteristics of the added accounts and their respective borrowers are not materially different from those in the existing trust. The idea is that adding accounts should not adversely affect the trust.

RECENT DEVELOPMENTS IN THE CREDIT CARD SECTOR

Weak Consumer Sector and Early Amortization Fears

After several years of economic growth characterized by declining charge-offs, the credit card sector has over the past two years been beset by rising losses owing to weakness in the consumer sector. Personal bankruptcies have risen to record high levels, at the same time that revolving consumer credit has grown exponentially.

The rise in bankruptcies and charge-offs have led to increasing fears among some investors about early amortization risk. Investors in AAA-rated credit card ABS in general are not concerned about principal risk on their securities. The greater risk for these investors is mark-to-market risk, in that early amortization fears may cause spreads to widen on their bonds.

There has been some reluctance among investors to step into the A-rated credit card sector, owing to both mark-to-market risk and perceived principal risk. In our view, the principal risk in A-rated credit cards is only marginally larger than in the AAA-rated cards. We have long recommended that investors can pick up incremental spread with only marginally greater risk by moving from AAA- to A-rated cards.

---

[13] See the Office of the Comptroller of the Currency, OCC Bulletin 96-52, "Securitization: Guidelines for National Banks," September 25, 1996.

Non-Dollar Transactions and Repackagings

Last year saw the development in the credit card market of a significant non-dollar sector. This included the first credit card transaction denominated in Deutsche marks (Citibank) and the first fixed rate Deutsche mark securitization (Capital One). In addition, the Batavia I and II transactions were the first non-dollar structures to reduce dramatically the chance of early amortization. These transactions converted Citibank floating rate collateral into fixed rate Dutch guilder and Deutsche mark notes. This basic structure was utilized by MBNA America European Structured Notes No. 1, a Dutch guilder deal that included the greatest swap counterparty event risk protection in a fixed rate non-dollar transaction.

These transactions follow MBNA's Chester Asset Receivables Deals, which are British pound Sterling securities backed by receivables denominated in Sterling. We expect to see more non-dollar transactions as the globalization of the ABS market continues.

CONCLUSION

Credit cards represent the largest and most mature sector of the asset backed securities market. Despite its maturity, it nonetheless continues to develop and evolve as new structures reflect, and appeal to, the increasingly global nature of the ABS investor base.

APPENDIX

Brief Profiles of Major Credit Card ABS Issuers*

Advanta

Advanta generates new accounts primarily through direct mail and telemarketing solicitation of potential card holders. Its marketing effort has centered on proprietary computer models that sift through credit bureau data to identify potentially profitable card holders who then are recruited through a focused direct mail effort. Generally, accounts are opened with an initial term of one year; at the anniversary date, accounts which meet certain criteria for usage and payment history are reissued for one to three year terms. Advanta also has a joint venture with the Royal Bank of Scotland to market credit cards in the United Kingdom.

American Express

The American Express card was introduced in 1958. The American Express card is not a credit card, but rather a charge card: a card holder's full balance is billed monthly and is due upon receipt of the billing statement and is not subject to finance charges. There is no pre-set spending limit on an American Express account. Every charge is subject to an approval process based on the card holder's past spending, payment patterns and financial resources. American Express has recently focused on building its Optima card portfolio, by issuing revolving credit cards with different features that appeal to various customer groups, such as a student card, a low-rate card, a golf card and several travel-oriented co-branded cards. In contrast to the American Express card being a charge card, the Optima card is a credit card, similar to VISA and MasterCard. The company is also rapidly expanding its card strategy abroad by issuing American Express credit cards in the United Kingdom, Canada, Hong Kong and Australia and continues to build its international charge card portfolio by offering the Platinum card in Switzerland, France and Italy.

AT&T Universal

AT&T Universal Card Services is a wholly-owned subsidiary of AT&T Corp. The AT&T Universal Card is a combination credit card and AT&T calling card, and is issued by Universal Bank and Columbus Bank and Trust. AT&T Universal began offering credit cards in 1990. The earliest card holders were offered cards with no annual fee for life, which tended to attract a high proportion of convenience users. AT&T has since broadened its solicitations to attract card holders who are more likely to carry balances, which would contribute to portfolio yield. Accounts are principally generated by pre-approved direct mailings to prospective card holders, as well as unsolicited telephone requests for applications, requests for applications

---

* The information in this appendix is obtained from company prospectuses, company information, and Morgan Stanley.

generated by telemarketing efforts or via the Internet, marketing on college campuses, non-pre-approved direct mailings, substitution of credit cards for single purpose calling cards and alternative AT&T channels, including AT&T WorldNet℠.

Bank of America

Bank of America is a subsidiary of BankAmerica Corporation, a multi-bank holding company. Bank of America's activities are primarily related to credit card lending. Bank of America issues VISA Classic, VISA Gold, Standard MasterCard and Gold MasterCard credit card accounts. Potential card holders are solicited via applications at Bank of America branch offices, non-pre-screened direct mail, pre-approved direct mail, applications mailed to Bank of America customers and consumer-initiated requests.

Capital One

Capital One Bank and Capital One F.S.B. are the principal subsidiaries of holding company Capital One Financial Corporation. Capital One Bank and Capital One F.S.B. offer financial products and services to consumers. Capital One Bank is the ninth largest issuer of MasterCard and VISA credit cards in terms of outstanding receivables. Capital One employs what it calls an Information Based Strategy, which combines information technology and analytical techniques to identify, manage and act upon business opportunities.

Chase

Chase's receivables include both those from credit cards originated by Chase Manhattan Bank and those from cards originated by the former Chemical Bank, which merged with Chase. The former Chemical Bank trust is now referred to as Chase Credit Card Master Trust, in contrast to the original Chase trust, which is referred to as Chase Manhattan Credit Card Master Trust. Credit card accounts were principally generated by prescreened and non-prescreened direct mail solicitations, applications mailed or made available at branches to existing customers, purchases of accounts from other credit card issuers, co-branded and affinity relationship marketing and consumer-initiated requests.

Citibank

Citibank is the largest credit card issuer in the United States. Citibank offers both non-premium and premium VISA and MasterCard accounts. Premium and non-premium accounts differ in terms of annual fees, periodic finance charges and late fees. The Citibank portfolio includes affinity and co-branded accounts, such as the American Airlines AAdvantage frequent flyer card and the Ford card, as well as accounts solicited through direct mail and telemarketing and those opened at Citibank branch offices. On January 1, 1996, the name of Citibank's master trust was changed from Standard Credit Card Master Trust to Citibank Credit Card Master Trust.

Discover

The Discover Card is issued by Greenwood Trust Co., a Delaware banking corporation indirectly owned by Dean Witter, Discover & Co. Dean Witter, Discover merged with Morgan Stanley & Co., in a transaction that closed in May 1997. The Discover Card is a general purpose credit card, first offered in 1985. The card can be used to purchase merchandise and services from establishments worldwide and also can be used to obtain cash advances at automated teller machines. One feature of the Discover Card is a cash back bonus in which Greenwood annually pays card members a percentage of their purchase amounts, ranging up to 1%, based on the amount of annual purchases. This amount is remitted to card holders from Greenwood and is not paid from the property of the Discover Card Master Trust.

First Bank System

First Bank issues charge cards through two programs, its Corporate Card and Purchasing Card programs. These programs issue non-revolving VISA card accounts to employees of corporations with annual travel and entertainment expenses of at least $1 million, and are not intended as a means of financing purchases. The Corporate Card program is designed for employee travel and entertainment expenses and is marketed to corporations with a large number of employees requiring a substantial number of corporate charge cards. The Purchasing Card is designed to accommodate a company's small dollar purchases and is issued directly to corporate employees whose job responsibilities require them to make routine small dollar purchases.

First Chicago NBD

First Chicago issues both Classic and Gold VISA cards and Standard and Gold MasterCard accounts. Cards include both co-branded and non-co-branded cards, with a significant co-branding relationship with the United Airlines Mileage Plus Program, for which card holders receive frequent flyer mileage credit for each dollar purchased with their card. First Chicago's accounts are principally generated via pre-approved direct mail solicitations; applications in financial institutions, retail outlets, college campuses and magazines; affinity marketing; and purchases of accounts from other issuers.

First Union

First Union National Bank of Georgia is a wholly owned subsidiary of First Union Corporation. It provides a wide range of commercial and retail banking services in Georgia. First Union offers both MasterCard and VISA credit cards, including both premium and standard, and with fixed and variable rates. First Union has an interest rebate program, in which after a period of 5 or 10 years, borrowers can recoup over a subsequent period 50% or 100% of their finance charges paid over the initial period. The rebate is absorbed by the seller's interest in the trust.

First USA

First USA Bank is a wholly-owned subsidiary of First USA Financial, Inc., which is a wholly-owned subsidiary of First USA, Inc. First USA markets over 1000 credit card products to customers throughout the United States. These include standard card products identified and developed through data analysis, as well as products developed and marketed through partnership relationships. Products include designs tailored to an individual's lifestyle, profession, or interests, as well as those built around affiliations, co-branded relationships and programs with financial institutions. First USA's strategy is to target customers through a combination of pricing, credit analysis and packaging. The products are generally marketed with low introductory and regular rates and no annual fee. First USA, Inc. and Banc One Corporation merged in mid-1997.

Household

Household has three different trusts: Household Affinity Credit Card Master Trust I, Household Credit Card Master Trust I and Household Private Label Credit Card Master Trust II. Household issues the General Motors (GM) credit card under a long-term contract. Card holders accumulate points by purchasing goods on the GM card and use the points to receive a discount on the purchase or lease of a GM car or truck. The GM points cannot be used for a car purchase unless the card holder maintains current payment status on their account. Receivables generated prior to September 1994 from the GM card are securitized in Household Affinity Credit Card Master Trust I.

In addition to the GM card, Household securitizes a portfolio of VISA and MasterCard accounts in Household Credit Card Master Trust I. This portfolio is made up of accounts generated by Household or purchased from other institutions. Household's third credit card portfolio is Household Private Label Credit Card Master Trust II. This is a portfolio of credit cards offered by Household under the name of a retailer.

MBNA America Bank, N.A.

MBNA is the country's second largest credit card lender. It has focused on providing credit cards to members of affinity groups that include professional and occupational associations, alumni and cause-related organizations and other groups of people who share a common interest. MBNA uses credit bureau reports to check the credit histories of applicants, but unlike most credit card issuers, it does not use automated credit scoring systems as its primary method of deciding whether to issue a card. Instead, decisions are made by credit analysts based upon customer applications, credit histories and additional information the analyst may gather. This process is referred to as a judgmental credit approval process. MBNA also offers credit cards in the United Kingdom and has securitized pound sterling-denominated receivables originated by its Chester, England, affiliate.

NationsBank

NationsBank is an indirect wholly-owned subsidiary of NationsBank Corporation, a multi-bank holding company. NationsBank is a national banking association which conducts nationwide consumer lending activities, principally comprised of credit card related activities. It issues Standard and Gold MasterCard and Classic and Gold VISA card accounts. NationsBank's credit card accounts are principally generated via applications at bank branches and outlets related to affinity and co-branded partners, pre-approved direct mail applications and purchases or other acquisitions of accounts from other credit card issuers.

People's Bank

People's Bank was formed in 1842 and is headquartered in Bridgeport, Connecticut. It is the 26th largest bank issuer of credit cards on the basis of outstanding receivables. People's Bank's credit card accounts were primarily generated via pre-screened direct mail applications, direct mail applications to existing bank customers, direct mail applications to members of affinity groups with a credit card program sponsored by People's Bank and consumer-initiated applications.

Providian

Providian's credit card and revolving line accounts were originated by First Deposit National Bank and Providian National Bank, both of which are subsidiaries of Providian Bancorp, Inc. Providian Bancorp had been a wholly-owned subsidiary of Providian Corporation, a publicly owned consumer financial services company, principally engaged in insurance, investment management and banking. In June 1997, Providian Corporation completed the merger of its insurance business with AEGON USA, a subsidiary of AEGON N.V., an international insurance company headquartered in the Netherlands, and spun off Providian Bancorp as a separate publicly held company. Providian Master Trust was formerly known as First Deposit Master Trust. Credit card accounts in the trust were originated primarily through direct mail and telemarketing.

Sears

The Sears Card is used exclusively to charge purchases at Sears, Roebuck & Co. stores. Sears is one of the largest retailers in the United States and has the largest receivables base among retailers. Its credit card carries a fixed rate and is the retail credit card with the largest amount of receivables; 60% of store purchases are charged on it. Sears has been in the credit business for 86 years. Sears credit card securitizations have been fixed rate and have employed principal paydown structures with 12- and 24-month controlled amortization periods.

Chapter 13

Credit Card "C-Pieces"

John N. Dunlevy, CFA
Chief Investment Officer
Beacon Hill Capital Advisers, LLC

INTRODUCTION

Credit card "C-pieces" are also commonly referred to as *collateral invested amounts* or CIAs. They are subordinate tranches, BBB-rated, and provide credit enhancement for the more senior bonds in the structure. C-pieces can be structured with either floating- or fixed-rate coupons and are most often bullet securities. C-pieces are unique in that they have increased credit enhancement as the collateral performance worsens. Further, these bonds are protected by a cash reserve fund which reduces the risk of downgrade and helps ensure the full return of principal.

HISTORY OF CREDIT CARD ABS STRUCTURES

In the earliest credit card transactions, a AAA rating was achieved by purchasing a letter of credit (most often from a highly rated foreign bank). This letter of credit could be drawn on to cover any losses resulting from the credit card portfolio. This structure was, unfortunately, heavily dependent on the credit risk of the LOC provider. When many foreign banks were downgraded in the late 1980s, several credit card deals were downgraded. Consequently, investors and issuers alike moved away from these structures.

The next structural enhancement was the use of the *cash collateral account* (CCA). This structure reduced the event risk potential since a pool of cash would be available to cover collateral losses. A CCA is essentially a pool of cash which earns interest and can only invest in A1/P1 rated money market investments. A diagram of this structure is shown in Exhibit 1. CCAs are funded by a loan from a third-party credit enhancer (usually a domestic or Yankee bank).

The third stage of structural development was the 2-tranche deal with two CCAs. This structure is shown in Exhibit 2. As in the single-tranche deal with CCA, total credit enhancement supporting the AAA bond is 18%. However, in this case it is comprised of 12% subordination (Class B) and 6% in a shared CCA. Total credit enhancement available to the Class B (A-rated) is 10% comprised of 6% in a shared CCA (a subordinated claim) and 4% in a CCA used only to support the Class B. This senior/subordinated execution was much more efficient since it reduces the need for a large CCA (the costs of maintaining a CCA are greater than the added costs of subordination).

The fourth phase of the market became popular around 1995. This was the further subordination of the structure by the creation of a C-piece. This C-piece was a better execution since it further reduced the need for outside credit enhancement such as CCAs. During this time period C-pieces were done as bank loans rather than 144-A style bonds. These C-pieces loans were placed privately with Yankee banks.

The fifth and most current phase of structural development is the 144-A style bond tranches. This structure has been popular since mid-1996. The C-pieces, both structured as loans and 144-A bonds, are internally credit enhanced through the use of excess spread and reserve accounts.

C-PIECE STRUCTURAL PROTECTIONS

The current C-piece bonds are protected by the following four structural features: (1) excess spread, (2) reserve accounts (Class D), (3) spread account triggers, and (4) early amortization triggers. Each of these features is discussed below.

Excess Spread

Excess spreads represents the current excess cash available to support the C-pieces and absorb losses on the collateral pool. The following is a simple example of an excess spread calculation.

Exhibit 1: Cash Collateral Account Structure

	% Deal
Class A (AAA)	82%
Class B (A)	8%
Class C (BBB)	10%

Structure	*Single Tranche with LOC*	*Single Tranche with CCA*	*2 Tranches with CCA*	*3 Tranches as Loan*	*3 Tranches as Bond*
Phase	1	2	3	4	5
Time Period	1986 to 1991	Early 1990s	1991 to Current	1995 to 1996	1996 to Current

Exhibit 2: Two-Tranche Deal with Two CCAs

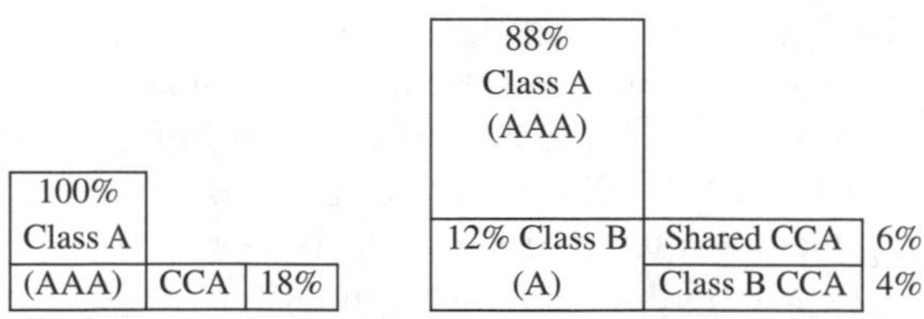

Exhibit 3: Excess Spreads of Major Issuers

Major Issuer	Sample Deal	Portfolio Yield	3-Month Average Excess SPD	Monthly Pay Rate
Advanta-II	96-E	17.66	1.66	11.71
Bank One	96-A	20.21	3.65	13.60
Capital One	96-3	20.86	5.21	10.81
Chase	97-1	18.50	2.31	11.88
Chevy Chase II	96-C	21.35	3.51	10.10
Citibank I	97-4	17.94	4.50	18.87
Discover I	96-5	19.62	4.03	14.16
First Chicago II	96-S	21.37	3.56	22.32
First USA	97-1	16.65	3.23	13.14
MBNA II	96-M	17.19	4.39	12.14
Providian	97-2	27.73	6.27	9.09
Sears	96-4	19.54	4.43	6.56

Source: Morgan Stanley 7/31/97

Gross portfolio yield	18.0%
Less charge-offs	(6.0)
Net portfolio yield	12.0
Less coupon expenses	(6.5)
Less servicing	(2.5)
Excess spread	3.5%

In this case, 350 basis points is available as a buffer against increased monthly losses. The recent excess spread levels available for the major card issuers is shown in Exhibit 3.

Reserve Account

Reserve account is a form of credit enhancement which can be used to protect the C-piece. This reserve account, sometimes called the "D-pieces," can be initially funded at closing. The rating agency will determine the initial size of the reserve account depending on the historical performance (i.e., portfolio yield, charge offs, and monthly payment rate) of the issuer. Additionally, the reserve account size will be increased or decreased depending on the ongoing performance of the collateral.

Spread Account Triggers

Spread (reserve) account triggers as excess spread deteriorates to a specified trigger level, the flow of excess spread (which normally flows back to the issuer) is interrupted and trapped in a separate reserve account. This reserve account is for the benefit of the C class and acts as a first loss position should excess spread deterioration lead to early amortization (discussed in the next section). Exhibit 4 provides an example of a reserve fund trigger for a First USA deal.

Exhibit 4: Reserve Fund Trigger for a First USA Deal

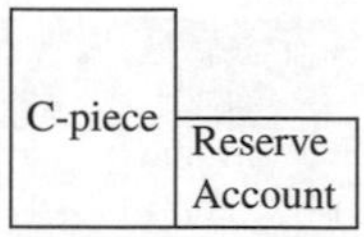

3-Month Average Excess Spread	Reserve Fund Target %A + B + C	Reserve Target % of Class C
>4.5	0.00	0.00
4.0 to 4.5	1.50	16.0
3.5 to 4.0	2.00	21.0
3.0 to 3.5	3.00	32.0
<3.0	4.00	42.0

Once trapped, cash cannot be released (if excess spread improves) for at least three months. Any initial reserve account funding may not be eligible for release (depending on the specific deal). The idea behind the reserve fund triggers is to increase the credit enhancement available to the C-piece as the collateral credit risk increases.

Early Amortization Triggers

Early amortization allows for the rapid return of principal in the event that the 3-month average spread falls to zero or less. When early amortization occurs, the credit card tranches are retired sequentially (i.e., first the AAA bond then the A rated bond, etc.). The length of time until the return of principal is largely a function of the monthly principal payment rate. For example, if the monthly payment rate is 11% then a typical AAA tranche would return principal over a 7.5 month (82%/11%) period (82% represents the AAA percent of the overall deal). Whereas an 18% monthly payment rate would return principal over a 4.5-month period (82%/18%).

Additionally, most indentures call for payout events for the triggers such as insolvency of the issuer or failure to maintain required seller's interest or reserve accounts.

RATING AGENCY CRITERIA

To date, credit card C-pieces have only been rated by a single rating agency — Fitch. Fitch determines the appropriate level of credit enhancement by stressing scenarios which reduce yields and monthly payment rates and increase charge-offs and investor coupons (for floating tranches). The extent of the stress scenario is determined by the structure, the quality of the portfolio, and potential basis risk.

As a benchmark, Fitch uses the performance of credit card portfolios originated in the depressed Northeast during the early 1990s as its BBB stress scenario. (It determined this to be a BB recession scenario.) The Fitch rating criteria for credit card stress scenarios is shown in Exhibit 5.

Exhibit 5: Fitch Rating Criteria for Credit Card Stress Scenarios

	A Class (AAA)	B Class (A)	C Class (BBB)
Charge-offs	4 to 5×	3×	2.25×
Portfolio yield	35% down	25% down	20% down
Monthly payment rate	45% down	35% down	20% down
New purchase rate	0%	0%	0%

Exhibit 6: Structural Risk Elements

Structural Risk:	Class A (AAA)	Class B (A)	Class C (BBB)
Servicer risk	AAA Std	AAA Std	AAA Std
Legal risk	AAA Std	AAA Std	AAA Std
Dilution	AAA Std	AAA Std	AAA Std
Commingling	AAA Std	AAA Std	AAA Std
Additions	AAA Std	AAA Std	AAA Std
Eligible investments	AAA Std	AAA Std	AAA Std

Fitch bases its rating on two main factors. First, it performs enhancement stress scenarios. As shown in Exhibit 5, a deal must be able to withstand an immediate reduction of yield and monthly payment rate of 20%. Next, a C-piece must also be able to withstand an increase in charge-offs of 2.0× to 2.5× over a 6-month period.

Second, Fitch sets its excess spread stress triggers to ensure an adequate build up of cash flow in the dedicated spread account. For issuers with more volatile patterns of excess spread, an up-front cash deposit in a reserve account is required.

Finally, Fitch requires the same protections for the C-piece as for the AAA class with regard to dilution and commingling risk. These structural risk elements are shown in Exhibit 6.

CASE STUDY

We have chosen a fairly recent deal as an example to illustrate the credit strengths of these transactions — First USA 1997-4. The deal is described below.

First USA 1997-4

Structure	%	Coupon	Avg Life
Class A	83.0	1-Mo LIBOR +21	9.8
Class B	7.5	1-Mo LIBOR +41	9.8
Class C	9.5	1-Mo LIBOR +95	9.8

Reserve fund deposit = 2% of deal balance

Further, the deal's spread targets are as follows:

3-Month Excess Spread	SPD Account Requirement
< 3.0%	4.0
3.0 to 3.5	3.0
3.5 to 4.0	2.0
4.0 to 4.5	1.5
4.5% >	0.0

Since in this example, the reserve account is initially funded with a 2.0% deposit, the reserve account can be built quickly. As shown below, the reserve an be completely funded in 3.5 months.

Assumptions

Portfolio yield	16.60%	
Coupon	(5.96)	
Servicing	(1.50)	
Charge-offs	(5.70)	
Excess spread	3.44	(which corresponds to a 3.0% target)

Excess SPD	Initial Reserve Bal % A + B+ C	Reserve Target	Reserve %C Class	No Months to Fund Reserve
3.44	2	3	31.5	3.5
3.00	2	3	31.5	4.0
2.75	2	4	42.1	8.7
2.50	2	4	42.1	9.6
2.00	2	4	42.1	12.0
1.75	2	4	42.1	12.7
1.50	2	4	42.1	16.0

We have a proprietary model that allows us to run various stress tests with regard to the building of the reserve fund. Additionally, the model allows us to stress test the following:

Factors:

- Portfolio yields
- Portfolio losses
- Monthly payment rates
- Tranche coupons
- Portfolio purchase rate

Below we repeat the results of our analysis involving these variables on our case study deal.

Portfolio Yields

The First USA portfolio can withstand a sharp instantaneous drop in portfolio yields without losing any C-piece principal. These scenarios are shown below:

Portfolio Yield (%)	Change in Portfolio Yield (bp)	Principal Returned (%)
16.60	0	100.0
15.60	–100	100.0
14.60	–200	100.0
13.60	–300	100.0
12.60	–400	100.0
11.60	–500	100.0
10.60	–600	100.0
9.60	–700	98.5

As shown above, the C-piece can absorb a large instantaneous decline in yield. In fact, even if yield declines from 16.60% to 9.60%, 98.5% of principal is still returned. This is the case since other key variables such as purchase rate, monthly payment rate, and portfolio losses were unchanged.

Portfolio Losses

The First USA 1997-4 C-piece also can withstand a sharp spike in portfolio losses. This is demonstrated below:

Charge-offs (%)	Change in Charge-offs (bp)	Principal Returns (%)
5.70	0	100.0
6.70	+100	100.0
7.70	+200	100.0
8.70	+300	100.0
9.70	+400	100.0
10.70	+500	100.0
11.70	+600	100.0
12.70	+700	98.0

As shown above, principal is returned in full to the C-piece in all scenarios, until an instant 700 basis point rise in portfolio charge-offs.

Monthly Payment Rates

Monthly payment rates are very important to the credit card structure since they dictate how quickly principal can be returned in the event of an early amortization. Generally, the faster the monthly payment rate the more credit protection is afforded the investor.

As shown above, at a slower monthly payment rate, principal losses are greater than in the base case. Conversely, at a higher monthly payment rate, a higher instantaneous portfolio loss can be absorbed.

Tranche Coupons

The impact of varying tranche coupons (i.e., for spikes in LIBOR) is the same as increasing portfolio charge-offs or cutting portfolio yields (i.e., impacts excess spread). This is shown below:

Monthly Payment Rate	Change from Base Case	Principal Returned @ 10.70% Loss	Principal Returned @ 12.70% Loss
13.00	0.0	100.0	98.0
6.00	−7.0	98.2	81.4
20.00	+7.0	100.0	100.0

Portfolio Purchase Rate

The impact of purchase rate is also similar to an increase in monthly payment rates. That is, an increase in purchase rates will improve the overall credit risk profile, while a decline in purchase rates will increase the risk.

OTHER RISK FACTORS

The other major risk in investing in this asset class is limited liquidity. That is, the size of the market — albeit growing rapidly — is around $1 billion as of August 1997. To date, 18 transactions have been completed with 15 being floating-rate bonds and three fixed rate. The average size of the typical C-piece bond is around $55 million. The four major issuers in this market to date are MBNA, First USA, Chevy Chase, and Providian.

Because these investments are 144-A securities, the following investment restrictions apply: (1) buyer must be qualified institutional buyer (QIB), (2) buyer must be U.S. taxpayer, (3) bonds not ERISA eligible, (4) limit of 100 owners per master trust, (5) minimum size $5 million per holder, and (6) issuer must approve transfers.

However, there are other factors which mitigate the risk of investing in C-pieces. First, the risk of early amortization is the same for all three tranches (AAA, A, and BBB). Thus, in that sense, that risk impacts the whole deal equally. The loss severity is the only difference among the tranches.

Second, the issuer has a large incentive not to have its excess spread trapped in the Master Trust. That is, any monies in the reserve account impact the issuer's earnings. Finally, credit card issuers have historically shown great support for their deals. For example, issuers have sold discounted receivables into the trust to prop up excess spread and avoid early amortization. As previously stated, only in an early amortization event is C-piece principal potentially at risk.

Chapter 14

Equipment-Financed ABS

James S. Anderson
Director, Asset-Backed Research
First Union Capital Markets

Scott H. Shannon
Director, Asset-Securitization Division
First Union Capital Markets

Steven A. Columbaro
Analyst, Fixed-Income Research
First Union Capital Markets

INTRODUCTION

The securitization of equipment leases began in 1985, when Sperry Lease Finance Corp. issued two deals backed by leases on computer equipment. This makes lease-backed paper among the first non-mortgage assets to be securitized. Subsequent to the Sperry transactions, volume from equipment issuers was sporadic, with most of the notable transactions through 1992 being computer-related. The past several years have witnessed significant growth in the types of leased assets being securitized. Large- and small-ticket medical, office, transportation, and essential-use industrial equipment are collateral types underlying recent asset-backed security ABS transactions.

The asset class had a watershed year in 1996 as GPA securitized in excess of $4 billion of aircraft and AT&T Capital entered the ABS market with a $3 billion transaction. Liquidity and investor acceptance of the asset class dramatically improved, as numerous institutions became educated on the characteristics of equipment ABS. Nominal spreads, which provided a significant 10-15 basis point pickup over alternative asset classes such as automobile and credit card ABS, narrowed on a relative basis and trended down over the year to a point where the equipment ABS traded in line with automobile ABS.

This trend continued in 1997 as several well-known issuers accessed the equipment-backed ABS market for the first time and investors, concerned with a general decline in consumer credit quality, looked to diversify. Because the collateral underlying equipment ABS generally represents commercial obligors, investors further embraced the asset class.

Exhibit 1: Business Trends in Equipment Lending

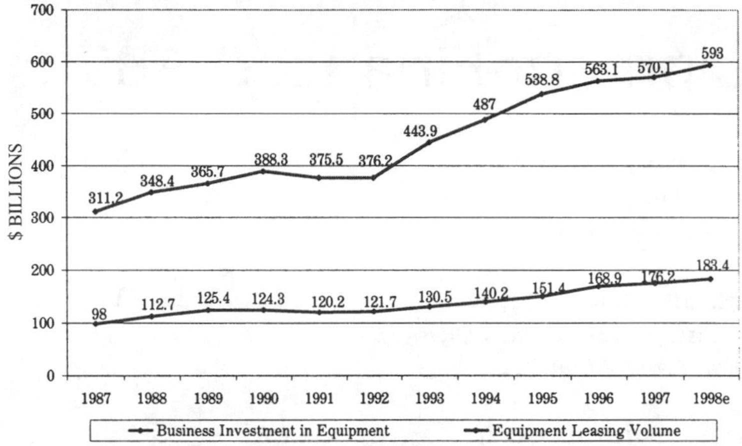

Source: U.S. Department of Commerce, Economics & Statistics Administration, Bureau of Economic Analysis, and Equipment Leasing Association, by permission.

This chapter explores the collateral underlying equipment ABS and the investment characteristics of the securities. It discusses the various types of originators and their motivation for issuance, as well as how investors should analyze particular structures. Finally, it discusses equipment ABS as a component of the broader ABS market.

THE EQUIPMENT LEASING INDUSTRY

Business investment in equipment has grown dramatically, with an estimated $582 billion coming into service in 1997.[1] Of this, approximately 31% was leased. An estimated 80% of corporations lease some or all of their equipment, either for cash flow reasons or in recognition that the productivity of equipment comes from use, not ownership. The U.S. Department of Commerce forecasts 6% annual growth through the year 2000, which translates to over $200 billion of lease volume per annum. This represents a huge pool of potential collateral for securitization.

Exhibit 1 displays the trends in new business investment in equipment and equipment leasing. Note the explosive growth coming out of the 1991-1992 economic slowdown.

Exhibit 2 breaks down the types of equipment by use. Various modes of transportation and computers are the two largest types of leased equipment. Within the computer group, the share of personal computers (PCs) and networks has been increasing vis-à-vis mainframes during the 1990s as lessees seek protection from technological obsolescence.

[1] Data in this section may be found on http://elaonline.com.

Exhibit 2: 1996 Equipment Leasing Volume by Type

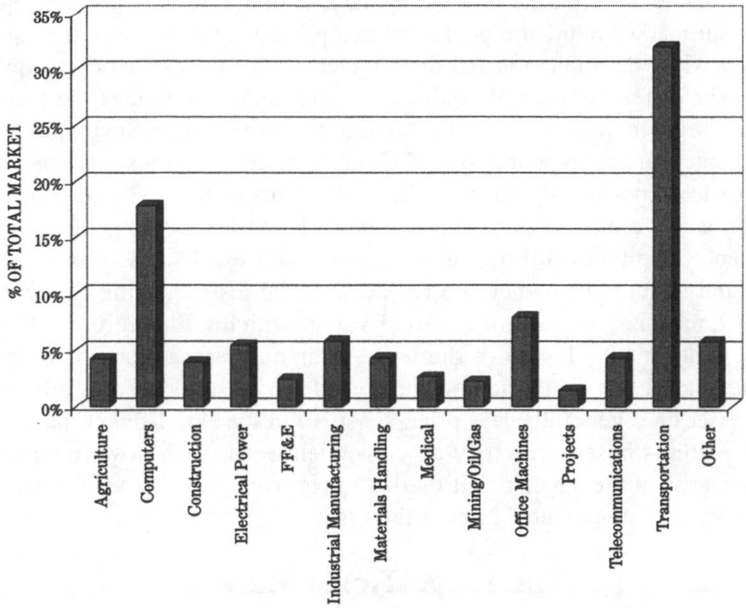

Source: 1997 ELA Survey of Industrial Activity, by permission.

Lease originators fall into four basic categories: banks, financial service companies (e.g., GECC), captive subsidiaries of equipment manufacturers (e.g., Case Credit Corporation), and independent leasing finance companies (e.g., Heller Financial and Newcourt Credit Group). Each originator may have different reasons to securitize its lease streams, which are discussed below.

Leasing companies compete on price, flexibility in structuring leases to customer requirements, their relationship with equipment vendors (whom they represent to the market), product knowledge, and service. Individual companies tend to specialize, whether by industry focus or equipment, lease or lessee type. The industry is fragmented, with over 2,000 leasing companies. Fragmented industries often benefit from access to ABS markets.

LEASING BASICS

A lease is essentially an agreement between an equipment owner (the lessor) and the equipment user (the lessee).[2] The lessee remits to the lessor a periodic payment in return for use of the equipment. The lessor continues to own the equipment and may

[2] For further discussion, see Terry A Isom, *et al*, *The Handbook of Equipment Leasing* (Salt Lake City, UT: Amembal & Isom, 1988) or Peter K. Nevitt and Frank J. Fabozzi, *Equipment Leasing: Third Edition* (Homewodd, IL: Dow-Jones-Irwin, 1988).

provide additional services such as routine maintenance or remarketing, if needed. At the end of the lease term, the lessee may have an option to purchase the equipment either at fair market value or a predetermined price; they may return the equipment, sometimes with a deinstallation and shipping fee; or they may re-lease the equipment.

The different types of equipment being financed divides the market into three core segments: small-, middle- and large-ticket leases. Small-ticket lessors focus on such products as copiers, PCs, facsimile machines, and the like, for which the lease period is generally short and terms of the lease generally mirror the functional life of the financed equipment. These leases are generally referred to as finance, capital or full payout leases, or conditional sales agreements. Obligations and benefits of ownership reside with the lessee during the lease term. There is a minimal amount of residual value, which is the value of the leased equipment at the conclusion of the lease term, and lessees may be able to purchase the underlying equipment at the end of the lease term for a minimal payment. Lessees are generally less price-sensitive in the small-ticket market, as the lease decision is based primarily on convenience and cash flow considerations. Lease balances in the small-ticket market range from $10,000-$100,000, depending on individual companies' interpretations.

The Large-Ticket Market

The large-ticket market is for capital equipment with an initial cost basis of at least $2 million. The underlying leases are generally operating leases, in which the lessee's payments do not cover the original equipment cost over the term of the lease. Thus, there is significant residual value in the underlying equipment, which is managed by the lessor. Additionally, obligations and benefits of ownership, including depreciation, stay with the lessor during the lease term. Operating leases are often thought of as usage leases, as opposed to finance leases, which are sometimes called ownership leases. An example of an operating lease would be one written on high-ticket medical equipment such as magnetic resonance imaging (MRI) or CAT scan machines.

Economic Risks and Rewards

The primary distinction between finance and operating leases is which party, the lessee or the lessor, bears the economic risks and rewards of owning the underlying equipment. To be classified as a finance lease for financial reporting purposes, one of the following statements must be true:

- The lease transfers title and ownership of the leased equipment to the lessee at the end of the lease term.
- The lease contains a bargain price option (e.g., "$1 buyout").
- The lease term at inception is at least 75% of the estimated life of the equipment leased.
- The present value of the minimum lease payments is at least 90% of the fair market value of the equipment at lease inception.

Exhibit 3: Equipment Finance New Issue Volume

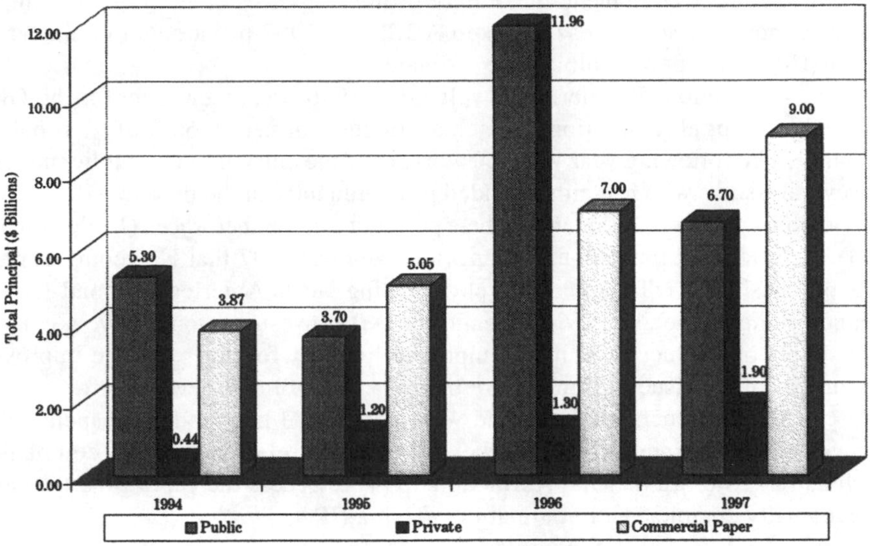

Source: First Union Capital Markets.

The Leveraged Lease

Another type of operating lease is the leveraged lease, in which the lessor borrows a significant portion of the equipment cost on a non-recourse basis and assigns the future lease payment stream to the lender. The lessor puts up a minimal amount of funds (the difference between the equipment cost and the present value of the lease stream), but is generally entitled to the full tax benefits of owning the equipment. Aircraft and railroad cars are usually leveraged leases. These types of assets are not the focus of the equipment ABS market and thus will not be discussed in this chapter.

The Middle Market

The middle market covers the ground between the aforementioned two groups. Predominantly finance leases, lessors in this segment tailor their lease terms to the needs of their customers, who may have specific tax considerations or cash flow needs that are addressed by the structure and terms of the lease. The equipment cost per item is higher. Computer networking equipment, application licenses (billing and payroll systems), and printing presses are examples of middle market leased equipment or systems.

GROWTH OF THE ABS EQUIPMENT MARKET

Exhibit 3 chronicles the growth of the equipment ABS market. We have included ABS issued by captive finance companies such as Case Credit Corporation and

Navistar Financial because we believe that although they are loans on agricultural and transportation equipment, the obligor profile and investor analysis are comparable to those for solely lease-backed ABS. The 1997 private and commercial paper (CP) numbers in Exhibit 3 are estimates.

As mentioned earlier, ABS volume in 1996 was noteworthy for the GPA and AT&T Capital transactions, which accounted for nearly 65% of total public issuance. The following year was noteworthy for the entry into the public markets of several issuers who had either funded predominantly in the private ABS market (Copelco Capital) or had financed their portfolio on-balance sheet (Heller Financial). Additionally, the announcement in November 1997 that Newcourt Capital was purchasing AT&T Capital, thereby creating North America's second-largest finance company behind GECC, meant that ABS investors would have a consistent supply of product to evaluate. Improved liquidity for investors and improved execution for the issuer/originator are likely because of these events.

Not all issuers are large and well established like Heller Financial. The growth of the equipment ABS market has enabled relatively young companies such as First Sierra Financial (formed in 1994) to access the capital markets and to eventually complete an initial public offering (IPO).

Reasons for Issuing ABS

Equipment finance companies use securitization as a funding tool for three basic reasons:

- Cheaper cost of funds than traditional sources such as bank loans.
- Securitization structured to remove the assets from the balance sheet, thereby accelerating income and improving traditional capital efficiency ratios such as return on assets and return on equity.
- Increasd liquidity by accessing an alternative funding source.

Depending on a company's access to varying funding sources, any or all of the above may be reasons to issue term ABS securities.

For a smaller company, securitization generally provides a cheaper cost of funds because the focus is on the asset quality of the underlying pool and not the investment ratings of the originator/seller-servicer. For established, investment-grade issuers such as Heller Financial, the maturation of the equipment ABS market with its more competitive spreads makes it a compelling alternative source of portfolio funding.

Balance Sheet Aspects

The off-balance-sheet aspect of securitization, along with the ability to manage the asset side of the balance sheet so as to recognize income from securitization, applies to large established companies as well as startups looking to achieve a history of profitability in preparation for an IPO.

Liquidity

The ability to increase corporate liquidity by accessing the equipment ABS market is another factor in the growth of the market. Although large originators may have multiple sources of funding — including corporate MTNs, CP, and bank lines — some at more attractive all-in levels than ABS, the rating agencies, in evaluating a corporation's liquidity, will likely look favorably on originators that have opened alternative funding sources by accessing the ABS market. When combined with the off-balance-sheet treatment noted above, the equipment ABS market becomes a compelling financing tool for larger companies as well.

Securitization Alternatives for Issuers

Equipment finance companies have three basic securitization alternatives:

- Issuance of term securities in the public ABS market.
- Issuance of term securities in the private ABS market
- Issuance of CP through either a bank-sponsored multi-seller CP conduit or a single-seller conduit.

Public Market

The public market is the largest and most liquid and typically offers the best pricing execution. The global investor base includes insurance companies, money managers, domestic and foreign banks, and pension funds. Upfront issuance costs can be somewhat higher owing to Securities and Exchange Commission filing costs and increased legal fees resulting from the greater disclosure requirements needed for a public offering. Issue size is generally at least $100 million, as investors will not pay up for issues perceived as too small for a liquid secondary market.

Private Placement

The private market, while less liquid than the public market, is nonetheless attractive for many issuers because the investor base is still large and disclosure requirements are somewhat less. Transactions can range from small, negotiated transactions with a single investor (often the strategy with newly formed companies) to large underwritings in the 144A market that price and trade much like public ABS.

Commercial Paper

The CP market can be accessed for either permanent financing through interest rate swaps to lock in a fixed rate or for warehouse financing prior to arranging permanent financing via a public or private ABS. Because all commercial paper needs to be fully supported by bank liquidity lines, this type of financing is essentially bank financing in another form. From an all-in cost perspective, CP can be extremely competitive. Although price competitive and offering certain flexibility, CP execution does not broaden a company's investor base because the conduits are bank sponsored and the underlying collateral is transparent to the CP buyer.

Active on All Fronts

Equipment is unique in that significant activity occurs in all three of these markets. Companies often use the asset-backed CP market to warehouse their originations prior to coming to market with a public term ABS. A recent trend is to access both the public and private markets simultaneously by issuing senior securities in the public market and subordinate securities in the private market.

STRUCTURE OF EQUIPMENT-BACKED ABS

Lease- and equipment-backed ABS differ somewhat from generic consumer loans in that the former do not have a specified loan balance and contract interest rate. Thus, they do not have a weighted-average coupon (WAC) and the concept of loan-to-value (LTV) does not apply. Instead, the lease contract between a lessor and lessee calls for a specified stream of payments over the life of the lease. Presumably, these payments adequately compensate the lessor, and it is this stream of payments that underlies the ABS.

Valuation

Valuation in equipment ABS is done by taking this stream of payments and discounting them at a rate equal to the weighted-average coupon of the securities plus ongoing expenses, which typically are servicing and trustee fees, as well as credit-enhancement fees, for which the transaction is "wrapped" (or insured by a third-party surety). Therefore, only after an issue's nominal spread is set can an exact principal amount of bonds be determined. This is why par amounts on a preliminary prospectus ("red herring") are approximate.

Allocation of Payments

Payments are allocated between principal and interest so that the remaining notional balance of the leases equals the net present value of the remaining stream of lease payments. To the extent that all leases in a pool are level pay throughout the term of the loan, the amortization of equipment ABS is similar to that of a pool of fixed-rate loans. Any particular securitization may contain cash flow variability owing to the presence of pre-funding or revolving accounts, irregular (i.e., non-monthly) lease payments or other variable cash flow features. The rating agencies evaluating the transaction structure perform analyses to ensure cash flow sufficiently supports monthly payments to bondholders. Because lease prepayments are infrequent (discussed in detail later), the cash flow characteristics of equipment ABS tend to be fairly stable and most closely resemble a generic amortizing security.

FRAMEWORK FOR EVALUATING EQUIPMENT ABS

For an investor in any type of asset- or mortgage-backed security, the first "law" should be to understand thoroughly the underlying collateral.[3] Whether evaluating the prepayment characteristics of agency MBS or assessing credit risk on a pool of subprime automobile loans, an understanding of the factors influencing the cash flows of the underlying collateral is paramount.

Primary Credit Risks

As in all classes of ABS, obligor (the lessee) delinquencies and defaults are the primary credit risks of equipment-backed deals. These can result in the disruption of anticipated cash flows. Structuring tools used in other ABS classes apply to equipment as well, such as excess spread, subordination, third-party surety guarantees, and trigger events. An originator's ability to demonstrate consistent realization of residual values is an additional source of credit enhancement for equipment ABS.

Market Insights

An understanding of the market niche the originator serves gives insight into the credit quality of the lessees and their susceptibility to cyclical economic conditions. Qualitative areas of focus for the rating agencies are management's experience, competitive strategies, financial resources, market segments served, and the types of leases/loans originated.

Analysis and Evaluation

To the extent that a pool of leases is originated via a vendor program in which the lease originator acts as a financing source for the manufacturer, an analysis is conducted by the rating agency to evaluate the vendor's ability to service and maintain the equipment. This service ensures the lessee remains willing to continue making payments on the lease. Many third-party originators have remarketing agreements with their vendors so that after termination of the lease, or repossession of the equipment in the event of lessee default, the anticipated residual value may be realized or the net loss (also known as loss-to-liquidation) will be minimized.

Concentration Risk

Concentration risk is also addressed during the structuring process. To the extent a particular pool has exposure to an industry or obligor, various structural requirements may be put into the transaction. For example, we have seen an originator agree to forego its servicing fee in the event any one of the three largest obligors

---

[3] The basics for this analysis come from *Standard & Poor's Equipment Leasing Criteria* (New York, NY, May 1996).

in the pool defaults prior to credit enhancement reaching certain levels. This is generally more of an issue in the middle- and large-ticket market because most small-ticket securitizations have a large number of obligors and sufficient diversification. When analyzing pool composition and concentrations, it is helpful to ascertain if the leased equipment is integral to the lessee's business. Lease payments are more likely to remain current for essential use equipment.

Rating agencies will evaluate a lessor's historical portfolio chargeoffs, preferably on a static pool basis. This shows likely performance over the life of the pool and may provide insight into crucial elements affecting portfolio performance, such as changes in underwriting guidelines and collections procedures. Static pool data are preferable to dynamic, or gross, portfolio data because growth can mask and dampen the true effects of defaults and losses. Static pool data may or may not be available in a prospectus supplement. If it is not available, investors should ascertain the expected default and net loss curve used in structuring the transaction. A related question investors should ask is what charge-off policy applies to the pool. The timing of the recognition of defaults and subsequent recoveries affects cash flow to the pool. Recoveries in lease-backed transactions can be significant owing to the secured nature of the obligations. The nature of the equipment being financed is a factor in determining the amount and timing of recovery recognition. For example, a copier is easier to repossess and re-lease or sell than a medical diagnostic center.

Residual Analysis

As mentioned earlier, residual values are unique to equipment transactions. When the lease is originated, the lessor books a residual value for the equipment. The amount is the lessor's estimate of the equipment's future value at the end of the lease. For finance leases with a nominal buy-out at the end of the lease, residual values are low. For operating leases, the amount can be significant.

If recognized residual cash flow is to be used as a credit enhancement to cover periodic losses or, more important, if some portion of the residual value is being financed through the issuance of ABS, it is essential that anticipated residual realizations meet or exceed the credit given them by the rating agencies. Generally, residual realization exceeds the booked value. In fact, leasing companies are generally very conservative in booking their residuals and have historically realized 1.1 to 1.5 times book value.

Rating agencies conservatively evaluate what credit should be given to residuals. Typically, no more than 50% of book value is given credit in an ABS structure. The agencies require seven to 10 years of historical residual realization data to evaluate how an originator has performed over an extended economic cycle. Obviously, to the extent historical residual realizations exceed the credit given by the rating agencies, investor credit support is enhanced. The more experience a lessor has with the particular industry, as well as any remarketing support from vendor affiliations, the greater the likelihood of adequate residual realization. The type of equipment being financed also has an impact on residual analysis. Shifts in demand for particular types of equipment, as well as the risk of technological obsolescence, may have an impact on residual realizations, so any concentrations in equipment types or industries serviced are part of a residual analysis.

Residuals by definition are back-end loaded, that is, they occur at the end of the lease. Typically, residuals flow through the deal structure in the month they are realized and are used to cover any shortfalls in cash. If no trigger events have occurred, which would require capturing excess cash or residual realizations, then the unused portion of the residual realized is released to the originator/issuer. Therefore, an analysis of the pool by lease expiration and amount of residual can provide insight into the timing of potential cash flow or credit support.

Prepayment Characteristics

Equipment ABS are much less negatively convex than other asset types in that little prepayment activity is rate-driven in this asset class. Also, structural considerations exist within most leases that mute prepayments.

Leases are generally written without a prepayment option and most contain a "hell or high water" provision whereby a lessee, if it chooses to make a prepayment, is obligated to make all contractual payments at the early termination of the lease. This provision is in effect to protect the lessor and by extension the investor. The lessee must unconditionally make all payments as specified in the lease contract. If the equipment fails, the lessee's claim is with the manufacturer, not the lessor. This is a powerful disincentive to prepay a lease.

There are still events in which lease prepayments occur and cash flow to the ABS is affected. The two primary sources of prepayments of equipment ABS are lessee defaults and equipment upgrades, under which the lessor allows a lessee to prepay one lease to upgrade to new equipment through a new lease. For example, if an owner-operator of a semitrailer upgrades to a larger and more powerful over-road system, it is not unusual for a lessor to allow an existing lease to be prepaid to facilitate the equipment swap. Our experience suggests that most lessees do not prepay early in the lease term (because they are still happy with their purchase) or late in the lease term (because the lease is almost paid off).

Pricing Speed

Issuers can substitute new lease collateral in the event the pool experiences prepayments. Copelco Capital is notable in that it has historically substituted new collateral in the event of a prepayment. From an investor's perspective, the substitution of new leases for prepaid leases ensures the pool's stability and the realization of the average life expected at the ABS pricing. Other issuers take the attitude that prepayments are a normal part of their business and are minimal in any event. An investor should seek historical prepayment information to verify whatever pricing speed is used.

Exhibit 4: ABS Spread Levels

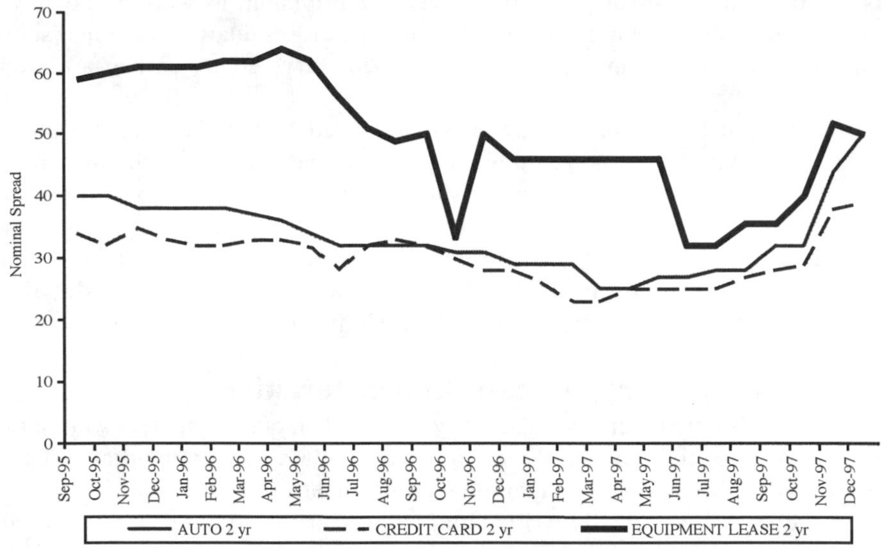

Source: First Union Capital Markets.

Average Life

In that the final maturity of loans and leases in equipment pools are usually five to seven years, the average lives of ABS structured from these pools are generally two to three years. An investor should look at the declination tables in the prospectus supplement to evaluate the average life stability of any particular ABS under varying prepayment scenarios. It will become apparent that the average life sensitivity to a change in CPR assumption is minimal, generally measured in fractions of a year. In addition, with the average deal size for equipment ABS increasing, the market has seen a move toward multiple tranches of pools, which further mitigates duration drift.

RELATIVE VALUE

Exhibit 4 shows the nominal spreads of equipment ABS vis-à-vis other ABS classes over the past several years. As with most fixed-income products during 1995-1997, spreads contracted during this period. The dramatic narrowing in late 1996 was the result of the aforementioned $3 billion AT&T Capital transaction, which brought a lot of new investors to the asset class.

As discussed throughout this chapter, many product attributes make equipment paper attractive for investors. Benign prepayment characteristics and a collateral base of commercial obligations make this asset class attractive for an investor seeking diversification from prepayment risk and consumer credit. That the collateral underlying equipment ABS is so stable makes it particularly attractive to investors looking to swap into LIBOR-based assets.

We believe that equipment ABS exhibit many of the characteristics of amortizing automobile ABS and should trade on top of, if not through, this competing asset class. Furthermore, we believe that this will be the case as the market evolves in size and number of issuers.

Chapter 15

Student Loan ABS

Karen Wagner, CFA
Director of ABS Research
Credit Suisse First Boston

Elen Callahan
Market Strategist
Credit Suisse First Boston

INTRODUCTION

In 1997, issuance of student loan-backed securities (SLABS) was $12.5 billion, representing 7% of the total ABS issuance. This is an impressive 30% increase over 1996 issuance and more than double 1995's issuance. SLABS have many structural features in common with other ABS. However, unlike most ABS products, the underlying collateral is either guaranteed by the federal government or a private guarantor. These guarantees make SLABS a highly creditworthy asset type. The purpose of this chapter is to discuss SLABS and the characteristics of the underlying loans.

THE PURPOSE OF STUDENT LOAN PROGRAMS

The single largest source of student financial aid in America is the Federally guaranteed student loan program. This program covers educational costs associated with different types of institutions — including 2- and 4-year colleges and universities, graduate school programs (including law and medical schools) and various vocational and trade schools.

History

The student loan program has existed in various forms since 1965. Due to the political nature of the program, the program changes, and is likely to change as

The authors would like to thank Phil Weingord and Wendy Williams for their contribution to this chapter. The authors also benefited from input provided by the following organizations: Dean, Blakely & Moskowitz; Fitch; IBCA; and, Moody's Investor Service.

each Administration changes. Fortunately for ABS investors, the dedication to the student loan program, in whatever form, has been a common thread throughout every Administration. Furthering the education of America's youth has never left the top of the government's agenda. Most of the changes have been motivated by budgetary demands or political struggles between advocates of direct loans and government guarantees.

Congress passed the Higher Education Act of 1965 (the HEA). Title IV, Part B, of the HEA established the guaranteed student loan program to provide assistance to lower- and middle-income college students and their families. The Federally regulated program relies on private sources of loan capital, with the Federal government subsidizing the interest rate and indirectly guaranteeing loan repayments. This program is known as the Federal Family Education Loan Program (FFELP) and loans originated under this program are known as FFELP loans. There are several types of FFELP loans. These include subsidized and unsubsidized Stafford, Parental Loans for Undergraduate Students (PLUS), Supplemental Loans to Students (SLS), and consolidation loans.[1]

The HEA is reauthorized periodically — with 1972 and 1976 reauthorizations being most noteworthy due to amendments made to the HEA at that time. The 1972 amendments extended Federal recognition to non-traditional educational programs and allowed proprietary schools to participate under Title IV of the HEA. Also under the 1972 amendments, Congress established the Student Loan Marketing Association (Sallie Mae) as a government-sponsored enterprise (GSE) and a stockholder-owned company to purchase student loans in the secondary market. The intent was to make it more attractive for lenders to originate student loans by providing liquidity via Sallie Mae.

The 1976 amendments provided for increased Federal incentives for states to establish loan guarantee agencies. The resulting proliferation of guarantors decentralized the program. Under the HEA, each state is required to establish its own guarantee agency or designate another agency (e.g., USA Group Guarantee Services which serves the states of Arkansas, Iowa, Louisiana, Maine, Michigan, Montana, New Mexico, Oklahoma, Oregon, and Rhode Island). Each guaranty agency is eligible to be reimbursed for guarantee payments by the U.S. Department of Education (DOE) under a Federal reinsurance agreement.

These guaranty agencies are required by law to set aside reserves to pay claims to lenders. Each guarantor's reserve ratio is determined by dividing its cumulative cash reserve by the original principal amount of the outstanding loans it has agreed to guarantee. These reserves are deemed by statute to be Federal property and can be recalled by the DOE if they exceed needed levels. In addition, however, the statute requires the DOE to step in and pay lender claims directly or reassign the guarantee obligation to another guarantor if a guarantor becomes insolvent.

---

[1] See the appendix to this chapter for a summary of FFELP student loan characterizations.

Exhibit 1: Annual Loan Volume by Fiscal Year

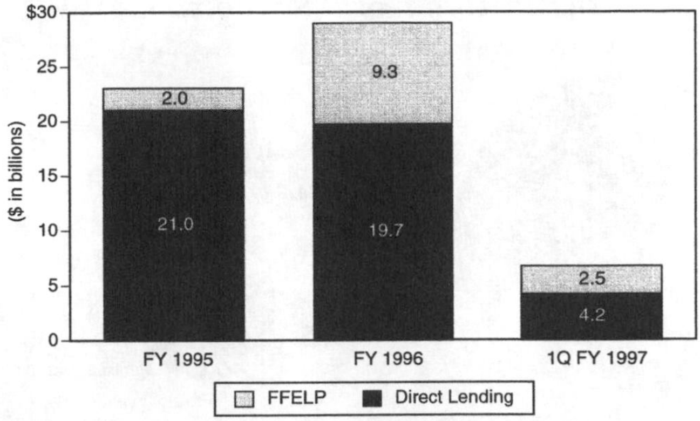

Source: Department of Education Office of Postsecondary Education: Policy, Planning and Innovation, "Loan Volume Update," May 1997.

Recent Developments

Direct Lending

Currently, student loans are originated under one of two programs, FFELP (discussed above) and the Federal Direct Student Loan Program (FDSLP), commonly referred to as direct lending. The FDSLP pilot program was established in 1992 under an HEA reauthorization by the Bush Administration. Exhibit 1 shows annual student loan origination volume since 1995.

Senator Kennedy of Massachusetts proposed the Federal Direct Student Loan Program (FDSLP) before President Clinton took office. It then became a key plank of the "New Democrats" — the Democratic Leadership Council with which President Clinton was involved with when he was Governor of Arkansas. In 1993, Congress, with Clinton's support, enacted legislation expanding the FDSLP, then only a pilot program, and in 1994 the U.S. Department of Education began making direct loans.

As the name implies, under the direct lending program, the Federal government lends money directly to students, thereby eliminating banks and other "middlemen." Congress approved a 5-year phase-in period for the program — 5% of total guaranteed loan volume was to be originated in academic year 1994–1995 via FDSLP, 40% in 1995–1996, 50% in 1996–1997, 50% in 1997–1998, and 60% in 1998–1999 and thereafter.

However, efforts by the Clinton Administration to reach these targets in 1996 and 1997 have fallen short. FDSLP currently enjoys approximately 34% of the student loan market, but that share is not increasing, probably due in part to recent dramatic improvements in customer service in the FFELP programs and the widening use of borrower benefit programs[2] that result in FFELP loans being offered at lower cost to borrowers than direct loans (see Exhibit 2).

[2] For example, many FFELP lenders have begun to offer reduced interest rates and lower fees to borrowers who make timely payments or who simply choose them over other lenders.

Exhibit 2: Direct Lending Participants Year 3 by Type of Institution (Total Schools: 354)

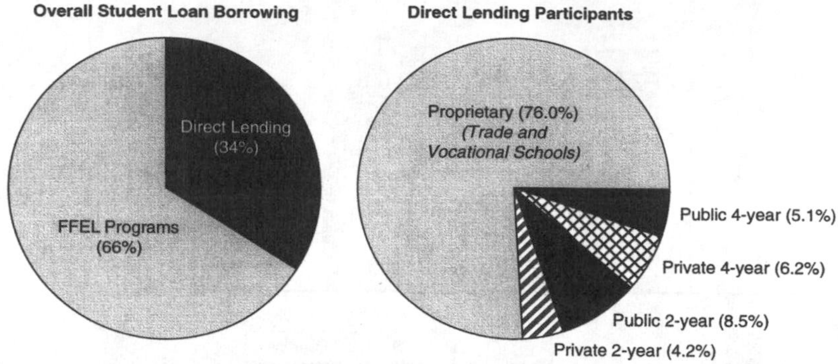

Advocates of FDSLP argue that direct lending helps students manage their debts better because the program gives students a wider array of repayment options and provides borrowers with a simpler process in terms of application and repayment. It is also argued that by eliminating the middleman, direct lending can promote competition in the student loan process, offer greater accountability (making the student loan business easier to monitor), and offer greater efficiency, which could ultimately mean lower cost. Supporters also contend that the combination of a simpler repayment and collection system and flexible repayment options will help reduce loan defaults going forward.

Detractors argue that the direct lending program will ultimately cost more and have a higher default rate. They doubt that the government can provide more efficient service and contend that the DOE "lacks the management personnel and experienced staff to operate the program."[3]

Opponents also argue that virtually the only schools moving toward the direct lending program have been for-profit trade and vocational schools (see Exhibit 2). For example, they cite that in 1995 "almost half the direct loans [were] to students of trade schools, with a third of all loans going to students of barber or beauty academies."[4] A 1995 Forbes article estimated that $725 million in loans were made to students of beauty schools.[5] Trade schools have historically had higher default rates than private or public 2- and 4-year institutions (see Exhibit 3). Additionally, most trade schools have guaranteed access to direct lending.[6] Experience indicates that the prevalence of trade schools in direct lending could mean higher default rates for direct lending going forward. Exhibit 4 compares the major differences of the two programs.

---

[3] Peter Hoekstra, "Direct Lending Works — No It Doesn't," *Trusteeship* (March/April 1997).

[4] Michael Fumento, *Direct Lending is Already Running out of Gas* (http://seldy.townhall.com:80/townhall/columnists/fumento/fume082295.html. August 22, 1995).

[5] Rita Koselka and Suzanne Oliver, "Hairdressers, Anyone? — Federal Student Loan Programme," *Forbes* (May 22, 1995).

[6] Schools with default rates over 15% are currently precluded from the program.

Exhibit 3: School Cohort Default Rates by Institutional Sector — Default Rates for First Year of Repayment*

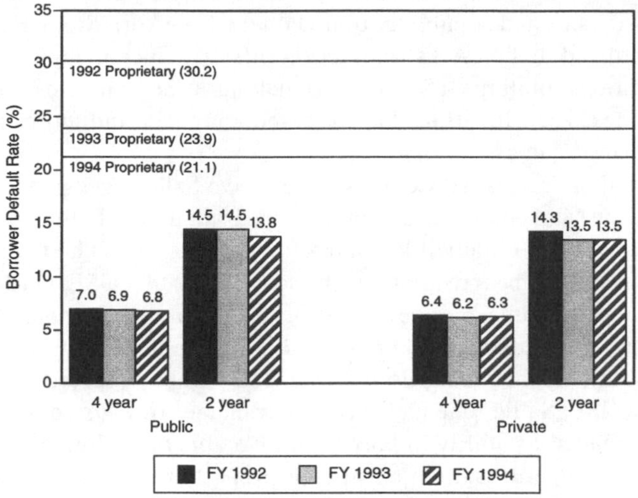

* FFELP only. An institution's FY 1994 cohort default rate is determined as follows:

$$\text{School's FY 1994 Cohort Default Rate} = \frac{\text{\# students who entered repayment in FY 1994 and defaulted on or before 9/30/95}}{\text{\# students who entered repayment in FY 1994}} \times 100$$

Source: Department of Education, Report to the President on Student Loan Default Initiative.

Exhibit 4: FDSLP versus FFELP: The Major Differences

	FDSLP	FFELP
Source of Funds	U.S. Government (DOE)	Private Lender
Application Process	1. Fill out Student Aid Application and Complete Promissory Note 2. School certifies application and note	1. Fill out Student Aid Application and Complete Separate Loan Application/ Promissory Note 2. School certifies application and note 3. Application sent to lender for evaluation, then to guarantor for guarantee
Repayment Plans	*Standard:* Fixed amount (up to 10 years) *Extended:* Extend loan payment (up to 30 years) *Graduated:* Lower payments at first, then increasing over time (up to 30 years) *Income Contingent:* Payment based on annual income; varies with income (up to 25 years; remaining balance after 25 years may be forgiven). Not available to Direct PLUS Borrowers.	*Standard:** Fixed amount (up to 10 years) *Graduated:* Lower payments at first, then increasing over time (up to 10 years) *Income Sensitive:* Payment based on annual income (up to 10 years). Minimum payment equals interest accrued during the month.
Funds Disbursed	DOE sends funds to school	Lender sends funds to school

* Excluding periods of deferment and forbearance.

Source: U. S. Department of Education. http://www.ed.gov/prog_info/SFA/StudentGuide/1997-8.

Privatizing Sallie Mae In 1972, Congress established the Student Loan Marketing Association (Sallie Mae) to purchase student loans in the secondary market. Similar to FNMA and FHLMC, Sallie Mae is a GSE, with implicit government support, and is publicly traded on the New York Stock Exchange. Sallie Mae securitized its first ABS transaction in 1995; since then, it has completed six securitizations totaling $15.8 billion, making it the bellwether issuer for the asset type. These securitizations have created a broader and more liquid market for student loans as an asset class.

Sallie Mae persuaded Congress to dissolve Sallie Mae's Federal charter in the Student Loan Marketing Association Reorganization Act of 1996. The Act authorized the restructuring of Sallie Mae into a fully private, state-chartered corporation without the line-of-business restrictions (or advantages) of a GSE. On July 31, 1997, shareholders elected a lineup of new directors and approved their plan for privatization. Pursuant to this privatization plan, Sallie Mae created a Delaware-chartered holding company, SLM Holding Corp.[7] This GSE will be dissolved by 2008.[8]

As a GSE, Sallie Mae had certain advantages over its competitors. These advantages included its ability to borrow at favorable rates, lower capital requirements than its competitors, and, except for property tax, state tax-exempt status for itself and its bondholders. Additionally, certain securities laws as well as state registration requirements for doing business did not apply to Sallie Mae.

However, there were obvious political risks inherent in having GSE status. Because of its implicit government support, Sallie Mae's charter was restricted and subject to change by Congress.[9] This limited Sallie Mae's ability to enter into new or expanded business lines to respond to Federal policy changes and programs. For example, direct lending, which took volume away from FFELP programs, affected Sallie Mae's business by reducing the amount of loans available for purchase. As a GSE whose charter was restricted by Congress, Sallie Mae was unable to shift its business focus to accommodate this shift in the market. Removal of this status will allow it to expand its business scope to better respond to the shifting lending landscape.

The Shifting Landscape of the SLABs Market

The SLABs market consists of two distinct types of issuers — for-profit (corporate) entities and not-for-profit (NFP) entities. Exhibit 5 lists the top players of each issuer type.

---

[7] The obligations of the holding company will not have GSE status.

[8] Until Sallie Mae's GSE status expires, on or before September 30, 2008, the legal status and attributes of all the GSE's debt obligations will be fully preserved. The GSE may issue debt with GSE characteristics, as long as the debt is due on or before September 30, 2008 (Moody's, "Privatizing Sallie Mae," December 1996.)

[9] Another policy change affecting Sallie Mae's profitability is the 1993 Omnibus Budget Reconciliation Act (OBRA). This act imposed a 30 basis point fee on loans held by Sallie Mae. Sallie Mae challenged the applicability of this policy to its securitized portfolio and on July 25, 1997 the DOE decided that the fee did not apply to securitized loans.

Exhibit 5: Public Taxable and Tax-Exempt SLABs Issuance by Major Issuers (as of December 1997)

	SLABs Issued ($MM)
Corporate Issuer	
Sallie Mae	$16,712
KeyCorp	3,087
The Money Store	1,289
Signet Bank	440
SMS	1,424
PNC Bank	1,030
Not-for Profit Issuers	
Brazos	517
Missouri Higher Education Loan Authority	508
Alternative Student Loans	
University Support Services	867
Nellie Mae	423

Source: Credit Suisse First Boston, Fitch, Bloomberg.

In 1996, the total corporate securitization market for student loans was approximately $9 billion, almost 70% ($6 billion) of which was issued by Sallie Mae. The total NFP market was about $3.5 billion in 1996, up from $2.4 billion in 1995. Generally, NFP issuance is tax-exempt and trades in the municipal bond market.

Other Events

Current legislation and legislative proposals continue to change the landscape of the student loan business.

91-Day Treasury Bill or 10-Year Treasury?

The Higher Education Act provides that, beginning July 1, 1998, the variable interest rates on *newly originated* Stafford and PLUS Loans (both direct and FFELP) will cease to be based on the 91-day Treasury bill and will instead be based on the "security with the comparable maturity," — determined to be the 10-year Treasury note. This change was driven by the assumption that, by 1998, the direct loan program would be source of the majority of student loan funds. The resulting borrower interest rate would more closely parallel the federal governments borrowing rate. The scheduled transition calls for the interest rate based on the 10-year Treasury note plus 1%.

Strong industry consensus exists on the need to repeal this provision due to the volatility of the 10-year Treasury note and the scarcity of matched funding options for private lenders. By introducing a "potentially expensive funding cost for private lenders," critics worry that the change will cause lenders to leave the program, thereby allowing the direct lending program to assume most, if not all, of student lending volume.[10]

More importantly, the new Stafford yield of 10-year Treasury note + 1%, is substantially lower than the existing yield of 91-day Treasury bill + margin of 2.5% to 3.1%. Thus, unless the yield curve steepens significantly, loans made after July 1, 1998 will carry a much lower yield than loans made at the beginning of 1998. Recommendations have been made to delete the provision and maintain the current interest rate structure. The issue is pending.

Nellie Mae: Not-For-Profits Conversion to For-Profit Entities

Partly in response to direct lending, Nellie Mae, the New England Education Loan Marketing Corp., a private not-for-profit corporation and a participant in FFELP, successfully lobbied for legislation that allows 150(d) not-for-profit corporations, like itself, to make a one-time conversion to "for-profit" entities. As other not-for-profit organizations convert to for-profit entities, the ABS market may see an increase in securitizations.

Nellie Mae was established by Massachusetts statute to purchase and hold student loans guaranteed by FFELP guaranty agencies and reinsured by the DOE. It is the largest not-for-profit holder, with total student loans receivables of $1.8 billion as of June 30, 1996. Nellie Mae also originates uninsured and privately insured loans to students with high academic credentials and from families with good credit histories. Nellie Mae issues both SLABs and, as an entity adhering to section 150(d) of the Internal Revenue Service code, Federally tax-exempt debt.

Budget Cuts

At the time of this writing, the White House and Congressional leaders agreed upon a budget resolution calling for a balanced budget by the year 2002. Included in the agreement for student loans are provisions calling for $1.763 billion in savings over five years, to be divided between the Federal Direct Student Loan and the Federal Family Education Loan Programs. The direct loan cuts will be derived from reductions in the direct loan administrative funds and the elimination of payment of a $10 per processed loan fee to institutions. FFELP cuts will come from the return of approximately $1 billion guaranty agency reserves. This agreement is likely to change as legislation implementing it moves through Congress in 1998.

The Tax Benefit Proposal

The Administration has recently proposed to enact the higher education tax proposals that President Clinton supported during the 1996 Presidential campaign and since his re-election. These proposals include a $1,500 tax credit for two years of postsecondary study, a tax deduction of up to $10,000 in educational expenses, and tax-free withdrawals from IRA accounts for educational expenses.

---

[10] Barbara Miles, "Student Loans: What is the Problem With Converting to the 10-Year Interest Rate Benchmark?" *CRS Report for Congress* (July 25, 1997).

As usual, these proposals have been the subject of numerous editorials and debates among members of Congress and the higher education community. Some believe that these tax benefits essentially will fuel tuition increases. If tuition prices do indeed increase as a result of the enactment of these proposals, demand for all student loans could increase, which could add supply to the SLABs market.

Other Proposals

An issue that has split the student loan community is President Clinton's proposal to radically restructure guaranty agencies. Under the Clinton proposal, guarantors would cease to share in the risk of default and would become in essence administrative entities for the Secretary of Education. This proposal coincides with the current consideration of possible subsidy cuts in the student loan program through reductions in guarantor reserves.

There has also been a movement by the higher education community and the student loan industry to restructure the Higher Education Act. Both factions endorse a major restructuring of the student aid delivery system (i.e., delivery of funds and service to borrowers). The student loan industry also proposes to change the role of guaranty agencies, reform the process for developing regulations, and expand payment options for borrowers. The higher education associations recommend an increase in loan limits and the continued concurrent existence of FDSLP and FFELP.

THE STUDENT LOAN BUSINESS

The Origination of Student Loans

The starting point for origination of student loans is the school's financial aid office (see Exhibit 6). A financial counsellor will determine whether the student qualifies for federal loans (based on financial need and loan limits). If federally insured funds are either unavailable or insufficient to meet the student's needs, private loans (underwritten more traditionally on ability-to-pay) can be used. The financial aid office assists the student in preparing the application, certifies the student's cost of attendance and financial need, and forwards completed applications to the lender(s).

There are more than 2,000 lenders — banks, thrifts, credit unions, state agencies, universities, and life insurance companies — and approximately 25 guarantee agencies participating in student loan underwriting. It is a fragmented origination business, with each lender typically originating relatively small loan volumes. However, a few large lenders plus the Student Loan Marketing Association (SLMA) account for the majority of ABS origination volume.[11]

In the case of federally insured (FFELP) loans, the lender submits a loan to a guarantee agency and applies to have it insured. If accepted, the lender pays a

---

[11] See Exhibits 9 and 10.

premium to the guarantor (typically 1%) to directly insure the loan against default. These guarantors are state or non-profit agencies designated by their respective state governments. The guarantors on federally insured loans are reinsured by the DOE for up to 98%[12] of the claims paid. The amount of such reinsurance payment to the guarantor is subject to reduction based upon the annual default claims rate of the federal guarantor.[13]

FFELP guarantors also oversee lenders, enforce servicing and origination guidelines, and pursue defaulted borrowers. (Recoveries on loans a guarantor has previously paid on are generally allocated 27% to the guarantor and 73% to the DOE.)[14] Private guarantors[15] are often unrated, with the exception of The Education Resources Institute (TERI[16]).

Bank originators usually hold student loans until just before they enter the repayment period,[17] at which point some banks sell their student loan portfolio. Before the loans enter repayment, the bank holds the loan to develop the borrower relationship, which could lead to additional lending opportunities. Servicing and collection are non-issues at this point because the interest is either deferred until repayment or interest is paid by the government (in the case of subsidized Stafford loans.)

Exhibit 6: Overview of the Student Loan Program

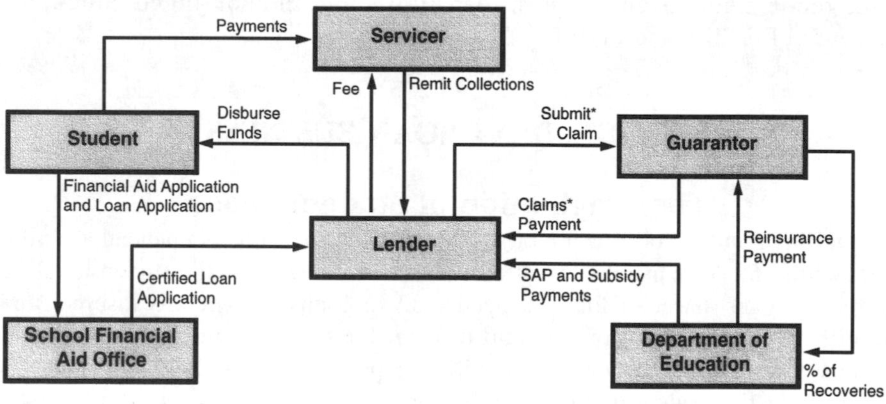

* Lender or servicer may submit claim.

[12] This applies to loans originated after October 1, 1993. For loans originated prior to this date, guarantors may be reinsured up to 100%.

[13] See Exhibit 20.

[14] The guarantor is compensated for acting as the government's collection agency.

[15] "Private guarantors" often refers to guarantors of non-FFELP loans (i.e., St. Paul Fire and Marine, TuitionGARD (Guarantee National). One of the difficulties in assessing the credit risk of private guarantors vis-a-vis SLABs is a lack of financial information and, often, unsegregated insurance reserves.

[16] TERI is a private, nonprofit organization founded in 1985 and is rated Baa/A by Moody's/Fitch. It is the oldest and largest guarantor of non-FFELP loans to students and primarily guarantees law, graduate, and undergraduate school loans.

[17] Repayment generally begins at the end of a 6 to 9 month grace period after the student's in-school period has ended.

For a number of reasons, once a loan enters repayment, many banks choose not to hold student loans for the long term. First, there is a ready market to sell student loans at up-front premiums. At spreads of 2.50% to 3.10% over 91-day Treasury bills (3.10% over 52-week Treasury bills on PLUS loans), and with generally 98% indirect guarantees by the DOE, this collateral is very attractive. Second, although credit risk is virtually moot for holders of insured student loans, student loans often have high delinquency rates. Banks are particularly concerned about the performance of their on-balance sheet assets; thus, from a regulatory standpoint, banks will tend to minimize their holdings of student loans. Further, banks find that due to the specialized and complex nature of servicing the broad array of student loan programs it is more economical to use third-party servicers. The use of third-party servicers makes holding the loans less valuable since the originator is not generating servicing fees and also makes the loans easier to sell by reducing servicing transfer complications.

The buyers of student loans are primarily student loan secondary markets, such as Sallie Mae, Student Loan Funding Corp., USA Group Secondary Market Services, Inc., Nellie Mae, and Brazos.

The Servicing of Student Loans

In most types of consumer lending, origination is as important or more important than servicing. In student loans, particularly federally insured student loans, there is minimal discretion in lending decisions (mainly in the form of price discrimination). Lenders must follow the processing and servicing guidelines set by the DOE. If proper procedures are not followed at origination, the guarantee may be void and the original lender is obligated to buy back the loan.[18] (In practice, this voiding of the guarantee virtually never happens.) Apart from this potential obligation, the quality of origination is far less an issue than the quality of servicing.

Since the existence of guarantees protects the owners of student loans from the lion's share of loss, the owners arguably have reduced incentive to exercise vigilance in servicing. The guarantors (ultimately, the DOE) need to dictate very specific servicing procedures to ameliorate such servicing risk. Failure to comply with these guidelines can result in a a rejected claim.

The percentage of claims rejected due to servicing violations, with respect to a given servicer, is termed the *gross rejection rate*. Many of these rejections are due to clerical errors and can be cured. (For example, a servicer may inadvertently exclude a copy of the original loan document; this defect can be cured by returning the claim with a copy of such loan document.) In such cases, the lender may be subject to an interest penalty (i.e., loss of interest for a prescribed period). After these clerical rejections are addressed, the remaining rejected claims are termed the *net rejections*.

---

[18] Because of the possible need for the lender to buy back a loan, rating agencies include in their analysis the likelihood of lender insolvency. Lender insolvency could impact on the originator's ability to perform under this obligation, as well as to make good on servicing errors. Also, there is less than total certainty over bankruptcy remoteness in SLABs.

Exhibit 7: Student Loan Time Line

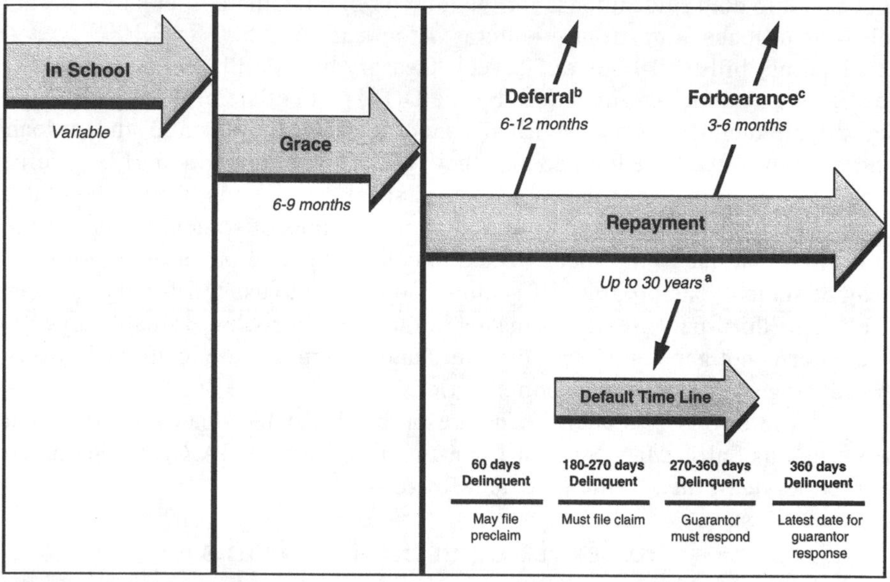

a. Generally repayment periods on student loans are 10 years. Consolidation loans can take up to 30 years depending on loan balances and certain other factors.
b. Granted for PLUS/SLS loans; may occur while in-school (MBA, etc.).
c. Up to 3 years on federal loans.

Among the servicers involved in the SLABs market, gross rejection rates generally range from 5% to 10% of claims submitted. Net rejection rates, however, typically are well under 1%. Assuming cumulative student loan defaults averaging less than 15%,[19] for example, the net rejection rate would lead to losses of approximately 15 b.p. [0.15 (15% defaults) × 0.01 (1% net rejection rate) = 0.0015 or 0.15%]. This compares very favorably to credit enhancement levels, which are typically in the 4% to 5% range for senior notes backed by pools of federally-insured student loans. Further, typically, the servicer is required to indemnify the issuer for any loss due to a rejected claim that is the result of an incurable servicing violation.

Claims that are accepted and paid by "federally insured" guarantors are then submitted to the DOE for reimbursement to the guarantor. Lenders and servicers of federally insured loans are audited annually to confirm that they are following federal servicing guidelines. Generally, the servicer conducts one annual audit for all customers. Lenders and servicers also must keep documentation of all collection activity.

Exhibit 7 shows a time line for student loan repayment and default.

[19] Average defaults for 4-year Stafford are approximately 15%; 2-year Stafford are 30%; Proprietary Stafford are 45%; 4-year PLUS are 13%; 2-year PLUS are 22%; Proprietary PLUS are 33%.

Exhibit 8: Student Loan ABS Issuance 1993-1997*

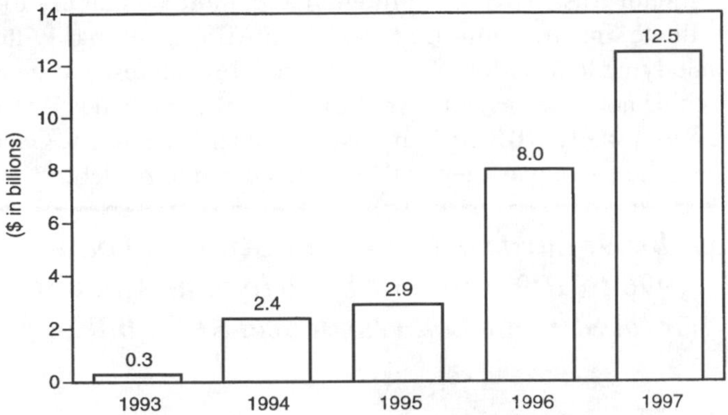

* Public taxable corporate issuance.

Source: Credit Suisse First Boston and Securities Data Corp.

STUDENT LOAN ABS

Securitization as a tool for financing has caught on with student lenders as much as it has in any other type of lending. Rule 3a(7), adopted in 1992 by the SEC, added student loans to the list of asset types exempt from the Investment Company Act of 1940's definition of an investment company. Prior to Rule 3a(7), issuance of student loan-backed securities was limited to those issues exempt from SEC registration (not-for-profit and state agencies). The largest holders of student loans, banks and Sallie Mae, had no such exemption and as result could not issue SLABs until Rule 3a(7) was adopted.

Another development that spurred ABS issuance was the development of "owner trust" ABS issuance vehicles. Such owner trusts facilitate many student loan securitization needs, such as prefunding accounts and mismatched indices. First Boston securitized the first SEC-registered student loan transaction in 1993. Society Student Loan Trust 1993-A (SSLT 1993-A) was a $220 million owner trust transaction rated Aaa by S&P and wrapped by CapMAC. The bonds are collateralized by federally insured FFELP loans and privately guaranteed alternative loans.

A history of the rapid growth of student loan ABS issuance is shown in Exhibit 8. Issuers include originators who traditionally held their student loan production, and originators who traditionally sold, as well as those that do not originate themselves but rather provide a secondary market. As Exhibits 9 and 10 show, Sallie Mae's pick-up in securitizations has fueled most of the growth in student loan ABS.

Structural Issues

Student loan ABS (SLABs) have many structural features in common with other ABS. Loans are sold into either trusts or special-purpose bankruptcy-remote corporations (SPCs). "True sale" and non-consolidation opinions are issued with respect to the entity issuing the securities. The trusts or SPCs issue SLABs both in the form of grantor trusts (for passthroughs) and, more commonly today, owner trusts (to facilitate time tranching). Student loan ABS are primarily floating rate, as are the underlying loans. Most SLABs pay monthly interest and quarterly principal. The senior notes are usually AAA-rated public securities, while subordinated classes are usually BBB or A and issued under Rule 144A. Generally both are ERISA eligible so long as they both are considered to be debt.[20]

Exhibit 9: Largest Issuers of Student Loan ABS 1996 to 1997 Percent by Principal Amount (Total Student Loan Issuance: $12.5 billion)

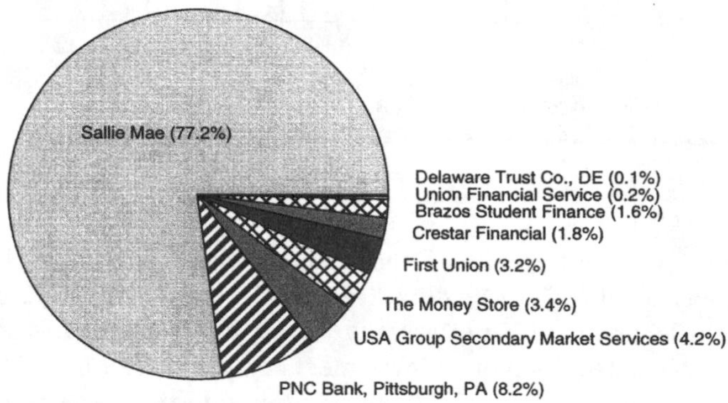

Source: Credit Suisse First Boston and Securities Data Corp.

Exhibit 10: Largest Issuers of Student Loan ABS 1989 to 1997 Percent by Principal Amount (Total Student Loan Issuance: $26.1 billion)

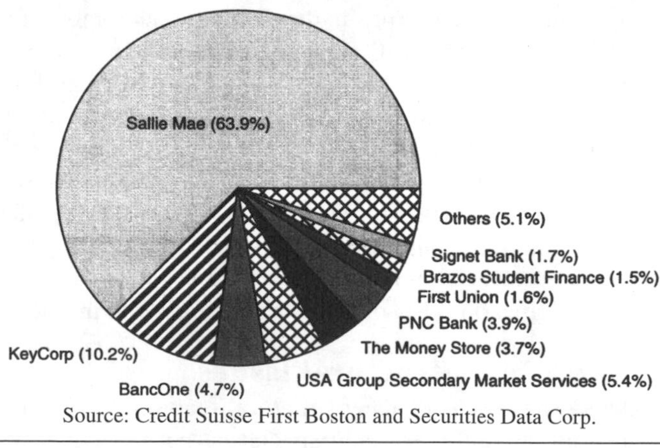

Source: Credit Suisse First Boston and Securities Data Corp.

[20] As opposed to a security representing the equity of the issuer which is generally not ERISA eligible.

Below, we discuss structural features in student loan ABS, including some that are unique to this asset class.

Sources of Credit Enhancement

The "raw material" used to create student loan ABS are highly creditworthy because of the guarantees discussed previously. However, credit protection is still necessary to cover the uninsured portion of defaults (typically 2% today), as well as to provide liquidity in the event that delays were to arise in the claim process, and to cover claims that are rejected.

The credit enhancement used in SLABs is typically comprised of three items:

- subordination (or overcollateralization, now less commonly)
- reserve funds
- excess spread (i.e., excess interest)

Subordinated classes range from 3% to 4% for deals backed purely by government guaranteed loans, and up to 20% or more for deals backed by all or some private loans. These subordinated tranches are often sold to investors. Subordinated tranches or "B-pieces" are protected by the reserve fund and excess spread, which typically can earn the subordinated class a A– or BBB-rating. In some cases the subordinate class may be wrapped by a surety bond as well (thus earning a AAA-rating).

Subordination and overcollateralization protect investors from losses, but they are not sources of cash to cover liquidity needs. For that, excess spread and reserve funds are used. The reserve fund is sometimes partially funded up front and then is fully funded over time out of excess spread. Alternatively, a reserve fund may be fully funded up front (as is often the case if the issuer is issuing bonds at a premium over the student loan collateral supporting the bonds). In addition to covering losses, the reserve fund insures that investors will receive timely interest payments, by providing liquidity over the period when defaulted student loans are submitted as claims and processed by the guarantor (usually a 3- to 6-month gestation period — see Exhibit 7). Reserve funds also provide liquidity for loans during the grace period — in the event of delays in the receipt of special payment allowance (SAP) and subsidy payments — and at times of high delinquency and during the forbearance period, which could result in no or partial cash flow. Reserve funds are typically sized by taking into account the percentage of loans fully guaranteed, the seasoning of the student loan pool, whether the bonds will be issued at par or with a premium, and whether the bonds will be LIBOR, Treasury-bill, or auction-rate based.

Excess spread on SLABs generally ranges from 170 to 220 basis points, depending on the weighted average margin (which may decrease as a result of increased loans that are in-school, grace period. In addition to providing liquidity, excess interest is the first part of the structure to absorb credit losses. During any revolving period (i.e., when no principal is returned to the investors), excess interest, and all principal collections, is often used to buy additional collateral (e.g., serial loans[21]) until parity is reached between the bonds and the collateral. If parity is not reached prior to the end of the revolving period, then excess interest is used to turbo[22] the bonds until parity is thereafter reached between the bonds and the collateral. Obviously, excess spread will vary based on prepayments and defaults, as well as servicing fees. An example of an annual excess interest calculation is shown in Exhibit 11.

Surety Bonds

In some instances, a surety bond is used to achieve a AAA-rating. For example, CapMAC and AMBAC have provided sureties for SLABs. In these cases, a combination of reserve fund, excess spread, and/or a subordinated class (retained by the issuer) is used to achieve the minimum BBB "natural" rating that surety providers must have before they wrap a deal. Surety bonds are somewhat more common in deals backed by private loans, since the credit enhancement requirements of those deals make the economics of procuring a surety wrap (5 to 10 basis points per annum) more attractive to the issuer than senior/subordinated structures. Where surety bonds are used, sometimes the AAA-rating is a maturity guarantee, which means that only ultimate, not timely, principal and interest is guaranteed.

Waterfall of Payments

Subordinated classes are subordinate to senior classes with respect to interest; thus, senior bondholders will always receive interest before any payment of interest is made to subordinate bondholders. Subordinated interest may or may not be senior to senior *principal* payments, depending on the deal. Generally, however, subordinate classes receive payments of interest prior to any payments of principal to senior noteholders. (This waterfall is necessary to provide the liquidity necessary to achieve the rating on the subordinate class.)

The senior classes are usually time tranched (sequential pay), into 2.5- and 7-year average life tranches (with an auction call). Five-year average life senior tranches exist, but are not as common. Subordinated classes usually have a 10-year average life. The priority of payments is shown in Exhibit 12.

Exhibit 11: Example of Excess Interest in SLABs*

Weighted Average Margin	3.10%
Servicing Fee Rate	(0.65%)
Administration Fee Rate	(0.04%)
Weighted Average Spread to T-bills on SLABs	(0.70%)
Amount of Excess Available	1.71%

* For transactions where servicing fee varies based on quantity of loans serviced, the servicing fee is often capped.

21 Serial loans are second, third, etc. loans made to existing borrowers in a pool, to fund successive years of education.

22 "Turboing" refers to using excess interest cash flows to pay down principal.

Exhibit 12: Student Loan ABS Waterfall of Payments

		Frequency
1.	Monthly Rebate Fee/Origination Fees	Monthly
2.	Servicing Fee	Monthly
3.	Administration Fee	Monthly
4.	Noteholders'[a] Interest Distribution Amount	Monthly/Quarterly[b]
5.	Certificateholders'[c] Interest Distribution Amount	Monthly/Quarterly[b]
6.	Purchase of Serial Loans (during Additional Serial Loan Funding Period)	Quarterly
7.	Noteholders'[a] Principal Distribution Amount	Quarterly
8.	Certificateholders'[c] Principal Distribution Amount	Quarterly
9.	Reserve Account funded to its specified balance	Quarterly
10.	Noteholders'[a] Interest LIBOR Carryover[d]	Quarterly
11.	Certificateholders'[c] Interest LIBOR Carryover[d]	Quarterly
12.	Excess Servicing[e]	Quarterly
13.	Remaining amount is released to the Seller	Quarterly

[a] "Noteholders" generally refers to senior tranches investors; "Certificateholders" often refers to subordinate tranche investors.
[b] Monthly if 1-month LIBOR-based coupon. Quarterly if 91-day Treasury-bill-based coupon.
[c] Certificateholders' interest is sometimes also subordinate to senior *principal.*
[d] "LIBOR Carryover" — see discussion of Available Funds Cap on LIBOR SLABs
[e] Excess servicing may be used to purchase additional loans (i.e., to bring a subparity deal to parity) or to turbo (paydown) the pool to create overcollateralization.

Auction Calls

Most SLABs issued today employ an auction call feature. SMS Student Loan Trust 1994-A was one of the first student loan transactions structured by Credit Suisse First Boston to use the auction call feature. The purpose of the auction call is to truncate the long cash flow tail that the underlying loans can have, especially with the possibility of consolidation loans. On the auction call date specified in the prospectus, the trustee must hold an auction. There must be a minimum of two bidders. The trustee accepts the highest bid, as long as the bid is at least the greater of (1) the unpaid balances and accrued interest on the loans and (2) the amount necessary to pay off the notes (both senior and subordinated), including accrued interest.[23]

Today, unsecuritized student loans trade at 3% to 4½% point premiums, once they have entered their repayment period. Most auction calls are 10 years. After 10 years, servicing costs (which are on a per loan basis, regardless of loan size) represent a higher percentage of the then smaller loan balances. However, losses on student loans are *de minimis* at this point. Therefore, it seems highly unlikely that 10-year seasoned student loans, which have floating coupons, could trade below par. Even in the event that changes in student loan programs were to make servicing less economical and hence student loans less valuable, we view the likelihood of an unsuccessful auction to be low. It is important to note, however, that the rating agencies do not rate the maturity that the auction call provides.

[23] Balances on loans may be different than on bonds (i.e., if a premium proceeds structure was used or if there have been principal or interest shortfalls). Capitalized interest after prefunding dollars used creates a difference, as well as timing differences between transfer dates and servicer activity.

Premium Proceeds Structure

In whole loan form, student loans, with their government guarantees and generally attractive margins (310 basis points over the 3-month Treasury bill as of this writing), trade at a premium. For those loan programs where interest is accrued rather than paid currently (i.e., by subsidized Stafford loans) prior to the repayment period, the accrued interest is capitalized, also resulting in premium dollar prices.

In order to provide greater efficiency for issuers, the "premium proceeds" or "sub-parity" structure was developed.[24] To understand the premium proceeds structure, assume a student loan lender (or secondary market maker) acquires $500 million par amount of student loans for a price of 103. In the past, the lender would issue $500 million in SLABs and fund the $15 million premium ($500 × 3%) from its own cash. However, because of the innately low-risk nature of the collateral — stable excess spread levels and relatively long life — the rating agencies have become comfortable with issuers issuing bonds where the face amount of the bond exceeds the face amount of the underlying collateral (a "premium proceeds" structure).

In effect, the bonds are *under*collateralized at the outset. Continuing our example, the issuer might be able to issue, say, $512.5 million in bonds backed by the $500 million in student loans. Over time, the application of excess spread to pay down ("turbo") the bonds or to reinvest in new collateral will bring the collateral balance in line with the bond balance (parity). Tax attorneys require parity to be reached by the end of the revolving period or soon thereafter.

All else equal, issuers who use a premium proceeds structure are likely to need slightly more credit enhancement to earn the same rating. The issuer benefits because the additional proceeds raised can be used to (1) fully fund the reserve fund,[25] (2) cover issuance expenses, or (3) recoup a portion of the premium that issuers paid for the collateral. We believe investors should be largely indifferent to premium proceeds versus par proceeds structure because the certainty of payment given the initial undercollateralization is evaluated in the rating process.

Prefunding Accounts

Many SLABs contain prefunding accounts. This simply means that a portion of the proceeds from the bond issue are put into a fund to buy additional student loans over time, including: (1) accrued interest to be capitalized; (2) serial loans; (3) consolidation loans; and, (4) new loans (i.e., to borrowers not already the trust).

The prefunding period may extend up to two years but deals are typically fully funded within the first year. At the end of the prefunding period, any amount remaining in the prefunding account is distributed to bondholders as prepayment of principal. The significance of such prefunding provisions for investors is that loans added to the pool could theoretically change the composition of the pool with respect to credit and/or maturity. However, in practice, the collateral pool

---

[24] Credit Suisse First Boston created the first premium proceeds structure for KeyBank USA in September 1996 (KeyCorp Student Loan Trust 1996-A).

[25] This is generally required in a premium proceeds structure.

does not materially change because the issuer is required to add loans substantially similar to the existing loan pool. In fact, the addition of serial and consolidation loans will generally improve the profitability of the pool. Consolidation loans typically perform better than most other loans since they are the only government loan subject to some credit underwriting criteria.

Revolving Period

An alternative to a prefunding account is the use of a revolving period. During this revolving period (typically 12 to 48 months), all collections not needed to pay interest and servicing fees are reinvested in new collateral. The revolving period may terminate early if certain excess spread, delinquency, or collateral composition triggers are hit. Revolving periods add stability and predictability to a transaction's amortization schedule.

In both prefunding and revolving periods, when principal is reinvested in new collateral, eligibility requirements must be met. These include maturity and yield consistent with the overall pool, and servicers and guarantors acceptable to the rating agencies. SMSLT 1996-A, underwritten by Credit Suisse First Boston, was the first student loan securitization done using the revolving feature. The use of a revolving period adds stability and predictability to the amortization schedule for investors, and offers issuers more flexibility in prefunding their originations.

Clean-up Calls

Clean-up calls allow for a par call of the ABS when the collateral has paid down to a certain level, generally 20% of the original balance. The concept of clean-up calls is unlike the traditional call features in corporate bonds, in that clean-up calls are not intended to provide issuers with an option to refinance. Rather, the purpose of clean-up calls in ABS is to allow issuers to call a deal in the event that the underlying collateral pays down to such an extent that the administrative costs (reporting, trustee fees, etc.) associated with keeping the issue outstanding are burdensome.

Withholding Taxes

Foreign investors purchasing senior notes should not be subject to withholding tax. For foreign investors purchasing BBB-rated subordinated bonds, certain U.S. tax code eligibility requirements may need to be met to ensure there is no withholding tax issue.

Coupon Basis

Treasury Bills versus LIBOR

From the first issuance of SLABs in 1993 until October 1995,[26] the coupon basis was LIBOR, in keeping with most of the floating-rate fixed income sector. However, a large market has since developed for Treasury bill (T-bill) based SLABs, as well.

[26] SLMA 1995-1 was the first student loan securitization indexed off the 91-day T-bill.

*Exhibit 13: Difference Between 1-Month and 91-Day T-Bills**

For the Last...	Average	Maximum	Minimum
6 months	0.59%	0.81%	0.42%
1 year	0.56%	0.98%	0.31%
2 years	0.50%	0.98%	0.23%
3 years	0.47%	0.98%	0.17%
5 years	0.42%	0.98%	0.11%
10 years	0.53%	1.58%	0.06%

* As of January 12, 1998.

Exhibit 14: Evaluating T-Bill Based SLABs (as of January 1998)

	3-month LIBOR		3-month T-bill
Index Level (6-month average)	5.78%	TED Spread -0.58%	5.20%
Investor Margin	0.15%	Swap Spread +0.60%	0.75%
Investor Coupon	5.93%	Difference +18b.p.	5.75%

Because the underlying student loans are based on T-bill rates, T-bill SLABs issuance is more attractive for issuers. There is no longer basis risk between the LIBOR-based coupon on the securities and the T-bill-based coupons on the underlying loans. This, in turn, reduces credit enhancement requirements because the rating agencies run very severe stress tests on the basis risk in a LIBOR-based transaction (i.e., using AAA scenarios) when they size the credit enhancement.

While some investors in the past have used swaps to go from T-bill into LIBOR, this has become less common. These swaps can be expensive, especially if they are balance guaranteed. In a balance-guaranteed swap, the swap counterparty agrees to adjust the notional amount of the swap in tandem with the actual balance on the bond over time. Investors who do not swap out of the T-bill index have gained comfort that the size and direction of the TED spread (the difference between LIBOR and T-bill rates) do not present considerable risk (see Exhibit 13). Obviously, this view can change with the markets. Exhibit 14 evaluates LIBOR based SLABS versus T-bill based SLABS.

Historically, floating-rate notes (FRNs) indexed to Treasury bills have experienced greater price volatility than issues based on LIBOR. This difference in volatility results from the difference in credit sensitivity of the indices — LIBOR is more sensitive to global credit risk than are Treasury bills. As a result, LIBOR has become the more popular index for investors wishing to link their coupon level to market rates. When investor confidence in the banking system is strong, this credit premium is reduced and the spread between LIBOR and Treasuries (the cash TED spread) narrows. Other factors that affect the cash TED spread are Treasury bill supply and economic and financial uncertainty.

Exhibit 15: The Cash TED Spread (Monthly Average: January 1985 to December 1997)

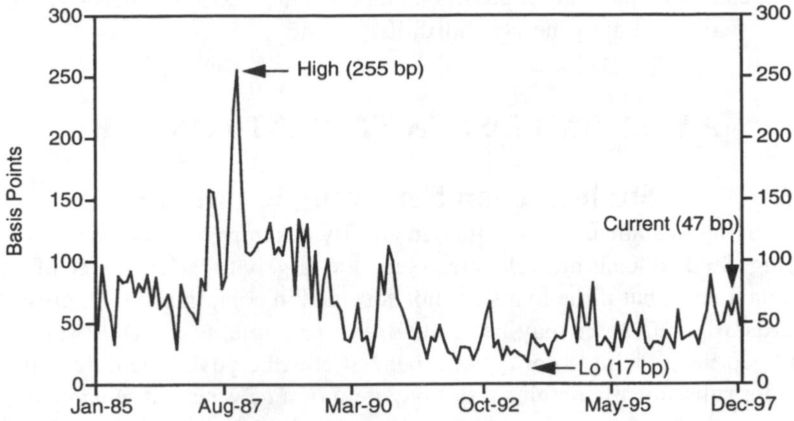

Source: Bloomberg Financial Markets

Typically, the supply of bills is not very sensitive to the general level of interest rates. Other factors can, however, affect the supply of Treasury bills, thereby affecting the yield levels. For instance, when Treasury funding needs decline due to higher-than-expected tax receipts, or when Federal debt ceiling limitations are approached, the supply of Treasury bills will often decline. In contrast, the elimination of the 7-year Treasury note and the reduction of issuance of 30-year bonds may result in higher bill yields than otherwise would have existed.

During periods of heightened economic or financial uncertainty, investors arc willing to pay a premium for safe and liquid assets. Because of their short maturities, liquidity, and government credit quality, Treasury bills are considered to be riskless securities. During these periods, bill yields generally decline. LIBOR, on the other hand, reflects the global banking community's cost of attracting deposits and includes a yield premium added to Treasury bills for credit risk. During periods of uncertainty, the effects of banks having to raise their bid levels to attract deposits and/or the increased demand for riskless securities lowering the rates on Treasury bills causes the spread between LIBOR and Treasury bills to widen.

As Exhibit 15 indicates, the cash TED spread widened dramatically during the 1987 stock market crash and the 1991 Gulf War, and was reasonably high throughout the late 1980s because of the S&L crisis. However, the cash TED spread has become increasingly more resilient to shocks in the banking community, possibly reflecting greater investor confidence in the ability of the banking system to withstand such crises.

Available Funds Caps on LIBOR SLABs

LIBOR-based SLABs have a floating cap tied to the blended average coupon of the loans (including SAP payments), less servicing fees. To the extent this cap is less than the indexed coupon in any given period, a LIBOR carryover shortfall results. This shortfall is recouped in future periods out of excess interest. The shortfall cannot be paid out of credit enhancement. Of course, Treasury bill based SLABs usually will not generate shortfalls.[27]

ANALYZING RISK IN STUDENT LOAN ABS

Student Loan Servicing is Unique

The servicing of student loans is fundamentally different from other types of loan servicing. Student loans are valuable assets due largely to the existence of government guarantees; but if the loans are not serviced in compliance with government standards, that guarantee may be vitiated. For example, under DOE standards, a 46-day gap in servicing a delinquent loan vitiates the guarantee unless and until the lender subsequently obtains a full payment or a new, signed repayment agreement from the borrower. The servicer, then, is arguably the focal point of risk analysis.

Because of its specialized nature, economies of scale in servicing student loans are important and, for this reason, third-party servicing is particularly common. The major third-party student loan servicers and the size of portfolio serviced are listed in Exhibit 16.

Exhibit 16: Student Loan ABS Servicers

Servicer	Description	Portfolio Size	Rating
Third Party Servicers (National Market)			
Pennsylvania Higher Education Assistance Agency (PHEAA)	Public corporation and a government instrumentality of Pennsylvania	$15 bn (9/97)	NR
USA Group Loan Services Inc.	Private, Nonprofit, nonstock membership corporation	$11 bn (6/97)	NR
UNIPAC Service Corporation	Nebraska Corporation headquartered in Colorado. Provides complete student loan administration.	$7.2 bn (10/97)	NR
AFSA Data Corporation	Wholly-owned subsidiary of Fleet Holding Corporation, a subsidiary of Fleet National Bank.	$32.8 bn (10/97)	A2
Third Party Servicers (Regional Market)			
Great Lakes Higher Education Corporation	Nonprofit Wisconsin corporation	NA	NR
SunTech Inc.	Mississippi business corporation established for student loan servicing operations of Mississippi Higher Education Assistance Corporation	$440 mm (11/97)	NR

[27] There are specific instances when PLUS loans are ineligible for SAP payments. This instances may result in shortfalls.

A great deal of consideration is given to servicer quality in the rating process. The rating agencies perform due diligence on management, systems and experience, human resources, and financial condition. They also will examine data on claims rejection rates and cure rates. Claims for payment on defaulted student loans can be rejected by student loan guarantors if proper servicing/collection procedures were not followed. In most cases, such breaches can be cured, which reinstates the guarantee. Gross rejected claims are rarely more than 5%to to 10% for major servicers and, of those, some 70% to 90% are cured.

As with most ABS, the rating agencies specify minimal levels of servicing expense and make that expense senior in the waterfall of payments. This helps to ensure that it will always be economically attractive for the servicer to service the loans or for a back-up servicer to step in.

Student Loan Defaults

While defaults are 98% guaranteed, excessive default rates can still pose risk to SLAB structures by reducing the life of the securities and hitting credit enhancement to cover the 2% loss.

Student loans are generally made without regard to the ability to repay and to individuals without credit history. They may be used to finance education at vocational and trade schools, 2-year and 4-year colleges and universities, and graduate schools including law and medicine. While students themselves are typically the obligors, loans are also made to parents or with parents as co-signors. Regardless, the resulting creditworthiness of the loan often has much to do with the quality of education received and the correlative effect on the individual's ability to generate income. While borrowers may develop poor money management habits or give priority to other creditors and as a result fall delinquent, they often default due to an *inability* to pay rather than an *unwillingness* to pay. Nevertheless, the government's power to administratively garnish wages and attach tax refunds of delinquent student loan borrowers, the reporting of defaults to credit bureaus, and the inability to discharge student loan debt in bankruptcy make defaulting an unattractive option.[28]

What Drives Defaults?

Two factors affect the ability to pay. One is general economic conditions, specifically unemployment levels. The other factor is the impact of the education dollars spent on the ability to repay. It is intuitive that the ability to pay will be greater for graduates who obtain advanced degrees from private schools than, for example, for graduates (or, for that matter, drop outs) of proprietary programs of shorter duration (e.g., "trade schools"). Consequently, the school-type breakdown of a

---

[28] Interestingly, the increased popularity of personal bankruptcy, which has led to large increases in losses for credit card issuers, poses no threat to investors in SLABs. For not only are student loans virtually non-dischargeable, but under some student loan programs, the federal guarantee is increased from 98% to 100% in the event of bankruptcy (as is also the case with death or disability).

portfolio has a large impact on the rating agencies' default assumptions. The experience from the DOE (see Exhibit 17) shows a downward trend in student loan defaults, resulting from successful efforts by the DOE and guarantors to crack down both on shady trade schools and recalcitrant borrowers, but also reflecting a strong labor market and generally buoyant U.S. economy.

The Student Loan Default Curve

As with most types of consumer loans, the incidence of defaults tends to follow a loss curve. In the case of student loans, the loans are often not yet in repayment at the time they are securitized (usually because the borrower is still in school, continuing their education, or in the initial grace period). Before a loan enters repayment, defaults are virtually non-existent. Student loans do exhibit a fairly high number of "first-payment" defaults, whereby the borrower defaults immediately upon entering repayment. These students may have never intended to pay their obligation, may be dissatisfied with the education they received, may have moved when employment is found (making them difficult to contact), or may simply have been unable to gain employment.

Exhibit 18 shows Credit Suisse First Boston's historical cumulative default analysis of loans in repayment by loan and school type. As the graphs show, a significant percentage of the total defaults occur within one year into repayment. After that point, losses tail off. The riskiest loans have already defaulted, so there is a positive survivor bias. It is also likely that over time the debt obligation has become a smaller part of the borrower's (growing) income.

The rating agencies front-end loss assumptions in order to be conservative in their rating process. Generally losses are assumed to be highest in the first 6 months to 1 year of repayment and virtually go to zero after being in repayment for 3 years. (See Exhibit 19 for Fitch's approach.)

*Exhibit 17: DOE Annual Cohort Default Rates**

Fiscal Year	A Number of Borrowers in Default	B Number of Borrowers Entering Repayment	A/B Cohort Default Rate
1987	418,717	2,381,087	17.6%
1988	440,790	2,561,183	17.2%
1989	542,158	2,700,446	20.1%
1990	551,208	2,460,102	22.4%
1991	380,346	2,135,595	17.8%
1992	299,881	1,994,925	15.0%
1993	212,052	1,826,626	11.6%
1994	199,233	1,866,420	10.7%

* Note that cohort default rates are annual rates for the first year after a cohort enters repayment. Defaults are highest in this first year. The DOE does not publish data on cumulative rates.

Source: U.S. Department of Education.

Exhibit 18: Credit Suisse First Boston's Historical Cumulative Default Analysis By Loan and School Type

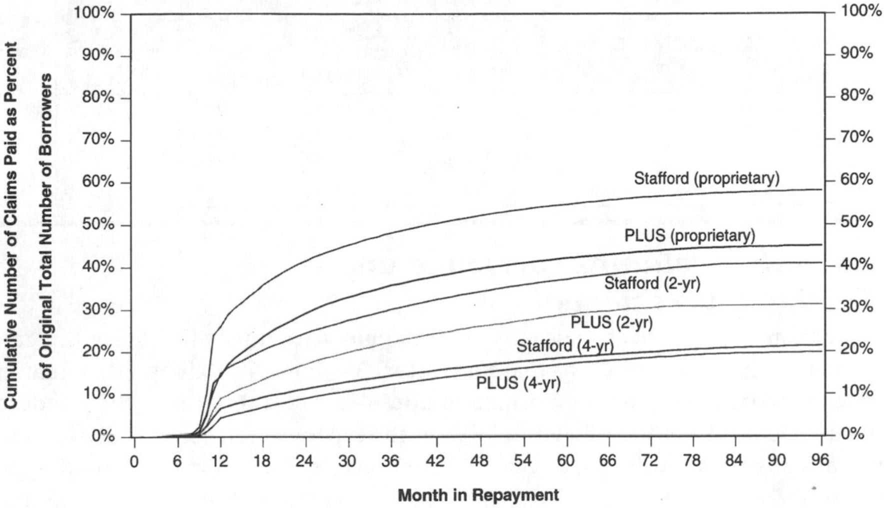

Source: Composite of Department of Education information and other Credit Suisse First Boston sources.

*Exhibit 19: Fitch's Basic AAA Cash Flow — Stress Scenario for Federal Loans**

1. Default rates are 3.0× – 5.0× historical levels.
2. Defaults occur during the first three years of repayment, with 75% of defaults occurring at the end of year one and 12.5% at the end of years two and three.
3. A 60-day lag on all student loan payments.
4. A 60-day lag on all interest subsidy and special allowance payments from the U.S. Department of Education.
5. The U.S. Department of Education reimburses defaulting loans 540 days after the last borrower payment on the loan. A servicer loss of 300 b.p. is assumed.
6. Interest must be capitalized on all eligible loans; cash flows must demonstrate sufficient liquidity to meet interest payments when interest is capitalized.
7. The reinvestment rate is equal to that of the 91-day U.S. Treasury bill or the investment agreement rate.
8. Forbearance and deferments are 2.0x – 3.0x historical rates.

* Fitch may apply different assumptions to transactions supported by supplemental loans.
Source: Fitch Investors Service, L.P., "A Primer on Rating Student Loan Bonds," October 22, 1997.

Exhibit 20: Effect of Default Experience in DOE Reimbursements to Guarantors

	Insurance Rate Paid to Loanholder from Guarantor		Reinsurance Rate to Guarantor from DOE	
Default Rate	Originations Post 10/1/93	Originations Pre 10/1/93	Originations Post 10/1/93	Originations Pre 10/1/93
≤ 5%	98%	100%	98%	100%
> 5% ≤ 9%	98%	100%	88%	90%
> 9%	98%	100%	78%	80%
Death, Disability, Bankruptcy	100%	100%	100%	100%

Guarantor Default Experience and DOE Reimbursements

If a guarantor experiences unusually high default rates, this will impact the government's reinsurance level for that guarantor. As shown in Exhibit 20, a guarantor with particularly poor performance could, conceivably, have their federal reinsurance cut from 98% down to 78% with respect to reinsurance claims submitted for the rest of the fiscal year.[29] This lower reinsurance rate would apply only to those default claims above the trigger level, not all claims. This sliding scale is an incentive for the guarantor to enforce origination and servicing guidelines and to diligently police schools participating in their programs.

How Do Defaults Impact SLABs?

Investors in SLABs have several sources of protection against credit losses. The lines of defense are shown in Exhibit 21. The combination of guaranties and structural features make SLABs exceptionally creditworthy as well as resistant to downgrades.

Internal Liquidity Risk

The path from the first delinquent payment to the receipt of the insured portion (98% or 100%) of principal and accrued interest from the guarantor takes several months — from 9 to 12 on average (see Exhibit 7). In order to have sufficient funds to make payments to noteholders even under high defaults (e.g., a AAA stress test), some type of provision must be made to provide liquidity over this time period. This is typically done with the use of a reserve fund.[30] There may also be liquidity needs if a guarantor should become insolvent. In the event of guarantor insolvency, however, the DOE is obligated to step in. The DOE did in fact step in once,[31] before it was required, and no delays occurred.

[29] Years ago, HEAF (Higher Education Assistance Fund) had its reinsurance cut to 80%. HEAF was ultimately liquidated by the DOE with obligations reassigned to other guarantors. Recently, no guarantor has gone below 88%.

[30] The size of the reserve fund is usually determined by the number of private loans in a pool. Typically, reserve funds are funded using excess spread and reach their required level within one year.

[31] HEAF required DOE assistance. See footnote 29.

Exhibit 21: Sources of Protection Against Credit Losses

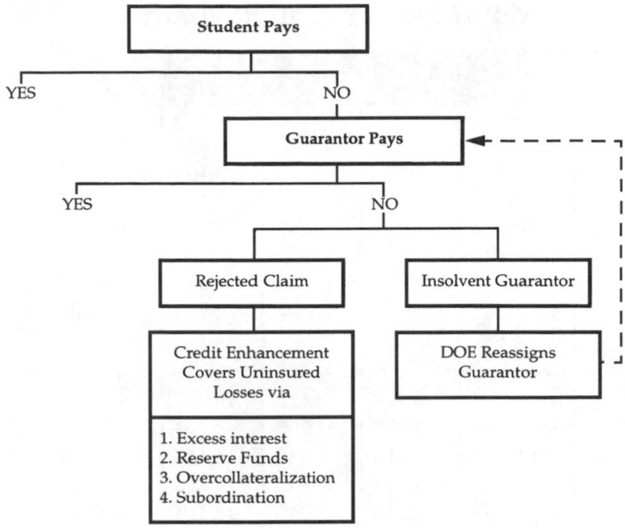

Cash Flow Variability

The cash flows on student loans vary based on defaults, prepayments, deferment, and forbearance and consolidation. This makes student loans more complex than other ABS collateral, where borrowers either pay as scheduled, default, or payoff in full. It is always important to see this cash flow variability as entirely distinct from the variability in mortgage and mortgage-like products. In contrast to mortgages, cash flow variability in student loans is largely independent of refinancing (except via consolidation), and hence cash flow variability is random and *not* interest-rate related.

Student loan borrowers are typically insensitive to interest rate fluctuations. Student loans are generally the cheapest source of consumer borrowing. This precludes refinancing of student loans with alternative debt, and student loan lenders do not provide refinancing into new student loans. Thus, student loan cash flows exhibit relatively minor random variation in life speeds (though month-to-month speeds can be volatile — see Exhibit 22) and are not correlated with interest rates. Most cash flow variability is likely to be default-related or due to loans being folded into consolidation loans.

Consolidation loans also present a source of cash flow uncertainty. Because student loans are made for a single school year, graduating students often have several loans outstanding. These loans can be consolidated at the weighted average of the underlying loans, rounded up to a full percent and subject to a minimum of 9%.[32] Consolidation loans are fixed under that formula. The term of the loan may be extended from the typical 10 years to up to 30 years.

[32] In addition to consolidating undergraduate and graduate student loans, student loans made to a borrower's spouse may also be consolidated by the borrower.

Exhibit 22: KeyCorp Student Loan Monthly Prepayment Analysis

Month	1995-A CPR	1994-B CPR	1994-A CPR	1993-A CPR
Jan-94			2.37%	2.10%
Apr-94			2.62%	1.89%
May-94			3.10%	1.50%
Jun-94			4.13%	0.82%
Jul-94			2.25%	0.68%
Aug-94			3.79%	2.21%
Sep-94			8.94%	8.52%
Oct-94			4.75%	12.10%
Nov-94			5.47%	3.53%
Dec-94		11.16%	7.07%	4.98%
Jan-95	6.12%	3.61%	10.98%	9.41%
Feb-95	3.73%	11.29%	9.84%	11.38%
Mar-95	7.91%	2.43%	14.47%	12.33%
Apr-95	4.44%	4.04%	15.81%	12.59%
May-95	6.24%	6.34%	13.32%	14.22%
Jun-95	4.02%	1.51%	10.20%	7.14%
Jul-95	2.88%	11.56%	1.45%	1.98%
Aug-95	16.51%	10.43%	13.68%	17.09%
Sep-95	14.34%	11.13%	13.36%	17.04%
Oct-95	12.95%	8.29%	13.12%	10.46%
Nov-95	9.43%	13.13%	8.16%	11.18%
Dec-95	8.56%	12.28%	9.71%	8.34%
Jan-96	13.11%	21.57%	12.19%	9.92%
Feb-96	20.78%	19.46%	12.66%	11.68%
Mar-96	17.38%	16.27%	0.00%	17.76%
Avg CPR	9.89%	10.28%	7.85%	7.98%

If consolidation loans are bought into the pool during the prefunding or revolving period, the longer repayment periods could extend the SLABs' average lives (though auction calls would typically offset this). After the refunding period, the borrower's option to restructure their debt into consolidation loans causes prepayments, which shorten the bond and shrink the amount of excess interest (a source of credit enhancement). At this writing, consolidation loans are a relatively minor force, as they represent a small share of most SLABs.

Keep in mind that, especially, in the years 1 through 3 when defaults are highest, defaults can be a significant source of prepayments of loans. The standard prepayment assumption (this includes involuntary "prepayments" caused by defaults) for student loan ABS is 7% CPR. CPR or conditional prepayment rate is the annualized or compounded monthly prepayment amount as a percentage of the previous month's outstanding balance, minus scheduled principal payment. In interpreting this data, note that the seasoning and repayment status of the loans are tied to prepayment speeds. So, prepayment speeds are low at the beginning of the transaction because most of the underlying loans have not entered repayment. Prepayment rates are high after entering repayment because defaults are high at that point.

Impact of Varying CPRs on SLABs

Average lives are not particularly volatile for SLABs. For example, we ran two recent representative SLABs, a senior note and a subordinated note, at CPRs from 0% to 17%. (See Exhibits 23 and 24.) The senior notes are locked out over a 3.7-year revolving period. Even under such dramatic and, we'd argue, unsustainable swings in CPR, the senior notes lengthen less than 9% (8 months) and shorten 11% (10 months) from the pricing assumption. The subordinated bond, which is locked out from prepayment until the senior bonds are retired, is unaffected. For both bonds the most significant impact on their average lives is the auction call.

The Importance of Reporting

The student loan ABS market does not yet enjoy industrywide excellence in investor reporting. This may be due to the lack of reporting standards and limited participation by many major servicers in the public rated market. Additionally, most third-party servicers lack the system enhancements necessary to support securitizations.

Data that is often missing from servicer reports include claim rejection rates, default rates, and updated loan characteristics. Unlike other ABS, where future losses may be estimated from current delinquencies, determining expected losses for student loans is dependent on an accurate claims rejection rate, or the number of defaulted loans that are rejected by the guarantors, and, ultimately, by the DOE. Unfortunately, a standard for reporting claim rejection rates has not been developed. Updating loan characteristics is an equally important measure of portfolio performance since cash flow to investors may be interrupted when borrowers in the repayment period enter forbearance or deferment.

Exhibit 23: Variability of Average Life of the Representative Securities

	0% CPR	4% CPR	7% CPR*	10% CPR	14% CPR	17% CPR
Senior Notes (years)	7.91	7.52	7.27	6.99	6.68	6.47
Subordinate (years)	10.23	10.23	10.23	10.23	10.23	10.23

* Pricing Assumption — Average life and expected final are calculated based on 10-year auction call.

Exhibit 24: Securities Characteristics at 7% CPR

	Average Life	Expected Final	Legal Final	Lockout	Window
Senior Notes	7.27 yrs	Jul 2007	Oct 2025	3.75 yrs	6.25 yrs
Subordinate Notes	10.23 yrs	Jul 2007	Oct 2028	10.0 yrs	0.25 yrs

Legislative Risk

Ratings address only the ability to receive interest up to the student loan rate cap. Federally insured floating-rate student loans are capped to the borrower. The borrower rate is reset annually in June and is capped at 8 to 10%. However, all Federally insured loans receive SAP (special allowance payments) from the DOE to augment below-market rates. SAP covers the shortfall between the indexed rate, which resets quarterly, and the cap. SAP is calculated and paid quarterly. For transactions which pay investors interest monthly, rating agencies require additional liquidity in the deal structure to handle the SAP delays. The eligibility for SAP is determined only once per year, based on whether the loan is above cap at reset.

APPENDIX
FFELP STUDENT LOAN CHARACTERISTICS

Date of First Loan	Origination Date	Maximum Repayment Term	Borrower Interest Rate	Borrower Interest Rate Cap	Borrower Interest Rate Reset Frequency	Subsidy
Stafford						
Prior to 1/1/81	Prior to 7/23/92	10 years	7.00%	N/A	N/A	Yes
Prior to 1/1/81	7/23/92–6/30/94	10 years	91-day T-Bill + 3.10%	7.00%	Annually, on each June 1	Yes
1/1/81–9/12/83	Prior to 7/23/92	10 years	9.00%	N/A	N/A	Yes
1/1/81–9/12/83	7/23/92–6/30/94	10 years	91-day T-Bill + 3.10%	9.00%	Annually, on each June 1	Yes
9/13/83–6/30/88	Prior to 7/23/92	10 years	8.00%	N/A	N/A	Yes
9/13/83–6/30/88	7/23/92–6/30/94	10 years	91-day T-Bill + 3.10%	8.00%	Annually, on each June 1	Yes
7/1/88–9/30/92	Prior to 7/23/92	10 years	8.00% through the four years after repayment; 91-day T-Bill + 3.25% thereafter	After four years of repayment: 10.00%	After four years of repayment: Annually on each June 1	Yes
7/1/88–9/30/92	7/23/92–6/30/94	10 years	91-day T-Bill + 3.10%	8.00% through the four years of repayment; 10.00% thereafter	Annually, on each June 1	Yes
10/1/92–6/30/94	Prior to 6/30/94	10 years	91-day T-Bill + 3.10%	9.00%	Annually, on each June 1	Yes
N/A	7/1/94–6/30/95	10 years	91-day T-Bill + 3.10%	8.25%	Annually, on each June 1	Yes
N/A	7/1/95–6/30/98	10 years	In school, grace or deferral: 91-day T-Bill + 2.50%; In repayment or forbearance: 91-day T-Bill + 3.10%	8.25%	Annually, on each June 1	Yes
N/A	After 6/30/98	10 years	Treasury security of comparable maturity + 1.0%	8.25%	N/A	Yes

APPENDIX (CONTINUED)

Date of First Loan	Origination Date	Maximum Repayment Term	Borrower Interest Rate	Borrower Interest Rate Cap	Borrower Interest Rate Reset Frequency	Subsidy
Unsubsidized Stafford						
N/A	10/1/92–6/30/94	10 years	91-day T-Bill + 3.10%	9.00%	Annually, on each June 1	No
N/A	7/1/94–6/30/95	10 years	91-day T-Bill + 3.10%	8.25%	Annually, on each June 1	No
N/A	7/1/95–6/30/98	10 years	In school, grace or deferral: 91-day T-Bill + 2.50%; In repayment or forbearance: 91-day T-Bill + 3.10%	8.25%	Annually, on each June 1	No
N/A	After 6/30/98	10 years	Treasury security of comparable maturity + 1.0%	8.25%	N/A	Yes
PLUS or SLS						
N/A	Prior to 10/1/81	10 years	9.00%	N/A	N/A	No
N/A	10/1/81–10/30/82	10 years	14.00%	N/A	N/A	No
N/A	11/1/82–6/30/87	10 years	12.00%	N/A	N/A	No
N/A	7/1/87–9/30/92	10 years	52 week T-Bill + 3.25%	12.00%	Annually, on each June 1	No
PLUS						
N/A	10/1/92–6/30/94	10 years	52 week T-Bill + 3.10%	10.00%	Annually, on each June 1	No
N/A	After 6/30/94	10 years	52 week T-Bill + 3.10%	9.00%	Annually, on each June 1	No
N/A	After 6/30/98	10 years	Treasury security of comparable maturity + 2.10%	9.00%	N/A	Yes
SLS						
N/A	10/1/92–6/30/94	10 years	52 week T-Bill + 3.10%	11.00%	Annually, on each June 1	No
N/A	After 6/30/98	10 years	Treasury security of comparable maturity + 2.10%	9.00%	N/A	Yes

APPENDIX (CONTINUED)

Date of First Loan	Origination Date	Maximum Repayment Term	Borrower Interest Rate	Borrower Interest Rate Cap	Borrower Interest Rate Reset Frequency	Subsidy
Consolidation						
N/A	Prior to 1/1/93	30 years	Wtd. Avg. of underlying loans rounded up to nearest whole percent, minimum 9%	N/A	N/A	No
N/A	1/1/93–8/9/93	30 years	Wtd. Avg. of underlying loans rounded up to nearest whole percent, minimum 9%	N/A	N/A	Yes
	8/10/93–6/30/94	30 years	Wtd. Avg. of underlying loans rounded up to nearest whole percent, minimum 9%	N/A	N/A	Yes, if all underlying loans received subsidy; Otherwise, No.
	After 6/30/94	30 years	Wtd. Avg. of underlying loans rounded up to nearest whole percent	N/A	N/A	Yes, if all underlying loans received subsidy; Otherwise, No.

Chapter 16

Securitization of Commercial and Industrial Loans

Anthony V. Thompson
Director of ABS Research
Goldman, Sachs & Co.

INTRODUCTION

Long before anyone had ever heard of a home equity loan or even a credit card, there were commercial and industrial loans. Surprisingly, this asset class — the bread and butter of many large commercial banks — has been slow to find its way into the multi-billion-dollar securitization market. But this is changing. A number of large financial institutions (some highly rated, others not) are rethinking how capital and funding should be allocated to their commercial and industrial (C&I) loan business. An estimated $34 billion of securities were issued in 1997 and the market is expected to grow significantly in 1998. While some structures look like traditional asset-backed securities, others have more in common with secured borrowings, credit derivatives, or CLO hybrids. None of them, however, are quite like anything the market has seen before.

Most of what we consider to be the traditional ABS market has been built on the securitization of consumer receivables (credit cards, autos, and home equities). These assets are relatively homogenous and easily repackaged. Rating agencies are generally comfortable assigning credit enhancement levels to deals because the large number of obligors is suited to a statistical analysis. Securitization of commercial loans has been slow to catch on, but this is changing and the market could be substantial. According to recent FDIC data, these assets represent over 25% of loans in the U.S. banking system (see Exhibit 1).

We see three factors behind the recent increase in activity in the sector. First, a number of financial institutions are looking to alleviate capital pressures through asset securitization; well-diversified pools of C&I loans (especially those to U.S. borrowers) are a logical starting point. Second, recent advances in securitization technology have enabled institutions to sell loan participations without borrower notification in a manner similar to traditional ABS deals. And third, with investor demand at a record high, the ability to execute C&I transactions at levels competitive to other, more traditional asset classes, is providing a further incentive to issuers.

Exhibit 1: U.S. Banking Industry: Loan Portfolio Summary

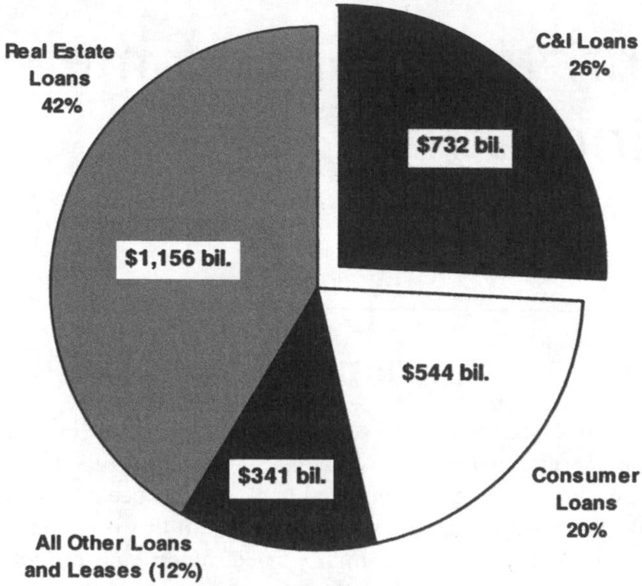

Loans and leases of insured commercial banks as of first quarter, 1997.
Source: FDIC

DISTINGUISHING COMMERCIAL LOAN SECURITIZATIONS FROM CLOs

The current generation of C&I loan securitization is quite different from its CLO/CBO predecessors, which may be more familiar to asset-backed investors. To understand C&I loan securitization, a brief review of their CBO/CLO cousins is in order. Broadly speaking, CBOs (collateralized bond obligations) and CLOs (collateralized loan obligations) are essentially secondary market arbitrage-driven securitizations. In a CLO or a CBO, a collateral manager establishes a bankruptcy-remote investment vehicle to purchase bank loans, corporate bonds, sovereign debt, or other high yielding securities. The vehicle issues asset-backed debt, and the collateral manager retains a layer of equity. The incentive for the collateral manager to do the transaction is driven by the return that can be earned on the equity layer; this will be based on the credit spread between the investment vehicle's assets (high yield loans and bonds) and its liabilities (higher quality asset-backed securities). The economics of the CLO are also influenced by the size and cost to fund the retained equity layer, as well as the market limitations associated with stringent rating agency guidelines.

There are two types of CBO/CLO transactions: cash flow and market value. In a cash flow transaction, the rating on the securities is derived from the ability to service bondholder interest and principal through cash generated by interest payments and redemptions on the underlying loans and bonds. In a market value transaction, securities issued by the investment vehicle are expected to be repaid through the sale of underlying collateral. Rating agencies require a regular marking to market of the securities in a market value transaction.

The first CBO was rated in 1988 (a transaction backed by high yield bonds); the first CLO was rated in 1990 (U.S. bank loans). Moody's estimates that about $70 billion of CBOs and CLOs have been issued to date, mostly in the private market. Volume has accelerated in recent years, fueled by low default experience in the high yield and emerging markets. And with other spread product at record tight levels, investors have been drawn to the attractive incremental yield and stable cash flows associated with CBOs and CLOs.

While CBOs and CLOs have been a part of the ABS market for quite some time, commercial loan securitizations are relatively new. Prior to 1996, securitizations of commercial loans in a traditional ABS format had been mostly limited to issuance by finance companies where the collateral is either small-business loans or secured by small and medium-size ticket equipment loans and leases. But these deals are quite different from the commercial bank loans that are now coming to market, where balances tend to be much larger, multilateral (or syndicated) facilities more common, and loan terms less standardized.

The first large-scale, non-arbitrage securitization of commercial bank loans took place at the end of 1996. The $5 billion deal was sponsored by NatWest and issued under the name R.O.S.E. Funding. A number of transactions have since followed. In our opinion, three points distinguish a commercial loan securitization from a traditional CLO transaction.

First, commercial loan securitizations are not driven by secondary market arbitrages; instead, the issuer is more likely to be motivated by capital efficiency created by funding the assets off balance sheet. These are the same reasons that would motivate a traditional ABS issuer to securitize.

Second, in a commercial loan securitization, the transaction sponsor is the underwriter/originator of the assets; in a CLO, loans are typically purchased in the secondary market. The sponsor of a commercial loan securitization therefore has a preexisting underwriting and servicing relationship with the borrower, similar to a typical consumer ABS deal. This is distinct from arbitrage CLO transactions, where the relationship between the collateral manager and the obligors is incidental and somewhat artificial based on availability of assets in the secondary market subject to rating agency diversity and credit criteria.

Third, in commercial loan securitizations, as in traditional ABS deals, loans are originated and serviced by a lender whose primary business is the granting and monitoring of credit. In a CLO, since the pool often has yet to be generated, there is more reliance on the credit quality criteria imposed by rating agencies (e.g., industry/obligor concentration limits) and the ability of the collateral manager to earn sufficient returns based on such criteria.

Exhibit 2: C&I Loan Securitization: Generic Structural Outline

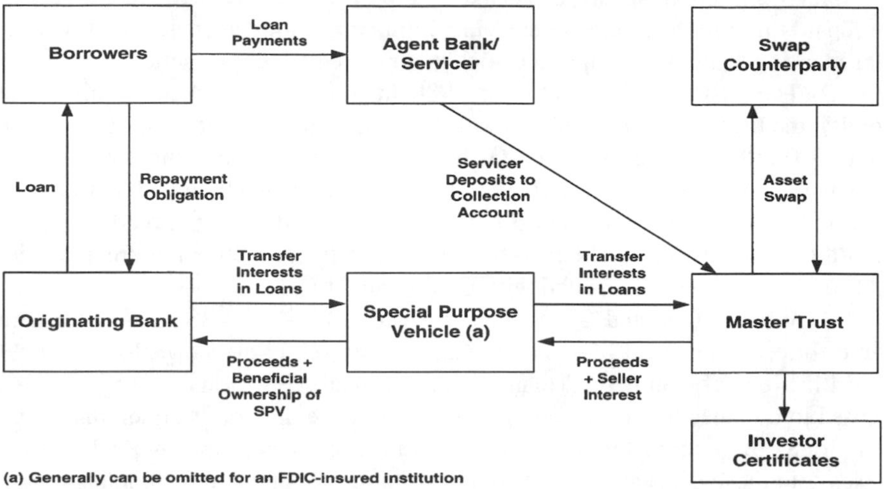

A SUMMARY OF STRUCTURAL AND CREDIT ISSUES TO LOOK FOR IN A COMMERCIAL LOAN SECURITIZATION

Much of the portfolio and structural analysis behind a commercial loan securitization is not unlike the analysis used to evaluate any other asset-backed deal. Here are a few key criteria.

Insolvency Risk

Not all commercial loan securitizations are alike when it comes to seller insolvency. For ABS investors seeking to reduce third-party risks, it is essential to understand to what degree the assets are insulated from the seller's insolvency. Several highly rated European banks have executed transactions with ratings tied to those of the underlying bank. Recent trends, however, have been toward more traditional ABS structures, where investors are "de-linked" from the seller (i.e., assets are isolated from the seller in the event of insolvency). For example, a bank not regulated by the FDIC (such as a branch of a foreign bank) would generally have to use a true-sale of assets to a special purpose, bankruptcy-remote vehicle in order to achieve Aaa/AAA ratings (see Exhibit 2).

Concentration Risk

Commercial loans typically have historical loss levels that are a fraction of consumer assets. However, the larger loan balances could expose investors to less-predictable risks if not properly managed. Many deals include limitations on borrower and industry concentrations. The limits would generally apply on an ongoing basis to current assets in the pool and to any new additions.

Servicing Risk

An inexperienced seller or servicer can adversely affect the performance of any asset-backed transaction. Generally, the servicing of C&I loans is less systems-intensive than consumer assets because of higher average loan balances. Furthermore, an active secondary market for commercial loans increases the ability to liquidate non-performing assets before a default occurs.

Multilateral Versus Bilateral

There are two basic types of C&I loans: loans where the lender is acting alone (bilateral) and loans where the lender is extending credit as part of a larger syndication with other banks (multilateral). Generally, multilateral facilities diversify underwriting risk among a larger pool of lenders.

Set-Off Risk

When a borrower has a loan from a bank where it also has a deposit, if the bank becomes insolvent and the deposit is lost, the borrower may be able to reduce ("set-off") the amount of its loan repayment by the size of the forfeited deposit. Lenders can obtain waivers from borrowers with respect to set-off. Any amounts subject to set-off can be addressed similar to dilution in a credit card deal, the risks of which can be reduced by appropriately increasing the seller's interest.

Interest Rate Mismatch Risk

There are two potential sources of mismatch in a C&I structure: basis risk and spread risk. *Basis risk* arises to the extent that there is a mismatch between interest rates on the underlying loans and the floating-rate asset-backed securities. Even in C&I portfolios that are predominately floating rate, a mismatch could still occur to the extent that loans are pegged to different floating-rate indexes with different reset dates. Also, many C&I loans carry spread risk because loan terms often provide for an increase or decrease in the loan rate if a borrower's financial condition changes. Both of these risks can be eliminated or substantially reduced through the use of a swap issued by a highly rated counterparty. To protect investors from deterioration in the counterparty, swap replacement clauses and amortization events can be incorporated that are similar to swap provisions in credit card structures.

Moral Hazard

Without sufficient incentive, a lender might be expected to let a loan portfolio deteriorate once it has been sold. In C&I securitizations, like other asset-backed transactions, this risk is offset by the lender's investment in the first loss tranche of the securitization, and its ongoing right to receive regular and excess servicing income. The desire to re-access the market also provides the lender with an incentive not to "abandon" a securitized pool.

A FEW POINTS ON RELATIVE VALUE

Liquidity Premium Relative to Generic ABS Product

The market for securitized C&I loans is still in its very early stages, and, until a standard template emerges, investors will command a premium for the deal-by-deal analysis. This will eventually change, as we believe issuers (especially those rated lower than double-A) will favor a standard ABS structure that provides investors with insolvency protection. Because most transactions are executed in the 144A market and are not uniformly eligible for ERISA, investors can command a several-basis-point premium relative to generic ABS product.

Cash Flow Stability

Many C&I loan portfolios have payment rates similar to those of credit cards. Using a master trust structure (revolving period followed by accumulation/amortization), investors can expect extremely predictable cash flows. In addition, as with credit card deals, C&I revolving structures contain early amortization events to protect investors from unforeseen credit deterioration in the pool or the servicer. The triggering of early amortization would reduce a security's average life; however, the investment impact should be less of a concern since most securities are likely to be issued as floating rate.

Asset Diversification

We see the growing market for commercial loans as an excellent diversification for floating-rate ABS buyers. In the past, third-party event risk has been a drawback for many investors, but we believe this is changing in light of structural innovations. Pools backing recent deals have exhibited solid fundamentals, and we think they are approaching the effective level of borrower diversification common to more generic ABS product.

Chapter 17

The Basics of CBO Investing

John N. Dunlevy, CFA
Chief Investment Officer
Beacon Hill Capital Advisers, LLC

Martin DeVito
Assistant Portfolio Manager
TCM Asset Management

INTRODUCTION

Collateralized bond obligations (CBOs) are special purpose vehicles that issue multi-tranche debt and equity backed by a highly diversified pool of below investment-grade bonds. These high-yield bond portfolios are backed by one or more of the following collateral groups: (1) high-yield corporate bonds, (2) emerging market bonds, and (3) bank loans. In this chapter, we will review CBOs and how to invest in them.

CBO BASIC STRUCTURE

The special purpose vehicle (SPV) created for the issuance of a collateralized bond obligation will be a stand-alone, bankruptcy remote entity whose assets are a portfolio of below investment-grade bonds. The pool of assets will be managed by a third-party asset manager with adequate experience and a successful track record within the asset class. The liability side of the balance sheet of a SPV typically consists of two debt tranches, usually of investment-grade credit quality and an equity tranche. Exhibit 1 gives a typical CBO structure.

Exhibit 1: Asset and Liability Structure of a CBO

SPV Balance Sheet

Assets		Liabilities
High Yield Assets	Hedges (Swaps and Caps)	Senior Debt Junior Debt Equity

Exhibit 2: Typical CBO Structure

Tranche	% Deal	Rating	Fixed/Floating	Typical Pricing
Senior Debt	70% to 80%	AA	Floating	LIBOR + 50
Junior Debt	10% to 15%	BBB–	Fixed	Tsy + 175
Equity	10% to 15%	NR	Variable	15% +

It is because of the redistribution of risk that the two bond tranches can obtain investment-grade ratings even though the underlying collateral consists largely of below investment-grade bonds. The rating agencies can gain comfort by requiring a large degree of diversification within the portfolio, and placing controls on the amount of trading which can be at the discretion of the asset manager. Additionally, the rating agencies require swaps and caps be used to hedge the basis risk between long-term fixed-rate assets (the collateral) and the CBO's floating-rate liabilities (the senior bonds). Finally, investment-grade ratings are achieved because of the excess cash flow available to cover any collateral shortfalls, as well as the transaction's built-in credit enhancement (i.e., subordination). Exhibit 2 shows a typical liability/equity structure of a CBO transaction.

CBO MARKET HISTORY AND SIZE

The first CBO transactions were done during the late 1980s, a period in which the junk bond market was hit hard. For example, the Chase high-yield index moved from a yield to worst of approximately 12% during the second half of 1988 to nearly 20% in December 1990. The underperformance of high-yield bonds over this period was a function of the following external factors:

- the RTC's liquidation of high-yield holdings by savings and loan associations
- introduction of risk-based capital for the insurance industry
- contraction of credit within the banking industry following record losses in real estate
- collapse of Drexel Burnham which was the market's largest underwriter and market-maker.

Since the first CBOs were market-value CBOs, which were actively managed (and which employed leverage), the downturn in the high-yield market lead to liquidations of portfolio holdings and poor overall returns. Consequently, the number of CBO transactions dropped sharply during the early 1990s. However, since the beginning of 1996, CBO popularity has skyrocketed.

RECENT CBO POPULARITY

One reason CBO activity has rebounded in recent years has been the increased simplicity of the current structures. That is, in the older *market value CBOs*, the cash required for interest and principal was generated by trading. The collateral was marked-to-market on a regular basis, allowing the rating agencies to monitor debt coverage ratios. The new structures are predominately *cash flow CBOs*. In a cash flow CBO, the payment of principal and interest is paid by simply passing through the cash flow from the underlying collateral. The deals are structured to have minimal cash flows which extend beyond the scheduled maturity dates of the bond tranches.

The cash flow CBO essentially has three phases. These phases are shown in Exhibit 3. The first phase, which is usually quite short, is known as the *ramp-up period*. This represents the time mandatory to invest in the required asset pool. The second phase, known as the *reinvestment period* is the time during which all principal received (including bond calls) must be reinvested in new assets. This reinvestment period is usually three years, but can be as long as five years. The third phase is known as the *pay-down period*. During this period, principal redemptions are used to repay principal of CBOs bond tranches. The CBOs bonds are retired in sequential order (i.e., the senior bonds are retired first).

The other major reason for the popularity of CBO is the alignment of interests of all parties involved in CBO issuance. That is, CBOs currently make sense for all three major parties involved — investors, Wall Street dealers, and the deal's asset managers. Each of the three CBO parties will be discussed below.

CBO Investors

As mentioned previously, there are typically three tranches involved in a CBO transaction. First is the *senior tranche*. This tranche is usually a AA-rated floating-rate bond. The senior tranche will drive the economics behind a CBO transaction since this bond, which represents about 75% of the deal, can be placed at LIBOR +40 to LIBOR +50. This senior tranche which equates to about Treasury +65 basis points versus the collateral spread of Treasury +300 basis points (for single-B average quality) produces the bulk of the *excess spread* which serves as the transaction's primary credit enhancement, as well as the source of cash flow to the equity investor. Despite the apparent richness of these bonds, the senior tranche represents a significant pick-up over many AA-rated, LIBOR-based bonds of industrial issuers, ABS bonds, and European MBS floaters. Therefore, institutional investors with a focus on US LIBOR investments have produced a strong demand for CBO floaters. These investors include banks, fund managers, corporations, and insurance companies.

Exhibit 3: Three Phases of a CBO

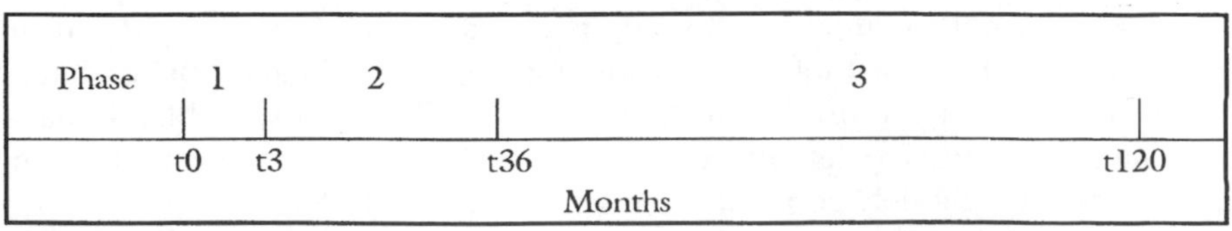

Exhibit 4: One-Year Default Rates for High-Yield Bonds: 1987 to 1996

1987	1988	1989	1990	1991	1992	1993	1994	1995	1996
3.77%	3.67%	5.99%	9.18%	10.67%	4.62%	3.49%	1.82%	3.28%	1.61%

Source: Moody's

The other debt obligations created in a CBO are the *junior bond tranches*. These tranches, which are issued as BBB bonds, are usually priced at Treasury +175 (LIBOR +140 to +150). They are also considered cheap versus corporates and asset-backed securities. The primary investors in these bonds are yield-oriented buyers such as insurance companies and money managers. Like the investors in the senior bonds, junior bond buyers continue to exhibit strong demand for additional CBO product.

The final tranche of the CBO is equity. Most equity tranches are structured to achieve 15% to 20% annualized returns on their original investment. Buyers of equity like to obtain exposure to the underlying asset class on a highly-levered basis. Frequent buyers of these tranches include the deal's asset manager (often required to own at least one-third of the CBO's equity), life insurers, banks, and high net worth individuals.

Wall Street Dealers

CBOs are very profitable for investment bankers. This is the case since bankers can earn fees for structuring the transaction, placing the debt and equity tranches, as well as earning the bid/offer spread for selling bonds into the deal. It is for these reasons that dealers have scrambled to broaden the investor base in this market.

Asset Managers

CBOs have become most popular with money managers. CBOs, like managing a closed-ended bond fund, allows the manager to lock-in the funds under management. Additionally, since the rating agencies limit the amount and scope of portfolio trading, the asset managers can often earn 35 to 50 basis point fees for merely overseeing the portfolio. Hence, CBOs offer the money managers a convenient way to build profitable and low maintenance assets under management.

RATING AGENCY PROCESS

The first step in the rating process is the analysis of the potential risk of default at the underlying collateral level. This step is called the calculation of *foreclosure frequency*. The foreclosure frequency among the three primary CBO collateral groups (high-yield corporate bonds, emerging market bonds, and bank loans) have had an impressive default experience. Exhibit 4 shows the actual default experience for high-yield corporate bonds from 1987 to 1996.

Exhibit 5: Ten-Year Weighted Average Cumulative Default Rates by Rating: 1971-1996

Rating	1	2	3	4	5	6	7	8	9	10
AAA	0.00	0.00	0.00	0.04	0.13	0.22	0.33	0.45	0.59	0.74
AA	0.03	0.05	0.10	0.25	0.40	0.57	0.73	0.91	1.04	1.13
A	0.01	0.07	0.22	0.39	0.57	0.76	0.96	1.18	1.44	1.73
BBB	0.12	0.39	0.76	1.27	1.71	2.21	2.79	3.36	3.99	4.61
BB	1.36	3.77	6.29	8.88	11.57	13.87	15.69	17.55	19.23	20.94
B	7.27	13.87	19.94	25.03	29.45	33.26	36.34	39.01	41.45	44.31

Source: Moody's 1971-1996 data

Exhibit 6: S&P Default Stress Levels

Rating	Level
AAA	2.50×
AA	2.00×
A	1.50×
BBB	1.25×
BB	1.00×

Additionally, the probability of a corporate default increases with time. Exhibit 5 shows the 10-year weighted average cumulative default rates by rating. The statistics in the exhibit confirm the importance of ratings as defaults increase consistently as a bond's rating is lowered. However, another reason for the popularity of CBOs recently is due to the decline in defaults. For example, during the 5-year period 1987 to 1992 the average annual default rate was 6.66% versus only 2.96% for the 1992 to 1996 period. Investors believe that future defaults should be lower, or more similar to the 1992 to 1996 default period for three reasons. First, the overall quality of junk credits has improved in recent years due to the demise of the hostile takeover and the highly leveraged transaction (HLT). Second, a strong IPO and equity market have made stock swaps the popular acquisition method. Third, the current strength of the domestic economy has made projected near-term defaults less likely.

Stress Levels

The rating agencies use historical defaults to set their credit enhancement levels. For example, Exhibit 6 shows how S&P sets its default stress levels. Moody's approach is similar as it uses a rating factor in determining default probability.

Default Timing

The agencies assume defaults will occur at various time intervals. The default timing intervals of S&P and Moody's are given in Exhibit 7. Many underwriters consider the Moody's assumption of 50% defaults in the first year unusually harsh.

Exhibit 7: Default Timing of S&P and Moody's

Year	S&P	Moody's
1	15%	50%
2	30%	10%
3	30%	10%
4	15%	10%
5	10%	10%
Total	100%	100%

Exhibit 8: S&P Recovery Rates

Position	Recovery Bonds	Rate Bank Loans
Senior secured	40%	50%
Senior unsecured	25%	25%
Subordinated	15%	15%

Loss Severity

The rating agencies used fixed recovery rates on their assumed defaults. These rates are based on collateral type and position on the debt within the capital structure. Exhibit 8 gives S&P's recovery rates. In contrast to the recovery rates in Exhibit 8, Moody's assumes a 30% recovery rate on all high-yield bond defaults. A higher recovery rate (i.e., 50%) is assumed on bank loans, while the recovery value for emerging market sovereign and corporate credits is assumed to be 25% and 10%, respectively.

Diversified Requirements

The agencies both require a highly diversified portfolio in order to lower the concentration risk and correlation risk of defaults among issuers in the same industry. S&P, for example, lists 39 industry groupings (see Exhibit 9) over which portfolio diversification can occur. Moody's, on the other hand, has a more concrete test called a *diversity score* which can be used to gauge portfolio diversification across deals.

Moody's breaks the corporate market into 32 industrial groups and includes two classifications for the emerging market sectors. CBO collateral pools must meet a minimum diversity score as specified in the prospectus for the deal. The collateral manager must maintain this level throughout the life of the deal. These levels also allow investors to quantify issuer and industry diversification in a given collateral pool.

Moody's diversity score is based upon the concept of diminishing marginal returns. That is, as a manager increases exposure to an industry, the diversity score will rise but at a diminishing level. For example, many recent CBOs have had diversity scores of 40 to 42 implying good diversification across industry sectors. Exhibit 10 shows Moody's diversity score criteria.

Exhibit 9: S&P CBO Industry Groupings

1. Aerospace and defense	21. Food/drug retailers
Aircraft manufacturer/components	22. Food products
Arms and ammunition	23. Food service
2. Air transport	Food service/restaurants
3. Automotive	Vending
Manufacturers	24. Forest products
Parts and equipment	Building materials
Tire and rubber	Paper products and containers
4. Beverage and tobacco	25. Health care
5. Broadcast radio and television	Medical equipment/supply
6. Brokerages/securities dealers/ investment houses	Hospital management
	26. Home furnishings
7. Building and development	Appliances
Builders	Furniture, fixtures
Land development/real estate	Housewares
Mobile homes	27. Hotels/motels/inns and casinos
REITs	28. Industrial equipment
8. Business equipment and services	Machinery
Graphic arts	Manufacturing/industrial
Office equipment/computers	Specialty instruments
Data processing service bureaus	29. Insurance
Computer software	30. Leisure
9. Cable television	Leisure goods
10. Chemical/plastics	Leisure activities/motion pictures
Coatings/paints/varnishes	31. Nonferrous metals/minerals
11. Clothing/textiles	Aluminum producers
12. Conglomerates	Other metal/mineral producers
13. Containers and glass products	Mining (including coal)
14. Cosmetics/toiletries	32. Oil and gas
15. Drugs	Producers/refiners
16. Ecological services and equipment	Gas pipelines
Waste disposal services and equipment	33. Publishing
17. Electronics/electric	34. Rail industries
Equipment	Railroads
Component	Rail equipment
18. Equipment leasing	35. Retailers (other than food/drug)
Auto leasing/rentals	36. Steel
Equipment leasing	37. Surface transport
Data processing equipment service/leasing	Shipping/shipbuilding
	Trucking
19. Farming/agriculture	38. Telecommunications/ cellular communications
Agriculture products and equipment	
Fertilizers	39. Utilities
20. Financial intermediaries	Electric
Banking	Local gas
Finance companies	Water

Source: Cash flow CBO/CLO Rating Criteria, S&P, October 1996.

Exhibit 10: Moody's Diversity Score Criteria

Number Bonds Held in Industry	Diversity Score Points
1	1.0
3	2.0
5	2.7
10	4.0
20	5.0

Source: Moody's

There is a separate diversity test for emerging markets. Moody's approach divides the world into five regions. Many investors have had trouble with the concept of an emerging market diversity score since there appears to be a high correlation between regions. Additionally, the historical default experience in emerging market credits is both limited and somewhat unreliable.

Minimum Rating Criteria

In order to maintain the credit quality of the collateral of a CBO, each of the rating agencies have developed formulas designed to produce a minimum rating level.

Moody's Minimum Rating Distribution Test assigns a numerical factor to each rating category, beginning with 1 for Aaa down to 10,000 for Ca (see Exhibit 11). By using these factors to weight each bond, based on its current principal amount, the entire collateral portfolio can be assigned a cumulative "rating," which must exceed a minimum level specified in the indenture. As an example, a typical CBO might require a maximum weighted average value of 2,675 which would represent a Moody's rating of between B1 and B2.

To illustrate Moody's Minimum Rating Distribution test, consider a CBO with the following pool of bonds.

Bond	Current Face	Rating	Factor
A	$2,000	A3	180
B	3,000	Baa3	610
C	5,500	Ba3	1,780
D	18,000	B3	3,490
Total	$28,500		

The weighted average rating factor is 2,625. Using the Moody's formula, our hypothetical pool with a Rating Factor of 2,625 would result in an equivalent rating of slightly above B2.

S&P employs a system of *Required Rating Percentages* to maintain the credit quality of the collateral pool. Rather than weight the portfolio as Moody's does, S&P specifies strict percentage limits for lower rated collateral (see Exhibit 12).

Exhibit 11: Moody's Minimum Rating Distribution Test

Moody's Rating	Rating Factor
Aaa	1
Aa1	10
Aa2	20
Aa3	40
A1	70
A2	120
A3	180
Baa1	260
Baa2	360
Baa3	610
Ba1	940
Ba2	1,350
Ba3	1,780
B1	2,220
B2	2,720
B3	3,490
Caa	6,500
Ca	10,000

Exhibit 12: S&P's Required Rating Percentages

Rating Category	Required Rating Percentage
BB– and above	10%
B+ and above	30%
B and above	75%
B- and above	95%

S&P and Moody's formulas share the same intention, namely preserving the integrity of the credit quality of the underlying pool. However, Moody's method, with its weighted approach, allows for more freedom in the mix of collateral since any combination of rating categories may be used as long as the overall "rating" of the pool exceeds the minimum guidelines.

Protective Covenants

CBO transactions are structured with protective covenants to protect the deal's bond tranches. Although these covenants will vary widely by deal, they generally will fall into the following categories:

- minimum levels of over collateralization must be maintained.
- minimum interest coverage ratios must be maintained.
- limitations of deals minimum rating, diversity score, weighted average coupon, weighted average life, maturity dates, etc.

Additionally, as previously mentioned, the agencies restrict the asset manager's ability to trade the portfolio by requiring that the criteria listed above be satisfied in order to maintain the deal's rating.

DEAL MONITORING

Deal monitoring, as in all credit-oriented securities, is a key part of achieving the best possible total returns. Investors should regularly monitor the credits held in the underlying portfolio. Most remittance reports allow investors to monitor the deal's diversity score, weighted average rating, and gross coupons. Moreover, investors should monitor the allocation of cash provided on the remittance reports. This report will show the cash flowing to the equity investor, the servicer, and the asset manager. By monitoring these cash flows the investor can see potential shortfalls.

The monitoring process is important because as the market liquidity for CBOs continues to improve, investors can trade out of potentially underperforming transactions.

CURRENT TRENDS IN CBO MARKET

We have seen two recent trends impacting the CBO market. First, the average deal size has been rising. This is largely due to combinations of two or more of the three collateral groups (high-yield corporate, bank loan, and emerging market debt) within the same transaction. This trend has resulted in deal sizes as large as $1 billion versus the typical deal size of $100 to $300 million in prior years.

Second, we are seeing a trend toward higher leverage within CBOs. This trend is occurring in two ways. The primary way is by the utilization of contingent interest CBO structures. In these deals, investment grade tranches are created with below market coupons and with a small participation in the equity upside. The other way leverage is increasing is through the sub-division of the equity tranche. By dividing the equity tranche into senior and junior pieces, the equity investor is able to get higher returns by subordinating a claim on the equity cash flow.

Chapter 18

Collateralized Loan and Bond Obligations: Creating Value Through Arbitrage

Ronald E. Thompson Jr.
Vice President
Citicorp Securities, Inc.

Eva F. J. Yun
Associate
Citicorp Securities, Inc.

INTRODUCTION

The collateralized loan obligation (CLO) and collateralized bond obligation (CBO) markets most clearly demonstrate the rapid innovation and development of the asset-backed securities market over the past few years. Structural nuances have developed, driven by why issuers created these securities in the first place and how they may be encouraged to ensure that the securities perform as expected.

Despite some concerns about these structural nuances and disclosures surrounding them, investors may find solid yield advantages in this relatively underdeveloped and evolving asset class, along with relatively stable average lives. As we explain in this chapter, these securities offer an opportunity to increase incremental yield without assuming undue risk.

CASH FLOW-BACKED INVESTMENTS: GROWTH OF THE MARKET

Both the CLO and CBO markets have undergone tremendous growth and garnered significant notice by the investment community. While CBOs have been around for some

---

The authors wish to thank David S. Blackwelder of Citicorp Securities, Inc., Darron Weinstein and Jennifer Wright of Citibank international, PLC for their helpful comments and suggestions. We also wish to thank Peg Pisani for her editorial guidance.

time as leveraged equity transactions, the development of a unified market for debt issued by these entities has increased markedly. Although the number of CLOs have increased dramatically, securitized loans have encompassed only either homogeneous consumer loans or large corporate loans. Over time, CLOs are expected to incorporate a broad range of loans, including small commercial and industrial (C&I) loans.

Bolstering the development of the CLO and CBO markets has been a strong investor appetite across the globe for investment products offering better yield value without incremental risk. Investors have sought alternatives to traditional markets, but often lack the resources to assess and monitor the risks embedded in these alternatives. Often, the CLO/CBO markets offer simpler methods through which investors may access higher returns, while hedging some of the exposures by using an experienced manager with economic incentives to temper risk.

Within the CLO submarket, two distinct lines have emerged based on transaction orientation: (1) the *investor-driven arbitrage transaction* and (2) the *balance sheet-driven transaction*. Investor-driven arbitrage transactions have long dominated the market (see Exhibits 1 and 2). These transactions have been prompted by investors' desire to increase yield through investments in other, riskier markets using skilled managers who purchase distressed or par loans in the secondary market. However, recently, as issuers have learned to apply securitization technology to large, high-quality loans, we have seen the rise of issuer/balance sheet-driven transactions. These issues tend to include loans that exhibit solid credit quality but pay below-hurdle yields for banks on-balance sheet. Banks have sought capital relief from carrying these loans by securitizing them and financing them off-balance sheet.

Exhibit 1: CLO, CBO, MV, and SLT Issuance, 1996 Versus 1997 YTD (Dollars in Billions)*

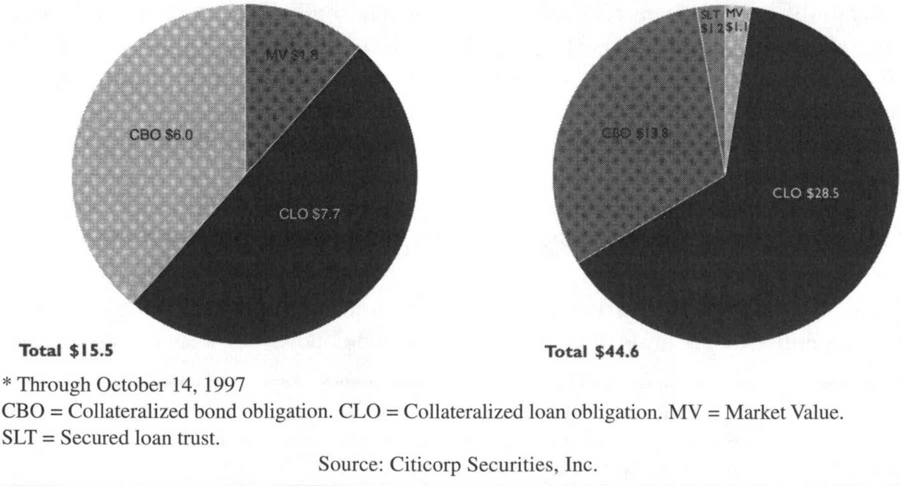

* Through October 14, 1997

CBO = Collateralized bond obligation. CLO = Collateralized loan obligation. MV = Market Value. SLT = Secured loan trust.

Source: Citicorp Securities, Inc.

Exhibit 2: CLO and CBO Transactions — Arbitrage- Versus Balance Sheet-Driven Structures

Arbitrage (Investor Driven)	Balance Sheet (Issuer Driven)
Assets generally bought out of the secondary market	Originator sells assets for off-balance sheet treatment
Generally more active trading	Regulatory rules act as catalyst; seller originates assets
Manager acts as investment advisor	Generally less active trading
Manager may take only a nominal economic stake in the transaction	Originator acts as investment advisor
	Originator generally retains a sizable economic stake in the transaction

Source: Citicorp Securities Inc.

The current capital weakness of the Japanese banks will foster future CLO/CBO market development through these issuer-driven transactions as the banks seek regulatory and GAAP capital relief by reducing assets. In our view, many of the European and U.S. banks will experience intensified earnings and shareholder pressures, forcing them to sell lower-yielding assets. Thus, although the CLO/CBO market will likely mature and stabilize over time, we foresee considerable growth ahead.

THE ECONOMICS OF CLOS AND CBOS

A CLO or CBO transaction is, at its essence, an arbitrage: either a market, capital, or regulatory arbitrage. For example, bank-issued CLOs are basically regulatory arbitrages. Banks are driven by regulatory discipline to maintain certain levels of capital to support their loan books; however, CLOs are driven by market discipline to develop and maintain sufficient capital or its market costs will rise. If market demands are lower than regulatory ones, a bank's return on capital is enhanced by securitizing assets for sale to investors.

The economics of a CLO or CBO are fairly simple. To examine a market arbitrage transaction, a transaction example may help explain the dynamics. We start with an investor that may wish to obtain return exposure to the high-yield market. While returns may be high, the investor may multiply the return by leveraging the investment and betting on default performance. The spread difference between the investment grade market and the high-yield market may be such that this leverage magnifies the return.

Exhibit 3 provides an example. In this example, we start with an investor who wants to place $40 million into the high-yield market. The investor works with an arranger to create a trust (usually in a tax-friendly country). Nominally capitalizing the trust, this investor seeds the newly created trust with the $40 million as a junior tranche (Class B) noteholder. The arranger seeks out investment grade investors looking for above-average yields, but highly-rated risk.

Exhibit 3: Example Economics of a Typical CBO Transaction

Transaction During Reinvestment Period (Dollars in Millions)

	Amount	Rate	Annual Income/(Expense)
Portfolio	$320	9.50%	$30.4
Assumed Defaults*		0.50%	(1.6)
Class A Notes	$280	6.75%	(18.9)
			$9.9
Expenses**			2.2
Residual Available to Class B Notes			$7.7
Annual Rate of Return			19.4%

Transaction During Reinvestment and Amortizatlon Periods (Dollars in Millions)

	Reinvest Period	Amortization Period			
	Years 1-5	Year 6	Year 7	Year 8	Year 9
Portfolio Balance	$320	$240	$160	$80	$0
Class A Notes	280	200	120	40	0
Portfolio Income	$30.4	$26.6	$19.0	$11.4	$3.8
Defaults*	(1.6)	(1.4)	(1.0)	(0.6)	(0.2)
Class A Note Interest	(18.9)	(16.2)	(10.8)	(5.4)	(1.4)
	9.9	9.0	7.2	5.4	2.3
Expenses**	(2.2)	(1.9)	(1.5)	(1.1)	(0.6)
Residual Available	$7.7	$7.1	$5.7	$4.3	1.6$
Annual Rate of Return	19.4%	17.7%	14.3%	10.9%	5.4%

* Defaults are assumed to be 50 bps of the average balance outstanding through the life of the transaction.
** Expenses are assumed to be 55bps of the outstanding portfolio plus $400,000.

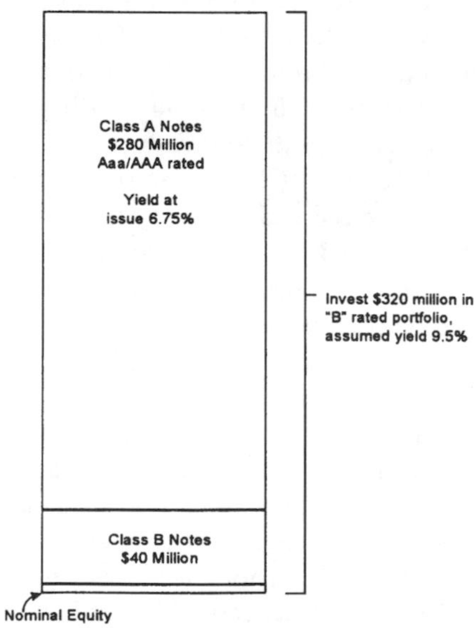

Source: Citicorp Securities Inc.

We assume that our exemplary trust has a reinvestment period of five years, with an expected 7-year average life. Principal is reinvested for five years, then paid out on straight-line basis, first to the Class A noteholders, then to the Class B noteholders. Using a debt-to-equity gearing of 7-to-1, the trust issues $280 million of senior notes, which are wrapped by a surety. The notes receive a Aaa/AAA rating because of the wrap and $40 million junior tranche. If the combined $320 million portfolio is assumed to earn 9.5% with defaults of 50 basis points and the Class A noteholders demand some premium to Treasuries, the transaction in our example yields the Class B investor $9.2 million annually during the portfolio's reinvestment period. After the reinvestment period, the returns drop and the effect of any portfolio deterioration is heightened as the transaction's leverage and resulting income fall.

If the Class B noteholder has the right to call the senior class, it often will call the senior notes to limit its exposure to losses. Also, as the transaction de-levers, the returns fall relative to the Class B principal outstanding. Therefore, investors in the senior securities generally look for a make-whole premium to offset a call.

CLOS AND CBOS: BLURRING DIFFERENCES

The CLO/CBO asset classes have evolved into several subclasses, although many of these lines are blurring. From a cash flow and a credit standpoint, the differences are sometimes more subtle than apparent between these two asset classes, but nonetheless, they remain important. For the most part, balance sheet-driven CLOs represent buy-and-hold investments in high-quality C&I loans that typically have lower default and loss severity rates than their leveraged loan and high-yield bond counterparts. However, investor-driven CLOs and CBOs generally represent more actively managed asset pools.

Often, the primary distinction between a CLO and a CBO is merely the dominant investment class in the pool. With both investments, investors may participate in the non-correlated returns offered by these markets versus more traditional asset classes without the commensurate investment in staff and analytics to track individual securities. Therefore, we believe investors may better distinguish structures through the motivation of the seller: either investor-driven arbitrage transactions or issuer-driven balance sheet transactions.

Structurally, arbitrage and balance sheet transactions tend to have similar characteristics. Most start with a special purpose vehicle that purchases loans or bonds directly from the issuers or from the secondary market (see Exhibit 4). This vehicle may take the form of a special purpose corporation, a limited liability corporation, or a limited partnership and is generally bankruptcy-remote from other entities that may arrange or support it. The vehicle usually has strict limitations on its activities, including borrowing funds and distributing dividends. Aside from investors in the trust structure, other parties to a transaction may include a portfolio manager and/or a servicer, a trustee for asset-backed bond holders, credit enhancer(s), and, as necessary, a swap provider.

Exhibit 4: Simplified CLO/CBO Structure

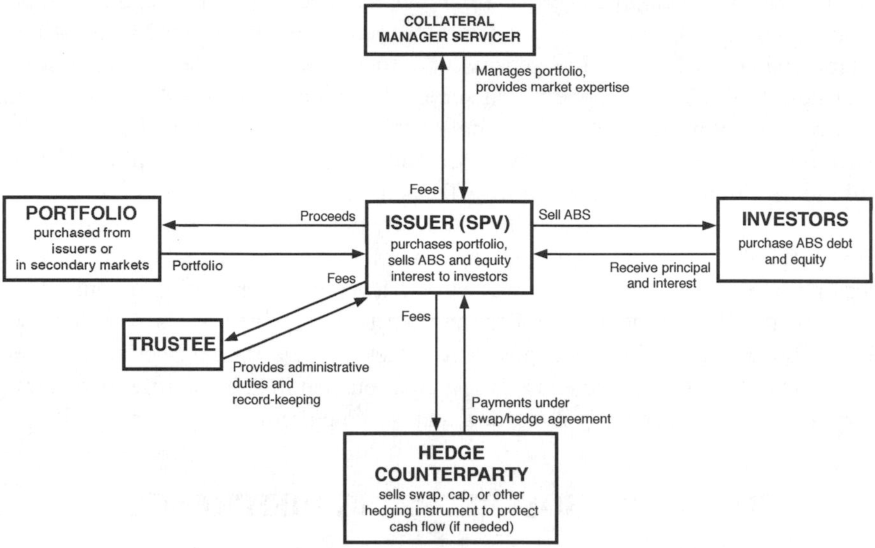

Source: Citicorp Securities Inc.

To support its capital structure, the vehicle may issue a number of classes of debt and an equity interest. Certain transactions have been structured with additional credit enhancements to bolster the rating value or to increase their marketability. Such credit enhancements may include additional equity, a mezzanine-type structure with junior lenders to the vehicle, or a surety wrap. In addition to credit enhancements, many transactions may have other protections, including excess spread or cash reserves, that bolster the credit quality of the vehicle.

The typical structure calls for a revolving period when the portfolio is actively managed, followed by an amortization period during which principal is paid to investors. To offer a more stable cash flow to investors, the structure may include a lock-out on principal payments, which builds cash reserves through excess spread generated by the cash flows in the vehicle. These structures generally restrict trading.[1] Many of the structures may offer partial or early-amortization triggers, which enhance principal protection but may increase reinvestment risk for investors.

Another type of structure, a so-called "market-value" transaction, derives its income not only from investment interest on invested assets, but also from trading strategies that may draw heavily on market timing and valuation. Because this asset class uses an actively managed, leveraged equity strategy, it deserves extensive analysis of the portfolio manager to perform in all types of markets and conditions within the manager's abilities and constraints. Under the market-value

[1] Trading in these types of CBOs and CLOs generally are limited to loan credit improvement, price improvement, or credit impairment.

structure, the underlying assets supporting the transaction will likely change dramatically from those present at the initial offering. These structures may purchase distressed loan assets in the secondary market and aggressively trade the loans based on potential price improvements. Many of these structures carry provisions to invest in various types of assets.

Another recent innovation is in the alternative collateral CLO or secured loan trust. This structure is similar to a CLO, but instead of buying loans for cash, it uses total return swaps with counterparties that are long a desired portfolio. This structure allows the counterparties to reduce exposures to particular markets without selling the portfolio. Conversely, the trust cuts execution costs by entering into swaps rather than purchasing the underlying assets.

AN ANALYTICAL FRAMEWORK

To examine the market, investors should use an analytical framework to identify relative value between issues (see Exhibit 5). In an analytical framework, investors may utilize a top-down analytical approach that focuses first on macro issues, then considers the peculiarities and nuances of each structure. We believe that this approach ferrets out the quality of the issue and enables the analyst to assign weights for pricing decisions. When analyzing CLOs and CBOs, most investors consider similar variables, but the reliance and weighting given to each factor differentiates CLOs from CBOs. While disclosure details vary from transaction to transaction, investors should try to evaluate as many of these as practicable. In any case, the analysis of the issuer/servicer and portfolio manager ranks as the primary fundamental factor or parties, followed by an analysis of the portfolio investment parameters and constraints.

Exhibit 5: CLO and CBO Investments — Analytical Framework

Balance Sheet CLO	*Arbitrage CLO/CBO*
Originator/Servicer/Manager	Portfolio Manager
Structure Analysis/Credit Enhancement Review	Structure Analysis/Credit Enhancement Review
Collateral Credit Analysis	Collateral Credit Analysis
Underwriting Criteria	Weighted-Average Credit Rating
Portfolio Heterogeneity	Weighted-Average Maturity
Event of Default Actions	Default Analysis
Weighted-Average Credit Rating	Default Probability
Weighted-Average Maturity	Default Severity
Default Analysis	Cash Flow Analysis
Default Probability	Amortization Trigger Events
Default Severity	Prefunding Amounts and Periods
Cash Flow Analysis	Redemption Rights (Optional/Mandatory)
Legal Considerations	Legal Considerations

Source: Citicorp Securities Inc., Duff and Phelps Credit Rating Co., Fitch Investors Service, LP, Moody's Investor Service, Inc., and Standard & Poor's

As with any asset-backed investment using a top-down strategy, investors generally focus the first analysis on the economic conditions that may drive or hinder the market for the underlying collateral. Next, investors evaluate several key areas pertinent to each transaction. We have outlined a number of these areas and an approach to evaluating each one:

Originator/Servicer/Portfolio Manager

Most investors focus first on the abilities of the asset manager or servicer. In arbitrage (investor-driven) CLO/CBO transactions, this analysis is crucial to establish potential manager risk from poor market timing and valuation decisions. In most balance sheet (issuer-driven) CLOs, much of the credit hinges on the issuing bank's ratings and its reputation risk if actions in the portfolio were to prove sour; thus, the question may arise whether the issuer is likely to intervene. Therefore, investors should feel comfortable with the quality and credit judgment of the issuing bank.

Structure Analysis/Credit Enhancement Review

After the investor is satisfied with the abilities of the portfolio manager or originator/servicer, the structure and attendant credit enhancement should receive solid scrutiny to ascertain cash flow waterfalls[2] for interest and principal, prepayment conditions and triggers, the rights and roles of senior tranches and credit enhancement, reserve account requirements, and allocation methods for defaults and recoveries. Credit enhancement generally takes several forms including excess spread, surety wraps, reserve accounts, and subordinate pieces.

Collateral Credit Analysis

The extent and type of collateral analysis depends on the type of structure analyzed. In balance sheet CLO transactions, portfolio collateral tends to be less heterogeneous and of higher quality than in investor-driven transactions and underlying assets trade less frequently, if at all. Therefore, investors need to focus on three areas: underwriting criteria and skills, portfolio heterogeneity, and actions undertaken on behalf of asset-backed holders in the event of default. Underwriting quality and parameters are fundamental to this analysis, but investors need to feel comfortable with the originating bank's approach, its markets, and its skill in curing defaults. Many of these CLO transactions have "lumpy" collateral. In many cases, the investors purchase increments smaller than the average loan size, and therefore, depend on the issuer's skill in selecting a diverse pool of loans. Conversely, in arbitrage-type CLO/CBOs, the collateral is generally traded and is unlikely to remain the same from period to period. Therefore, investors should examine the investment parameters and restrictions on the portfolio manager and his track record with similar constraints.

---

[2] "Cash flow waterfall" is a descriptive term in asset-backed securities used to refer to the allocation of interest and principal to each tranche in a series. If excess cash flows are allowed to be shared with other series, then the cash flows are reallocated through the "waterfall," cascading back through the tranches.

Weighted-Average Credit Rating and Maturity

As part of CLO and CBO reviews, investors focus next on loss rates that could stress the portfolio. This analysis determines the proper size of the credit enhancement, but also points out stress scenarios that may trigger early-amortization events. Under early amortization, investors may face reinvestment risk as the portfolio pays out. Therefore, several default scenarios should be run, examining the effect of the credit enhancement and on the prepayment triggers.

Prepayment events would not be as highly correlated with interest rates as negatively convex products such as mortgage passthroughs, but a recessionary environment may cause credit deterioration while prompting declining interest rates. Compounding the issue may be embedded calls by issuers. Therefore, investors should review these events in light of several interest rate scenarios in their cash flow analysis.

Default Analysis

We recommend that investors use a combination of Moody's and Standard & Poor's approaches to develop default scenarios. Both approaches segregate the two underlying factors fundamental to default analysis: (1) probably of default, and (2) severity. While the first factor is easy to conceptualize, the latter incorporates recovery rates by asset type (senior bank loans rank higher in priority after defaults and therefore have higher recovery rates than unsecured debt, for example). This second variable may be expanded or contracted based on economic outlook. However, the combination of probability and severity determine cash flows within the trust and may accelerate or extend the expected maturity.

Another component of the Moody's approach incorporates a diversity score, in an attempt to evaluate the underlying collinearity of the credits in the pool. Each credit in the portfolio is classified by industry groupings — a total of 32 groups under the Moody's model — which are loosely correlated. For the first credit in each industry group, a certain value is assigned. Each subsequent credit in the same industry is assigned a diminishing value. For example, five different credits in five different industries may be each assigned a value of one point for a total diversity score of 5.00 points. Each second credit added to each industry may be assigned a value of 0.50 points, and each third credit added to an industry group may be assigned a value of 0.25 points, and so on.

A higher value in this diversity index indicates greater diversity within the underlying collateral pool. Balance sheet transactions are constructed to obtain greater diversity than arbitrage deals, because they are less actively managed. Typically, balance sheet deals have indexes of 70-80, while arbitrage deals typically start with indexes of 35-40. Investors should be cautious about relying only on diversity scores because diversity scores are not dollar-weighted and may lead to credit concentrations despite the appearance of a balanced portfolio; therefore, investors should ascertain and evaluate portfolio exposure limits to any one industry or credit. While most transactions do not let investors monitor individual credits in the managed pool, investors can and should monitor diversity scores and adherence to portfolio guidelines.

A recent innovation with CBOs is to establish single industry concentrations, as portfolio managers with industry specialties may outperform broader portfolio management styles. While this concentration may pose greater benefits for the subordinate class in a CBO, the senior tranche becomes exposed to greater risk through reliance on a single industry to perform as expected. Therefore, the typical single-industry CBOs should retain more protection for the senior classes than multiple-industry CBOs.

Cash Flow Analysis

Incorporating many of the default parameters and remedies, investors generally next focus on cash flow scenario analysis, ensuring that the effects of cash flow waterfalls in normal and distressed scenarios are tested and compared against total returns in varying interest rate scenarios. While this process is generally less vigorous for floating-rate transactions than for fixed-rate ones, investors look at forward rates to determine reinvestment risk expectations.

Other Considerations

For many transactions, investors consider the implications of other features, such as prepayment triggers for ratings or default changes, bankruptcy remoteness of the vehicles, dependence on issuer ratings, prefunding amounts, whether CBO securities are callable and by whom, and rights for investors under stressful scenarios to change portfolio managers or to collapse the structure.

BALANCE SHEET- DRIVEN CLO MARKET: OFFERING A CAPITAL AND MARKET ARBITRAGE FOR BANKS

The CLO market has undergone tremendous growth as banks have sought to arbitrage their risk-based capital requirements for markets where investors require less equity. While banks have other constraints such as tax, legal, confidentiality, and accounting practices, the primary driver for issuers lies in the capital required to support loans. Many of the structures target 2%-3% "capital" through the sale of a junior tranche or retention of the seller's equity piece.

In bank balance sheet securitizations, issuers structure the CLO to obtain regulatory and/or GAAP capital relief, targeting 2%-3% "equity" versus 8% for on balance sheet. Under Bank of International Settlements (BIS) risk-based capital requirements, banks must hold capital against assets based on risk weighting. Currently, banks must hold 8% Tier I capital (a combination of tangible common equity and certain types of preferred securities) against loans, which are counted with a 100% risk weighting.

In the United States, the Federal Financial Institutions Examination Council recently proposed changing the capital allocation rules for banks holding investment-grade and other rated securities. This change may accelerate the development of these securitizations because of banks' ability to arbitrage the capital rules for loans. To generate a 15% return for shareholders, a bank using an 8% equity-to-assets ratio must produce a 1.2% return on assets. If banks are able to hold a 20% risk asset for a AAA-rated CLO versus a 100% risk asset for a loan, the required return drops from 1.2% to 0.3% on regulatory accounting principles (RAP) assets. This lower funding cost enables banks to rechannel resources to seek out higher-risk assets for origination and portfolio.

Credit-Linked Notes: Regulatory Relief But No GAAP Benefit

Recently, the traditional CLO market began to include new asset types such as derivatives and fee receivables. Many of these exposures are linked to the trust through credit-linked notes rather than a true sale of assets. This sale of notes provides Regulatory Accounting Principles (RAP) capital relief, but offers no GAAP benefit. However, other benefits (see Exhibit 6), such as no borrower approval requirements, create for issuers a simpler and cleaner structure than that of traditional CLOs. These structures are similar to issuer-offered credit derivatives, but allow for a blended "sale" of exposure in an investor-blind pool.

SBC Warburg launched the first of these synthetic CLOs in 1997 with a $1.7 billion offering of a vehicle known as SBC Glacier Finance Ltd. (see Exhibit 7). Through the offering, SBC Warburg sold credit exposure to a portfolio referenced to more than 100 of its investment-grade borrowers in a 5-tranche structure. This structure references credit exposures through the trust, rather than sell participations in bank loans in the traditional structure. In both structures, investors bear risk to the pooled risk, but, for the credit-linked notes structure, they do not own the bank loans, merely the references to them. No "true-sale" opinion, which is critical to obtaining off-balance sheet treatment for GAAP purposes, may be obtained because the credit-linked notes reference the loans as opposed to owning an interest in them. Therefore, the strength and ratings of credit-linked notes structure depend heavily on the strength and ratings of the issuer.

Exhibit 6: Credit-Linked Note Sale to Issuers — Advantages and Disadvantages

Advantages	Disadvantages
BIS capital relief	Rating linked to originator/issuer
Administratively simple/flexible	Unsecured debt capacity diminished
Funding costs comparable to a participation-interest CLO	Structure only for highly rated banks
	More expensive than "true sale" CLO
No borrower notification requirement	No GAAP benefit

Source: Citicorp Securities Inc.

Exhibit 7: SBC Glacier Finance Ltd. — Credit-Linked Note Program Structure

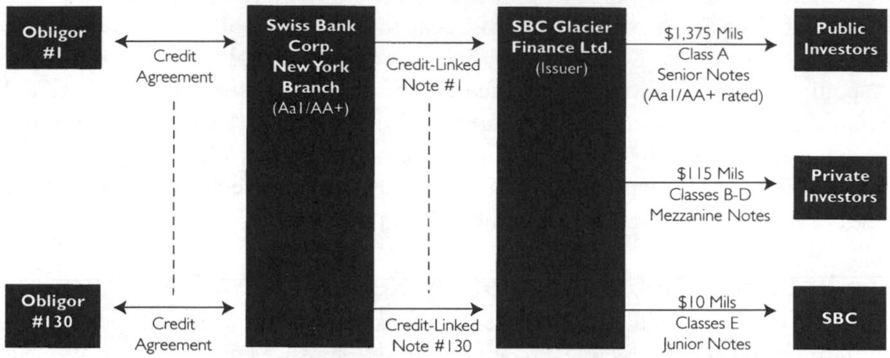

CONCLUSION

Investors looking to gain exposure to alternative market sectors or asset classes can use CBOs or CLOs to create cost-effective returns from these markets. Using a portfolio manager to focus on a particular sector where the investor lacks expertise can improve yields, without incurring incremental costs to establish and maintain large infrastructures to manage alternative investment risk. Accordingly, high-grade investors can access incremental yields through this market without incurring substantial incremental risk.

Chapter 19

Utility Stranded Costs Securitization

Charles N. Schorin
Principal
Director of ABS Research
Morgan Stanley

Kevin Roach
Principal
Corporate Bond Research
Morgan Stanley

INTRODUCTION

The term stranded costs refers to utility company investments, principally in power generation projects, made in a regulated environment that are likely to be uneconomical in a deregulated competitive market. These investments include power generating plants and related tax assets, power purchase contracts, and remnants of public policy programs. Utility companies made many of these investments in response to energy shortages in the 1970s, when their regulators mandated them to seek alternative sources of power. While these costs would be recoverable in a regulated environment, they generally would not in a competitive market — hence, the term "stranded." Securitization can accelerate the recovery of these costs, and facilitate a utility's transition to a competitive marketplace.

As part of the restructuring of respective state's utilities, the companies will submit plans to their regulators for charging and securitizing their stranded costs. These charges are often referred to as competitive transition charges (CTCs). The utility presents a rate plan that shows that customers would achieve lower utility rates. The rate reduction is achievable because securitization allows the utility to lower its overall cost of capital, by substituting relatively costly equity and corporate debt with less expensive secured, AAA-rated asset-backed securities.

This chapter provides the fundamentals of stranded asset securitization. We first examine the legislation that provides for the restructuring and then turn to the securitization. Issues involved with securitization include cash flow stability, credit enhancement, legal structure, servicing and use of proceeds. We then consider stranded costs in the ABS arena and turn to some remaining uncertainties and risks. Finally, we look at some other securitizations with which to compare the stranded costs transactions.

LEGISLATION

The Energy Policy Act of 1992 authorized the Federal Energy Regulatory Commission to order transmission-owning utilities to provide wholesale transmission service to new competing generators. This opened up wholesale markets and interstate transmission networks to competition. State regulators are now examining retail competition on a state-by-state basis. The result will be permitting customers to choose power suppliers and, perhaps, an unbundling of the power generation, transmission and distribution processes.

States that have passed restructuring legislation that creates the ability to securitize stranded costs include California, Pennsylvania, Illinois, Massachusetts, Rhode Island, and Montana. States that currently are considering legislation in various forms include Michigan, New Hampshire, New York, Ohio, and New Jersey, of which all are looking at stranded cost recovery via securitization. California, Massachusetts, and Illinois laws all specify rate cuts of 10% to 15%, which is to be generated in part by securitization savings. Pennsylvania law allows the regulators to determine the appropriate rate cut, but requires savings from securitization to be passed along to customers.

The key element of legislation pertaining to securitization is that it converts a regulatory asset[1] into a statutory asset. The regulatory asset in this case arises from the decision by the regulatory body to allow utilities to recover some of their stranded assets. The statutory asset, however, specifically establishes the property rights to the assets, provides for these rights to be transferred or assigned and commits future regulatory commissions to honor these rights. This statutory asset is intangible property separate and distinct from any physical generation plant assets. These property rights will ultimately be assigned to a special purpose vehicle that will issue the ABS.

The legislation also explicitly provides for securitization as a mechanism for recovering the stranded costs, as well as for the competition transition charge — the CTC — to be explicitly carved out of ratepayers' bills to service the debt. The CTC generally would be based on customer usage (charge per kilowatt hour) or capacity, but could be a flat charge per customer. The charge is non-bypassable, meaning that if a customer switches power generation companies (but remains on the same distribution line), the second company must collect the CTC on behalf of the first. With the expense of their uneconomic investments recovered, utilities are in a position to pass on certain savings in the form of lower rates to customers, as well as perhaps a rate cap for a specified period of time. Note that despite sometimes being referred to as a tariff, the CTC is carved out of customers' current bills — it is *not* an add-on charge or surcharge.

---

[1] The term "regulatory asset" is used here in its non-technical sense to include the uneconomic portion of generation plant assets and long term power purchase contracts. Typically, the term "regulatory asset" is used to refer to certain deferred taxes and charges that are present on a utility's balance sheet due to their inclusion in the rate base by regulation.

Exhibit 1: Electric Utility Usage has Grown at a Remarkably Stable Rate Through Various Economic Environments

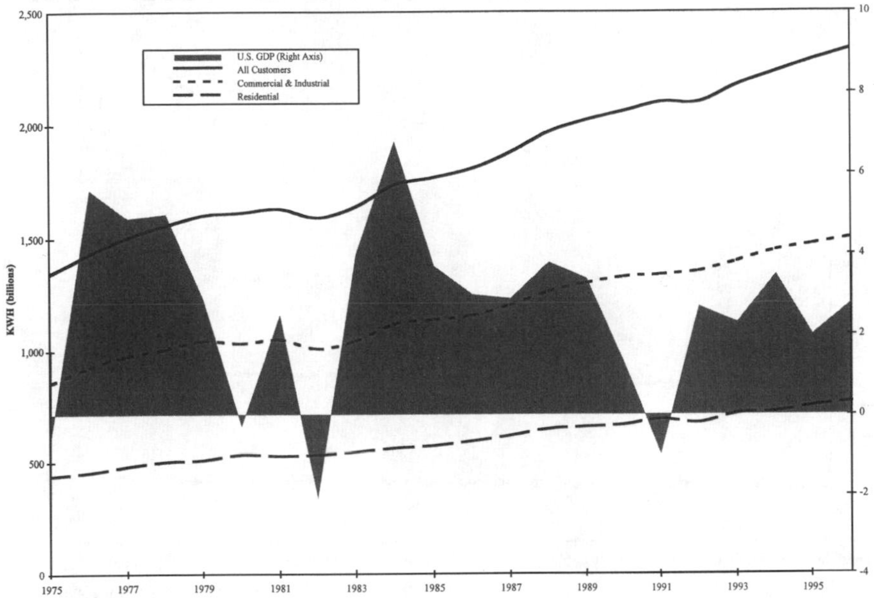

Source: Edison Electric Institute, *Statistical Yearbook of the Electric Utility Industry 1996*

Legislation also generally provides for a "true-up" mechanism, by which the CTC could be adjusted periodically — once a year in the case of California — in the event that CTC collections deviate from those projected. This will ensure that cash flows to the bondholder will remain intact and very stable.

SECURITIZATION

Transactions backed by stranded assets are likely to have final maturities of 10 to 15 years, with 5- to 8-year average lives. The cash flows probably will be tranched to provide investors with various short, intermediate, and long average life bonds. The bonds should be amortizing securities and could be either fixed or floating rate.

Cash flows generated from utilities' customers tend to be extremely stable. Exhibit 1 shows energy sales by investor-owned utilities in terms of kilowatt hours, compared to changes in U.S. real gross domestic product (GDP). The total sales data — labeled "all customers" in Exhibit 1 — are broken down into residential and commercial and industrial use. It is clear that through various economic scenarios — both expansion and recession — energy usage has grown at a remarkably stable rate. This has clear positive implications for securitizing charges of utility customers.

Exhibit 2: Average Annual Kilowatt Use Per Customer Has Been Very Steady

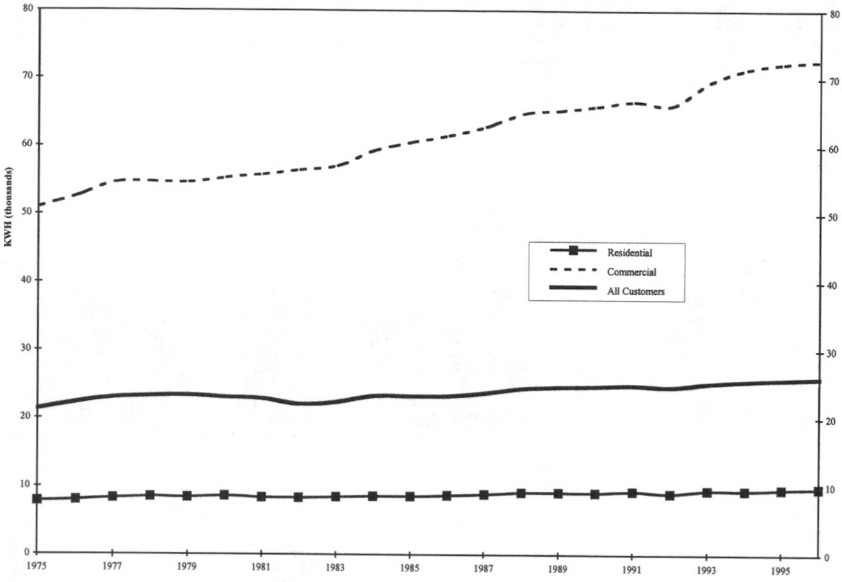

Source: Edison Electric Institute, *Statistical Yearbook of the Electric Utility Industry 1996*

It also is noteworthy that usage per customer has been remarkably steady (Exhibit 2). This suggests that if the utility can forecast the *number* of users — which should be relatively straightforward, given population trends and economic cycles — it should be able to forecast t*otal usage* very accurately.

The stable underlying cash flows from customer utility bills should result in positive convexity for the asset-backed securities. This is because whatever the seasonal variation in utility usage over the course of a year or change in the pattern of power consumption over time, it is not related to interest rates. This would make stranded cost securitizations one of the few amortizing assets that would actually reduce the negative convexity of investors' portfolios.

Credit Enhancement

Credit enhancement will be provided predominantly through the periodic adjustment of the transition charges to ensure timely recovery of the transition costs and payment in full of interest and principal on the securities — the true-up mechanism. Since the transition charge is based on energy consumption, shortfalls in required collections will be adjusted by increasing the kilowatt per hour charge to customers or increasing the allocation of the existing CTC to ABS bondholders.

Also, credit enhancement is expected to be in the form of quite modest over-collateralization, because the payment histories of the utilities exhibit extreme stability and low losses. Note that this enhancement effectively is supporting just the longest tranche in the deal for just the last year of the transaction's life, since potential shortfalls in years prior to the last would be corrected by turning to the true-up mechanism and increasing the CTC. In addition to the tune-up mechanism and overcollateralization, there are likely to be reserve accounts and capital accounts to provide for intra-year cash flow stability. The reserve fund would absorb payments in excess of schedule, as the average life of the securities does not shorten. The capital account would be funded upfront and provide cash to investors in the event payments are less than scheduled, so the average life of the securities does not extend.

In contrast to most new asset classes, where collateral performance data usually is minimal, utilities generally possess decades of customer payment histories on their collateral. Utilities also have the ability to discontinue customer service for failure of customers to pay their bills, providing them with substantial leverage over customers. Finally, legislatively imposed exit fees make it very difficult for customers who leave a utility's generation service to escape its tariff. Customer migration is probably only a risk pertaining to the largest users.

Legal Structure

Utilities will attempt to achieve non-recourse financing, with a true sale for bankruptcy purposes and debt-for-tax treatment.[2] One stumbling block for accounting sale treatment is the Securities and Exchange Commission (SEC). Three large California utilities — Pacific Gas & Electric, Southern California Edison and San Diego Gas & Electric — requested sale treatment for their prospective asset backed securitizations. The SEC denied their request, citing the lack of a contractual obligation between utility customers paying their bills and the utility receiving the payments. On the bright side for the utilities, not receiving sale treatment makes it easier for them to obtain a debt-for-tax opinion.

The credit implication of not receiving accounting sale treatment is that utilities typically will show more leverage than would be the case if they were allowed sale treatment, assuming that securitization proceeds are used in part to reduce equity. Even without receiving accounting sale treatment, however, the special purpose vehicles issuing the securities would still be bankruptcy remote from the utility. This is achievable because the legislation creating the statutory asset deemed the asset as property. That, coupled with the usual ABS type of legal bankruptcy opinion that considers whether the utility retains an economic benefit or risk and whether the transaction is more of a sale or financing, would result in bankruptcy remoteness. Note that ratings agencies require a very strong bankruptcy opinion for them to confer a AAA rating on the asset backed security. The secured, bankruptcy remote structure of the financing should enable rating agencies to exclude this debt from their corporate financial ratio analysis. The eco-

---

[2] "Debt-for-tax" stated more formally is "debt financing for tax purposes."

nomic result of the transaction, rather than the accounting result, should drive credit analysis.[3,4] We expect the economic result to be positive for most utilities.

Debt-for-tax treatment would allow the utility to avoid an upfront tax associated with the securitization. Each utility is expected to establish a bankruptcy remote special purpose corporation to facilitate the issuance of the securities at a higher rating level than the utility. Whereas most utilities are rated in the neighborhood of A-to-BBB, the asset backed transactions will seek AAA ratings.

Servicing

Utilities are expected to perform their own servicing. This should provide the most efficient servicing, since the utilities already are collecting payments from their ratepayers. Utilities should receive a fee for servicing that is sufficient to compensate a substitute servicer, if necessary.

Use of Proceeds

Proceeds from the securitization could be used for general corporate purposes, but the use most beneficial would likely be to shrink its capital structure — this is specified in the Pennsylvania and Illinois legislation. Most utilities are financed 50%-50% with equity and debt. A securitization would raise funds that would allow the utility to pay off some of its relatively high cost corporate debt, as well as engage in a stock buyback program.

STRANDED COSTS IN THE ABS ARENA

Stranded asset securitization will be about $6 billion in 1997. The first transaction was a $2.9 billion securitization by Pacific Gas & Electric in November 1997. The other two large Californian utilities — Southern California Edison and San Diego Gas & Electric — came to market in November 1997 with transactions totalling $3.1 billion.The big surge in output probably will not occur until 1998, when utilities in Pennsylvania, New Jersey, Illinois, and Michigan may come to market. Issuance in 1998 will likely be on the order of $15-20 billion. Even conservative estimates of stranded asset securitization would result in a significant asset class, comparable in size to manufactured housing and student loans, and in future years comparable to credit card, automobile, and home equity loans.

---

[3] Standard & Poor's recently stated that it "will make adjustments to recognize the economic, as opposed to the accounting, reality. If structured as a 'true sale' for legal purposes, associated nonrecourse debt and carrying costs associated with stranded assets will be backed out of utilities' financial statements for analytical purposes." Standard & Poor's *CreditWire*, "SEC Rejects FAS 125 for Electric Utility Stranded Assets," February 26, 1997.

[4] Moody's, however, warns that utility corporate bondholders could be worse off if securitization proceeds dilute remaining cash flows. Moody's Investors Service, "Stranded Utility Investments Can Support Highly Rated Structured Transactions," March 19, 1997.

Stranded asset ABS would most probably trade similar to securitized automobile loans and credit cards. The resemblance to auto loan ABS is due to the amortizing nature of the stranded assets, without interest rate sensitivity. The analogy to credit cards is based on their extremely predictable cash flows, although the utilities represent a better credit asset.

These securities should have excellent liquidity owing to the large size of the transactions. There are 37 utilities in the United States with estimated stranded costs exceeding $1 billion. If a utility has in excess of $1 billion in stranded costs, even if the entire amount is not securitizable or is securitized in more than a single transaction, there should be excellent liquidity in its product.

UNCERTAINTIES

Despite extremely stable, predictable and high quality cash flows, there are some risks and uncertainties with stranded cost securitization. One is the risk that future legislation may repeal or cut back on the allowable carve out of CTCs from utility bills. Investors should look toward states that have explicitly and strongly pledged through their enabling legislation that stranded costs will be funded in the future. In addition, to the extent that consumers' utility bills are lowered via competition and utilities are able to write down their stranded costs, it is unlikely that there would be political motivation to overturn the carve outs.

Another risk is that there could be a dramatic change in energy consumption, due either to the exodus of a large portion of a state's population or to the development of an alternative energy source that causes demand for electric utility output to plummet. As for the former, the tune-up mechanism provided in the legislation adjusts the rates that consumers pay to make up for reduced electricity demand. As for new energy sources, this should be more of a concern over a longer period of time. Most of the utility transactions are expected to have 10 to 15 year final maturities, and while it cannot be ruled out, it is unlikely that there will be an alternative energy source that would largely supplant electric utility production over the next 10-15 years.

PREVIOUS TRANSACTIONS

The previous transaction that most closely approximates the stranded costs securitizations is the Puget Sound Power & Light deal in 1995. This was a $202 million pass-through securitizing customer charges for utility conservation expenditures, not recovery of stranded costs. The State of Washington passed legislation in 1994 permitting utilities to finance new or existing conservation expenditures that were approved by the Washington Utilities and Transportation Commission. The legislation provides for a true-up mechanism if collected amounts varied by more than 2% from the amount necessary to pay down the bonds on schedule. It also makes the rights of the bondholders irrevocable for as long as the bonds are outstanding.[5]

Two other transactions did allow for stranded costs recovery. These were bonds issued to recover costs resulting from Italian and Spanish nuclear moratoria and issued by Orchid Securities, Ltd. and Fondo de Titulazacion de Activos Resultantes de la Moratoria Nuclear, respectively. Unlike the prospective transactions in the United States, the Italian and Spanish bonds securitize customer surcharges, rather than carve outs of existing bills. Whereas Puget Sound and Orchid were enhanced primarily by overcollateralization, the Spanish nuclear moratorium bonds are guaranteed by the Republic of Spain.

Another utility transaction involved securitizing customer utility bills from Cleveland Electric Illuminating Company and Toledo Edison Company, which are wholly owned by Centerior Energy Corp. This, however, was not a stranded assets transaction, but rather involved securitizing revolving trade receivables from customers' entire utility bills. The purpose, as with any non-utility receivables securitization, was to monetize future cash flow. This deal sometimes is mentioned in the same breath as the stranded assets deals simply because it involved a utility.

CONCLUSION

Deregulation of the utility industry will create a new asset class for the ABS market. Securitization of utilities' stranded assets is likely to be on the order of $50-$75 billion by the turn of the century, rivaling in size the major asset classes of the ABS market.

The legislative mandate, cash flow stability, true-up mechanism, collateral quality, and transaction sizes should allow stranded costs asset backeds to trade at levels comparable to auto loan and credit card ABS.

---

[5] Fitch Investors Service, "Guidelines for Rating Debt Backed by Regulatory Assets," *Structured Finance Special Report*, September 30, 1996.

Chapter 20

Catastrophe-Linked Securities

Sunita Ganapati
Associate
Lehman Brothers

Mark Retik
Associate
Lehman Brothers

Paul Puleo
Senior Vice President
Lehman Brothers

Beth Starr
Senior Vice President
Lehman Brothers

INTRODUCTION

Catastrophe-linked securities (CLS), an emerging class of structured insurance risk products, offer returns that are linked to the occurrence of catastrophic events such as earthquakes and hurricanes. These securities can provide investors with diversification from corporate and asset-backed securities at comparable or wider spreads. Issued through special-purpose vehicles, these securities offer an opportunity to participate directly in catastrophe risk without having to assume the operational risks inherent in securities issued by property and casualty insurance and reinsurance companies that underwrite this risk. Investing in "pure" catastrophe risk can also improve the risk/return profile of a diversified portfolio of assets because this risk is generally uncorrelated with the systematic risks present in other securities markets.

An outgrowth of the need for additional reinsurance capacity following Hurricane Andrew (1992) and the Northridge Earthquake (1994), which in combination produced $29 billion in industrywide insured losses,[1] CLS provide insurers with a new form of reinsurance protection. In exchange for a reinsurance premium (i.e., interest on the securities), investors assume financial exposure to the risk that a catastrophe will strike and will generate insured losses above a certain

[1] A.M. Best.

level. If such a catastrophe occurs, CLS investors would receive a reduced yield and/or lose part or all of their principal, and the insurer would receive a reinsurance claim payment. By transferring catastrophe risks to the capital markets in this manner, insurance companies are supplementing their use of traditional reinsurance and internal loss management mechanisms to reduce volatility in their financial statements and preserve overall liquidity.

As the CLS market develops, we believe that spreads will tighten considerably, similar to the way corporate high yield spreads have responded as that market has matured. Tightening will result as liquidity increases in the market and CLS investors become increasingly sophisticated at valuing catastrophe risk.

In this chapter, we discuss catastrophes and the role that reinsurance has traditionally played in mitigating catastrophic losses. We describe developments in the capital markets that have led to catastrophe risk securitization and outline typical CLS structures. We then discuss the use of simulation models to conduct CLS analysis and consider related rating agency approaches. Finally, we provide a framework for assessing relative valuation and offer our outlook for this emerging asset class.

CATASTROPHE RISK MANAGEMENT

Economic Impact of Catastrophes

Catastrophes are low probability natural events that cause widespread property damage; they include earthquakes, hurricanes, hailstorms, and floods. (Appendix A provides a description of earthquakes and hurricanes, the two types of catastrophes that have historically caused the most insured losses.) Though the timing of a catastrophe is inherently unpredictable, the insurance industry uses sophisticated mathematical models to estimate the probability of occurrence of an event and expected losses.

Insured losses from catastrophes have been increasing since 1970 (see Exhibit 1), coinciding with population migration toward high-risk coastal regions during the same period. From 1970 to 1990, population in the Pacific and South Atlantic coastal states increased by 51% and 45%, respectively, far more than the countrywide increase of 24% over the same period.[2] This population shift has increased the demand for insured dwellings in these areas and consequently has increased the potential for insured loss.

After Hurricane Andrew in 1992, the insurance industry took various measures to counter increased exposure to losses. Major U.S. personal lines insurers attempted to reduce their risk concentration by limiting issuance of new policies in high risk areas. Additional measures included increases in policy premiums and deductibles. Insurers also sought to hedge their balance sheets and earnings against catastrophes by increasing coverage from traditional reinsurance and exploring other financial alternatives, particularly for low probability, high severity events.

---

[2] *Statistical Abstract of the U.S.*, 1992, National Data Book.

Exhibit 1: Industrywide Insured Issues, 1970-1996

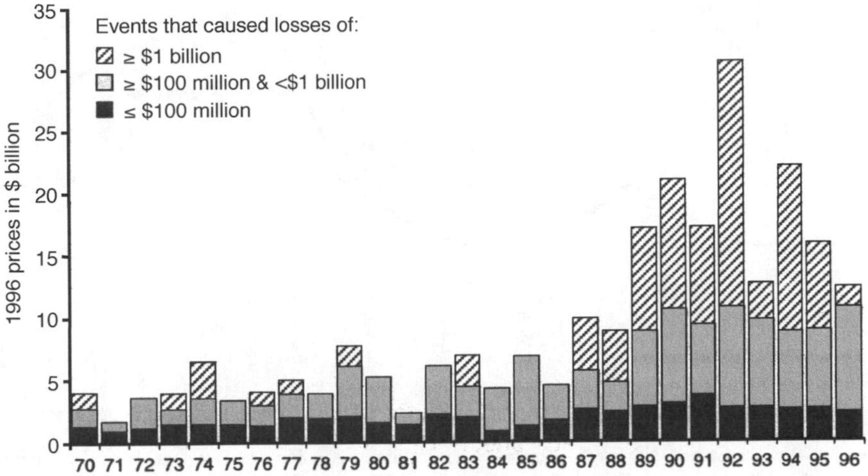

Source: Swiss Re, sigma no. 3/1997.

Exhibit 2: Key Reinsurance Terms

Excess-of-loss contracts cover against losses over an *attachment point*, up to a predetermined limit. For example, a reinsurance contract with an attachment point of $100 million and a limit of $150 million covers the insurance company for the first $50 million of losses in excess of $100 million.

Quota-share or pro-rata contracts provide coverage against a predetermined percent of catastrophic losses. Under this type of agreement, the reinsurer assumes a percentage of the insurance company's premiums and losses.

Retention is the amount of losses for which the primary insurer is responsible — $100 million in the preceding example.

Exposure is the amount ceded to the reinsurer — $50 million in the preceding example.

Rate-on-line is the premium paid by the insurer to purchase reinsurance as a percentage of the exposure.

Traditional Reinsurance

Reinsurance gives an insurer the ability to transfer risk with the primary purpose of either smoothing its income stream or protecting its balance sheet. Catastrophe management is an essential component of a reinsurance program for large property insurers. Risk can be transferred in one of two ways — excess-of-loss reinsurance and quota-share or pro rata reinsurance. Exhibit 2 provides a summary of key reinsurance terms. Catastrophe reinsurance is typically written on an excess-of-loss basis.

Exhibit 3: Paragon Catastrophe Price Index, 1984-July 1996

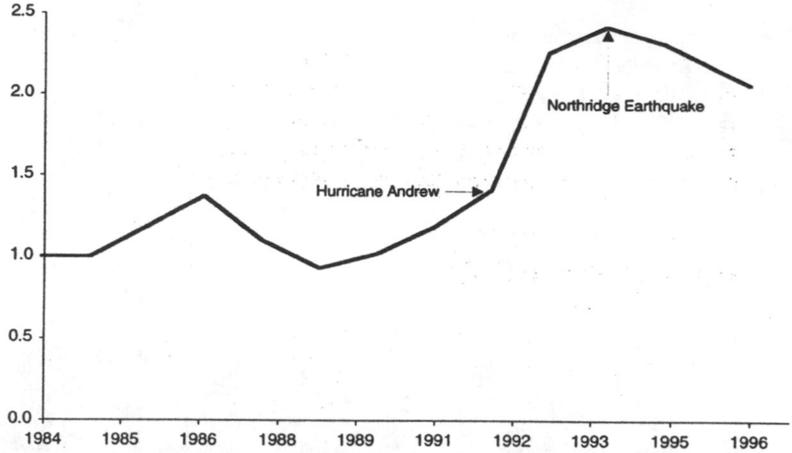

Note: The Paragon Catastrophe Price Index reflects reinsurance premiums of 300 companies and includes an estimated 60% of insurance industry premiums.

After Hurricane Andrew, reinsurance companies changed the structure of contracts by raising their attachment points, and capping their aggregate exposures, thus reducing the overall amount of coverage provided. At the same time, insurers were seeking increased reinsurance coverage. This raised reinsurance pricing above historical levels in the early 1990s as shown by the Paragon Catastrophe Price Index (see Exhibit 3). However, reinsurance premiums have been falling since 1994 with the additional capacity injected by Bermuda reinsurers (see Appendix B for a discussion of Bermuda reinsurers) and the re-entry of Lloyd's syndicates into the reinsurance market. Further, no single catastrophe has caused extraordinary losses (such as Hurricane Andrew or the Northridge earthquake) since 1994. However, initial indications are that reinsurance capacity today is still inadequate to meet potential losses from large catastrophes; the shortfall in reinsurance is estimated at $30-$50 billion for an event that causes $60-$80 billion[3] in insured losses. As a result, many insurance companies need to supplement the capacity of the current reinsurance market with the capacity potentially available in the capital markets (the estimated size of the fixed income markets is $10 trillion[4]).

Catastrophe Risk Layers

Catastrophe risk can be viewed as composed of layers of risk from events with decreasing probability of occurrence and increasing magnitude of losses. Sophisticated modeling efforts have shown that catastrophic events occur in random intervals of time and less severe catastrophes occur with more frequency. Risk

[3] Lehman Brothers estimate.

[4] Estimate based on market value of the Lehman Brothers Global Family of Indices.

management of catastrophe losses varies from one insurer to another. Exhibit 4 shows a probability distribution of insured losses and the sources of risk capital that an insurer may use to manage its catastrophe exposure.

Catastrophes resulting in gross insured losses of less than 5% of a major property insurer's statutory surplus, occur frequently and are assumed to be part of the normal course of business. Losses from these events are absorbed by an insurer's operating cash flow, policyholders' surplus, or "working layer" reinsurance program. Events that cause losses between 5% and 10% of surplus are generally covered by purchasing traditional reinsurance contracts.

As insurers have increased use of advanced catastrophe modeling to predict losses, they have tended to purchase coverage equal to their probable loss under a severe loss scenario or, at a minimum, for losses in excess of 10% of their capital. However, large insurers find that protecting their balance sheet against an infrequent but large catastrophe is currently priced too high due to lack of capacity in the reinsurance industry for covering this type of risk. Hence, insurers are seeking capital market solutions to bridge this gap in capacity and to create a more efficient risk transfer mechanism.

RECENT CAPITAL MARKETS DEVELOPMENTS

As insurers explore alternative solutions for gaining additional reinsurance coverage, they have participated in several creative capital market developments including government initiatives, exchange-traded derivatives, and CLS.

Exhibit 4: An Illustration of Insurer Catastrophe Risk Management

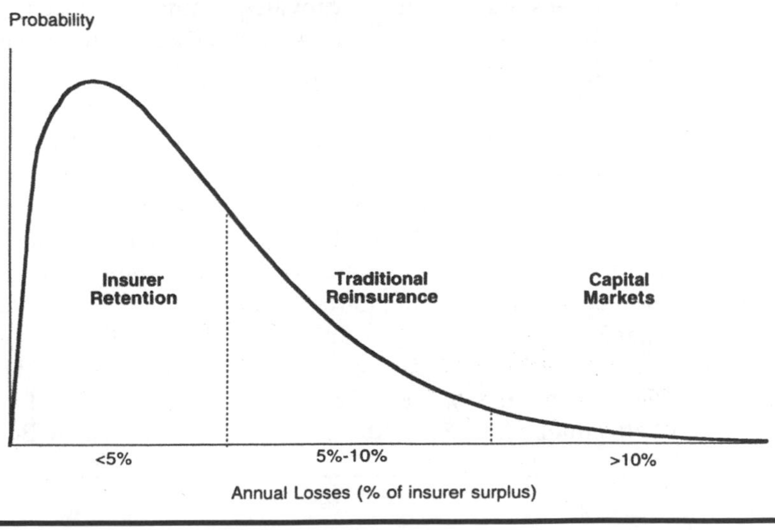

Government Initiatives

In response to reduced property insurance availability after Hurricane Andrew, the U.S. and state governments created various funds to provide additional capacity in the event of a catastrophe. These include the Florida Hurricane Catastrophe Fund, the California Earthquake Authority, the Hawaii Hurricane Relief Fund, and others. These funds are set up to access the capital markets immediately after an event to provide additional funding either directly to homeowners or to insurance companies.

The California Earthquake Authority (CEA) is the largest of these funds, providing up to $12.5 billion of support to insurers in California. The program was designed to include a combination of letter of credit facilities, reinsurance policies directly from reinsurers, and the capital markets. In 1996 the CEA attempted to issue a catastrophe-linked security similar to the structure described in more detail below for an additional $1.5 billion of coverage in excess of $7 billion. Because of the high pricing of that issue relative to prevailing reinsurance rates, Berkshire Hathaway's reinsurance subsidiary purchased the entire transaction.

The Florida Hurricane Catastrophe Fund provides reinsurance capacity to all primary insurers writing homeowner policies in Florida. The fund collects annual premiums from these insurers and holds these payments for future claims. The fund intends to meet any additional capacity requirements following an event by raising capital in the fixed income markets. A bond issue after a substantial hurricane would be paid entirely by assessing surcharges on the primary insurers in Florida.

The Hawaii Hurricane Relief Fund took yet another approach. Because its funding needs are smaller than those of other states, it relies on a letter of credit syndicated through various commercial banks. This fund assesses homeowners directly, instead of assessing primary insurers as in Florida, and uses the assessments to repay any future draws on the letter of credit.

These special funds are expected to provide incremental capacity to the property-casualty industry and potentially bridge part of the gap in reinsurance supply.

Exchange-Traded Options and Swap Contracts

The introduction of exchange-traded catastrophe risk contracts in 1995 marked the entry of insurance risk products into the capital markets. Derivative contracts are offered on the Chicago Board of Trade (CBOT), Catex, and Bermuda Commodities Exchange. A description of the contracts appears in Appendix C.

These developments are meaningful steps in achieving incremental risk transfer for reinsurance, but the exchanges have so far met with limited success. Although trading volumes at the CBOT have grown over the last year, the total value of catastrophe exposure that has been hedged since the beginning of 1996 is estimated at only $40 million.[5] Trading on the Catex has been thin and the Bermuda

---

[5] Chicago Board of Trade.

Commodities Exchange was launched in November 1997. Lack of liquidity in the market, relatively small transaction size, and concerns about basis risk[6] have deterred insurance companies and potential investors from entering the market. These exchanges could develop into reasonable ways to supplement reinsurance if investors outside the insurance and reinsurance industry begin to participate.

Securitization of Catastrophe Risk

Securitizing insurance risk is the transfer or sale in the form of an investment security, of part of the underwriting risks associated with a group of insurance policies. Insurance companies expect that securitizing insurance risk will play a significant role in meeting the shortage in reinsurance capacity. Investing in CLS is akin to issuing a reinsurance contract where the investor covers the insurer for a fixed amount of losses over a specified value (the attachment point or trigger). Several issues of catastrophe-linked securities have been marketed in 1997, and approximately six issues have been placed in the private markets.

As with any new capital market product, structures are still evolving. The transactions that have been placed have had varying structures and have covered catastrophe and other types of insurance risk. Exhibit 5 provides a list of transactions.

STRUCTURE OF CATASTROPHE-LINKED SECURITIES

Catastrophe-linked securities are issued for an expected maturity with the payment of coupon and retirement of principal dependent on occurrence of a catastrophic event with losses greater than a specified trigger during a defined risk or loss-occurrence period. As in other asset-backed transactions, the issuer sets up a special purpose vehicle (SPV) that is bankruptcy remote. The vehicle is generally set up offshore for regulatory and tax reasons and issues securities that carry the risk of catastrophe losses over a specified level. It then issues a back-to-back reinsurance contract to the insurer, thus providing the reinsurance protection.

Exhibit 5: Transactions as of February 1998

Issuer/Sponsor	Deal Size	Securitized Risks
USAA Residential Re	$477 million	U.S. eastern seaboard hurricane risk
Hannover Re	$125 million	Various U.S., European, Japanese, Australian, and Canadian perils
Swiss Re	$137 million	California earthquake risk
Winterthur	$290 million	Weather-related automobile claims in Switzerland
St. Paul Re	$70 million	Various insurance risks in revolving facility

[6] Basis risk is the risk of exposure differences between the value of losses estimated by the underlying index such as the Property Claims Services index and the value of loss claims from the insurer's book of policies.

The security, like reinsurance, can be structured as a quota-share or an excess-of-loss issue. In the quota-share structure, the issuer shares with investors a fixed percentage of losses over the attachment point. A recently placed issue by Hannover Re was structured so that the risk of losses and ultimate returns on the company's entire portfolio over a predefined level was shared proportionately by investors and the issuer. In an excess-of-loss structure, investors absorb losses over the attachment point for the total amount of the issue (equivalent to exposure amount in a reinsurance contract). Such a structure was used in the USAA Residential Re transaction. By issuing a security with an excess-of-loss structure and retaining a portion of the security, issuers can also create hybrid structures.

The underlying catastrophe can either be one type of event, such as earthquakes as in the CEA deal, or a mix of events, as in the Hannover Re deal, which involved seven types of risk. Risks can be spread across geographic region, type of event, or underlying property type (residential, commercial, industrial, etc.). Only events that occur prior to the end of the specified loss occurrence period and result in losses in excess of the attachment point are considered loss events for the securities. Underlying losses in any specific transaction can be based either on the insurer's book of policies or on a basket of risks as measured, for example, by the PCS index.[7]

The SPV invests cash raised from the issue in high quality, liquid, fixed income instruments (typically U.S. Treasuries or AAA rated securities). This short-term portfolio is used to cover losses from events or to repay investors on maturity of the bond, and to provide a minimum rate of return (e.g., LIBOR, Treasury bill). The contract is structured like a cash-collateralized reinsurance contract, and unlike traditional reinsurance contracts, does not carry any credit risk of the reinsurer. The coupon on the CLS includes a spread over the minimum rate earned by the short-term portfolio. The insurer pays the spread to the SPV, which passes through the total coupon payment to investors (see Exhibit 6).

The maturity of the security is based on the period during which a loss event can occur, called the risk period (or the loss occurrence period), and the time for computation of losses, called the *development period*. The development period may be up to one year, during which time the company receives final claims, surveys its policyholders' properties and determines total damage claims. Typically, loss estimates 2 to 3 months after the catastrophe give an indication of whether losses from the event have exceeded the trigger. However, the actual amount of losses is determined after the development period (i.e., after final claims are received). The CLS may be structured with a fixed maturity after the end of the specified loss occurrence period that includes an estimated development period, or may have a scheduled maturity date that can be extended for a maximum period equal to the development period, thus exposing investors to some extension risk.

---

[7] The PCS index is described in Appendix C.

Exhibit 6: Illustrative CLS Structure

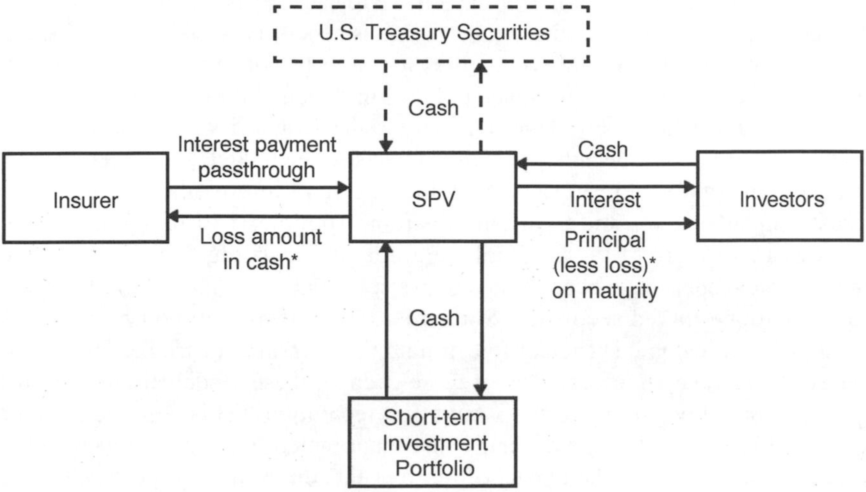

* In case of loss trigger.

To attract a wider investor base, some structures provide protection of principal, with only coupon at risk. This is accomplished by establishing a structural feature (as detailed in the dashed box in Exhibit 6) which provides the investor with U.S. Treasury STRIPS with a par value equal to the principal value of the CLS, upon occurrence of a qualifying catastrophe. The USAA Residential Re transaction included such a principal-protected structure. Since principal for these securities is backed by U.S. Treasuries, these securities will generally be rated higher than CLS with principal at risk. Nevertheless, investors face the risk of earning little or no yield for the remaining period of the STRIPS. A related structure which has been considered involves swapping U.S. Treasury securities held by the SPV for surplus notes or equity of the insurer upon occurrence of a qualifying catastrophe.

SIMULATION MODELING OF CATASTROPHE-LINKED SECURITIES

Evaluating principal-at-risk catastrophe-linked securities is conceptually similar to evaluating other fixed income securities with a material risk of default, such as corporates or subordinated ABS. Estimating the performance of a particular security requires assessing the likelihood of default, and the loss of principal and interest associated with such a default. Default risk on a corporate bond is assessed by examining historical corporate default probabilities, industry- and issuer-specific credit considerations, and the security's relative position in the issuer's capital structure. Default risk on most asset-backed securities (such as those backed by credit card receivables, auto loans, etc.) is based on an actuarial analysis of a large pool of receivables.

Default on a catastrophe-linked security, on the other hand, is generally triggered by a catastrophe of sufficient magnitude to cause a specified level of losses on insured properties. To assess the default risk, it is necessary to estimate the likelihood and intensity of catastrophic events, the susceptibility of insured properties to the effects of these events, the insurance policies in effect, and the specific terms of the transaction. Each factor contributes uniquely to the default risk of the security.

Over the past decade, specialized catastrophe models have been developed to assist insurance and reinsurance companies and intermediaries in analyzing catastrophe exposures and in pricing insurance policies.[8] Virtually all reinsurers rely on one or more of these models to guide underwriting decisions.[9] In recent years, these models have been refined to assist in evaluating the prospect for default on catastrophe-linked securities. Since historical information on hurricanes and earthquakes alone is insufficient to estimate the current catastrophe loss potential (based on the relative infrequency of these events), these models use an alternative approach based on sophisticated simulation techniques. This approach simulates catastrophic events in terms of their constituent meteorological or seismic characteristics and determines the impact of these events on insured properties. Engineering and actuarial analyses are then used to estimate the level of catastrophe-related losses — expressed as a probability distribution — on each individual insured property for a given period of time. Running a large number of simulations ensures that the probability distribution of catastrophe losses will converge to a stable, representative distribution and therefore produce statistically robust results.

Modeling companies employ various methodologies to estimate catastrophe loss distributions, and techniques to estimate hurricanes are distinct from those used for earthquakes. However, a common set of elements is incorporated in all the models. Exhibit 7 shows how the parts of a catastrophe model fit together. We describe each part, discuss the resulting catastrophe loss distribution, and explore how these tools can assist investors in making prudent investment decisions.

Catastrophe Likelihood Model

The likelihood that a catastrophe will strike during the term of the catastrophe-linked security will directly affect the ultimate probability of security default (if a catastrophe does not occur then principal and interest will be fully preserved). The first step in the catastrophe model is to predict the likelihood of zero, one, or more catastrophes occurring in a given year. Historical data on catastrophe frequency, coupled with statistical smoothing techniques, are used to select an appropriate probability distribution and estimate its parameters. Most modeling companies use either Poisson or negative binomial distributions to estimate hurricane frequency. Exhibit 8 shows a sample distribution of annual hurricane occurrences for all categories of hurricane severity.

---

[8] Some of the specialized catastrophe modeling firms include Applied Insurance Research, Equecat, Impact Forecasting, Risk Management Solutions, and Tillinghast/Towers Perrin.

[9] One important implication of the widespread use of catastrophe models is that pricing of the debt and equity securities issued by insurers and reinsurers implicitly reflects the results of these models.

Exhibit 7: Catastrophe Model Schematic

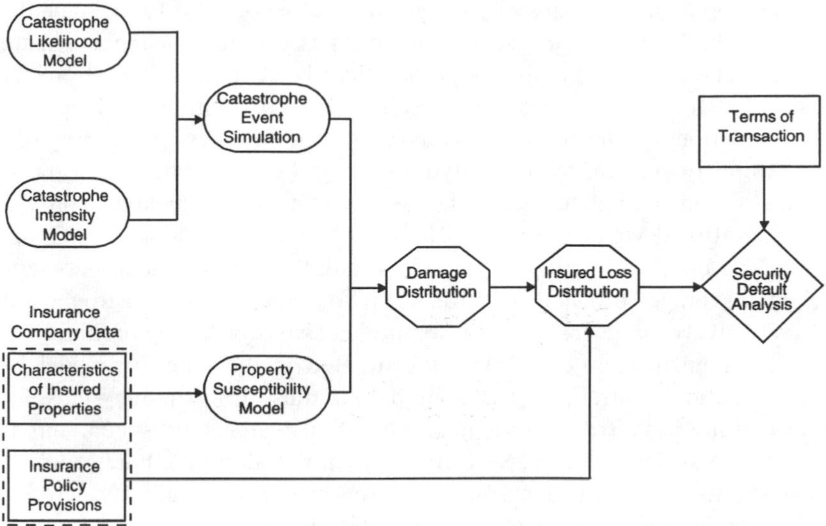

Exhibit 8: Sample Probability Distribution of Annual Number of Hurricane Occurrences

All Hurricane Strength Categories

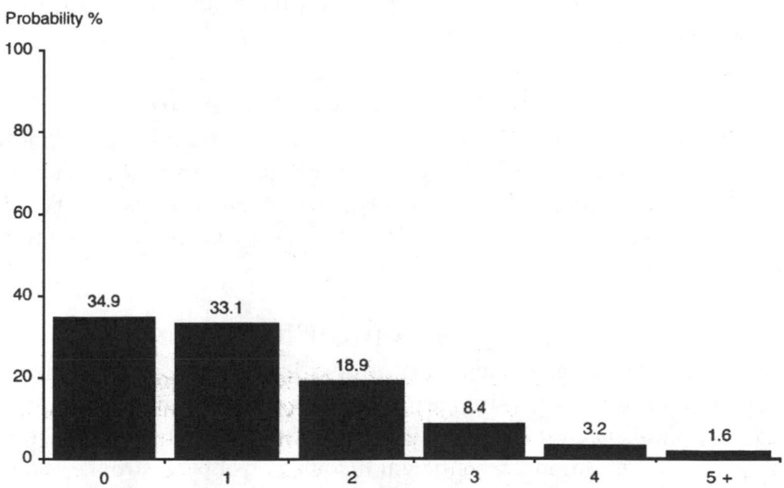

Note: This distribution of annual hurricane occurrences is depicted using a negative binomial distribution (with parameters s= 5 and p = 0.81).

Catastrophe Intensity Model

The catastrophe intensity model predicts an event's potential for damage. Similar to catastrophe likelihood, catastrophe intensity is estimated using a probabilistic approach. The model uses separate probability distributions for location of initial catastrophe strike, movement following initial strike, dispersion, length of time until dissipation, and level of severity at each location. These probability distributions explicitly account for virtually all potential catastrophe scenarios, setting parameters using complete historical seismic and meteorological data provided by the U.S. National Weather Service, National Hurricane Center, U.S. Geological Survey, and other industry groups. This simulation-driven technique generates "weighted average" probability distributions for each salient catastrophe attribute and, collectively, produces a robust, comprehensive catastrophe profile.

For hurricanes, the attributes estimated in the intensity model include landfall location, central pressure along path, radius of maximum winds, forward velocity along path, track angle, maximum over-water wind speed, and adjustments due to surface friction. Severity at any point along the hurricane's path is generally measured in terms of central pressure or, equivalently, wind speed. These measures can be translated into escalating category values 1 through 5 on the Saffir-Simpson hurricane intensity scale, the meteorological industry standard (see Appendix A).

In earthquake intensity models, the key attributes affecting intensity include regional seismicity, regional geology, attenuation of seismic energy, local soil conditions, and potential hazards including landslide, liquefaction, and fire. Quake intensity at each site is rated 1 to 12 on the Modified Mercalli Intensity scale (see Appendix A).

Catastrophe Event Simulation

Catastrophe likelihood and intensity profiles in combination fully characterize annual catastrophic event activity. Melding the output from the likelihood and intensity models permits a complete catastrophe event simulation. Typically, at least several thousand years of catastrophic event activity are simulated to enhance the statistical significance of results.

Property Susceptibility Model

The specific residential and commercial properties covered by CLS have varying levels of susceptibility to catastrophe. To the extent that properties are more resilient, catastrophe-related damages will be mitigated. Damages will also be lessened if properties are located at sufficient distances from catastrophe-prone areas. The property-specific attributes determine vulnerability. In the property susceptibility model, insurance company data on the attributes of insured properties are combined with engineering analysis to define relationships between catastrophe severity and damage for insured properties. Key to the robustness of the property susceptibility model is the calculation of separate damage ratios for each insured property covered by the transaction. These relationships are typically expressed as a damage ratio, which is the percentage of the property value that is damaged for a given level of catastrophe intensity. This analysis is necessarily conducted separately for each construction class (e.g., wood frame, masonry, etc.) and for different building code specifications.

Damage Distribution

The results from the catastrophe event simulation and property susceptibility models are then linked to produce a probability distribution of annual catastrophe-related damages. This distribution represents the probability that, given the annual frequency and intensity of catastrophes and the vulnerability of properties to catastrophe-related events, damages on a particular property will equal a certain amount over the course of one year.

Insured Loss Distribution

Once the damage distribution has been computed, the insurance policy provisions in place on each property covered under the transaction are then superimposed to determine a distribution of insured losses. Insured losses on a property are almost always less than total damages on the property due to policy requirements that limit claim payments in the event of a catastrophe. Policy deductibles and depreciated cost provisions are two examples of such limitations. Properties carrying full replacement cost policy riders, on the other hand, will have insured loss distributions that more closely approach their associated damage distributions. Individual insured loss distributions on each property are then summed to arrive at an aggregate insured loss distribution on the whole block of insured properties.

Security Default Analysis

Investors can use the aggregate insured loss distribution in conjunction with the specific terms of the transaction to ascertain the probability of default on the catastrophe-linked security in question. For transactions structured as excess-of-loss reinsurance arrangements, the annual probability of security default will equal the annual probability that insured losses exceed the attachment point. This number — frequently referred to as the annual probability of exceedance — is the area under the insured loss distribution curve to the right of the attachment point value (see Exhibit 9). This statistic can be compared to default probabilities on other securities to draw conclusions on relative creditworthiness.

The insured loss distribution can be used to derive other statistics that are helpful to investors. Examples are the expected annual losses, expected recovery rate, maximum likelihood amount of annual losses, 99% confidence interval of annual losses, and number of years on average between which losses of a certain magnitude are expected to occur (the so-called return period). This information can assist investors in assessing the risk associated with particular catastrophe-linked securities.

Exhibit 9: Sample Probability of Default on an Excess-of-Loss Catastrophe-Linked Security

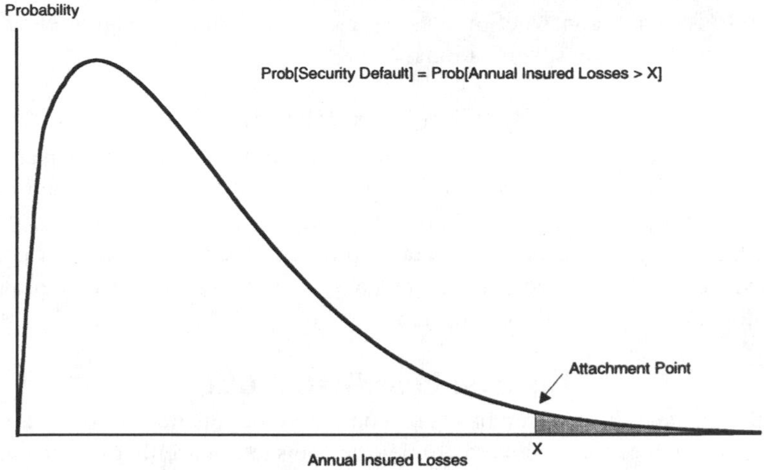

RATING AGENCY CONSIDERATIONS

The four major rating agencies have all developed criteria for rating catastrophe-linked securities and are furnishing ratings on transactions. At present, the methodology used by each agency is similar — though each is being continually refined, reflecting the relative newness and prospect for growth of this asset class.[10] The approaches used to rate principal-at-risk and principal-protected catastrophe-linked securities are different.

Principal-at-Risk Securities

The agencies rate principal-at-risk catastrophe-linked securities to reflect loss and timing risks to both principal and interest. Because this approach is also used to rate corporate credits and ABS structures, it is possible to draw conclusions on relative creditworthiness between these securities and catastrophe-linked securities based on ratings.

In analyzing principal-at-risk securities, the rating agencies consider structural and insurance risks. The structural analysis is essentially the same as the analysis used to rate any structured security, and is identical to the approach

[10] This section is based on discussions with analysts at S&P and Moody's, along with publications on catastrophe-linked security rating approaches from S&P ("Behind the Ratings — Structured Finance Alternative to Reinsurance," *Standard & Poor's CreditWeek*, November 13, 1996), Fitch (Structured Finance and Catastrophic Risk, *Fitch Financial Institutions Special Report*, February 3, 1997), and DCR (*DCR's Approach to Rating Catastrophe Bonds*, Duff & Phelps Credit Rating Co., January 1997).

used to rate principal-protected catastrophe-linked securities (discussed below). This analysis focuses on the transaction's legal structure, the quality of collateral, the bankruptcy-remote status of the SPV issuer, the flow of funds, and the market, counterparty and legal risks inherent in the transaction.

Although structural risk is an important element in the rating methodology, the key risk that the rating agencies analyze is insurance risk. Principal-at-risk catastrophe-linked securities are subject to the risk that insured losses on properties related to the specific transaction will exceed some attachment point (for an excess-of-loss type of reinsurance structure, for example).

The rating agencies rely on the results of simulation-driven catastrophe models to assign their ratings. However, the agencies first validate the analytic integrity of the model and test the quality of the insurance company data used by the model.

These "stress tests" are conducted through a due diligence process. This process typically involves assessing the appropriateness of the probability distributions employed by the model to simulate catastrophe frequency and intensity. Both the underlying density functions and parameters are considered. Occasionally, a rating agency will request a modification of the probability distribution to generate more conservative results (e.g., it might ask to recalculate the insured loss distribution using twice the assumed catastrophe frequency).

In addition, property damage vulnerability relationships are examined. Vulnerability functions are considered for each property characteristic (e.g., construction type, elevation, building usage, etc.) using engineering and actuarial analysis. In all cases, consistency with published industry and academic literature is tested. Some rating agencies retain the services of outside meteorological or seismic experts to assist in evaluating the model.

The insurance company data used by the model are reviewed by the rating agencies for accuracy. These data include both the book of insured properties and the policy provisions in place on each property. Conservative adjustments are made to account for incomplete data in each case.

Finally, certain indirect factors are sometimes also accounted for in the rating analysis. These include demand surge (the effect of a catastrophe on local equilibrium prices for building materials and wages), growth and change of mix in the insured book of business over the course of the security's term, and the insurance company's claims handling and loss management/settlement procedures.

Principal-Protected Securities

The approach used to rate principal-protected catastrophe-linked securities is consistent with the approach for other structured securities that offer principal protection. The rating agencies traditionally provide ratings for certain structured securities that reflect the loss and timing risks associated with default on principal only. That is, the risk that interest is not paid on a timely basis is not explicitly taken into account in the rating.[11] As a result, the approach that rating agencies are taking on principal-protected catastrophe-linked securities is to rate only the principal component. The rating assigned will reflect the quality of the underlying collateral that is providing the principal protection. For this reason, structures supported by U.S. Treasuries or STRIPS are expected be rated AAA. On the other hand, if the issuing insurer's surplus notes are providing the principal protection, then the structure is expected to be assigned the rating on the surplus notes. This is consistent with the rating agencies' "look-through" approach to rating all principal-protected structured transactions.

RELATIVE VALUE

Framework for Pricing

Catastrophe-linked securities are expected to trade at a significant spread over Treasuries. This spread has two components: the base spread and the risk premium. The base spread reflects the minimum spread an investor should require on CLS to break even relative to an investment in comparable maturity risk-free assets (i.e., U.S. Treasuries). This component accounts for the expected loss of principal and interest on CLS. The second component, the risk premium, represents compensation for the uncertainty of estimated losses on CLS and the fact that it is a new asset class. Another way of viewing the risk premium is as the additional return investors should receive for researching the catastrophe risk associated with these securities (in the same way as investors are compensated for research on other ABS).

The CLS base spread can be computed, using the insured loss distribution for the transaction, as the annual probability of exceedance (as defined above) multiplied by one minus the expected recovery rate. The recovery rate on CLS reflects the percentage of principal recovered in the event of default. This rate will depend on the magnitude of insured losses from the catastrophe and can range from 0% (insured losses exceed total value of issued securities) to 100% (insured losses less than or equal to attachment point). The CLS risk premium can then be calculated as the offered spread on the security minus the base spread.

Spreads on corporate bonds can be similarly decomposed. The base spread on a corporate reflects the probability of default times one minus the expected recovery rate, and the risk premium is the offered spread in excess of the base spread. Exhibit 10 shows corporate 1-year default rates and indicative spreads. The default rates reflect historical corporate defaults between 1970-1996 based on a recent Moody's study, and can serve as an estimate of the future probability of corporate defaults. Recovery rates on corporate bonds are estimated by Moody's at 40% of par on average. Together these can serve as the basis for comparison with expected losses on CLS.

---

[11] One exception is Standard & Poor's convention of providing an "r" suffix on ratings of certain securities to reflect yield volatility.

Exhibit 10: Default Rates and Indicative Spreads of Corporate Bonds

Rating	One-Year Defaults 1970-1996*	Expected Loss (% of par)**	Indicative Spreads to Treasury (bp)*** 5/15/97
Aaa	0.00%	0.00%	20
Aa	0.03	0.02	21
A	0.01	0.01	27
Baa	0.12	0.07	42
Ba	1.36	0.82	135
B	7.27	4.36	300

* *Historical Default Rates of Corporate Bond Issuers, 1920-1996*, Moody's Investors Service, January 1997.
** Assumes 40% recovery rate
*** 2-year spreads used as proxy for 1-year spreads.

Comparing spreads and expected losses on CLS with similarly rated corporates can provide an indication of relative value. CLS relative value versus corporate bonds with the same rating can be assessed in one of two ways. In the first case the base spread on the CLS can equal the base spread on the corporate (i.e., the expected loss on the two securities is the same), yet the risk premium is higher on the CLS. For example, if a Ba rated CLS has a base spread of 82 bp (annual probability of exceedance of 1.36% multiplied by one minus expected recovery rate of 40%) and is offered at a spread greater than 135 bp (the indicative spread of a corporate bond with the same probability of default and expected recovery rate), then the CLS offers relative value.

The second case where a CLS offers relative value is when the offered spread on the two securities are equal but the expected loss on the CLS is less than that of the corporate bond (as a result of either a lower probability of default or a higher recovery rate or both). In our example, if the CLS and corporate are both offered at a spread of 135 bp but the expected loss on the CLS is less than 0.82%, then the CLS offers relative value.

Spread Outlook

We expect that current CLS issues will be priced more attractively than future issues, since investors are likely to demand a premium for the lower liquidity associated with a new product. Additionally, some insurance companies may be willing to pay an initial premium over reinsurance rates to develop new sources of reinsurance capital, in the expectation that a long-term, stable alternative could potentially improve the efficiency in the market. Spreads are likely to narrow as understanding of the underlying risk grows, liquidity increases, and investor acceptance broadens. A parallel is distinguishable in the corporate market. Exhibit 11 illustrates that, although the corporate market is cyclical, there has been a long-term tightening of spreads as appetite for high yield corporate bonds has grown and the risk is better understood.

Exhibit 11: High Yield Corporate Spreads by Credit Quality, 1987-April 30, 1997

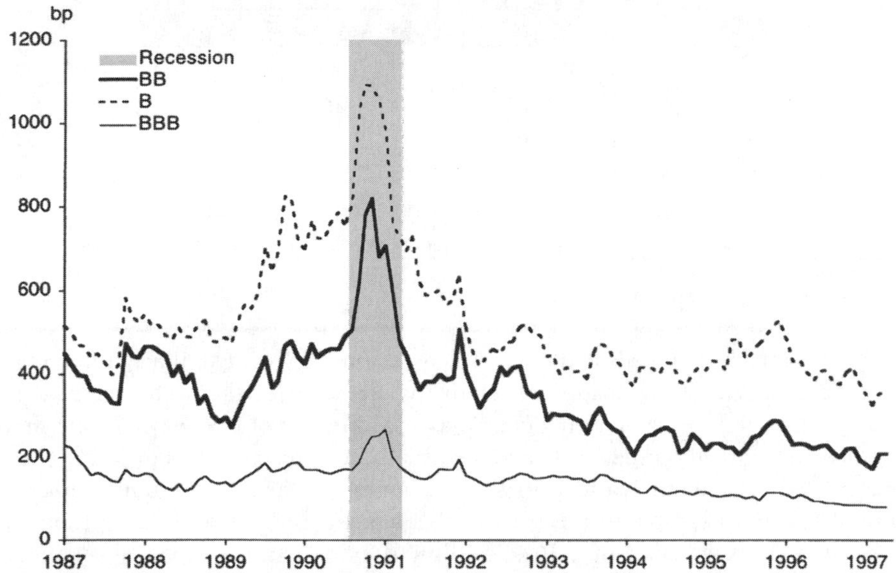

An additional consideration is that for an issue affected by underlying seasonal events (floods, hurricanes, hailstorms, etc.) that has a maturity date occurring after the season, there is a strong possibility that spreads will tighten if no trigger event occurs before the end of the season. This tightening should reflect the substantially reduced probability of default on the securities.

An Uncorrelated Asset Class

CLS offer investors the unique opportunity to invest exclusively in catastrophe risk and may provide potential diversification benefits. Although investors can invest in catastrophe risks by buying insurance and/or reinsurance company equity and debt, these investments are not a perfect substitute for the pure catastrophe exposure inherent in CLS. First, CLS do not carry the idiosyncratic[12] risks associated with an investment in securities of an insurance or reinsurance company. CLS also allow investors to avoid principal-agent risks (such as the risk that equity-holders may have incentives to restructure the debt or increase the overall riskiness of the company, to the disadvantage of bondholders) inherent in a corporate security.

Second, the occurrence and magnitude of natural hazards are expected to be uncorrelated with movements in the stock and bond markets. On the other

[12] Idiosyncratic or nonsystematic risk is the diversifiable risk of a security.

hand, insurance and reinsurance company securities do involve a significant portion of systematic risk. A recent study by Canter, Cole, and Sandor[13] shows that a portfolio of ten prominent catastrophe reinsurance companies has a strong positive correlation (beta of 0.83) with stock market movements. As a result, buying reinsurance company equity does not bring significant diversification benefits. In this respect, CLS offer better diversification opportunities since they are expected to have near zero betas. The correlation between the yearly percentage change in the S&P 500 index and the yearly percentage change in the PCS index over the period 1976-1996 is statistically insignificant (see Exhibit 12).

Modern portfolio theory states that an uncorrelated asset would be an attractive addition to a well diversified portfolio even at a required rate of return that is equal to the risk free rate of return. If CLS offer returns in excess of the risk-free rate (Treasury bill rate) and do not exhibit systematic risk, then investing in these securities can improve overall portfolio performance on a risk-adjusted basis. Investors who purchase CLS can potentially receive an attractive expected return and improve the diversification of their current portfolio.

Exhibit 12: Correlation of PCS Index and S&P 500 Index

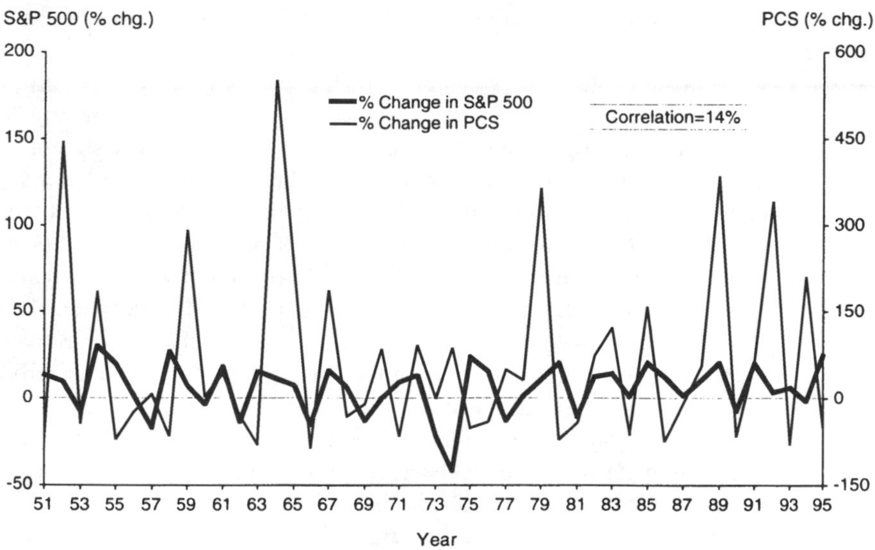

Source: CBOT

[13] Michael S. Canter, Joseph B. Cole, and Richard L. Sandor, "Insurance Derivatives: A new asset class for the capital markets and a new hedging tool for the insurance industry," *Journal of Derivatives* (Winter 1996), pp. 89-104.

A study by Froot, Murphy, Stern, and Usher[14] based on pricing and claims on actual catastrophe reinsurance contracts brokered by the reinsurance intermediary, Guy Carpenter & Company Inc., draws three valuable conclusions. First, the correlation of catastrophe risk with stocks and bonds is statistically indistinguishable from zero. Second, assuming that returns on reinsurance contracts provide a reasonable proxy for expected returns on CLS, the study shows that investment in such a portfolio of catastrophe reinsurance contracts from 1970-1994 would have generated returns 200 bp above the Treasury bill rate. Third, adding the portfolio of reinsurance contracts improves the efficiency of a diversified portfolio. Using a base portfolio of 70% domestic assets (70% stocks, 30% bonds) and 30% foreign assets (70% stocks, 30% bonds), the study shows that the "reward to risk ratio"[15] grows from 26% to 30% as the addition of catastrophe risk goes from 5% to 25%. Even though the past is no guarantee for future results, historical data provide strong evidence that catastrophe-linked securities offer portfolio opportunities to investors.

OTHER CONSIDERATIONS

In evaluating CLS, in addition to conducting a thorough relative value analysis, it is important for investors to examine several transaction-specific criteria, including these:

- *Insurer Coparticipation:* In CLS, since insurers could potentially take action that affects the value of the transaction (e.g., increase risk profile of policies, reduce deductibles, improperly adjudicate claims, etc.) risk of moral hazard exists. One method of mitigating this risk is to structure quota-share transactions, where the insurer shares losses proportionately with investors. An excess-of-loss structure lowers the risk to the extent that losses from lower layers are absorbed by the insurer's own capital. Hybrid structures may also be used to achieve insurer coparticipation objectives.
- *Quality of Insurer:* Catastrophe-linked securities isolate the underlying catastrophe risk from credit risk of the insurer. Nevertheless, the quality of the insurer is important since it determines the company's ability to implement pricing changes, collect accurate policy level data, and influence the quality of the underlying pool of policies.
- *Diversification of Underlying Events:* To the extent that occurrences of one catastrophic event is independent of another event, a pool of underlying

---

[14] Kenneth Froot, Brian Murphy, Aaron Stern, and Stephen Usher, "The Emerging Asset Class: Insurance Risk," *Guy Carpenter & Company Inc.'s Review of Catastrophes Exposures and the Capital Markets*, July 1995.

[15] Measured as the realized return minus the risk-free return divided by the standard deviation of the portfolio return.

policies that is diversified across regions or types of events (earthquakes, hurricanes, floods, etc.) or index-based (using the PCS Index, for example) may be less risky than one without this diversification.

- *Quality of the Modeling Company:* The security is priced and rated based on the probability of default, which in turn depends on probability of exceedance as calculated by the modeling company. It is therefore important for the company to be well-regarded in the industry.

OUTLOOK

We think that the CLS market is likely to develop within the context of a general trend toward securitization of insurance risk. Innovative investment choices will be introduced that will enable investors to buy insurance risk products tailored to their particular risk/return preferences. Securitization of life insurance risks (e.g., mortality, lapsation, etc.) and other property risks (e.g., space satellite launches, pipelines, etc.) will likely follow. Investors will be able to choose from securities subject to one risk (e.g., California earthquake), a diversified pool of risks (e.g., Japan earthquake and Florida hurricane), and/or risks measured by a recognized industry index. Multiyear structures will also be introduced, and OTC insurance derivatives will supplement the use of cash instruments in these securitizations.

We believe that the market for CLS will grow significantly in the years ahead, driven by the fundamental need of the insurance industry to create additional catastrophe reinsurance capacity and investor desire to achieve uncorrelated excess returns relative to comparably rated corporate and ABS investments. As the market matures and investors become more comfortable assuming catastrophe risk, spreads on these securities will likely tighten. Based on the existing gap in reinsurance capacity required to cover a $60 billion industrywide catastrophe, we believe that annual CLS issuance could reach $40 billion.

APPENDIX A
A DESCRIPTION OF HURRICANES AND EARTHQUAKES

Earthquakes[1]

Earthquakes are vibrations, sometimes violent, of the earth's surface caused by abrupt releases of energy in the earth's crust. They occur along preexisting fault lines, or zones of fracture in the earth's crust composed of crushed rock between blocks of rock that form naturally weak areas. When stress in the earth's outer layer builds up, it causes rocks on either side of the fault line to move relative to each other. This results in a sudden slippage, which releases energy in waves that travels through the rocks and produces shaking. Hazards that may result include landslide, liquefaction (solid soil liquefying), and fire.

The United States Geological Survey uses a 12-level scale known as the Modified Mercalli Intensity (MMI) scale to identify the intensity of quakes (i.e., their surface-level effects). Lower values on the MMI scale are derived from human and structural response to shaking, while higher intensities are based on permanent ground distortion. Though the Richter scale is a widely used measure of earthquake intensity, all the catastrophe models are based on the Mercalli intensity scale.

Earthquakes occur primarily in three zones of the earth. The largest earthquake belt, along which roughly 81% of the world's largest earthquakes occur, is known as the circum-Pacific seismic belt. As its name suggests, the belt runs around the rim of the Pacific Ocean, from Chile north to Alaska, west to Japan, and south to New Zealand. The second largest belt, which accounts for about 17% of the world's largest earthquakes, is known as the Alpide. It extends from Java to Sumatra, through the Himalayas and the Mediterranean, and out into the Atlantic. The third prominent belt follows the submerged mid-Atlantic Ridge. Within the United States, the largest earthquake belt runs from north to south in California where the Pacific and North American techtonic plates meet. The boundary between the plates is the San Andreas fault, an 800-mile-long fault system that extends to depths of at least 10 miles. This system, which produces thousands of small earthquakes every year, was responsible for the San Francisco earthquake of 1906 that caused landscape offsets up to 21 feet and registered intensities as high as 11 on the MMI, as well as the Northridge earthquake.

Hurricanes[2]

Hurricanes are part of a family of weather systems known as "tropical cyclones." A hurricane begins as a disorganized storm system that forms over warm, tropical waters. If and when the storm system becomes more organized, it is classified as a "tropical depression" and given a number by the National Hurricane Center. If the winds in a tropical depression grow in intensity to 40 mph, it is reclassified as a

[1] Source: U.S. Geological Survey; National Earthquake Information Center

[2] Source: U.S. Department of Commerce, National Oceanic and Atmospheric Administration.

"tropical storm" and given a name. When the winds in the storm reach 74 mph, the storm is upgraded to hurricane status.

The winds of a hurricane are structured around a central "eye," which is an area free of clouds and relatively calm. A band of strong winds and precipitation, known as the maximum radius of winds, develops outside the eye of the storm. As these winds wrap around the eye in a counterclockwise motion, air flow moves toward the center of the storm. Energy in the form of moist air and vapor is released as the air flow spirals upward, widening the difference between the pressure at the hurricane's center and its perimeter — the central pressure difference. An increasing central pressure difference increases the maximum wind speed, which ultimately determines the storm's potential to inflict damage.

Hurricane intensity is measured on the Saffir-Simpson scale on the basis of sustained wind speed (see Exhibit A-1).

All Atlantic and Gulf coastal areas are subject to hurricanes or tropical storms. For the U.S., the peak hurricane threat exists from mid-August to late October, although the official hurricane season extends from June 1 through November 30.

Exhibit A-1: Saffir-Simpson Scale for Hurricane Intensity

Saffir-Simpson Category	Sustained Wind Speed (mph)	% of Occurrences since 1900*	Examples (States Affected)
1	74-95	2.6%	1988: Florence (LA); Charley (NC)
2	96-110	41.0	1985: Kate (FL); 1991: Bob (RI)
3	111-130	35.9	1983: Alicia (TX); 1993: Emily (NC)
4	131-155	17.9	1989: Hugo (SC); 1992: Andrew (FL)
5	155 +	2.6	1935: Labor Day Hurricane (FL); 1969: Camille (LA/MS)

* Source: Applied Insurance Research.

APPENDIX B
CATASTROPHES AND THE BERMUDA MARKET

Raising more private or public equity capital is one alternative to expand resources available to cover catastrophe risk. Primarily in response to Hurricane Andrew, the island of Bermuda has flourished into an accepted insurance market. Investment banks, commercial banks, hedge funds, insurers, and reinsurers all sought to capitalize on the returns available in the catastrophe reinsurance market. By the middle of 1994, roughly $4 billion of new capital was available in Bermuda for catastrophe reinsurance. Shortly thereafter, Bermuda's insurance regulatory climate became more structured, adding legitimacy to a budding insurance market. With a wealth of capital, Bermuda is now a recognized force in the reinsurance market. Several companies have rapidly captured market share (28% of world insurance premiums) and recently contributed $700 million to the California Earthquake Authority in reinsurance contracts. The return that these insurers has earned have been exceptional. As a group, the eight reinsurers earned a 51.9% gross margin and 22% return on equity in 1995 (see Exhibit B-1). The companies have made such superior returns that their invested capital rose to $5 billion in 1995. Many of these companies are using excess capital to buy back stock or to diversify product lines.

But the Bermuda market does not possess the capacity to meet all the catastrophe demands of the U.S. market's major personal lines insurers in high risk regions. One concern is that the balance sheets of the Bermuda reinsurers have not been put through the necessary stress of a massive natural event (the last one was the 1994 Northridge earthquake, which occurred before many of these companies were set up), and hence their ability to withstand such an event is still undetermined.

Exhibit B-1: Bermuda Reinsurers

Reinsurance Company	Invested Capital ($ mill.)*	Return on Equity (1995)**
Centre Cat	312	15.5%
Global Capital Re	425	22.0
International P/C Re	309	19.0
LaSalle Re	200	19.2
Mid Ocean Re	700	20.5
Partner Re	950	19.1
Renaissance Re	240	44.0
Tempest Re	500	15.1
Total	3,636	22.0

* Institutional Investor

** Standard & Poor's, *Bermuda Catastrophe Reinsurance Market Report*, February 1997.

APPENDIX C
EXCHANGE TRADED DERIVATIVE CONTRACTS

The Chicago Board of Trade has offered since 1992 a catastrophe futures contract based on an index provided by the Insurance Services Office (ISO). This contract was not popular because the ISO index was based only on losses of the top 25 companies and hence was not considered reliable in predicting catastrophe losses. In 1995, the CBOT began offering option contracts with underlying indices computed by Property Claims Services' (PCS); these indices have gradually become the industry accepted standards. Contracts trade based on each of the PCS indices (see Exhibit C-1).

The PCS indices are based on surveys of insurance companies and their estimates of claims after the occurrence of an event. The losses can occur during a risk period (quarterly or annually depending on the seasonality of the catastrophe), at the beginning of which the index is set to zero. Each point on the index translates to a $100 million loss. The loss data are collected during a loss development period that can extend from six to twelve months. Contracts trade in the risk and development period of the index.

At the CBOT, investors can buy and sell standardized call/put option contracts, where the underlying index is a PCS Catastrophe Index. A buyer can purchase either a small-cap option with strike of 0-195 (aggregate losses up to $20 billion) or a large-cap contract with strike of 200-495 (losses of $20-$50 billion). By simultaneously buying call options with a lower strike and selling calls with a higher strike, a buyer can synthetically create an excess-of-loss reinsurance contract. On expiration, the buyer of an in-the-money call option receives the difference between the final index value and the strike, multiplied by $200. The settlement is in cash and is limited by the loss cap of 195 or 495. The buyer of the contract pays a premium that is quoted as points per spread contract, which is similar to the rate on line in a reinsurance contract.

Catex Swaps

Another recently introduced mechanism for diversifying catastrophe risk is provided by the Catex exchanges in New Jersey and Bermuda, set up in late 1996. The exchange in New Jersey is restricted to insurers, reinsurers, and self-insurers, whereas the Bermuda exchange allows for nontraditional investors, such as hedge funds and investment banks. Through the exchange, subscribers can swap catastrophe risk exposures over a nationwide computer system. An insurer can diversify its exposure to catastrophes by exchanging a basket of its own risks for a different basket of risks. For example, if an insurance company determines that its portfolio has an over-concentration of risk in Florida hurricanes, it can enter into an agreement with another market participant to swap California earthquake risk for its Florida risk. Inasmuch as Catex swaps help insurers diversify their balance sheets, the swaps reduce the need for capital, thus indirectly adding to the risk capacity in the industry.

Exhibit C-1: PCS Indices

National
Eastern
Northeastern
Southeastern
Midwestern
Western

Chapter 21

ABS-Backed Index Amortizing Notes

Charles N. Schorin
Principal
Director of ABS Research
Morgan Stanley

Steven Weinreich
ABS Research
Morgan Stanley

INTRODUCTION

Index amortizing notes (IANs) backed by asset-backed securities have become an important new product, bridging the agency, corporate bond, mortgage, and asset-backed markets. Since the CARCO 97-1 transaction backed by Chrysler dealer floorplans, there have been $2.5 billion in public ABS-backed IANs. There has been an additional $1.9 billion of private ABS-backed IANs. We expect this financing tool to continue to be used as market conditions warrant.

Index amortizing structures have been in the market since 1993. These structures have sometimes taken the form (and name) of index amortizing swaps, in which notional amortization is based upon an index such as LIBOR or CMT, and mortgage notes, mortgage swaps, and CMO swaps, in which amortization is based upon a reference pool of MBS collateral. ABS-backed IANs are conceptually similar to these other structures, with the exception that the AAA rating is based upon AAA-rated ABS employed as collateral for the IAN and the amortization is actual rather than notional.

RELATIVE VALUE

ABS-backed IANs offer value relative to competing products. Exhibit 1 compares the option-adjusted spread (OAS) on CARCO 97-1 with CMO PAC bonds, 15-year conventional passthroughs, and 7-year conventional balloon passthroughs on October 21, 1997. Note that the ABS-backed IAN has a 7-year absolute final, similar to the balloons, and a PSA range over which cash flows meet a constant schedule, similar to the PAC bond; the advantage of the IAN, however, is that its PAC range is not subject to band drift. In addition, the 2-year hard lockout on the IAN means that fast prepayments on collateral actually are a benefit, whereas they are a detriment to the CMO PAC. The reason is that fast collateral prepayments can cause the PAC range on the CMO PAC bonds to deteriorate; not only does the PAC range on the IAN not change, but fast prepayments can be a benefit for the IAN because it leads to burnout of the collateral. This means that when the lockout period ends after two years, the reference collateral pool is likely to have more stable prepayments, actually improving the convexity characteristics of the IAN.

As indicated in Exhibit 1, the OAS advantage of the CARCO IAN on October 21, 1997 was 6 basis points over the balloons, 14 bp relative to the 15-year passthroughs, and 9 bp over the discount PAC. Exhibit 2 compares the CARCO IAN with callable agency securities at various constant volatilities. The OAS advantage of the CARCO IAN is more than 30 bp.

INDEX AMORTIZING NOTE MECHANICS

Exhibit 3 uses CARCO 97-1 as an example of an ABS-backed IAN. This structure has a 4-year average life, 2-year principal lockout, and 7-year absolute final maturity.

Exhibit 1: ABS-Backed IANs versus Competing MBS

Bond	Type	Price[a]	OAS[b] (bp)	Zero Vol (bp) Spread	Option Cost (bp)	Effective Duration
CARCO 97-1	IAN	99-28	36	84	48	2.9
15-year Gold 6.5s	TBA Pass-thru	99-7+	22	60	38	3.8
15-year Gold 7s	TBA Pass-thru	100-29+	20	73	53	3.0
7-year Balloon 6.5s	TBA Pass-thru	99-26	25	52	27	3.3
7-year Balloon 7s	TBA Pass-thru	101-3	30	67	37	2.9
FHLMC 1471 F	PAC[c]	100-10+	11	40	29	2.3
FHLMC 1603 F	PAC[d]	97-24+	27	38	11	3.1

[a] Price is closing price on 10/21/97 for corporate settlement.
[b] OAS calculation employs term structure of volatility.
[c] FHLMC 1471 is backed by 15-year Gold 7s, with a current effective PAC range of 165-255 PSA.
[d] FHLMC 1603 is backed by Gold 7s, with a current effective PAC range of 110-415 PSA.

Source: Morgan Stanley

Exhibit 2: ABS-Backed IANs versus Agency Callables

	OAS in Basis Points at Various Constant Volatilities				
	12%	14%	16%	18%	20%
CARCO 97-1	54	45	35	25	13
7-year Non-Call 2 Agency	23	13	2	−8	−19

Source: Morgan Stanley

Exhibit 3: ABS-Backed Index Amortizing Note Example CARCO 97-1 at Origination

Final Maturity	7 years
PAC Range	225-325 PSA
Average Life in PAC Range	4.00 years
Lockout Period	2 years
Reference Collateral	FHLMC Gold 8s originated in 1995
Ratings(Moody's/S&P)	Aaa/AAA
Mandatory Cleanup Call	10%
Credit Enhancement	10% subordinated seller's interest, which increases to 11% if Chrysler Financial Corporation's long-term rating is lowered below BBB– and 35 bp ($1.75 million) reserve account

After the 2-year lockout period, the prepayment speed on the aggregate grouping of 1995 issue FHLMC Gold 8s is determined in a given month. The PSA for the reference collateral in a given month corresponds to a percentage paydown of security principal for that month as indicated by the monthly amortization rate (MAR) in Exhibit 4. For example, if 1995 issue Gold 8s prepay at 150 PSA in a given month (after the lockout period), the security pays down 3.006% of its outstanding principal balance. For PSAs between the values shown in Exhibit 4, the MAR is determined by linear interpolation.

Exhibit 4: Reference Pool PSA for IAN Example CARCO 97-1 at Origination

	0-100	125	135	150	225-325	375	450	575+
Monthly Amort. Rate (MAR) %	0.027	0.164	1.233	3.006	3.543	6.938	12.678	22.402
Approx. Avg. Life in Years	6.95	6.75	5.50	4.25	4.00	3.00	2.50	2.25
First Principal Pay	8/15/99	8/15/99	8/15/99	8/15/99	8/15/99	8/15/99	8/15/99	8/15/99
Last Principal Pay	8/15/04	8/15/04	8/15/04	8/15/04	8/15/04	4/15/02	12/15/00	5/15/00
BEY %	6.783	6.783	6.783	6.783	6.783	6.783	6.783	6.783
Spread (bp)/Treasury* (years)	+69/6.95	+70/6.75	+72/5.50	+78/4.25	+80/4.00	+87/3.00	+90/2.50	+92/2.25

* Using yield curve at pricing on July 24, 1997.

Mechanics of the transaction are as follows: the investor receives a fixed-rate coupon of 80 basis points over the 4-year Treasury at the pricing date. Principal payments are locked out for two years. Thereafter, it depends upon actual prepayments on a reference pool of collateral, in this case 30-year Federal Home Loan Mortgage Corp. (FHLMC or Freddie Mac) Gold 8s issued in 1995. Prepayment rates on the reference collateral pool map into amortization rates of the security's principal, as shown in Exhibit 4. For example, if 1995 issue Gold 8s prepay at 150 PSA in a given month, then the outstanding balance of the security is reduced by 3.006% in that month.

The MAR determines the average life of the security. If 1995 Gold 8s prepay each month at 150 PSA, then the average life of the IAN will be 4.25 years. If prepayments on 1995 Gold 8s are between 225 and 325 PSA each month, then the IAN has an average life of 4.00 years. In this sense, the IAN resembles a PAC bond with a PAC range of 225 to 325 PSA, except with the advantage that the PAC band of the IAN structure does not experience PAC band drift. The maximum final maturity of the IAN in any prepayment scenario is seven years. Exhibit 4 shows details of a reference pool for the example of CARCO 97-1.

SIGNIFICANCE OF ABS COLLATERAL

Previous mortgage-linked IANs often were issued by government agencies. The agency carries an implied AAA rating, which gets extended to the IAN.

In contrast to an agency guarantee, ABS-backed IANs employ AAA-rated ABS collateral to provide principal with AAA certainty. The ABS collateral also allows the IAN to be offered at wider spreads than agency-guaranteed IANs. The issuer is able to tap a relatively inexpensive source of financing for its securitized program.

STRUCTURAL OVERLAY ON ABS COLLATERAL

IANs may impose some structural overlays to mitigate some of the potential risks of the ABS collateral. For example, in CARCO 97-1, most of the early amortization events in a typical (i.e., non-IAN) CARCO floorplan transaction are reinvestment events. Instead of returning principal to investors, the principal is accumulated into a trust account and invested in A-1+/P-1 securities. The negative carry resulting from the difference between the interest received on the A-1+/P-1 commercial paper and that paid on CARCO 97-1 is absorbed first by a yield supplement account, and if that is insufficient, then by the AAA-rated swap counterparty.

OTHER STRUCTURAL FEATURES

Other structural features include early amortization protection, early amortization events, and reinvestment events. We discuss each below.

Early Amortization Protection

Early amortization protections includes:

- In the case of a reinvestment event, principal received by the trust will be accumulated into a trust account and invested in A-1+/P-1 securities and payments to certificateholders will proceed as before.
- Negative carry will be assumed by the yield supplement account, and if this is insufficient, then by the swap counterparty
- Yield supplement account is initially 0.25% of initial invested amount and declines as follows:

$$[0.0025 \times (84 - \text{Months Elapsed}) \div 84) \times \text{Current Invested Amount}]$$

Early Amortization Events

All amortization events typical in a CARCO transaction will be reinvestment events, except for the following:

- The trust becomes an investment company, as per the Investment Company Act of 1940.
- The occurrence of certain insolvency events relating to the trust or U.S. Auto Receivables Company.
- Swap counterparty and contingent counterparty default.
- Non-zero balance at expected final maturity date.

Reinvestment Events

With the exception of the four early amortization events described above, typical CARCO early amortization events will result in reinvestment events, where the wholesale floorplan receivables will be invested in A-1+/P-1 instruments. The following constitute reinvestment events:

- Failure of the servicer to make a payment or deposit as required.
- Breach of representation or warranty by the seller.
- Occurrence of certain events of bankruptcy, insolvency or receivership related to Chrysler Financial Corporation or Chrysler.
- Failure of U.S. Auto Receivables Company to convey receivables to the trust.
- Available subordinated amount is less than the required subordinated amount.
- Servicer default with respect to CARCO 1997-1.
- Used vehicles exceed 20% of pool balance.
- Average monthly payment rate declines to less than 20% for three preceding months.
- Any carryover amount is outstanding on six consecutive payment dates.

BRIDGING THE MARKETS

Index amortizing notes backed by ABS collateral bridge the corporate bond, agency, mortgage, and asset-backed markets. Investors who take the effort to learn about the security and the collateral can earn incremental spread relative to competing product.

Section III:

Mortgage-Related ABS Products

Chapter 22

Mortgage-Backed Securities

Frank J. Fabozzi, PhD., CFA
Adjunct Professor of Finance
School of Management
Yale University

INTRODUCTION

Mortgage-backed securities (MBS) are securities backed by a pool (collection) of mortgage loans. A pool of residential or commercial mortgage loans can be used as collateral for an MBS. Our focus in this chapter is on MBS in which the underlying loans are residential mortgages. An MBS in which the underlying pool of loans includes commercial loans is discussed in Chapter 29.

Residential mortgage loans can be classified as first liens or junior liens. Our focus in this chapter is on securities backed by first liens. In Chapters 23 through 26 we look at securities backed by home equity loans. The typical loan for these securities has a junior (i.e., second or third) lien, although there may be first liens in some pools.

MBS include the following securities: (1) mortgage passthrough securities, (2) collateralized mortgage obligations, and (3) stripped MBS. The latter two MBS are referred to as "derivative MBS." The issuers of MBS include an agency of the U.S. government (the Government National Mortgage Association, nicknamed Ginnie Mae), two government sponsored enterprises (the Federal National Mortgage Association, nicknamed Fannie Mae, and Federal Home Loan Mortgage Corporation, nicknamed Freddie Mac), and private entities. Securities issued by Ginnie Mae, Fannie Mae, and Freddie Mac are called *agency MBS* and securities issued by private entities are called *nonagency MBS*.

MORTGAGES

We begin our discussion with the raw material for an MBS — the mortgage loan. A mortgage loan, or simply mortgage, is a loan secured by real estate property which obliges the borrower to make a predetermined series of payments. The interest rate on the mortgage loan is called the *mortgage rate* or *contract rate*. The frequency of payment is typically monthly.

When the lender makes the loan based on the credit of the borrower and on the collateral for the mortgage, the mortgage is said to be a *conventional mort-*

gage. The lender may require the borrower to obtain mortgage insurance to guarantee the fulfillment of the borrower's obligation. Some borrowers can qualify for mortgage insurance which is guaranteed by one of three U.S. government agencies: the Federal Housing Administration (FHA), the Veteran's Administration (VA), or the Rural Housing Service (RHS). There are also private mortgage insurers.

Mortgage Designs

There are many types of mortgage designs available in the United States. A mortgage design is a specification of the interest rate, term of the mortgage, and manner in which the borrowed funds are repaid. Below we describe the three most popular mortgage designs: (1) the fixed-rate, level-payment, fully amortized mortgage, (2) the adjustable-rate mortgage, and (3) the balloon mortgage.

Fixed-Rate, Level-Payment, Fully Amortized Mortgage

The basic idea behind the design of the fixed-rate, level payment, fully amortized mortgage is that the borrower pays interest and repays principal in equal installments over the life of the loan. Each monthly mortgage payment for this mortgage design is due on the first of each month and consists of:

1. interest of ⅟12th of the annual interest rate times the amount of the outstanding mortgage balance at the beginning of the previous month, and
2. a repayment of a portion of the outstanding mortgage balance (principal).

The difference between the monthly mortgage payment and the portion of the payment that represents interest equals the amount that is applied to reduce the outstanding mortgage balance. The monthly mortgage payment is designed so that after the last scheduled monthly payment of the loan is made, the amount of the outstanding mortgage balance is zero (i.e., the mortgage is fully repaid or amortized). Over the life of the mortgage, the portion of the monthly mortgage payment applied to interest declines each month and the portion applied to reducing the mortgage balance increases.

The cash flow in each month is reduced by the servicing fee. The dollar amount of the servicing fee declines over time as the mortgage amortizes. This is true for not only the mortgage design that we have just described, but for all mortgage designs.

Adjustable-Rate Mortgages

An *adjustable-rate mortgage* (ARM) is a loan in which the mortgage rate is reset periodically in accordance with a specified reference rate. The mortgage rate at the reset date is equal to the reference rate plus a spread.

Two categories of reference rates have been used in ARMs (1) market-determined rates and (2) calculated cost of funds for thrifts. The reference rate will have an important impact on the performance of an ARM and how it is priced. The most popular reference rate is a market-determined rate — the weekly average yield of constant maturity 1-year Treasuries.

The cost of funds index for thrifts is calculated based on the monthly weighted average interest cost for liabilities of thrifts. The most popular is the Eleventh Federal Home Loan Bank Board District Cost of Funds Index (COFI). The Eleventh District includes the states of California, Arizona, and Nevada. The cost of funds is calculated by first computing the monthly interest expense for all thrifts included in the Eleventh District. The interest expenses are summed and then divided by the average of the beginning and ending monthly balance. The index value is reported with a one month lag. For example, June's Eleventh District COFI is reported in July. The mortgage rate for a mortgage based on the Eleventh District COFI is usually reset based on the previous month's reported index rate. For example, if the reset date is August, the index rate reported in July will be used to set the mortgage rate. Consequently, there is a two month lag by the time the average cost of funds is reflected in the mortgage rate. This obviously is an advantage to the borrower when interest rates are rising and a disadvantage to the investor. The opposite is true when interest rates are falling.

The monthly mortgage payments of an ARM are affected by other features — periodic caps and lifetime rate caps and floors. Periodic caps limit the amount that the mortgage rate may increase or decrease at the reset date. The periodic rate cap is expressed in percentage points. The most common rate cap on annual reset loans is 2%. Most ARMs have an upper limit on the mortgage rate that can be charged over the life of the loan. This lifetime loan cap is expressed in terms of the initial rate. For example, if the initial mortgage rate is 7% and the lifetime cap is 5%, the maximum interest rate that the lender can charge over the life of the loan is 12%. Many ARMs also have a lower limit (floor) on the interest rate that can be charged over the life of the loan.

Balloon Mortgages

A variant of the adjustable-rate mortgage is the *balloon mortgage*. The primary difference between a balloon mortgage design and an ARM is that the mortgage rate is reset less frequently. In this mortgage design the borrower is given long-term financing by the lender but at specified future dates the mortgage rate is renegotiated. Thus, the lender is providing long-term funds for what is effectively a short-term borrowing, how short depending on the frequency of the renegotiation period. Effectively it is a short-term balloon loan in which the lender agrees to provide financing for the remainder of the term of the mortgage. The balloon payment is the original amount borrowed less the amount amortized.

Prepayments and Cash Flow Uncertainty

In projecting the cash flows of a mortgage loan, an investor must recognize that the homeowner may pay off all or part of the mortgage balance prior to the scheduled repayment date. Payments made in excess of the scheduled principal repayments are called *prepayments*. We'll look more closely at the factors that affect prepayment behavior later in this chapter.

The effect of prepayments is that the amount and timing of the cash flows from a mortgage are not known with certainty. This risk is referred to as *prepayment risk*. For example, all that the investor in a $100,000, 8.125% 30-year FHA-insured mortgage knows is that as long as the loan is outstanding, interest will be received and the principal will be repaid at the scheduled date each month; then at the end of the 30 years, the investor would have received $100,000 in principal payments. What the investor does not know — the uncertainty — is for how long the loan will be outstanding, and therefore what the timing of the principal payments will be.

MORTGAGE PASSTHROUGH SECURITIES

A mortgage passthrough security is a security created when one or more holders of mortgages form a pool (collection) of mortgages and sell shares or participation certificates in the pool. A pool may consist of several thousand or only a few mortgages. When a mortgage is included in a pool of mortgages that is used as collateral for a mortgage passthrough security, the mortgage is said to be securitized.

The cash flows of a mortgage passthrough security depend on the cash flows of the underlying mortgages — interest, the scheduled repayment of principal, and any prepayments. Payments are made to security holders each month. Neither the amount nor the timing, however, of the cash flows from the pool of mortgages are identical to that of the cash flows passed through to investors. The monthly cash flows for a passthrough are less than the monthly cash flows of the underlying mortgages by an amount equal to servicing and other fees. The other fees are those charged by the issuer or guarantor of the passthrough for guaranteeing the issue. The coupon rate on a passthrough, called the *passthrough coupon rate*, is less than the mortgage rate on the underlying pool of mortgage loans by an amount equal to the servicing fee and guarantee fee. The latter is a fee charged by an agency for providing a guarantee of the principal and interest payments.

The timing of the cash flows is also different. The monthly mortgage payment is due from each mortgagor on the first day of each month, but there is a delay in passing through the corresponding monthly cash flow to the security holders. The length of the delay varies by the type of passthrough security.

Not all of the mortgages that are included in a pool of mortgages that are securitized have the same mortgage rate and the same maturity. Consequently, when describing a passthrough security, a weighted average coupon rate and a weighted average maturity are determined. A *weighted average coupon rate*, or WAC, is found by weighting the mortgage rate of each mortgage loan in the pool by the amount of the mortgage balance outstanding. A *weighted average maturity*, or WAM, is found by weighting the remaining number of months to maturity for each mortgage loan in the pool by the amount of the mortgage balance outstanding.

Agency passthrough securities include loans that meet underwriting standards set forth by the particular agency with the approval of Congress. These underwriting standards involve limitations on the amount of the loan, the amount of seasoning, the variation in the mortgage rates in the pool, and whether or not the loans must be insured or conventional. Loans that do not qualify for inclusion because they do not satisfy the underwriting standards established by the agencies are securitized by private entities. Such loans are said to be *nonconforming loans*.

Agency passthrough securities can provide one of two types of guarantee. One type is the timely payment of both interest and principal, meaning the interest and principal will be paid when due, even if any of the mortgagors fail to make their monthly mortgage payments. The second type guarantees both interest and principal payments; however, it only guarantees the timely payment of interest. The scheduled principal is passed through as it is collected with a guarantee that the scheduled payment will be made no later than a specified date. All Ginnie Mae and Fannie Mae passthroughs have the first type of guarantee. While passthroughs currently issued by Freddie Mac have the first type of guarantee, there are outstanding issues that have the second type of guarantee.

Nonagency passthroughs have no explicit or implicit government guarantee. The credit risk of an issue is determined by one or more of the nationally recognized statistical rating organizations (i.e., rating agencies). As explained in other chapters in this book, the pool of loans will be credit enhanced to obtain the desired rating of the issuer. Credit enhancement for nonagency MBS will be discussed later in this chapter.

Prepayment Conventions and Cash Flows

In order to value a passthrough security, it is necessary to project its cash flows. The difficulty is that the cash flows are unknown because of prepayments. The only way to project cash flows are to make some assumption about the prepayment rate over the life of the underlying mortgage pool. The prepayment rate is sometimes referred to as the *speed*. Two conventions have been used as a benchmark for prepayment rates — conditional prepayment rate and Public Securities Association prepayment benchmark.

Conditional Prepayment Rate

One convention for projecting prepayments and the cash flows of a passthrough assumes that some fraction of the remaining principal in the pool is prepaid each month for the remaining term of the mortgage. The prepayment rate assumed for a pool, called the *conditional prepayment rate* (CPR), is based on the characteristics of the pool (including its historical prepayment experience) and the current and expected future economic environment.

The CPR is an annual prepayment rate. To estimate monthly prepayments, the CPR must be converted into a monthly prepayment rate, commonly referred to as the *single-monthly mortality* rate (SMM). A formula can be used to determine the SMM for a given CPR:

$$SMM = 1 - (1 - CPR)^{1/12}$$

Suppose that the CPR used to estimate prepayments is 6%. The corresponding SMM is:

$$SMM = 1 - (1 - 0.06)^{1/12}$$
$$= 1 - (0.94)^{0.08333} = 0.005143$$

An SMM of $w\%$ means that approximately $w\%$ of the remaining mortgage balance at the beginning of the month, less the scheduled principal payment, will prepay that month. That is,

$$\text{Prepayment for month } t = \text{SMM} \times (\text{Beginning mortgage balance for month } t - \text{Scheduled principal payment for month } t)$$

For example, suppose that an investor owns a passthrough in which the remaining mortgage balance at the beginning of some month is $290 million. Assuming that the SMM is 0.5143% and the scheduled principal payment is $3 million, the estimated prepayment for the month is:

$$0.005143 \times (\$290{,}000{,}000 - \$3{,}000{,}000) = \$1{,}476{,}041$$

PSA Prepayment Benchmark

The Public Securities Association (PSA) prepayment benchmark is expressed as a monthly series of CPRs.[1] The PSA benchmark assumes that prepayment rates are low for newly originated mortgages and then will speed up as the mortgages become seasoned.

The PSA benchmark assumes the following prepayment rates for 30-year mortgages:

- a CPR of 0.2% for the first month, increased by 0.2% per year per month for the next 30 months when it reaches 6% per year
- a 6% CPR after month 30

This benchmark, referred to as "100% PSA" or simply "100 PSA," is graphically depicted in Exhibit 1. Mathematically, 100 PSA can be expressed as follows:

- if $t \leq 30$ then $CPR = \dfrac{6\% t}{30}$
- if $t > 30$ then $CPR = 6\%$

where t is the number of months since origination.

[1] This benchmark is commonly referred to as a prepayment model, suggesting that it can be used to estimate prepayments. Characterization of this benchmark as a prepayment model is inappropriate. It is simply a market convention describing a possible behavior pattern for prepayments.

Exhibit 1: Graphical Depiction of 100 PSA

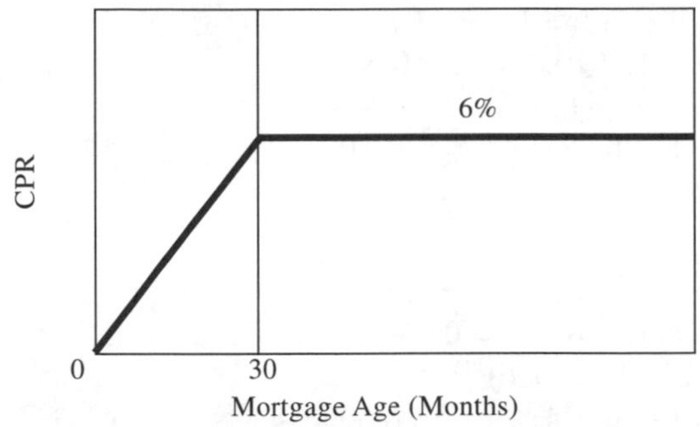

Slower or faster speeds are then referred to as some percentage of PSA. For example, 50 PSA means one-half the CPR of the PSA benchmark prepayment rate; 150 PSA means 1.5 times the CPR of the PSA benchmark prepayment rate; 300 PSA means three times the CPR of the benchmark prepayment rate. A prepayment rate of 0 PSA means that no prepayments are assumed.

The CPR is converted to an SMM using the formula given above. For example, the SMMs for month 5, month 20, and months 31 through 360 assuming 100 PSA are calculated as follows:

for month 5:

$$\text{CPR} = 6\% \ (5/30) = 1\% = 0.01$$
$$\text{SMM} = 1 - (1 - 0.01)^{1/12}$$
$$= 1 - (0.99)^{0.08333} = 0.000837$$

for month 20:

$$\text{CPR} = 6\% \ (20/30) = 4\% = 0.04$$
$$\text{SMM} = 1 - (1 - 0.04)^{1/12}$$
$$= 1 - (0.96)^{0.08333} = 0.003396$$

for months 31-360:

$$\text{CPR} = 6\%$$
$$\text{SMM} = 1 - (1 - 0.06)^{1/12}$$
$$= 1 - (0.94)^{0.08333} = 0.005143$$

The SMMs for month 5, month 20, and months 31 through 360 assuming 165 PSA are computed as follows:

for month 5:

$$\begin{aligned} \text{CPR} &= 6\% \ (5/30) = 1\% = 0.01 \\ 165 \text{ PSA} &= 1.65 \ (0.01) = 0.0165 \\ \text{SMM} &= 1 - (1 - 0.0165)^{1/12} \\ &= 1 - (0.9835)^{0.08333} = 0.001386 \end{aligned}$$

for month 20:

$$\begin{aligned} \text{CPR} &= 6\% \ (20/30) = 4\% = 0.04 \\ 165 \text{ PSA} &= 1.65 \ (0.04) = 0.066 \\ \text{SMM} &= 1 - (1 - 0.066)^{1/12} \\ &= 1 - (0.934)^{0.08333} = 0.005674 \end{aligned}$$

for months 31-360:

$$\begin{aligned} \text{CPR} &= 6\% \\ 165 \text{ PSA} &= 1.65 \ (0.06) = 0.099 \\ \text{SMM} &= 1 - (1 - 0.099)^{1/12} \\ &= 1 - (0.901)^{0.08333} = 0.00865 \end{aligned}$$

Notice that the SMM assuming 165 PSA is not just 1.65 times the SMM assuming 100 PSA. It is the CPR that is a multiple of the CPR assuming 100 PSA.

Illustration of Monthly Cash Flow Construction

We now show how to construct a monthly cash flow for a hypothetical passthrough given a PSA assumption. For the purpose of this illustration, the underlying mortgages for this hypothetical passthrough are assumed to be fixed-rate, level-payment, fully amortized mortgages with a WAC of 8.125%. It will be assumed that the passthrough rate is 7.5% with a WAM of 357 months.

Exhibit 2 shows the cash flow for selected months assuming 165 PSA. The cash flow is broken down into three components: (1) interest (based on the passthrough rate), (2) the regularly scheduled principal repayment, and (3) prepayments based on 100 PSA. Let's walk through Exhibit 2 column by column.

Column 1: This is the month.

Column 2: This column gives the outstanding mortgage balance at the beginning of the month. It is equal to the outstanding balance at the beginning of the previous month reduced by the total principal payment in the previous month.

Column 3: This column shows the SMM for 165 PSA. Two things should be noted in this column. First, for month 1, the SMM is for a passthrough that has been seasoned three months. That is, the CPR is 0.8% for the first month times 1.65. This is because the WAM is 357. Second, from month 27 on, the SMM is 0.00865 which corresponds to a CPR of 9.9% (6% times 1.65).

Exhibit 2: Monthly Cash Flow for a $400 Million Passthrough with a 7.5% Passthrough Rate, a WAC of 8.125%, and a WAM of 357 Months Assuming 165 PSA

(1) Month	(2) Outstanding Balance	(3) SMM	(4) Mortgage Payment	(5) Net Interest	(6) Scheduled Principal	(7) Prepayment	(8) Total Principal	(9) Cash Flow
1	$400,000,000	0.00111	$2,975,868	$2,500,000	$267,535	$442,389	$709,923	$3,209,923
2	399,290,077	0.00139	2,972,575	2,495,563	269,048	552,847	821,896	3,317,459
3	398,468,181	0.00167	2,968,456	2,490,426	270,495	663,065	933,560	3,423,986
4	397,534,621	0.00195	2,963,513	2,484,591	271,873	772,949	1,044,822	3,529,413
5	396,489,799	0.00223	2,957,747	2,478,061	273,181	882,405	1,155,586	3,633,647
6	395,334,213	0.00251	2,951,160	2,470,839	274,418	991,341	1,265,759	3,736,598
7	394,068,454	0.00279	2,943,755	2,462,928	275,583	1,099,664	1,375,246	3,838,174
8	392,693,208	0.00308	2,935,534	2,454,333	276,674	1,207,280	1,483,954	3,938,287
9	391,209,254	0.00336	2,926,503	2,445,058	277,690	1,314,099	1,591,789	4,036,847
10	389,617,464	0.00365	2,916,666	2,435,109	278,631	1,420,029	1,698,659	4,133,769
11	387,918,805	0.00393	2,906,028	2,424,493	279,494	1,524,979	1,804,473	4,228,965
12	386,114,332	0.00422	2,894,595	2,413,215	280,280	1,628,859	1,909,139	4,322,353
13	384,205,194	0.00451	2,882,375	2,401,282	280,986	1,731,581	2,012,567	4,413,850
14	382,192,626	0.00480	2,869,375	2,388,704	281,613	1,833,058	2,114,670	4,503,374
15	380,077,956	0.00509	2,855,603	2,375,487	282,159	1,933,203	2,215,361	4,590,848
16	377,862,595	0.00538	2,841,068	2,361,641	282,623	2,031,931	2,314,554	4,676,195
17	375,548,041	0.00567	2,825,779	2,347,175	283,006	2,129,159	2,412,164	4,759,339
18	373,135,877	0.00597	2,809,746	2,332,099	283,305	2,224,805	2,508,110	4,840,210
19	370,627,766	0.00626	2,792,980	2,316,424	283,521	2,318,790	2,602,312	4,918,735
20	368,025,455	0.00656	2,775,493	2,300,159	283,654	2,411,036	2,694,690	4,994,849
21	365,330,765	0.00685	2,757,296	2,283,317	283,702	2,501,466	2,785,169	5,068,486
22	362,545,596	0.00715	2,738,402	2,265,910	283,666	2,590,008	2,873,674	5,139,584
23	359,671,922	0.00745	2,718,823	2,247,950	283,545	2,676,588	2,960,133	5,208,083
24	356,711,789	0.00775	2,698,575	2,229,449	283,338	2,761,139	3,044,477	5,273,926
25	353,667,312	0.00805	2,677,670	2,210,421	283,047	2,843,593	3,126,640	5,337,061
26	350,540,672	0.00835	2,656,123	2,190,879	282,671	2,923,885	3,206,556	5,397,435
27	347,334,116	0.00865	2,633,950	2,170,838	282,209	3,001,955	3,284,164	5,455,002
28	344,049,952	0.00865	2,611,167	2,150,312	281,662	2,973,553	3,255,215	5,405,527
29	340,794,737	0.00865	2,588,581	2,129,967	281,116	2,945,400	3,226,516	5,356,483
30	337,568,221	0.00865	2,566,190	2,109,801	280,572	2,917,496	3,198,067	5,307,869
100	170,142,350	0.00865	1,396,958	1,063,390	244,953	1,469,591	1,714,544	2,777,933
101	168,427,806	0.00865	1,384,875	1,052,674	244,478	1,454,765	1,699,243	2,751,916
102	166,728,563	0.00865	1,372,896	1,042,054	244,004	1,440,071	1,684,075	2,726,128
103	165,044,489	0.00865	1,361,020	1,031,528	243,531	1,425,508	1,669,039	2,700,567
104	163,375,450	0.00865	1,349,248	1,021,097	243,060	1,411,075	1,654,134	2,675,231
105	161,721,315	0.00865	1,337,577	1,010,758	242,589	1,396,771	1,639,359	2,650,118
200	56,746,664	0.00865	585,990	354,667	201,767	489,106	690,874	1,045,540
201	56,055,790	0.00865	580,921	350,349	201,377	483,134	684,510	1,034,859
202	55,371,280	0.00865	575,896	346,070	200,986	477,216	678,202	1,024,273
203	54,693,077	0.00865	570,915	341,832	200,597	471,353	671,950	1,013,782
204	54,021,127	0.00865	565,976	337,632	200,208	465,544	665,752	1,003,384
205	53,355,375	0.00865	561,081	333,471	199,820	459,789	659,609	993,080

Exhibit 2 (Concluded)

(1) Month	(2) Outstanding Balance	(3) SMM	(4) Mortgage Payment	(5) Net Interest	(6) Scheduled Principal	(7) Prepayment	(8) Total Principal	(9) Cash Flow
300	$11,758,141	0.00865	$245,808	$73,488	$166,196	$100,269	$266,465	$339,953
301	11,491,677	0.00865	243,682	71,823	165,874	97,967	263,841	335,664
302	11,227,836	0.00865	241,574	70,174	165,552	95,687	261,240	331,414
303	10,966,596	0.00865	239,485	68,541	165,232	93,430	258,662	327,203
304	10,707,934	0.00865	237,413	66,925	164,912	91,196	256,107	323,032
305	10,451,827	0.00865	235,360	65,324	164,592	88,983	253,575	318,899
350	1,235,674	0.00865	159,202	7,723	150,836	9,384	160,220	167,943
351	1,075,454	0.00865	157,825	6,722	150,544	8,000	158,544	165,266
352	916,910	0.00865	156,460	5,731	150,252	6,631	156,883	162,614
353	760,027	0.00865	155,107	4,750	149,961	5,277	155,238	159,988
354	604,789	0.00865	153,765	3,780	149,670	3,937	153,607	157,387
355	451,182	0.00865	152,435	2,820	149,380	2,611	151,991	154,811
356	299,191	0.00865	151,117	1,870	149,091	1,298	150,389	152,259
357	148,802	0.00865	149,809	930	148,802	0	148,802	149,732

Note: Since the WAM is 357 months, the underlying mortgage pool is seasoned an average of three months. Therefore, the CPR for month 27 is 1.65 × 6%.

Column 4: The total monthly mortgage payment is shown in this column. Notice that the total monthly mortgage payment declines over time as prepayments reduce the mortgage balance outstanding. There is a formula to determine what the monthly mortgage balance will be for each month given prepayments.[2]

Column 5: The monthly interest paid to the passthrough investor is found in this column. This value is determined by multiplying the outstanding mortgage balance at the beginning of the month by the passthrough rate of 7.5% and dividing by 12.

Column 6: This column gives the regularly scheduled principal repayment. This is the difference between the total monthly mortgage payment [the amount shown in column (4)] and the gross coupon interest for the month. The gross coupon interest is 8.125% multiplied by the outstanding mortgage balance at the beginning of the month, then divided by 12.

Column 7: The prepayment for the month is reported in this column. The prepayment is found as follows:

SMM × (Beginning mortgage balance for month *t*
  − Scheduled principal payment for month *t*)

[2] The formula is presented in Chapter 20 of Frank J. Fabozzi, *Fixed Income Mathematics: Analytical and Statistical Techniques* (Chicago: Probus Publishing, 1993).

Column 8: The total principal payment, which is the sum of columns (6) and (7), is shown in this column.

Column 9: The projected monthly cash flow for this passthrough is shown in this last column. The monthly cash flow is the sum of the interest paid to the passthrough investor [column (5)] and the total principal payments for the month [column (8)].

Average Life of a Mortgage-Backed Security

Unlike a bullet maturity security such as a Treasury security, an MBS is an amortizing security. This means that principal is repaid over time. Consequently, it makes little sense to talk about the maturity of an MBS. Instead, practitioners use as a measure of the life of an MBS the security's *average life.*

The average life of a mortgage-backed security is the average time to receipt of principal payments (scheduled principal payments and projected prepayments), weighted by the amount of principal expected. Specifically, the average life is found by first calculating:

$$\begin{aligned}
&1 \times (\text{Projected principal received in month 1})\\
&+ 2 \times (\text{Projected principal received in month 2})\\
&+ 3 \times (\text{Projected principal received in month 3})\\
&+ \ldots\\
&+T \times (\text{Projected principal received in month } T)
\end{aligned}$$

The above sum is the weighted monthly average of principal received where T is the last month that principal is expected to be received. Then the average life is found as follows:

$$\text{Average life} = \frac{\text{Weighted monthly average of principal received}}{12(\text{Total principal to be received})}$$

The average life of a passthrough depends on the PSA prepayment assumption. To see this, the average life is shown below for different prepayment speeds for the passthrough we used to illustrate the cash flows for 165 PSA in Exhibits 2:

PSA speed	50	100	165	200	300	400	500	600	700
Average life	15.11	11.66	8.76	7.68	5.63	4.44	3.68	3.16	2.78

COLLATERALIZED MORTGAGE OBLIGATIONS

Passthrough securities or whole loans can be used as collateral for the creation of a *collateralized mortgage obligation* (CMO). Before we describe CMOs, we will look at the motivation for their creation by taking a closer look at prepayment risk.

An investor who owns passthrough securities does not know what the cash flows will be because of prepayments. As we noted earlier, this risk is called prepayment risk. To understand the significance of prepayment risk, suppose an investor buys a passthrough with a 10% passthrough rate at a time when mortgage rates are 10%. Let's consider what is likely to happen to prepayments if mortgage rates decline to, say, 6%. There will be two adverse consequences. First, a basic property of fixed income securities is that the price of an option-free bond will rise. But in the case of a passthrough security, the rise in price will not be as large as that of an option-free bond because a fall in interest rates will give the borrower an incentive to prepay the loan and refinance the debt at a lower rate.[3] Thus, the upside price potential of a passthrough security is truncated because of prepayments. The second adverse consequence is that the cash flows must be reinvested at a lower rate. These two adverse consequences when mortgage rates decline are referred to as *contraction risk*.

Now let's look at what happens if mortgage rates rise to 15%. The price of the passthrough, like the price of any bond, will decline. But again it will decline more because the higher rates will tend to slow down the rate of prepayment, in effect increasing the amount invested at the coupon rate, which is lower than the market rate. Prepayments will slow down because homeowners will not refinance or partially prepay their mortgages when mortgage rates are higher than the contract rate of 10%. Of course this is just the time when investors want prepayments to speed up so that they can reinvest the prepayments at the higher market interest rate. This adverse consequence of rising mortgage rates is called *extension risk*.

Therefore, prepayment risk encompasses contraction risk and extension risk. Prepayment risk makes passthrough securities unattractive for certain individuals and financial institutions to hold for purposes of accomplishing their investment objectives.

Basic Principles of a CMO

Some investors are concerned with extension risk and others with contraction risk when they invest in a passthrough. An investor may be willing to accept one form of prepayment risk but seek to avoid the other. For example, an investor who seeks a short-term security is concerned with extension risk. An investor who seeks a long-term security, and wants to avoid reinvesting unexpected principal prepayments should interest rates drop, is concerned with contraction risk.

By redirecting how the cash flows of passthrough securities are paid to different bond classes that are created, securities can be created that have different exposure to prepayment risk. When the cash flows of mortgage-related products are redistributed to different bond classes, the resulting securities are called collateralized mortgage obligations. The creation of a CMO cannot eliminate prepayment risk, it can only redistribute the two forms of prepayment risk among different classes of bondholders.

---

[3] This characteristic is popularly referred to as *negative convexity.*

The basic principle is that redirecting cash flows (interest and principal) to different bond classes, called *tranches*, mitigates different forms of prepayment risk. It is never possible to eliminate prepayment risk. If one tranche in a CMO structure has less prepayment risk than the mortgage passthrough securities that are collateral for the structure, then another tranche in the same structure has greater prepayment risk than the collateral.

CMOs are referred to as paythroughs or multi-class passthroughs. A security structure in which collateral is carved into different bond classes is not uncommon. Similar paythrough or multi-class passthrough structures are discussed for other asset-backed securities in other chapters in this book.

Agency CMOs

There are agency and nonagency CMOs. The same three entities that issue agency passthrough securities (Freddie Mac, Fannie Mae, and Ginnie Mae) issue agency CMOs. Agency CMOs are backed by pools of passthrough securities. Unlike an agency CMO which exposes an investor to prepayment but not credit risk, a nonagency CMO exposes an investor to credit risk as well as prepayment risk. In this section we focus on agency CMOs to see how prepayment risk can be redistributed among the tranches in a CMO structure. Later in this chapter we look at how prepayment risk and credit risk can be redistributed among the tranches in a nonagency CMO structure.

There is a wide-range of CMO structures. We review the major structures below. Rather than just provide a definition, it is useful to see how the various types of CMOs are created.

Sequential-Pay Tranches

The first CMO was structured so that each tranche would be retired sequentially. Such structures are referred to as sequential-pay CMOs.

To illustrate a sequential-pay CMO, we discuss FAF-01, a hypothetical deal made up to illustrate the basic features of the structure.[4] The collateral for this hypothetical CMO is a hypothetical passthrough with a total par value of $400 million and the following characteristics: (1) the passthrough rate is 7.5%, (2) the WAC is 8.125%, and (3) the WAM is 357 months. This is the same passthrough that we used earlier in this chapter to calculate the cash flows assuming 165 PSA.

From this $400 million of collateral, four tranches are created. Their characteristics are summarized in Exhibit 3. The total par value of the four tranches is equal to the par value of the collateral (i.e., the passthrough security). In this simple structure, the coupon rate is the same for each tranche and also the same as the collateral's coupon rate. There is no reason why this must be so, and, in fact, typically the coupon rate varies by tranche.

---

[4] All CMO structures are given a name. In our illustrations we use FAF.

Exhibit 3: FAF-01: A Hypothetical Four-Tranche Sequential-Pay Structure

Tranche	Par Amount	Coupon Rate (%)
A	$194,500,000	7.5
B	36,000,000	7.5
C	96,500,000	7.5
D	73,000,000	7.5
Total	$400,000,000	

Payment rules:

1. *For payment of periodic coupon interest:* Disburse periodic coupon interest to each tranche on the basis of the amount of principal outstanding at the beginning of the period.
2. *For disbursement of principal payments:* Disburse principal payments to tranche A until it is completely paid off. After tranche A is completely paid off, disburse principal payments to tranche B until it is completely paid off. After tranche B is completely paid off, disburse principal payments to tranche C until it is completely paid off. After tranche C is completely paid off, disburse principal payments to tranche D until it is completely paid off.

Now remember that a CMO is created by redistributing the cash flow — interest and principal — to the different tranches based on a set of payment rules. The payment rules at the bottom of Exhibit 3 set forth how the monthly cash flow from the passthrough (i.e., collateral) is to be distributed to the four tranches. There are separate rules for the payment of the coupon interest and the payment of principal, the principal being the total of the regularly scheduled principal payment and any prepayments.

In FAF-01, each tranche receives periodic coupon interest payments based on the amount of the outstanding balance. The disbursement of the principal, however, is made in a special way. A tranche is not entitled to receive principal until the entire principal of the tranche before it has been paid off. More specifically, tranche A receives all the principal payments until the entire principal amount owed to that tranche, $194,500,000, is paid off; then tranche B begins to receive principal and continues to do so until it is paid the entire $36,000,000. Tranche C then receives principal, and when it is paid off, tranche D starts receiving principal payments.

While the payment rules for the disbursement of the principal payments are known, the precise amount of the principal in each period is not. This will depend on the cash flow, and therefore principal payments, of the collateral, which depends on the actual prepayment rate of the collateral. An assumed PSA speed allows the monthly cash flow to be projected. Assuming that the collateral does prepay at 165 PSA, the cash flows available to distribute to all four tranches of FAF-01 will be precisely the cash flows shown in Exhibit 2.

To demonstrate how the payment rules for FAF-01 work, Exhibit 4 shows the cash flow for selected months assuming the collateral prepays at 165 PSA. For each tranche, the exhibit shows: (1) the balance at the end of the month, (2) the principal paid down (regularly scheduled principal repayment plus prepayments), and (3) interest. In month 1, the cash flow for the collateral consists of a principal payment of $709,923 and interest of $2.5 million (0.075 times $400 million divided by 12). The interest payment is distributed to the four tranches based on the amount of the par value outstanding. So, for example, tranche A receives $1,215,625 (0.075 times $194,500,000 divided by 12) of the $2.5 million. The principal, however, is all distributed to tranche A. Therefore, the cash flow for tranche A in month 1 is $1,925,548. The principal balance at the end of month 1 for tranche A is $193,790,076 (the original principal balance of $194,500,000 less the principal payment of $709,923). No principal payment is distributed to the three other tranches because there is still a principal balance outstanding for tranche A. This will be true for months 2 through 80.

Exhibit 4: Monthly Cash Flow for Selected Months for FAF-01 Assuming 165 PSA

	Tranche A			Tranche B		
Month	Balance	Principal	Interest	Balance	Principal	Interest
1	194,500,000	709,923	1,215,625	36,000,000	0	225,000
2	193,790,077	821,896	1,211,188	36,000,000	0	225,000
3	192,968,181	933,560	1,206,051	36,000,000	0	225,000
4	192,034,621	1,044,822	1,200,216	36,000,000	0	225,000
5	190,989,799	1,155,586	1,193,686	36,000,000	0	225,000
6	189,834,213	1,265,759	1,186,464	36,000,000	0	225,000
7	188,568,454	1,375,246	1,178,553	36,000,000	0	225,000
8	187,193,208	1,483,954	1,169,958	36,000,000	0	225,000
9	185,709,254	1,591,789	1,160,683	36,000,000	0	225,000
10	184,117,464	1,698,659	1,150,734	36,000,000	0	225,000
11	182,418,805	1,804,473	1,140,118	36,000,000	0	225,000
12	180,614,332	1,909,139	1,128,840	36,000,000	0	225,000
75	12,893,479	2,143,974	80,584	36,000,000	0	225,000
76	10,749,504	2,124,935	67,184	36,000,000	0	225,000
77	8,624,569	2,106,062	53,904	36,000,000	0	225,000
78	6,518,507	2,087,353	40,741	36,000,000	0	225,000
79	4,431,154	2,068,807	27,695	36,000,000	0	225,000
80	2,362,347	2,050,422	14,765	36,000,000	0	225,000
81	311,926	311,926	1,950	36,000,000	1,720,271	225,000
82	0	0	0	34,279,729	2,014,130	214,248
83	0	0	0	32,265,599	1,996,221	201,660
84	0	0	0	30,269,378	1,978,468	189,184
85	0	0	0	28,290,911	1,960,869	176,818
95	0	0	0	9,449,331	1,793,089	59,058
96	0	0	0	7,656,242	1,777,104	47,852
97	0	0	0	5,879,138	1,761,258	36,745
98	0	0	0	4,117,880	1,745,550	25,737
99	0	0	0	2,372,329	1,729,979	14,827
100	0	0	0	642,350	642,350	4,015
101	0	0	0	0	0	0
102	0	0	0	0	0	0
103	0	0	0	0	0	0
104	0	0	0	0	0	0
105	0	0	0	0	0	0

Exhibit 4 (Concluded)

	Tranche C			Tranche D		
Month	Balance	Principal	Interest	Balance	Principal	Interest
1	96,500,000	0	603,125	73,000,000	0	456,250
2	96,500,000	0	603,125	73,000,000	0	456,250
3	96,500,000	0	603,125	73,000,000	0	456,250
4	96,500,000	0	603,125	73,000,000	0	456,250
5	96,500,000	0	603,125	73,000,000	0	456,250
6	96,500,000	0	603,125	73,000,000	0	456,250
7	96,500,000	0	603,125	73,000,000	0	456,250
8	96,500,000	0	603,125	73,000,000	0	456,250
9	96,500,000	0	603,125	73,000,000	0	456,250
10	96,500,000	0	603,125	73,000,000	0	456,250
11	96,500,000	0	603,125	73,000,000	0	456,250
12	96,500,000	0	603,125	73,000,000	0	456,250
95	96,500,000	0	603,125	73,000,000	0	456,250
96	96,500,000	0	603,125	73,000,000	0	456,250
97	96,500,000	0	603,125	73,000,000	0	456,250
98	96,500,000	0	603,125	73,000,000	0	456,250
99	96,500,000	0	603,125	73,000,000	0	456,250
100	96,500,000	1,072,194	603,125	73,000,000	0	456,250
101	95,427,806	1,699,243	596,424	73,000,000	0	456,250
102	93,728,563	1,684,075	585,804	73,000,000	0	456,250
103	92,044,489	1,669,039	575,278	73,000,000	0	456,250
104	90,375,450	1,654,134	564,847	73,000,000	0	456,250
105	88,721,315	1,639,359	554,508	73,000,000	0	456,250
175	3,260,287	869,602	20,377	73,000,000	0	456,250
176	2,390,685	861,673	14,942	73,000,000	0	456,250
177	1,529,013	853,813	9,556	73,000,000	0	456,250
178	675,199	675,199	4,220	73,000,000	170,824	456,250
179	0	0	0	72,829,176	838,300	455,182
180	0	0	0	71,990,876	830,646	449,943
181	0	0	0	71,160,230	823,058	444,751
182	0	0	0	70,337,173	815,536	439,607
183	0	0	0	69,521,637	808,081	434,510
184	0	0	0	68,713,556	800,690	429,460
185	0	0	0	67,912,866	793,365	424,455
350	0	0	0	1,235,674	160,220	7,723
351	0	0	0	1,075,454	158,544	6,722
352	0	0	0	916,910	156,883	5,731
353	0	0	0	760,027	155,238	4,750
354	0	0	0	604,789	153,607	3,780
355	0	0	0	451,182	151,991	2,820
356	0	0	0	299,191	150,389	1,870
357	0	0	0	148,802	148,802	930

Exhibit 5: Average Life for Collateral and the Four Tranches of FAF-01

Prepayment speed (PSA)	Average life for				
	Collateral	Tranche A	Tranche B	Tranche C	Tranche D
50	15.11	7.48	15.98	21.02	27.24
100	11.66	4.90	10.86	15.78	24.58
165	8.76	3.48	7.49	11.19	20.27
200	7.68	3.05	6.42	9.60	18.11
300	5.63	2.32	4.64	6.81	13.36
400	4.44	1.94	3.70	5.31	10.34
500	3.68	1.69	3.12	4.38	8.35
600	3.16	1.51	2.74	3.75	6.96
700	2.78	1.38	2.47	3.30	5.95

After month 81, the principal balance will be zero for tranche A. For the collateral the cash flow in month 81 is $3,318,521, consisting of a principal payment of $2,032,196 and interest of $1,286,325. At the beginning of month 81 (end of month 80), the principal balance for tranche A is $311,926. Therefore, $311,926 of the $2,032,196 of the principal payment from the collateral will be disbursed to tranche A. After this payment is made, no additional principal payments are made to this tranche as the principal balance is zero. The remaining principal payment from the collateral, $1,720,271, is disbursed to tranche B. According to the assumed prepayment speed of 165 PSA, tranche B then begins receiving principal payments in month 81.

Exhibit 4 shows that tranche B is fully paid off by month 100, when tranche C now begins to receive principal payments. Tranche C is not fully paid off until month 178, at which time tranche D begins receiving the remaining principal payments. The maturity (i.e., the time until the principal is fully paid off) for these four tranches assuming 165 PSA is 81 months for tranche A, 100 months for tranche B, 178 months for tranche C, and 357 months for tranche D.

The *principal pay down window* for a tranche is the time period between the beginning and the ending of the principal payments to that tranche. So, for example, for tranche A, the principal pay down window would be month 1 to month 81 assuming 165 PSA. For tranche B it is from month 81 to month 100. The window is also specified in terms of the length of the time from the beginning of the principal pay down window to the end of the principal pay down window. For tranche A, the window would be stated as 81 months, for tranche B 20 months. In confirmation of trades involving CMOs, the principal pay down window is specified in terms of the initial month that principal is expected to be received to the final month that principal is expected to be received.

Let's look at what has been accomplished by creating the CMO. First, earlier we saw that the average life of the passthrough is 8.76 years, assuming a prepayment speed of 165 PSA. Exhibit 5 reports the average life of the collateral and the four tranches assuming different prepayment speeds. Notice that the four tranches have average lives that are both shorter and longer than the collateral thereby attracting investors who have a preference for an average life different from that of the collateral.

There is still a major problem: there is considerable variability of the average life for the tranches. We'll see how this can be tackled later on. However, there is some protection provided for each tranche against prepayment risk. This is because prioritizing the distribution of principal (i.e., establishing the payment rules for principal) effectively protects the shorter-term tranche A in this structure against extension risk. This protection must come from somewhere, so it comes from the three other tranches. Similarly, tranches C and D provide protection against extension risk for tranches A and B. At the same time, tranches C and D benefit because they are provided protection against contraction risk, the protection coming from tranches A and B.

Accrual Tranches

In FAF-01, the payment rules for interest provide for all tranches to be paid interest each month. In many sequential-pay CMO structures, at least one tranche does not receive current interest. Instead, the interest for that tranche would accrue and be added to the principal balance. Such a tranche is commonly referred to as an *accrual tranche* or a Z bond (because the tranche is similar to a zero-coupon bond). The interest that would have been paid to the accrual tranche is then used to speed up pay down of the principal balance of earlier tranches.

To see this, consider FAF-02, a hypothetical CMO structure with the same collateral as FAF-01 and with four tranches, each with a coupon rate of 7.5%. The difference is in the last tranche, Z, which is an accrual tranche. The structure for FAF-02 is shown in Exhibit 6.

Exhibit 6: FAF-02: A Hypothetical Four-Tranche Sequential-Pay Structure with an Accrual Bond Class

Tranche	Par Amount	Coupon rate (%)
A	$194,500,000	7.5
B	36,000,000	7.5
C	96,500,000	7.5
Z (Accrual)	73,000,000	7.5
Total	$400,000,000	

Payment rules:

1. *For payment of periodic coupon interest:* Disburse periodic coupon interest to tranches A, B, and C on the basis of the amount of principal outstanding at the beginning of the period. For tranche Z, accrue the interest based on the principal plus accrued interest in the previous period. The interest for tranche Z is to be paid to the earlier tranches as a principal paydown.
2. *For disbursement of principal payments:* Disburse principal payments to tranche A until it is completely paid off. After tranche A is completely paid off, disburse principal payments to tranche B until it is completely paid off. After tranche B is completely paid off, disburse principal payments to tranche C until it is completely paid off. After tranche C is completely paid off, disburse principal payments to tranche Z until the original principal balance plus accrued interest is completely paid off.

The inclusion of the accrual tranche will shorten the expected final maturity for tranches A, B, and C. The final payout for tranche A would be 64 months rather than 81 months; for tranche B it is 77 months rather than 100 months; and for tranche C it is 112 months rather than 178 months. The average lives for tranches A, B, and C are shorter in FAF-02 compared to FAF-01 because of the inclusion of the accrual tranche. For example, at 165 PSA, the average lives are as follows:

Structure	Tranche A	Tranche B	Tranche C
FAF-02	2.90	5.86	7.87
FAF-01	3.48	7.49	11.19

The reason for the shortening of the non-accrual tranches is that the interest that would be paid to the accrual tranche is being allocated to the other tranches. Tranche Z in FAF-02 will have a longer average life than tranche D in FAF-01.

Thus, shorter-term tranches and a longer-term tranche are created by including an accrual tranche. The accrual tranche has appeal to investors who are concerned with reinvestment risk. Since there are no coupon payments to reinvest, reinvestment risk is eliminated until all the other tranches are paid off.

Floating-Rate Tranches

A floating-rate tranche can be created from a fixed-rate tranche by creating a floater/inverse floater combination. We will illustrate the creation of a floating-rate and an inverse floating-rate tranche using the hypothetical CMO structure FAF-02, which is a four tranche sequential-pay structure with an accrual tranche. We can select any of the tranches from which to create a floating-rate and an inverse floating-rate tranche. In fact, we can create these two securities for more than one of the four tranches or for only a portion of one tranche.

In this case, we create a floater and an inverse floater from tranche C. The par value for this tranche is $96.5 million, and we create two tranches that have a combined par value of $96.5 million. We refer to this CMO structure with a floater and an inverse floater as FAF-03. It has five tranches, designated A, B, FL, IFL, and Z, where FL is the floating-rate tranche and IFL is the inverse floating-rate tranche. Exhibit 7 describes FAF-03. Any reference rate can be used to create a floater and the corresponding inverse floater. The reference rate selected for setting the coupon rate for FL and IFL in FAF-03 is 1-month LIBOR.

The amount of the par value of the floating-rate tranche will be some portion of the $96.5 million. There are an infinite number of ways to cut up the $96.5 million between the floater and inverse floater, and final partitioning will be driven by the demands of investors. In the FAF-03 structure, we made the floater from $72,375,000 or 75% of the $96.5 million. The coupon rate on the floater is set at 1-month LIBOR plus 50 basis points. So, for example, if LIBOR is 3.75% at the coupon reset date, the coupon rate on the floater is 3.75% + 0.5%, or 4.25%. There is a cap on the coupon rate for the floater (discussed later).

Exhibit 7: FAF-03: A Hypothetical Five-Tranche Sequential-Pay Structure with Floater, Inverse Floater, and Accrual Tranche

Tranche	Par amount	Coupon rate
A	$194,500,000	7.50%
B	36,000,000	7.50%
FL	72,375,000	1-mo. LIBOR + 0.50
IFL	24,125,000	28.50 – 3 × (1-mo. LIBOR)
Z (Accrual)	73,000,000	7.50%
Total	$400,000,000	

Payment rules:

1. *For payment of periodic coupon interest:* Disburse periodic coupon interest to tranches A, B, FL, and IFL on the basis of the amount of principal outstanding at the beginning of the period. For tranche Z, accrue the interest based on the principal plus accrued interest in the previous period. The interest for tranche Z is to be paid to the earlier tranches as a principal paydown. The maximum coupon rate for FL is 10%; the minimum coupon rate for IFL is 0%.
2. *For disbursement of principal payments:* Disburse principal payments to tranche A until it is completely paid off. After tranche A is completely paid off, disburse principal payments to tranche B until it is completely paid off. After tranche B is completely paid off, disburse principal payments to tranches FL and IFL until they are completely paid off. The principal payments between tranches FL and IFL should be made in the following way: 75% to tranche FL and 25% to tranche IFL. After tranches FL and IFL are completely paid off, disburse principal payments to tranche Z until the original principal balance plus accrued interest is completely paid off.

Unlike a floating-rate note whose principal is unchanged over the life of the instrument, the floater's principal balance declines over time as principal repayments are made. The principal payments to the floater are determined by the principal payments from the tranche from which the floater is created. In our CMO structure, this is tranche C.

Since the floater's par value is $72,375,000 of the $96.5 million, the balance is the inverse floater. Assuming that 1-month LIBOR is the reference rate, the coupon reset formula for an inverse floater takes the following form:

$$K - L \times (\text{1-month LIBOR})$$

In FAF-03, K is set at 28.50% and L at 3. Thus, if 1-month LIBOR is 3.75%, the coupon rate for the month is:

$$28.50\% - 3 \times (3.75\%) = 17.25\%$$

K is the cap or maximum coupon rate for the inverse floater. In FAF-03, the cap for the inverse floater is 28.50%.

The L or multiple in the coupon reset formula for the inverse floater is called the *coupon leverage*. The higher the coupon leverage, the more the inverse floater's coupon rate changes for a given change in 1-month LIBOR. For example, a coupon leverage of 3 means that a 1-basis point change in 1-month LIBOR will change the coupon rate on the inverse floater by 3 basis points.

As in the case of the floater, the principal paydown of an inverse floater will be a proportionate amount of the principal paydown of tranche C.

Because 1-month LIBOR is always positive, the coupon rate paid to the floating-rate tranche cannot be negative. If there are no restrictions placed on the coupon rate for the inverse floater, however, it is possible for the coupon rate for that tranche to be negative. To prevent this, a floor, or minimum, can be placed on the coupon rate. In many structures, the floor is set at zero. Once a floor is set for the inverse floater, a cap or ceiling is imposed on the floater. In FAF-03, a floor of zero is set for the inverse floater. The floor results in a cap or maximum coupon rate for the floater of 10%.

Planned Amortization Class Tranches

A *planned amortization class* (PAC) tranche is one in which a schedule of principal of payments is set forth in the prospectus. The PAC bondholders have priority over all other bond classes in the structure with respect to the receipt of the scheduled principal payments. While there is no assurance that the principal payments will be actually realized so as to satisfy the schedule, a PAC tranche is structured so that if prepayment speeds are within a certain range, the collateral will throw off sufficient principal to meet the schedule of principal payments.[5]

The greater certainty of the cash flow for the PAC tranches comes at the expense of the non-PAC classes, called the *support* or *companion tranches*. It is these tranches that absorb the prepayment risk. Because PAC tranches have protection against both extension risk and contraction risk, they are said to provide two-sided prepayment protection.

To illustrate how to create a PAC tranche, we will use as collateral the $400 million passthrough with a coupon rate of 7.5%, an 8.125% WAC, and a WAM of 357 months. From this collateral a PAC tranche with a par value of $243.8 million will be created. The second column of Exhibit 8 shows the principal payment (regularly scheduled principal repayment plus prepayments) for selected months assuming a prepayment speed of 90 PSA, and the next column shows the principal payments for selected months assuming that the passthrough prepays at 300 PSA.

The last column of Exhibit 8 gives the minimum principal payment if the collateral speed is 90 PSA or 300 PSA for months 1 to 349. (After month 349, the outstanding principal balance will be paid off if the prepayment speed is between 90 PSA and 300 PSA.) For example, in the first month, the principal payment would be $508,169.52 if the collateral prepays at 90 PSA and $1,075,931.20 if the collateral prepays at 300 PSA. Thus, the minimum principal payment is $508,169.52, as reported in the last column of Exhibit 8. In month 103, the minimum principal payment is also the amount if the prepayment speed is 90 PSA, $1,446,761, compared to $1,458,618.04 for 300 PSA. In month 104, however, a prepayment speed of 300 PSA would produce a principal payment of $1,433,539.23, which is less than the principal payment of $1,440,825.55 assuming 90 PSA. So, $1,433,539.23 is reported in the last column of Exhibit 8. In fact, from month 104 on the minimum principal payment is the one that would result assuming a prepayment speed of 300 PSA.

[5] For home equity loan ABS, these tranches are called senior non-accelerating bonds. See Chapter 25.

Exhibit 8: Monthly Principal Payment for $400 Million Par 7.5% Coupon Passthrough with an 8.125% WAC and a 357 WAM Assuming Prepayment Rates of 90 PSA and 300 PSA

			Minimum principal payment
Month	At 90% PSA	At 300% PSA	PAC schedule
1	$508,169.52	$1,075,931.20	$508,169.52
2	569,843.43	1,279,412.11	569,843.43
3	631,377.11	1,482,194.45	631,377.11
4	692,741.89	1,683,966.17	692,741.89
5	753,909.12	1,884,414.62	753,909.12
6	814,850.22	2,083,227.31	814,850.22
7	875,536.68	2,280,092.68	875,536.68
8	935,940.10	2,474,700.92	935,940.10
9	996,032.19	2,666,744.77	996,032.19
10	1,055,784.82	2,855,920.32	1,055,784.82
11	1,115,170.01	3,041,927.81	1,115,170.01
12	1,174,160.00	3,224,472.44	1,174,160.00
13	1,232,727.22	3,403,265.17	1,232,727.22
14	1,290,844.32	3,578,023.49	1,290,844.32
15	1,348,484.24	3,748,472.23	1,348,484.24
16	1,405,620.17	3,914,344.26	1,405,620.17
17	1,462,225.60	4,075,381.29	1,462,225.60
18	1,518,274.36	4,231,334.57	1,518,274.36
101	1,458,719.34	1,510,072.17	1,458,719.34
102	1,452,725.55	1,484,126.59	1,452,725.55
103	1,446,761.00	1,458,618.04	1,446,761.00
104	1,440,825.55	1,433,539.23	1,433,539.23
105	1,434,919.07	1,408,883.01	1,408,883.01
211	949,482.58	213,309.00	213,309.00
212	946,033.34	209,409.09	209,409.09
213	942,601.99	205,577.05	205,577.05
346	618,684.59	13,269.17	13,269.17
347	617,071.58	12,944.51	12,944.51
348	615,468.65	12,626.21	12,626.21
349	613,875.77	12,314.16	3,432.32
350	612,292.88	12,008.25	0
351	610,719.96	11,708.38	0
352	609,156.96	11,414.42	0
353	607,603.84	11,126.28	0
354	606,060.57	10,843.85	0
355	604,527.09	10,567.02	0
356	603,003.38	10,295.70	0
357	601,489.39	10,029.78	0

Exhibit 9: FAF-04 CMO Structure with One PAC Tranche and One Support Tranche

Tranche	Par amount	Coupon rate (%)
P (PAC)	$243,800,000	7.5
S (Support)	156,200,000	7.5
Total	$400,000,000	

Payment rules:
1. *For payment of periodic coupon interest:* Disburse periodic coupon interest to each tranche on the basis of the amount of principal outstanding at the beginning of the period.
2. *For disbursement of principal payments:* Disburse principal payments to tranche P based on its schedule of principal repayments. Tranche P has priority with respect to current and future principal payments to satisfy the schedule. Any excess principal payments in a month over the amount necessary to satisfy the schedule for tranche P are paid to tranche S. When tranche S is completely paid off, all principal payments are to be made to tranche P regardless of the schedule.

Actually, if the collateral prepays at any speed between 90 PSA and 300 PSA, the minimum principal payment would be the amount reported in the last column of Exhibit 8. For example, if we had included principal payment figures assuming a prepayment speed of 200 PSA, the minimum principal payment would not change: from month 11 through month 103, the minimum principal payment is that generated from 90 PSA, but from month 104 on, the minimum principal payment is that generated from 300 PSA.

This characteristic of the collateral allows for the creation of a PAC tranche, assuming that the collateral prepays over its life at a constant speed between 90 PSA and 300 PSA. A schedule of principal repayments that the PAC bondholders are entitled to receive before any other tranche in the CMO is specified. The monthly schedule of principal repayments is as specified in the last column of Exhibit 8, which shows the minimum principal payment. While there is no assurance that the collateral will prepay at a constant rate between these two speeds, a PAC tranche can be structured assuming that it will.

Exhibit 9 shows a CMO structure, FAF-04, created from the $400 million 7.5% coupon passthrough with a WAC of 8.125% and a WAM of 357 months. There are just two tranches in this structure: a 7.5% coupon PAC tranche created assuming 90 to 300 PSA with a par value of $243.8 million, and a support tranche with a par value of $156.2 million. The two speeds used to create a PAC tranche are called the initial PAC collars (or initial PAC bands). For FAF-04, 90 PSA is the lower collar and 300 PSA the upper collar.

Exhibit 10 reports the average life for the PAC tranche and the support tranche in FAF-04 assuming various actual prepayment speeds. Notice that between 90 PSA and 300 PSA, the average life for the PAC tranche is stable at 7.26 years. However, at slower or faster PSA speeds the schedule is broken and the average life changes, lengthening when the prepayment speed is less than 90 PSA and shortening when it is greater than 300 PSA. Even so, there is much greater variability for the average life of the support tranche.

Exhibit 10: Average Life for PAC Tranche and Support Tranche in FAF-04 Assuming Various Prepayment Speeds

Prepayment rate (PSA)	PAC Tranche (P)	Support Tranche (S)
0	15.97	27.26
50	9.44	24.00
90	7.26	18.56
100	7.26	18.56
150	7.26	12.57
165	7.26	11.16
200	7.26	8.38
250	7.26	5.37
300	7.26	3.13
350	6.56	2.51
400	5.92	2.17
450	5.38	1.94
500	4.93	1.77
700	3.70	1.37

Exhibit 11: FAF-05 CMO Structure with Six PAC Tranche and One Support Bond

Tranche	Par amount	Coupon rate (%)
P-A	$85,000,000	7.5
P-B	8,000,000	7.5
P-C	35,000,000	7.5
P-D	45,000,000	7.5
P-E	40,000,000	7.5
P-F	30,800,000	7.5
S	156,200,000	7.5
Total	$400,000,000	

Payment rules:
1. *For payment of periodic coupon interest:* Disburse periodic coupon interest to each tranche on the basis of the amount of principal outstanding at the beginning of the period.
2. *For disbursement of principal payments:* Disburse principal payments to tranches P-A to P-F based on their respective schedules of principal repayments. Tranche P-A has priority with respect to current and future principal payments to satisfy the schedule. Any excess principal payments in a month over the amount necessary to satisfy the schedule for tranche P-A are paid to tranche S. Once tranche P-A is completely paid off, tranche P-B has priority, then tranche P-C, etc. When tranche S is completely paid off, all principal payments are to be made to the remaining PAC tranches in order of priority regardless of the schedule.

Most CMO PAC structures have more than one class of PAC tranches. Exhibit 11 shows six PAC tranches created from the single PAC tranche in FAF-04. We will refer to this CMO structure as FAF-05. Information about this CMO structure is provided in Exhibit 11. The total par value of the six PAC tranches is equal to $243.8 million, which is the amount of the single PAC tranche in FAF-04.

Exhibit 12: Average Life for the Six PAC Tranches in FAF-05 Assuming Various Prepayment Speeds

Prepayment rate (PSA)	PAC Tranches					
	P-A	P-B	P-C	P-D	P-E	P-F
0	8.46	14.61	16.49	19.41	21.91	23.76
50	3.58	6.82	8.36	11.30	14.50	18.20
90	2.58	4.72	5.78	7.89	10.83	16.92
100	2.58	4.72	5.78	7.89	10.83	16.92
150	2.58	4.72	5.78	7.89	10.83	16.92
165	2.58	4.72	5.78	7.89	10.83	16.92
200	2.58	4.72	5.78	7.89	10.83	16.92
250	2.58	4.72	5.78	7.89	10.83	16.92
300	2.58	4.72	5.78	7.89	10.83	16.92
350	2.58	4.72	5.94	6.95	9.24	14.91
400	2.57	4.37	4.91	6.17	8.33	13.21
450	2.50	3.97	4.44	5.56	7.45	11.81
500	2.40	3.65	4.07	5.06	6.74	10.65
700	2.06	2.82	3.10	3.75	4.88	7.51

Exhibit 12 shows the average life for the six PAC tranches and the support bond in FAF-05 at various prepayment speeds. From a PAC tranche in FAF-04 with an average life of 7.26, we have created six PAC tranches with an average life as short as 2.58 years (P-A) and as long as 16.92 years (P-F) if prepayments stay within 90 PSA and 300 PSA.

As expected, the average lives are stable if the prepayment speed is between 90 PSA and 300 PSA. Notice that even outside this range the average life is stable for several of the PAC tranches. For example, PAC P-A is stable even if prepayment speeds are as high as 400 PSA. For the PAC P-B, the average life does not vary when prepayments are between 90 PSA and 350 PSA. To understand why this is so, remember that there are $156.2 million in support tranches that are protecting the $85 million of PAC P-A. Thus, even if prepayments are faster than the initial upper collar, there may be sufficient support tranches to assure the satisfaction of the schedule. In fact, as can been from Exhibit 12 if prepayments are at 400 PSA over the life of the collateral, the average life is unchanged. Now consider PAC P-B. The support tranches are providing protection for both the $85 million of PAC P-A and $93 million of PAC P-B. The exhibit shows that even if prepayments are 350 PSA, the average life is still unchanged. From the exhibit it can be seen that the degree of protection against extension risk increases the shorter the PAC. Thus, while the initial collar may be 90 to 300 PSA, the effective collar is wider for the shorter PAC tranches.

As we have emphasized, the creation of a mortgage-backed security cannot make prepayment risk disappear. This is true for both a passthrough and a CMO. Thus, the reduction in prepayment risk (both extension risk and contraction risk) that a PAC offers must come from somewhere. Where does the prepayment protection come from? It comes from the support tranches. It is the support tranches that forego principal payments if the collateral prepayments are slow; support tranches do not receive any principal until the PAC tranches receive the scheduled principal repayment. This reduces the risk that the PAC tranches will extend. Similarly, it is the support tranches that absorb any principal payments in excess of the scheduled principal payments that are made. This reduces the contraction risk of the PAC tranches. Thus, the key to the prepayment protection offered by a PAC tranche is the amount of support tranches outstanding. If the support tranches are paid off quickly because of faster-than-expected prepayments, then there is no longer any protection for the PAC tranches. In fact, in FAF-05, if the support tranche is paid off, the structure is effectively reduced to a sequential-pay CMO. In such cases, the schedule is unlikely to be maintained, and the structure is referred to as a busted PAC.

It should be clear from these observations that the initial collars are not particularly useful in assessing the prepayment protection for a seasoned PAC tranche. This is most important to understand, as it is common for CMO buyers to compare prepayment protection of PACs in different CMO structures, and conclude that the greater protection is offered by the one with the wider initial collars. This approach is inadequate because it is actual prepayment experience that determines the degree of prepayment protection going forward, as well as the expected future prepayment behavior of the collateral.

The way to determine this protection is to calculate the *effective collar* for a PAC tranche. This is the lower and the upper PSA that can occur in the future and still allow maintenance of the schedule of principal repayments. The effective collar changes every month. An extended period over which actual prepayments are below the upper range of the initial PAC collar will result in an increase in the upper range of the effective collar. An extended period of prepayments slower than the lower range of the initial PAC collar will raise the lower range of the effective collar. This is because it will take faster prepayments to make up the shortfall of the scheduled principal payments not made plus the scheduled future principal payments.

The PAC schedule may not be satisfied even if the actual prepayments never fall outside of the initial collar. This may seem surprising since our previous analysis indicated that the average life would not change if prepayments are at either extreme of the initial collar. However, recall that all of our previous analysis has been based on a single PSA speed for the life of the structure. If we vary the PSA speed over time rather than keep it *constant* over the life of the CMO, we can see what happens to the effective collar if the prepayments are at the initial upper collar for a certain number of months. Exhibit 13 shows the average life two years from now for the PAC bond in FAF-04 assuming that prepayments are 300 PSA for the first 24 months. Notice that the average life is stable at six years if the prepayments for the following months are between 115 PSA and 300 PSA. That is, the effective PAC collar is no longer the initial collar. Instead, the lower collar has shifted upward. This means that the protection from year 2 on is for 115 to 300 PSA, a narrower band than initially, even though the earlier prepayments did not exceed the initial upper collar.

Exhibit 13: Average Life Two Years from Now for the PAC Tranche of FAF-04 Assuming Prepayments of 300 PSA Initially

PSA from Year 2 on	Average Life
95	6.43
105	6.11
115	6.01
120	6.00
125	6.00
300	6.00
305	5.62

Notional IOs

In our previous illustrations, we used a CMO structure in which all the tranches have the same coupon rate (7.5%) and that coupon rate is the same as the collateral. In practice, the same coupon rate would not be given to each tranche. Instead, the coupon rate would depend on the term structure of interest rates and the average life of the tranche, among other things.

In the earlier CMO deals, all of the excess interest between the coupon rate on the tranches and the coupon interest on the collateral was paid to an equity class referred to as the CMO residual. This is no longer the practice today. Instead, a tranche is created that receives the excess coupon interest. This tranche is called a *notional interest-only class*, or *notional IO*.

To see how a notional IO is created, consider the CMO structure shown in Exhibit 14, FAF-05. This is the same structure as FAF-02 except that the coupon rate varies by tranche and there is a class denoted "IO" which is the class of interest to us. Notice that for this structure the par amount for the IO class is shown as $52,566,667 and the coupon rate is 7.5%. Since this is an IO class there is no par amount. The amount shown is the amount used to determine the interest payments, not the amount that will be paid to the holder of this bond. Therefore, it is called a *notional amount*.

Let's look at how the notional amount is determined. Consider first tranche A. The par value is $194.5 million and the coupon rate is 6%. Since the collateral's coupon rate is 7.5%, the excess interest is 150 basis points (1.5%). Therefore, an IO with a 1.5% coupon rate and a notional amount of $194.5 million can be created from tranche A. But this is equivalent to an IO with a notional amount of $38.9 million and a coupon rate of 7.5%. Mathematically, this notional amount is found as follows:

$$\text{Notional amount for 7.5\%} = \frac{\text{Tranche's par value} \times \text{Excess interest}}{0.075}$$

where

$$\text{Excess interest} = \text{Collateral coupon rate} - \text{Tranche coupon rate}$$

Exhibit 14: FAF-05: A Hypothetical Five Tranche Sequential-Pay with an Accrual Tranche, an Interest-Only Tranche, and a Residual Class

Tranche	Par amount	Coupon rate (%)
A	$194,500,000	6.00
B	36,000,000	6.50
C	96,500,000	7.00
Z	73,000,000	7.25
IO	52,566,667 (Notional)	7.50
Total	$400,000,000	

Payment rules:
1. *For payment of periodic coupon interest:* Disburse periodic coupon interest to tranches A, B, and C on the basis of the amount of principal outstanding at the beginning of the period. For tranche Z, accrue the interest based on the principal plus accrued interest in the previous period. The interest for tranche Z is to be paid to the earlier tranches as a principal pay down. Disburse periodic interest to the IO tranche based on the notional amount at the beginning of the period.
2. *For disbursement of principal payments:* Disburse principal payments to tranche A until it is completely paid off. After tranche A is completely paid off, disburse principal payments to tranche B until it is completely paid off. After tranche B is completely paid off, disburse principal payments to tranche C until it is completely paid off. After tranche C is completely paid off, disburse principal payments to tranche Z until the original principal balance plus accrued interest is completely paid off.
3. *No principal is to be paid to the IO tranche:* The notional amount of the IO tranche declines based on the principal payments to all other tranches.

For example, for tranche A:

Excess interest = 0.075 – 0.060 = 0.015

Tranche's par value = $194,500,000

Similarly, from tranche B with a par value of $36 million, the excess interest is 100 basis points (1%) and therefore an IO with a coupon rate of 1% and a notional amount of $36 million can be created. But this is equivalent to creating an IO with a notional amount of $4.8 million and a coupon rate of 7.5%.

Support Tranches

The support tranches are the tranches that provide prepayment protection for the PAC tranches. Consequently, support tranches expose investors to the greatest level of prepayment risk. Because of this, investors must be particularly careful in assessing the cash flow characteristics of support tranches to reduce the likelihood of adverse portfolio consequences due to prepayments.

The support tranche typically is divided into different tranches. All the bond classes we have discussed earlier are available, including sequential-pay support tranches, floater and inverse floater support tranches, and accrual support tranches.

The support tranche can even be partitioned so as to create support tranche classes with a schedule of principal payments. That is, support tranches that are PAC tranches can be created. In a structure with a PAC tranche and a support tranche with a PAC schedule of principal payments, the former is called a PAC I tranche or Level I PAC tranche and the latter a PAC II tranche or Level II PAC tranche. While PAC II tranches have greater prepayment protection than the support tranches without a schedule of principal repayments, the prepayment protection is less than that provided PAC I tranches.

There is more that can be done with the PAC II tranche. A series of PAC IIs can be created just as we did with the PACs in FAF-05. PAC IIs can also be used to create any other type of bond class, such as a PAC II inverse floater or an accrual tranche, for example.

The support tranche without a principal repayment schedule can be used to create any type of bond class. In fact, a portion of the non-PAC II support tranche can be given a schedule of principal repayments. This tranche would be called a PAC III tranche or a Level III PAC tranche. While it provides protection against prepayments for the PAC I and PAC II tranches and is therefore subject to considerable prepayment risk, such a tranche has greater protection than the support tranche without a schedule of principal repayments.

STRIPPED MORTGAGE-BACKED SECURITIES

A passthrough security divides the cash flows from the underlying pool of mortgages on a pro rata basis to the security holders. A *stripped mortgage-backed security* is created by altering that distribution of principal and interest from a pro rata distribution to an unequal distribution. The result is that the securities created will have a price/yield relationship that is different from the price/yield relationship of the underlying passthrough security.

In the most common type of stripped mortgage-backed securities all the interest is allocated to one class (called the interest only or IO class) and all the principal to the other class (called the principal only or PO class). The IO class receives no principal payments.

The PO security is purchased at a substantial discount from par value. The return an investor realizes depends on the speed at which prepayments are made. The faster the prepayments, the higher the investor's return. For example, suppose there is a mortgage pool consisting of 30-year mortgages with $400 million in principal, and that investors can purchase POs backed by this mortgage pool for $175 million. The dollar return on this investment will be $225 million. How quickly that dollar return is recovered by PO investors determines the actual return that will be realized. In the extreme case, if all homeowners in the underlying mortgage pool decide to prepay their mortgage loans immediately, PO investors will realize the $225 million immediately. At the other extreme, if all homeowners decide to remain in their homes for 30 years and make no prepayments, the $225 million will be spread out over 30 years, which would result in a much lower return for PO investors.

Let's look at how the price of the PO would be expected to change as mortgage rates in the market change. When mortgage rates decline below the coupon rate, prepayments are expected to speed up, accelerating payments to the PO holder. Thus, the cash flows of a PO improve (in the sense that principal repayments are received earlier). The result is that the PO price will increase when mortgage rates decline. When mortgage rates rise above the coupon rate, prepayments are expected to slow down. The cash flows then deteriorate (in the sense that it takes longer to recover principal repayments). The price of a PO will fall when mortgage rates rise.

An IO has no par value. In contrast to the PO investor, the IO investor wants prepayments to be slow. The reason is that the IO investor receives interest only on the amount of the principal outstanding. When prepayments are made, less dollar interest will be received as the outstanding principal declines. In fact, if prepayments are too fast, the IO investor may not recover the amount paid for the IO. This is an important point since there have been reported losses by some investors who thought that since the IO was created from a passthrough either guaranteed by the U.S. government or government sponsored enterprise, there would be no loss. The guarantee only specifies that if there is a mortgage outstanding there is a guarantee that interest due will be paid.

Let's look at the expected price response of an IO to changes in mortgage rates. If mortgage rates decline below the coupon rate, prepayments are expected to accelerate. This would result in a deterioration of the expected cash flows for an IO. Typically there will be a decline in the price of an IO. If mortgage rates rise above the coupon rate, the expected cash flows improve and within a certain range of interest rates the price of an IO will increase. Thus, we see an interesting characteristic of an IO: its price tends to move in the same direction as the change in mortgage rates.

Both POs and IOs exhibit substantial price volatility when mortgage rates change. The greater price volatility of the IO and PO compared to the passthrough is due to the fact that the combined price volatility of the IO and PO must equal the price volatility of the passthrough.

NONAGENCY MORTGAGE-BACKED SECURITIES

Our focus thus far has been on agency MBS. Consequently, there was no concern with credit risk. An investor in a nonagency MBS is exposed to credit risk. These products are therefore sometimes referred to as *credit-sensitive mortgage-backed securities*.

As we explained earlier in this chapter, the underlying loans for agency securities are those that conform to the underwriting standards of the agency issuing or guaranteeing the issue. That is, only conforming loans are included in pools that are collateral for an agency mortgage-backed security. The three main underwriting standards deal with (1) the maximum loan-to-value ratio, (2) the maximum payment-to-income ratio, and (3) the maximum loan amount. A nonconforming mortgage loan is one that does not conform to the underwriting standards established by any of the agencies.

Nonconforming mortgage loans that fail to qualify for inclusion because the amount of the loan exceeds the limit established by the agencies are called *jumbo loans*. Jumbo loans do not necessarily have greater credit risk than conforming mortgages. Loans that fail to qualify because of the first two underwriting standards expose the lender to greater credit risk. In general, lenders classify borrowers by credit quality. Borrowers are classified as A borrowers, B borrowers, C borrowers, and D borrowers. A borrowers are those that are viewed as having the best credit record. These borrowers are referred to as *prime borrowers*. Borrowers rated below A are viewed as *subprime borrowers*. Unfortunately, there is no industrywide classification system for prime and subprime borrowers.

Differences Between Agency and Nonagency Securities

Nonagency securities can be either passthroughs or CMOs. In the agency market, CMOs are created from pools of passthrough securities. In the nonagency market, a CMO can be created from either a pool of passthroughs or mortgage loans that have not been securitized. It is uncommon for nonconforming mortgage loans to be securitized as passthroughs and then the passthroughs carved up to create a CMO. Instead, in the nonagency market a CMO is typically carved out of mortgage loans that have not been securitized as passthroughs. Since a mortgage loan is commonly referred to as a whole loan, nonagency CMOs are commonly referred to as *whole-loan CMOs*.

In addition to the absence of any explicit or implicit government guarantee, the major differences between agency and nonagency securities have to do with dispersion of the characteristics of the underlying collateral, servicer advances, and compensating interest. We discuss each below.

Dispersion of Characteristics of Underlying Collateral

While both agency and nonagency securities are backed by 1- to 4-single family residential mortgages, the underlying loans for nonagency securities will typically be more heterogeneous with respect to coupon rate and maturity of the individual loans. For example, a nonagency security might include both 15-year and 30-year mortgages in the same mortgage pool. The greater dispersion of the coupon rate means that it is more difficult to predict prepayments based on the weighted average coupon. As explained later in this chapter, the WAC is a key factor used to determine prepayments since it indicates the opportunity for homeowners to refinance.

Servicer Advances

When there is a delinquency by the homeowner, the investor in a nonagency security may or may not be affected. This depends on whether a servicer is required to make advances. Thus, the financial capacity of the servicer to make advances is critical. The servicer recovers advances when delinquent payments are made or the property is foreclosed and proceeds received.

There are different forms of advancing: (1) mandatory advancing, (2) optional advancing, and (3) limited advancing. The strongest form from the investor's perspective is mandatory advancing wherein failure to advance by a servicer is an event of default. However, a servicer need not advance if it can show that there is not a strong likelihood of recovery of the amount advanced when the property is ultimately disposed of. In an optional or a voluntary advancing, the servicer is not legally obligated to advance so that failure to do so is not an event of default. In a limited advancing the issuer is obligated to advance, but the amount it must advance is limited.

Compensating Interest

An additional factor to consider which is unique to nonagency securities is compensating interest. Mortgage passthroughs and CMOs pay principal and interest on a monthly basis. While homeowners may prepay their mortgage on any day throughout the month, the agencies guarantee and pay investors a full month of interest as if all the prepayments occur on the last day of the month. This guarantee does not apply to nonagency securities. If a homeowner pays off a mortgage on the tenth day of the month, he will stop paying interest for the rest of the month. Because of the payment delay (for example, 25 days), the investor will receive full principal but only 10 days of interest on the 25th of the following month.

This phenomenon is known as payment interest shortfall or *compensating interest* and is handled differently by different issuers. Some issuers will only pay up to a specified amount and some will not pay at all. Actually, it the servicers who will pay any compensating interest. The servicer obtains the shortfall in interest from the servicing spread. The shortfall that will be made up to the investor may be limited to the entire servicing spread or part of the servicing spread. Thus, while an investor has protection against the loss of a full month's interest, the protection is limited.

For a nonagency security in which there is compensating interest, typically prepayments of the entire outstanding balance are covered. Curtailments (i.e., partial prepayments) are not covered.

In an agency CMO and nonagency CMO, the interest is paid to each tranche on the basis of the distribution rules for interest. In a nonagency CMO, as explained below there are tranches within credit classes. When there is a shortfall in the full month's interest, typically the shortfall is prorated among the credit classes based on the outstanding principal balance. Then, for each tranche within a credit class, the shortfall is prorated based on the interest that would be due.

In a nonagency CMO structure, the economic value of compensating interest depends on the level of prepayment and the types of CMO tranches. Generally, the faster the prepayments and the greater the coupon for the tranche, the higher the economic value of compensating interest.

Exhibit 15: Assumed Default Frequencies

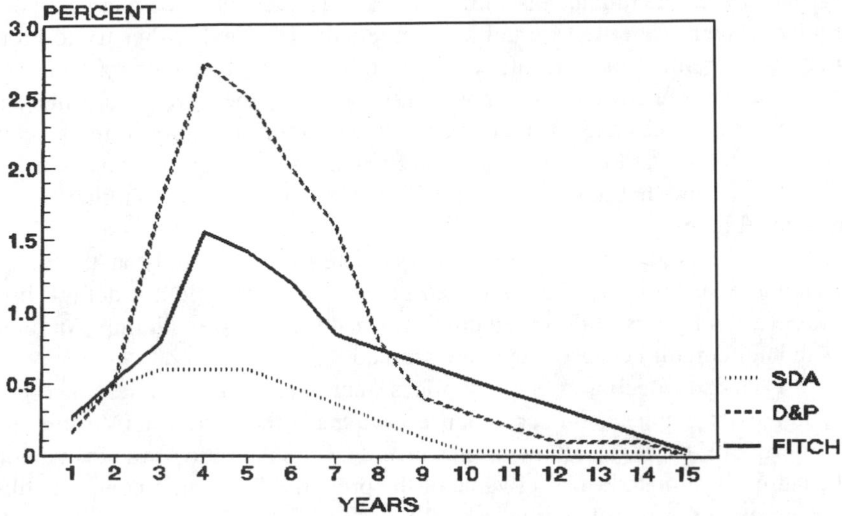

How Rating Agencies View Credit Risk[6]

In assigning ratings, rating agencies evaluate the magnitude of potential losses of a pool of loans to determine the amount of credit support the issuer needs to achieve a desired credit rating. There are four factors considered in assigning ratings: (1) frequency of default; (2) severity of loss given default; (3) pool characteristics or the structure of the pool; and (4) credit enhancement or the structure of the security.

Frequency of Default

There is ample evidence suggesting that most homeowners default relatively early in the life of the mortgage. Exhibit 15 shows the effect of seasoning assumed by two rating agencies and the Public Securities Association. These seasoning curves are based on default experience of so-called "prime loans" — a 30-year fixed-rate mortgage with a 75% to 80% loan-to-value (LTV) ratio that is fully documented for the purchase of an owner-occupied single-family detached house. These characteristics describe the most common mortgage type generally associated with the lowest default rates. Loans with almost any other characteristic generally are assumed to have a greater frequency of default.

Loan-to-Value Ratio/Seasoning A mortgage's LTV ratio is the single most important determinant of its likelihood of default and therefore the amount of

[6] This section is adapted from Douglas L. Bendt, Chuck Ramsey, and Frank J. Fabozzi, "The Rating Agencies' Approach: New Evidence," Chapter 8 in Frank J. Fabozzi, Chuck Ramsey, Frank Ramirez, and Michael Marz (eds.), *The Handbook of Nonagency Mortgage-Backed Securities* (New Hope, PA: Frank J. Fabozzi Associates, 1997).

required credit enhancement. Rating agencies treat loans with LTVs above 80% as a negative factor. The rationale is straightforward. Homeowners with large amounts of equity in their properties are unlikely to default. They will either try to protect this equity by remaining current, or if they fail, sell the house or refinance it to unlock the equity. In any case, the lender is protected by the buyer's self-interest.

On the other hand, if the borrower has little or no equity in the property, the value of the default option is much greater. This argument is consistent with the long-held view that default rates for FHA/VA loans are much higher than for conventional loans.

Until recently, rating agencies considered the LTV only at the time of origination. Seasoning was an unalloyed good — if a loan did not default in the first three to four years, it deserved credit for making it past the hump. And many loans did not default because they were prepaid.

Periods of declining housing prices, increased volume of seasoned product, and greater emphasis on surveillance have made the current LTV rather than the original LTV the focus of attention. *Current LTV* is the ratio of the loan amount to the current (estimated) market value of the property. Seasoning now is as likely to be a negative for a pool as it is to be a plus. It is little comfort to own a pool of original 80% LTV mortgages from California originated in 1990 because many of the borrowers will owe more than their houses are worth; their LTVs will exceed 100%. Moreover, the prepayment option has been taken away for these borrowers.

Mortgage Term Amortization increases the equity a homeowner has in a property, which reduces the likelihood of default. Because amortization schedules for terms less than 30 years accumulate equity faster, all the rating agencies view this as a positive factor.

Mortgage Type Fixed-rate mortgages are considered "prime" because both the borrower and the lender know the monthly payment and amortization schedule with certainty. Presumably, the loan was underwritten considering this payment stream and the borrower's current income.

Both lender and borrower are uncertain about the future payment schedule for adjustable-rate mortgages (ARMs). Because most ARMs have lower initial ("teaser") rates, underwriting usually is done to ensure that the borrower will be able to meet the monthly payment assuming the rate adjusts up to the fully indexed rate at the first reset date. Beyond that first date, however, there is uncertainty both about the future stream of payments and the borrower's ability to meet higher payments. Future payment schedules for balloon mortgages are known, but uncertainty about borrowers' income still exists. All non-fixed-rate mortgages are viewed as a negative by the rating agencies.

Transaction Type Mortgages taken out for cash-out refinancings are considered riskier than mortgages taken out for purchases, chiefly because the homeowner is reducing the equity in the home. In addition, the fact that the homeowner is taking out cash may be an indication of need, which could indicate shakier finances, and the homeowner's monthly payment will increase. On the other hand, a no-cash refinancing — in which the rate is reduced — lowers the monthly payment and speeds the rate of amortization, so there are no penalties for such mortgages in the view of rating agencies.

Documentation "Full" documentation generally means that the borrower has supplied income, employment, and asset verification sufficient to meet Fannie Mae/Freddie Mac underwriting standards. "Low," "alternative," or "reduced" documentation means at least one form was not supplied, perhaps, for example, because the borrower is self-employed. In this case, because the income stream is likely to be more volatile, the borrower is more likely to default.

"No" documentation loans generally are made as "hard money" loans; that is, the value of the collateral is the most important criterion in the lending decision. Typically, lenders require larger down payments for these types of loans.

Occupancy Status Property owners obviously have a greater vested interest in not defaulting on a mortgage on a house in which they live. Thus, mortgages for second homes or rental property are a negative factor.

Property Type Generally, single-family detached houses are the most desirable properties because they are larger, more private, and include more land. Moreover, the supply of condominiums or townhouses is more likely to become overbuilt in a local area with the addition of a single large project, potentially increasing the volatility of prices and the length of time needed to sell a property.

Mortgage Size/House Price As noted earlier in this chapter, most mortgages that are used in nonagency securities have loan balances that exceed the agency conforming limits. The rating agencies make the strong presumption that higher-valued properties with larger mortgages are much riskier.

Credit Worthiness of the Borrower Although loan originators place a great deal of emphasis on borrowers' credit histories, these data are not available to the rating agencies. The Fair Credit Reporting Act restricts access to such information to parties involved in a credit extension decision. As a result, the agencies use credit proxies such as the debt-to-income ratio, the mortgage coupon rate, past delinquencies or seasoned loans, or originators' scores from credit scoring models.

Severity of Loss

In the case of default, foreclosure, and ultimate property sale, lenders incur two costs: (1) direct foreclosure costs and (2) market decline. These costs may be mitigated to the extent there is equity in the property, i.e., lower LTVs will reduce the severity of loss.

Direct Foreclosure Costs Once a lender begins the foreclosure process — often as soon as a borrower becomes 60 days delinquent — it begins to incur significant direct costs. The direct foreclosure costs include unpaid interest, property taxes, management fees, and legal fees. Unpaid interest results because the lender stops accruing interest on the mortgage as income, instead adding it to the unpaid balance of the loan. Thus direct foreclosure costs include the coupon rate of the mortgage per year.

Property taxes are a foreclosure cost because the lender becomes responsible for paying taxes to preserve its first lien position. This cost can be up to 2% or more of the house price annually. Management fees are incurred because the property must be maintained so as to preserve its value for sale. The cost can average 6% of the house price annually. Legal fees are a variable cost.

Market Decline When a house is sold out of foreclosure, the lender is unlikely to obtain market value. Potential buyers know that the seller is distressed and know the size of the mortgage on the property. One common bidding strategy is to bid for the amount of the outstanding mortgage, figuring it is the seller's obligation to cover the out of pocket costs. The price received on a foreclosure sale depends greatly on local economic conditions and future housing prices, both of which are unknown at the time a rating agency is evaluating a loan. The range of assumed losses is 25% to 45%.

Pool Characteristics

Rating agencies draw upon general portfolio theory that diversification reduces risk and concentration increases risk. They typically consider two characteristics of the overall pool composition in setting credit enhancement levels: (1) size of the pool and (2) geographic composition/location.

Pool Size Pools with fewer than 300 loans are penalized by three of the four rating agencies, while larger pools are viewed positively. The rationale is that smaller pools are not sufficiently diversified to take account of (unspecified) desirable statistical properties.

Geography The first kind of geographic consideration is again a question of diversification: "too many" loans concentrated in a single zip code or small local area. For example, a lender might finance an entire subdivision, townhouse development, or condominium project that might be exposed to a common, special risk such as a single plant closing or an environmental hazard.

The second kind of geographic consideration is generally broader in scope, such as a pool with a high concentration in Southern California that is exposed to risks not of a single plant but of a single industry. In special cases such as Boeing in Seattle, the risk is both industry-specific and company-specific.

PSA Standard Default Assumption Benchmark

With the increase in nonagency security issuance, a standardized benchmark for default rates was introduced by the Public Securities Association. The PSA standard default assumption (SDA) benchmark gives the annual default rate for a mortgage pool as a function of the seasoning of the mortgages. The PSA SDA benchmark, or 100 SDA, specifies the following:

1. the default rate in month 1 is 0.02% and increases by 0.02% up to month 30 so that in month 30 the default rate is 0.60%;
2. from month 30 to month 60, the default rate remains at 0.60%;
3. from month 61 to month 120, the default rate declines from 0.60% to 0.03%;
4. from month 120 on, the default rate remains constant at 0.03%.

This pattern is consistent with the default data reported in Exhibit 15.

As with the PSA prepayment benchmark, multiples of the benchmark are found by multiplying the default rate by the assumed multiple. A 0 SDA means that no defaults are assumed.

Calculating Credit Enhancement Levels

Pool characteristic risks are cumulative; that is, if a loan has two or more adverse characteristics, the factors are multiplied to determine the relative degree of the frequency of default. Then one calculates an expected loss equal to the discounted probability of default times the expected loss severity. After performing these calculations on a loan-by-loan basis, the overall pool characteristics are taken into account.

Credit enhancement levels are determined relative to a specific rating desired for a security. Specifically, an investor in a triple A rated security expects to have "minimal," that is to say, virtually no chance of losing any principal due to defaults. For example, Standard & Poor's requires credit enhancement equal to four times expected losses to obtain a triple A rating.

Lower-rated securities require less credit enhancement for four reasons. First, the loss coverage ratio is lower. Second, some of the factors may be less stringent. Third, the base case frequency of default may be lower. And fourth, the severity of loss may be less.

Credit Enhancements

The rating agencies consider the factors just described in rating a nonagency security. Typically a double A or triple A rating is sought for the most senior tranche. The amount of credit enhancement necessary depends on rating agency requirements. There are two general types of credit enhancement structures: external and internal. We describe each type below.

External Credit Enhancements

External credit enhancements come in the form of third-party guarantees that provide for first loss protection against losses up to a specified level, for example, 10%. The most common forms of external credit enhancements are (1) a corporate guarantee, (2) a letter of credit, (3) pool insurance, and (4) bond insurance.

Pool insurance policies cover losses resulting from defaults and foreclosures. Policies are typically written for a dollar amount of coverage that continues in force throughout the life of the pool. However, some policies are written so that the dollar amount of coverage declines as the pool seasons as long as two conditions are met: (1) the credit performance is better than expected and (2) the rating agencies that rated the issue approve. Since only defaults and foreclosures are covered, additional insurance must be obtained to cover losses resulting from bankruptcy (i.e., court mandated modification of mortgage debt — "cramdown"), fraud arising in the origination process, and special hazards (i.e., losses resulting from events not covered by a standard homeowner's insurance policy). Bond insurance provides the same function as in municipal bond structures. Typically, bond insurance is not used as the primary protection but to supplement other forms of credit enhancement.

A nonagency security with external credit support is subject to the credit risk of the third-party guarantor. Should the third-party guarantor be downgraded, the issue itself could be subject to downgrade even if the structure is performing as expected. This is based on the "weak link" test followed by rating agencies. According to this test, when evaluating a proposed structure, credit quality of the issue is only as good as the weakest link in credit enhancement regardless of the quality of underlying loans. For example, in the early 1990s, mortgage-backed securities issued by Citibank Mortgage Securities Inc. were downgraded when Citibank, the third-party guarantor, was downgraded. This is the chief disadvantage of third-party guarantees. Therefore, it is imperative that investors monitor the third-party guarantor as well as the collateral.

External credit enhancements do not materially alter the cash flow characteristics of a CMO structure except in the form of prepayment. In case of a default resulting in net losses within the guarantee level, investors will receive the principal amount as if a prepayment has occurred. If the net losses exceed the guarantee level, investors will have a shortfall in the cash flows.

Internal Credit Enhancements

Internal credit enhancements come in more complicated forms than external credit enhancements and may alter the cash flow characteristics of the loans even in the absence of default. The most common forms of internal credit enhancements are reserve funds and senior/subordinated structures.

Reserve Funds Reserve funds come in two forms, cash reserve funds and excess servicing spread. Cash reserve funds are straight deposits of cash generated from issuance proceeds. In this case, part of the underwriting profits from the deal are deposited into a hypothecated fund which typically invests in money market instruments. Cash reserve funds are typically used in conjunction with letters of credit or other kinds of external credit enhancements.

Excess servicing spread accounts involve the allocation of excess spread or cash into a separate reserve account after paying out the net coupon, servicing fee, and all other expenses on a monthly basis. For example, suppose that the gross weighted average coupon (gross WAC) is 7.75%, the servicing and other fees are 0.25%, and the net weighted average coupon (net WAC) is 7.25%. This means that there is excess servicing of 0.25%. The amount in the reserve account will gradually increase and can be used to pay for possible future losses.

The excess spread is analogous to the guarantee fee paid to the issuer of an agency MBS except that this is a form of self-insurance. This form of credit enhancement relies on the assumption that defaults occur infrequently in the very early life of the loans but gradually increase in the following two to five years.

Senior/Subordinated Structure The most widely used internal credit support structure is by far the senior/subordinated structure. Today a typical structure will have a senior bond and several junior bonds. The junior bonds represent the subordinated bonds of the structure. The issuer will seek a triple A or double A rating for the senior bond. The junior bonds will have lower ratings — investment grade and non-investment grade. Typically, the most junior bond — called the first loss piece — will not be rated.

Exhibit 16 shows a hypothetical \$200 million structure with a senior bond representing 92.25% of the deal and five junior bonds representing 7.75% of the deal. The first loss piece in this hypothetical deal is bond X5. The subordination level in this hypothetical structure is 7.75%. The junior classes will absorb all losses up to \$15.5 million and the senior class will start to experience losses thereafter. So, if there is a \$10 million loss, no loss will be realized by the senior bond. If, instead, there is a \$20 million loss, the senior bond will experience a loss of \$4.5 million (\$20 million minus \$15.5 million) or a 2.4% loss (\$4.5/\$184.5).

Exhibit 16: Hypothetical \$200 Million Senior/Subordinated Structure

Bond	Rating	Amount (\$ in millions)	Percent of deal(%)
Senior	AAA	\$184.50	92.25
Junior			
X1	AA	4.00	2.00
X2	A	2.00	1.00
X3	BBB	3.00	1.50
X4	BB	4.00	2.00
X5*	Not rated	2.50	1.25

* First loss piece.

In the case where the loss is $10, the first loss piece (bond X5), bond X4, and bond X3 absorb $9.5 million. These bonds will realize a loss experience of 100%. Bond X2 will realize a loss of $0.5 million, thereby having a loss experience of 25% ($0.5/$2.0). Bond X1 will not realize any loss. If the loss is $20 million, all junior bonds will have a loss experience of 100%.

This setup is another form of self-insurance wherein investors in the senior bond are giving up yield spread to the investors in the junior classes. This form of credit enhancement still does not affect cash flow characteristics of the senior class except in the form of prepayment. To the extent that losses are within the subordination level, investors in the senior tranche will receive principal as if a prepayment has occurred.

Note that all that has been done in this structure is credit tranching. The senior or any of the junior bonds can then be carved up to create CMO tranches.

Almost all existing senior/subordinated structures also incorporate a *shifting interest structure*. A shifting interest structure redirects prepayments disproportionally from the subordinated classes to the senior class according to a specified schedule. An example of such a schedule would be as follows:

Months	Percentage of prepayments directed to senior class
1-60	100%
61-72	70%
73-84	60%
85-96	40%
97-108	20%
109+	pro rata

The rationale for the shifting interest structure is to have enough insurance outstanding to cover future losses. Because of the shifting interest structure, the subordination amount may actually grow in time especially in a low default and fast prepayment environment. This is sometimes referred to as “riding up the credit curve.” Using the same example of our previous $200 million deal with 7.75% initial subordination and assuming a cumulative paydown (prepayments at 165 PSA and regular repayments) of $40 million by year 3, the subordination will actually increase to 10.7% [$15.5/($184.50 – $40)] without any net losses. Even if the subordinated classes have experienced some losses, say, $1 million, the subordination will still increase to 9.3% [($15.5 – $1)/($184.50 – $40)].

While the shifting interest structure is beneficial to the senior bond from a credit standpoint, it does alter the cash flow characteristics of the senior bond even in the absence of defaults. A 7.75% subordination with the shifting interest structure will shorten the average life of the senior bond to 8.41 assuming 165 PSA and no defaults. The size of the subordination also matters. Larger subordinated bonds result in the redirecting of a higher proportion of prepayments to the senior bond, thereby shortening the average life even further.

It may be counter-intuitive that the size of the subordination should affect the average life and cash flows of the senior bond more than the credit quality. The reason is that the size of the subordination is already factored into the rating. The rating agency typically requires more subordination for lower credit quality loans to obtain a triple A rating and less subordination for better credit quality loans. From a credit standpoint, the investor may be indifferent between a 5% subordination on a package of good quality loans and a 10% subordination on a package of lower quality loans as long as the rating agency gives them the same rating. However, the quality of the underlying loans will determine the default rate and therefore the timing of the cash flows.

WAC Interest-Only and Principal-Only Securities

In our discussion of agency CMOs, we saw how a notional interest-only tranche can be created. This is done by stripping the excess interest between the coupon rate of the passthrough securities that are the collateral for the CMO and coupon rate for a particular tranche. In the case of stripped MBS, we saw how principal-only and interest-only securities can be created.

Because of the wide dispersion of the coupon rates on the underlying mortgages for a nonagency security, a different type of IO and PO security can be created. This is done by the issuer first establishing the rate that it wants to pay on the issue. This is called the *remittance rate*. Then from all underlying mortgages with a coupon rate that is in excess of the remittance rate, the excess interest is stripped off to create an IO security. This IO security is called a *WAC IO*. A principal-only security is created from the underlying mortgages for which the coupon rate is less than the remittance rate. The resulting PO security is called a *WAC PO*.

FACTORS AFFECTING PREPAYMENT BEHAVIOR

There have been extensive studies of the factors that affect prepayments on agency MBS. The same factors as well as several others affect prepayments on nonagency MBS.

Prepayments on Agency MBS

The following four factors have been found to affect prepayment behavior on agency MBS: (1) prevailing mortgage rate, (2) characteristics of the underlying mortgage pool, (3) seasonal factors, and (4) general economic activity. We discuss each below.

Prevailing Mortgage Rate

The single most important factor affecting prepayments because of refinancing is the current level of mortgage rates relative to the borrower's contract rate. The more the contract rate exceeds the prevailing mortgage rate, the greater the incentive to refinance the mortgage loan. For refinancing to make economic sense, the interest savings must be greater than the costs associated with refinancing the mortgage. These costs include legal expenses, origination fees, title insurance, and the value of the time associated with obtaining another mortgage loan. Some of these costs — such as title insurance and origination points — will vary proportionately with the amount to be financed. Other costs such as the application fee and legal expenses are typically fixed.

Historically, it has been observed that when mortgage rates fall to more than 200 basis points below the contract rate, prepayment rates increase. However, the creativity of mortgage originators in designing mortgage loans such that the refinancing costs are folded into the amount borrowed has changed the view that mortgage rates must drop dramatically below the contract rate to make refinancing economic. Moreover, mortgage originators now do an effective job of advertising to make homeowners cognizant of the economic benefits of refinancing.

The historical pattern of prepayments and economic theory suggest that it is not only the level of mortgage rates that affects prepayment behavior but also the path that mortgage rates take to get to the current level. To illustrate why, suppose the underlying contract rate for a pool of mortgage loans is 11% and that three years after origination, the prevailing mortgage rate declines to 8%. Let's consider two possible paths of the mortgage rate in getting to the 8% level. In the first path, the mortgage rate declines to 8% at the end of the first year, then rises to 13% at the end of the second year, and then falls to 8% at the end of the third year. In the second path, the mortgage rate rises to 12% at the end of the first year, continues its rise to 13% at the end of the second year, and then falls to 8% at the end of the third year. If the mortgage rate follows the first path, those who can benefit from refinancing will more than likely take advantage of this opportunity when the mortgage rate drops to 8% in the first year. When the mortgage rate drops again to 8% at the end of the third year, the likelihood is that prepayments because of refinancing will not surge; those who can benefit by taking advantage of the refinancing opportunity will have done so already when the mortgage rate declined the first time. This prepayment behavior is referred to as *refinancing burnout* (or simply, burnout).

In contrast, the expected prepayment behavior when the mortgage rate follows the second path is quite different. Prepayment rates are expected to be low in the first two years. When the mortgage rate declines to 8% in the third year, refinancing activity and therefore prepayments are expected to surge. Consequently, burnout is related to the path of mortgage rates.

Our focus so far has been on the factors that affect prepayments caused by refinancing. Prepayments also occur because of housing turnover. The level of mortgage rates affects housing turnover to the extent that a lower rate increases the affordability of homes.

Characteristics of the Underlying Mortgage Loans

The following characteristics of the underlying mortgage loans affect prepayments: (1) the contract rate, (2) whether the loans are FHA/VA-guaranteed or conventional, (3) the amount of seasoning, (4) the type of loan, for example, a 30-year level payment mortgage, 5-year balloon mortgage, etc., and (5) the geographical location of the underlying properties.

Seasonality

There is a well-documented seasonal pattern in prepayments. This pattern is related to activity in the primary housing market, with home buying increasing in the spring, and gradually reaching a peak in the late summer. Home buying declines in the fall and winter. Mirroring this activity are the prepayments that result from the turnover of housing as home buyers sell their existing homes and purchase new ones. Prepayments are low in the winter months and begin to rise in the spring, reaching a peak in the summer months. However, probably because of delays in passing through prepayments, the peak may not be observed until early fall.

Macroeconomic Factors

Economic theory would suggest that general economic activity affects prepayment behavior through its effect on housing turnover. The link is as follows: a growing economy results in a rise in personal income and in opportunities for worker migration; this increases family mobility and as a result increases housing turnover. The opposite holds for a weak economy.

Prepayments on Nonagency MBS[7]

In the agency MBS market, prepayment analysis typically has been limited to the value of the prepayment option as determined chiefly by the gap between the mortgage's coupon rate and the prevailing mortgage rate and, to a lesser extent, the impact of loan age or seasoning along with macroeconomic factors. However, analysts know that prepayment models ideally should discriminate between a homeowner's decision to refinance an existing mortgage — whether to obtain a lower rate or to obtain cash — and the decision to sell the property. Modeling these decisions accurately would require much more data, such as information on the homeowner's family composition, life style stage, and overall financial situation. Hence, the existing models with only the factors just noted are only proxies for the "real" model.

These model imperfections are not the result of any lack of creativity, but rather the limitations of the data released by Fannie Mae, Freddie Mac, and Ginnie Mae. The agencies release only aggregate information such as weighted average coupon/maturity (WAC/WAM) by quartile and geographic concentrations at the state level, average loan age, and average loan size. Moreover, prepayments are not reported by type.

---

[7] This section is adapted from Douglas L. Bendt, Chuck Ramsey, and Frank J. Fabozzi, "Prepayment Analysis of Nonagency Mortgage-Backed Securities," Chapter 13 in *The Handbook of Nonagency Mortgage-Backed Securities.*

Issuers of nonagency securities are much more forthcoming with data, generally releasing loan-level detail for the collateral backing their deals. These data generally are in a standard format such as the one developed by the Public Securities Association. This detail makes it possible to do much more complete prepayment analysis to answer the following kinds of questions:

- Is the prepayment function for loans taken out to purchase a house different from the function for loans that refinance a previous mortgage?
- What is the effect of homeowners' equity and changing property values on prepayments?
- Do alternate documentation or low/no-doc loans prepay differently from fully documented loans?

Traditional Agency/Nonagency Prepayment Comparisons

Several research reports have found that prepayments for nonagency securities tend to be faster than "comparable" agency securities. (The quotation marks are necessary because some analysts control only for the WAC and the WAM of the pools being compared.) Among the factors cited for the faster speeds are that:

1. Greater variation in loan composition, such as greater WAC dispersion, can make WAC/WAM comparisons inadequate.
2. Larger loan sizes tend to prepay faster because the same size prepayment option in percentage terms is worth more in dollar terms.
3. More affluent borrowers tend to be more mobile.
4. California — traditionally a fast-prepaying state — is overrepresented in nonagency securities.

Other analysts correct for some of these factors. Adjusting for collateral diversity and geographic concentrations, Prudential finds prepayments speeds to average around 50% faster except during the depths of the last recession, when nonagency securities prepaid slower than agency securities.

Adjusted Agency/Nonagency Prepayment Comparisons

Often, prepayment rates for nonagency securities are cited as a multiple of expected prepayment rates on agency securities. Rather than compare nonagency and agency prepayment rates, it would be preferable to make such comparisons on a loan-level basis. This analysis would effectively remove the effects of WAC/WAM discrepancies and dispersions, allowing the effects of other factors to be seen more clearly.

With agency data, such comparisons are normally impossible. The data provided by Dow Jones/Telerate's Advance Factor Service, however, clearly show the effects of analyzing prepayments by pool coupon compared to analyzing prepayments using the actual mortgage rate. Using loan-level data, one study finds that the average "multiplier" for new-issue, lower coupons is about 2.5 — well above the range cited by analysts at the time — while multipliers for older, higher-rate collateral are about 1.5 — right in the middle of the range cited by other analysts at the time.[8]

The higher multipliers for the lower coupons that were observed in the study were measuring the effects of the refinancing wave in 1992 and 1993. For example, the barriers to refinancing have been lowered substantially with the increasing popularity of no-points mortgages. Thus, the value of the prepayment option for jumbo borrowers has increased in dollar terms relative to the value of the option for agency borrowers, given the same size of rate decrease.

Besides coupon and seasoning, there are three major influences on prepayment rates for nonagency securities. In order of importance, they are (1) homeowners' equity; (2) transaction type (purchase versus refinance); and, (3) level of documentation.

Homeowners' Equity A homeowner's equity depends chiefly upon two major factors: (1) the initial down payment and (2) changes in home prices. Together, these factors determine the current LTV ratio. Amortization and partial prepayments are of lesser importance.

Homeowners with lower LTVs — greater equity — have more home financing choices. Most importantly, they could sell their houses to unlock the equity to use as a down payment on another house. Second, they could do a cash-out refinancing to unlock the equity even if they don't want to move or interest rates are not any lower. And finally, if interest rates are lower so that the prepayment option has value, there is no constraint on taking advantage of the lower interest rate.

The study cited earlier finds a clear pattern of faster speeds among mortgages with lower current LTVs where current market values are estimated by using indexes of home price changes. This pattern helps explain California's reputation for being a fast-prepaying state throughout the 1980s. Housing prices exploded, allowing many homeowners to do equity-takeout refinancings and to trade up to bigger homes. With housing prices having dropped in the early 1990s in most areas of California, prepayments have slowed dramatically.

Transaction Type Mortgages taken out to purchase homes tend to be prepaid more slowly than mortgages taken out to refinance previous higher-rate mortgages. Refinance transactions in which the homeowner takes out cash tend to be more like purchase transactions. The study cited earlier finds this pattern is especially clear for mortgages originated in the 1992-1993 and the 1986-1987 periods, when rates were low.

Homeowners refinancing an existing mortgage are different from homeowners who just purchased a house in two important ways. First, they have lived

[8] Bendt, Ramsey, and Fabozzi, "Prepayment Analysis for Non-Agency Mortgage-Backed Securities."

in their house for some amount of time. Therefore, they are more likely to have moved to a new stage in their life cycle and to require a different type of house. And second, the fact that they have refinanced their mortgage once already may make them more sensitive to future rate drops because they realize how easy the process can be. Mortgage brokers are more likely to be more aggressive with previous refinancers as well.

Level of Documentation Nonagency mortgages that are fully documented are loans that would qualify for sale to the agencies, but for the fact that the loan amount is higher than the agencies' limits. (Loans may not qualify for sale to the agencies for other underwriting characteristics such as debt ratios as well, but these reasons are much less common.) Borrowers are required to submit forms verifying income and employment with W-2 forms, pay stubs, tax forms, and lenders verify the sources of the assets to be used for the down payment.

Loans that are deficient in at least one of these areas qualify under "alternative" or "low" documentation programs, usually at a slightly higher interest rate and a lower cap on the permissible LTV. In the extreme, no documentation may have been required as a trade-off for a higher rate and/or an even lower LTV.

The study found that borrowers who qualified for full documentation programs in 1993 and 1994 have had higher prepayments. First, the spectrum of lenders who will lend to such borrowers is wider; fewer lenders have a low or no-doc program than in the past because of higher default experience. Second, borrowers who qualified under a less-than-full-doc program are more likely to have fluctuations in their income — many are self-employed — that may limit their ability to refinance or trade up.

Chapter 23

Home Equity Loan-Backed Securities

Charles N. Schorin
Principal
Director of ABS Research
Morgan Stanley

INTRODUCTION

This chapter provides investors with an introduction to home equity loan-backed securities. In order to better understand securities backed by home equity loans, it is necessary to understand fundamental aspects of the loans themselves: loan attributes, borrower characteristics, loan purposes, underwriting criteria and loan performance.

The term "home equity loan" covers a broad array of products. While included in this term is the traditional second mortgage, "home equity loan" now encompasses, and often primarily refers to, first mortgages to borrowers unable to obtain funding from conventional mortgage lenders. Sometimes referred to as B and C loans, their primary purpose generally is for debt consolidation or other consumer expenses, and rarely to purchase a home.

Home equity loans can take several forms. There are closed-end home equity loans (HEL), where the loan amount and term to maturity are known at origination, and open-end revolving loans, where the borrower receives a home equity line of credit (HELOC) that can be (partially or completely) drawn down and (partially or completely) paid back over time. HELs are primarily fixed rate, although adjustable-rate loans also comprise a significant share. HELOCs carry floating rates.

Advanta Mortgage provided Morgan Stanley considerable loan level information on its home equity program, allowing us to draw conclusions about the behavior of home equity borrowers. This chapter frequently uses Advanta as a benchmark for the home equity market.

Exhibit 1: Annual Issuance of Home Equity Loan ABS & Home Equity Share of Total ABS Issued

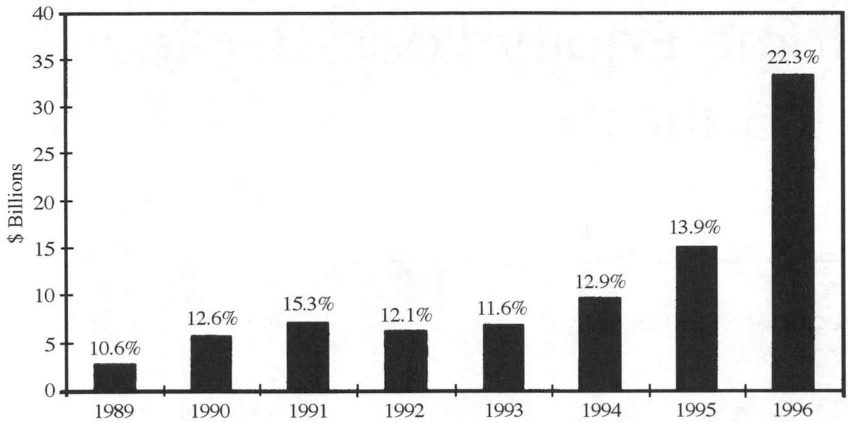

Source: Morgan Stanley

HOME EQUITY MARKET OVERVIEW

We estimate that there have been approximately $400 billion of home equity loans originated. Of this, $225 billion are closed end loans and $175 billion are revolving lines of credit. Of the home equity loans originated, over 20% (about $85 billion) have been securitized. Netting out prepayments and scheduled paydowns, the outstanding amount of securitized home equity loans as of early 1997 was about $55 billion, of which about three-quarters were closed end loans.

Exhibit 1 reports annual issuance of home equity loan asset backed securities since 1989, with home equity's share of total ABS issuance indicated. As ABS issuance has mushroomed, home equity loans have comprised an increasing market share. The breakdown between fixed- and floating-rate home equity ABS has been roughly equal. The majority of floating-rate home equity ABS are collateralized by home equity lines of credit. However, there also are floating-rate ABS that are backed by closed end adjustable- and fixed-rate loans.

The largest issuers of home equity loan ABS through 1996 are shown in Exhibit 2. The product of some issuers, such as Beneficial and Household, consists almost entirely of lines of credit. Other issuers, such as Advanta, securitize primarily closed end loans, the vast majority of which are fixed rate. This chapter focuses on fixed-rate closed end loans. The largest issuers of closed end fixed-rate home equity loan ABS through 1996 are displayed in Exhibit 3.[1]

[1] Large home equity originators, such as Long Beach and Option One, that sell their product rather than securitize it directly under their name, are not included in Exhibit 3.

Exhibit 2: Largest Issuers of Home Equity Loan ABS: Cumulative Issuance

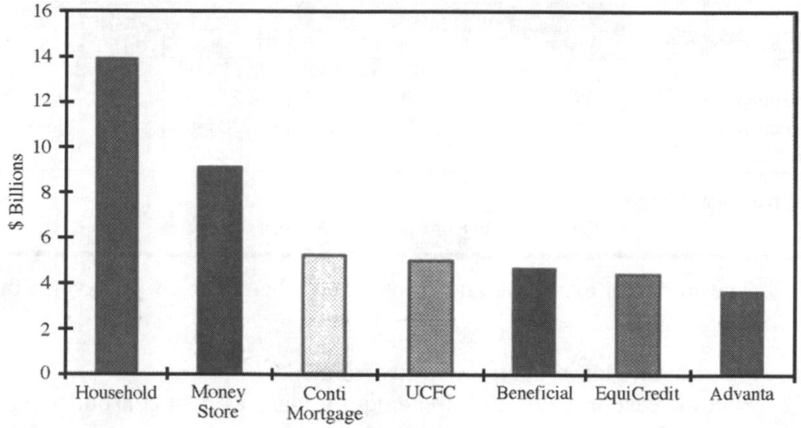

Source: Morgan Stanley

Exhibit 3: Largest Issuers of Fixed Rate Home Equity Loan ABS: Cumulative Issuance

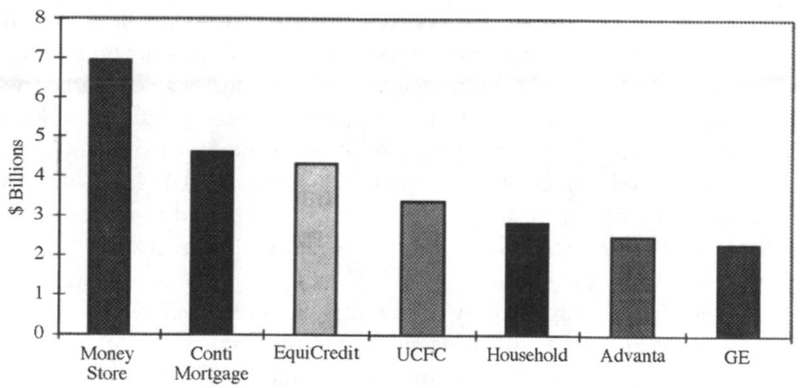

Source: Morgan Stanley

EVOLUTION OF THE HOME EQUITY MARKET

Through the late 1980s and early 1990s, the home equity market was characterized by relatively small balance, second lien loans. The market, however, has evolved dramatically in the past few years toward larger loans that are first liens and with longer maturities. The changed nature of the home equity market is indicated in Exhibit 4 by a comparison of the collateral characteristics for Advanta 91-1 and 96-3. The tendency toward first liens, longer maturities and larger loan balances is clear.

Exhibit 4: Home Equity Market Has Moved Toward First Liens, Longer Maturities and Larger Loan Balances

	Advanta 91-1		Advanta 96-3*	
Characteristic	Average	Range	Average	Range
Loan Size	$41,116	$4,499-$260,508	$57,199	$3,574-$598,395
Remaining Term	173 mos.	32-180 mos.	226 mos.	33-360 mos.
Original Term	180 mos.	180 mos.	228 mos.	36-360 mos.
First Lien	24%		87%	

* Fixed rate collateral pool

Source: Advanta prospectuses, Morgan Stanley

The market's evolution and growth have been fueled by several factors, including

- a generally lower interest rate environment
- an increase in the use of home equity loans as debt consolidation instruments
- an increase in the number and volume of B and C lending programs
- a change in tax laws making mortgage debt the only remaining tax deductible form of consumer debt.

Low rates allow homeowners to refinance their first lien and take out equity or consolidate debt more cheaply than with a non-mortgage consumer loan. The cost effectiveness of mortgage versus non-mortgage consumer debt has increased since tax laws changed to make mortgage debt the only tax deductible form of consumer debt. The acceptance by homeowners of using equity in their home to increase their financial flexibility and consolidate debt has grown tremendously. As homeowners have sought to consolidate debt and as A quality conventional lenders saw their traditional lines of business diminish, they developed B and C programs to fill the void.

B and C grade home equity borrowers tend either to have had some blemishes on their credit records that prevent them from qualifying for A quality conventional mortgages or else have debt-to-income ratios (or some other loan parameters) that disqualify them from conventional loans. Tapping the equity in their homes provides their readiest access to credit, which often is used to consolidate other consumer debt (such as credit card or automobile debt), or for home improvements, medical or education expenditures. Borrower classification by lenders into various credit grades is discussed in the next section.

HOME EQUITY LOAN UNDERWRITING

Lenders classify borrowing applicants by their credit quality. Specific criteria for a credit grade sometimes differ among lenders, so that one lender's B applicant may be another's C candidate. Within the home equity arena, however, A quality finance company borrowers either do not generally possess as strong personal credit profiles or do not meet certain loan parameters, such as debt-to-income ratio, as required for standard conventional mortgages.

Exhibit 5 shows guidelines that Advanta uses when evaluating its borrowing applicants. The difference between credit grades can result in substantially different mortgage rates offered to borrowers (see Exhibit 6).

Borrower credit grades have significant implications for home equity loan prepayments. Less-than-A quality borrowers can achieve considerable reductions in their mortgage rates if they can improve their credit record and achieve a personal rating "upgrade." They may be able to obtain an upgrade by being current on their mortgage for 12 months. As indicated in Exhibit 6, moving from grade C to B could lower a borrower's rate by about 200 basis points. Note that this savings would occur with no change in market interest rates. This will be addressed in more detail in the section on prepayments below.

Exhibit 5: Advanta Conduit Program Underwriting Matrix

Grade	Quality	Credit History and Ratios
A	Good	• No more than 2 mortgage or rent delinquencies in past 12 months • Non-mortgage debt: majority paid as agreed, limited 30- and isolated 60-day delinquencies • Bankruptcies acceptable with 2 years re-established major credit • Maximum debt/income ratio of 45% • Maximum LTV* of 85%
B	Satisfactory	• No more than 3 mortgage or rent delinquencies in past 12 months • Non-mortgage debt: pattern of 30-day and limited 60-day delinquencies, isolated 90-day delinquencies with explanation • Bankruptcies acceptable with 2 years re-established major credit • Maximum debt/income ratio of 50% • Maximum LTV* of 85%
C	Fair	• No more than 4 30-day mortgage or rent delinquencies, or 3 30-day and 1 60-day delinquencies, in past 12 months • Non-mortgage debt: cross-section of 30-, 60-, and 90-day delinquencies with some major derogatory ratings • Bankruptcies acceptable with 2 years re-established major credit (less with compensating factors) • Maximum debt/income ratio of 55% • Maximum LTV* of 75%
D	Poor	• No more than 120-day mortgage or rent delinquency in past 12 months. Property cannot be in foreclosure. • Non-mortgage debt: Major derogatory ratings, delinquent or charged off accounts acceptable • Bankruptcies acceptable if discharged or dismissed • Maximum debt/income ratio of 60% • Maximum LTV* of 65%

* Full documentation loans on single-family units

Source: Advanta Mortgage

Exhibit 6: Mortgage Rate Differentials by Borrower Credit Grade: Advanta Mortgage

	Range of Rate Differential	
Grade	From Next Highest Grade	From A Borrower
A	NA	NA
B	0.875 - 1.875%	0.875 - 1.875%
C	1.625 - 2.125	2.500 - 4.000
D	2.625 - 3.125	5.125 - 7.125

Source: Advanta Mortgage

Exhibit 7: Home Equity Loan Issuer Summary

Banks
• Excellent credit quality: A/B credits
• Lending on ability to repay
• Low delinquency and loss experience
• Relatively low interest rates
• Relatively high CLTV
Finance Companies
• Good to average credit quality: B/C credits
• Lending on ability to repay and equity
• Average level of delinquencies and losses
• Moderately high interest rates
• Moderate CLTV
"Hard Money" Lenders
• Poor or riskier credit quality: C/D credits
• Lending primarily on homeowner equity
• Highest level of delinquencies and losses
• Relatively high interest rates
• Relatively low CLTV

Source: Morgan Stanley

A broad summary of the types of issuers and their products is presented in Exhibit 7. While any particular issuer or product may not fit precisely into the table, it nonetheless provides a general illustration of lenders' guidelines.

Credit Scoring

Mortgage lenders have moved in the past few years towards credit scoring their borrowing candidates. Credit scoring attaches a quantitative measure to candidates based upon their personal credit history. It is used by many home equity lenders as an additional piece of information to that in the underwriting matrix in Exhibit 5.

For example, some home equity lenders will not lend to applicants who score below a particular numerical threshold.[2] Other lenders use the score as an additional piece of information — which could offset other borrower data that are

[2] On the other hand, borrowers with credit scores above a given level probably are not applicants for finance company loans.

either positive or negative — in determining the overall quality of the borrower and affecting the credit decision.

LOAN SERVICING

Servicing loans to B and C borrowers is markedly different from servicing loans to A quality conventional borrowers. B and C borrowers generally require active attention by servicers to maximize the likelihood of payment. The quality and effectiveness of servicing can have a substantial impact on the performance of a home equity loan pool.

Loan servicers who have extensive experience with A borrowers have found that their expertise in that arena does not necessarily, or even generally, carry over into the B and C sector. The cost of servicing B and C loans could easily be double that of servicing A loans.

Some of the larger lender/servicers, such as Advanta, perform servicing for other lenders on a contract basis. These large operations allow servicers to achieve scale economies. When loans are serviced on a contract basis, the servicer may not give a preference in servicing to either its owned portfolio or its contracted servicing.

PERFORMANCE OF HOME EQUITY LOAN ABS

Home equity loan ABS performance depends upon both voluntary prepayments and defaults on the underlying home equity collateral. Prepayments may be classified as either responding to interest rate refinancing incentives or seasoning as the loans age.

Factors affecting the interest rate sensitivity of home equity loans include borrower credit grade, loan size, lien position, and combined loan-to-value (CLTV) ratio. The rate at which a pool of loans seasons also will be related to most of these parameters, as well as to whether the loans are premiums, discounts, or current coupons. These factors, as well as whether the loan is fixed or adjustable rate, may affect the likelihood of delinquency and default. Each of these influences is discussed in this section for fixed-rate home equity loans.[3] We drew our conclusions on home equity loan performance from loan level data provided to Morgan Stanley by Advanta Mortgage.

Prepayments on Fixed-Rate Home Equity Loans

Cash flows on securities backed by fixed-rate closed end home equity loans are heavily dependent on the prepayment characteristics of the underlying loans. The

[3] HELOCs are relatively rate insensitive because their rates adjust according to an index. ARM HEL prepayments may be sensitive to teaser rates rolling off and periodic caps.

prepayment behavior of the loans, in turn, is closely related to the characteristics of the borrower.

Home equity loans are typically used to

- consolidate consumer debt in a lower rate, tax deductible form
- reduce a homeowner's monthly mortgage payment by extending the loan's term
- finance home improvements
- monetize equity in the home
- finance temporary liquidity needs, such as for education or medical expenses.

Accessing equity in the home is typically the least expensive and most readily available means of financing for the borrower. Aside from credit card lines — which usually charge interest at rates that are several hundred basis points higher than home equity note rates and that is not tax deductible — home equity borrowers generally do not have access to other forms of credit. Borrowers who have consolidated debt or taken cash out to meet an expense frequently consolidate again after their debt burden re-accumulates. This behavior is especially achievable if home values rise over time. This pattern of reconsolidation keeps the life of these loans considerably shorter than their maturity. Finance company home equity loan borrowers tend to be more sensitive to monthly dollar payments than the interest rates on the loans, *per se*.

Interest Rate Sensitivity

Exhibit 8 shows a spectrum of refinancing sensitivity to interest rate movements of various mortgage products. Large balance (jumbo) conventional loans have the strongest response, followed by agency conforming mortgages. After this are home equity loans, with loans to A borrowers the most responsive and those to D borrowers the least responsive.

One of the reasons that home equity loans display less interest rate refinancing sensitivity than conventional loans is that home equities typically have smaller loan balances. The smaller home equity loan balances mean that it requires a larger interest rate move for the borrower to achieve a substantial monthly dollar savings from refinancing.[4] Small balances also make these loans less of a target to lenders that solicit refinancings, for which larger loans are more profitable.

[4] As an example, consider a $50,000 home equity loan. It may require points and origination fees of perhaps 5%, which typically would be financed. At an 11% note rate on a 30-year loan, the borrower's monthly payment would be $499.97 (assuming points are financed). If, after this loan has been outstanding for three years, rates fall 100 basis points, the borrower could refinance his $51,705.85 loan balance and pay $476.44 per month (assuming origination fees and points are financed). This 100 basis point reduction in rates would save the borrower only $23.53 per month. By comparison, a 100 basis point reduction after three years from 8.50% to 7.50% for a $300,000 non-conforming loan would reduce the borrower's monthly payments by $261.00 per month.

Exhibit 8: Mortgage Products Interest Rate Sensitivity Spectrum

Most Sensitive					Least Sensitive
Jumbo Mortgages	Agency Conforming Mortgages	"A" Quality Home Equity	"B" Quality Home Equity	"C" Quality Home Equity	"D" Quality Home Equity

Source: Morgan Stanley

Exhibit 9: Home Equity Loans Have Less Interest Rate Sensitivity than Conventional Mortgages

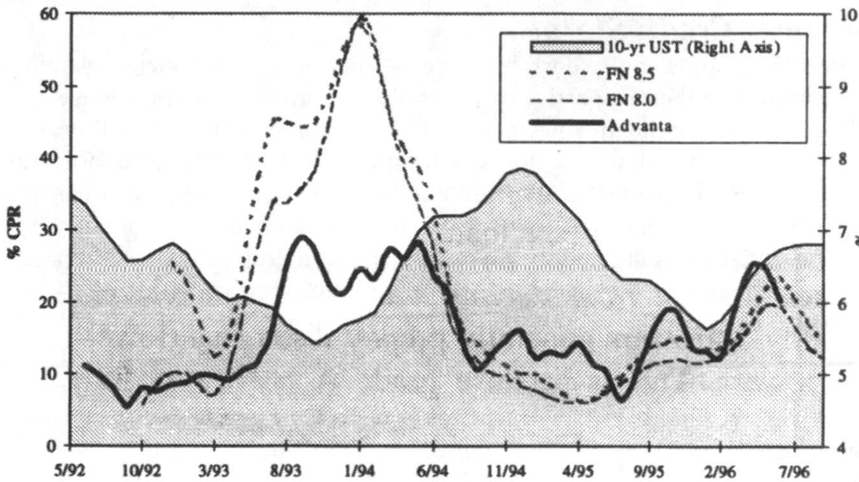

Source: Advanta Mortgage, Morgan Stanley

As an illustration of interest rate refinancing sensitivity, Exhibit 9 compares prepayment rates on home equity loans to those on conventional mortgages. The home equity data are derived from loan level detail from Advanta Mortgage. These loans are 15-year, fixed rate, fully amortizing first liens that Advanta originated in 1992 as A quality loans. The conventionals are represented by 15-year FNMA 8% and 8.5% passthrough coupons that also were originated in 1992.[5] Exhibit 9 displays prepayments on a 3-month average basis to smooth volatility in the 1-month CPR series.

It is clear from Exhibit 9 that when interest rates fell dramatically in 1993, conventional pass-throughs responded with prepayment speeds in the neighborhood of 60% CPR, whereas home equity prepayments on a 3-month average basis barely pierced 30% CPR. Moreover, when the 1994 bear market hit, home equity prepayment speeds declined less than the conventional loans: the

[5] The FNMA pass-throughs are backed by 15-year, fixed rate, fully amortizing first liens.

FNMA 8s in Exhibit 10 prepaid on a 3-month average basis between 6% and 10% CPR in the fourth quarter of 1994 and the first half of 1995, whereas the home equity loans prepaid between 10% and 16% CPR over this period.[6] This combination of less refinancing in market rallies, as well as a smaller prepayment slowdown in bear markets, combine to give home equities a more stable prepayment profile across interest rate scenarios than conventional mortgages. Securities backed by home equity loans, then, have less optionality than those backed by conventional mortgages.

The following subsections address various influences on interest rate sensitivity of home equity loans: borrower credit status, loan size, lien position, and combined loan-to-value ratio.

Borrower Credit Status

The profile of home equity borrowers means that their prepayment behavior is closely related to their respective credit grade. C borrowers could achieve a significant drop in their monthly payments if they were to be upgraded to B or A levels. For a C borrower with a 30-year loan of $50,000 at an 11% note rate, receiving a credit upgrade to B would cut the borrower's monthly payment by about $58.[7] Grade A borrowers, already in the highest rated class, cannot achieve a meaningful savings in monthly payments, absent a drop in interest rates or an extension of loan term.[8] In addition to voluntary prepayments, lower credit grade borrowers are more likely to experience defaults than higher grade borrowers,[9] which will affect prepayments on home equity loan backed ABS.[10] Therefore, *in the absence of interest rate shifts* (i.e., in the base case rate scenario), lower quality borrowers generally display faster prepayments than higher quality borrowers, all else equal.

---

[6] The FNMA 8.5s prepaid between 6% and 13% CPR over this period, and between 6% and 10% CPR for the first half of 1995.

[7] This example assumes a $50,000, 11% loan with 5 points of origination fees that are financed. If the borrower is able to improve his credit record by being current for one year, he may be able to achieve a personal rating upgrade, which would reduce his rate by about 200 basis points. After one year, his balance would be $52,263.68, which at the lower rate, would result in monthly payments (after financing 5 points) of $441.55, a saving of $58.42 per month.

[8] Grade A borrowers could also lower their rates if they were to improve their financial position sufficiently so as to qualify for a conventional loan. However, this is likely to be more difficult than a B or C borrower improving to a higher grade within the finance company rankings.

[9] The lower credit grade borrowers are more likely to experience defaults than higher credit grades, but if the loans are priced appropriately, the excess spread on these loans should be similar to those on loans to higher grade borrowers. Note also that lenders require lower LTVs on lower credit grade loans to mitigate losses in the event of default.

[10] The Advanta home equity prepayment data from which we draw conclusions in Exhibits 9 through 19 are based on home equity *loans*, not securities backed by home equity loans. The difference is that loan level prepayment data represent voluntary prepayments, whereas security level prepayments would include defaults, also. Using loan level detail, however, allows us to isolate relationships between prepayments and various borrower parameters, which would not be possible in the highly aggregated deal level information.

Exhibit 10: Lower Credit Grade Borrowers Have Less Interest Rate Sensitivity than Higher Grade Borrowers

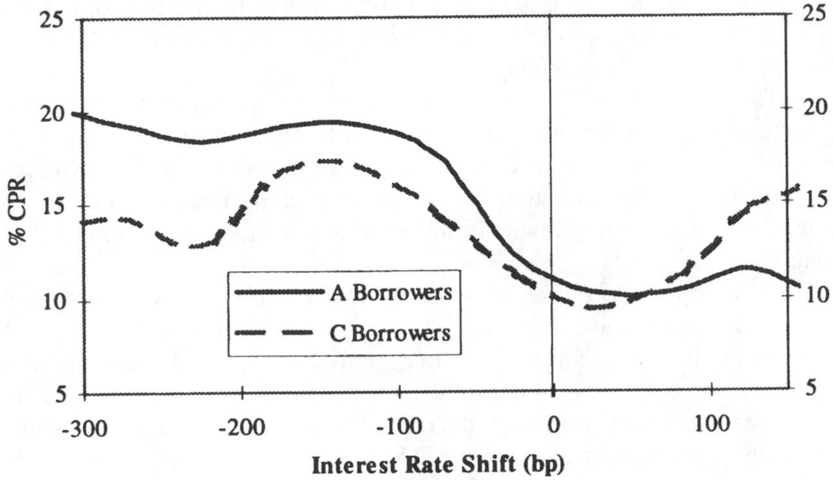

Source: Advanta Mortgage, Morgan Stanley

Another cause of relatively fast base case prepayment speeds for home equity borrowers traces back to their reason for borrowing. Many of these borrowers have used their home equity loan to consolidate other consumer debt. It is often the case, however, that three to five years after taking out a home equity loan to consolidate debt, the borrower again is in need of cash and looks either to consolidate the debt that has accumulated since the previous consolidation or to extend the loan term to reduce monthly payments. This results in a prepayment of the original home equity loan and the origination of a new loan.

When *interest rates decline substantially*, however, higher quality borrowers generally prepay faster than lower quality borrowers. This is because grade A borrowers have more financing options available to them than C borrowers and are able to take advantage of market rallies.

To summarize the interest rate sensitivity of home equity loans: the ability of some home equity loan borrowers to achieve a credit upgrade, as well as the debt consolidation behavior described above, contribute to *base case* prepayment speeds on home equity loans to B and C borrowers to be *faster* than on conforming conventional mortgages. The blemished credit status of these borrowers, especially those who do not achieve a credit upgrade, causes the *interest rate sensitivity* of home equity loans to be *less* than agency conventional mortgages.

This behavior is demonstrated in Exhibit 10, which compares the relative interest rate sensitivity of home equity loans for Advanta A and C borrower credit categories. (For clarity of presentation, B borrowers were excluded from the graph.) As discussed, the lower the credit grade of the borrowers, the weaker their responsiveness to an interest rate refinancing opportunity. In environments where interest rates have fallen since loan origination (the negative values on the horizontal axis), prepayments for A borrowers were higher than those for C borrowers. On the other hand, we see that C borrowers prepaid faster than A borrowers when both were out-of-the-money.

The behavior of C borrowers — fairly fast speeds when interest rates have *not* fallen — is noteworthy. It is important to realize that even though to the right of the vertical axis borrowers faced interest rates higher than at origination, the C borrower who was able to achieve a personal credit upgrade to B still could have received, in a rising rate environment, a loan with a lower rate than he had originally.

An exception to our conclusion that lower grade borrowers prepay relatively fast in the base case is given by Advanta D borrowers. Exhibit 11 adds D borrowers to Exhibit 10, and shows that D borrowers displayed almost no interest rate refinancing sensitivity — not totally unexpected — but also prepaid in the base case considerably more slowly than A or C borrowers. The likely explanation for this is that the credit histories of the D borrowers have been so impaired that it is difficult for them to recover sufficiently[11] to either respond to a refinancing opportunity or to achieve a personal ratings upgrade that would lower their note rate without a change in market rates.

Exhibit 11: Lowest Credit Grade Borrowers Have Almost No Interest Rate Sensitivity and Prepay More Slowly than Higher Grade Borrowers When Out-of-the-Money

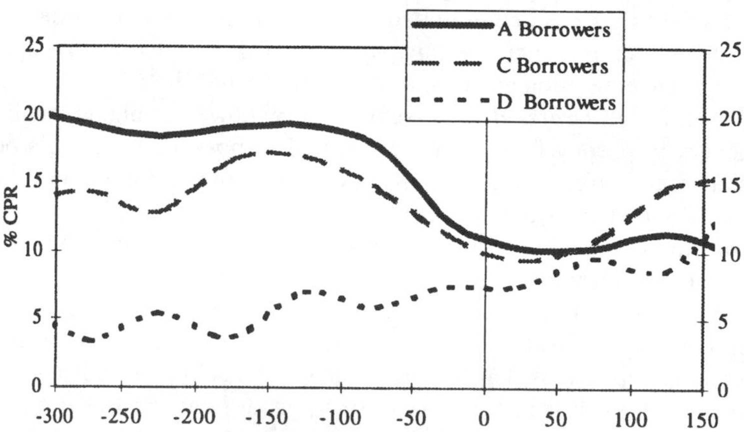

Source: Advanta Mortgage, Morgan Stanley

[11] For example, see the underwriting matrix for D borrowers in Exhibit 5.

Exhibit 12: Smaller Loan Balances Have Less Interest Rate Sensitivity than Larger Loan Balances

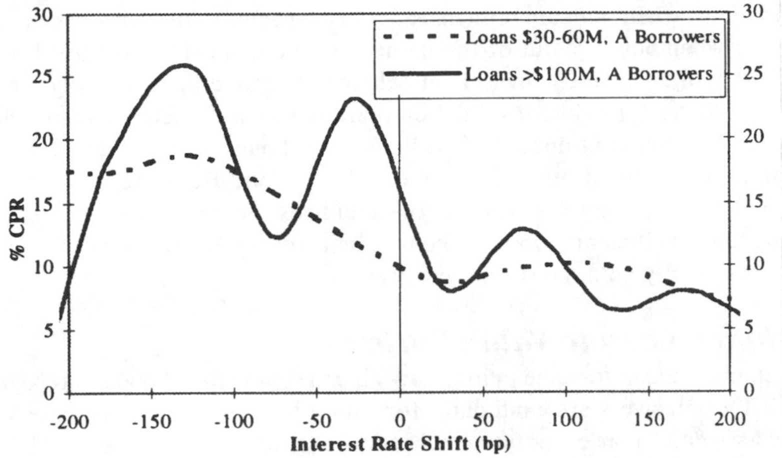

Source: Advanta Mortgage, Morgan Stanley

Loan Size

Exhibit 12 compares the relative interest rate sensitivity by loan size for Advanta A borrowers. The exhibit displays prepayments for various interest rate shifts for borrowers with loan balances between $30,000 and $60,000, compared to prepayments for balances greater than $100,000. Even though there is considerable volatility in the plus-$100,000 balance series, it still appears that in general, the smaller the loan balance, the less the sensitivity to interest rates. As noted earlier, this is because it requires a larger interest rate move to provide a meaningful dollar savings in the borrower's monthly payments. In addition, these lower balance borrowers are less likely to be solicited for refinancings.

Lien Position

Since most finance company home equity loans are now first liens, lien position is perhaps a less important factor for prepayments than other parameters. Nonetheless, some transactions still consist of a considerable percentage of second liens, so the relationship of lien position to interest rate moves still is worth considering.

Exhibit 13 considers interest rate sensitivity by lien position. The data are first and second lien B quality loans originated by Advanta. *We would have expected a priori* that second liens would prepay at least as fast as first liens. This is because in falling interest rate environments, a higher proportion of first liens are originated, as borrowers tend to refinance all their debt — including outstanding second mortgages — into new first liens. In a rising rate environment, there are more second liens originated as borrowers try to preserve the relatively low rate on the first lien and take out a higher rate on the marginal debt added (second lien). Given the higher interest rates on second liens, borrowers have an incentive to pay off this loan and *we would expect them* to be prepaid faster than first liens.

Exhibit 13, however, shows that while Advanta second liens prepay faster than first liens when both are refinanceable (as expected), first liens appear to prepay faster when both are out-of-the-money. This counter-intuitive result may be explained by the generally lower loan balance of second liens, making them less likely candidates for debt consolidation than first liens. When out-of-the-money, debt consolidation continues, as first liens are refinanced to extract equity from the home to pay down other consumer debt. Second liens are backed by less equity in the home and so are less likely candidates for debt consolidation, if rates have not fallen sufficiently. In fact, the first liens for the B borrowers in Exhibit 13 display essentially no interest rate sensitivity.

Combined Loan-to-Value Ratio

A low combined loan-to-value ratio (CLTV) increases the likelihood of prepayments. Low CLTV borrowers are candidates for future borrowings against equity (they already have done it once) for future debt consolidation or equity takeout. These borrowers also have greater ability to trade up to a better home or refinance into a lower note rate since it is easier for low CLTV borrowers to obtain favorable financing.

Exhibit 14 reports this relationship for Advanta's A quality borrowers. While there is considerable variability in the high CLTV data, it nonetheless is clear that the loans in the lower CLTV range (51-70%) are, on average, more able to take advantage of refinancing opportunities than those in the higher CLTV group (more than 80%).

Exhibit 13: Second Liens Are More Interest Rate Sensitive than First Liens

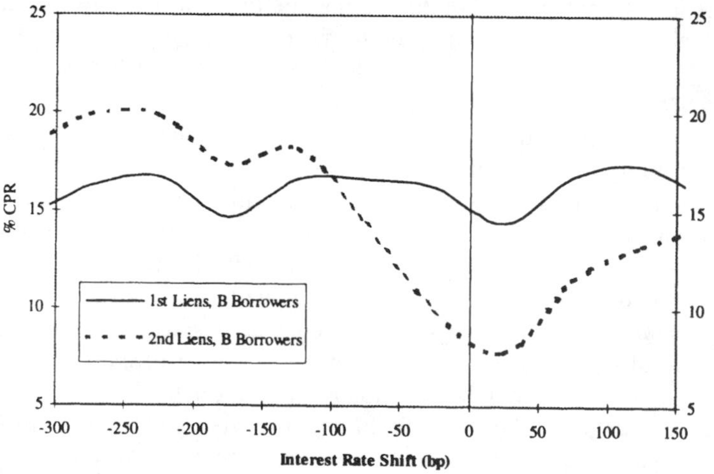

Source: Advanta Mortgage, Morgan Stanley

Exhibit 14: Higher CLTV Loans Have Less Interest Rate Sensitivity than Lower CLTV

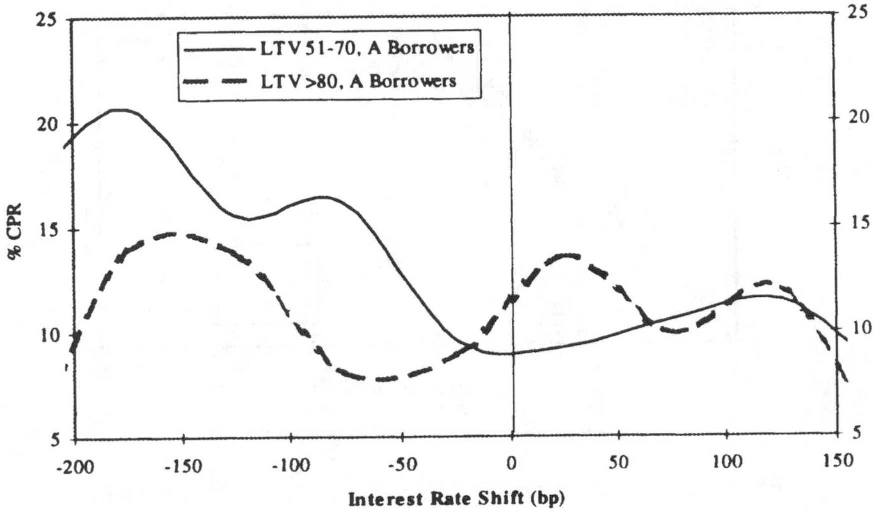

Source: Advanta Mortgage, Morgan Stanley

Seasoning

Here we consider the factors that cause prepayments on home equities to ramp upward as the loans age and reach their long term base case speed, or fully seasoned prepayment rate. The elements affecting seasoning are borrower credit status, relationship of loan rate to market rate, CLTV ratio and lien position. This section uses 3-month average CPRs to smooth volatility in the monthly CPR series.

Borrower Credit Status

Exhibit 15 shows home equity loan seasoning by credit category for Advanta. As expected, the C grade loans season faster than the B loans, which in turn, season faster than the A loans. It makes sense that the C borrowers would season fastest, as they have the most to gain from upgrading their credit status. The lower grade loans also generally maintain their faster speed after all categories reach their respective plateau levels, although these data indicate a slight slowdown in the C data from its peak level.

There is an exception to our conclusion that lower grade loans season faster than higher grade loans. This is the case of Advanta D borrowers. These borrowers season more slowly and reach lower plateau prepayment levels than A, B and C borrowers. This probably is because the D borrowers have such impaired credit records that they are generally unable to recover as fast as, and to the extent of, C or B borrowers. It also is the case that Advanta has extended relatively few loans to D borrowers. It is conceivable that a larger sample of D borrowers would provide additional information or a somewhat different seasoning pattern.

Exhibit 15: Home Equity Loans to Lower Credit Grade Borrowers Season Faster than Loans to Higher Grade Borrowers

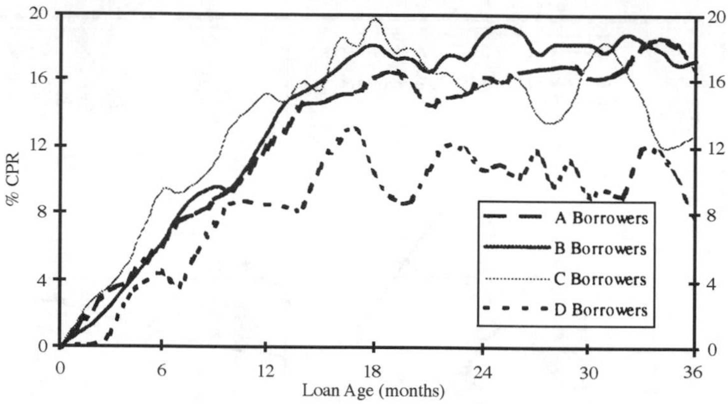

Source: Advanta Mortgage, Morgan Stanley

Exhibit 16: Premium Loans Season Faster than Current Coupon and Discount Home Equity Loans

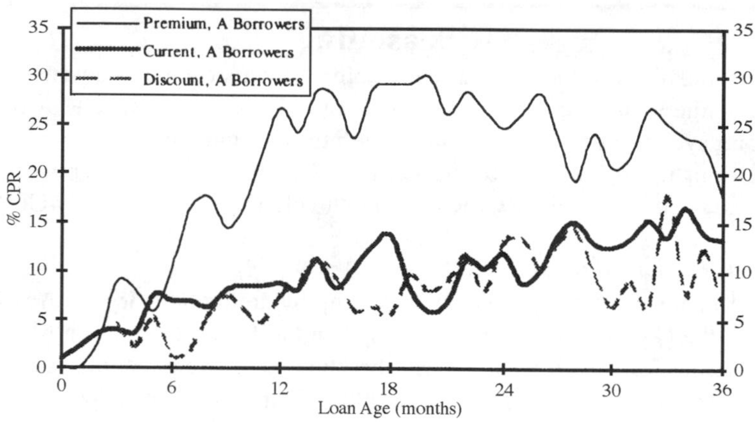

Source: Advanta Mortgage, Morgan Stanley

Premium, Discount or Current Coupon

Even though home equity loans have less interest rate sensitivity than conventional mortgages, there still is some responsiveness to rate moves. This enables premium loans to season faster than current coupon and discount loans. Exhibit 16 displays this relationship for 15-year Advanta A grade home equity loans.

It is apparent that premiums prepay faster and reach their peak sooner than discounts and current coupons. What is interesting is that discounts and current coupons season similarly. In the conventional mortgage arena, current coupons season faster than discounts: holders of below-market rate loans have a disincentive to move to another home because moving would require them to take out a new mortgage at the higher market rate. In the home equity arena, however, homeowner mobility is *not* often a reason for prepayment and borrowers are more dollar payment sensitive than rate sensitive, *per se*. Therefore, current coupon and discount borrowers perceive the lack of prepayment opportunity similarly.

CLTV Ratio

Loans with lower CLTVs season faster than those with higher CLTVs, for given credit grade. This behavior is because borrowers with lower CLTVs have more equity in their homes that they again can tap. Exhibit 17 shows this general behavior for Advanta A category mortgages, although there is considerable volatility in the data series.

Lien Position

We would expect that second liens season faster than first liens. This is because borrowers with second liens have more incentive to prepay because the second lien's interest rate is likely to be higher than that on the first lien. As soon as market circumstances allow, these borrowers will refinance both first and second liens into a new first lien loan. Exhibit 18 compares prepayments on Advanta A loans by lien position.

It is interesting, however, that for Advanta C borrowers, *first* liens season faster than second liens (Exhibit 19). A likely explanation is the following: the ability of C borrowers to achieve personal credit upgrades on *first* liens causes these to prepay faster than C borrowers' *second* liens.[12] Since A borrowers cannot, by definition, achieve a ratings upgrade, their first lien prepayments do not embody this component and they prepay more slowly than grade A second liens.

Exhibit 17: Low CLTV Loans Season Faster than High CLTV Loans

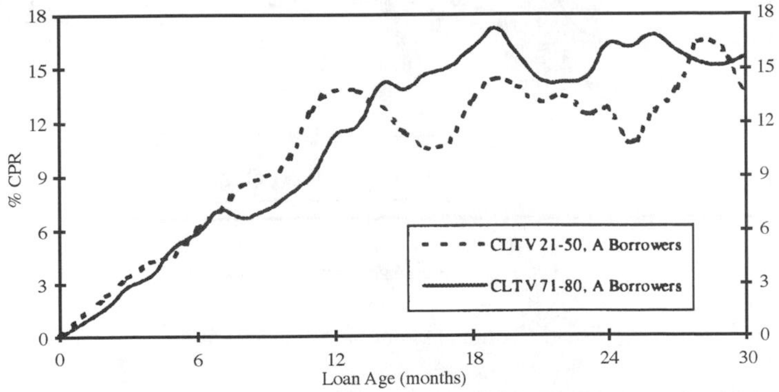

Source: Advanta Mortgage, Morgan Stanley

[12] It is likely that the generally larger loan size of first liens makes them more likely candidates for prepayment related to borrower upgrades, as well as for future debt consolidations.

Exhibit 18: Second Liens Season Faster than First Liens for Grade A Borrowers

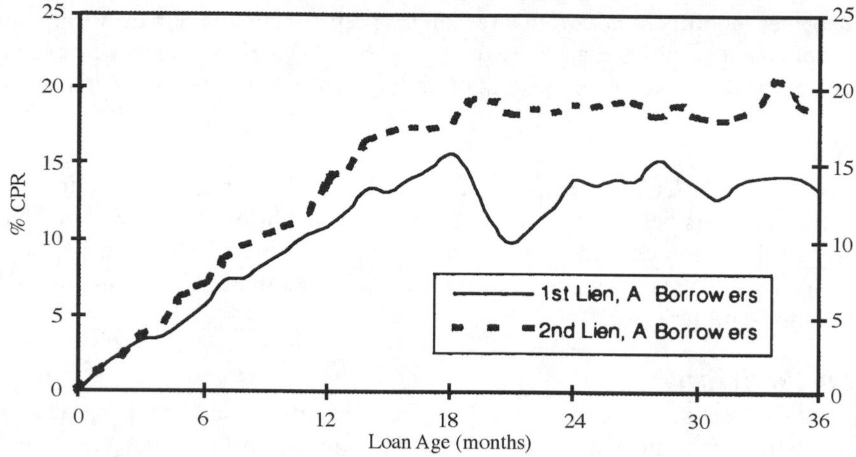

Source: Advanta Mortgage, Morgan Stanley

Exhibit 19: First Liens Season Faster than Second Liens for Grade C Borrowers

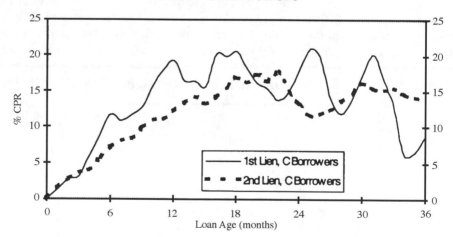

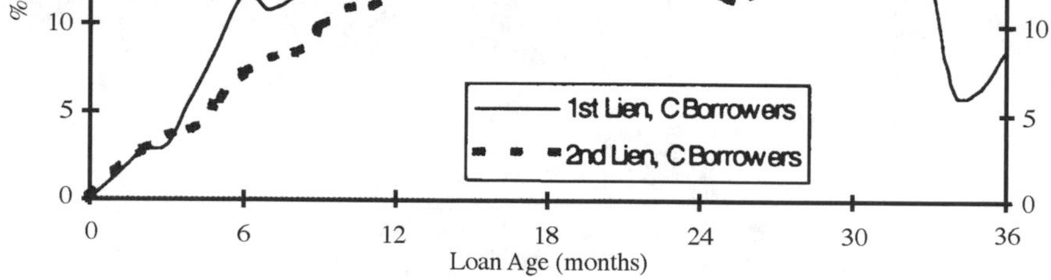

Source: Advanta Mortgage, Morgan Stanley

Exhibit 20: Delinquency Frequency by Borrower Credit Grade
Percent of Loans Delinquent For Indicated Number of Days

Loan Type	30-59 Days	60-89 Days	90-179 Days	≥ 180 Days
All Loans	6.00-6.50%	1.00-1.25%	1.00-1.25%	2.25-2.75%
A Borrowers	4.50-4.75	0.50-1.00	0.50-0.75	1.25-1.50
B Borrowers	8.25-8.50	1.25-1.50	1.50-1.75	3.25-3.75
C Borrowers	9.75-10.00	2.25-2.50	2.00-2.50	4.75-5.00
D Borrowers	11.75-12.25	2.75-3.00	2.50-3.00	9.50-9.75

Source: Advanta Mortgage, Morgan Stanley

Delinquencies and Defaults

This section relates various loan and borrower characteristics to the frequency of delinquency and default in Advanta's home equity portfolio. We consider the borrower credit status, lien position, rate type (fixed or adjustable) and CLTV ratio. The data provide a snapshot as of July 31, 1996.

Delinquent loans are grouped according to their tenure of delinquency: 30-59, 60-89, 90-179, and at least 180 days. The latter group — at least 180 days delinquent — gives a measure of default frequency. Ranges are provided for each category to indicate that there is variation around these values. The ranges nonetheless provide an indication of the relative and absolute magnitudes of various loan parameters as they relate to delinquencies.

Borrower Credit Status

A few items in Exhibit 20 are interesting. One is that 30-day delinquencies are relatively high, but 60- and 90-day delinquencies are considerably more modest. Active servicing of the loans can prevent the delinquencies from translating into defaults. In addition, with the exception of the D grade borrowers, defaults are much lower than one may expect for borrowers with blemished credit records. That delinquencies beyond 30-days and defaults are relatively low is testimony to the high quality of Advanta's loan servicing.

Exhibit 20 shows that lower credit grade borrowers experience higher delinquency and default rates than those of higher credit quality. Despite higher default rates, however, lower quality loans should have higher recovery rates in the event of default because they generally would be originated with lower loan-to-value ratios. If these lower grade loans are priced appropriately, they still should be profitable.

Lien Position

As evidenced by Exhibit 21, lien position appears unrelated to the likelihood of serious delinquency or default.

Exhibit 21: Delinquency Frequency by Lien Position
Percent of Loans Delinquent for Indicated Number of Days

Loan Type	30-59 Days	60-89 Days	90-179 Days	≥ 180 Days
All Loans	6.00-6.50%	1.00-1.25%	1.00-1.25%	2.25-2.75%
First Liens	6.50-7.00	0.75-1.25	1.00-1.25	2.25-2.75
Second Liens	5.25-5.75	1.00-1.50	0.75-1.25	2.50-2.75

Source: Advanta Mortgage, Morgan Stanley

Exhibit 22: Delinquency Frequency by Fixed/ARM Type
Percent of Loans Delinquent for Indicated Number of Days

Loan Type	30-59 Days	60-89 Days	90-179 Days	≥ 180 Days
All Loans	6.00-6.50%	1.00-1.25%	1.00-1.25%	2.25-2.75%
Fixed Rate	5.75-6.00	1.00-1.25	1.00-1.25	2.25-2.75
ARM	10.00-10.25	1.25-1.50	1.25-1.50	2.75-3.00

Source: Advanta Mortgage, Morgan Stanley

Exhibit 23: Delinquency Frequency by CLTV Ratio
Percent of Loans Delinquent For Indicated Number of Days

Loan Type	30-59 Days	60-89 Days	90-179 Days	≥ 180 Days
All Loans	6.00-6.50%	1.00-1.25%	1.00-1.25%	2.25-2.75%
CLTV Range				
< 50%	4.00-4.25	0.50-1.00	0.25-0.75	1.25-1.75
50% to < 70%	6.00-6.25	1.25-1.50	1.00-1.50	3.25-3.50
70% to < 80%	6.75-7.00	1.00-1.50	1.00-1.25	2.75-3.00
≥ 80%	6.75-7.00	1.00-1.25	1.00-1.50	2.00-2.25

Source: Advanta Mortgage, Morgan Stanley

Fixed Rate versus ARM

ARMs exhibit higher 30-day delinquency rates than fixed rate loans (see Exhibit 22), but interestingly, do not register appreciably more serious delinquency or default rates. It should be noted, however, that ARMs constitute a relatively small share of Advanta's product.

CLTV Ratio

Higher CLTV loans generally have higher delinquency rates than lower CLTV loans. (See Exhibit 23.) Interestingly, the highest default rates — as indicated by delinquencies greater than 180 days — are in the 50-70% CLTV range, followed by the 70-80% CLTV range. This is probably because of the correlation between credit grades and allowable CLTVs. Lower credit grade borrowers must maintain lower CLTVs than higher grade borrowers, but as seen above, lower grade borrowers also tend to have higher default rates. Somewhat offsetting the higher default rates of the lower grade borrowers is their higher recovery rates in the event of default, due to their lower CLTVs.

CONCLUSION

The home equity market has undergone a sea change in the past few years. Whereas home equity loans previously were primarily relatively small balance, second lien loans, the market today is characterized predominantly by relatively large balance first liens. Despite changes in loan size and lien position, the characteristics of the home equity borrower and the reasons for the loans have remained fairly constant.

We examined several factors that affect home equity prepayments and determined that the following characteristics generally result in less interest rate *sensitivity*: lower credit grade borrower, smaller loan balance, more senior lien position and higher CLTV.

In addition to their relative interest rate insensitivity, home equities generally prepay faster than conventional mortgages when rates have *not* fallen. We found that the following parameters generally imply faster *seasoning* prepayments: lower credit grade borrower, above-market rate loan and lower CLTV. The influence of lien position on seasoning depends upon the borrower's credit status.

The relatively fast base case speeds and limited interest rate sensitivity result in loans that have much more stable cash flows than conventional mortgages. These relatively stable cash flows provide investors in home equity backed securities with instruments demonstrating markedly more favorable convexity characteristics than securities backed by conventional mortgages.

Chapter 24

Prepayment Modeling and Valuation of Home Equity Loan Securities

Dale Westhoff
Senior Managing Director
Financial Analytics & Structured Transactions Group
Bear, Stearns & Co., Inc.

Mark Feldman
Managing Director
Financial Analytics & Structured Transactions Group
Bear, Stearns & Co., Inc.

INTRODUCTION

Understanding and valuing prepayment risk is a fundamental concern for most investors in the rapidly expanding home equity securities market. Yet conducting even a rudimentary prepayment analysis can be a difficult task because of the diversity of loan and borrower attributes at the deal level. In addition, there is often little historical prepayment information available to investors on new deals or on deals with similar collateral profiles. While the current market prepayment convention centered on issuer specific prepayment curves (similar to the PSA curve) is useful in establishing a static pricing speed assumption, it lends little insight into the underlying causes of home equity prepayments and is generally inadequate as a valuation tool. In this chapter we present a home equity prepayment model developed from historical observations on nearly 300,000 individual loans provided by leading issuers of home equity securities. The multi-issuer database used is unique in both the breadth of its coverage and in its loan-level detail, which includes information on a borrower's credit status. For the first time, the underlying forces that govern home equity loan prepayments can be analyzed

The authors would like to thank the issuers listed in Exhibit 1 for their cooperation in providing data for this study.

and statistically measured, all at the loan level. Our model, developed entirely from this new data, incorporates several innovative features:

- Given that borrowers of different credit quality exhibit fundamentally different prepayment behavior, our model is constructed as a composite forecast from three functionally independent sub-models, each representing a distinct level of borrower credit.
- Each model was estimated on a loan by loan basis using a discrete choice estimation to preserve all loan and borrower attributes (no data aggregation was performed).
- The borrower's current equity position, a key determinant of home equity prepayment behavior, is dynamically updated and measured using proprietary regional home price indices.
- Users have the ability to assess the joint effects of changes in home prices and interest rates on home equity loan prepayments.
- Borrower adverse selection, responsible for "burnout" and other path dependent prepayment behavior, is implicitly accounted for by the loan-level specification and sub-model structure of our forecasting framework.

THE LOAN-LEVEL HOME EQUITY DATABASE

A prepayment model is only as good as the data set employed in its estimation. In contrast to pool-specific data like that from FNMA/FHLMC and GNMA, loan-level information greatly enhances the precision and scope of variables available to the modeler. Bear Stearns has assembled one of the largest and most comprehensive loan-level home equity databases in the asset-backed industry. The database targets finance company fixed rate, closed-end home equity issuers and incorporates statistics on a borrower's credit status, property location, original combined loan-to-value ratio (CLTV), updated CLTV, lien position, loan size, rate, and term. The database contains ten years of historical prepayment information, including the important prepayment experience from the 1992 and 1993 prepayment cycles.

In general, there is a high level of dispersion in the loan attributes of finance company issues since the loans are made to a broad spectrum of borrowers (most with lower than A credit ratings). Home equity securities from different issuers can exhibit very different prepayment behavior owing to disparities in the credit quality of the underlying borrowers and the specific underwriting criteria imposed by an issuer. To date, most home equity prepayment studies have focused on data from a single issuer and are applicable to a relatively small universe of securities with similar collateral characteristics. By drawing our database from a representative cross-section of issuers we can minimize issuer specific effects and isolate the common loan and borrower characteristics that are responsible for the observed differences in prepayments across issuers and deals. This is particularly important given that several issuers have recently altered their product mix for strategic reasons or in response to current market opportunities. A model constructed from this data is more robust and can be applied to a wider array of securities than a model based on data from a single issuer.

The disparity in loan attributes at the issuer level is evident in the summarized issuer data shown in Exhibit 1. For example, issuers originating a greater portion of loans to higher credit quality borrowers tend to have much lower average loan rates and higher average combined loan-to-value ratios. Two observations can be made regarding the data in Exhibit 1.

First, a traditional analysis based on a stratification of home equity securities by weighted average coupon (WAC) may produce very misleading results because it ignores the substantial credit premium associated with lower credit borrowers. A high WAC often indicates the presence of credit impaired borrowers who exhibit prepayment behavior that is fundamentally different from borrowers with better credit ratings. Second, to the extent that an issuer targets loan production to a particular segment of borrowers, the prepayments of that issuer will be subject to any prepayment patterns that are unique to that sub-population.

THE DETERMINANTS OF HOME EQUITY PREPAYMENTS: IDENTIFYING THE RISKS

From the investor's perspective, the most attractive feature of home equity securities is that they are less negatively convex[1] when compared to securities backed by conventional purchase money mortgages. Indeed, historical observations indicate that finance company home-equity borrowers are relatively insensitive to changes in interest rates. For example, during the severe 1992 and 1993 refinancing cycles, most home equity securities experienced prepayments that were considerably slower (rarely above 35 CPR for more than one period) than similar mortgage-backed securities (MBS). Conversely, home equity securities did not extend as much as MBS when interest rates rose in 1994. This pattern is clearly evident in Exhibit 2, a comparison of historical prepayments between the 1990 issue FNMA 9.0% 15-year MBS and a typical B/C home equity deal (Fleet Finance 90-1). Given this experience, investors have embraced home equity issues as an attractive alternative to traditional mortgage securities since they have the advantage of limited call and extension risk. In addition, investors have found that home equity securities make a reasonable substitute for short average life CMOs since they offer PAC-like average life stability without the premium paid for a CMO structure.

---

[1] Negatively convex securities tend to shorten in duration when interest rates fall and increase in duration when rates rise.

Exhibit 1: The Bear Stearns Home Equity Database

Contributing Issuer	Number of Loans	Average Loan Rate	Average Loan Size	Credit Distributions			Lien Position		OLTV Distribution			
				A	B	C	First	Second	≤ 60%	60%-70%	70%-80%	> 80%
GE	55,832	10.54	54,968	88%	12%	0%	49%	51%	26%	18%	42%	14%
Conti	47,037	11.66	55,276	57%	29%	14%	66%	34%	31%	21%	42%	6%
Equicredit	101,709	12.30	39,306	46%	35%	19%	57%	43%	20%	18%	50%	12%
Advanta	69,200	13.39	33,710	49%	41%	10%	39%	61%	24%	14%	32%	30%
Alliance Funding	32,504	14.04	51,104	15%	40%	45%	47%	53%	67%	26%	6%	1%
Totals	306,282	12.31	44,601	53%	30%	17%	53%	47%	29%	18%	39%	14%

Exhibit 2: Historical MBS and Home Equity Prepayments

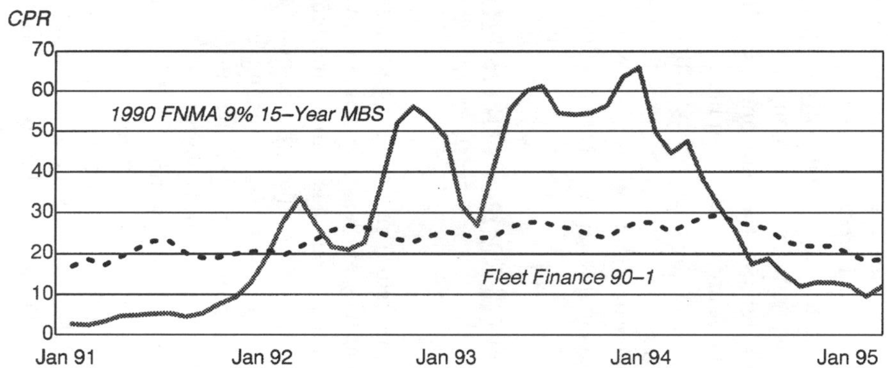

*Exhibit 3: Home Equity Pricing Speeds Versus Actual Prepayments**

			Actual CPR	
Date	Issuer	Pricing Speed	3 Months	6 Months
21-Feb-91	ADVANTA 91-1	18	21.00	20.30
31-Jul-91	AFC 91-3	20	29.40	22.20
10-Sep-91	ADVANTA 91-3	22	20.80	18.10
25-Oct-91	AFC 91-4	20	23.20	24.00
29-Jan-92	AFC 92-1	20	28.60	25.90
13-Mar-92	ADVANTA 92-1	22	19.40	17.20
26-Mar-92	OSCC 92-1	21	25.70	22.90
5-Jun-92	OSCC 92-2	25	19.90	18.70
16-Jun-92	TMS 92B	22	22.20	19.10
18-Jun-92	AFC 92-3	20	24.40	20.70
11-Sep-92	ADVANTA 92-3(14)	23	23.90	20.60
17-Sep-92	AFC 92-4	20	24.70	25.40
26-Oct-92	OSCC 92-4	25	21.50	18.80
4-Dec-92	TMS 92D	23	16.30	N/A
16-Dec-92	AFC 92-5	20	22.00	23.70
2-Mar-93	ADVANTA 93-1	23	12.30	12.30
12-Mar-93	TMS 93A	23	15.00	14.30
27-May-93	ADVANTA 93-2	23	17.90	16.20
10-Jun-93	TMS 93B	23	10.70	9.90
28-Jul-93	TMS 93C	23	14.70	N/A
16-Nov-93	First Alliance 93-2	25	29.80	22.90
16-Feb-94	TMS 94A	23	10.70	10.30
3-Mar-94	ADVANTA 94-1	23	15.60	12.20
10-Mar-94	Equicon 94-1	23	20.00	19.70
24-May-94	TMS 94B	22	13.50	11.80
25-May-94	EQCC 94-2	25	22.60	19.10
8-Jun-94	ADVANTA 94-2	22	18.90	14.90
20-Jun-94	Contimortgage 94-3 (16)	26	18.30	14.30
9-Sep-94	ADVANTA 94-3	23	20.30	16.30
13-Sep-94	EQCC 94-3	24	26.90	22.80
18-Oct-94	Equicon 94-2	23	29.00	19.30
2-Dec-94	Contimortgage 94-5	20	20.70	16.20
8-Dec-94	ADVANTA 94-4	20	12.40	9.90
8-Mar-95	ADVANTA 95-1	20	10.60	8.20

* Actual prepayments as of September 1995.

Source: Moody's Asset Credit Evaluations Report

With broad investor acceptance there has been little differentiation in deal pricing speeds. The vast majority of deals have been priced to a long term speed of between 20 and 25 CPR with various permutations on the seasoning ramp. However, a comparison of the pricing speed assumptions to actual 6-month prepayments (see Exhibit 3) suggests that more deal differentiation is needed. Key loan and borrower attributes, like borrower credit quality, that influence the seasoning ramp and long-term level of home equity prepayments must be identified and accounted for at pricing. No single ramp standard (or ramp multiple) can explain the disparity evident across deal prepayments.

Exhibit 4: Model Inputs and Prepayment Risk

Model Input	Lower Prepayment Risk (more prepayment stable)	Higher Prepayment Risk (more prepayment sensitive)
Borrower Credit Status	C Borrower	A Borrower
Borrower Credit Premium	High	Low
Loan Age	Seasoned Loans	New Loans
Combined Loan-to-Value	High CLTV	Low CLTV
Lien Position	Second Lien	First Lien
Loan Size	Small	Large
Level of Interest Rates (Exogenous)	Neutral	Declining
Level of Home Prices (Exogenous)	Stable/Declining	Rising

More importantly, within the home equity universe investors must be compensated for securities whose prepayments are more likely to be correlated to changes in interest rates. Although the market may be justified in pricing two deals to similar static long term prepayment speeds, there may still exist substantial differences in the negative convexity of the securities. Consider the extreme case of First Interstate Bank of California (FICAL) 90-1, GE 91-1 and Fleet Finance 90-1. Although all three deals were priced between 20 and 23 CPR, actual prepayments through the 1992 and 1993 interest rate cycles proved to be radically different. For example, during the period from January 1992 to December 1993 the three deals peaked at 62 CPR, 42 CPR and 30 CPR, respectively. Obviously, not all home equity securities are created equal. Nevertheless, the task of identifying deals that are more vulnerable to interest rate swings has been onerous due to the heterogeneous mix of borrower and loan attributes. In addition, the trend by finance companies to originate home equity first lien mortgages has clouded the distinction between a traditional purchase money mortgage[2] and a home equity loan. For instance, should we expect a home equity security backed by A credit borrowers with large balance, first lien loans to exhibit the same prepayment behavior as a deal backed by C credit borrowers with small balance, second mortgages? Clearly, the answer is no; however, until now valuing the impact of these disparities has been virtually impossible.

The Bear Stearns home equity model addresses the need for a prepayment forecast consistent with the underlying mix of borrower and loan characteristics present in a deal. The model inputs include six loan attributes and two exogenous variables whose independent and joint effects explain home equity loan prepayment behavior. Each of these parameters and their values as they relate to increasing prepayment risk is provided in Exhibit 4. A more detailed discussion of our findings with respect to each of these parameters follows.

[2] A purchase money mortgage is used exclusively to finance the initial purchase of a home.

Exhibit 5: Representative Finance Company Home Equity Obligor

Age	40-45 years
Employment	8-10 years; Blue collar/light-white collar
Residence	8-10 years
Income	\$40K
Credit	5-6 cards
Home Value	\$100-\$125K

STRUCTURAL CONSIDERATIONS

There are three structural factors that suppress the interest rate sensitivity of finance company fixed rate home equity loan securities: small loan sizes, short amortization schedules, and below A borrower credit quality. First, smaller average loan sizes greatly reduce the economic benefit of a refinancing opportunity. In our sample, the average loan balance was \$45,000 compared to \$124,000 for a standard purchase money mortgage. As a rule of thumb, interest rates must fall two to four times further in the home equity market before the interest cost savings of a refinance breaks even to the interest cost savings realized from a standard purchase money refinance. It should be noted, however, that this effect is partially negated for second lien home equity loans because second liens are subject to the full refinancing risk of the underlying first mortgage.

Second, the 10-year to 15-year amortization schedule of most home equity loans limits the average life variability and price sensitivity of HEL securities. For example, a 10 CPR increase in prepayments will shorten the average life of a 30-year security by approximately 4.7 years compared to only 2.2 years for a 15-year security.[3] Third, credit impaired home equity borrowers tend to be cash-strapped and, consequently, more payment sensitive (less interest rate sensitive) than purchase money borrowers. Exhibit 5 profiles a representative finance company home equity obligor. The combination of these three factors produces a return profile that is intrinsically more stable and less interest rate sensitive than that of a standard purchase money mortgage security. Nevertheless, within the home equity universe, there still exist significant disparities in the rate of seasoning, long-term level, and interest rate sensitivity of prepayments.

BORROWER CREDIT QUALITY IS THE MOST IMPORTANT DETERMINANT OF HOME EQUITY LOAN PREPAYMENTS

Different levels of borrower credit quality expose investors to different levels of prepayment risk. The typical home equity security is backed by borrowers across a broad spectrum of credit ratings. Intuitively, the A credit borrowers are the most likely to

[3] Assuming a 9.0% gross coupon and an initial base speed of 8% CPR.

prepay their loans when interest rates fall because they can usually qualify for a new loan and are more likely to be in a financial position to pay transaction costs. Less credit worthy borrowers are less likely to refinance because they are less financially "able" to pay transaction costs and usually have fewer refinancing alternatives available to them. Lenders will generally underwrite lower credit borrowers at higher spreads and with more points and fees to offset their increased exposure to default. Moreover, during a refinancing cycle, lenders will target better credit borrowers with large balance loans before lower credit borrowers. Thus, the refinancing economics for B/C rated borrowers are usually much less attractive than for A borrowers. In effect, these constraints act as a prepayment penalty imposed on low credit borrowers.

Historical observations confirm the "credit effect" on prepayments. For example, Exhibit 6 tracks the historical prepayment experience of four separate deals, each selected to represent a different level of borrower credit quality. The highest credit borrowers populate the bank issue (FICAL 90-1) followed by A- borrowers (GE Capital 91-1), B/C borrowers (Fleet Finance 90-1), and finally D borrowers (Goldome Credit 90-1). During the refinancing waves of 1992-93, the range of prepayments across these different issues of home equity securities was extraordinary. The bank issue exhibited refinancing levels that rivaled any security in the conventional MBS market while the finance company issues, populated by more credit impaired borrowers, exhibited a much more restrained response to lower interest rates.

The degree to which prepayments were unresponsive to lower rates can be linked directly to the level of borrower credit. In the case of the Goldome issue (D borrowers) prepayments were completely uncorrelated to changes in interest rates. Moving up the credit spectrum, the Fleet Finance issue (B/C borrowers) exhibited a modest correlation to interest rates while the GE issue (A- borrowers) spiked above 35 CPR on three separate occasions; each spike was coincident with a new low in interest rates. The strong relationship between borrower credit status and prepayments was again evident in 1994 when interest rates moved higher, only this time prepayments slowed and securities extended. In the absence of a refinancing incentive, the bank home equity security became the slowest paying issue, followed by GE and then Fleet Finance. Once again, Goldome showed no response to the movement in interest rates.

Exhibit 6: Historical Prepayments on Selected Home Equity Issues

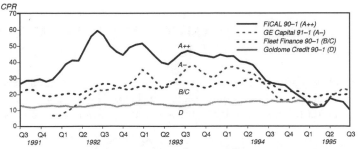

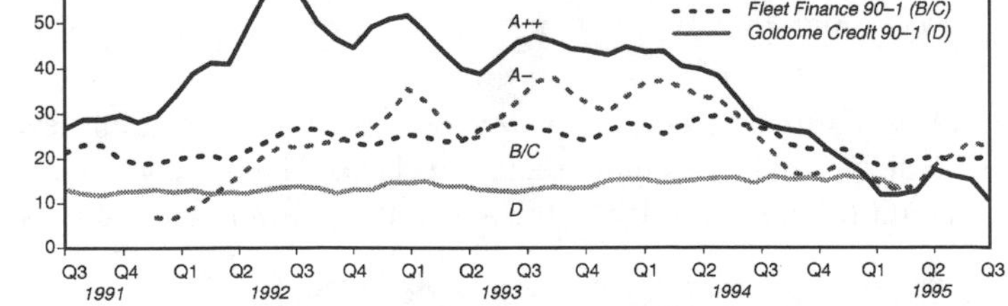

Exhibit 7: Finance Company Issuer Credit Ratings

Classification	Meaning
A	Good to excellent credit Maximum of 2 30-day delinquencies in past 12 months No bankruptcies in past 5 years
B	Satisfactory credit Maximum of 3 30-day delinquencies in past 12 months No bankruptcies in past 3 years
C	Fair/poor credit Maximum of 4 30-day and 1 60-day delinquencies in past 12 months No bankruptcies in past 2 years

The greater contraction and extension risk exhibited in securities backed by higher credit quality borrowers makes them more negatively convex than securities backed by credit impaired borrowers. Indeed, securities backed by the lowest credit borrowers remained positively convex through the prepayment cycles of 1992 and 1993. The radically different prepayment behavior evident across different credit "domains" underscores the importance of developing a sound methodology to model the influence of credit on home equity prepayments. We have accomplished this by constructing our model as a composite forecast from three independent, credit based sub-models. Loans are first stratified by credit designation, then directed to the appropriate sub-model where a separate forecast is made based on loan-level attributes. The individual forecasts are then re-combined to form the final aggregate projection. We found that this approach produced the most accurate aggregate projection for securities that are often backed by a diverse collection of borrowers. The first step in this process, however, is to identify the level of credit.

TWO MEASURES OF BORROWER CREDIT QUALITY: ISSUER RATING AND CREDIT PREMIUM

A reliable measure of credit quality is essential for an accurate prepayment forecast in the home equity sector. Unfortunately, generating a consistent measure of a borrower's credit quality can be problematic because of the lack of standardized underwriting criteria for each credit designation among issuers. To overcome this problem, each loan in our database is indexed in two ways: first by its credit designation (supplied by the issuer) and second by a measure based on a "credit premium" paid by the borrower at origination. Despite differences in underwriting guidelines, we found that the credit history criteria applied to a particular credit designation were relatively uniform. Therefore, in lieu of discarding the issuer supplied credit rating we use it as a broad indication of a borrower's recent credit standing, and account for differences in issuer underwriting limits for CLTV, loan size, etc., by directly measuring them at the loan level. Exhibit 7 summarizes the most common credit history criteria applied to each of the classifications.

Exhibit 8: Home Equity Credit Premiums

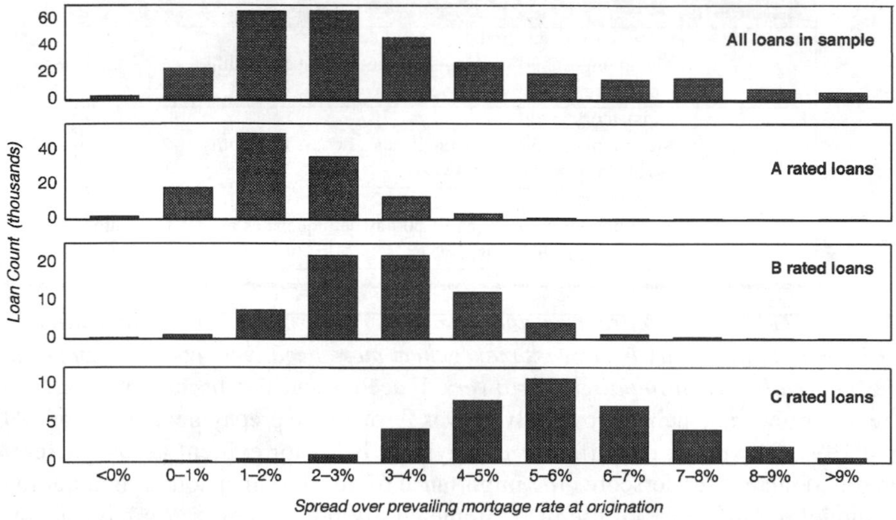

Within a given credit class we further stratify the loans by calculating a credit premium. It is based on the spread between the prevailing conforming rate (we use the FHLMC commitment rate) and the home equity contract rate on the day that each loan was originated. While this measure ignores the possibility that a borrower "buys" the rate down, it has proven to be strongly correlated to the actual credit quality of each borrower, i.e., the higher the credit premium, the lower the credit quality of the borrower. Exhibit 8 conclusively shows that in our loan sample the average credit premium is substantially higher for lower credit classes.

For example, the average credit premium for all A, B, and C designated loans is 1.89%, 3.32% and 5.68%, respectively. In addition, the variation in premium within a credit class, particularly the C's, indicates numerous sub-levels of credit. The credit premium provides a mechanism to statistically measure the various gradations of credit quality within a credit class. Estimation results validate the credit premium as an explanatory variable; after loan age it was the most statistically significant variable in our sub-models.

THE SEASONING OF HOME EQUITY LOANS OCCURS IN TWO PHASES

One of the most important aspects of home equity loan prepayments is how rapidly prepayments increase or "season" with loan age. Given that prepayments are less correlated to interest rates, the most common mistake at pricing is a misspecification of the slope and leveling point of the seasoning ramp. In general, the seasoning period for home equity loans is much shorter than that exhibited in the purchase money market (measured to be 30 months by the PSA standard). Home equity deals can season in as little as 10 months or as many as 30 months depending on the credit mix of the borrowers and the loan attributes of the deal. Moreover, we have found that the aging process actually consists of two distinct phases: an initial period that is characterized by rapid seasoning and an eventual plateau in prepayments, followed by a longer second period of steadily declining prepayments.

Phase 1: Rapid Seasoning and the "Credit Cure" Effect

Our research indicates that in a neutral interest rate environment, lower credit quality loans tend to season much more rapidly and plateau at a higher level than better credit loans, all else equal (see Exhibit 9). For example, in a no-change interest rate scenario A loans season in approximately 30 months, leveling between 18 and 20 CPR; B loans season in 15 to 18 months leveling near 24 CPR; and C loans season in 12 to 15 months leveling near 30 CPR. It should be noted that the actual aging profiles shown in Exhibit 9 are conditional on age only and, thus, independent of interest rate levels. Consequently, there is some distortion in the A profile since prepayments are heavily influenced by interest rates. This will be addressed in more detail in the next section. In contrast, there is minimal interest rate distortion in the B/C aging profiles shown in Exhibit 9, since there is less correlation to interest rates. We have identified several factors that contribute to Phase 1 of the seasoning process (in order of significance):

Exhibit 9: Historical Prepayments Conditional on Loan Age and Credit Domain (All Issuers, 1988-Present)

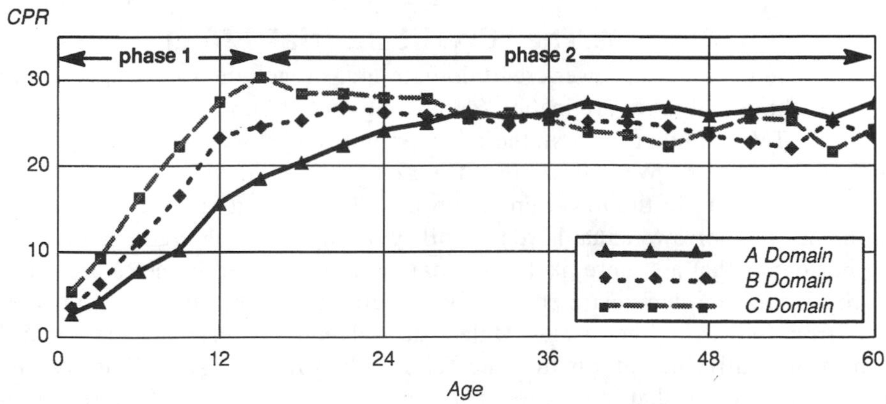

The "Credit Cure" Effect

As some of the lower credit borrowers improve the timeliness of their payments, they become eligible for a lower rate loan in a higher credit domain. Many brokers monitor the status of low credit home equity borrowers and solicit a refinance when their credit status improves. We have seen previously that there is a substantial difference in credit premium between adjacent credit domains. For example, a C rated borrower will reduce his rate by an average of 2.36% simply by qualifying for a B rated loan, while a B rated borrower will improve his rate by only 1.43% by qualifying for an A rated loan. Therefore, the lower the credit quality of borrowers in a deal, the greater the potential for a "credit cure" effect and the steeper the seasoning ramp. Furthermore, we found that once borrowers attain an A rating, credit curing is much less pronounced. The lack of a credit cure effect in the A credit domain causes a seasoning pattern that is more akin to the purchase money market (a 30 month seasoning ramp like the PSA curve). While A rated borrowers as a group remain more sensitive to interest rates, they will season at a substantially slower rate than lower credit loans when there is no incentive to refinance.

Higher Margin Loans Attract More Broker Competition

With brokers often working to originate loans 7 to 8 points above the FHLMC commitment rate, there is naturally more latitude for competition in the lower credit sector. In addition, lenders often try to offset declines in refinancing volumes by competing more aggressively in the B/C sector.

Higher Default Rates On Lower Credit Loans

While this is a marginal contribution to overall prepayments (a maximum of 2 or 3 CPR in the early months of the seasoning process), low credit domain loans experience higher default rates.

Phase 2: The "Credit Inertia" Effect

We also found that after lower credit domain loans reach their peak speed in the 10th to 20th month after origination (depending on the joint effects of credit premium, CLTV, and other factors), there is a pronounced slowdown in prepayments lasting 3 to 4 years. We believe this effect can be explained by a self-selection among borrowers in the lower credit groups. The "credit cure" effect quickly eliminates the borrowers that have the ability to improve their credit status, leaving borrowers that are more likely to remain credit impaired in the future. These borrowers have a demonstrated history of delinquency behavior that prevents them from improving their status. Unless they change this behavior there is little chance of qualifying for a better rate. The probability of a "cure" decays as a function of time so that in a period of three to four years most of the remaining borrowers are either habitually delinquent or have some other constraint (such as equity) that prevents a prepayment. We call this process the "credit inertia" effect because it characterizes the growing inability of the remaining borrowers in the population to change their status, improve their rate, or take out more equity. This puts a downward pressure on prepayments that is clearly visible in Exhibit 9 (in the B/C credit domain). The A credit domain, on the other hand, exhibits little credit inertia.

PURE INTEREST RATE EFFECTS: WHAT THE DATA TELL US

To analyze pure interest rate effects on home equity prepayments one must adjust for the higher credit premium imposed on lower credit borrowers. One common mistake made by market participants is to perform a simple WAC stratification of historical prepayments to assess the sensitivity to interest rates. Although commonly used in the MBS market, this approach can have very misleading results in the home equity market because it masks the true sensitivity to interest rates. Indeed, we often find that home equity securities behave in a manner exactly opposite to that of securities backed by conforming purchase money mortgages, i.e., prepayments from the highest WAC home equity deals are the least sensitive to low interest rates. Stratifying historical prepayments by WAC alone with no adjustment for credit premium tends to produce a flat prepayment profile and a false picture of call protection. To correct for the credit premium, Exhibit 10 plots actual home equity prepayment rates partitioned by credit domain and conditional on how much rates have risen or fallen since each loan was originated. Once these adjustments are made a more reliable picture of pure interest rate effects emerges.

Exhibit 10: Historical Prepayments Conditional on Changes in Interest Rates, and Credit Domain

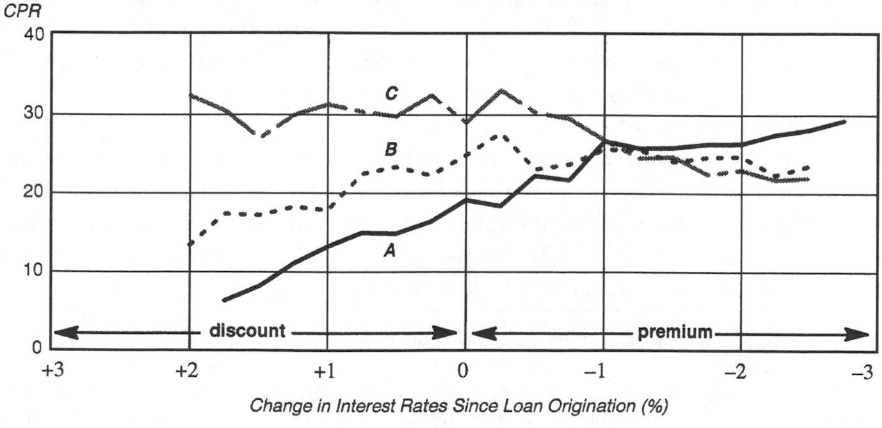

Each point on a curve in Exhibit 10 represents the average prepayment rate for only seasoned[4] loans that map to a specific credit domain and change in rates. Several well-defined trends emerge from the prepayment curves shown in Exhibit 10.

- Prepayments of A domain loans are highly correlated to the level of refinancing incentive. Loans that are deeply out-of-the money prepay on average slightly less than 10 CPR (only 2 to 3 CPR faster than the baseline level of a discount conventional MBS) while loans with the largest refinancing incentive have an average prepayment rate that is approximately 30 CPR.
- B domain loans are less correlated to interest rate changes than A loans, increasing from approximately 14 CPR on loans well out-of-the-money and leveling at around 25 CPR for loans well in-the-money.
- C domain loans range between 22 and 32 CPR but exhibit little correlation to interest rates. In fact, C loans with a positive refinancing incentive have historically prepaid modestly slower than loans with no incentive.

The curves shown in Exhibit 10 are average prepayment rates across all periods and loans within each credit domain. Actual prepayments at the deal level may be faster or slower than shown in the exhibit depending on specific loan attributes. The slightly inverted C domain profile can be explained by recent competitive forces in the B/C sector that have accelerated the discount prepayment observations in Exhibit 10. For example, in 1994 the B and C domains displayed a rapid acceleration in prepayments despite rising interest rates. A closer examination of the data in the exhibit confirms that the discount region (left side of the horizontal axis) is dominated by observations from the 1994/95 backup in interest rates, while the premium observations are more dispersed across time with burnout helping to suppress the speeds in the highest premium regions. Recent notable entrants include Residential Funding Corporation under its Alternet A program and Option One Mortgage offering adjustable rate home equity loans. In addition, when interest rates rise, refinancing business dries up and existing lenders look to other areas, like B and C loans, to offset the drop in loan production.

Another view of pure interest rate effects in A credit loans is shown in Exhibit 11. It stratifies the A credit domain by current, premium, or discount[5] and plots historical prepayments conditional on loan age. Once again, the data confirms a clear segmentation by rate incentive. Loans in the current coupon region ramp to just under 20 CPR in approximately 30 months, while the premium loans ramp to 30 CPR and the discounts to just above 10 CPR.

---

[4] For this analysis, seasoned loans in the A, B and C domains constitute loans older than 18, 15, and 12 months, respectively.

[5] The "current" sector is defined as loans with rates within 50 basis points of the actual current coupon; "premium" designates all loans with rates at least 50 basis points above current; "discount" designates all loans with rates at least 50 basis points below current coupon.

Exhibit 11: "A" Credit Home Equity Prepayments Partioned by Current, Premium, And Discount Loans

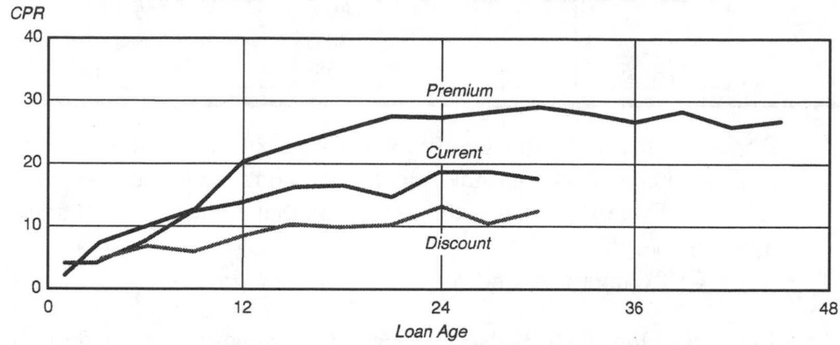

Exhibit 12: Home Equity Originations by Loan Purpose

Purpose	Percentage
Debt Consolidation	39%
Refinance	44%
Purchase Money	2%
Other	15%

A final stratification of our database by loan purpose reveals the substantial contribution to prepayments caused by either changing interest rates or credit curing. Although the population and definition of the loan purpose field varied from issuer to issuer, the general breakdown provided in Exhibit 12 confirms that home equity loans are often used to consolidate debt. However, an even higher percentage of existing loans is refinanced as a result of normal credit curing or rate and term refinancing.

COMBINED LOAN-TO-VALUE AND GEOGRAPHIC EFFECTS

After credit domain and loan age, the combined loan-to-value (CLTV)[6] ratio is the most important explanatory variable in our model. An inverse relationship exists between the CLTV and home equity loan prepayments. A low CLTV increases the probability of a prepayment for the following reasons:

- Existing home equity borrowers with substantial equity remaining in their homes are much more likely to take out additional equity in the future, whether on their own or through broker solicitation. These borrowers not only possess the necessary equity to take out a new loan but also have a demonstrated willingness to borrow against their equity.

[6] The CLTV is calculated by adding the balances of the first and second liens and dividing the total by the value of the house.

Exhibit 13: Common CLTV Underwriting Limits

Credit Domain	Maximum Allowable CLTV	CLTV Threshold
A	≈ 85%	75%
B	≈ 80%	70%
C	≈ 75%	60%

- Borrowers that use home equity loans to consolidate debt are predisposed to another consolidation if their debt levels continue to increase.
- A low CLTV ratio increases the likelihood that a borrower will trade-up to a new home.
- A low CLTV improves a borrower's ability to refinance.

Although a low CLTV also reduces the probability of a default, any potential decline in prepayments from lower default rates is overwhelmed by the four factors cited above. Naturally, the strength of a regional economy can have a significant impact on prepayment behavior because it changes a borrower's equity position. For example, a vigorous local economy tends to increase borrower mobility and strengthen home prices, lowering CLTVs and increasing prepayments. Conversely, a sluggish local economy lowers mobility and weakens home prices, slowing prepayments. Consider California, once the fastest prepayment state in the country, where a housing recession has severely eroded home prices and slowed prepayments to a level that is currently 15% below the national average. In general, investors should prefer geographically disperse collateral because it reduces exposure to regional economic volatility.

To account for regional loan concentrations, we dynamically update CLTVs in our home equity database by applying our proprietary regional home price indices to the original CLTV supplied by the issuer. In this way prepayment forecasts remain consistent with current home price trends across the nation. In addition, by modifying our baseline appreciation assumption, investors can assess the joint effects of changes in home prices and interest rates on the prepayment and return profile of their portfolios.

We also found that the CLTV threshold that suppresses prepayments in the home equity sector varies by credit domain. Exhibit 13 shows common CLTV underwriting limits for each credit domain followed by the approximate CLTV threshold where there is a measurable impact on prepayments. Loans with CLTVs above the thresholds listed in Exhibit 13 tended to be slower than identical loans with lower CLTVs. Bear in mind that there has been a recent trend towards relaxing CLTV standards as lenders struggle to maintain market share. It is not uncommon today for lenders to underwrite loans with CLTVs even higher than those listed in Exhibit 13. In the short term, this will put an upward pressure on prepayments as brokers canvas the existing universe of equity-rich borrowers to take out additional equity. However, the trend will ultimately slow prepayments (but increase defaults) as new limits are reached and borrowers are left with lower overall levels of equity.

CHANGES IN THE UNDERLYING BORROWER MIX AFFECT FUTURE PREPAYMENT BEHAVIOR

The unique seasoning and refinancing patterns evident in each of the borrower credit domains implies that, over time, the underlying composition of the borrowers will also change. This can have a profound impact on the future prepayment behavior of home equity securities. For example, one type of altered behavior results when lower interest rates remove the most rate sensitive borrowers from a pool of mortgages. Widely referred to as burnout, this particular type of evolution in the mix of borrowers tends to temper interest rate related prepayments in the future. From a broader perspective, the mix of borrowers at any point in time is a function of the prior interest rate path and the prepayment experience along that path. We believe home equity securities are particularly vulnerable to the "path dependent" aspect of prepayments because of the diverse mix of borrower credit quality and refinancing abilities present in most deals.

Path dependency is often the most challenging aspect of mortgage prepayment modeling owing to the complex processes at work. In the absence of loan-level data, there is no mechanism available to keep track of the remaining borrowers in a pool (modelers are forced to treat an entire pool of loans as if it were one mortgage); consequently, proxies[7] for path dependent behavior must be developed. One of the remarkable features of a loan-level model is that it automatically accounts for the borrower self-selection that is responsible for "burnout" and many other path dependent changes in prepayment behavior. Having access to loan level data allows us to model actual borrower behavior, and avoid the need to develop variables to "simulate" this behavior. We believe a loan-level model produces a superior forecast because it directly models the fundamental cause of path dependent prepayment behavior, i.e., a change in the composition of the underlying borrowers.

To the extent that borrowers are self-selected over time, our composite forecast will begin to take on the prepayment characteristics of the surviving borrowers. For example, an initially disperse credit base will shift toward B/C borrowers and more stable prepayments after a low interest rate cycle since A borrowers are much more likely to refinance out of a pool (our A domain submodel will forecast a very fast prepayment rate, eroding the A component of the pool). Conversely, the concentration will shift toward A borrowers and more interest rate sensitive prepayments in a neutral to high interest rate cycle since B/C borrowers tend to pay faster than A borrowers in a non-refinancing environment.

LIEN POSITION AND LOAN SIZE

A significant percentage of recent home equity originations have been first liens. This trend tends to be correlated with interest rates, i.e., during low interest rate

[7] Often survivorship (the percentage of a pool that has not prepaid) is used to measure the degree of burnout.

cycles many home equity borrowers prefer to refinance all of their debt (including their first mortgage) at the more attractive prevailing rate. Conversely, in a rising rate environment homeowners preserve the low rate on their first mortgage by opting to take out a second lien home equity loan. A comparison of prepayments between first lien and second lien home equity loans indicates that second liens tend to prepay systematically faster than first liens in the high credit domains. Exhibits 14, 15, and 16 compare historical first and second lien prepayments in the A domain for the discount, current and premium sectors, respectively.

An important distinction between first and second lien home equity loans is that second liens are subject to the full prepayment risk of the underlying first mortgage. A second lien must always be refinanced when the first is refinanced to avoid subordination of the new first lien to the old second lien. Therefore, if homeowners elect to refinance their first mortgages when interest rates fall, second liens will exhibit a matching increase in prepayments. In addition, a borrower may elect to refinance his second lien independently of his first lien at any time.

For credit worthy second lien borrowers, the relative ease of refinancing the underlying purchase mortgage in the era of "frictionless" refinancing may have contributed to the speed differential exhibited in Exhibits 14, 15, and 16. Indeed, as Exhibit 6 illustrated, second lien borrowers with no credit impairment (represented by the FICAL issue) prepaid as fast as comparable MBS through the 1992/1993 prepayment cycle.

Exhibits 14, 15, and 16 illustrate several key differences between first and second lien prepayments.

- The prepayment difference is most pronounced in the discount sector, where second lien prepayments may be accelerated by higher turnover levels and some additional refinancing of the underlying first mortgage (which may itself be in the money).
- The prepayment difference narrows in the premium sector.
- There is more extension risk in first lien home equity loans.

Although on the surface first lien home equity loans "look" more like traditional purchase money mortgages, we found that they do not prepay like them if (1) the borrowers have a lower than A credit rating, (2) equity is taken out of the transaction, and (3) average balances remain below standard purchase money levels. One benefit of first lien home equity transactions is that investors have complete information to determine refinancing risk. There is generally no information on the attributes of the underlying first mortgage in a second lien transaction. Our models explicitly account for the observed differences in prepayment behavior between first and second lien home equity securities. In the lower credit domains there was little systematic divergence between first and second lien home equity prepayments. Less credit worthy borrowers were probably less able and less willing to take advantage of refinancing opportunities, whether they held a first lien or a second lien home equity loan.

Exhibit 14: Discount Sector Home Equity Prepayments Conditional on Age and Lien Position

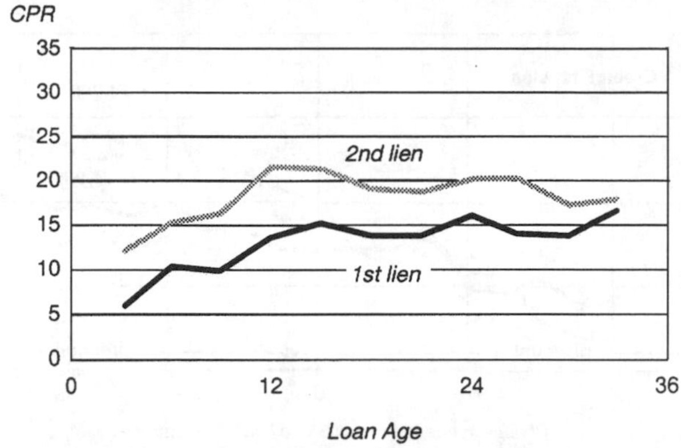

Exhibit 15: Current Sector Home Equity Prepayments Conditional on Age and Lien Position

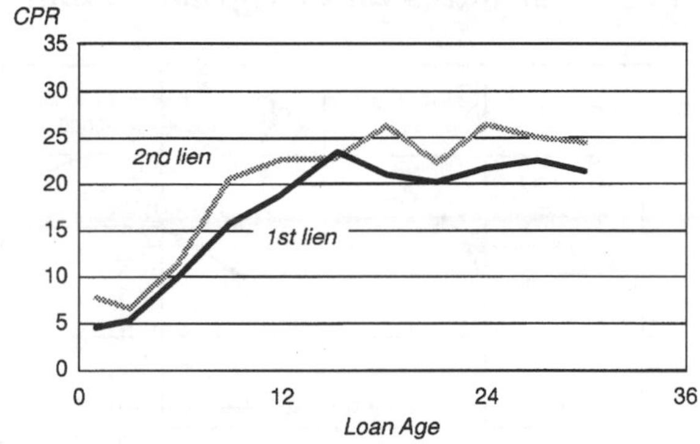

Exhibit 16: Premium Sector Home Equity Prepayments Conditional on Age and Lien Position

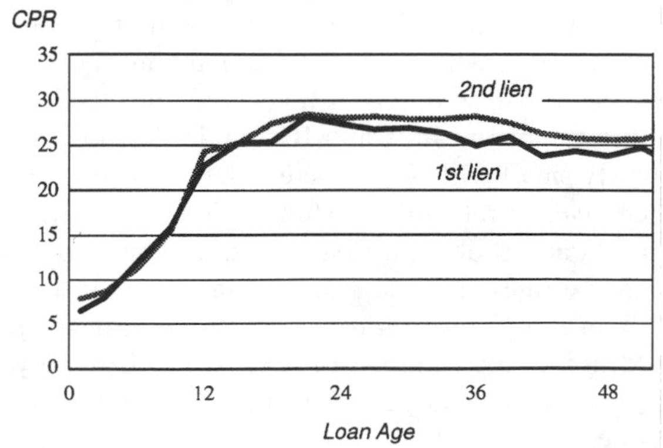

Exhibit 17: Historical Prepayments Conditional on Changes in Interest Rates and Original Amount

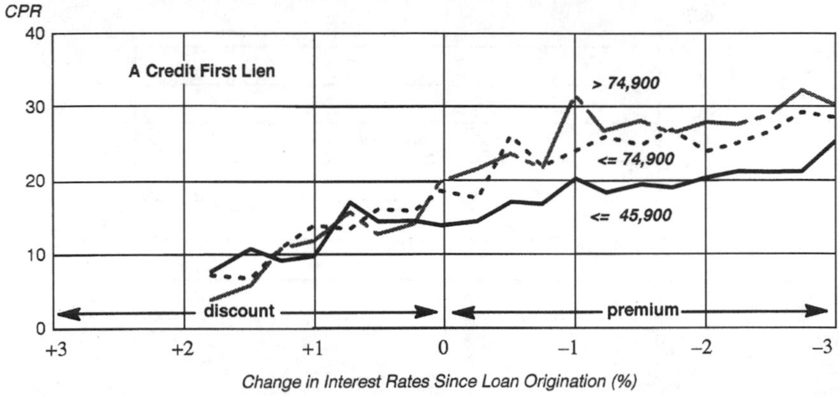

Exhibit 18: Historical Prepayments Conditional on Changes in Interest Rates and Original Amount

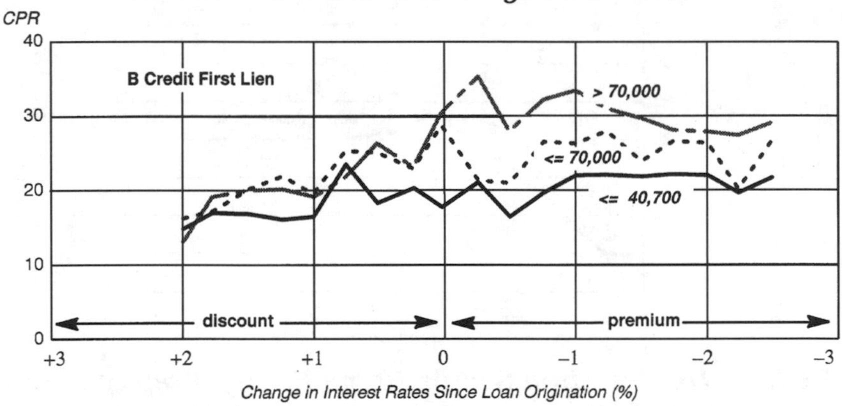

We also found a statistically significant relationship between loan balance and prepayments, i.e., with a positive refinancing incentive large balance loans tended to prepay consistently faster than small balance loans. The influence of loan size was most apparent in A and B domain first lien loans. Second lien loans were uniformly small with an average balance of just $35,100, restricting any economic incentives to refinance. Exhibits 17 and 18 plot historical prepayments for seasoned A and B domain first lien loans conditional on loan amount and changes in interest rates. The clear segmentation evident by loan amount in Exhibits 17 and 18 reflects the greater dollar cost savings of refinancing large balance loans. In addition to the economic benefits, credit worthy borrowers with large loans are the most likely targets of broker solicitations to refinance when interest rates decline.

Exhibit 19: The Default Contribution to CPR by Credit Domain

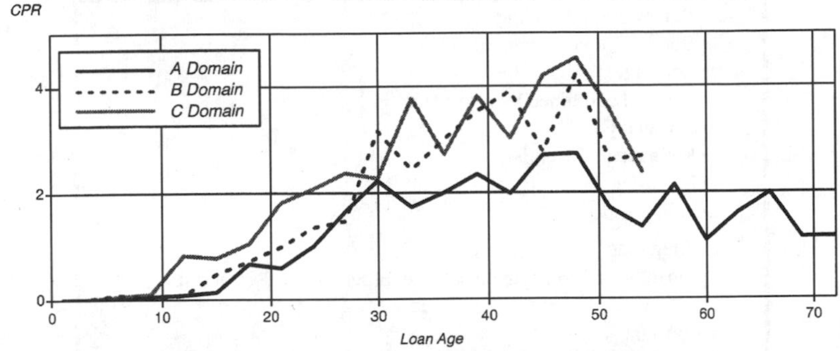

PARTIAL PREPAYMENTS AND DEFAULTS

We found that curtailments (partial prepayments) and defaults play a relatively minor role in home equity loan prepayments. Low curtailments may seem counter-intuitive given that home equity loan rates are so much higher than purchase money rates. Clearly, borrowers have an economic incentive to reduce their home equity debt service. However, by definition many of the finance company home equity borrowers are cash-strapped and unable or unwilling to make payments above the scheduled amount. This may have contributed to curtailments that were uniformly low, averaging about 1% CPR. Nevertheless, as a borrower's economic situation improves over time, we would expect higher curtailment rates to reflect a greater capacity to pay down debt over time.

Similarly, the default contribution to prepayments was relatively small but increased over time, with the maximum impact occurring between months 30 and 50 and then declining thereafter (see Exhibit 19). Lower credit domain loans experienced a higher default rate that peaked at approximately 4.5 CPR between month 40 and month 50. "A" credit domain loans exhibited a similar pattern but peaked at only 2.5 CPR. Despite these relatively low default levels, we anticipate that defaults will play a larger role in the future as increased competition pushes CLTV limits higher.

STATISTICAL ESTIMATION AND MODEL STRUCTURE

Each sub-model was developed entirely from loan level data; no data aggregation was performed. Direct measurements of WAC, age, credit rating, CLTV, and balance were available from the issuer data on a loan by loan basis. A discrete choice estimation was selected because it utilizes all loan level information, modeling the probability that a given home equity borrower will either prepay or not prepay his loan in any given period. We assumed that the probability of prepayment was a non-linear function of the independent variables with a probability distribution that follows a modified logistic curve. Prepayments were explained by the individual and joint effects of the independent variables listed in Exhibit 20.

Exhibit 20: Independent Variables

- Borrower credit rating
- Borrower credit premium
- Loan age
- Original combined loan-to-value
- Updated CLTV
- Refinancing incentive
- Loan size
- Lien position

Assuming that:
the probability of prepayment = C * exp(beta) / [1 = exp(beta)]
where:
C = Constant
beta = sum (coefficient[i] * Independent variable[i])

Exhibit 21: Prepayment Model Structure

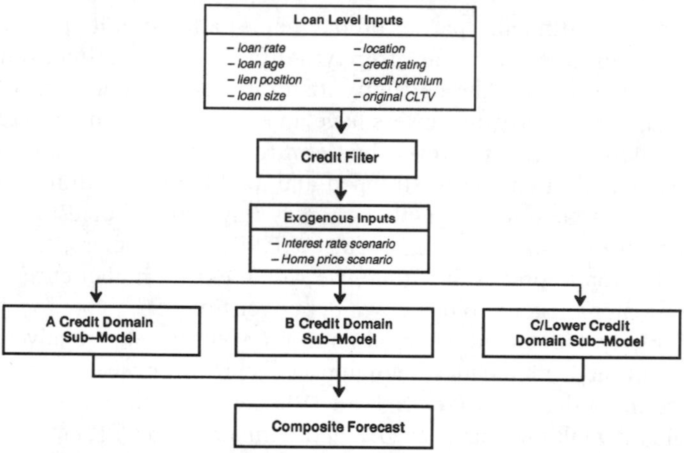

As previously mentioned, the impact of borrower adverse selection is implicitly accounted for by the loan level specification and sub-model structure of our forecast. Having access to loan level data allows us to model behavior at the borrower level and eliminate the need to develop variables that "simulate" behavior at the aggregate level. There are other potential variables that could be added to our home equity model; however, it is our experience that a more parsimonious approach focusing on the correct identification and specification of the key determinants of prepayments, leads to a more robust and predictive model. Furthermore, while adding variables always improves the fit, it often increases the complexity of a model with little improvement in predictive power.

The implementation of our model is straightforward, as shown in Exhibit 21. Loan level data are direct inputs and can originate from either actual deal data or hypothetical user inputs. Once loan attributes have been supplied, cash flows can be generated for various interest rate scenarios.

Exhibit 22: Baseline Forecasts for A, B, and C Domain Home Equity Loans

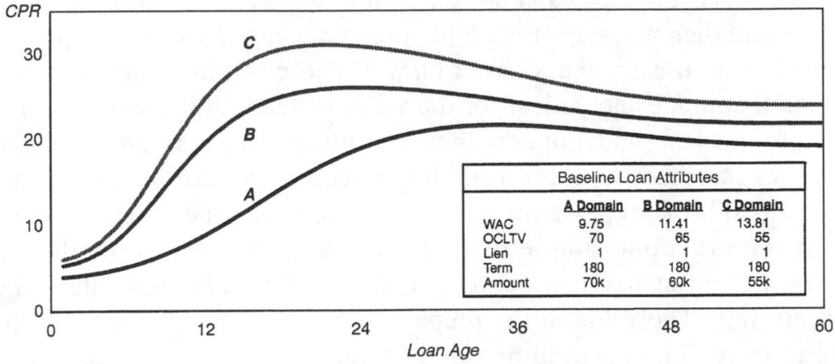

Exhibit 23: Interest Rate Sensitivity Forecast for A Domain Home Equity Loans

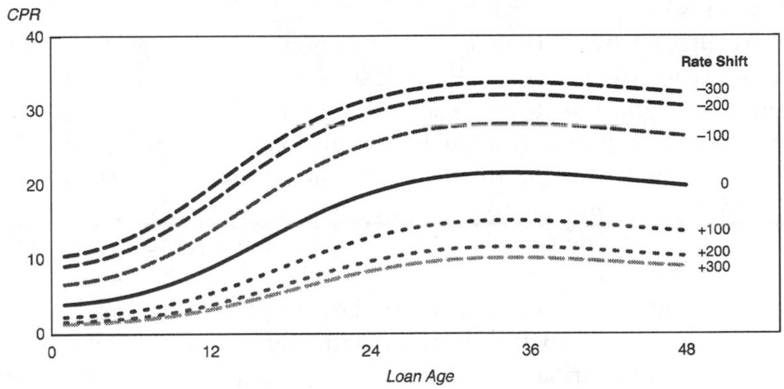

Projections

Exhibit 22 shows our flat rate scenario forecast for representative loans in each credit domain. Baseline loan attribute assumptions are shown in the accompanying box in Exhibit 22. As discussed earlier, under neutral interest rate conditions the forecasts exhibit seasoning profiles that are unique to each credit class. To the extent that loan attributes deviate from our baseline loan assumptions, actual forecasts may be faster or slower than those shown in Exhibit 22. In addition, the higher the concentration of A domain loans backing a given home equity security, the more sensitive it will be to a change in the interest rate assumption. For example, Exhibit 23 shows our forecasts under plus and minus 300 basis point interest rate shocks (in 100 bp increments) assuming a 100% A domain concentration. The prepayment variation caused by these extreme interest rate shocks totals approximately 26 CPR (low extreme to high extreme) in the A domain and 18 CPR in the B domain for seasoned loans with baseline attributes.

Valuation

In general, home equity securities have been priced and traded on an average life spread basis. This approach calculates a cash flow yield using a static prepayment assumption and then measures the yield spread differential to the equivalent average life point on the Treasury yield curve. The obvious disadvantage of this approach is that it does not adjust for the value of the prepayment option. A well-specified prepayment model in conjunction with an option based pricing methodology allows investors to determine the expected reduction in the static yield spread as a result of prepayment volatility. The option adjusted spread (OAS), derived from a random sample of interest rate paths, measures the expected spread over the entire Treasury curve adjusted for future interest rate and prepayment uncertainty. The value of the prepayment option, usually referred to as the "convexity cost," is measured as the difference between the static cash flow spread (0% volatility OAS) and the OAS assuming market volatilities. OAS analysis has generally proved to be the best framework to value a bond with interest rate contingent cash flows, improving the accuracy of duration, convexity and return measures.

We present two sets of complete option adjusted spread valuations in Exhibit 24 (synthetic deals) and Exhibit 25 (actual deals). In both tables, the reduction in the static cash flow spread (0% volatility OAS) measured by the convexity cost column is primarily a function of the loan and borrower-level inputs to the prepayment model and the volatility assumption used in the OAS model. Our results confirm that home equity securities have less negative convexity (lower convexity costs) than comparable agency MBS, but are more negatively convex than credit cards and autos.

In Exhibit 24 and 26, we quantify the influence of credit quality on valuation results using three hypothetical deals with identical sequential structures but with different credit distributions. We assume Synthetic Deal #1 is comprised of 100% A credit domain loans; Synthetic Deal #2 is equally distributed across A/B/C credits; and Synthetic Deal #3 is an equal split between B/C credits with 0% A concentration. Once again we assume baseline loan attributes for each credit domain. Exhibit 26 illustrates the flattening in the projected prepayment profile caused by a heavy concentration of B and C loans. Note that each point on a curve in Exhibit 26 represents the constant life speed that corresponds to the projected monthly vector of speeds at that specific interest rate assumption. In the no change scenario, Synthetic Deals #2 and #3 accelerate above Deal #1 because of the "credit cure" effect. However, Deal #1 is faster in the down 200 and 300 basis point scenarios because of additional rate refinancing.

OAS results from our synthetic deal analysis (see Exhibit 24) are intuitive and support our empirical findings. Several important observations can be made regarding the results shown in Exhibit 24:

Exhibit 24: Home Equity Valuation Results (Synthetic Deals)

				Prepayment Forecast (CPR)						Static Analysis				Option Adjusted Spread				
Security				−200	−100	0	+100	+200	Tranche	Price	Yield	Avg Life	A.L. Sprd	Dur.	Convex.	Cash Flow Sprd	OAS	Convex. Cost
Synthetic Deal #1				26.26	23.40	18.31	12.67	9.13	A1	99.821	5.99	1.30	84.72	1.19	−0.20	81.75	63.69	18.05
Collateral:	Credit	lien	%	WAC	age	rtrm	size	oltv	A2	99.815	6.21	3.23	93.71	3.43	−0.32	91.05	45.15	45.89
	A	1	100.0	9.75	0	180	70K	70	A3	99.733	6.54	4.92	110.76	5.19	−0.23	105.78	49.26	56.52
									A4	99.226	7.00	6.65	145.93	6.23	−0.20	145.94	87.96	47.98
									A5	98.788	7.40	10.83	163.34	7.73	0.20	158.72	134.16	24.55
Synthetic Deal #2				25.70	24.43	21.54	17.44	14.62	A1	99.816	5.98	1.21	84.01	.89	−0.07	77.47	72.22	5.25
Collateral:	Credit	lien	%	WAC	age	rtrm	size	oltv	A2	99.948	6.15	2.89	90.86	2.66	−0.16	89.83	66.56	23.27
	A	1	33.3	9.75	0	180	70K	70	A3	99.714	6.54	4.28	116.74	4.45	−0.22	114.10	80.92	33.18
	B	1	33.3	11.41	0	180	60K	65	A4	100.318	6.77	5.73	128.67	5.71	−0.09	122.27	86.73	35.54
	C	1	33.3	13.81	0	180	55K	55	A5	98.915	7.39	9.56	166.80	7.74	0.25	160.20	140.00	20.21
Synthetic Deal #3				25.44	24.94	23.31	20.28	18.06	A1	99.808	5.98	1.16	84.16	.82	−0.06	76.78	74.16	2.63
Collateral:	Credit	lien	%	WAC	age	rtrm	size	oltv	A2	99.929	6.15	2.73	92.27	2.33	−0.08	91.56	78.09	13.47
	B	1	50.0	11.41	0	180	60K	65	A3	99.869	6.49	3.98	114.73	3.92	−0.11	113.94	93.77	20.17
	C	1	50.0	13.81	0	180	55K	55	A4	100.747	6.66	5.29	120.42	5.26	−0.04	116.63	93.29	23.34
									A5	99.072	7.37	8.85	169.23	7.58	0.25	160.47	144.77	15.70

Exhibit 25: Valuation Results For Selected Home Equity Deals

Security	Prepayment Forecast (CPR) -200	-100	0	+100	+200
AAMES 95C	21.63	21.08	19.64	17.02	14.65

Collateral:

Credit	lien	%	WAC	age	rtrm	size	oltv
A	1	20.1	10.2	2	303	90K	66
	2	5.0	12.0	2	232	38K	60
B	1	17.8	10.8	2	335	86K	62
	2	3.0	12.2	2	208	27K	64
C	1	49.7	12.3	2	351	85K	62
	2	4.4	13.5	2	222	31K	61

Historical CPR speeds: 1 Mo 4.9, 3 Mo NA

Tranche	Static Analysis Price	Yield	Avg Life	A.L. Sprd	Option Adjusted Spread Dur.	Convex.	Cash Flow Sprd	OAS	Convex. Cost
AA	100.688	6.16	2.18	97.80	1.56	–0.14	80.65	64.14	16.52
AB	100.953	6.66	5.21	121.24	4.62	–0.27	123.00	89.08	33.91
AC	100.828	7.29	9.03	159.87	7.11	0.05	159.24	131.00	28.24

Security	Prepayment Forecast (CPR) -200	-100	0	+100	+200
FNMA 95W1	29.62	27.49	23.10	17.06	11.90

Collateral:

Credit	lien	%	WAC	age	rtrm	size	oltv
A	1	51.6	10.0	13	172	61K	69
	2	35.7	10.2	21	159	34K	67
B	1	8.6	10.6	17	170	64K	67
	2	4.1	10.9	19	161	32K	65

Historical CPR speeds: 1 Mo 20.1, 3 Mo 18.2

Tranche	Static Analysis Price	Yield	Avg Life	A.L. Sprd	Option Adjusted Spread Dur.	Convex.	Cash Flow Sprd	OAS	Convex. Cost
A2	101.891	6.18	1.21	103.95	0.59	–0.13	69.57	65.73	3.84
A3	103.047	6.19	1.97	102.81	1.40	–0.34	87.63	70.42	17.21
A4	103.750	6.36	2.72	113.66	2.15	–0.32	112.40	78.11	34.29
A5	104.422	6.49	3.48	119.75	3.03	–0.62	126.03	84.36	41.67
A6	105.312	6.82	5.06	137.87	4.50	–0.36	146.61	95.19	51.42
A7	105.249	7.45	9.42	173.59	6.90	0.03	179.47	145.75	33.72

Security	Prepayment Forecast (CPR) -200	-100	0	+100	+200
FNMA 95W4	27.59	25.86	22.08	16.22	10.92

Collateral:

Credit	lien	%	WAC	age	rtrm	size	oltv
A	1	60.7	9.9	6	187	70K	71
	2	28.3	10.7	12	170	31K	68
B	1	8.1	10.7	10	184	68K	70
	2	2.9	11.4	12	170	31K	67

Historical CPR speeds: 1 Mo 22.3, 3 Mo 17.5

Tranche	Static Analysis Price	Yield	Avg Life	A.L. Sprd	Option Adjusted Spread Dur.	Convex.	Cash Flow Sprd	OAS	Convex. Cost
A2	101.625	6.19	1.81	103.00	1.51	–0.29	87.20	67.39	19.81
A3	102.031	6.33	2.88	108.58	2.88	–0.37	107.08	61.43	45.66
A4	102.609	6.43	4.11	136.04	4.40	–0.47	110.09	50.05	60.04
A5	102.641	6.87	6.10	136.04	6.00	–0.35	136.27	78.37	57.90
A6	100.949	7.40	9.66	167.02	7.64	0.21	165.15	132.67	32.49

Exhibit 25 (Continued)

Security	Prepayment Forecast (CPR) -200	-100	0	+100	+200
FNMA 95W5	23.80	21.27	15.53	10.97	7.33

Collateral:

Credit	lien	%	WAC	age	rtrm	size	oltv
A	1	82.6	9.0	2	199	76K	72
	2	17.4	10.0	4	180	29K	71

Historical CPR speeds: NA, newly issued deal

Tranche	Static Analysis Price	Yield	Avg Life	A.L. Sprd	Dur.	Convex.	Option Adjusted Spread Cash Flow Sprd	OAS	Convex. Cost
A1	100.250	5.94	1.95	77.31	1.98	–0.32	71.73	31.21	40.52
A2	100.359	6.18	3.77	85.25	4.37	–0.65	85.03	20.07	64.96
A3	100.141	6.45	5.51	98.16	5.81	–0.44	91.55	24.53	67.02
A4	99.844	6.85	7.89	122.89	7.27	–0.03	113.06	58.29	54.77
A5	99.062	7.25	11.29	147.20	8.05	0.12	140.61	110.79	29.83

Security	Prepayment Forecast (CPR) -200	-100	0	+100	+200
GEHEL 951	26.61	24.13	19.38	13.59	9.39

Collateral:

Credit	lien	%	WAC	age	rtrm	size*	oltv
A	1	66.7	9.2	10	180	77K	72
	2	23.5	10.4	13	171	50K	70
B	1	8.1	10.1	9	183	77K	70
	2	1.7	11.0	12	180	39K	70

* Non balloons only

Historical CPR speeds: 1 Mo 18.3, 3 Mo 12.1

Tranche	Static Analysis Price	Yield	Avg Life	A.L. Sprd	Dur.	Convex.	Option Adjusted Spread Cash Flow Sprd	OAS	Convex. Cost
A1	100.422	6.17	1.02	103.46	0.65	–0.14	74.22	67.48	6.73
A2	101.125	6.34	2.71	111.73	2.47	–0.39	104.74	64.84	39.90
A3	101.250	6.65	4.46	125.75	4.52	–0.47	126.38	65.13	61.26
A4	101.271	7.05	6.18	153.90	5.74	–0.39	151.49	91.59	59.90
A5	101.270	7.40	10.09	164.72	7.42	0.09	164.72	129.50	35.21

Definitions and Assumptions:

CPR: Average Life equivalent prepayment speed projected by Bear Stearns' Econometric Prepayment Model.

Yield: Bond Equivalent Yield calculated using projected CPR.

Average Life: Weighted average time to principal return, in years, using projected prepayment speed.

Average Life Spread: Yield spread of security to interpolated Treasury with equal average life.

Duration: Price sensitivity of the security, expressed as the percentage price change, given a 100 basis point move in interest rates.

Convexity: A measure of the sensitivity of duration to changes in interest rates.

Cash Flow Spread: 0% volatility OAS.

Convexity Cost: Difference between OAS at 0% volatility and OAS with observed volatility.

Volatility: Volatility is calculated by first pricing an at the money 10 year libor cap and then solving for the implied volatility that gives the same cap price. Our implied volatility assumption is 19.8%. The volatility is *internally* translated for calculations using mean reversion. At 5% mean reversion the equivalent mortgage rate volatility is approximately 12.77%

Pricing: Bid side as of 1/12/96

Yield Curve:	3 mo	6 mo	12 mo	2 yr	3 yr.	5 yr.	7 yr.	10 yr.	30 yr.
	5.18	5.18	5.13	5.16	5.25	5.44	5.56	5.75	6.16

Exhibit 26: Projected Life Prepayment Speeds

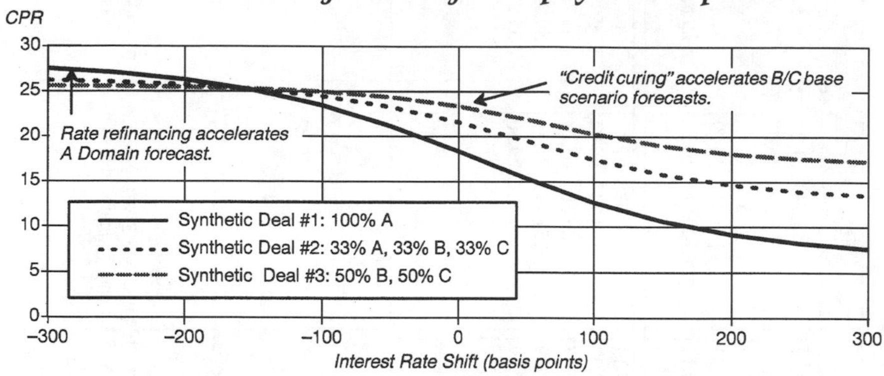

- Synthetic Deal #1 (100% A credit) has inherently more volatile prepayments than the other synthetic deals, as evidenced by substantially higher levels of convexity cost across all average life points on the Treasury curve. In the most sensitive tranche, prepayment volatility reduces the static yield spread by over 55 basis points.
- Synthetic Deal #3, backed by the most credit-impaired borrowers (50/50 B/C split), was the least negatively convex security. Convexity cost levels remained below 25 basis points even in the most volatile tranches.
- In general, finance company securities backed by the highest credit quality borrowers are two to three times more negatively convex than deals backed by the lowest credit borrowers (as measured by convexity cost). For the average deal with a relatively disperse credit profile, investors should be compensated an additional 20 to 40 basis points for prepayment uncertainty depending on the average life of the security.
- In the long average life sector, risk/reward favors the last tranche where convexity costs are lowered by the additional call protection of preceding tranches, less overall extension risk, and more stable long-dated cash flows. Convexity costs tended to drop by 30% to 40% in these issues. The most volatile tranches (highest convexity costs) tended to be concentrated in the 4 to 6 year average life sector of the curve.

We also present full option adjusted spread analytics in Exhibit 25 for 25 actual home equity securities from 5 recently issued deals. Note that differences in projected base case speeds can be explained by either a difference in seasoning or a difference in credit quality. For example, the FNMA-95W5 issue has a slower base speed than FNMA-95W1 or FNMA-95W2 since it is at the beginning of its seasoning ramp. In addition, projections for the 95W1 and 95W4 issues are propped up by today's lower interest rates (relative to when they were issued). The results in Exhibit 25 are consistent with our findings from the synthetic deal analysis presented in Exhibit 24. The reduction in static yield spread due to prepayment volatility ranged from just several basis points in the shortest average life securities to well over 60 basis points in the 5 to 7 year average life securities backed by A credit borrowers. The most notable drop in convexity cost was evident in the AAMES issue, a result of the heavy concentration of B/C loans. In contrast, FNMA-95W5 was penalized by the heavy concentration of A domain loans and the newness of the issue. Once again, risk/reward favored the long dated tranches where convexity costs were cut by 30% to 40% relative to preceding tranches.

CONCLUSION

To address the need for a more sophisticated and robust valuation framework, we have presented the results of a comprehensive prepayment study derived from borrower level information on over 300,000 home equity loans. The result of our efforts is a prepayment model that accounts for the key determinants of home equity prepayment behavior. Linked to our option adjusted spread model, our prepayment model allows investors to differentiate and value the prepayment uncertainty inherent in home equity securities with very disperse loan and borrower attributes. Using this technology, investors can make informed and reliable cross-sector relative value decisions as well as anticipate the market response to changing interest rates and home prices. It also provides the basis for superior hedging capabilities, including option adjusted duration and convexity measurements.

Chapter 25

Non-Accelerating Senior Home Equity Loan ABS

Ralph DiSerio
First Vice President
Global Fixed Income Research Department
Merrill Lynch & Co.

Ryan Asato
Vice President
Global Fixed Income Research Department
Merrill Lynch & Co.

Chris Flanagan
Director
Global Fixed Income Research Department
Merrill Lynch & Co.

INTRODUCTION

Investors in the asset-backed securities market have increasingly taken on prepayment risk as a means to earn satisfactory returns. Investors employing this strategy can mitigate some of the additional risk inherent in mortgage-related ABS by selecting transactions that employ strong cash flow structures. An important recent structural innovation in the home equity loan (HEL) sector has been the creation of *lockout tranches*, commonly called *non-accelerating senior (NAS) bonds*. HEL NAS bonds are structured specifically to provide investors with greater cash flow stability. Relative to other amortizing ABS, such as manufactured housing (MH) securities, HEL NAS bonds can offer investors the chance to pick-up yield while enhancing weighted average life stability and total-rate-of-return performance. The superior cash flow qualities of HEL NAS bonds, however, come at the expense of some of the remaining tranches in the structure.

Exhibit 1: Typical NAS Structures

Month	140% Structure	300% Structure
0-36	0	0
37-60	45	45
61-72	80	80
73-84	100	100
85+	140	300

Exhibit 2: Original WAL Stability of AFC NAS versus AFC Sequentials

	Percent Pricing Prepayment Assumption		
	50%	100%	150%
AFC 96-4 A-4 (5 year seq.)	10.16	5.27	3.59
AFC 96-4 A-5 (7 year seq.)	13.34	7.07	4.56
AFC 96-4 A-7 (NAS)	9.27	7.30	6.22

HEL NAS STRUCTURES

In order to provide investors with greater cash flow stability, HEL NAS bonds are typically locked out for three years and then receive a varying percentage of their pro-rata share of principal. To date, the two NAS structures illustrated in Exhibit 1 have dominated the market. The 140% NAS structure shown in Exhibit 1 is typical of the original NAS offerings brought to market. Under this structure, the NAS bond receives no principal for three years. In years 4-5, the NAS bond receives 45% of its pro-rata share of principal. The percentage of pro-rata principal received increases to 80% in year 6, 100% in year 7, and 140% thereafter. More recent NAS offerings have employed the 300% NAS structure, where a 300% pro-rata share distribution is utilized in years 8 and beyond. This structure enhances the efficiency of execution by increasing the amount of NAS bonds available as well as by shortening the NAS bond's weighted average life.

ENHANCED WEIGHTED AVERAGE LIFE STABILITY

As a result of their principal lockout and distribution schedules, NAS bonds exhibit more stable weighted average life characteristics than their sequential counterparts under various prepayment environments. As shown in Exhibit 2, the original weighted average life profile of the NAS bond in AFC 1996-4 varies 3.05 years between 50% and 150% of the pricing prepayment assumption, while the original weighted average life profiles of sequential 5 year and 7 year bonds in AFC 1996-4 vary 6.57 and 8.78 years, respectively.

Exhibit 3: Total Return Analysis: HEL NAS versus MH Sequential (As of May 6, 1997)

	WAL	Duration	Yield	Z Spread
AFC 96-4 A-7	6.404	4.893	7.20%	60
GT 95-8 A-5	6.483	5.003	7.13%	53

	Total returns				
	-200 bps	-100 bps	Base	+100 bps	+200 bps
AFC 96-4 A-7	14.87%	11.26%	7.42%	3.43%	–0.68%
WAL	4.90	5.17	5.40	5.65	5.92
GT 95-8 A-5	13.85%	11.15%	7.17%	3.25%	–0.90%
WAL	3.79	4.96	5.48	5.71	5.89
Pickup	102 bps	11 bps	25 bps	18 bps	22 bps

CHEAP RELATIVE TO SEQUENTIAL MH SECURITIES

Although HELs exhibit more negative convexity than MH contracts, comparing the weighted average life and total-rate-of-return profiles of a HEL NAS class to a similar weighted average life sequential MH class under various interest rate scenarios illustrates the potential superior performance of the lockout structure. Exhibit 3 shows this comparison for the ABS listed at the top of Exhibit 3 — AFC 96-4 A-7 and GT 95-8 A-5. As interest rates increase 200 basis points (bps), Merrill Lynch's prepayment models project GT 95-8 speeds will decrease 1% CPR and AFC 96-4 speeds will decrease 6% CPR. Although a greater slowdown is projected for the HEL collateral, the HEL NAS bond and the MH bond both extend approximately 5-6 months. When interest rates fall 200 bps, the models project GT 95-8 prepayments to increase 4% CPR and AFC 96-4 prepayments to increase 5% CPR. Despite the faster speeds projected for the HEL collateral, the AFC bond only shortens by 6 months while the Green Tree bond shortens by almost 1.7 years. This is due, in large part, to the HEL class being locked out for the first three years of the transaction. This relative weighted average life stability makes the HEL NAS bond an attractive alternative to the sequential MH bond without exposing it to the additional prepayment risk associated with HEL collateral. As illustrated in Exhibit 3, the AFC NAS bond offers investors a 7 bps pick-up in yield and a superior one year total-rate-of-return profile relative to the Green Tree sequential payer. The total-rate-of-return advantage can be significant, ranging from 11 bps to 102 bps under the interest rate scenarios provided.

PURE SEQUENTIAL TRANCHES ATTRACTIVE RELATIVE TO NAS SEQUENTIAL TRANCHES

If the NAS bond is more stable and the overall prepayment risk is constant, then, by definition, the structure has shifted risk to some of the non-lockout tranches.

Exhibits 4, 5, and 6 display the principal redirections to the NAS bond under a variety of prepayment scenarios. These exhibits assume a generic transaction which utilizes a 45%/80%/100%/140% NAS structure.

In effect, the structure causes some of the sequential classes to act as support bonds for the NAS tranche. As shown, different sequential classes can provide support to the NAS bond as prepayment speeds vary. At 15% CPR, for example, classes A-3 through A-8 provide support to the NAS bond, while at 35% CPR, only classes A-6 through A-8 provide support to the NAS bond. The level of support provided by a sequential class to the NAS bond can also change as prepayment speeds vary. Class A-6, for example, provides little support to the NAS bond at 35% CPR because its payment window coincides with a period when only a relatively small portion of principal is redirected to the NAS bond. At 15% CPR, however, class A-6 provides considerable support to the NAS Bond because its payment window coincides with a period when a relatively large portion of principal is redirected to the NAS bond.

At various prepayment speeds, the payment windows on all of the sequential tranches can either coincide with or be mutually exclusive of the NAS schedule. At the pricing speed classes A-1 through A-3 do not provide support to the NAS bond. Exhibit 7 shows how far prepayment speeds have to fall in order for the payment windows on these short tranches to intersect with the NAS schedule. Prepayment speeds would have to fall to 3% CPR and 10% CPR, respectively, for the payment windows on class A-1 and A-2 to extend past month 36. At the pricing speed, classes A-4 through A-8 provide support to the NAS bond.

Exhibit 4: Principal Cash Flows in Typical NAS Structure at Pricing Speed

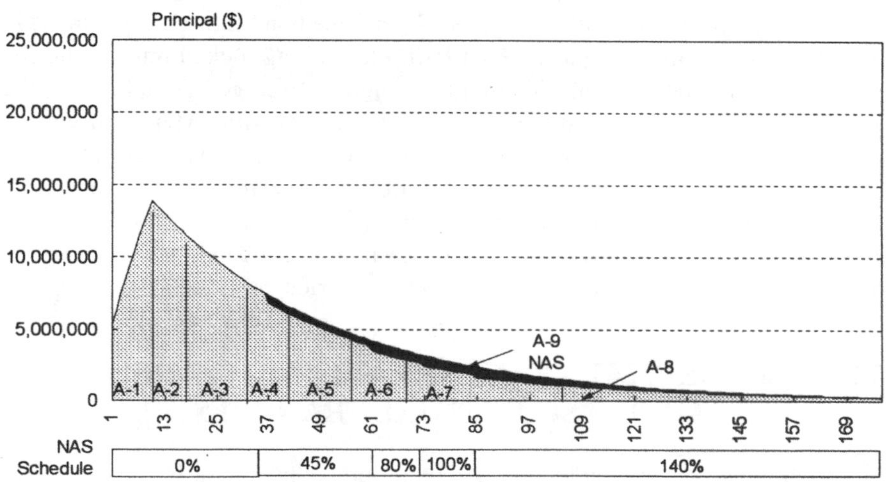

Exhibit 5: Principal Cash Flows in Typical NAS Structure at 15% CPR

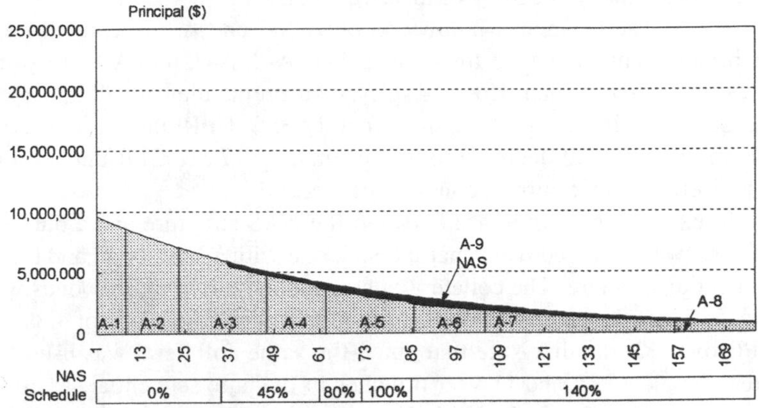

Exhibit 6: Principal Cash Flows in Typical NAS Structure at 35% CPR

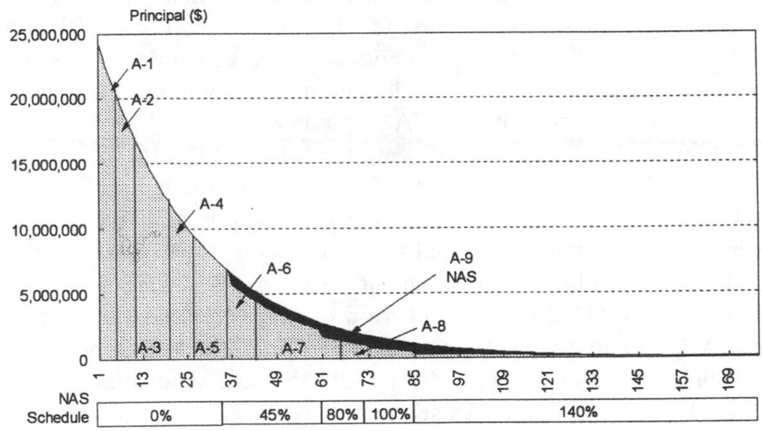

Exhibit 7: Break-Even Prepayment Speeds

Tranche	Prepayment Speed
A-1	3%
A-2	10%
A-3	20%
A-4	26%
A-5	33%
A-6	39%
A-7	48%
A-8	57%

Exhibit 8 also shows how far prepayment speeds have to rise in order for the payment windows on these longer tranches to end prior to the start of the NAS schedule. Prepayment speeds would have to rise to 48% CPR and 57% CPR, respectively, for the payment windows on class A-7 and A-8 to end before month 36. The break-evens displayed for classes A-1, A-2, A-7, and A-8 are somewhat remote as the Merrill Lynch Home Equity loan prepayment model projects prepayment speeds will increase to approximately 35% CPR under a down 300 bps scenario and speeds will decrease to approximately 17.5% CPR under an up 300 bps scenario for generic current coupon collateral.

To examine the difference between the NAS structure and a pure sequential structure, we compared two generic deals: one with a NAS bond and the other a pure sequential structure. The collateral was tranched out to create bonds with 0.5, 1, 2, 3, 4, 5, 7, and 11-year WALs based on an initial pricing speed of 4.8% CPR to 24% CPR over 12 months. Note that since the same collateral was used for both structures, the 3, 4, 5, 7, and 11-year tranches in the pure sequential structure were slightly larger so that the total bond balances under both structures were identical.

Exhibit 8 examines the weighted average life sensitivity of the 3, 4, 5, 7, and 11-year pure sequential tranches versus the 3, 4, 5, 7, and 11-year NAS sequential tranches under various prepayment scenarios. As shown, the NAS sequential tranches can exhibit increased weighted average life sensitivity relative to the pure sequential tranches. In general, the magnitude of this increased weighted average life sensitivity will depend upon how the sequential tranche's payment window coincides with the NAS schedule.

For example, if prepayments were to slow to 15% CPR, the pure sequential 7-year tranche extends 3.64 years while the NAS sequential 7-year tranche extends 4.36 years. As seen in Exhibit 5, the sequential bond in the NAS structure extends more than the pure sequential bond because a larger share of principal is redirected to the NAS bond as prepayments slow. At the pricing speed, class A-7 is exposed to the 80%/100%/140% portion of the NAS schedule, while at 15% CPR class A-7 is exposed only to the 140% portion of the NAS schedule.

If prepayments speed up to 35% CPR, the pure sequential 7-year tranche shortens 2.59 years, while the NAS sequential 7-year tranche shortens 3.02 years. As seen in Exhibit 6, the sequential bond in the NAS structure shortens more than the pure sequential bond because a smaller share of principal is redirected to the NAS bond as prepayments rise. At the pricing speed, class A-7 is exposed to the 80%/100%/140% portion of the NAS schedule, while at 35% CPR class A-7 is exposed to the 45%/80% portion of the NAS schedule.

As of this writing, investors have not clearly differentiated between similar weighted average life tranches that are part of a NAS structure and those that are part of a pure sequential structure. Although the weighted average life variability under various interest rate scenarios is somewhat limited, some spread differential is necessary for the added volatility associated with the sequential tranches in a NAS structure.

Exhibit 8: WAL Stability of 3, 4, 5, 7, and 11-Year Sequentials With and Without NAS Structure

	15% CPR	20% CPR	Pricing	30% CPR	35% CPR
NAS (Lockout)					
WAL	8.34	7.53	7.01	6.37	5.96
Sequential 3 Year					
A-4 (w/ NAS)					
WAL	4.64	3.41	3.08	2.17	1.81
Change from Base	1.56	0.33		–0.91	–1.27
Payment Window	48-65	35-47	32-42	23-30	19-25
A-4 (w/o NAS)					
WAL	4.54	3.40	3.08	2.18	1.82
Change from Base	1.46	0.32		–0.90	–1.26
Sequential 4 Year					
A-5 (w/ NAS)					
WAL	6.38	4.64	4.08	2.90	2.39
Change from Base	2.30	0.56		–1.18	–1.69
Payment Window	65-91	47-65	42-56	30-40	25-33
A-5 (w/o NAS)					
WAL	6.14	4.61	4.08	2.97	2.46
Change from Base	2.06	0.53		–1.11	–1.62
Sequential 5 Year					
A-6 (w/ NAS)					
WAL	8.46	6.07	5.20	3.72	3.05
Change from Base	3.26	0.87		–1.48	–2.15
Payment Window	91-113	65-81	56-69	40-49	33-40
A-6 (w/o NAS)					
WAL	7.90	5.96	5.20	3.85	3.22
Change from Base	2.70	0.76		–1.35	–1.98
Sequential 7 Year					
A-7 (w/ NAS)					
WAL	11.36	8.36	7.00	4.90	3.98
Change from Base	4.36	1.36		–2.10	–3.02
Payment Window	113-164	81-124	69-104	49-72	40-57
A-7 (w/o NAS)					
WAL	10.64	8.11	7.00	5.27	4.41
Change from Base	3.64	1.11		–1.73	–2.59
Sequential 11 Year					
A-8 (w/ NAS)					
WAL	15.05	12.96	11.39	8.42	6.58
Change from Base	3.66	1.57		–2.97	–4.81
Payment Window	164-229	124-192	104-178	72-167	57-141
A-8 (w/o NAS)					
WAL	14.80	12.69	11.21	8.74	7.34
Change from Base	3.59	1.48		–2.47	–3.87

Exhibit 9: Break-even Spread Tightening of Tranches in Pure Sequential Structure

Tranche	WAL	Break-even Spread Tightening	Principal Payment Window
A-1	0.51	0	1-10
A-2	1.15	0	10-18
A-3	2.08	0	18-32
A-4	3.08	−1	32-42
A-5	4.09	−1	42-57
A-6	5.20	−2	57-68
A-7	7.02	−4	68-106
A-8	11.35	−3	106-178

To examine this premise, we compared the duration weighted all-in yields of a NAS structure with a pure sequential structure that has comparable weighted average life tranches. If the pure sequential tranches are priced to the same spread levels as the NAS sequential tranches, the all-in yield of the pure sequential structure is 2 bps higher. In order for both structures to result in the same execution, spreads on the pure sequential structure would need to tighten 1 to 4 bps. As illustrated in Exhibit 9, this tightening was distributed based on the relative impact that cash flow redirection has on each corresponding sequential tranche in the NAS structure.

SUMMARY

Non-accelerating senior bonds are a recent structural innovation in the HEL ABS market which are designed to provide investors with greater cash flow stability. Relative to other amortizing ABS, such as manufactured housing securities, HEL NAS bonds can offer investors a pick-up in yield, greater weighted average life stability, and an enhanced total-rate-of-return profile. Superior cash flow properties of HEL NAS bonds come at the expense of the remaining tranches in the structure.

Chapter 26

Adjustable-Rate Home Equity Loan ABS

Chris Flanagan
Director
Global Fixed Income Research Department
Merrill Lynch & Co.

Ralph DiSerio
First Vice President
Global Fixed Income Research Department
Merrill Lynch & Co.

Ryan Asato
Vice President
Global Fixed Income Research Department
Merrill Lynch & Co.

INTRODUCTION

Adjustable-rate home equity loans (HELs) are emerging as an increasingly important segment of the ABS market. As shown in Exhibit 1 the sector was almost non-existent in 1994, but has grown impressively ever since. The sector remains poised for growth. Increased market share of HELs is anticipated as lenders continue to use low rate teaser adjustable-rate HELs as a means of attracting borrowers particularly from fixed-rate HEL refinancings.

COLLATERAL

With fierce competition developing in the HEL market in recent years, adjustable-rate products have been developed to broaden the borrower base and increase loan originations. These products have been utilized as a means to qualify more borrowers by lowering their respective debt-to-income ratios as a result of calculating underwriting ratios based on either a teased rate or by extending the term of the loan Consequently, the average terms and balances observed in the adjustable-rate HEL market are generally significantly higher than those seen in the fixed-rate HEL market. For example, the adjustable-rate portion of ContiMortgage HEL Trust 1997-3 had an average remaining term of 358 months and an average loan balance of $80,399, while its fixed-rate portion only had an average remaining term of 220 months and an average loan balance of $60,304.

Issuers have also developed alternative products with various indices, reset periods, and teased periods to appeal to different market niches, as well as to help manage their risk. In particular, originators have begun to add hybrid products (such as 2/28 and 3/27 loans) and prepayment penalties to their loan offerings to help reduce exposure to fast prepayment speeds on adjustable-rate HELs and enhance their residual values.

Supply

In 1994, there were only 10 originators issuing adjustable-rate HEL ABS. Total volume for the year was only $958 million spread over 22 deals, resulting in an average deal size of only $44 million. Leading the pack was the Money Store with $280 million and First Alliance with $210 million in securitizations. In comparison, through December 15, 1997 volume reached $22.3 billion and was spread among 37 issuers. Over 102 adjustable-rate HEL deals have been priced through December 15, 1997, with an average deal size of $219 million. Exhibit 2 shows adjustable-rate HEL issuers and their 1997 securitization volumes.

Exhibit 1: Home Equity ABS by Product Type

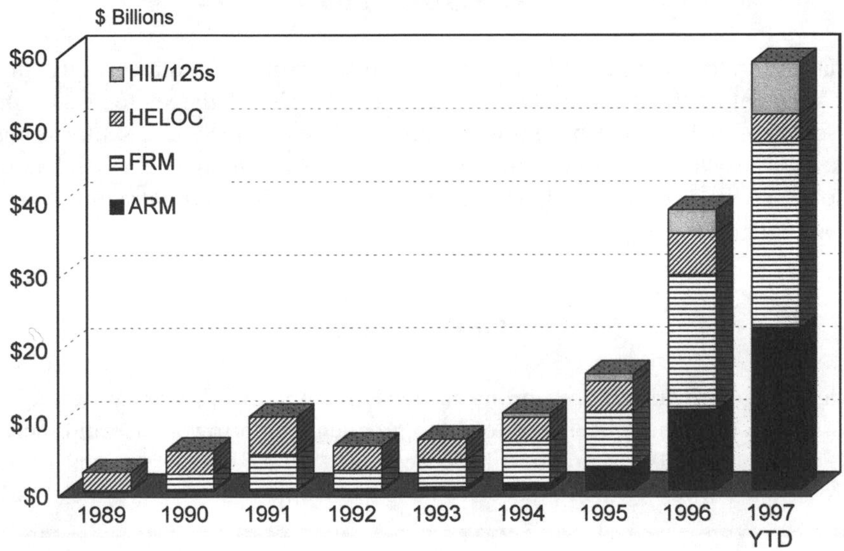

* Through December 15, 1997

Exhibit 2: Adjustable Rate HEL Issuers
*1997 Originations**

Issuer	Amount ($ 000)	% ARMs of Total HEL Issuance
ContiMortgage	$2,180	38.35%
United Companies	1,475	54.63%
Amresco	1,460	63.73%
Aames Financial	1,431	64.22%
Industry Mortgage Company	1,420	31.21%
ADVANTA	1,365	44.76%
The Money Store	1,330	35.05%
Saxon Mortgage	1,071	69.95%
Residential Funding	1,015	71.73%
Southern Pacific	947	72.83%
Long Beach Mortgage	770	82.64%
Alliance Funding Company	723	63.94%
Merrill Lynch Credit Corp.	633	63.50%
Provident Bank	603	55.47%
WMC Mortgage Corp.	600	100.00%
New Century Financial	595	64.03%
First Franklin Financial Corporation	555	100.00%
Countrywide	552	39.71%
EquiCredit	467	20.22%
Ocwen	398	95.74%
NationsBank	367	100.00%
Access Financial Corp.	352	53.49%
Green Tree Financial Corp.	317	11.60%
Delta Funding	247	20.00%
NovaStar	212	100.00%
First Alliance Mortgage	204	60.03%
Block Mortgage Finance	147	46.28%
Cityscape Financial Corp.	130	12.90%
American Financial Corp	120	100.00%
Equivantage	113	31.35%
Transamerica	112	66.52%
PacificAmerica Money Center Inc.	100	100.00%
CIT Group Holdings Inc.	90	18.18%
Independent National Mortgage Corp.	87	35.41%
Irwin Home Equity	70	30.43%
Life Savings Bank	62	13.01%
Home Loan & Investment of Rhode Island	16	29.98%

* Through 12/15/97

Exhibit 2 also shows the percentage of adjustable-rate collateral to total originations. Several issuers such as Long Beach, New Century, RFC, and First Franklin primarily originate adjustable-rate product while others such as Conti, IMC, and The Money Store continue to originate primarily fixed-rate product.

Exhibit 3: Adjustable Rate HEL Collateral Characteristics

			Weighted Average								
Deal	Loan Type	% ARM Pool	Coupon	Margin	Teased Period Cap	Next Period Cap	Life Cap	Life Floor	Months to Roll	Adjust Freq
Conti 1996-1	6 M LIBOR	100%	10.32%	6.82%	1.00%	1.00%	16.42%	10.37%	3	6 mo
Conti 1997-3	6 M LIBOR	53%	9.99%	6.71%	1.01%	1.00%	16.22%	9.90%	3	6 mo
	2/28 LIBOR	41%	10.38%	6.27%	2.98%	1.08%	16.70%	10.34%	22	2yr fixed /6mo
	3/27 LIBOR	7%	10.61%	6.39%	3.28%	1.01%	16.68%	10 56%	34	3yr fixed /6 mo
Total 1997-3			10.19%	6.51%	1.96%	1.04%	16.45%	10.13%	13	

Product Types

Adjustable-rate HEL collateral has typically been first lien, 30-year fully amortizing conventional product. The vast majority of loans are indexed off 6-month LIBOR, while a small percentage of loans reset either off a 1-year constant maturity Treasury (1-year CMT) index or prime index. The 6-month LIBOR loans typically reset every 6 months while the 1-year CMT loans reset every 12 months.

Six-month LIBOR loans have generally had an initial teased period of 6 months. Recently, however, more lenders have been offering hybrid fixed/adjustable products such as 1/29, 2/28, 3/27, 4/26, and 5/25 loans. These loans accrue interest at a fixed rate for 1, 2, 3, 4, or 5 years, respectively, then adjust every 6 months thereafter based on 6-month LIBOR.

Each loan has a specified gross margin which is added to the index to determine the borrower's interest rate. At each rate adjustment, the payment will be changed to an amount that will fully amortize the outstanding mortgage balance over the remaining term at the new rate. As with other ARMs, periodic and lifetime caps and floors constrain the adjustments.

Exhibit 3 shows collateral characteristics for two ContiMortgage transactions, 1996-1 and 1997-3. The evolution in collateral composition is evident. The 1996-1 transaction was backed by 100% 6-month LIBOR loans with a 6 month teaser period. In contrast, 1997-3 was backed by 53% 6-month LIBOR, 41% 2/28, and 7% 3/27 loans.

Assuming a 6-month LIBOR rate of 6%, we can examine how deeply teased each of the product type was at origination. For Conti 1997-3, if the 6-month LIBOR loans were fully indexed, their rate would be 12.71% compared to their initial rate of 9.99%. This provides the mortgagor with a rate 2.72% lower than the fully indexed rate. With a periodic cap of 1%, it would take 18 months before the loan would be fully indexed. If rates remain flat or even if 6-month LIBOR decreases by up to 1.7%, the 6-month LIBOR loans will immediately reset 1% higher at their first reset date.

The 2/28s and 3/27s have initial rates 1.89% and 1.78% below their respective fully indexed rates The first periodic caps, which constrain the adjustment at the end of fixed-rate period, average 2.98% and 3.28%, respectively. After the initial adjustment, most of these loans have a 1% periodic cap. These borrowers have slightly higher initial rates than the 6-month LIBOR loans. In return, they are able to lock in this rate for a 2 to 3-year period. Based on the 6-month LIBOR prepayment experience, we think that the impact of the eventual "payment shock" incurred on the first reset date may drive prepayments to peak in the 50% or 60% CPR range, especially if borrowers face up to a 3% increase in their rates.

Many issuers have also been adding prepayment penalties to stem high prepayment rates. Prepayment penalties usually take the form of 6 months interest on 80% of the loan, i.e., borrowers are allowed to make a curtailment of up to 20% before they are penalized. The penalties are typically in effect for 1 to 3 years. In the prepayment section we examine the impact of prepayment penalties on collateral speeds.

Periodic/Life Caps

Adjustable-rate HELs have caps and floors which limit the amount the borrower's rate can increase or decrease at each adjustment date and for the life of the loan. Periodic caps limit the amount the mortgage rate can increase or decrease at each adjustment date. These usually range from 1% to 1.5%. Hybrid fixed/adjustable loans, however, have higher initial periodic caps (usually 2% to 3%) for the first adjustment date to allow the loans to move closer to market levels if rates have increased during the 2 to 5-year teased period. The loans have floors commonly set at the initial teased rate. In essence, the mortgagor is long a series of periodic caps and a life cap and short a floor. Investors in adjustable-rate HEL ABS, in contrast, are short a series of periodic caps and a life cap, while the residual holder is long a floor.

The periodic and life caps of the underlying loans impact both the payments received and the valuation of adjustable-rate HEL ABS because adjustable-rate HEL ABS investors are paid interest based on the lesser of an index (typically 1-month LIBOR) plus a spread, or the weighted average net available funds cap (as defined below). If interest rates increase to the point where periodic and/or life caps are hit, or if the bond and mortgage indices become mismatched, investors may be adversely affected. Investors need to consider the underlying collateral including:

- Teaser amount
- Teaser period
- Teaser (first reset) periodic cap
- Subsequent periodic caps
- Basis risk and reset mismatch of 1- and 6-month LIBOR.[1]

Exhibit 4 shows the initial available funds cap for Conti 1997-3. To determine the available funds cap, we subtract the trust expenses, which includes the servicing fee, trustee fee, and an I/O strip, from the weighted average gross collateral coupon of the underlying loans. For transactions that are wrapped by a monoline insurer, the surety fee is also subtracted from the gross margin. As shown, for the initial period, the net available funds cap is 9. 18% with 3.25% of excess spread.

[1] The basis risk will be discussed in the next section.

Exhibit 4: Conti 1997-3 Available Funds Cap and Life Cap

Initial Available Funds Cap		Life Cap	
Weighted Avg Gross Coupon	10.19%	Weighted Avg Life Cap	16.45%
Less Servicing Fee	0.50%	Less Servicing Fee	0.50%
Less Trustee Fee	0.01%	Less Trustee Fee	0.01%
Less I/O Strip	0 50%	Less I/O Strip	0.50%
Net Available Funds Cap	9.18%	Net Available Funds Cap	15.44%
Weighted Avg Bond Coupon	5.93%	Weighted Bond Spread	0.28%
Initial Excess Spread	3.25%	Maximum 1-month LIBOR Rate Before Hitting life Cap	15.16%
		Current 1-month LIBOR	5.64%
		Maximum increase in LIBOR	9.52%

Exhibit 5: Conti 1997-3 Net Available Funds Cap

Period	Net Available Funds Cap	Period	Net Available Funds Cap
1	9.18%	13	10.24%
2	9.21%	14	10.27%
3	9.27%	15	10.33%
4	9.45%	16	10.50%
5	9.61%	17	10.67%
6	9.71%	18	10.76%
7	9.71%	19	10.77%
8	9.74%	20	10.80%
9	9.80%	21	10.86%
10	9.98%	22	11.03%
11	10.14%	23	12.41%
12	10.24%	24	12.50%

* Assumes 30% CPR

The net life cap is calculated in the same manner. In order for investors to hit the life cap, 1-month LIBOR has to rise from the current level of 5.64% to 15.16%, an increase of 9.52%. Currently, the periodic caps under 2 years are effectively worthless because they are so far out of the money. For example, Conti 1997-3 initially had 325 bps of available excess spread to cushion any increase in 1-month LIBOR. Using option pricing technology, the life cap and periodic caps 2 years and out were found to be worth approximately 4 bps.

As the loans season and reset, the available funds cap will increase. Exhibit 5 shows the increase in the available funds cap for Conti 1997-3. Note that as the 2/28 loans start to reset, the net available funds cap increases from 10.80% in period 20 to 12.50% in period 24. By period 53, when all the loans have fully reset, the maximum net available funds cap is defined by the life cap, which for this transaction is 15.44%. However, investors need to recognize that the mix of loans, and hence the available funds cap, may change as loans prepay. The net available funds cap may actually decrease over time if loans that are due to reset, prepay, leaving a higher percentage of teased coupon 2/28 and 3/27 loans.[2]

Basis Risk

Most adjustable-rate HEL ABS are indexed off l-month LIBOR. However, the collateral backing these securities is generally indexed off 6-month LIBOR. Thus, if 1-month LIBOR moves out of sync with 6-month LIBOR, the value of the caps will change. If the LIBOR yield curve inverts or if 1-month LIBOR converges toward 6-month LIBOR, the value of the cap will increase.

The rate reset periods of the collateral and the securities are mismatched as well. Most adjustable-rate HEL ABS reset monthly, while the underlying collateral may reset every 6 or 12 months (depending on the index). Complicating matters is the introduction of fixed/adjustable hybrid products that have fixed coupons for anywhere from 1 to 5 years.

Exhibits 6-9 the historical relationship between l-month LIBOR and 6-month LIBOR (lagged 6 and 24 months) and the historical relationship between 1-month LIBOR and 1-year CMT (lagged 12 months). For the most part, when 6-month LIBOR is lagged by 6 months, it tracks fairly closely with 1-month LIBOR. The largest negative difference in the past 12 years was 1.63%. This is well within the 325 bps initial excess spread that we saw in Conti 1997-3. However, when 6-month LIBOR is lagged 24 months to approximate the impact of 2/28 loans, the maximum difference with 1-month LIBOR was 3.81%.

Similarly, when 1-year CMT is lagged 12 months to approximate the impact of collateral that resets yearly, the maximum difference with l-month LIBOR was 3.65%. Although these last two product types in a worse case scenario could potentially cap the securities, most pools have a mix of loan types and roll dates that help to mitigate some of the basis risk. Healthy levels of excess spread and a variety of structural mechanisms (discussed later in the structure section) can also help mitigate basis risk.

Exhibit 6: Basis Risk

	Average	Max	Min	Std Dev
6M Libor Lagged 6 Months—1M Libor	0.30%	2.63%	−1.63%	0.74%
6M Libor Lagged 24 Months—1 M Libor	0.60%	5.25%	−3.81%	2.38%
1Y CMT Lagged 12 Months—1M Libor	0.20%	3.03%	−3.65%	1.42%

[2] We add further discussion on prepayments by loan product type in the prepayment section.

Exhibit 7: Basis Risk: 6-Month LIBOR Loans

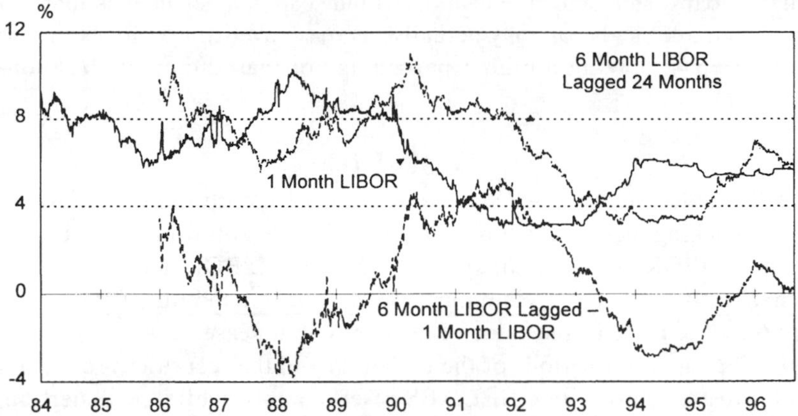

Exhibit 8: Basis Risk: 2/28 LIBOR Loans

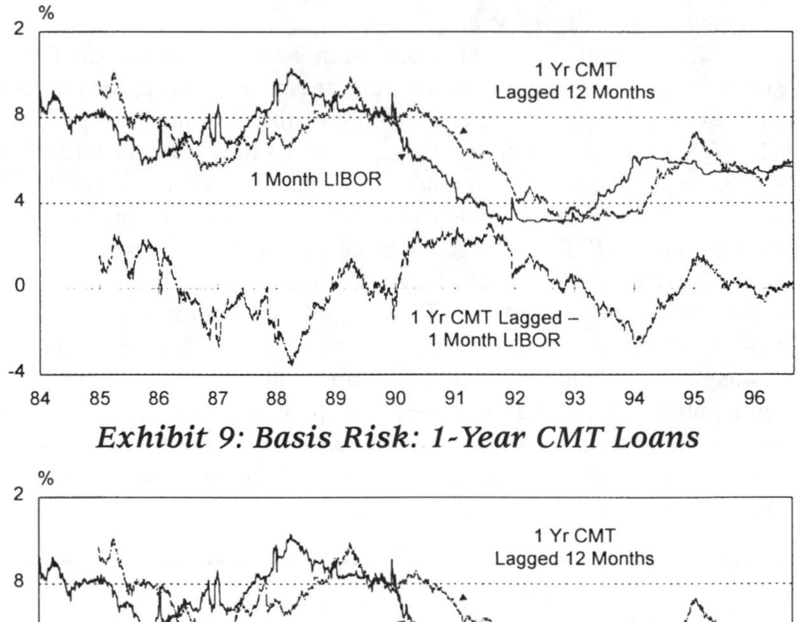

Exhibit 9: Basis Risk: 1-Year CMT Loans

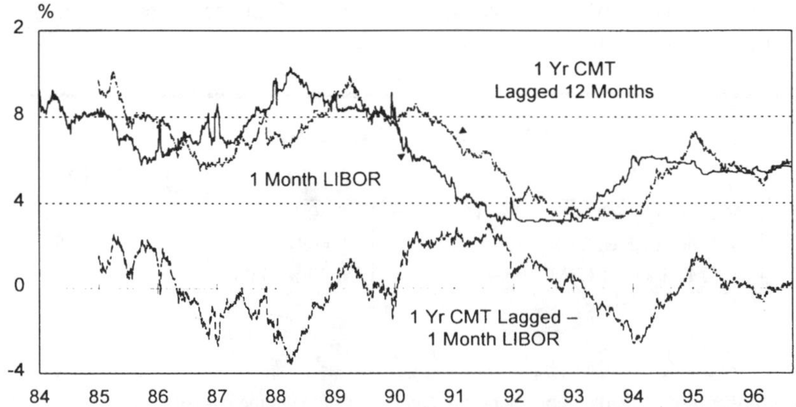

Exhibit 10: Projected Baseline Adjustable-Rate HEL Prepayment Curve
6-Month LIBOR Loans

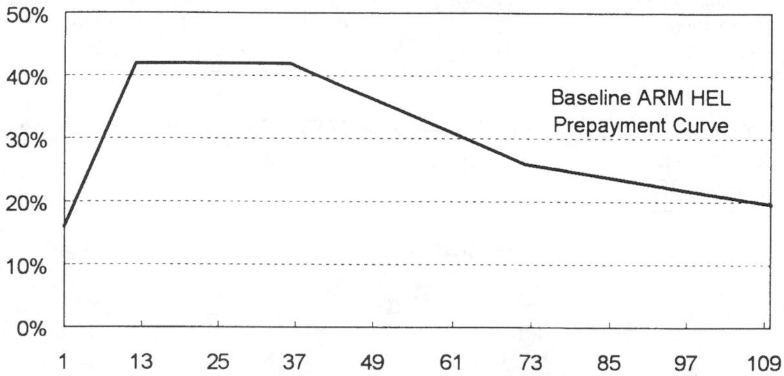

PREPAYMENTS

In the past, adjustable-rate HEL ABS investors did not focus heavily on prepayment speeds since the securities are short-duration assets that reset every month. With the price of the securities remaining close to par, prepayments have relatively little impact on the securities' yield. Investors actually benefited from fast prepayment speeds relative to pricing by getting a shorter security with less periodic and life cap risk while still being compensated based on a longer weighted-average life.

However, with the addition of hybrid fixed/adjustable products, the prepayment as well as the periodic and life cap profile of the pool could change more dramatically over time. This is especially true if the 6-month LIBOR loans were to exit the pool via prepayments, leaving behind the 2/28, 3/27, 4/26, and 5/25 hybrid loans.

In the following sections, we present a baseline 6-month LIBOR HEL prepayment curve, examine prepayment speeds for different product types, and then discuss the impact of prepayment penalties.

Baseline Adjustable Rate HEL Prepayment Curve

Adjustable-rate HEL collateral has been prepaying extremely quickly, in some cases above 50% CPR! This experience arises from refinancing opportunities available due to heavy competition, the use of teaser rates, and credit curing. Exhibit 10 shows the projected baseline prepayment curve for 6-month LIBOR loans. The curve starts at 16% CPR in month 1. As the loans near their first and second reset dates, prepayments ramp up to 42% CPR by month 12. This portion of the ramp reflects the payment sensitive nature of adjustable-rate HEL borrowers. As teaser rates approach their reset date, these borrowers have a built in bias to refinance. Prepayments are projected to remain at 42% CPR until month 36. At that point, we expect that burnout will cause prepayments to decrease to 26% until month 72 and then to 20% CPR thereafter.

Exhibit 11: Adjustable-Rate HEL Prepayment Rates

Deal	1 Mo CPR	3 Mo CPR	6 Mo CPR	Original Pricing	Current Pricing
Alliance Funding 1996-1	52.10%	48.80%	47.88%	20% CPR	26% CPR
ContiMortgage 1996-1	57.30%	52.30%	57.30%	18% CPR	30% CPR
Saxon 1996-1	61.90%	43.80%	47.91%	18% CPR	30% CPR

Exhibit 12: Adjustable-Rate HEL Prepayment Rates

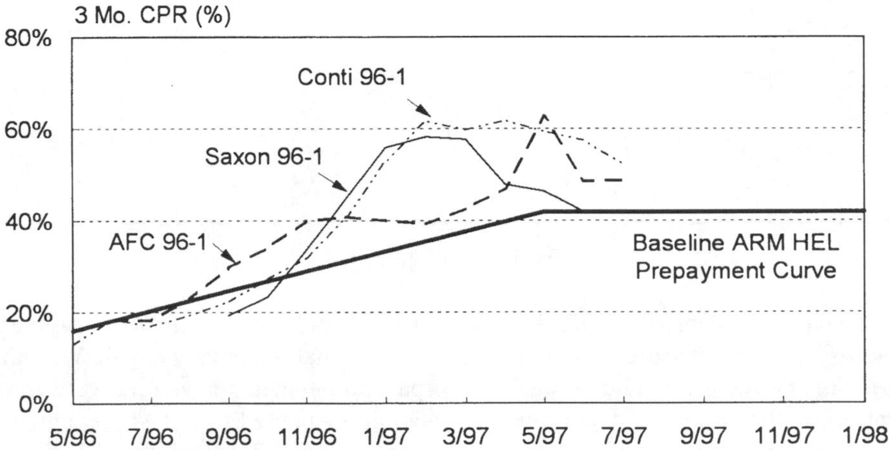

At the baseline prepayment curve, over 60% of the pool would pay down after two years, with 80% prepaying by the end of the third year.

Exhibits 11 and 12 show prepayment rates for three 1996 adjustable-rate pools from ContiMortgage, Alliance Funding, and Saxon Mortgage. The Alliance deal was priced to a 20% CPR while the ContiMortgage and Saxon deals were priced at 18% CPR. However, at the time of this writing, these deals have been coming in closer to 50% CPR over the prior six months, more than 2.5 times the original pricing speeds. The majority of the loans in these pools were either 6-month LIBOR or 1-year CMT with most loans resetting within 6-months of the deal cut-off date. We expect these prepayment rates to persist for at least another 12 months, before showing signs of burnout.

Adjustable-Rate HEL Product Types and Prepayments

Given the sector's relative lack of history, adjustable-rate HEL prepayment data are in short supply, particularly for 2/28 and 3/27 product. To look at prepayment speeds for different loan types, we examined the adjustable-rate loans from Saxon 1996-1 and 1996-2. Although the majority of Saxon's 1996 originations were 6-month LIBOR, the pools did contain over \$108 million of 1-year CMT, \$32 million of 2/28, and \$33 million of 3/27 loans.

Exhibit 13: Prepayment Speeds by Adjustable Rate HEL Collateral Type

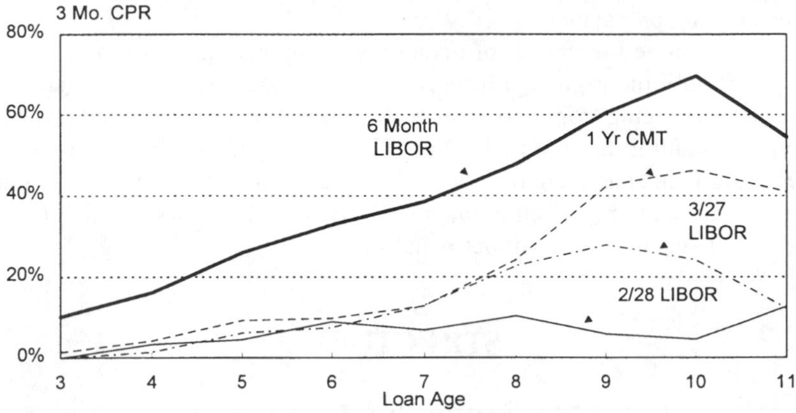

Exhibit 13 shows 3-month CPRs for the different product types. The results, not surprisingly, show that the 6-month LIBOR loans ramped up most quickly, peaking at an extraordinary 1-month speed of 77% CPR in month 9. After 11 months of seasoning, over 39% of the 6-month LIBOR loans had prepaid. Since the majority of the loans were teased, these borrowers immediately reset to a higher rate at their first adjustment date. By refinancing into another teased loan, the borrowers could reduce their monthly payment. If the borrowers had to pay points to refinance, their monthly payments could still be less than the reset loan even if the points were financed.

The 1-year CMT loans started off slowly, but sped up as the loans neared their reset date. The 2/28 loans prepaid extremely slowly, averaging 1-month speeds under 10% CPR. Even though the 3/27 loans prepaid significantly slower than the 6-month LIBOR and the 1-year CMT loans, it was somewhat unexpected that those loans prepaid at a rate over 20% CPR after 8 months. However, upon closer examination of the loans, over 40% of those that prepaid were B and C borrowers who probably were able to refinance at a lower rate due to credit curing.

While the 2/28 and 3/27 loans may exhibit relatively slow prepayment rates during their teaser periods, we expect them to eventually behave like the non-hybrid loans. In particular we look for them to exhibit a spike in prepayments as they come out of their teaser periods and the borrowers face a 2% to 3% increase in their rates.

Prepayment Penalties

Another way HEL issuers are trying to stem high initial prepayment speeds has been the introduction of prepayment penalties. As discussed earlier, penalties usually take the form of 6 months interest on 80% of the outstanding loan balance for full prepayments. These penalties are in force generally from 1 to 3 years after which the borrower can prepay without penalty. Since the use of penalties has been a recent trend, limited historical data exists for assessing the impact of penalties on slowing prepayments.

To examine the impact of penalties, we looked at a pool of 1,250 loans totaling $150 million originated in 1996. Of these loans, $51 million had prepayment penalties ranging from 1 to 3 years. Although the loans included a variety of loan types including 6-month LIBOR, 2/28, and 1-year CMT, and a variety of borrower and loan characteristics, we still can draw the basic conclusion that the penalties do have an impact on prepayments. Exhibit 14 shows the historical prepayments of loans with and without penalties.

STRUCTURE

Available Funds Cap Carryforward

One of the structural changes introduced into adjustable-rate HEL transactions to reduce cap risk is the available funds cap carryforward mechanism. The carryforward mechanism is used if the passthrough rate of the adjustable-rate tranche is based on the available funds cap. The difference between the available funds cap and the passthrough rate calculated based on the bond's index and margin is carried forward to subsequent periods The carryforward amount will also accrue interest at the current passthrough rate. This amount will be repaid with any future excess cash. However, if the carryforward amount is not reimbursed by the termination of the trust, either at the cleanup call or final maturity it is not recoverable.

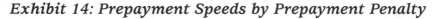

Exhibit 14: Prepayment Speeds by Prepayment Penalty

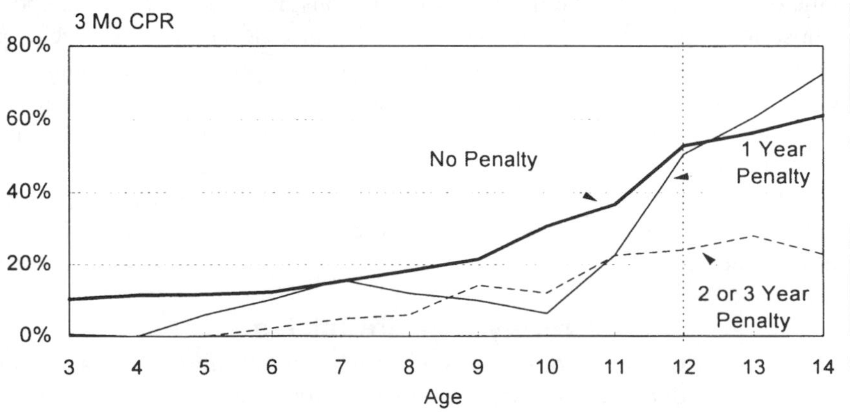

Exhibit 15: Available Funds Cap Carryforward

Issuer	Series	Carry Forward	Covered By
Alliance Funding	1997-2	No	
Amresco	1997-2	Yes	Excess Cash
ContiMortgage	1997-3	No	
First Franklin	1997-FF2	Yes	FSA til 6/99
Long Beach	1997-LB3	Yes	Excess Cash
Money Store	1997-B	Yes	Excess Cash
Saxon	1997-2V	Yes	Excess Cash
UCFC	1997-B	Yes	Reserve Fund

Exhibit 16: Excess Cash FLow Waterfall — Saxon 1997-2

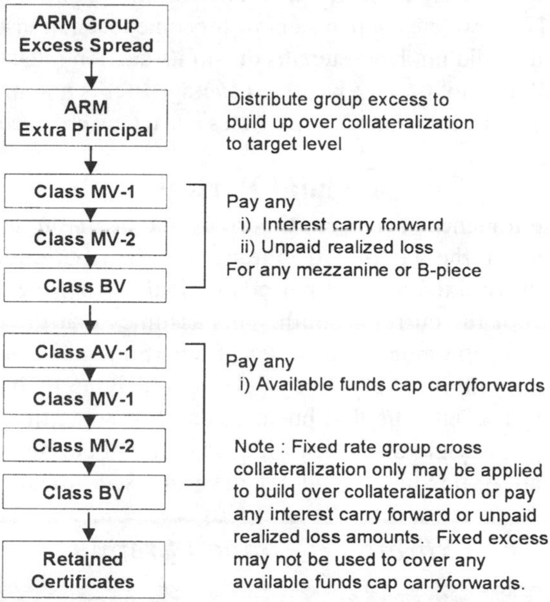

Exhibit 15 shows various 1997 second quarter transactions, indicating which transactions are structured with a carryforward mechanism and how the carryforward is reimbursed. Alliance Funding and ContiMortgage did not have the carryforward mechanism in place. First Franklin, due to the predominance of 2/28 product in their pool, bought a cap from FSA to cover any available funds shortfalls until all of the loans reset in 6/99. After 6/99, any available fund shortfall is not covered as no carryforward mechanism is structured in this transaction.

Exhibit 16 shows the excess cash flow waterfall for Saxon 1997-2. Any excess cash from the adjustable-rate group is first applied to build overcollateralization to the required levels. Then any regular interest carry forwards or unpaid realized losses are paid. Excess cash is then used to cover any available funds cap carryforwards. The remaining excess spread is then distributed to the residual holder. Note that the fixed rate cross collateralization does not apply to any available funds cap carryforward amounts as the carryforward can only be reimbursed by future excess spread from the adjustable-rate group.

Coupon Stepups

In order to increase the probability that the issuer or residual holder will exercise the cleanup call, most adjustable-rate HEL tranches allow for the coupon to stepup if the call is not exercised. Typically, the spread on the senior tranches will double if the deal is not called on the first eligible date. By increasing the bond coupon, in effect, the issuer or residual holder is incented to call the deal since the stepup decreases the amount of excess spread that is passed back to the residual holder. This coupon stepup mitigates some of the extension risk inherent in these transactions.

Exhibit 17 shows the coupon stepups for some recent transactions. Note that the Money Store deal did not have stepups due to its auction rate structure. The first tranche of the deal, due to its short weighted average life, is not affected by the call. The call also doesn't affect the auction rate notes since they arc auctioned monthly.

Accrual Period

Most floating-rate tranches have accrual periods that begin on the previous remittance date and end on the day prior to the current distribution date. However, a few transactions have fixed accrual periods typically from the 15th of the prior month to the 14th of the current month. This assumes that the distribution date occurs on the 15th of the month. However, if the 15th occurs on a weekend or a holiday, investors would incur a 1-3 day delay in receiving their payment as payments are not remitted until the first business day following the weekend or holiday. The impact on the yield of the securities is minimal but nonetheless investors should be cognizant of this potential delay in certain securities.

Exhibit 17: Coupon Stepup

Issuer	Series	Class	Coupon	Stepup
Alliance Funding	1997-2	2A-1	1ML+24	1ML+64
Green Tree	1997-C	A-1A	1ML+23	1ML+46
ContiMortgage	1997-3	A-10	1ML+21	1ML+42
		M-1A	1ML+34	1ML+51
		M-2A	1ML+58	1ML+87
		B-1A	1ML+100	1ML+150
First Franklin	1997-FF2	A	1ML+24	1ML+48
Money Store	1997-B	A-9	1ML+10	N/A
		A-10	Auction	N/A
Saxon	1997-2V	A-1	1ML+21	1ML+42
		M-1	1ML+35	1ML+52.5
		M-2	1ML+56	1ML+84
		B	1ML+97	1ML+145.5

SUMMARY

Adjustable-rate HELs are emerging as an increasingly important segment of the ABS market. The sector remains poised for growth. Originators have introduced hybrid adjustable-rate products (2/28 and 3/27 loans) and prepayment penalty features that not only appeal to a wide borrower base, but also help alter the prepayment rates and, consequently, the cap schedules of mixed adjustable-rate HEL pools. Hybrid adjustable-rate products may expose investors to additional available funds cap risk during teaser periods, but structural innovations such as available funds cap carryforward mechanisms mitigate this risk.

Chapter 27

Manufactured Housing Securitization

Paul N. Watterson Jr., Esq.
Partner
Schulte Roth & Zabel LLP

Shlomo C. Twerski, Esq.
Partner
Schulte Roth & Zabel LLP

Craig S. Stein, Esq.
Associate
Schulte Roth & Zabel LLP

INTRODUCTION

Securities backed by manufactured housing contracts are marketed as asset-backed securities (ABS) because of their underwriting, prepayment, default, and recovery patterns. However, securities backed by manufactured housing contracts share many of the legal characteristics of mortgage-backed securities (MBS). For example, some manufactured home financings are secured by mortgages or deeds of trust. Manufactured housing securitizations are generally structured as real estate mortgage investment conduits (REMICs) for tax purposes. The securities laws treat manufactured housing contracts as interests in real estate and, therefore, classify most manufactured housing securitizations with MBS transactions. The securities backed by manufactured housing contracts are typically tranched in ways more common in MBS transactions. The purpose of this chapter is to examine how the dichotomy between MBS and ABS affects the structuring and legal issues involved in securitizing manufactured housing contracts.

WHAT IS A MANUFACTURED HOME?

Manufactured homes are single-family residences constructed on a chassis at a factory and transported to a site in one or more components (single-section or multisection). Unit sizes range from about 400 square feet to more than 2,000 square feet.[1] Upon delivery to the site, the wheels are removed and the unit is placed on a concrete pad. Most manufactured homes are expected to remain at the site indefinitely; their wheels are simply a built-in means of transportation to the home site. The sites for manufactured homes are generally manufactured housing parks or private lots that are owned or rented.

MANUFACTURED HOUSING SECURITIZATION MARKET

In 1997, approximately $7.5 billion securities backed by manufactured homes were issued.[2] While Green Tree has been the largest issuer in this market, a number of other large finance companies are active issuers in this market.

In most of these transactions, the securitization is structured as a sale of the manufactured housing contracts by the originating finance company, directly or through a special purpose subsidiary, to a newly formed trust. The trust then issues several classes of senior and subordinate certificates of beneficial interest in the trust, and a single residual class which in most cases is held by the seller or its affiliate. Additional credit enhancement may be provided by a reserve account or spread account. In a rare case, manufactured housing contracts (particularly land-and-home contracts, discussed below) and residential mortgage or home equity loans may be included in the same offering.

TYPES OF RECEIVABLES

Most manufactured housing contract receivables are installment sales contracts or installment loan contracts. The installment sales contract creates a security interest in the manufactured home. However, some manufactured housing contract receivables are "land-and-home" or "land home" contracts. Originators of land-and-home contracts require the obligor to execute a mortgage or deed of trust creating a first lien on the real estate on which the manufactured home is affixed to secure the manufactured housing contract.

A land-and-home contract is similar to a residential mortgage loan. The mortgage or deed of trust is recorded in the real estate records, title insurance usually is obtained, and, after a default by an obligor on its manufactured housing contract, foreclosure procedures similar to procedures for a residential mortgage loan may be commenced. A land-and-home contract may finance the acquisition of both the manufactured home and the land; in some contracts (a "land in lieu" contract), the obligor already owns the site and gives a mortgage on it to the lender in lieu of a downpayment on the manufactured home.

---

[1] "Manufactured Housing's Changing Landscape," Fitch Investors Service, L.P., July 15, 1996.

[2] *Asset-Backed Securities Week*, Vol. 4, No. 1 (January 5, 1998).

Most manufactured housing contracts are "three party paper" in which a dealer originates an installment sales contract to finance a consumer's purchase of a manufactured home and assigns the installment sales contract to a finance company, usually at the time of funding. However, an increasing number of manufactured housing contracts are being financed through direct origination by the finance company.

PROTECTION OF TRUST'S INTEREST IN MANUFACTURED HOUSING CONTRACTS

Chattel Paper: Perfection by Filing or Possession

Manufactured housing contracts are generally classified as chattel paper under the Uniform Commercial Code (UCC). Chattel paper is defined in Section 9-105(b) of the UCC as "a writing or writings which evidence both a monetary obligation and a security interest in or lease of specific goods." Each installment sales contract evidences the debt and the grant of a security interest in the related manufactured home.

Generally, UCC financing statements are filed to perfect the sale of the manufactured housing contracts to the trust. Under Section 9-308 of the UCC, "a purchaser of chattel paper ... who gives new value and takes possession of it in the ordinary course of business has priority over a security interest in the chattel paper" which was perfected by filing, if the purchaser "acts without knowledge that the specific paper ... is subject to a security interest." Thus, unless the trust has possession of the manufactured housing contracts, it is possible for the seller, through mistake or fraud, to transfer the manufactured housing contracts to a third party.

In order to evidence the trust's ownership of the manufactured housing contracts and to make it difficult for any purchaser to claim that it had no knowledge of the trust's interest in the manufactured housing contracts, the manufactured housing contracts can be stamped to reflect their sale to the trust. Alternatively, the trust could protect its interests by taking possession of the manufactured housing contracts. But it is customary in most securitizations of this type for the manufactured housing contracts to be held by the seller/servicer as custodian for the trust to enable it to perform the necessary servicing duties.

Additional steps may be taken to protect investors in the case of land-and-home contracts. The seller is more likely to deliver the land-and-home contracts to a third-party custodian, similar to the practice in MBS transactions.

Protection of Trust's Security Interest in Manufactured Homes

Under the laws of most states, manufactured homes constitute personal property, perfection of a security interest in which may be obtained by filing a UCC financing statement. In some states, manufactured homes are covered by certificate of title laws. In these states, perfection of a security interest requires delivery of the certificate of title or notation of the lien on the certificate of title of the manufactured home.

Because of the cost and administrative inconvenience involved, the practice in manufactured housing securitizations is not to amend the certificates of title of the manufactured homes to reflect the trust's lien, even though such amendment is required in some states to render the assignment of the originator/seller's security interest in the manufactured home to the trust enforceable against third-party creditors (including a trustee in bankruptcy) of the obligor under the contract. Instead, the originator/seller represents at closing that it has obtained a first priority security interest in the manufactured homes underlying the manufactured housing contracts. Investors rely on this representation and the good servicing practices of the servicer to protect the trust's security interest in the manufactured homes.

Land and Home Contracts: Filing in Real Estate Records

For land-and-home contracts the practice is different, because a mortgage or deed of trust is involved. First, the originator/seller records the mortgage or deed of trust in the real estate records. The mortgage or deed of trust is then assigned to the trust, together with the manufactured housing contract.

There are three basic approaches with respect to the assignment to the trust of the mortgage or deed of trust. One approach is to record the assignments of mortgage to the trustee in the real estate records. Another approach is not to deliver the assignments of mortgage at closing, but to establish triggers (for example, a decline in the credit rating of the seller) in the transaction documents which, if they occur in the future, will require the seller to deliver assignments of mortgage to the trustee for recording. The third approach, which is the most common, is to deliver assignments of mortgage to the trustee in recordable form, but not to record them at closing because of the cost involved. Instead, the transaction documents establish triggers which, if they occur in the future, will require the trustee to record the assignments of mortgage. Under the laws of many states, the recording of the assignments is not required to protect the interests of the trust.

Consequences of Change of Location of Manufactured Home and Permanent Attachment to the Site

There are two additional problems with manufactured homes that do not exist in MBS transactions. Like automobiles, manufactured homes can be moved to another state and retitled. This can result in the loss of the trust's lien on the manufactured home unless the servicer receives notice of the move and follows the proper procedure in the new state to protect the trust's lien on the manufactured home.

Another risk is that the manufactured homes can become permanently affixed to the real estate. Under the laws of some states once the manufactured home becomes "affixed" to the real estate, it becomes a "fixture" and, thus, becomes part of the real estate to which the manufactured home is attached. At the time the manufactured home becomes a fixture it becomes subject to the real estate title and recording laws, in which case perfection of the trust's interest would require recordation in the real estate records. Failure to record may result in the loss of the trust's lien on the manufactured home or the loss of the trust's first priority position against third parties (e.g., the obligor's real estate lender) that may have filed a mortgage in the real estate records. Manufactured housing contracts generally prohibit the obligor from attaching the manufactured home permanently to the site.

Filing of Continuation Statements

The UCC requires that a creditor file continuation statements every five years or lose its security interest in the manufactured home. Since manufactured housing contracts have terms of 25 to 30 years, this requires four or five filings to protect the trust's interest in the manufactured home. Proposals are now under consideration to amend the UCC so that continuation statements need not be filed for manufactured housing contracts.[3]

TRANSACTION STRUCTURES

The structure of manufactured housing securitizations is driven primarily by tax considerations. Because of the Internal Revenue Code's "taxable mortgage pool" rules, most receivables secured by an interest in real estate can be securitized only in a multiple-class or tranched offering if a REMIC or financial asset securitization investment trust (FASIT) is used. A multiple class or tranched offering is desirable so that subordinated securities can provide credit enhancement for senior securities and so that the cash flows can be tailored to investors' average life requirements. This tailoring, in turn, broadens the investor base and improves the pricing of the transaction.

To qualify as a REMIC, each manufactured housing contract in the pool must be considered to be principally secured by an interest in real property. For these purposes, the Internal Revenue Code provides that a manufactured housing unit is to be treated as real property if it has at least 400 square feet of living space, is more than 102 inches wide, and is of the type customarily used at a fixed location. Most manufactured housing units meet this test and the contracts thereon are therefore secured by interests in real property, even if the manufactured housing contract is not secured by a mortgage, deed, or trust on the site.

Under a 1996 IRS private ruling, an ANSI (American National Standards Institute) unit was also considered real property and a contract secured by such a

---

[3] See The National Conference of Commissioners on Uniform State Laws, Drafts of Uniform and Model Acts Official Website (October 1997 draft contains a proposal to amend Section 9-502(b) of the UCC to provide that if the financing statement states that it is filed in connection with a manufactured home transaction, the financing statement may indicate that its effectiveness will be extended for a total effective period of 10, 20 or 30 years).

unit was permitted to be included in a REMIC. An ANSI unit is at least 375 square feet, more than 102 inches wide, has the wheels removed, is anchored to the ground, and has additions attached to the unit. Contracts secured by units that are not treated as real property cannot be securitized as part of a REMIC.

A FASIT may hold a pool consisting of one or more types of debt instrument, whether secured or unsecured. Using a FASIT would allow the securitization of a pool containing contracts secured by any type of manufactured housing units, together with other types of qualifying receivables.

Because most manufactured housing contracts are considered to be interests in real property, most issuers have structured the securitization as a REMIC. Although some manufactured housing securitizations have been structured as grantor trusts, this structure is used infrequently because grantor trusts cannot have "fast pay/slow pay" or sequential classes of securities and can have only limited subordination of classes.

A trust that elects to be a REMIC (or a FASIT) is permitted to issue multiple classes of securities with senior/subordinate and fast-pay/slow-pay features. Usually, the trust issues senior classes of securities to investors and one or more junior classes that may be sold to investors or retained by an affiliate of the originator. The trust issues a single residual class in a REMIC (or a FASIT), which is usually retained by the originator/seller.

CREDIT ENHANCEMENT

In all securitizations, including those backed by manufactured housing contracts, there is the risk that obligors will default on the payments due under their contracts or will not make their payments on time. Credit enhancement seeks to minimize the risk that nonpayment by the obligors will cause a loss to the securityholders. Credit enhancement comes in many forms. It may be provided by the originator/seller or by a third party. The size of the credit-enhancement facility required to obtain the desired rating from the rating agencies for each class of securities is dependent on a number of factors, including the historical delinquency and loss experience of similar pools of manufactured housing contracts and the structure of the transaction.

Generally, qualifying credit enhancements may be included in a REMIC or a FASIT without adversely affecting the entity's tax status.

Senior/Subordinate Structure

The primary form of credit enhancement used in manufactured housing contract securitizations is the subordination of one or more of the classes of securities issued by the trust. These subordinated class(es) of securities serve as credit support for the more senior classes of securities issued by the trust. In a typical senior/subordinated transaction, the rights of the holders of the subordinated securities to receive distributions in respect of principal and interest are subordinated to the rights of the holders of the senior securities to receive such distributions. The subordination feature may also be accomplished by the allocation among the classes of securities of certain types of payments, losses or delinquencies on the manufactured housing contracts or the payments from reserve accounts or a guarantee.

The subordinated securities are sometimes held by the originator/seller. In this circumstance, the attorneys delivering the opinion that there has been a "true sale" of the manufactured housing contracts to the trust must consider whether the originator/seller has divested itself of the risks of loss on the pool of manufactured housing contracts.

Overcollateralization

Credit support may consist of overcollateralization whereby the aggregate principal balance of the manufactured housing contracts exceeds the principal balance of the securities on the closing date. Overcollateralization may be created after the closing date through the use of the interest collected on the manufactured housing contracts (in excess of the amounts necessary to pay the interest rate on the securities) to pay principal on the securities. Overcollateralization can be created in this way because the weighted average interest rate on the manufactured housing contracts is usually significantly greater than the weighted average interest rate on the securities. This "excess spread" is used to pay principal on the securities, thus creating overcollateralization as the principal balance of the securities is reduced faster than the principal balance of the pool of manufactured housing contracts.

Guaranty

Payments on a class of securities, deficiencies in principal or interest payments on the manufactured housing contracts, or liquidation losses on the manufactured housing contracts may be supported by a guaranty. The guarantor may be the originator/seller, an affiliate of the originator/seller or a third party financial institution. The guarantor may be required to make deposits to an account, make advances, or purchase defaulted manufactured housing contracts. The scope, amount, and allocation of payments made under and pursuant to a guaranty will vary from transaction to transaction. The rating on the class of securities supported by the guaranty will be contingent on the maintenance of the guarantor's credit rating.

Reserve Account

Credit enhancement for the securities or some classes of the securities may be provided by a reserve account. The purpose of a reserve account is to protect the trust from credit losses on the manufactured housing contracts. Funds on deposit in the reserve account may be withdrawn for distribution to holders of designated (or all) classes of the securities at times specified in the transaction documents.

Funds on deposit in the reserve account may be invested in eligible investment securities; and future funding of the reserve account may be secured by a letter of credit, guaranty, or demand notes. A reserve account may be funded at closing from the proceeds of the issuance of the securities, or the account may be funded from the "excess spread" generated by the manufactured housing contracts after the closing (in which case it may be referred to as a "spread account").

Subordination of Servicing Fee

The servicer typically receives its servicing fee prior to the securityholders receiving any distributions. However, in many manufactured housing securitizations, the originator/seller may agree that, so long as it or its affiliate is the servicer, the servicing fee will be subordinated and will be paid only if all payments then due to the holders of the securities have been made.

Other Forms of Credit Enhancement

Two other forms of credit enhancement frequently used in ABS transactions are not often seen in manufactured housing securitizations. In a few transactions, credit support has been provided by the issuance of a letter of credit from a third-party financial institution to support timely payments on the securities, to provide protection against losses on the manufactured housing contracts, to provide a source of funding for a reserve account or to secure the servicer's obligations. As in the case of a guarantee, the credit rating of the securities supported by the letter of credit will be tied to the credit rating of the issuer of the letter of credit.

Alternatively, a surety "wrap" may be obtained from an insurer to provide credit support for one or more classes of securities. This insurance product generally guarantees to securityholders the payment of interest and principal to which securityholders would be entitled. Again, the credit rating of the insurer will affect the rating on the securities.

LIQUIDITY ENHANCEMENT

Even if obligors ultimately make the payments due under their manufactured housing contracts, there is the risk that the timing of their payments may be such that the trust will not have sufficient funds on a distribution date to pay all amounts due to the securityholders. Liquidity enhancement seeks to minimize this risk by providing an alternative source of funds with which to pay the securityholders, pending receipt of the payments under the manufactured housing contracts.

Servicer Advances

The servicer typically agrees to help maintain a regular flow of scheduled interest payments to securityholders by making servicer advances to the trust. Such advances are usually made in the amount of the delinquency of each obligor on his interest payment (or, in some cases, his full scheduled payment) under his manufactured housing contract. The servicer is obligated to make the advance only if it believes that it will be recoverable from future payments by the obligor or through the proceeds of liquidation of the collateral. Such advances are reimbursed to the servicer out of late payments made by the obligor or the insurance proceeds or liquidation proceeds of the manufactured home; or, if the servicer determines that the advance is not recoverable from payments on other manufactured housing contracts in the pool.

Compensating Interest

If a manufactured housing contract is prepaid in advance of the final scheduled due date on the manufactured housing contract, the trust may receive less interest on such contract for a particular collection period than it would have otherwise received had such contract not been prepaid. The servicer may make a payment to the trust (but only to the extent of its servicing fee for such collection period) equal to the excess of the amount of interest that would have been due on such contract for the full collection period had the prepayment not been made over the amount of interest actually received for such collection period.

The amount paid by the servicer is sometimes referred to as compensating interest. The servicer often agrees to make this type of advance (as well as advances to cover suspensions of payments on contracts pursuant to laws protecting obligors performing military service) without any right to reimbursement.

Prefunding and Capitalized Interest Accounts

A manufactured housing securitization — whether structured as a REMIC, FASIT, grantor trust, or otherwise — may include a prefunding account. In such a transaction, the original principal amount of securities issued by the trust exceeds the principal balance of the manufactured housing contracts initially sold to the trust, and a portion of the proceed of the securities is deposited into a prefunding account. This account is used to purchase additional manufactured housing contracts during a short period, usually three months, after the initial closing date. In this instance, a capitalized interest account typically is established to protect against the negative arbitrage resulting from the investments in the prefunding account earning interest at a lower rate than the interest rate on the securities.

There are other circumstances in which a capitalized interest account may be required. For example, the monthly payments on some manufactured housing contracts sold to the trust may not commence prior to the date interest is due on the securities. A capitalized interest account may be established to cover the "lost interest" on these manufactured housing contracts.

SECURITIES LAWS

SEC Registration

Manufactured housing securitizations are treated to a large extent under the federal securities laws as MBS. Unless all classes of the securities are offered pursuant to a private placement exempt from registration under the Securities Act of 1933 (the "1933 Act"), the securities must be registered under the 1933 Act pursuant to a registration statement.

A stand-alone registration statement of securities backed by manufactured housing contracts typically was filed on Form S-11. This form is used for securities issued by issuers whose business is primarily that of acquiring and holding investment real estate or interests in real estate. Manufactured housing contracts are considered to be interests in real estate for this purpose.

Rule 415 under the 1933 Act, which permits shelf registrations of securities to be offered on a delayed or continuous basis, is limited to certain kinds of public offerings, including "mortgage related securities" and "asset backed securities." Securities backed by manufactured housing contracts can qualify for shelf registration under either rubric. A shelf registration for a manufactured housing securitization may be filed on Form S-11 or Form S-3 if the securities qualify as "mortgage related securities" under the standard discussed below.

Alternatively, a shelf registration may be filed on Form S-3 if they qualify as "asset backed securities" with "investment grade" ratings. An "asset-backed security" is "a security that is primarily serviced by the cashflows of a discrete pool of receivables or other financial assets, either fixed or revolving, that by their terms convert into cash within a finite period plus any rights designed to assure the servicing or timely distribution of proceeds to the securityholders."[4] A security is an investment-grade security if, at the time of sale, at least one nationally recognized statistical rating organization has rated the security in one of its generic rating categories that signifies investment grade; typically the four highest rating categories (within which there may be subcategories or gradations indicating relative standing) signify investment grade.[5]

SMMEA

If the manufactured housing contract-backed securities are rated double-A or better and the contracts in the pool satisfy certain requirements, they will constitute "mortgage related securities"[6] for purposes of the Secondary Mortgage Market Enhancement Act of 1984 (SMMEA). As such, the securities will be exempt from many requirements under state blue sky and legal investment laws.

Investment Company Act of 1940

As in most ABS and MBS offerings, a trust does not register under the Investment Company Act of 1940 (the "1940 Act") when it issues securities backed by manufactured housing contracts. Issuers of securities backed by manufactured housing contracts are excepted from the definition of an investment company under Section 3(c)(5)(C) of the 1940 Act. Section 3(c)(5)(C) of the 1940 Act provides that

[4] Form S-3, general instructions parts I.A.4. and I.B.5.

[5] Form S-3, general instructions Part I.B.2.

[6] See Section 3(a)(41) of the Securities and Exchange Act of 1934, as amended.

any person primarily engaged in the business of purchasing or otherwise acquiring mortgages and other liens on and interests in real estate is not an investment company under the 1940 Act.

Moreover, issuers of securities backed by manufactured housing contracts are exempt under Rule 3a-7. Rule 3a-7 exempts any issuer engaged in the business of purchasing, or otherwise acquiring, and holding "eligible assets" provided that the securities meet other requirements specified in the rule. Eligible assets are defined as financial assets, either fixed or revolving, that by their terms convert into cash within a finite time period. Manufactured housing contracts qualify as eligible assets, and the other requirements of Rule 3a-7 usually are easily met in a typical manufactured housing securitization.

CONCLUSION

Manufactured housing securitizations should be analyzed using both ABS and MBS concepts. An increasing portion of each pool of manufactured housing contracts is mortgages or deeds of trust and additional steps should be taken to protect the trust's interest in the mortgages or deeds of trust. Since most manufactured housing securitizations are structured as REMICs, a familiarity with MBS structures is helpful in analyzing the cash flow and class structure of the transaction and understanding the legal issues.

Chapter 28

Manufactured Housing Securitization and Prepayments

Steven Abrahams
Principal
Mortgage Research
Morgan Stanley

Howard Esaki
Principal
Mortgage Research
Morgan Stanley

Robert Restrick

INTRODUCTION

Securitization of manufactured housing loans has grown dramatically in recent years. The purpose of this chapter is to discuss this sector of the market. Specifically, we will cover the following topics: (1) the market for manufactured housing; (2) the market for the securitized loans; (3) credit risk; and, (4) prepayment risk.

THE MARKET FOR MANUFACTURED HOUSING

Manufactured homes are single-family detached homes constructed off-site and transported to an individual plot of land or to a manufactured housing community. There are eight million manufactured homes in the United States, representing about 7% of all homes and more than 10% of the housing stock in some southern states. About one-third of manufactured homes are located in manufactured housing communities,[1] with the remainder located on individually owned or rented

[1] See for example, Howard Esaki and Robert Restrick, "Manufactured Housing Communities: Outlook and Risk Assessment," *Morgan Stanley Mortgage Research*, October 1995 and Eric Hemel and Steve Sakura, "Manufactured Housing REITs," *Morgan Stanley U.S. Investment Research* (May 26, 1995).

Mr. Restrick was employed by Morgan Stanley at the time this chapter was written.

plots of land. According to the Census Bureau, manufactured homes are the fastest growing type of housing, increasing by 57% in the 1980s. In the same period, the number of one-family houses increased by 13%.

Although manufactured homes are sometimes called "mobile homes," most are moved infrequently and are expensive to transport. For example, the average homeowner stay in a manufactured housing community is seven years. The home is likely to stay in the community for a much longer period. Costs of transporting a manufactured home range from $2,000 to $6,000, depending on the size of the home and location. In recent years, manufactured housing has come to more closely resemble site-built housing, containing many of the amenities of standard single-family detached homes. Newer "double-wide" homes are twice the size of older manufactured homes and are similar in size to standard homes with an average of 1,525 square feet of living space. In addition, federal government standards established in 1976 for manufactured homes have helped to improve the overall quality of this housing type.

Size, Cost and Buyer Demographics

Exhibits 1 and 2 provide cost and demographic characteristics for manufactured homes. On average, manufactured housing is less expensive and smaller than site-built housing. In 1993, the average sales price of a manufactured home was about one-fourth the cost of a site-built home, excluding land cost. The average manufactured home is about 60% of the size of the average site-built home. Since 1980, the average sales price of a manufactured home has fallen by 10% in real terms, while the price of a site-built home has risen by 13% in real terms. Manufactured housing occupants are, on average, younger and have lower incomes than site-built housing residents.

Exhibit 1: Cost Comparison: Manufactured Homes versus Site-Built Homes

	1980	1993
Manufactured Homes:		
Average sales price*	$33,900	$30,500
Average square footage	1,050	1,295
Average cost/square foot*	$32.29	$23.55
Site-Built Homes:		
Average sales price*	$130,900	$147,700
Land sales price	$26,200	$36,925
Sales price without land	$104,700	$110,775
Average square footage	1,740	2,095
Average cost/square foot*	$60.17	$52.88

*in 1993 dollars

Source: U.S Department of Commerce and Bureau of the Census cited in Daniel Friedman "Manufactured Housing: It Just Keeps Rolling Along," Balcor Consulting Group.

Exhibit 2: Demographic Characteristics: Manufactured Housing versus Non-Manufactured Housing
(in percent, except for income)

	Manufactured	Non-Manufactured*
Median Household Income	$21,052	$36,785
Age:		
Under 25	5.2	0.8
25-34	22.2	13.9
35-54	33.4	42.2
55-74	28.2	32.5
Over 75	11.0	10.6
Race:		
White	92.1	89.8
Non-White	7.9	10.2

*includes multifamily housing

Source: U.S Department of Commerce and Bureau of the Census cited in Daniel Friedman, "Manufactured Housing: It Just Keeps Rolling Along," Balcor Consulting Group.

Exhibit 3: Top 10 Growth States for Manufactured Homes, 1980 to 1990

State	Percent Growth (in units)
South Carolina	91.2
Georgia	87.9
North Carolina	80.6
Texas	80.5
Alabama	75.4
Rhode Island	75.4
Mississippi	75.3
Louisiana	75.3
Oklahoma	73.9
Arkansas	70.6

Source: Bureau of the Census

Geographic Location

Almost 60% of all manufactured homes in the US are located in the South Atlantic and South Central geographical census regions. Florida alone accounts for 10% of all units nationwide. The top three growth states for manufactured housing are also in the South Atlantic, with more than 80% growth from 1980 to 1990. Exhibit 3 lists the top ten growth states for manufactured housing. Exhibit 4 shows the top ten metropolitan areas for manufactured housing, by number of units. Most of these areas are in the Sunbelt, with the exception of the Seattle and Detroit metropolitan areas.

Exhibit 4: Top 10 Metro Areas by Number of Manufactured Homes (thousands of units), 1990

Los Angeles-Anaheim-Riverside, CA	217.3
Tampa-St. Petersburg-Clearwater, FL	147.0
Phoenix, AZ	86.0
Houston-Galveston-Brazoria, TX	68.8
San Francisco-Oakland-San Jose, CA	68.1
Dallas-Ft. Worth, TX	61.8
Seattle-Tacoma, WA	59.2
Detroit-Ann Arbor, MI	58.0
Lakeland-Winter Haven, FL	51.8
Miami-Ft. Lauderdale, FL	46.5

Source: American Demographics, January 1993

Exhibit 5: Total Issuance of Manufactured Housing Securities, 1987 to 1995

Issuer	Issues	Original Balance ($ Millions)	Market Share (%)
CFAC Grantor Trust	1	306	2
CIT Group Securitization Corporation	2	279	1
Green Tree Financial Corporation	25	9,961	52
Merrill Lynch Mortgage Investors, Inc.	41	5,774	30
Oakwood Mortgage Investors, Inc.	3	468	2
RTC	3	616	3
Security Pacific Acceptance Corp.	6	919	5
USWFS Manufactured Housing Contract	1	214	1
Vanderbilt Mortgage Finance	3	539	3
Total	85	19,076	100

Source: Bloomberg

THE MARKET FOR SECURITIES BACKED BY MANUFACTURED HOUSING LOANS

Over $19 billion of securities backed by manufactured housing loans have been issued since 1987. Exhibit 5 lists the total issuance of manufactured housing securities from 1987 to 1995. About 90% of these loans are on the value of the manufactured home itself, with 10% to 20% including the land. Green Tree Financial Corporation, through Merrill Lynch Mortgage Investors, Inc. and its own shelf, accounts for about two-thirds of total issuance.

With the exception of a few early deals, the majority of manufactured housing loan asset-backed securities (ABS) are composed of AAA-rated, sequential-pay classes. Credit enhancement is usually provided by excess servicing and subordination. The excess servicing strip, which represents the difference between the weighted average coupon on the bonds and the higher coupons on the mortgages, may be 350 basis points per year or more at issue. This strip covers losses first, and allows the rating agencies to assign investment grade ratings to 100% of the bonds issued. Mezzanine and subordinate classes, rated AA, A, and BBB, or some combination thereof, provide additional enhancement for the AAA classes. The mezzanine classes are typically locked out from receiving any principal for four or more years. Many recent manufactured housing loan ABS now pay principal pro rata to the senior classes and to certain of the mezzanine classes after the initial 4-year lockout period.

Exhibit 6 shows the characteristics of the ten most recent Green Tree manufactured housing loan transactions. The average size of the Green Tree transactions was $454 million, backed by an average of more than 15,000 loans. More than 80% of the loans are on new manufactured homes. The weighted average loan-to-value ratio was 87.2%. About 42% of the loans were on single-wide homes; the remainder were on double-wides or other sizes. About one-third of the loans were on homes located in manufactured housing communities. The largest state concentrations were North Carolina (9.6%), Texas (9.5%), and Florida (6.7%). Credit support for the senior classes has averaged 19.7%. Exhibit 7 shows the characteristics of the two CIT manufactured housing loan transactions.

Indicative spread to Treasury levels as of October 15, 1995 for the asset-backed securities issued in a sample Green Tree transaction, 1995-8, are shown in Exhibit 8. Spread levels on manufactured housing loan ABS have been fairly constant over the prior year.

RATING AGENCY VIEW OF MANUFACTURED HOUSING

Rating agencies have a generally favorable view of the manufactured housing industry and securities backed by manufactured housing loans. For example, Moody's recently wrote that "the recent favorable operating environment for the manufactured housing industry — along with an improved product line and new financing options — should provide for continued growth for the industry over the short-to-intermediate term." [2]

The credit performance of securities backed by manufactured housing loans is among the best of any type of mortgage- or asset-backed security. As can be seen from Exhibit 9, of the 70 asset-backed classes upgraded by Moody's since 1986, 38 are on deals backed by manufactured housing loans. Twenty-four of the manufactured housing upgrades were based on collateral performance and 14 were because of upgrades of third-party credit enhancers or Green Tree Financial Corporation.

---

[2] Mark Stancher, "Manufactured Housing Collateral and Structural Aspects: A Solid Foundation," *Moody's Investors Service*, January 27, 1995.

Exhibit 6: Characteristics of the Ten Mid-1990s Green Tree Issues

Series	1994-6	1994-7	1994-8	1995-1
Issue Date	Sep-94	Nov-94	Dec-94	Feb-95
Original Balance ($ mil.)	463.9	353.5	523.2	378.3
Number of Loans	17,515	12,723	18,430	12,805
Average Balance ($)	26,485	27,784	28,388	29,546
WAM (Years)	18.1	18.6	18.8	19.9
WAC	11.48	11.46	11.57	11.91
Ratings (Moody's/S&P/Fitch)				
Seniors	Aaa/AAA/NR	Aaa/AAA/NR	Aaa/AAA/NR	Aaa/AAA/NR
Subordinates				
Class M-1	Aa3/AA+/NR	Aa3/AA/NR	Aa3/AA/NR	AA/Aa3/NR
Class B-1	Baa1/A-/NR	Baa1/BBB+/NR	Baa1/BBB+/NR	Baa1/BBB+/NR
Class B-2	Baa1/A/NR	Baa1/A/NR	Baa1/A/NR	Baa1/A/NR
Credit Support (%)				
Seniors	21.0	21.0	21.0	19.0
Subordinates (%)				
Class M-1	12.0	11.5	11.5	10.0
Class B-1	6.5	6.0	6.0	6.0
Class B-2	Limited Guarantee from Green Tree Financial Corporation			
Sep-95 CPR (MHP)				
1mo	7.6 (156)	6.5 (144)	7.4 (161)	6.9 (157)
3mo	7.7 (161)	7.0 (150)	6.0 (133)	6.3 (146)
Life	4.8 (111)	5.2 (122)	n/a	6.2 (149)
Loan to Value (%)				
<80	16.1	16.2	18.9	11.2
80-85	11.8	12.2	12.9	11.4
85-90	42.7	41.9	39.3	35.5
90-95	28.8	29.2	28.2	32.1
95-100	0.7	0.6	0.7	9.8
Est. Wtd Avg.	87.3	87.2	86.4	85.2
Manufactured Homes (%)				
New	82	83	83	84
Single-Wide	45	41	39	37
Double-Wide/Other	55	59	61	63
Location (%)				
Park Property	33	32	29	27
Privately Owned	51	52	55	56
Nonpark Rental	16	16	16	17
State Percentage>5%				
Texas	10.3	8.9	8.3	8.7
Florida	6.3	6.1	6.8	7.5
North Carolina	9.0	9.0	9.6	10.8
Michigan	—	6.9	5.8	6.2
Georgia	5.6	5.2	5.5	6.9
South Carolina	—	—	5.3	—
Alabama	—	—	5.2	—

Source: Morgan Stanley, Fitch, Bloomberg

Exhibit 6 (Continued)

Series	1995-2	1995-3	1995-4	1995-5
Issue Date	Mar-95	May-95	Jun-95	Jul-95
Original Balance ($ mil.)	328.3	502.2	320.0	451.2
Number of Loans	11,738	18,112	11,138	14,283
Average Balance ($)	27,966	27,727	28,730	31,593
WAM (Years)	20.5	20.8	21.2	22.3
WAC	12.10	11.67	11.19	10.65
Ratings (Moody's/S&P/Fitch)				
Seniors	Aaa/AAA/AAA	Aaa/AAA/AAA	Aaa/AAA/AAA	Aaa/AAA/AAA
Subordinates				
Class M-1	Aa2/AA–/AA–	Aa2/AA–/AA–	Aa3/AA–/AA–	Aa3/AA–/AA–
Class B-1	Baa1/BBB+/BBB	Baa1/BBB+/BBB+	Baa1/BBB+/BBB+	Baa1/BBB+/BBB+
Class B-2	Baa1/A–/A	Baa1/A–/A	Baa1/A–/A	Baa1/A–/A
Credit Support (%)				
Seniors	18.0	18.0	17.0	17.0
Subordinates (%)				
Class M-1	9.0	9.0	8.0	8.0
Class B-1	5.0	4.5	4.0	4.0
Class B-2	Limited Guarantee from Green Tree Financial Corporation			
Sep-95 CPR (MHP)				
1mo	5.3 (123)	4.8 (118)	2.7 (68)	7.5 (191)
3mo	5.4 (129)	4.6 (114)	4.5 (116)	4.0 (106)
Life	5.5 (135)	4.5 (113)	4.5 (116)	6.5 (166)
Loan to Value (%)				
<80	13.8	13.0	15.1	16.7
80-85	12.5	11.3	11.0	10.9
85-90	35.9	30.3	29.0	26.6
90-95	36.3	43.4	42.7	43.9
95-100	1.5	2.1	2.2	2.0
Est. Wtd Avg.	88.1	88.8	88.2	87.7
Manufactured Homes (%)				
New	81	80	81	83
Single-Wide	43	45	44	39
Double-Wide/Other	57	55	56	61
Location (%)				
Park Property	34	36	36	31
Privately Owned	49	45	45	54
Nonpark Rental	17	19	19	15
State Percentage>5%				
Texas	10.8	10.1	9.1	7.9
Florida	6.9	6.7	6.9	6.9
North Carolina	9.5	10.0	9.0	8.2
Michigan	5.2	—	—	7.0
Georgia	6.1	5.9	6.1	5.0
South Carolina	6.2	6.2	5.9	5.4
Alabama	5.1	—	5.1	—

Source: Morgan Stanley, Fitch, Bloomberg

Exhibit 6 (Continued)

Series	1995-6	1995-7	1995-8	Average
Issue Date	Aug-95	Sep-95	Oct-95	
Original Balance ($ mil.)	396.7	347.8	479.9	424.9
Number of Loans	12,591	10,785	14,708	15,221
Average Balance ($)	31,506	32,244	32,628	27,916
WAM (Years)	22.4	22.6	22.9	19.4
WAC	10.27	10.12	10.11	11.7
Ratings (Moody's/S&P/Fitch)				
Seniors	Aaa/AAA/AAA	Aaa/AAA/AAA	Aaa/AAA/AAA	
Subordinates				
Class M-1	Aa3/AA-/AA	Aa3/AA-/AA	Aa3/AA-/AA	
Class B-1	Baa2/BBB+/BBB+	Baa1/BBB+/BBB+	Baa1/BBB+/BBB+	
Class B-2	Baa1/A-/A	Baa1/A-/A	Baa1/A-/A	
Credit Support (%)				
Seniors	17.0	17.0	17.0	19.7
Subordinates (%)				
Class M-1	9.5	9.5	9.5	10.6
Class B-1	4.5	4.0	4.0	5.7
Class B-2	Limited Guarantee from Green Tree Financial Corporation			
Sep-95 CPR (MHP)				
1mo	7.8 (205)	—	—	
3mo	—	—	—	
Life	7.8 (205)	—	—	
Loan to Value (%)				
<80	16.5	16.7	17.4	15.0
80-85	11.3	11.2	10.8	12.0
85-90	26.8	26.5	26.3	37.5
90-95	43.8	43.7	43.9	33.0
95-100	1.6	1.9	1.6	2.4
Est. Wtd Avg.	87.7	87.6	87.6	87.2
Manufactured Homes (%)				
New	82	83	82	82
Single-Wide	39	39	37	42
Double-Wide/Other	61	61	63	58
Location (%)				
Park Property	32	31	32	32
Privately Owned	52	53	52	51
Nonpark Rental	16	16	16	17
State Percentage >5%				
Texas	7.0	6.5	5.9	9.5
Florida	6.4	5.6	6.1	6.7
North Carolina	9.1	8.3	9.3	9.6
Michigan	6.4	7.2	7.5	3.7
Georgia	5.3	5.3	—	5.8
South Carolina	5.9	6.3	5.6	3.1
Alabama	—	—	—	1.7

Source: Morgan Stanley, Fitch, Bloomberg

Exhibit 7: Characteristics of CIT Issues

Series	1993-1	1995-1*
Issue Date	Jul-93	Feb-95
Original Balance ($ mil.)	155.0	84.6
Number of Loans	4,598	2,152
Average Balance ($)	33,719	39,297
WAM (Years)	17.1	19.9
WAC	10.61	11.32
Ratings (Moody's/S&P/Fitch)		
Seniors	NR/AAA/NR	Aaa/NR/NR
Subordinates		
Mezzanine	NA	Aa3/NR/NR
Subordinate	NR/BBB+/NR	Aa3/NR/NR
Credit Support (%)		
Seniors	15.8	16.5
Subordinates (%)		
Mezzanine	NA	8.5
Subordinate	1.8	Limited Guarantee
Aug-95 CPR (MHP)		
1mo	12.8 (213)	7.6 (176)
3mo	10.6 (177)	7.5 (179)
Life	12.5 (210)	5.8 (143)
Loan to Value (%)		
<80	30.0	12.4
80-85	30.8	10.6
85-90	29.2	24.5
90-95	9.1	32.4
95-100	0.9	19.2
Manufactured Homes (%)		
New	84	93
Double-Wide/Other	—	74
State Percentage>5%		
Texas	—	26.4
Arizona	—	10.8
Washington	6.8	—
California	18.8	—
Nevada	6.7	—
Oregon	7.3	—

* Based on initial contracts sold to the Trust.

Source: Morgan Stanley, Fitch, Bloomberg

Exhibit 8: Pricing Spread Levels on Green Tree 1995-8

Class	Average Life (years)	Nominal Spread (bp) Over Benchmark	Benchmark U.S. Treasury
A-1	1.05	45	5.27% of 10/17/96
A-2	3.05	45	3 year
A-3	5.05	55	5 year
A-4	7.08	70	6 3/8% of 8/02
A-5	10.29	92	10 year
A-6	17.07	140	10 year
M-1	13.35	135	10 year
B-1	8.75	135	10 year
B-2	17.44	168	10 year

Source: *Asset Sales Report*, Morgan Stanley, yields as of October 15, 1995

Exhibit 9: ABS Rating Changes by Moody's, 1986-1995

	Upgrades		Downgrades	
Asset Type	#	$ (Mil)	#	$ (Mil)
Autos	17	1,087	27	14,416
Credit Cards	7	372	14	4,750
Home Equity	4	359	7	21,607
Manufactured Housing	38	3,149	2	413
Other	4	216	6	1,139
Total	70	5,182	56	42,324

Source: Moody's

Only two classes of ABS backed by manufactured housing have been downgraded by Moody's, both related to downgrades of third-party credit enhancement providers. The upgrade to downgrade ratio for manufactured housing transactions (19 to 1) is greater than for any other type of ABS. As a comparison, the residential MBS upgrade downgrade ratio is about 2 to 1 for 1995. Fitch and Duff and Phelps have also upgraded several manufactured housing transactions.

Going forward, we believe credit performance will remain strong as the rating agencies continue to maintain strict standards for ratings of manufactured housing securities. Moody's notes, "..since most securities in the asset-backed market are rated Aaa initially (and therefore cannot be upgraded), we expect that there will be relatively more downgrades in this market than in the total corporate bond market." The average rating in the corporate bond market is close to BBB/Baa, leaving more opportunities for upgrades. However, Moody's also points out that, "...given the predominance of high initial ratings and the relatively short maturities, ...relatively few of [manufactured housing] securities will end in default."[3]

[3] Andrew Silver, "A Historical Review of Rating Changes in the Public Asset-Backed Securities Market, 1986-1995," *Moody's Investors Service*, October 20, 1995.

PREPAYMENT RISKS

Prepayments in manufactured housing arise from the same major sources as in other mortgage-backed bonds: refinancings, housing turnover, and defaults. Because of their smaller average loan balance, manufactured housing prepayment speeds, nonetheless, tend to be lower and much more stable than speeds on mortgages on site-build homes. In fact, prepayments on manufactured housing loans are arguably more stable than prepayments on higher-balance home equity loans.

Refinancings

As in other mortgage-backed securities, refinancing of manufactured housing loans represents the most volatile component of prepayments. Refinancings can double or triple prepayments on manufactured homes within a few months, sending speeds from 6% CPR to 18% CPR. Refinancings in site-built homes, however, can generate a tenfold jump in speeds from 6% CPR to 60% CPR.

A handful of factors drive the refinancings of most manufactured housing loans:

Primary
- Interest rate incentives
- Loan size

Secondary
- Loan age
- Seasonality

Tertiary
- The economy
- Competition among lenders

Exhibit 10 summarizes the factors driving refinancing on manufactured housing loans.

Primary Refinancing Risks

Falling interest rates represent the single most important driver of prepayments. Lower rates create opportunities for borrowers to refinance their loans and capture a stream of future monthly savings. The greater the drop in financing rates below the borrower's rate, the larger the absolute stream of potential savings. Monthly savings are also directly proportional to loan size, with small and large loans producing correspondingly small and large savings. (See Exhibit 11.)

As an example, take the savings from refinancing the average 80% LTV, 15-year manufactured housing loan of $24,400. If the borrower starts with a 9% interest rate, refinancing into an 8% interest rate only saves $14.30 a month. Refinancing into a 6% interest rate only saves $41.58 a month.

Refinancing the average 80% LTV, 15-year loan on a site-built home and land, by contrast, would save much more. With an average balance of $118,160, refinancing a site-built's loan from a 9% interest rate to an 8% rate saves $69.26 a month, and refinancing to a 6% rate saves $201.36 a month — nearly five times the potential savings from refinancing the smaller manufactured housing loan.

Because mortgages on manufactured homes are roughly one-fifth the size of conventional loans for site-built homes and land, the manufactured housing loans show much less interest-rate sensitivity. For small manufactured housing loans, monthly savings from refinancing may seem small against the upfront, fixed costs of attorney's fees, title searches, and the like. Prepayments from 1992-93 suggest that prepayment rates on seasoned par manufactured housing loans would rise from 6% to 10% CPR-to-life to 16% to 20% CPR-to-life if rates dropped 300 bp. In contrast, CPR-to-life speeds on conventional par 30-year agency mortgages could rise from 6% CPR to 49% CPR, according to Morgan Stanley prepayment models.

Exhibit 10: Factors Driving Refinancings in Manufactured Housing Loans

		Proportional Prepayment Impact (% CPR)				
		Interest Rates Shift (bp from loan mortgage rate)				
Factor	Factor Levels	0	−50	−100	−200	−300
Refinancing	$18,000 balance (< avg size loan)	6	7	9	12	14
Incentive	$24,000 balance (avg size loan)	6	8	10	13	16
and Loan Size	$30,000 balance (> avg size loan)	6	9	12	14	17
Loan Age	< 24 Months	80% of average life speed				
	> 24 Months	105% of average life speed				
Seasonality	January, February	80% of average life speed				
	Other Months	105% of average life speed				
The	0.8 Million New Home Sales	Slower				
Economy	1.0 Million New Home Sales	Average				
	1.2 Million New Home Sales	Faster				
Lender	More	Raises prepayments				
Competition	Less	Lowers prepayment				

Source: Morgan Stanley

Exhibit 11: Savings from Refinancing

	Loan Size	
Monthly Payment At:	$24,400	$118,160
9% Interest Rate	$247	$1,198
8% Interest Rate	$233	$1,129
7% Interest Rate	$219	$1,062
6% Interest Rate	$205	$997
Monthly Savings From Refinancing A 9% Interest Rate Loan to a:		
8% Interest Rate	$14.30	$69.26
7% Interest Rate	$28.17	$136.41
6% Interest Rate	$41.58	$201.36

Source: Morgan Stanley

Secondary Refinancing Risks

Even in the event of falling interest rates, refinancing risk falls in the first two years of a loan made on a new manufactured home. During these two years, the underlying home typically depreciates, raising its loan-to-value ratio to levels unacceptable to many lenders. Refinancings in the first 24 months of a loan run slowly relative to their long-run average.

Seasonality influences refinancings as well. Refinancings on manufactured housing loans typically fall in January and February to 80% of their annual average. Conventional agency mortgages show the same pattern. Refinancings typically slow in January and February as borrowers recover from year-end holiday spending.

Tertiary Refinancing Risks

The economy and employment also shape prepayment risk. Robust economies with more jobs allow more applicants to build the job histories, credit, and assets to qualify for refinancing or upgrade to another home. A bad economy brings the opposite. Using new single-family home sales as an economic benchmark, an annualized pace of 1.2 million sales has coincided with refinancings running above their long-run average. A 0.8 million sales pace has coincided with speeds running well below their long-run average, and a 1.0 million sales pace typically has kept refinancings at their long-run mean.

Finally, competition among lenders can influence refinancing activity as well. To the extent that lenders get more aggressive either through lower rates or their efforts to inform borrowers of refinancing options, prepayments could become more interest-rate sensitive.

Housing Turnover

For borrowers holding mortgages with below-market rates of interest, housing turnover drives prepayments. Most of that turnover reflects borrowers trading up to larger manufactured housing units or into site-built homes, or moving out of the home to another area altogether.

A handful of factors again predict most of the pattern of turnover:

Primary

- Loan age
- Economic conditions

Secondary

- Seasonality
- Setting for the manufactured home

Exhibit 12 shows the factors driving turnover in manufactured housing loans.

Exhibit 12: Factors Driving Turnover in Manufactured Housing Loans

Factor	Factor Levels	Prepayment Impact
Loan Age	Month 1	3.7% CPR
	Months 2-23	Increases 0.1% CPR a month
	Months 24 and beyond	6.0% CPR
The Economy	0.8 Million New Home Sales	Slower
	1.0 Million New Home Sales	Average
	1.2 Million New Home Sales	Faster
Seasonality	January Low	80% of average annual speed
	July High	120% of average annual speed
Setting	On Borrower-Owned Land	Seasons over 36 Months
	In an MH Park	Seasons over 24 Months

Source: Morgan Stanley

Exhibit 13: 100% MHP

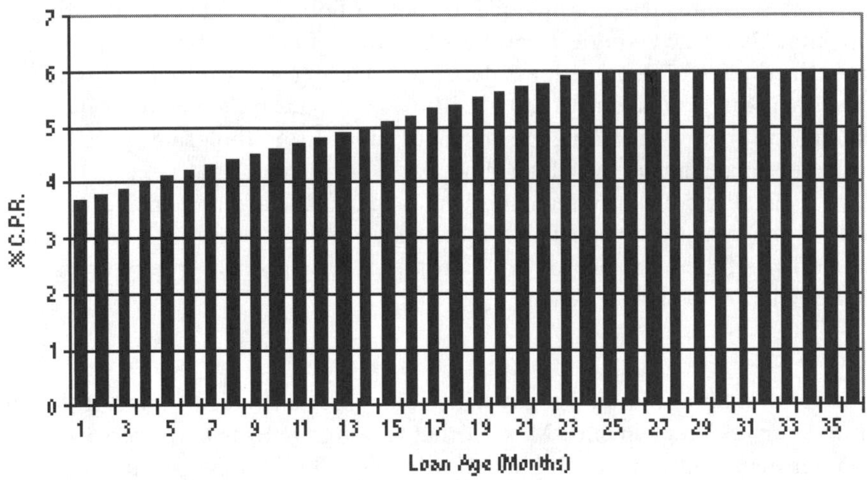

Source: Morgan Stanley

Primary Turnover Risks

As in mortgages on traditional homes, prepayments on manufactured homes rise with age. Some investors have settled on a standard *manufactured housing prepayment* curve (MHP) to describe the rising speeds. The 100% MHP curve starts at 3.7% CPR in the first month after origination and rises 0.1% CPR monthly to 6.0% CPR in the 24th month, remaining constant thereafter. This is depicted in Exhibit 13. Manufactured housing prepayment speeds can be described as multiples of the MHP curve, the same way that other sectors of the mortgage market use the PSA curve. Like the PSA curve, the MHP curve is a yardstick for prepayments rather than a forecast or a predictor. Actual seasoning can differ from 100% MHP due to changing rates of home depreciation, economic conditions, interest rates, and other factors.

The economy can have a significant influence on rates of manufactured housing turnover, beyond its already important impact on refinancing. Robust economies with strong employment tend to draw migration, raising demand for all housing. In addition, improving employment prospects for existing homeowners allow them to move easily and trade up to better homes.

Secondary Turnover Risks

Borrowers' tendency to move at the end of the school year, and with the arrival of summer weather, drives turnover toward an annual high in July, and a low in January. July's pace typically runs at 120% of its annual average, with January coming in at 80%, the same pattern as other mortgages.

The physical location of the manufactured home also helps predict turnover. Homes located on the borrower's own property turnover more slowly than homes in manufactured housing parks. The homes on owned property take roughly 36 months to fully season, rather than the normal 24. Presumably, borrowers located on owned property have a longer-term commitment to living in that area.

Defaults

Defaults constitute a larger component of manufactured housings' prepayments than of prepayments in site-built homes. Defaulted loans eventually become prepayments when the financed property is liquidated and principal returned to the investor. However, they show limited month-to-month variability. In many manufactured housing securitizations, monthly defaults constitute a steady 0.1% to 0.2% of original principal, roughly equivalent to 2% to 3% CPR a year.

CONCLUSION

The recent growth in securitized manufactured housing loans and current investor appetite for less negatively convex securities makes manufactured housing loans an attractive alternative. The small loan size, at least relative to conventional mortgage-backed securities, historically has made borrowers less sensitive to refinancing opportunities. Moreover, credit support in securitized deals has proven to be more than adequate historically, and should continue to cover reasonable credit risk.

Chapter 29

Commercial Mortgage-Backed Securities

Joseph F. DeMichele
Vice President
Conseco Capital Management, Inc.

William J. Adams, CFA
Assistant Vice President
Massachusetts Finance Services

INTRODUCTION

Commercial mortgage-backed securities (CMBS) are collateralized by loans on income-producing properties. The CMBS market has grown dramatically from its modest beginnings in the mid-1980s. Issuance, liquidity, and the number of investors participating in the CMBS market have all increased throughout the 1990s. This chapter gives a brief overview of the history and composition of the CMBS market. It also provides an introduction to the risks involving structure, optionality, and credit quality of CMBS that investors must be aware when allocating assets to this market sector.

HISTORY

During the 1980s, a strong economy, the deregulation of the financial services industry, and preferential tax treatment led to an explosion in the level of capital flows into the commercial real estate markets. Total commercial debt outstanding grew from over $400 billion in 1982 to approximately $1 trillion by 1990. Inevitably, extreme overbuilding caused the bubble to burst, and the boom of the 1980s was followed by a severe recession in the commercial property markets during the early 1990s. From 1990 to 1993, returns on income-producing properties fell by 28% as reported in the NCREIF Property Index.[1]

---

[1] Jonathan Adams, "CMBS Structures and Relative Value Analysis," Chapter 13 in Anand K. Bhattacharya and Frank J. Fabozzi (eds.), *Asset-Backed Securities* (New Hope: Frank J. Fabozzi Associates, 1996).

During the 1980s, the primary sources of commercial real estate funding were tax shelter syndicates, savings institutions, commercial banks, and life insurance companies. The Tax Reform Act of 1986 withdrew many real estate tax benefits and eliminated the tax shelter syndicates as a major source of funds. The severe devaluation of commercial property values in the early 1990s resulted in sizable losses among thrifts, banks, and insurance companies and led to a major retrenchment of lending activity by these traditional sources of commercial real estate funds. Two significant developments were born of this commercial real estate cycle downturn, one major and one minor, which precipitated the securitization of commercial loans.

The biggest contributing factor leading to the maturation of the CMBS market was the creation of the Resolution Trust Corporation (RTC). The RTC was created by Congress to facilitate the bailout of the ailing thrift industry. The mandate handed down from Congress was for the RTC to liquidate assets it acquired from insolvent thrifts as quickly and efficiently as possible. A large portion of the assets inherited by the RTC from the thrifts it acquired consisted of commercial mortgage loans. The RTC turned to the CMBS market to monetize its "investment." Between 1991 and 1993 it issued nearly $15 billion multi-family and mixed property CMBS. The large number of loans in each deal led to a high level of diversification much like what was found in the widely-accepted residential MBS market. The presence of an over-abundant level of credit protection through subordination, often in the form of cash, made the securities very attractive to investors.

The other occurrence, albeit minor, was the introduction of stricter risk-based capital charges for insurance companies at year-end 1993. These guidelines required insurance companies to hold larger capital reserves for whole-loan commercial mortgages than for securitized commercial mortgages, thus incentivising insurance companies to securitize their commercial mortgage holdings.

As can be seen in Exhibit 1, issuance has continued to expand since1993, although the contribution from the RTC has fallen dramatically. As the RTC finished its job of liquidating insolvent thrifts, other issuers opportunistically stepped in to continue the growth of the CMBS market.

Witnessing the success of the RTC's foray into the CMBS market, many insurance companies, pension funds, and commercial banks began to use the CMBS market as a means of restructuring their balance sheets. Institutions began to utilize the CMBS market, as a means of liquidity for disposing of unwanted assets, to receive better regulatory treatment for holding securities in lieu of whole loans, or even simply to raise capital for underwriting more loans. As commercial real estate valuations have rebounded since the last recession, these traditional lenders have stepped up their commercial lending programs and have been a consistent source of issuance in the CMBS market.

The emergence of the commercial mortgage conduits also has fueled the expansion of CMBS issuance. Almost every major investment bank has established a conduit arrangement with a mortgage banker to originate commercial loans for the specific purpose of securitization. The number of commercial mortgage conduits providing real estate funding increased from less than five at the start of 1993 to over 30 at the start of 1995.[2] Conduit issuance has steadily grown as a percentage of total CMBS issuance (see Exhibit 2).

Exhibit 1: Private Label CMBS Issuance: 1987-1997

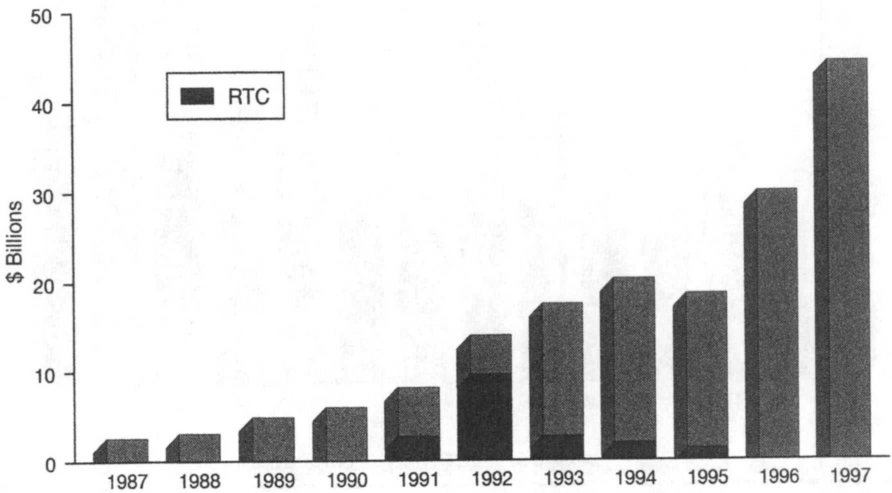

Source: Morgan Stanley, *Commercial Mortgage Alert*, Hoboken, N.J.

Exhibit 2: Conduit Issuance: 1993-1997

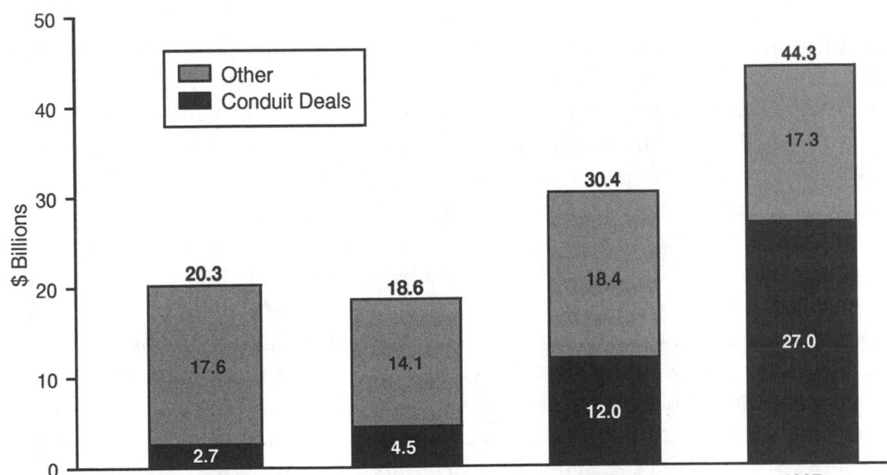

Source: Morgan Stanley, *Commercial Mortgage Alert*, Hoboken, N.J.

[2] John Mulligan and Diane Parsley, *Commercial Mortgage-Backed Securities A Market Update* (New York: Donaldson, Lufkin, and Jenrette Securities Corp., February, 1995).

*Exhibit 3: Multifamily Agency Issuance: 1985-1997**

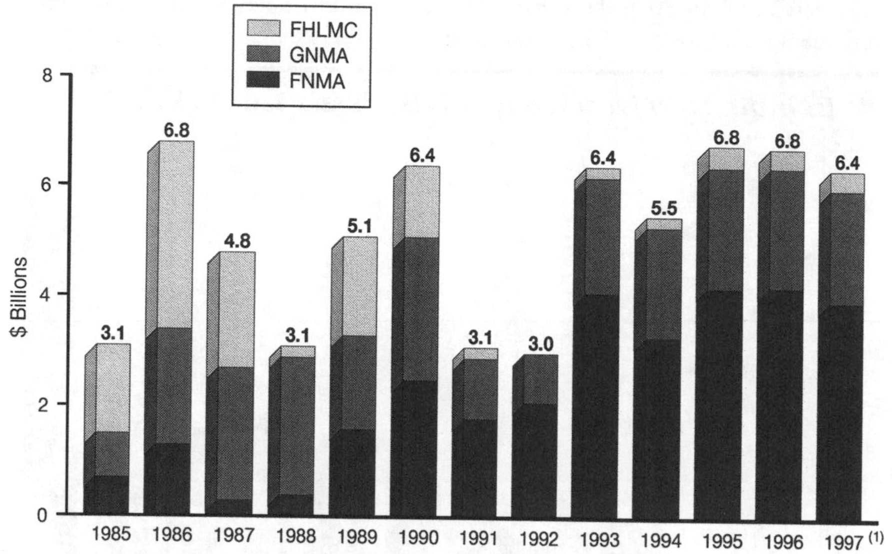

* Through September 1997.

Source: Morgan Stanley, GNMA, FNMA, FHLMC

TYPES OF CMBS IN TODAY'S MARKET

Agency

All three of the government's housing-related agencies (GNMA, FNMA, FHLMC) issue forms of CMBS. Because the mission of each of these agencies is to provide funding for residential housing, they have been involved in the issuance of multi-family housing loan securitizations. GNMA also issues securities backed by loans on nursing home projects and healthcare facilities. All agencies have issued these types of securities since 1985 (see Exhibit 3).

GNMA issues passthrough securities backed by loans on commercial projects insured by the Federal Housing Authority (FHA). GNMA guarantees full and timely payment of principal and interest. Most GNMA project loans are backed by a loan on a single facility, thereby negating any diversification effect that a pool of loans would provide. Any default on the underlying loan would be passed on to the investor as a prepayment. The FHA has established numerous multi-family insurance programs since its inception. Each GNMA project pool will vary depending on the underlying FHA insurance program. Specific characteristics such as project type, loan limit, prepayment features, or the presence of rent subsidies, will affect the performance of a GNMA project pool.

FNMA also has recently increased its activity in the multi-family market. FNMA issues CMBS through two programs. The first is its Alternative Credit

Enhancement Structure (ACES) Program. Private lenders originate loans that qualify for this program. A senior/subordinate structure is used with a FNMA guarantee for payment of principal and interest on the senior portion, usually around 90 percent. The other, more popular FNMA securities, are issued under the Delegated Underwriting and Servicing (DUS) Program. Specific underwriting guidelines are set by FNMA for designated eligible lenders to originate loans. These loans are sold to FNMA, which then issues securities. Pools of one to five loans can be issued. The stringent call provisions have led FNMA to market these securities as substitutes for its bullet-pay agency debentures.

FHLMC issues multi-family securities through its Participation Certificate (PC) Program. The agency purchases qualifying loans and issues PCs in the same manner as its residential PC program. FHLMC was the dominant player of the three agencies before 1990. The commercial real estate recession led to a decrease in issuance from FHLMC. Recently, FHLMC issued a multi-family PC that resembles a larger, more diverse FNMA DUS pool. Backed by over 40 loans of strong credit quality, the pool provides more diversification than a DUS pool. Continued issuance of this type is expected.

Private Label

The majority of CMBS issued today are nonagency or private label securities. Some are collateralized by pools of seasoned commercial loans. The RTC deals were examples of CMBS backed by seasoned collateral. Newly-issued deals backed by seasoned collateral are generally the result of balance sheet restructuring by banks or insurance companies. As the commercial real estate market continues to rebound, the percentage of total issuance collateralized by seasoned loans will further decline. Many seasoned pools are characterized by a wide range of coupons and loan types and by widely varying prepayment protection.

Currently, more private label CMBS are backed by newly originated loans. These CMBS fall into two major categories: those backed by loans made to a single borrower, and those backed by loans made to multiple borrowers. Single borrower deals can involve one property or a group. Single property deals represent a small portion of the CMBS market (17% in 1997 according to *Commercial Mortgage Alert*), and many are done as private placements. Usually, they are backed by large properties such as office buildings or regional malls. Although the transactions obviously lack diversity, information is generally more current and comprehensive. Insurance companies are the most common buyer, since many have the necessary real estate lending expertise to evaluate these deals. The attractiveness of the lower reserving requirement for CMBS over commercial whole loans also entices insurance companies.

Single borrower deals with a variety of properties are more common. Properties are run by a single management company. Real Estate Investment Trusts (REIT) sometimes issue this type of CMBS. Typically all the properties backing a particular deal are *cross-collateralized* and *cross-defaulted*. Should one property in the pool experience an impediment to cash flow, the cash generated from the other properties is used to support it. Should one property experience a default, all the remaining properties are defaulted. This is a strong disincentive against defaulting, preventing the borrower from walking away from lower quality properties. In essence, this feature allows the cash flow from stronger properties to support weaker ones. Another important characteristic of single borrower pools is the presence of release provisions. A *release provision* requires a borrower to prepay a percentage of the remaining balance of the underlying loans if it wishes to prepay one of the loans and remove the property from the pool. Thus the bondholders are protected from the borrower being able to remove the strongest properties from the pool.

The most common type of private label CMBS is backed by loans underwritten by more than one unrelated borrower on various property types. Conduit deals are the most prevalent example of multiple borrower deals in today's market. Because the loans are underwritten with the intent of securitization, conduit deals possess certain characteristics that are favorable to investors. Loan types tend to be more homogeneous, and call protection is strong. They also have more uniform underwriting standards, and information on credit statistics is generally readily available. According to *Commercial Mortgage Alert*, multiple borrower conduit deals represented 83% of all deals as of 1997.

Another kind of CMBS deal found today is one backed by leases on a property. These *triple-net lease* or *credit tenant loan deals* are collateralized by lease agreements between the property owner and a tenant. As long as the lease cannot be terminated, the CMBS created have the same credit as any debt obligation of the underlying tenant. Additionally the bonds are secured by the property. The majority of these securities have been collateralized by mortgages on retail stores with lessees, such as Wal-Mart and Circuit City, who are rated by one of the nationally recognized rating organizations. Recently, mortgages on large office buildings with publicly rated tenants such as Merrill Lynch and Chubb have also been securitized.

STRUCTURE OF CMBS

Senior/Subordinate Structure

The majority of private label CMBS created today utilize a *senior/subordinate structure*, whereby the cash flow generated by the pool of underlying commercial mortgages is used to create distinct classes of securities. Monthly cash flow is first used to pay the class with the highest priority, the senior classes. After interest and scheduled principal is paid to the senior classes, the remaining classes are paid in order of stated priority. Should cash flow collected from the pool be insufficient to pay off the bonds designated senior, the loss will be incurred first by the class with the lowest priority.

Exhibit 4: Hypothetical CMBS Structure

Class	Rating	Size ($MM)	Description	Credit Support (%)	WAL (Years)	Principal Window
A1	AAA	343.00	Senior	32.55	7.00	1/97-7/05
B1	AA	30.60	Mezzanine	26.50	9.70	7/05-8/06
B2	A	30.60	Mezzanine	20.50	9.80	8/06-9/06
B3	BBB	25.50	Mezzanine	15.50	9.90	9/06-10/06
B4	BBB-	12.70	Mezzanine	13.00	9.90	10/06-10/06
B5	BB	30.60	Subordinate	7.00	10.00	10/06-11/06
C	B	17.80	Subordinate	3.50	10.00	11/06-11/06
D	NR	17.77	First Loss	NA	13.70	11/06-11/16
IO	AAA		IO			

In a senior/subordinate structure the lower priority classes provide credit enhancement for the senior securities. The amount of subordination is determined in conjunction with the rating agencies in order to obtain the desired rating on the senior securities. Exhibit 4 shows an example of a hypothetical CMBS structure with subordination levels typical in the market as of the end of 1996. Note that the majority of securities created are senior classes. Subordination levels are set to attain a AAA credit rating on the senior class. This is the highest rating given by the rating agencies, and signifies bonds deemed to have minimal credit risk. Issuers set subordination levels such that the senior classes will receive this rating, thus being more attractive to investors. Rating agencies determine the appropriate amount of credit enhancement based on an analysis of the credit quality of the pool of commercial loans. This will be discussed in more detail later in the chapter.

In industry jargon, those non-senior securities receiving investment grade ratings are known as *mezzanine bonds*. Those rated non-investment grade are known as subordinate or "B" pieces. The class with the lowest payment priority is called the *first loss piece*. Any shortfall of cash flow on the commercial loan pool would affect this class first, thus putting it at the highest risk of a loss of principal. The risk profile of the other classes changes inversely to the priority of payment schedule.

A unique feature of the senior/subordinate structure is the fact that credit enhancement can grow over time. Since principal is paid to the senior classes first, if no losses occur these classes will pay down faster than the mezzanine or subordinate pieces. This has the effect of increasing the amount of non-senior classes as a percentage of the entire deal and thus providing more enhancement to the remaining senior classes.

Additional forms of credit enhancement are available. For some deals, such as the RTC originated transactions, a cash account, known as a *reserve fund*, will be maintained to absorb losses and protect investors. *Overcollateralizing* is another form of credit enhancement. It refers to the excess of the aggregate balance of the pool of commercial loans over the aggregate balance of the bond classes created. Like a reserve fund, losses would be absorbed by the amount of excess collateral before affecting any of the bond classes.

Exhibit 5: Hypothetical CMBS Structure with Sequential Pay

Class	Rating	Size ($MM)	Description	Credit Support (%)	WAL (Years)	Principal Window
A1	AAA	130.00	Senior	32.55	5.70	1/97-7/05
A2	AAA	213.00	Senior	32.55	9.40	7/05-7/06
B1	AA	30.60	Mezzanine	26.50	9.70	7/06-8/06
B2	A	30.60	Mezzanine	20.50	9.80	8/06-9/06
B3	BBB	35.50	Mezzanine	15.50	9.90	9/06-10/06
B4	BBB-	12.70	Mezzanine	13.00	9.90	10/06-10/06
B5	BB	30.60	Subordinate	7.00	10.00	10/06-11/06
C	B	17.80	Subordinate	3.50	10.00	11/06-11/06
D	NR	17.77	First Loss	NA	13.70	11/06-11/06
IO	AAA		IO			

Paydown Structures

The most common principal paydown method used in CMBS is the *sequential-pay method.* All principal paydowns, both scheduled and prepaid, are allocated entirely to the most senior class outstanding. Occasionally, a variant of the sequential-pay structure is used. The pool of loans may be segregated into loan groups with each loan group collateralizing a specific set of bond classes. In either pay down structure, principal payments can be designated further to create different bonds within the same class. In Exhibit 5, we have altered slightly our hypothetical CMBS to illustrate this technique. The senior class has been further tranched to create two bonds, A1 and A2. Principal is allocated to A1 before A2, thus creating two senior bonds with different average lives.

Interest Payments

In a CMBS structure, all interest payments generated by the underlying commercial loans can be used to pay either interest or principal payments on the created securities. One alternative is to have all the interest received used to pay interest on the bonds. The principal weighted-average coupon on the bonds can be set to equal the principal weighted-average coupon on the pool of loans. In this case, as different loans with different coupons in the pool pay down, the principal weighted-average coupon on the pool will change. In turn, the amount of cash flow available to pay interest on the bonds will vary. Thus, the coupons on the bonds will be variable. CMBS classes from this structure are said to have *WAC coupons*.

In order to create fixed coupon bonds, the most common method used in CMBS structures is to set the highest coupon on the securities lower than the lowest coupon of the underlying loans. This will ensure that there will be a sufficient amount of interest payments generated by the pool to make all interest payments on the securities. This will lead to a higher level of interest cash flow from the pool of loans than is required to pay interest on the bonds. This extra cash flow is known as *excess interest.*

In some cases excess interest is used to paydown principal on the most senior bonds outstanding. Under this type of structure the more senior classes will amortize at a rate faster than the junior classes, thus leading to overcollateralization and providing additional credit enhancement for the deal.

More frequently, the excess interest is used to form an *interest-only* or *IO class*. The IO class receives no principal. Its yield is determined solely by the interest cash flow generated by the pool of loans. If the principal balance of a loan is paid prior to its maturity, the yield of the IO will fall. Should a principal payment extend beyond maturity for a loan, the yield will rise.

Underlying Mortgage Type

There are several mortgage loan types that back CMBS deals. The most common are fully amortizing loans, amortizing balloon loans, and interest-only balloons. All else being equal, the faster the amortization of the loan, the faster equity is built up in the property, and the less risk of default. Fully amortizing loans provide the best credit profile. Balloon mortgages also introduce the notion of extension risk, which will be discussed later.

Commercial mortgage loans may have fixed or variable interest rates. If variable rate loans are uncapped, and rates rise substantially, the income generated by the property may not be enough to service the debt. Also, if variable rate mortgages are used to structure CMBS with fixed rate classes, basis risk will exist, and interest on the loans may not cover coupon payments on the bonds.

OPTIONALITY

Prepayment Risk

As with most mortgage-backed securities, CMBS have inherent prepayment risk. The underlying commercial mortgages may be prepaid by the borrower. Prepayments on CMBS will affect the yield and average lives of the bonds issued, particularly interest-only securities. Fortunately for investors, most commercial mortgages have explicit provisions that preclude borrowers from prepaying.

The most onerous to a borrower is the *prepayment lock-out*. Written into the loan agreement, a lock-out is a provision preventing any prepayments for a set time period. The time may vary, but generally will range from three to five years.

Another form of prepayment protection in CMBS structures is called *yield maintenance*. The yield maintenance provision is designed to create a disincentive for the borrower to prepay. If the borrower chooses to prepay, the lender must be compensated for any lost yield. If market interest rates are lower than when the loan was originated, the borrower must reimburse the lender for any lost interest income. The yield maintenance penalty would be equal to the income that would have been earned by the lender less what would now be earned by reinvesting the prepaid proceeds at the risk-free Treasury rate.

A third form of prepayment protection is the prepayment penalty in the case of a prepaid loan. This will typically take the form of a fixed percentage of the remaining principal balance of the loan. The most common penalty in today's market is the "5-4-3-2-1" penalty. During the first year of the penalty period, the prepayment penalty would be equal to 5% of the unpaid principal balance of the loan. In year two, the penalty would decline to 4%, and so on.

Today, most commercial mortgages backing CMBS possess some combination of these three prepayment provisions. However, many loan agreements allow for prepayment penalties to decrease over time with the loans becoming freely prepayable during the last six to nine months of the life of each loan.

During the time that these prepayment provisions are in place, the predominant cause of prepayments will be defaults. After these provisions have expired the prevailing interest rate environment will become a determinant of prepayments as in the residential mortgage market. Other factors, such as retained equity, will affect the level of prepayments. If capital improvements are needed and cheaper financing cannot be found, the owner will most likely prepay the loan in order to refinance. If the property has appreciated sufficiently in value or net operating income has grown enough to cover additional leverage, the owner will most likely do an equity take-out refinancing.

Unfortunately, the amount of data available on prepayments in the CMBS market pales in comparison to the residential mortgage market. Data available are mostly from the RTC deals. Underwriting standards as well as the current real estate market environment are much different today and bring the validity of comparisons on prepayments into question. Additionally, the lack of a dominant, measurable variable such as interest rates makes option analysis much more difficult than with residential mortgage-backed securities. Fortunately, the call protection provided by the various prepayment provisions in CMBS helps to significantly offset these factors.

Extension Risk

The majority of CMBS issued today are collateralized by balloon mortgages. In order to meet the balloon principal payment the borrower will have to either sell the property or refinance the loan. Should neither be possible, the servicer usually has the option to extend the loan beyond the balloon date. The extension option varies but typically cannot exceed three years. Rating agencies generally require the stated final maturity of the bond to be four or five years beyond the maturity of the underlying loans. This would allow time for foreclosure and workout should refinancing be unavailable.

Factors that affect extension risk are loan-to-value (LTV) and the interest rate environment at the balloon date. Should property values fall, LTV will rise, and refinancing will be more difficult, thus increasing extension risk. Likewise, if interest rates are high enough such that the income produced by the property does not generate an acceptable debt service ratio, refinancing may not be obtainable.

EVALUATING CREDIT QUALITY IN COMMERCIAL MORTGAGE-BACKED SECURITIES

As the commercial mortgage-backed securities market continues to grow in both dollar amount and investor acceptance, a move toward an acceptance of standardization appears evident. This may prove to be an alarming trend if investors in these securities are lowering credit standards or reducing their level of analysis in exchange for yield and favorable regulatory treatment. Prudent investors must remember that these securities require a consistent level of credit and cash flow analyses, well beyond that of standardized structured collateral. The best analysis for the securities must combine elements of both structured finance and fundamental collateral and credit analyses. Therefore, in this section, we attempt to build a basic, analytical framework for CMBS transactions, which starts with the previously discussed development and appreciation of the forces which created this market. Next, the inherent volatility and cash flow variability of the underlying commercial mortgages are described. Finally, a means of dealing with the unique characteristics of the collateral, including underwriting standards and structural features, is presented. The point of this section is to focus investor attention on relative value and issues affecting the quality of various CMBS transactions in the market.

Earlier, we discussed the development of liquidity in the CMBS market from direct real estate lending to securitization. Readily available capital for the asset class led to excessive development which culminated in the early 1990s real estate recession. The RTC was created to monetize problem commercial real estate. It did so through structured securities, thereby broadening the investor base and creating many of the structural and legal features of the market today. During this time, a black cloud formed over commercial real estate as an investment. Traditional real estate investors left the market, creating both a liquidity crisis for any new and/or existing financing and an over-supply of additional product due to a reduction in exposure to the asset class. In this void, Wall Street's expertise and capital was required, thereby fueling the CMBS market as we know it today.

The current commercial real estate market combines the two elements described above: the RTC's structure and Wall Street's capital. In the mid-1990s, commercial real estate appears to have recovered from its recent problems. The RTC's role is diminishing to zero, fewer banks and insurers are selling the asset class (in fact, many traditional long-term real estate investors have returned to the market), and, most important, Wall Street's capital remains in the market in the form of conduits. Conduits are now the (re)financing vehicle of choice for real estate owners and developers starved for regular sources of capital. Conduits originate and then securitize real estate loans, rather than maintain the credit risk on their own balance sheet. Typically, conduits take the form of mortgage brokers/bankers backed by an investment bank or commercial banks. Mortgage brokers originate and underwrite commercial mortgages using the capital, warehousing, and distribution channels of the investment bank. A commercial bank provides all such functions, thereby offering it a viable commercial real estate operation, while maintaining significantly lower levels of direct real estate exposure on its balance sheet.

As the CMBS market has evolved, the commercial mortgage market has taken an interesting turn (or return, in this case). With traditional real estate lenders returning to the market along with the capital provided by real estate investment trusts, the highest quality properties (Class A) are rarely available for conduit programs. As such, most commercial real estate underwritten by conduits is average, at best, typically Class B and C quality. Historically, this asset class was the domain of the S&Ls. Wall Street's capital, therefore, is filling a financing void left by the S&Ls, while securitization is transferring risks. These two points are key. It is important to understand the issues and reasons why S&L collateral became RTC collateral and avoid those mistakes again. By structuring commercial real estate mortgages, investors best suited to manage real estate risks are those investors getting paid for it, while investors without the necessary real estate analysis capabilities receive the benefits of the asset class without having to staff a complete real estate operation.

While this brief description of the evolution of commercial real estate lending is clearly simplified, we discuss the nature and role of conduits to raise specific points about evaluating CMBS. This is a highly competitive business involving many constituencies with conflicting interests. The competition is likely causing both spread compression (cheaper capital) and lower quality underwriting standards and/or property quality; these are two inconsistent forces. However, demand for the securities from the investment community remains strong, and, as such, issuance is likely to continue its current rapid pace. Therefore, within this environment, it is even more important to provide a proper framework for credit analysis for CMBS.

THE UNDERLYING COMMERCIAL REAL ESTATE MORTGAGES

If Wall Street's conduit programs have truly replaced S&L's historical financing role, obviously the historical performance of this class of commercial mortgage assets should be assessed when analyzing today's conduit product. However, the lack of historical information on the CMBS market is problematic. The traditional real estate asset is far from standardized, varying significantly by property type, market, transaction, and ownership structure. As such, consistent and standardized historical performance information is not available to the market, and, therefore, credit ratings and valuation decisions are often driven largely by generalizations about the collateral, near-term performance of the assets, and analysis of small, non-uniform portfolio characteristics. While this market is often standardized under the CMBS heading, it is crucial to consider the significant differences amongst the variety of assets found in a pool, as well as the resulting differences in underwriting criteria demanded. Thus, investors will have a better sense of the differences found in today's CMBS pools and the stability of the individual cash flows and valuations.

Multi-Family

Multi-family housing generally is considered to be a more stable real estate investment. Cash flows typically are quite consistent, and valuations are much less volatile than other types of income producing properties, due to the stable demand for rental housing. However, the asset also is tends to be the most commodity-like income-producing property type, making it more susceptible to competitive pressures and rapid changes in supply and demand. Multi-family properties are unique in that they combine elements of both commercial, income-producing real estate, and residential housing. As such, the traditional analysis of commercial real estate (location, property quality, market dynamics, etc.) is an important consideration for the properties, while the impact of its residential characteristics also needs to be recognized.

The primary difference between multi-family properties and other types of income-producing properties involves the lease term of the typical tenant, and the diversification provided by the large number of available units for rent relative to office or retail space. Residents in multi-family properties are obligated on short-term leases, ranging from six months to two years. This is a positive characteristic of the projects in that it permits the property to adjust quickly to improving market conditions, and also provides owners with regular opportunities to pass through increased operating costs. However, the inverse is also true, as multi-family properties are susceptible to increased supply or competitive pressures and weakening economic or demographic trends within market. This is especially true in strong multi-family markets, as the barriers to entry are low enough for multi-family developers to quickly bring supply into any given market.

These characteristics demand an understanding of key housing trends in the local geographic areas, and the age and condition of the individual property, as well as its ability to remain competitive within its market. Property owners and underwriters must allocate money for maintenance spending. Absent such upkeep, apartments can quickly deteriorate and show significant underperformance of cash flows. Also, consider historical performance of the market (boom/bust versus conservative capital allocation) as well as the outlook for markets in which the pool is heavily weighted. One year's operating performance is the typical underwriting period for multi-family properties, often completed with little sense of the past or expected market conditions going forward.

Retail/Shopping Center

Retail real estate ranges from large super-regional malls to smaller neighborhood shopping centers. As implied by the names, this space is differentiated by its size.

Regional and super-regional malls are typically enclosed structures, ranging from 500,000 square feet to upwards of 3 million square feet. These properties generally are well-known, high quality shopping centers within the property's given market and surrounding area. The malls are anchored by nationally-recognized department stores and retail tenants, and maintain significant fill-in, small shop space. The assets are primarily the domain of long-term, direct real estate investors (such as insurers or pension funds) or equity REITs, and are rarely found in pooled CMBS transactions; those assets in the CMBS market primarily are in the form of single asset transactions. Given the unique positioning and retail exposure of most large malls, as well as high barriers to entry, cash flows are often quite stable for this asset class.

Community and neighborhood shopping centers are more likely to be found in today's conduit transactions, and these properties' cash flows can prove to be more volatile. The properties are usually an open-air format, ranging in size from under 100,000 square feet to 500,000 square feet, serving a smaller market area than the larger malls. The properties often are anchored by necessity-based retailers, such as national and regional discount chains, grocery markets and drug stores. Smaller centers are sometimes unanchored. The anchors serve as a drawing point for customer traffic to the smaller, in-line stores, which also are often characterized by necessity shopping and convenience (banks, dry cleaners, video rental, small restaurants, for instance). The properties are standardized, nondescript neighborhood convenience centers, which implies that an accessible location is a key valuation feature. Also, the properties are susceptible to competition and new development, so regular maintenance spending is important in keeping the centers competitive.

When evaluating retail real estate, an investor should consider the following: the age and quality of the property, the presence and quality of anchors tenants in the center, location and accessibility, sales volume on a square foot basis, competitive development, sales trends, and occupancy costs in relation to sales volumes. Recognize the excessive growth in retail real estate space over the past ten years. According to some national surveys, the growth of retail space in the United States over the past decade increased almost 40%, exceeding annualized population growth by more than a full percentage point. Certainly, some space has been removed from service over this time as well. However, the growth trends remain striking. Of particular interest for conduit investors is the above-average growth of neighborhood and community centers. As stated earlier, retail exposure in today's conduit transactions is typically neighborhood and community centers in the Class B and Class C quality range.

Office

Office space is a unique component of the commercial real estate market. Office buildings comprise over 25% of real estate space in the United States, but the exposure is highly fragmented and diverse. Significant differences between various classes of space exist, ranging from renowned Class A landmarks to poorly located, aging Class C space in need of both deferred maintenance spending and capital improvements. Properties are also classified by location, ranging from the central business district (CBD) to suburban space. CBD settings are tightly grouped on small parcels of land, typically representing the "downtown" business districts of the representative market. Suburban space, on the other hand, is more widely dispersed on larger areas of land often grouped in the business park setting. During the past decade nearly 70% of office space constructed in the United States was built in a suburban setting, due in part to cheaper construction and lower priced land costs, as well as the continued "suburbanization" of corporate America. These facts along with excellent, decentralized distribution locations will likely keep suburban office space competitive over the long term.

The office sector also presents unique credit issues to analyze. The sector experienced significant overbuilding in the 1980s and also proved susceptible to corporate downsizing. Rental rates are extremely volatile and occupancy levels can swing dramatically. The properties typically are subject to longer-term leases and require significant spending for maintenance and improvements, tenant build-outs, and leasing commissions. Information regarding lease rollover schedules, tenant quality and retention rates, down time between leases, and rental stream forecasting (effective rent versus straight line rents in periods of free rent and over/under market rent conditions) are necessary to understand the performance of office properties. Future market conditions are also important to consider, since markets can change dramatically with the addition of new, large projects. Given this cash flow volatility, both investors and rating agencies continue to demand strong debt service coverage ratios and adequate credit enhancement for office properties within conduit pools.

Other Operating Properties

Recent CMBS transactions are beginning to include other non-traditional real estate investments, characterized by higher cash flow volatility, as well as an operating/business component. Hotels, for instance, continue to represent a growing component of transactions, as do self-storage centers and health care facilities. While a detailed description of these commercial assets is not appropriate for this analysis, some description of the issues affecting property quality and volatility is important. These properties maintain a high correlation with the macro-economic forces shaping property performance, are very susceptible to increased competition and supply, and possess high operating leverage. Volatility of the cash flows can be as high as 30% to 50%, from peak to trough; therefore, rating agencies and investors demand higher underwriting standards and credit enhancement for these assets. Additionally, the operating business component results in volatile income due to typical real estate forces affecting commercial properties, but also as a result of management's ability to operate and maintain the property's competitiveness.

UNDERWRITING CRITERIA

One method analysts use to evaluate cash flow volatility among different property types and property qualities is mortgage underwriting standards. Clearly, the credit quality of any commercial mortgage pool is determined by the underlying collateral's ability to function as an income producing, debt servicing property over a defined time period. Several financial ratios are available for determining the credit quality of the property, including a ratio of cash flow to the required debt service (DSC) and a ratio of the mortgage loan amount to the value of the property (loan to value or LTV).

In many ways, debt service coverage is a more important credit analysis tool available for real estate securities than is valuation. This cash flow ratio compares a property's net operating income (NOI) to its required debt service payments, with NOI defined as income less property operating expenses and an allowance for maintenance capital spending or replacement reserves. Typically, NOI also will include other recurring expense items demanded by an individual property, such as leasing commissions for retail properties or tenant buildout costs for office properties. The data are often calculated on a trailing 12-month basis. However, shorter reporting periods are annualized or longer reporting periods averaged. Whatever the case, a true picture of normalized operating performance is required to understand the property's ability to service its debt load. More often than not, a reporting period may overstate NOI due to above-market leases, stronger than expected occupancy levels, or leasing commissions/tenant buildout costs not commensurate with the existing lease rollover schedule. In such a case, it is imperative to normalize operating cash flow, and consider its impact on the credit profile of the individual property or collateral pool.

The credit rating agencies attempt to quantify the process of normalizing cash flow by reporting the agency's variance figure. Expressed on a percentage basis, the variance figure calculates the rating agency's re-underwritten (or normalized) cash flow figure relative to the cash flow reported by the mortgage originators. Recently, the rating agencies have "haircut" reported NOI for a variety of reasons, including above-market rents and occupancy levels, below-market mortgage interest rates, normalized amortization, management fees, tenant buildout costs, leasing commissions, replacement reserves, and deferred maintenance. Potentially volatile cash flows derived from a property or the pool must be accounted for in the initial valuation of the CMBS transaction. Additionally, when armed with both underwritten and normalized NOI, investors can determine the appropriate level of DSC for a given property or pool to account for volatility in the cash flows and its ability to service debt. This figure can be as low as 1.1× to 1.15× for stable properties with a positive outlook to 1.6× to 1.7× for properties subject to highly volatile cash flows.

Loan to value is another analytical tool used to compare the property's debt level to its current valuation, as well as its loan balance at maturity. While third-party appraisals are used in this process, which are subject to significant interpretation, a general sense of a property's or pool's loan to value ratio allows one to address refinancing risks. Clearly, lenders and investors should require equity, in line with the property's quality and cash flow volatility. Equally important is an acceptable level of debt amortization over the life of the loan. In doing so, investors protect themselves from shifts in valuation, whether driven by true changes in cash flows or the required rate of return demanded for the asset class. The equity portion of a property's capitalization also tends to incent property owners to properly maintain the asset. Finally, investors protect themselves at maturity by reducing the LTV ratio over the life of the loan through amortization, thereby increasing the likelihood of refinancing the property when the loan is due. If refinancing at maturity is unlikely, then investors must factor in principal shortfalls or extension risks. To repeat, standards for LTV ratios vary by property type with stable multi-family units pressing the 75% level and riskier hotels or offices sometimes as low as 50% to 55%.

Portfolio Issues

CMBS investors also must focus on a number of portfolio issues, especially those involving the composition of the total collateral pool. The benefits of the CMBS structure derive from an ability to make real estate investments without the risks associated with direct mortgage or equity placements (i.e., diversification by property type, loan size and type, geography, borrower, and tenant). As discussed, diversification by property type should be evident, as a well-mixed pool clearly will overcome the cash flow volatility of any one property type. Geographic diversification is also important, because commercial real estate performance is a function of local and regional economics, demographics, and employment conditions. Higher state concentrations increase the correlation amongst properties, thus offsetting the benefits of diversification. Loan size and borrower/tenant concentration are also important features of a well-diversified mortgage pool, as greater loan diversity by size or borrower diminishes investor reliance upon and exposure to any one property, set of properties, or individual borrower or tenant performance.

STRUCTURING — TRANSFERRING RISKS AND RETURNS

We have attempted to provide a continuum of stability amongst the various property types typically found in today's CMBS transactions, as well as the resulting underwriting issues created by cash flow variability. As discussed, the standard structure in today's conduit deals is a senior/subordinate structure which transfers significant risk to the underlying equity and support bonds. This risk is typically borne by the master or special servicers or some other real estate professionals, which will be discussed in more detail later. On a portfolio level, these issues are manifested by the level of credit enhancement demanded by the rating agencies for any given rating category. Therefore, one must recognize that varying levels of credit enhancement and the subsequent differences in valuation from one security to the next represent the ratings agencies' and investment community's attempt to cope with the cash flow and valuation variability of the underlying collateral. As such, excessive credit enhancement for a pool is not necessarily a good investment characteristic, but could indicate high expected cash flow volatility and/or poor property quality.

Compare standardized residential mortgage pools requiring 6% to 8% credit support at the AAA level, versus 28% to 34% credit support often found in commercial mortgage pools. The CMBS level of credit support is designed specifically to recognize the lack of standardization of the underlying collateral, cash flow volatility, and the higher default frequency and loss severity on commercial mortgage securities. As stated, some commercial properties require DSC ratios as high as 1.6× to 1.7×, indicating cash flow variability in excess of 40%. The property's ability to service its debt load is driven by any number of controllable and non-controllable factors. Residential housing, on the other hand, is owned by its occupants and holds a much more meaningful position to its occupants, other than holding a put option on the property. As such, volatility is significantly higher for commercial mortgages, and the level of credit support required to protect senior investors is more substantial.

Default frequency and loss severity are also important issues to consider when investing in commercial mortgage securities. Typically, individual assets are structured in bankruptcy-remote entities or some other type of isolation from third-party bankruptcy risks. Therefore, there is no recourse to the borrower's assets beyond the equity in the property. While low LTV ratios alleviate some risks in this scenario, maintaining equity value when a commercial mortgage has reached the point of default is often futile. Often, property level cash flows have fallen, and, for properties underwritten with a low DSC ratio, debt service requirements may exceed cash flow. Additionally, property cash flow problems which are driven by macro-economic issues (over-building or weakening economic conditions, for instance) will have a substantial impact on valuations. In this environment, equity withers and properties that do not cover debt service become uneconomical. Borrowers without a contractual obligation, incentive and/or an ability to fund losses are forced to default, and the decision to do so is certainly easier than that of a residential mortgage.

Loss severity on the typical commercial real estate default is also impacted in this scenario and is often higher than residential mortgage losses. Valuation drops as the property's performance weakens. However, this loss is exacerbated by market forces which demand either higher rates of return on the asset class and/or stronger equity coverage (i.e., more mortgage losses on the original loan balance). Finally, the costs of liquidating commercial mortgages exceeds those of residential mortgages. The assets are large and unique, and often in need of capital improvements or deferred maintenance. The investor population is smaller, more sophisticated and specialized, while there are costs associated with the property (taxes, insurance, etc.) that must be carried often for extended marketing periods. As such, loss severities approaching 60% or 70% are not unreasonable. Clearly, for this asset class, the original cash flows, debt service coverage, and loan to value ratios are the mitigant to these risks, and, therefore, must be thoroughly analyzed and understood when the transactions are originated.

Master and Special Servicers

A final important structural feature of CMBS transactions is the presence of both master and special servicers. Master servicers manage the routine, day-to-day administration functions required by all structured securities or collateralized transactions, while special servicers are used to handle delinquent loans and work-out situations. Assigned the task of maximizing the recovery on a defaulted loan, special servicers play an important role in CMBS transactions as both defaults and work-outs are frequent and specialized. Often, the servicer's interests are aligned with investors as servicers are now investing in non-rated and subordinate bonds within the deals they service. Thus, it is important to assess the quality and competency of the servicer. Investors should consider the level of latitude and advancing capabilities provided the servicer in a work-out situation, its financial condition, historical performance and experience within the commercial real estate asset class (and in work-out situations, if applicable), and the monitoring, reporting and servicing capabilities (including cash management and collections operations). Investors must be comfortable with the servicer's ability to function effectively in that role, as well as the outlook for the servicer's continued viability.

Regulatory Issues

Increasingly, CMBS have been afforded favorable regulatory treatment. The National Association of Insurance Commissioners (NAIC) recognizes CMBS as securities rather than real estate. This allows for a capital reserve requirement ranging from 0.03% to 1.0% for investment grade fixed-income securities compared with 3.0% for commercial mortgages. Bank regulators currently are considering lowering the risk-based capital weighting on AAA rated CMBS to 20%. Currently, the risk weighting is 100%. The Department of Labor also is continuing to study the possibility of granting an ERISA exemption to CMBS. Should this change occur, ERISA-guided pension plans would be able to purchase investment grade CMBS. Clearly, the growing CMBS market would benefit from these new investors, as new capital would support the securities, increase coverage and improve liquidity.

CONCLUSION

In this chapter, we presented an overview of the development of the CMBS market and a discussion of the current issues facing investors today. Commercial real estate lending is evolving into sophisticated, structured securities that represent a growing portion of the fixed income market. Despite trading under the general CMBS heading, the securities and the underlying collateral are specialized and unique, thereby presenting investors with new challenges, as well as potentially higher return. As pointed out, the securities must be recognized for the individual characteristics which differentiate them, thereby demanding prudent analysis. If recent issuance is any indication, this market should continue to expand, and new investors will continue to enter the market. With the continued expansion of available securities and investors, as well as new performance data, the market likely will differentiate the securities by quality. This chapter presents an introduction to those issues and security types which affect the quality of CMBS transactions and the market's investment potential going forward.

Chapter 30

Understanding Prepayments in CMBS Deals

Da Cheng
Development Associate
Wall Street Analytics, Inc.

Adrian R. Cooper, Ph.D.
Vice President
Wall Street Analytics, Inc.

Jason Huang
Structuring Associate
Wall Street Analytics, Inc.

INTRODUCTION

One of the most important and least understood aspects of CMBS deals is their behavior under prepayments. In residential deals the bondholders are protected against prepayments solely by the cash flow distribution structure. For commercial deals, call protection at the loan level leads to a greater cash flow certainty, and this has led some investors to grossly misprice CMBS tranches by ignoring the allocation of prepayment risk. Within a rising rate environment, which is often coupled with a booming real estate market, a thorough analysis of the prepayment risks become especially important.

The prepayment protection in commercial deals comes from both the call protection available at the loan level, and also from the CMBS structure. The call protection is provided by a combination of prepayment lockouts, prepayment penalties, and yield maintenance, so it is important to understand the way that these interact with the structure of the deal. The purpose of this chapter is to provide a comprehensive catalog of the methods commonly used for prepayment protection in CMBS deals.

LOCKOUTS AND PREPAYMENT PENALTIES

The simplest method of affording call protection is to require that for some period after the loan is originated, no prepayments be allowed to occur. This is known as a *lockout*, and has the advantage that it is simple to model and provides complete protection against prepayments. A lockout typically only covers the first few years of a loan, and CMBS deals that use them almost invariably combine them with at least one other method.

The next simplest form of call protection is a *prepayment penalty.* This represents an additional penalty that the borrower must pay when he chooses to prepay the loan. It is expressed as a percentage of the prepayment amount, and generally declines over time. Prepayment premiums are often substantial, and may be used in conjunction with lockouts. A commonly used schedule is shown in Exhibit 1.

In a typical CMBS deal, the prepayment penalties will be distributed separately from other funds. The rules by which they are allocated are obviously crucial for assessing the risk exposure of various bonds. There is a common misconception amongst investors that prepayment premiums are a relatively ineffective means of providing call protection. However, as we will see below, in a rising rate environment they may significantly outperform yield maintenance.

YIELD MAINTENANCE

In addition to lockouts and prepayment premiums, most CMBS deals also use a far more complex form of call protection. This is known as *yield maintenance* (YM), and perhaps represents the most misunderstood aspect of commercial deals. At the current time there is a peculiar stratification of the CMBS marketplace. On the one hand, since yield maintenance is generally too complex to be modeled on spreadsheets, many buyers are forced to ignore it. Those with more sophisticated systems, however, are able to correctly price even the most volatile tranches, giving them a significant investing advantage. More surprisingly, perhaps, even issuers are finding that their in-house systems are able to handle only the simplest methods of yield maintenance. In fact, one major investment bank was recently embarrassed when they discovered that the language in their prospectus didn't agree with their own yield maintenance model. At this point — long after issuing the deal — they were forced to invent a new type of yield maintenance to match the prospectus, and to acquire a new analytical system that allowed them to model it.

Exhibit 1: Commonly Used Prepayment Penalty Schedule

Year after lockout	Prepayment Penalty
1	5% of prepayment amount
2	4%
3	3%
4	2%
5	1%
6 and after	no penalty

Yield Maintenance Defined

The basic concept behind yield maintenance is quite simple: When a borrower prepays his loan, he must pay the lender an additional *yield maintenance charge* (or *make-whole charge*). The amount of the charge is calculated so that the lender becomes indifferent to prepayments. So the question is, what is a fair compensation to the lender for receiving a prepayment?

To illustrate this point, imagine that we make a loan in January with a maturity date in May. The first couple of months go by without event and we receive our principal and interest payments as scheduled. Suddenly in March the borrower informs us that he wishes to prepay. How much should we charge him for this privilege? A fair approach would be to require that the total check that we receive in March be equal to the value of all the remaining payments we were due to receive in order to "make us whole." In other words, he must pay us a yield maintenance charge given by

YM charge = Value of future scheduled payments – Amount prepaid

Our intention is that by reinvesting the prepayment amount and the yield maintenance charge, we could reproduce the future cash flow that we'd been scheduled to receive from the original bond. At this level, the concept of yield maintenance is very simple. The complexity comes from determining exactly how the value of future scheduled payments should be computed, or equivalently from deciding how the prepayment proceeds can be reinvested. In the following sections we shall explore the rather daunting variety of yield maintenance methods in the marketplace today. These have generally evolved from differing assumptions about the available reinvestment options, although some of their variants have arisen as mere historical accidents.

Having decided on the YM penalty that should be paid by the borrower, a further complication arises when we realize that the prepaying loan is part of a CMBS deal. Even after the YM charge has been computed, the question remains as to how it should be distributed amongst the bondholders. We shall discuss the various allocation methods that are currently used, and describe in particular how *bond yield maintenance* is used to make whole the individual tranche holders.

The Importance of Analyzing Yield Maintenance

Before discussing the details of yield maintenance, we give a brief example of the magnitude of its effects. These will generally be most significant for an IO strip. To illustrate this, we take an actual CMBS deal and plot the yield of the IO against prepayment speed both with and without the effects of yield maintenance. The results are shown in Exhibit 2.

It is important to stress that the beneficial effects to the bondholder of yield maintenance may be either less than or greater than those of a simple prepayment lockout, depending on the precise form of YM used and the scenario under consideration.

Exhibit 2: Class I-1 Pre-Tax CBE Yield Without and With Yield Maintenance*

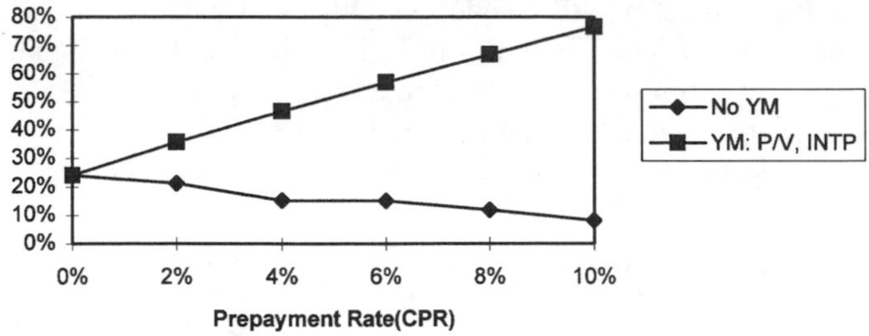

* From Mortgage Capital Funding, Inc., Multifamily/Commercial Mortgage Pass-Through Certificates, Series 1994-MC1

COLLATERAL YIELD MAINTENANCE

In the following, as is typical in CMBS deals, we assume that when a loan prepays it prepays completely, so that *prepaid amount* is equal to the outstanding balance of the loan at the date of prepayment. It is a simple matter to allow partial prepayment of loans instead. The basic philosophy behind all the methods is to compare the value of the cash flow that would have occurred in absence of prepayments to the value of the cash flow after the prepayment has occurred. Although the details of many of the methods may seem rather convoluted and artificial, they have all been used in actual CMBS transactions, and so must be understood and modeled by anyone wishing to accurately price commercial deals.

The Simple Model

The most straightforward form of yield maintenance (generally referred to as the *simple model*) estimates the value of future scheduled cash flows by adding up future scheduled payments. The YM charge then becomes

$$\sum \text{Future scheduled payments} - \text{Prepaid amount}$$

or equivalently

$$\sum \text{Future scheduled interest payments}$$

The lender in this case will clearly be overcompensated since there is no discounting of the future value of cash flows. For this reason it is not commonly used in today's deals.

The Bullet Model

A slightly more complex variant of the previous method is the *bullet model*. For this, the YM charge is given by

$$\text{Prepaid amount} \times \text{Remaining term} \times (\text{Loan coupon} - \text{YM coupon})$$

where *loan coupon* represents the coupon of the loan at origination, and *YM coupon* is a prevailing interest rate at the prepayment date. The interpretation behind this is that at the date of prepayment we pretend that the loan represented a single bullet that would come due on its maturity date, and in the meantime paid interest at the *loan coupon* rate. We next assume that the prepaid amount can be invested in a similar bullet bond, bought at par, and paying interest at YM coupon. As in the case of the simple model, we ignore discounting and take the difference between the two cash streams to give the *YM charge*.

The bullet method ignores both the loan amortization and the discounting of future cash flows. For loans with a short balloon period, this assumption will be less inaccurate.

The Single Discount Factor Model

The *single discount factor model* is a little more sophisticated and gives the YM charge as

$$\sum_t \frac{\text{Future scheduled payment}_t}{(1 + \text{YM yield})^t} - \text{Prepaid amount}$$

where the summation index t represents the number of months after the prepayment date. The model computes the net present value of the future scheduled cash flows discounted back at a constant rate of *YM yield*. This rate will typically be chosen as the yield of a Treasury of comparable maturity, plus some hand-picked spread. If there were no spread, then the YM charge would allow the lender to exactly reproduce the future scheduled cash flow with a risk-free Treasury portfolio, which is clearly an overcompensation.

The Multiple Discount Factor Model

The *multiple discount factor model* is similar to the single discount factor model, but the discounting of future cash flows is taken with respect to the Treasury spot curve and gives the YM charge as:

$$\sum_t \frac{\text{Future scheduled payment}}{(1 + \text{Treasury spot rate}_t + \text{YM spread})^t} - \text{Prepaid amount}$$

Again the summation index t represents the number of months after the prepayment date.

With *YM spread* set to zero, this model is known as *Treasury flat yield maintenance*, and provides a sufficient charge for the lender to reproduce the future scheduled cash flow by purchasing a Treasury portfolio. This is clearly an overcompensation, since a Treasury portfolio would be risk free. With a non-zero value of YM spread, the charge would be sufficient to allow the lender to reproduce the scheduled cash flow by purchasing a portfolio of investments with a spread *YM spread* over the Treasury curve. Its value is therefore chosen to represent the expected spread of bonds with a similar risk profile to the original loan. With YM spread of 150 basis points, this model is generally known as a "T+150" yield maintenance premium.

In many ways this model represents the most sensible definition of yield maintenance, and the others described here can be thought of as approximations to it.

The Interest Difference Model

For the interest difference model, the YM charge is given as the present value of the difference between the scheduled interest payments, and the scheduled interest payments that would have been due with the same amortization schedule but with the coupon of the loan replaced by the coupon of a Treasury bond of comparable maturity. More precisely it is

$$\sum_t \frac{\text{Scheduled interest}_t - \text{Scheduled interest at YM yield}_t}{(1 + \text{Treasury spot rate}_t)^t}$$

where *YM yield* is chosen as the yield of a Treasury bond of comparable maturity to the loan, plus a possible hand-picked spread. The justifying assumption behind this approach is that upon receiving the prepayment, the lender can reissue bonds with an identical amortization schedule. The (fixed) coupon of these new loans will equal some spread over a comparable Treasury. The difference between the present value of the two cash flows produces the YM charge.

As a slight variant of this method, YM yield is occasionally based upon the yield of a Treasury bond whose maturity is comparable to the remaining average life of the loan at the prepayment date, rather than its remaining term. In another variation, the Treasury spot rate in the denominator is replaced by a single discount factor.

The Truncated Interest Difference Model

Unfortunately, the preceding model has spawned a rather confusing mutation in which the YM charge is given by

$$\sum_t \frac{\text{Max}(\text{Scheduled interest}_t - \text{Prepaid amount}_t \times \text{YM yield}, 0)}{(1 + \text{YM yield})^t}$$

where again YM yield is chosen as the yield of a Treasury bond of comparable maturity to the loan, plus a possible hand-picked spread. Roughly speaking, the assumption behind this is that the prepayment can be reinvested in a non-amortizing bond that pays YM yield for some period of time (however, the duration of this period has no sensible interpretation). The resulting cash flows are discounted at a single rate of YM yield.

Exhibit 3: Different YM Allocation Rules

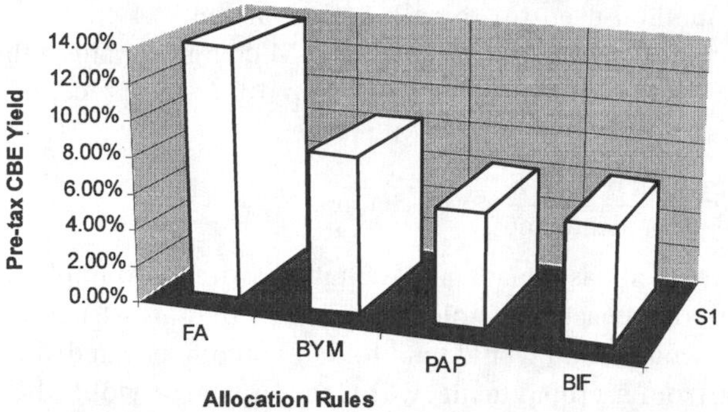

This IO certificate is part of the Nationslink Funding Corporation, Commercial Mortgage Pass-Through Certificates, Series 1996-1. Its price is 3% excluding accrued interests. All mortgage loans balloon 60 month from the cut-off date.

FA	Full Allocation of yield maintenance to IO certificate
BYM	Bond Yield Maintenance method
PAP	Principal Allocation method
BIF	Base Interest Fraction method

Source: Statistical results generated by the Structured Financing Workstation by Wall Street Analytics, Inc.

Yield Maintenance Floors

For most of the methods described above, the YM charges will decrease in a rising interest rate environment. In order to provide additional protection to lenders, they are often supplemented with *yield maintenance floors*. These impose a minimum value for the YM charge as follows:

$$\text{YM charge} = \text{Max (Raw YM charge, Prepaid amount} \times \text{YM floor rate)}$$

where *Raw YM charge* represents the charge before the floor is taken into account.

ALLOCATION OF YIELD MAINTENANCE CHARGES

In the previous sections we have discussed various methods of implementing Yield maintenance on the collateral side. It is now necessary to consider how the resulting YM charges will be allocated amongst the bondholders of a CMBS deal.

It is important to realize that under many circumstances although the YM charge is computed so as to protect the whole loan against prepayments, it may be insufficient to protect all of the bonds. In other words the sum of the make-whole amounts for the bonds will not equal the make-whole amount for the collateral. Given this discrepancy, it is obviously extremely important to model the allocation of the YM charges completely. To further illustrate this point, Exhibit 3 shows how switching between some commonly used allocation methods may dramatically affect the yield of a bond.

The Principal Allocation Percentage Method

The simplest method used for the allocation of the YM charge is the *principal allocation percentage method.* For this, the YM charge is paid to the bonds in proportion to the amount of prepayment principal that they receive. Specifically, a bond X receives as its share of the YM charge

$$\frac{\text{Prepayment paid to } X}{\text{Total prepaid amount}} \times \text{YM charge}$$

This method has the advantage that it is simple to implement, although it tends to undercompensate the holders of bonds that are structurally locked out. Moreover, a discount bond would tend to be overcompensated since it would generally benefit from a prepayment, while the converse would be true of a bond bought at a premium. As an extreme example of this consider the case of a PO strip. If the entire collateral prepaid one month after the deal had been issued, then the PO holder would obviously be delighted. There is obviously no reason to compensate him further with a portion of the YM charge.

The Base Interest Method

The base interest method provides a far more complex, though somewhat arbitrary, means of distributing the YM charge. When a mortgage M prepays, the amount of the YM charge distributed to a bond X is given by

$$\frac{(\text{Principal paid to } X)}{(\text{Total principal paid})} \times \frac{\text{Max}(\text{Coupon of } X - \text{YM coupon}, 0)}{\text{Net coupon of } M - \text{YM coupon}} \times \text{YM charge}$$

with all excess YM charge being distributed to the IO strip.

This method has an advantage over the previous method in that it treats premium and discount bonds more fairly. In particular, a PO strip will receive no portion of the YM charge. A complete analysis of the deal would be required to tell whether a particular bond was fairly compensated.

Bond Yield Maintenance Method

Perhaps the most logical method for allocating the YM charge is to use *bond yield maintenance.* This is somewhat analogous to the process of calculating collateral yield maintenance. The concept is that a bondholder should be "made whole" for the disruption in cash flow that he suffers for receiving a prepayment. For a particular bond, the fair value for this is

$$\text{Bond YM amount} = \sum_t \frac{\text{Scheduled bond payment}_t - \text{Actual bond payment}_t}{(1 + \text{Bond YM yield})^t}$$

where *Scheduled bond payment*$_t$ represents the total payment that the bond would receive at time t if the prepayment had not occurred, and *Actual bond payment*$_t$ is the total payment that the bond would receive at time t after taking into account the effects of the prepayment (but ignoring any YM distributions). *Bond YM yield* is set equal to the Treasury spot rate for a maturity comparable to the bond, plus a spread. This spread may be the same as the current bond spread at the time of prepayment. Alternatively, if it is expected that the bond will be upgraded, a lesser spread might be used. (This will generate a higher bond YM amount, which is obviously reasonable if the bond has become more valuable.)

As an extension to this method, if the prepayment has the effect of changing the bond's risk profile, then different discount spreads may be used for computing the two present values. In other words,

$$\text{Bond YM amount} = \sum_t \frac{\text{Scheduled bond payment}_t}{(1 + \text{Bond YM yield}_1)^t} - \frac{\text{Actual bond payment}_t}{(1 + \text{Bond YM yield}_2)^t}$$

where *Bond YM yield*$_1$ is the Treasury rate corresponding to the scheduled maturity (or average life) of the bond, plus a spread appropriate to the scheduled term and risk profile. Similarly, *Bond YM yield*$_2$ is the Treasury rate corresponding to the scheduled maturity of the bond after taking into account the prepayment, plus a spread appropriate to this term and risk profile. The exact values of these spreads will be negotiated between issuer and buyer.

The bond YM amount computed above would give the bondholder a fair compensation for receiving a prepayment. However, as we have mentioned before, there is no guarantee that the total YM charge collected from the borrowers will be sufficient to pay each of the bondholders their fair bond YM amount. Instead, a bond *X* will receive as its share of the YM charge an amount equal to

$$\frac{\text{Bond YM amount for } X}{\sum_{\text{all tranches}} \text{Bond YM amounts}} \times \text{YM charge}$$

This is effectively the "best that we can do" with the available YM charge.

From a purely practical standpoint, the correct modeling of bond yield maintenance can prove extremely difficult. For a scenario with n prepayments, the deal must be run n+1 separate times. However, a good structuring or modeling tool should be able to perform these calculations automatically.

Defeasance

For completeness, we should also mention the most precise form of call protection. This is known as *defeasance*. From the point of view of the borrower, it is equivalent to Treasury-flat yield maintenance. However, the proceeds generated from the YM charges are not distributed directly to the bondholders, but are instead invested by the servicer in a Treasury portfolio. By design, this generates the same future cash flows that would have been obtained in absence of prepayments, and these are distributed to the bondholders as if no prepayments had occurred. This has the advantage of imposing no extra taxes due to the distribution of YM charges, and also maintains a higher level of credit on the remaining assets.

SPECIAL CONSIDERATIONS FOR IOS

While prepayment considerations are important for all bonds in a CMBS deal, their most dramatic effect can generally be seen on the IO. In this section we briefly review the necessity of the IO strips, and discuss their risk profiles in more detail.

Typically, a CMBS deal will contain collateral with a wide range of coupons. Since different loans will amortize at different rates, and some may prepay or default, the weighted average coupon (WAC) for the collateral will tend to change over time. The presence of this *coupon dispersion* obviously makes it impossible to structure a deal with only fixed rate bonds. Sometimes this is dealt with by creating one or more *WAC bonds* whose coupon changes with the collateral. In effect, the dispersion is passed through to the bondholders. An alternative approach is to allocate any excess interest payments over some specified cutoff to an IO strip, thus giving the collateral a constant effective passthrough rate. This strip may be taken either directly from the collateral, in which case the technique is referred to as *ratio stripping*, or it can be taken from the bonds.

An IO that has been stripped directly from the underlying loans will obviously be influenced the most by high coupon loans. These loans will have a higher coupon either because they were originated earlier when rates were higher, or because they are loans on riskier asset types. The former type will be particularly subject to prepayment risk, while the latter will be subject to credit risk, so it may seem that such an IO would be at high risk from both defaults and prepayments. In a well structured deal, however, the allocation of prepayment premiums will protect it against calls. Moreover, since the servicer is generally required to advance principal and interest, prepayments and defaults will tend to affect this type of IO similarly.

In contrast, an IO that has been stripped from a senior bond will be affected very differently by prepayments and defaults. Because of the subordination structure, it will be relatively insensitive to defaults risk. However, the same subordination structure will cause it to be highly sensitive to prepayment risk.

When investing in IOs, it is especially important to realize that a deal using yield maintenance does not always provide the best call protection. For many of the methods discussed in this chapter, the YM charge may be reduced to zero in an upward rate environment. A prepayment could then cause the IO to disappear, without any distribution of YM charges to compensate. In contrast, a lockout or prepayment premium would provide far better protection. This highlights the point that when analyzing an IO, there is no substitute for thoroughly modeling the entire yield maintenance provisions of the deal, and performing analysis runs for multiple scenarios.

CONCLUSION

In this chapter we have provided a catalog of the different techniques that are used to provide prepayment protection in CMBS deals, and have illustrated the dramatic effect that they can have on the risk-return profiles of bonds. This emphasizes the importance to investors of completely modeling the call provisions of a CMBS deal and performing analyses under several scenarios.

Within residential CMOs, it is the payment structure of the deal that protects tranches against prepayments. This is often achieved with considerable complexity and may involve multiple layers of PAC classes and accrual bonds. In contrast, CMBS deals typically have a far simpler bond structure. They instead achieve call protection by imposing various prepayment lockouts and fees on the collateral, the most complex of which is yield maintenance. In this, a borrower who chooses to prepay is subject to an additional charge that is intended to fairly compensate the lender for any loss of investment yield. This penalty is then distributed to the bondholders in such a way as to render them indifferent to the prepayment.

We have examined the different ways in which the yield maintenance charge may be defined, and have also listed the current methods for allocating it amongst tranches.

As the market evolves, it seems inevitable that the methods of CMBS call protection discussed in this chapter will become supplemented by some of the techniques used in residential deals. In this case we can look forward to deals that combine PAC bonds, Z bonds, and bond yield maintenance within a single structure. It is obviously important that anyone building a CMBS structuring or analysis model designs it with enough flexibility to allow for this future expansion.

Chapter 31

An Option-Theoretic Approach to the Valuation of Multifamily Mortgage Loans and Securities

Michael D. Youngblood, Ph.D.
Managing Director — Mortgage Research
Chase Securities Inc.

INTRODUCTION

Issuance of multifamily and commercial mortgage securities accelerated briskly in the 1990s, from a meager \$5.7 billion in 1990 to \$20.3 billion in 1994, before slipping to \$19 billion in 1995. However, issuance has rebounded and should set a new record in 1996. Renewed issuance of mixed-collateral commercial securities by dealer conduits, which totaled \$12.7 billion, or 60.9% of the total, has led this rebound. Such vigorous issuance has provided investors with a wide range of opportunities, spanning virtually all investment grades (from AAA to NR), intermediate and long maturities, fixed and floating interest rates, and property types. In addition, it has enlarged the secondary market for multifamily and commercial mortgage securities, although the intemperate demand for new securities usually produces odd-lot allocations that impede subsequent secondary trading.

Nevertheless, the proliferation of multifamily and commercial mortgage securities should not obscure the risks to which they expose investors. Greater liquidity does not necessarily mean lower risk, as the markets for high-yield securities and syndicated bank loans attest. The primary risks facing investors are prepayment or default of one or more of the underlying mortgage loans. These events could result in reinvestment of principal at lower interest rates and/or in outright loss of expected interest or principal, or both. Even if a subordinated class or cash reserve fund should absorb any loss, the elevated cash flow variability or the reduction in available credit enhancement could widen yield spreads and undermine performance. These are,

---

I wish to express my gratitude to my colleagues, Dr. Eugene Xu and Sangam Pande, for their expert assistance in the preparation of this chapter.

obviously, the primary risks of single-family mortgage securities as well, although the much larger size of the underlying loans and the much smaller number of them magnify these risks for multifamily and commercial mortgage securities.

Consider the most salient examples of the risk of prepayment and default of these securities in recent years:

- One $122 million privately-placed floating-rate multifamily security, issued in June 1993 and maturing in August 1998, was refinanced two years later. Ironically, in July 1996 the borrower used the same collateral to support a new $125 million fixed-rate security, maturing in 2015.
- Cumulative losses have exhausted the $122.2 million reserve fund of Resolution Trust Corporation, Series 1991-M2, leaving a single $51.9 million subordinated class to protect $151.6 million of senior classes from future losses (as of the July 1996 remittance report). In light of the vulnerability of the senior classes, Moody's Investors Service and Standard & Poor's Rating Group have sliced the original ratings from Aa1/AA or Aa2/AA to Baa3/B.
- The first two non-RTC multifamily securities issued in the 1990s have effectively failed. The rating of the very first security tumbled from AA in 1991 to D (Standard & Poor's) in July 1996, as the most senior class incurred losses of $1.7 million, or 3.1% of the unpaid principal balance, after the utter depletion of the subordinated classes. To forestall potentially huge investor losses, the issuer of the second nonagency security of 1991 repurchased all of its senior classes in 1994. The ratings on this security and one other, which was also repurchased, were withdrawn before they could be cut.

The poor performance of these landmark issues, three of which contributed prominently to re-establishing the nonagency multifamily market in 1991, after its virtual dissolution in the late 1980s, highlights the risks inherent in multifamily and commercial securities.

In this chapter, we show how to evaluate the risks of prepayment and default of multifamily mortgage loans and securities through the same option-theoretic approach that has evolved to evaluate them for single-family mortgage loans and securities. This approach has evolved from the seminal work of Black and Scholes, Merton, and Cox, Ingersoll, and Ross, and from continuous refinements by practitioners over the past decade.[1] We focus here on prepayment and default of multifamily mortgage *loans* rather than *securities* because the former necessarily leads to the latter. And the operation of nonagency credit enhance-

[1] See Fischer Black and Myron Scholes, "The Pricing of Options and Corporate Liabilities," *Journal of Political Economy*, 81 (1972), pp. 637-54; Robert Merton, "Theory of Rational Option Pricing," *Bell Journal of Economics and Management Science*, 4 (1973), pp. 141-83; and J.C. Cox, J.E. Ingersoll, Jr., and S.A. Ross, "A Theory of the Term Structure of Interest Rates," *Econometrica*, 53 (1985), pp. 385-407.

ment in absorbing losses on the loans underlying multifamily securities requires no explanation to institutional investors. While using a common option-theoretic approach, we need to adjust for certain fundamental differences between multifamily and residential loans, borrowers, and properties. By adjusting for these differences, we can specify the multifamily (and, without loss of generality, commercial) prepayment and default functions that allow optional valuation under Monte Carlo or binomial simulation of an interest rate process.

DIFFERENCES BETWEEN MULTIFAMILY AND SINGLE-FAMILY LOANS

Multifamily and residential mortgage loans differ fundamentally in their terms and conditions. Multifamily mortgage loans generally amortize over terms of 240 to 360 months, with a final balloon payment of principal due in 60 to 240 months. Some loans amortize fully over terms of 300 to 360 months, with no balloon payment. Some loans do not amortize at all, but pay only interest until the final maturity date. Most loans have significant constraints on prepayment before maturity, which can take many forms:

- Lock-out periods which absolutely prohibit prepayment and which may be succeeded by further constraints.
- Yield maintenance premiums that require the borrower to pay the present value of the change in the yield of a specified Treasury note between closing date and prepayment date, depriving the borrower of any pure interest-rate incentive to refinance; variations in calculating these premiums may reduce the borrower's disincentive.
- Prepayment penalties, expressed as a percentage of the unpaid principal balance of the loan, which typically decline as the loan approaches maturity.

Loans that do allow the borrower to prepay, subject to constraints like these, usually require payment in full and explicitly prohibit partial payment. In contrast, the huge majority of single-family mortgage loans, whether fixed-rate or adjustable-rate, amortize over 15- or 30-year terms. (Of course, the comparatively small number of residential balloon loans amortize over 360 months, with final payments of principal due in five or seven years.) Single-family loans generally permit prepayment in full or in part at any time without penalty.

THE OPTION TO PREPAY WITH TRANSACTION COSTS

The multifamily borrower has invested equity in and raised debt on the security of the apartment property solely to obtain the after-tax real financial returns that it generates, in the form of periodic income and ultimate proceeds from sale. In maximizing the return on equity, the borrower, who is rarely an individual and usually a partnership or corporation, will act rationally to prepay or to default on the mortgage loan. In contrast, residential borrowers usually derive housing services as well as financial returns from the equity and debt invested in a house; the physical or emotional value of housing services may outweigh the investment returns. Hence, the residential borrower may not act rationally to maximize return on investment. Moreover, individuals generally lack access to the full information about alternative returns from investment or costs of debt that institutional borrowers generally possess, which ignorance may contribute to evidently irrational actions.

The multifamily borrower will generally prepay the mortgage loan, subject to the constraints set forth in the related note or deed of trust, when the present value of the scheduled payments exceeds the present value of payments on a new loan under whatever terms may prevail in the future, plus transaction and other costs. If the borrower seeks to prepay when yield maintenance or prepayment penalties are required by the note, then these payments will effectively increase the present value of the alternative loan. Similarly, the borrower will incur substantial upfront costs in refinancing a multifamily mortgage loan, which will overtly increase the present value of the alternative loan.

These expenses include (1) the fees to the commercial loan broker who located the lender of the new loan (1% to 3% of the new loan amount); (2) commitment fees and other "inducements" to the lender (2% to 5%); (3) the title insurance policy or its equivalent (1%); (4) fees for a FFIEC-eligible appraisal, engineering report, and Phase I environment assessment; and, (5) legal fees, including those for recordation. The last two typically represent 0.50% of the new loan amount. One estimates that borrowers incur transaction costs, on average, of 5% of the new loan amount. These average transaction costs are roughly equivalent to an additional 1% on the annual interest rate of a 10-year non-amortizing balloon mortgage loan. In sharp contrast, residential borrowers can obtain new loans for average points and fees of 1.50%, or less, of the loan amount.

Furthermore, the engineering report and Phase I environment assessment may reveal deferred maintenance, or violations of building codes, or environmental hazards. These may range from the innocuous, i.e., potholes in the parking lot, to the pathological, i.e., friable "popcorn" asbestos sprayed on a significant proportion of the interior surface of an apartment building. If these conditions impair the current or future value of the building, then the lender will routinely require the borrower to cure these conditions. The lender will always require cure of building code violations, without which the borrower cannot obtain a certificate of occupancy. The lender may not agree to advance any or all of the funds needed to cure these conditions, which would present the borrower with additional upfront expenditures, further inflating the present value of alternative credit. Together, prepayment penalties, transaction costs, and deferred maintenance expenditures set a high threshold on prepayment that can deter the borrower from prepayment.

Prepayment Function

In light of these considerations, we can define the *prepayment function* as the relationship between the present value of the existing loan under the terms set forth in the mortgage note, and the present value of an alternative mortgage loan under whatever terms lenders may offer in the future. The prepayment function discounts the principal and interest payments scheduled under the original loan by current interest rates, plus the average risk premium or yield spread that lenders currently charge for comparable loans. Mathematically this is expressed as follows:

$$\Pi_0 = \sum_{i=0}^{T} (P_i + I_i)\left(1 + \frac{r_0 + s}{2}\right)^{-2t_i} \tag{1}$$

where

Π_0 = the original loan amount
P_i = the scheduled principal payment of period i
I_i = the scheduled interest payment of period i
T = the final period
r_0 = the base rate at origination (month 0)
t_i = the time to receive principal and interest payments of period i
s = the risk premium

The prepayment function also discounts the principal and interest payments scheduled under the alternative loan by the interest rates that prevail in the future, plus the same risk premium, and then adds prepayment penalties, transaction costs, and deferred maintenance expenditures as shown below:

$$\sum_{i=0}^{T} (P_i + I_i)\left(1 + \frac{r_{i0} + s}{2}\right)^{-2(t_i - t_{i0})} > \Pi_{i0} + PP_{i0} + PTC_0 + DM_0 \tag{2}$$

where:

r_i = the discount rate at i_0
Π_{i0} = the alternative loan amount at i_0
PP_{i0} = the prepayment penalty at i_0
PTC_0 = the prepayment transaction cost
DM_0 = deferred maintenance expenditures

and T, t_i, s, P_i, and I_i are as defined in equation (1).

If the value of first term of the inequality, the existing loan, exceeds that of the second term, the alternative loan, then the borrower should prepay, presumably in the following month.

The rationality of the borrower simplifies this part of the valuation of multifamily loans relative to that of residential loans. One does not need to introduce an econometric model to estimate the likelihood or rate of non-rational prepayment as one does with residential loans. One need only to solve the prepayment function in conjunction with an appropriate interest-rate process.

THE OPTION TO DEFAULT WITH TRANSACTION COSTS

Unlike the residential borrower who acquires a house as a shelter and as an investment, the multifamily borrower acquires an apartment property only as an investment. He or she acquires the property, with a mixture of equity and debt in order to receive the monthly net operating income and the proceeds from eventual sale that it will generate. Net operating income is the cash that remains after deducting the opportunity cost of vacant units and the operating expenses of a property from its gross possible income.[2] It does not include deductions for accounting depreciation or debt service payments. Most real estate investors calculate the expected return on equity and debt from net operating income and sale proceeds using one of the many forms of *the discounted cash flow approach.*

However, the borrower does not receive net operating income, but rather the residual cash that remains after payment of scheduled principal and interest and of escrows for property taxes, insurance premiums, replacement reserves, and other impounds. Indeed, multifamily loans sometimes require the apartment manager to remit all rents, late payment penalties, deposit forfeitures, and other collections directly to a lock box which the lender controls. The lender will remit to the borrower only the residual amount that remains after payment of all amounts due. Similarly, the borrower does not receive all of the proceeds from the eventual sale of the property, but rather the residual cash after repaying the unamortized loan amount. No lender will release the title on sale of a property until payment of the remaining loan amount, any interest accrued but not yet paid, and any late payment penalties outstanding.

Therefore, the borrower should expect to receive the present values of the monthly net income from the property and the net proceeds from sale. The present values of the net income and the net proceeds will jointly determine the borrower's decision each month over the life of the mortgage loan either to make principal and interest payments, and other mandatory payments, or to default. Understanding this monthly decision is essential to the analysis that follows: *the valuation of the borrower's option to default depends on both the net income and the net proceeds.* Unless net income falls below zero (when net operating income is less than principal and interest payments), the borrower will not default, even if the present value of net proceeds is negative (when the market value of the property is less than the loan amount). Monthly net income must fall below zero *and* the market value of the property must fall below that of the loan balance.

Furthermore, the borrower will include transaction costs in the monthly decision to pay or to default on the loan. Whereas one can quantify the transaction

[2] See Charles Wurtzebach and Mike Miles, *Modern Real Estate* (New York: John Wiley, 1991), pp. 206-211.

costs incurred in the prepayment decision, one cannot precisely quantify those incurred in default because they include the following three components that vary widely among borrowers: (1) decreased availability and increased cost of future debt and equity; (2) lender recourse to the borrower; and, (3) federal income tax liability.

First, some lenders do not extend credit to real estate borrowers with a history of uncured defaults. Those who do extend credit to such borrowers routinely impose more stringent terms; these terms may become onerous for borrowers with a history of opportunistic default. Second, fewer loans originated in the 1990s than heretofore allow recourse to the borrower in the event of default. The declining popularity of recourse provisions belongs, in part, to fierce competition from conduits and other non-traditional lenders and, in part, to the legal form of many borrowers. If the borrower takes the legal form of a limited partnership or a special purpose corporation, the mortgaged property may be the only asset. Where recourse provisions exist, the borrower must weigh the likelihood of the loss of other assets in addition to those explicitly pledged in the mortgage note. One cannot measure the value of these assets, or the lender's ability to locate and attach them. Third, the borrower will incur a federal income tax liability equal to the difference between the loan amount and the property value. The value of this difference to the borrower depends upon his or her marginal income tax rate and other considerations, which one does not know.

Nevertheless, one can estimate the loss of operating funds, the forfeiture of property, and certain expenses. The expenses include (1) operating income from the property until definitive foreclosure; (2) working capital, accounts receivable, and escrows; (3) furniture, fixtures, and equipment used to furnish or manage the property; (4) management fees for operating the property; and (5) legal fees, which increase if the borrower also files for bankruptcy. Offsetting these costs, the borrower may retain rents, late payment fees, and other miscellaneous income collected over several months until the lender can accelerate the mortgage note and take control of the property. We estimate that these transaction costs average 7% of the loan amount.

Default Function

In light of these considerations, one can define the *default function* from two simultaneous relationships:

(1) monthly net operating income less scheduled principal and interest, and other payments over the term of the *loan*.

(2) the present value of monthly net operating income over the life of the *property*, plus transaction costs, less the present value of scheduled principal (including the final balloon) and interest, and other payments over the term of the loan.

As long as the first relationship remains positive, the borrower will not default. He or she has sufficient income to pay monthly debt service, and, bolstered by the endemic optimism of real estate investors, will continue to make scheduled payments even if the second relationship has turned negative. As long as the second relationship remains positive, the borrower will not default. He or she retains the excess of the property value over the loan amount, or positive equity. If the first relationship turns negative, then he or she can sell the property, repay the outstanding loan, thereby avoiding default, and realize the amount of positive equity. This relationship reveals an important aspect of the default option on mortgage loans: the loan amount represents the price at which the borrower can sell, in effect, the property to the lender at any time in the future, should equity become negative. When the first and second relationships turn negative, the borrower will default. He or she lacks the income to pay scheduled monthly principal and interest, while the future value of the property, plus transaction costs, has fallen below the loan amount, leaving negative equity.

Rents, Vacancies, and Operating Expenses

The default function of the first relationship compares net operating income to scheduled payments of principal and interest, and escrows. Hence, it requires projection of net operating income as the sum of gross possible rents, the opportunity cost of vacant units, and operating expenses, for each month over the term of the loan. We project future rents as a function of employment growth, income growth, population growth, household formation, housing affordability, net change in the stock of apartments, the natural vacancy rate — all from the housing sub-market in which the property is located — and future 10-year Treasury rates. We estimate the opportunity cost of vacant units from the *natural vacancy rate*, as developed by Rosen and Smith as an equilibrium function of historical rents and operating expenses.[3] Last, we project future operating expenses from their historical correlation with rents. Like the prepayment function, the default function discounts the scheduled principal and interest payments, and other payments, on the loan by the interest rates that prevail in the future, plus the initial risk premium or spread charged by the lender. Therefore, we can project both the net operating income from the property, over the life of the property, and the scheduled payments, over the term of the loan, given an interest rate process.

Similarly, the default function of the second relationship discounts monthly net operating income over the life of the property by the interest rates that prevail in the future, plus the multifamily risk premium. We project net operating income as before over the expected *economic life* of the property, which we obtain the from the mandatory FFIEC-eligible appraisal or engineering report. A new apartment property has an expected economic life of 50 years, assuming that rehabilitation does not extend it, but most of the apartment properties underlying

---

[3] Kenneth Rosen and Lawrence B. Smith, "The Price-Adjustment Process for Rental Housing and the Natural Vacancy Rate," *American Economic Review*, 73 (1983), pp. 779-786, and Lawrence B. Smith, "A Note on the Price Adjustment Mechanism for Rental Housing," *American Economic Review*, 64 (1974), pp. 478-481.

multifamily (and mixed-property commercial) securities are not new, which reduces the term over which they can generate net operating income.

The default function of the second relationship discounts the net operating income by the interest rates expected to prevail in the future, plus a multifamily risk premium. The multifamily risk premium is the entrepreneurial return that the borrower requires for investing equity and debt in the apartment property. We measure it by the spread between the yield capitalization rate of the property and the interest rates that prevailed at origination of the mortgage loan. The yield capitalization rate is the internal rate of return that equated the appraised or sales value of the apartment property, at the time of the origination of the mortgage loan, to the future net operating income that it may generate over its economic life, assuming no rehabilitation.[4]

Therefore, default occurs in any month i_0 over the term of the mortgage loan, if both of the following relationships are satisfied:

$$NOI_{i_0} < P_{i_0} + I_{i_0} + E_{i_0} \tag{3}$$

$$\sum_{i=i_0}^{EL} NOI_i \left(1 + \frac{r_{i_0} + ycr}{2}\right)^{-2(t_i - t_0)} + DTC_0 - \sum_{i=i_0}^{T-1} (P_i + I_i + E_i) \left(1 + \frac{r_{i_0} + s}{2}\right)^{-2(t_i - t_0)} < 0 \tag{4}$$

where

NOI_{i0}	=	a (future) payment of net operating income, from the rent process, at period i
r_{i0}	=	the discount rate at period i_0
ycr	=	the discount mortgage risk premium
P_i	=	the scheduled principal payment of period i
I_i	=	the scheduled interest payment of period i
T	=	the final period in the term of the mortgage loan
EL	=	the final period in the economic life of the property
r_0	=	the base rate at origination (month 0)
t_i	=	the time to receive principal and inters payments of period i
s	=	the risk premium
DTC_i	=	default transaction costs at period i

Alternatively, we can rewrite equation (4) such that default occurs if the following inequality obtains:

[4] See Kenneth M. Lusht and Jeffrey D. Fisher, "Anticipated Growth and the Specification of Debt in Real Estate Value Models," *AREUEA Journal*, 12 (1984), pp. 1-11.

$$\frac{\sum_{i=i0}^{EL} NOI_i \left(1+\frac{r_{i_0}+ycr}{2}\right)^{-2(t_i-t_0)} + DTC_0}{\sum_{i=i_0}^{T-1} (P_i+I_i+E_i)\left(1+\frac{r_{i_0}+s}{2}\right)^{-2(t_i-t_0)}} < 1 \tag{5}$$

If the ratio of present value of the property, plus default transaction costs, to the present value of the mortgage loan falls below 1 and if the relationship in equation (3) is less than zero, then the borrower will default.

INTERPRETING PREPAYMENT AND DEFAULT FUNCTIONS

The default and prepayment functions assume the same interest rate process, which generates the future interest rates that discount both the principal and interest payments of the mortgage loan and the net operating income of the apartment property. For the interest rate process, we employ a proprietary variant of the one-factor model proposed by Cox, Ingersoll, and Ross. Our variant precludes certain extreme results, for example, negative interest rates.

We begin with the discount rate of the on-the-run 1-month Treasury bill and generate a series of 1-month arbitrage-free forward rates that extend over the entire Treasury yield curve, i.e., over 360 months. We calibrate these rates so that they recover, or produce the exact prices of, the on-the-run Treasury coupon curve. These are the future interest rates described in the prepayment and default models described earlier. Generating these rates requires the on-the-run Treasury yield curve and a measure of interest-rate volatility for each of the 360 months. To provide the monthly volatilities, we interpolate the term structure of volatility from the series of average implied volatilities of puts and calls on (U.S. dollar) interest rate swaps, which range from one week to ten years in term. Furthermore, we can generate a full path of 360 arbitrage-free riskless discount rates for any sequence of 360 monthly volatilities that we may produce with Monte Carlo or other methods.[5]

By applying the default and prepayment functions simultaneously to the path of forward discount rates generated by this process, we can simulate the borrower's decision to default on or prepay any multifamily loan in the present or any future month. Indeed, we can value the borrower's options to default and to prepay by simulating these decisions over all possible paths of forward discount rates. While this comprehensive simulation would require infinite calculations, we can achieve equivalent valuation of the borrower's options by simulating a finite set of

[5] See Frank J. Fabozzi, *Valuation of Fixed Income Securities and Derivatives* (New Hope, PA: Frank J. Fabozzi Associates, 1995), pp. 131-154.

paths of forward discount rates that achieves a lognormal distribution, using established tests with appropriate size and power for the lognormal distribution.

To value the options to default and to prepay, we simulate the borrower's rational decisions over a sufficiently large set of discount rate paths in the following sequence:

- Decompose the loan amount into its scheduled monthly payments of principal and interest over months (t) of its remaining term, and its balloon payment, if any, at term (T);
- Reprice the loan, using the appropriate on-the-run Treasury note, plus a risk premium, which is the average yield spread charged by lenders on comparable loans for the same term;
- Solve for the zero-volatility spread (Z-spread) of the loan using current forward discount rates;
- Calculate the present value of the loan over every month in its term with the associated forward discount rate plus the Z-spread;
- Over every path, calculate the present value of the loan over every month with the associated forward discount rate plus the Z-spread;
- Compare the present value of the loan, obtained using current rates, with the present value of the loan (plus prepayment penalties, prepayment transaction costs, and deferred maintenance expenditures) in each path, using path-specific rates; if the conditions of equations (1) and (2) obtain in any month in any path, prepay the unamortized principal balance;
- Decompose the property value into its projected net operating income over months (t) of its expected economic life (EL);
- Solve for the yield capitalization rate and the related Z-spread of the mortgaged property, using the contemporary appraised value or sales price, and current forward discount rates;
- Calculate the present value of the property over every month with the associated forward discount rate plus the Z-spread;
- Compare the present value of the property, obtained using current rates (plus default transaction costs) with the present value of the loan in each path, using path-specific rates; if the conditions of equations (3) and (4) or (3) and (5) obtain in any month in any path, default the mortgage loan;
- Integrate the principal and interest payments over every month and every path and then solve for that risk-adjusted spread to the discount rates in every path that produces an average loan price equal to price of the loan.

CREDIT-ADJUSTED OAS, EFFECTIVE DURATION, AND CONVEXITY

This approach to the simultaneous valuation of the borrower's options to prepay and default enables us to solve for the option-adjusted spread (OAS) or, more precisely, the credit risk option-adjusted spread (CROAS) of a multifamily mortgage loan. Solution of CROAS requires only two steps, assuming the prior simulation of arbitrage-free forward discount rates along a sufficiently large number of paths.

First, we integrate the principal and interest payments that result from allowing rational prepayment and default in every month over the term of the loan and over every path of forward discount rates. One series of payments, from origination to termination of the loan, corresponds to each path of discount rates. Second, we solve iteratively (by trial and error) for the *spread*, that added to the forward rates along each path, will discount each series of monthly payments to its present value, the average of which equals the current price of the loan (plus accrued interest). The semiannual bond-equivalent of this spread is the CROAS. This is expressed mathematically as follows:

$$P + I = \sum_{i=0}^{N} \sum_{j=0}^{T} (PF_{i,j} + IF_{i,j}) \times D_i \times \prod_{i=d}^{i+d} \left(1 + \frac{r_{i,j} + s'}{12}\right)$$

$$s = 2 \times \left[\left(1 + \frac{y' + s'}{12}\right)^6 - \left(1 + \frac{y}{2}\right)\right] \tag{6}$$

where

P = the price
I = the accrued interest
N = the number of paths
T = the number of months to maturity
$PF_{i,j}$ = the principal cash flow in *i*th path and *j*th month
$IF_{i,j}$ = the interest cash flow in *i*th path and *j*th month
D_i = the extra discount factor in *i*th path due to fractional month of the cash flow's timing
$r_{i,j}$ = the 1-month Treasury rate (30/360) in *i*th path and *j*th month
y' = the mortgage-equivalent 10-year
s' = the CROAS expressed in mortgage equivalent terms (12 month compounding)
y = the bond-equivalent 10-year Treasury yield
s = the CROAS expressed in bond equivalent term (semi-annual compounding)

This CROAS is directly comparable to the OAS of any mortgage or non-mortgage security evaluated using the same interest rate process.

Furthermore, we can calculate the first and second derivatives of the price and CROAS of the multifamily loan with respect to the term structures of interest rates and volatility: *effective duration*, *convexity*, *volatility sensitivity*, *volatility convexity*, and so on. We calculate these additional parameters of value by numerical methods, changing the term structures of interest rates or of (average implied swaption) volatility.

For *effective duration*, we increase the term structure of discount rates by any arbitrary magnitude, for example, 25 basis points, for all paths and solve for the average price that results. We then decrease the term structure by the same magnitude for all paths and solve for the average price that results. The difference between the two average prices that result, scaled by the change in basis points and the current price, is the effective duration of the mortgage loan. Effective duration measures the sensitivity of the price of the loan to a change in the term structure of interest rates.[6] The second derivative of price with respect to the term structure of interest rates, *convexity*, follows directly from this calculation. It is the effective duration scaled by the current price multiplied by the square of the same change in interest rates.[7] We calculate the volatility sensitivity and the volatility convexity of the mortgage loan in the same way.

The formulas for duration and convexity are given below.

$$D = \frac{\Delta P}{2P\Delta y} = \frac{P_+ - P_-}{2P\Delta y} \tag{7}$$

$$C = \frac{\Delta^2 P}{100P\Delta y^2} = \frac{P_+ - 2P + P_-}{100P\Delta y^2} \tag{8}$$

where

D = the duration
C = the convexity
Δy = shift in yield curve
P = the current price
P_+ = the projected price when the yield curve is up by Δy
$P-$ = the projected price when the yield curve is down by Δy

VALUING A MULTIFAMILY MORTGAGE LOAN

Consider the example of a representative multifamily mortgage loan, which was underwritten to FNMA DUS standards and originated in August 1996. FNMA's underwriting standards for the DUS program are representative of those employed by most institutional lenders; indeed, most conduit lenders have openly embraced these standards for their multifamily programs for the expedient reason that the rating agencies and institutional investors generally accept them. The lender furnished the following limited information about the loan and the related property:

---

[6] Effective duration differs from modified duration in that the latter does not allow for how changes in the term structure affect a security's cash flow.

[7] Andrew Kalotay, George Williams, and Frank J. Fabozzi, "A Model for Valuing Bonds and Embedded Options," *Financial Analysts Journal* (May-June 1993), pp. 35-46, and Fabozzi, *Valuation of Fixed Income Securities and Derivatives*, pp. 93-130.

Property city, state, and zip code	Houston, TX 77077
Principal balance amount	$8,000,000
Mortgage interest rate	8.42%
Maturity date	8/1/2006
Original amortization term	30 years
Prepayment premium option	Yield maintenance
Yield maintenance period	7.0 years
U.S. Treasury yield rate	5.625%
Security due date	2/1/2006
Total number of units	436
Annual net operating income	$951,904
Loan-to-value ratio	79.21%
Appraised value	$10,100,000
Occupancy	92%
Debt service coverage ratio	1.29x

From our own analysis of the Briar Forest sub-market, where this property is located, and our econometric models of the apartment market in metropolitan Houston, we add the following to FNMA's information:

Risk premium of DUS Tier II loans	1.67%
Yield capitalization rate	13.00
Long-term rent growth rate	3.26
Long-term rent volatility	6.86
Natural vacancy rate	11.20
Prepayment transaction costs	5.00
Default transaction costs	7.00

From this information and our projections of rent growth, rent volatility, and the natural vacancy rate for the apartment property, we calculate the following parameters of risk and value:

Frequency of prepayments	11.3%
Average months to prepayment	83
Average prepayment price	107-04 (32s)
Option cost	9 b.p.
Frequency of defaults	20.7%
Average months to default	82
Average loss severity	27.1%
Option cost	45 b.p.
Z-spread	166 b.p.
Prepayment and default option cost	54 b.p.
CROAS	112 b.p.
Effective duration	6.08 years
Convexity	0.30

This multifamily mortgage loan has an 11.3% probability of prepaying and a 20.7% probability of defaulting over its 10-year term. The probabilities of prepayment and default combine to reduce the nominal and Z-spreads of this mortgage loan by 54 basis points to a CROAS of 112 basis points. Similarly, the effective duration of the loan, which reflects the combined risks, is 6.08 years, whereas the modified duration of the loan, which assumes neither prepayment nor default, is somewhat longer, 6.25 years.

It is striking that the frequency of default and the average severity of loss projected on this multifamily loan, which was underwritten to common institutional standards, fall within the ranges of default and loss experienced historically by mainstream institutional lenders. From his most recent study of the historical performance of commercial mortgage loans originated by life insurance companies in the years 1972-1991, Snyderman finds a aggregate lifetime rate of default of 13.8%.[8] However, Snyderman concedes that the historical default rate is artificially low, because many of the loans in the insurance company sample remain outstanding — they have yet to default or mature. After adjustment, he projects an 18.3% lifetime default rate. Similarly, on reviewing Snyderman's first two studies, Fitch Investors Service noticed that the widespread restructuring of loans by life companies reduced the frequency of default.[9] Based on this review and a separate study of the commercial mortgage portfolios of 11 life companies, Fitch projects a much higher lifetime default rate of 30%. This level forms the baseline for its rating of commercial mortgage securities. It is also consistent with the default rate projected on the representative multifamily mortgage loan.

In addition, Snyderman finds that the severity of loss of commercial mortgage loans (measured as a percentage of the unpaid principal balance) varies widely by the origination year, from a low of –7% in 1972 to a high of 96% in 1984. He concludes that the severity of loss averaged 33% in the 1970s and 45% in the 1980s; the average yield cost of default was 50 basis points. Fitch adopts the average loss severity of the 1980s, projecting a loss factor of 40% to 50% for defaulted commercial mortgage loans. As with default frequency, the loss severity projected on the representative multifamily loan is consistent with the historical experience of mainstream commercial lenders. Indeed, Snyderman's estimate of the yield cost of default of 50 basis points is virtually the same as the yield cost of default of 45 basis points on this multifamily loan.

THE PARAMETERS OF CROAS

We can explore the risks of this multifamily mortgage loan in greater depth by calculating the sensitivity of the CROAS to its salient parameters: loan-to-value ratio, debt service coverage ratio, term to maturity of the loan, long-term rent

[8] Mark Snyderman, "Update on Commercial Mortgage Defaults," *Real Estate Finance Journal* (Summer 1994), pp. 22-32.

[9] Fitch Investors Service, Inc., "Commercial Mortgage Stress Test," *Structured Finance* (June 8, 1992), pp. 1-12.

growth rate, long-term rent volatility, and natural vacancy rate. By exploring the partial derivatives of these parameters to CROAS, we expose the influence on the likelihood of prepayment and default of the underwriting criteria, the terms and conditions of the loan itself, and the local property market. (See Exhibit 1.) Accordingly, we vary each parameter across a wide, but arbitrary, range of values and record the CROAS that results, in terms of basis points and price. We hold all other parameters and the price of the loan constant. We find that:

- Increases in the loan-to-value ratio (LTV), by diminishing the borrower's equity and increasing his or her leverage, decrease CROAS modestly. A decline in LTV from 79.8% to 55% increases CROAS from 112 basis points to 136 basis points. Decreases in LTV increase CROAS symmetrically.
- Increases in the debt service coverage ratio (DSCR) increase CROAS slightly less than the given changes in LTV. An increase from 1.29× to 2.5× DSCR would increase CROAS from 112 basis points to 131 basis points. Decreases in DSCR also affect CROAS symmetrically.
- Term to maturity affects CROAS inversely: the longer the term of the loan, the lower the CROAS. This inverse relationship reflects the operation of volatility; the longer a loan remains outstanding, the broader the range of rental growth rates, including negative rates, that may occur. Term to maturity affects most options in this fashion, especially the short-term exchange-traded financial options that the Black-Scholes or Black futures model evaluate accurately. Indeed, given the unambiguously positive influence that shorter terms have on CROAS, its is paradoxical that the four rating agencies penalize loans with them, requiring more credit enhancement than for otherwise identical loans with longer terms.

Exhibit 1: Sensitivity of Parameters and Terms of Multifamily Mortgage Loan Expressed as CROAS
(In Basis Points and Price in 32s)

						Base				
LTV (%)	100	95	90	85	79.8	75	70	65	60	55
CROAS (bp)	83	91	99	106	112	120	125	129	133	136
CROAS (32s)	4-24	4-10	3-27	3-15	3-05	2-21+	2-14	2-05	1-30+	1-25
DSCR	0.90	1.00	1.10	1.20	1.29	1.40	1.50	1.75	2.00	2.50
CROAS (bp)	94	102	109	110	112	116	117	122	126	131
CROAS (32s)	4-02+	3-21	3-09	3-07	3-05	2-30	2-27	2-19	2-12	2-03+
Term (Years)	30	25	20	15	10	7	5	3	2	1
CROAS (bp)	52	54	59	76	112	128	130	143	184	229
CROAS (32s)	5-24+	5-21+	5-11	4-18+	3-05	2-17+	2-11	1-19	0-23+	0-08+
Rent Growth (%)	−1.0	0.0	1.0	2.0	3.3	4.0	4.5	5.0	5.5	6.0
CROAS (bp)	42	64	81	98	112	123	127	131	134	137
CROAS (32s)	15-28+	5-20+	4-25+	3-28	3-05	2-16	2-08+	2-02	1-29	1-22+
Rent (Vol.)	25.0	20.0	15.0	10.0	6.9	5.9	4.9	3.9	2.9	1.9
CROAS (bp)	−8.3	−35	11	77	112	128	137	144	150	154
CROAS (32s)	12-21	10-14	8-08	5-00	3-05	2-07+	1-23+	11-10+	0-29+	0-23+

- The long-term rent growth rate affects CROAS strongly and asymmetrically. An increase from 3.26% to 6.0% increases CROAS from 112 basis points to 137 basis points, but a decrease to –1% drops CROAS to 42 basis points. It is noteworthy that the rent growth rate crosses a threshold of sensitivity below 2%. From 2% to 0%, the rent growth rate cannot overcome the influence of the projected 6.9% volatility, which propagates enough simulated negative growth rates to render CROAS consistently negative. Of course, below 0%, negative growth rates predominate with commensurate effects on CROAS.
- Long-term rent volatility affects CROAS even more strongly than the rent growth rate. It governs the range of potential growth rates associated with the simulated forward discount rates, in effect, raising or lowering the influence of interest rates on rents. High levels of volatility will propagate over time broader ranges of rent growth rates, including negative rates, that ultimately turn CROAS negative.
- The natural vacancy rate acts asymmetrically on CROAS. Increasing vacancy rates diminish CROAS more than increasing this rate inflates CROAS. It is particularly striking that CROAS declines very rapidly once the vacancy rate exceeds 25%.

The influence of these parameters on CROAS reveals its acute vulnerability to the initial equity and leverage of the borrower, and to the conditions of the local market. Investors will need to scrutinize carefully loans with LTVs above 85% or DSCRs below 1.2%, and loans with underlying properties located in volatile real estate markets.

VALUING A MULTIFAMILY MORTGAGE SECURITY

The analysis of the representative multifamily mortgage loan discussed in the previous section leads directly to that of nonagency multifamily and, by extension, commercial mortgage securities. It enables one to quantify the risks of prepayment and default of the underlying mortgage loans, and to measure the adequacy of the credit enhancement provided by the security.

Consider a truly exemplary multifamily mortgage security, the Evans Withycombe Finance Trust, which was issued in August 1994 by a special purpose Delaware limited partnership, which is, in turn, wholly-owned by Evans Withycombe, Inc., a publicly-held real estate investment trust. The multifamily security consists of four classes, one senior (A-1) and three subordinate (A-2, A-3, and A-4), all totaling $131 million. (See Exhibit 2.) The three subordinated classes, which total $29 million and represent 22.1% of the principal balance, protect the senior class against loss from default on the underlying mortgage notes. Each class receives payment of interest sequentially at a 7.98% annualized rate; class A-1 receives interest, then class A-2, and so on. The securities do not amortize and mature in August 2001; they cannot be prepaid in whole or in part until March 2001. Unusually, the servicer has no obligation to advance interest in the event that the borrower fails to pay on any due date.

Exhibit 2: Structure of Evans Withycombe Finance Trust, August 1994 (Dollars in Millions)

Class	Amount	Coupon (%)	Maturity	Call Date
A-1 (Senior)	102.0	7.98	8/1/2001	3/1/2001
A-2 (Sub.)	15.0	7.98	8/1/2001	3/1/2001
A-3 (Sub.)	9.0	7.98	8/1/2001	3/1/2001
A-4 (Sub.)	5.0	7.98	8/1/2001	3/1/2001

The underlying collateral consists of 22 apartment properties which are located in the Phoenix and Tucson metropolitan areas. They incorporate 5,380 apartments units, with 4.88 million square feet of rentable space. The average apartment size is roughly 907 square feet. The borrower describes the properties as "oriented to upscale residents seeking high levels of amenities, such as clubhouses, exercise rooms, tennis courts, swimming pools, therapy pools, and covered parking." The units rented for an average of $606 a month in the 12 months ending May 31, 1994, subject to a 92% economic occupancy rate. The apartments units were constructed between 1984 and 1990, leaving little scope for economic or functional obsolescence. A subsidiary of Evans Withycombe. Inc. manages the properties on behalf of the special purpose partnership. The underwriters estimated a debt service coverage ratio of 1.68× and a loan-to-value ratio of 54% at issuance of the security. After updating this information for current apartment market conditions in Phoenix and Tucson, we project a long-term rental growth rate of 2.3% on these properties, a long-term volatility of the rental growth rate of 4.3%, and a natural vacancy rate of 10%.

Assuming that dealers would offer the senior class A-1 at a nominal spread of 75 basis points over an interpolated Treasury note with a 4.7-year maturity, we calculate a CROAS of 74 basis points. (See Exhibit 3.) We estimate a zero probability of prepayment, given the absolute prohibition against it until March 2001, and a zero probability of default, given the high DSCR, low LTV, and favorable rental growth and volatility rates of the properties. Arbitrarily reducing the initial DSCR to 1.20× and raising the initial LTV to 80% would produce a 17.7% probability of default and an 11% expected loss rate; the CROAS of class A-1 falls by six basis points to 68 basis points. Under this scenario, losses of 1.95% of the principal balance of the mortgage notes, or $2.55 million, would result. Losses of this magnitude would eliminate 51% of the A-4 subordinated class, but leave classes A-2 and A-3 intact. Arbitrarily reducing the initial DSCR to 1.0× and raising the initial LTV to 100% would produce a 47.5% probability of default and a 12.3% expected loss rate; the CROAS of class A-1 would fall by 106 basis points to –32 basis points. Under this scenario, losses of 5.84% of the principal balance of the mortgage notes, or $7.65 million, would result. Losses of this magnitude would eliminate the A-4 subordinated class entirely, and 29.5% of the A-3 class, but leave the A-2 class intact. The senior class would not suffer actual loss, but rather an erosion of relative value such that it would yield substantially less than a comparable Treasury note. Since extreme conditions must occur to undermine the performance of class A-1 to such an extent, we conclude that the credit enhancement for class A-1 more than compensates for the likely risk of default and may render class A-1 a candidate for upgrading from AA by Standard and Poor's.

CONCLUSION

The approach to joint valuation of the prepayment and default options of multifamily loans that we developed in this chapter offers important advantages over other approaches. First, it unifies the valuation of multifamily and commercial mortgage loans and securities with that of single-family mortgage loans and securities by means of a common interest rate process. The simulation of arbitrage-free forward discount rates using the term structure of (average implied swaption) volatility along a sufficiently large number of paths by Monte Carlo methods provides the framework for discounting all monthly (or other periodic) future cash flows, whatever their source, commercial or residential, by appropriate risk premia. Hence, one can directly compare the usual first and second derivatives of price, rate, and volatility across the various types of loans and securities.

Second, the approach unifies the valuation of the mortgage loan and the related apartment property, by a more complex application of the common interest rate process. It discounts all future monthly cash flows, from loan or from property, by the same set of forward discount rates, plus respective risk premia. It offers thereby a framework capable of valuing a wide variety of financial instruments, not only mortgage loans and securities. Furthermore, it simulates the future net operating income from an apartment property as a function of economic and demographic variables, drawn from the local real estate sub-market, and the yield of the 10-year Treasury note. It creates thereby a direct link to forward 10-year discount rates and an indirect link through dynamic covariance coefficients for each economic and demographic variable to the 10-year rate. These coefficients will vary in size, sign, and lag. Hence, we can simulate the future net operating income for a property consistently with the simulation of future interest payments on alternative mortgage loans, which could lead to prepayment. In contrast, most other approaches simulate the value of the loan separately from the value of the property, using distinct stochastic processes. Accordingly, they may randomly associate future states of the property with future discount rates, propagating potentially aberrant relationships; one could find a very high growth rate or high variability of property price inflation associated with a very low discount rate.

Exhibit 3: Scenario Performance of Evans Withycombe Finance Trust, Class A-1

Scenario (DSCR / LTV)	Nominal Spread	CROAS	Loss Frequency (%)	Loss Severity (%)
1.68 / 54	75	74	0.0	0.0
1.20 / 80	75	68	17.7	11.0
1.00 / 100	75	−32	45.7	12.3

Third, the approach estimates the value of the property by the function described above for each month of the term of the related loan, including the final balloon payment. Thus, it avoids recourse to an externally-specified value of the property at maturity of the loan. The continuous internal determination of property value overcomes a critical weakness in the discounted cash flow approach that many lenders, borrowers, and appraisers use to value multifamily loans and properties: the arbitrary choice of the value of the property at maturity of the loan. Amid its countless variations, the discounted cash flow approach generally applies a constant discount rate, usually the yield of a comparable Treasury note plus a risk premium, to the projected annual net operating income and to the final sale price or market value of property, as of the maturity of the loan. This value is determined by capitalizing the projected net operating income in the last year at a projected rate. The projected capitalization rate is seldom derived by any methodology; rather, appraisers and others often use a rule of thumb, adding 1% or more to the initial capitalization rate, which is itself an average of capitalization rates sampled from recent sales or loans.[10] The discounted cash flow method, thus, founders at a critical point in any valuation by arbitrary, if not randomly, selecting terminal property value.

The fourth advantage is that the continuous internal determination of the value of a specific property overcomes a critical weakness in the valuation of multifamily properties: the arbitrary choice of the rate of return or "building-payout rate." Those who evaluate the property by a pure stochastic process often assume that it will offer the same rate of return as did equity real estate investment trusts (REITs), i.e., 8%, over some arbitrary period of time such as 1980-1987. This choice of rate of return invites numerous objections. REITs provide investors with valuable *liquidity*, which permits a higher valuation and lower rate of return on the properties that they own. REITs represent many different property types, so that any average return will not reflect a return specific to apartment properties. REITs own different types of properties in different markets, allowing a smoothing of return by the natural covariance of returns across property types and markets, which again leads to imprecision in valuing an individual apartment property. REITs typically use much less debt than other real estate investors; lower leverage implies lower risk and, appropriately, lower returns to investors. Also, REITS provide professional management of income-producing properties that small apartment properties (36 units or less) may not, which would motivate investors generally to require higher returns and expect higher variance of returns from them. In contrast, our approach infers the yield capitalization rate of a specific property and the risk premium to current interest rates implied by this rate. It then adds the property-specific risk premium to the forward discount rates across all paths, which produces a different series of capitalization rates for each path. Therefore, our approach provides greater specificity as well as greater flexibility in the valuation of mortgaged properties.

---

[10] See D. Richard Wincott, "Terminal Capitalization Rates and Reasonableness," *The Appraisal Journal* (April 1991), pp. 253-260.

The fifth advantage is the approach estimates the incidence of default and loss on foreclosure by the same function. Default occurs when the two conditions of the default function occur simultaneously. The number of paths on which default occurs automatically furnishes the frequency of default. The delay between default and final foreclosure and sale, which we obtain by random draws from a normal distribution that assumes an average of 24 months and variance of five months, permits calculation of the accrued interest foregone. (To the accrued interest, we add additional foreclosure costs of 5% the loan balance, and deduct net operating income received from the property over the foreclosure period.) The loss on foreclosure of the property derives from the difference between the property value, 24 months or so after default, and the unpaid principal balance of the loan. Hence, the magnitude of loss arises from the internal operation of our approach to value. Of course, one can compare the incidence of default and severity of loss projected on any loan to the historical experience of comparable loans originated by life insurance companies, RTC-administered financial institutions, or agency multifamily portfolios.

Finally, our approach offers a compromise in the persistent debate on the subject of *ruthless* versus *non-ruthless* default. Some contend that a borrower will rationally default on a property whenever its present value falls below that of the related mortgage loan, without consideration of transaction costs — hence, ruthless default. Any delay by the borrower in defaulting on the loan arises from his or her unwillingness to forego the persistent value of the option to default in the future, since the property value may continue to decline. (This decline magnifies the borrower's implicit gain and the lender's loss, because the loan amount fixes the strike price or tacit sales price of the property to the lender.) However, others contend that a borrower will rationally default on a property whenever its present value falls below that of the related loan, but will include transaction costs in assessing its value; hence, non-ruthless default. The borrower will not default as soon as the present value of the property falls below that of the loan, eliminating equity, but waits until negative equity should accumulate to the amount of observable and unobservable transaction costs.

While our approach clearly incorporates transaction costs in anticipating the borrower's rational decision, it also tenders a compromise to the opponents in the debate. We contend that the borrower should default in any month when two conditions occur: when net operating income falls below scheduled debt payments and when property value falls below loan amount, eliminating the borrower's equity. In practice, the second condition occurs before the first. The present value of expected net operating income falls below the present value of scheduled mortgage payments before income falls below scheduled payments. Property value declines faster than loan value, in part, because net operating income is discounted with a much higher risk premium than is the mortgage payment. Accordingly, the borrower may have sufficient cash flow to make scheduled payments even though the property value has fallen below the loan amount, plus transaction costs. He or she will rationally delay default as long as net operating income continues to exceed scheduled monthly payments, even though equity is negative. Therefore, the future option to default consists only of the option to default before these cash flows decline to zero. Our approach conflates the value of the present and future options to default.

Furthermore, those who conclude that the borrower has an option to default in the present and in the future must ignore the presence of the lender, who should act as rationally as the borrower. While few mortgage notes give the lender the ability to act unilaterally when the borrower's equity turns negative, all lenders have the legal right to accelerate the note and begin foreclosure as soon as the borrower fails to pay. The separate assignment of rents enhances the lender's ability to collect rents as soon as default occurs. Indeed, the lender will attempt to take possession of the property in order to forestall the borrower from optimizing the value of the option to default! The lender endeavors to obtain the property before its value falls below that of the loan, minimizing the value of default to the borrower. In most states, within three months of the first failure to pay scheduled principal and interest, the lender can obtain possession of, if not title to, the property and begin to receive net operating income. In conclusion, if a value to default in the future does exist, it consists either of the option to receive cash flow until it turns negative, or an option on property value from the month that cash flow turns negative until the lender assumes control of the property. These options have little time or intrinsic value, and we already incorporate them within our approach to valuation.

Chapter 32

Evaluating the Risk of Commercial Mortgage-Backed Securities

George J. Pappadopoulos
Director of Debt Research
Property & Portfolio Research, Inc.

Jeff Fisher, Ph.D.
Director, Center for Real Estate Studies
Professor of Finance and Real Estate
Indiana University

INTRODUCTION

During the 1990s we have witnessed a dramatic shift in the source of debt capital used to finance commercial real estate as Wall Street learned to package commercial real estate mortgages in loan pools with different classes of securities. As often happens in the evolution of securities markets, new products are issued and purchased by investors long before we truly understand how to evaluate their risk![1] In the case of commercial mortgage-backed securities (CMBS), there has been a lack of research dealing with the relationship between the riskiness of a pool of mortgages and the riskiness of the underlying collateral. In effect, there has been a disconnect between the way Wall Street typically analyzed *credit risk* versus the way Main Street evaluates *property risk.*

Real estate counselors and other analysts who better understand this relationship are in a better position to evaluate how changes in property markets are likely to ultimately affect pools of mortgages whose value is inextricably linked to the value of the underlying collateral. In assessing the true risk exposure of CMBS, numerous uncertainties must be properly addressed, and gauging default is certainly a major factor underlying this assessment.

Commercial mortgages are typically "non-recourse" loans that give the borrower the "option" to default if the value of the property falls below the bal-

---

[1] It now seems hard to believe that there was a time that stock options were traded without the Black and Scholes Option Pricing Model or that portfolios were constructed without using modern portfolio theory. But there was!

ance of the mortgage. In effect the borrower has a "put option" that can be exercised if it is to the borrower's benefit to do so. Thus, analytical tools that attempt to address the possible consequences of the borrower's embedded default put option must appropriately adjust for the key factors that drive default. Unfortunately, there are analysts who often make simplifying assumptions about the possibility of mortgage default that may lead to grossly misleading results.

One approach used is to estimate a "conditional default rate" (CDR) which makes the nonviable assumption that a fixed percentage of each outstanding loan defaults in each year. This approach makes no attempt to consider differences in the outlook for different geographic markets that determine the probability of each individual loan defaulting. Treating all loans in the same manner is a major shortcoming as loans that appear to be very similar may have drastically differing risk profiles. In fact, it is highly likely that individual loans will have very different susceptibilities to default. Thus, the use of CDR is virtually a guarantee for the erroneous evaluation of CMBS risk.

Attempts have also been made to use the more sophisticated Monte Carlo simulation technique to evaluate default risk for CMBS. Although Monte Carlo simulation can evaluate default on a loan-by-loan basis and may adjust for contract terms, analysts using this approach assume that differences in the performance of individual properties is random rather than dependent on a forecast of local market conditions. This approach does not take into account the underlying economic factors that move individual markets and property types cyclically, yet often independently.

Market level economic factors are a major driver of default, and should therefore be incorporated into any CMBS analysis. Differences at the MSA and property type levels will significantly affect property level performance, and thereby impart drastically different values for tranched bonds. Although this may seem obvious, many models do not properly address this critical influence on bond performance.

By utilizing a model that appropriately incorporates the effects on CMBS of the multiplicity of real world market behaviors, we will clearly illustrate why this should be an issue of concern for any CMBS investor. Basically, the following analysis will quantify bond price differences as a direct result of changes across: (1) markets, (2) loan contract terms, (3) origination cohorts, and (4) property types, all critical factors in CMBS issues.

THE MODEL

The model used in this chapter links the cash flows of the security directly to the cash flows of the underlying real estate, as shown by Exhibit 1. Distinct market behaviors drive real estate cash flows and valuation that affect resultant mortgage cash flows via the borrower's default decision. Next, these cash flows directly impact the overall loan pool which, in turn, affect the tranched securities. Cash flow from the loan pool flows to the different classes (tranches) of securities according to their priority. Class A has first claim on the payments, followed by Class B and then Class C. The C Class is most susceptible to default because it only receives payments if there is sufficient funds to repay the Class A and Class B securities.

It is important to note that in the model the link begins by first modeling the real estate on a market by market, property type by property type basis. The benefit of this approach lies in accurately outlining the substantive differences in the underlying economic fundamentals that occur between individual real estate markets that therefore affect the security.

A key difference in the approach used by the model in this chapter and techniques used by others is to use explicit forecasts of expected changes in the value of properties and the level of cash flows in different metropolitan areas by property type. In this chapter we use projections for changes in property value levels calculated by Property & Portfolio Research (PPR) in Boston. PPR uses an econometric model to project indices of changes in levels of NOI and property value for each property type and each metropolitan area. As we will show, it is important to have such a forecast as a starting point for this type of analysis. This provides a rigorous and thorough environment for forecasting individual loan, mortgage portfolio, and security performance. At the mortgage level, default is now viewed within the context of current, localized market pricing information, and is based on contemporaneous pricing ratios. These factors are crucial to the borrower's own financial decision regarding the loan, and our increased understanding of this information is therefore crucial to the accurate assessment of the securities.

Exhibit 1: Model Flow

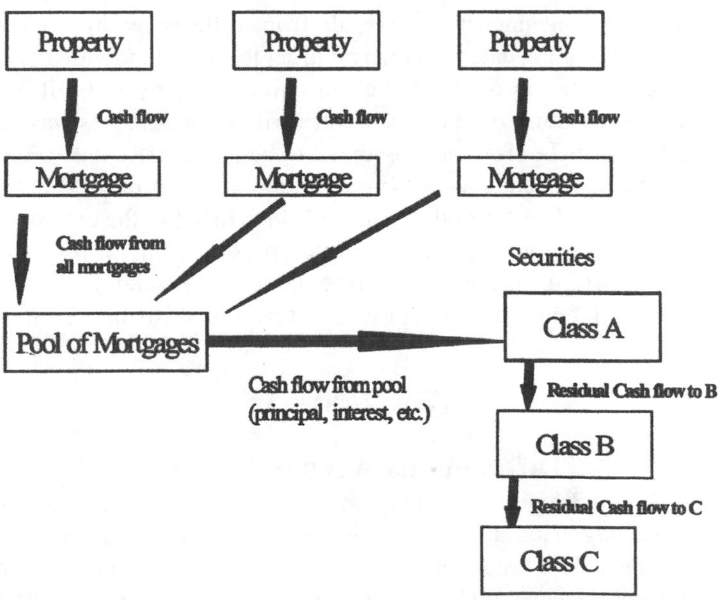

The unique, performance adjusted, loan cash flows are then pooled and distributed according to the specific structure of the CMBS being analyzed. Additionally, this approach allows the model to forecast critical rating ratios and thereby enable the appropriate application of time and risk sensitive interest rate spreads. The reward is a complete time-series forecast of mark-to-market pricing of each class (tranche) in the CMBS.

THE PARAMETERS

To properly illustrate the pricing effects surrounding differences in market location, property type, origination date, and loan contract terms, nine stylized loan pools were analyzed. To ease direct comparison, each pool contains individual loans that are all $25 million in size. Although principal payments in each case are scheduled over a 30-year amortization period, all notes are balloons with outstanding principal due in full 10 years after origination, and no further term extension is considered. Finally, all loan interest payments are calculated at an annual rate of 9.50% of the outstanding mortgage balance, and both scheduled principal and interest are due quarterly.

Exhibit 2 outlines the scenarios surrounding these base loans, and each applied change is highlighted. Static sensitivity analysis was performed by independently varying four key parameters that effect the probability of loan default: the geographic location of the properties in the loan pool, the property type, the origination date of the loan, and the loan-to-value ratio. In general, a higher risk timeframe for origination was used to aid the illustration of these critical pricing issues.

Actual pricing impacts that result from differences in market location, property type, origination date, and loan contract terms are individually outlined in the exhibits presented in the next section and overall by Exhibit 3. A typical sequential pay, subordinated tranche structure with three tranches was used for the analysis, and the tranche sizes were assumed to be 70%, 20%, and 10% of the loan pool. Additionally, tranches were assigned contract rates of 9.00%, 9.50%, and 10.00% respectively. The "Default Adjusted Price" listed in the exhibits represents the ratio between the contract rate discounted present value of the actual default impacted cash flows versus the original face value of the bond. In other words, the ratio captures the default impact on price as a result of shifts in the parameters.

THE RESULTS

Differences Across Markets

Scenarios 1, 2, and 3 represent equally sized pools comprised entirely of loans on office properties originated at the same point in time with identical contract terms and underwriting ratios. As a result, these three pools would look virtually identical when analyzed by most financial models. In other words, even though the underlying real estate assets are located in different markets, traditional analysis would produce indistinguishable pricing differences and offer no opinion on which may be the better pool.

Although each of these three pools incorporate "typical/acceptable" characteristics for geographic diversification, the econometrically based model of each market's performance suggests that each pool is in fact characterized by distinctly different default risk profiles. A slight shift in pool geographic mix produces variances in both loss severity and loss timing. In other words, the unique economic cycles of each market produce a different set of defaults and foreclosure losses for otherwise equal loan pools.

Exhibit 2: Scenario Outline

Scenario	Pool	Propert Type	Origination Date	Loan to Value	Debt Service Coverage	Projected Foreclosure Date
1	Atlanta 2 Boston 2 Salt Lake City 2 *San Francisco 2*	Office	3/31/88	70%	1.40	12/31/92
2	Atlanta 2 Boston 2 *Los Angeles 2* Salt Lake City 2	Office	3/31/88	70%	1.40	12/31/92 9/30/92
3	*Hartford 2* *Kansas City 2* *Phoenix 2* *San Francisco 2*	Office	3/31/88	70%	1.40	9/30/95 9/30/92
4	Hartford 2 Kansas City 2 Salt Lake City 2 San Francisco 2	Office	3/31/88	*70%*	*1.40*	9/30/95
5	Hartford 1 Kansas City 1 Salt Lake City 1 San Francisco 1	Office	3/31/88	*75%*	*1.30*	9/30/94 9/30/93 6/30/93
6	Atlanta 1 Kansas City 1 Salt Lake City 1 San Francisco 1	Office	*3/31/88*	75%	1.30	9/30/92 9/30/93 6/30/93
7	Atlanta 4 Kansas City 4 Salt Lake City 4 San Francisco 4	Office	*3/31/90*	75%	1.30	3/31/93
8	Boston 1 Hartford 1 San Francisco 1	*Office*	3/31/88	75%	1.30	9/30/94
9	Boston 3 Hartford 3 San Francisco 3	*Apartment*	3/31/88	75%	1.30	

Exhibit 3: Bond Pricing Across All Scenarios

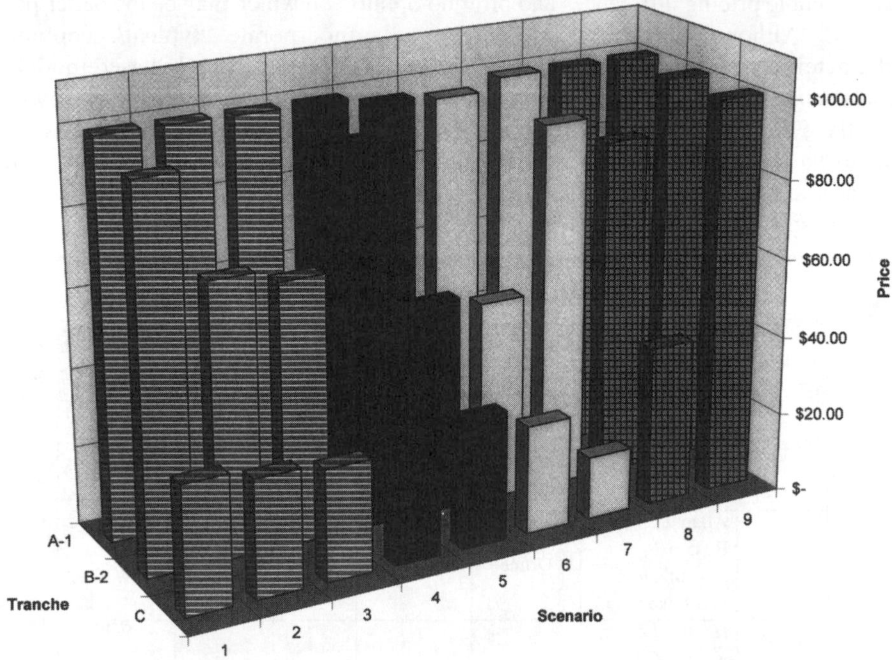

For example, the only change between the pool of Scenario 1 and that of Scenario 2 is the substitution of a loan from Los Angeles for one underwritten in San Francisco. Yet Scenario 1 experiences only one foreclosure in late 1992, while Scenario 2 gets hit by the 1992 foreclosure as well as by an additional foreclosure almost three years later in the third quarter of 1995. Furthermore, the pool of Scenario 3 encompasses four different, geographically dispersed markets and has yet a third type of experience.

It is clear that the market cycle differences that affect the underlying collateral flow through to affect the bonds. Moreover, it is evident from reviewing Exhibit 4 that even the senior "A-1" tranche is not necessarily immune from the effects of these differences. The single default of Scenario 1 is not enough to affect the A-1 tranche, but the second default produced by the pools of Scenarios 2 and 3 does produce a slight negative value impact, even for this "safe" tranche.

Although there is no loss of actual principal for the bond as a result of the second foreclosure loss, there is a shortfall of incoming loan contract payments during the delayed foreclosure process. We have made the general assumption that the servicer will not make any advances, and as a result the senior bond suffers because there is not enough current cash flow to cover the full interest payment during this foreclosure lag period.

Exhibit 4: Bond Pricing Across Markets

Tranche	Delta	Scenario	Initial Size	Default Adjusted Value	Default Adjusted Price
		1	$70,000	$70,000	$100.00
A-1	MSA	2	70,000	69,962	99.95
		3	70,000	69,973	99.96
		1	$20,000	$19,136	$95.68
B-2	MSA	2	20,000	13,862	69.31
		3	20,000	13,196	65.98
		1	$10,000	$3,321	$32.21
C	MSA	2	10,000	2,964	29.64
		3	10,000	2,813	28.13

This cash flow shortfall also causes a problem for the B-2 tranche under the first three scenarios. Until the proceeds from the foreclosure are available to pay down the senior tranche, there is not enough cash flow to cover the interest due to the mezzanine B-2 tranche. Once the A-1 tranche principal has thus been reduced, its interest payment requirements decrease, and there then is enough cash flow to cover the current interest due to the B-2 tranche.

The second default that occurs in both Scenarios 2 and 3 does much more damage to the mezzanine tranche. The principal of this tranche absorbs some of the foreclosure loss under both of these scenarios due to the fact that the first loss "C" tranche is eliminated prior to bond maturity. The effect on B-2 is evidenced in its drastically reduced pricing.

The junior "C" tranche is the first to absorb any foreclosure losses, and this is evidenced by its extremely low pricing for all of the first three scenarios. More importantly, we continue to see material pricing contrasts as a result of market cycle differences underlying each scenario.

It is also worth noting the pricing differences between Scenario 2 and Scenario 3. Here lies a situation in which there are two defaults in each case, yet pricing discrepancies still exist. The disparity is explained by disparities in market cycles. The pricing variance is due not only to the differences in timing between the defaults of these two scenarios, but also due to differences in the severity of the loss for each particular foreclosure.

Actual loss severity, being a function of property value, is of course strongly affected by market economic cycle. The model we describe in this chapter captures loss severity as a function of contemporaneous property value forecast on a market-by-market basis that more realistically captures the factors that affect the risk and value of a CMBS.

Since Tranche A-1 does not directly shoulder any of the foreclosure losses, the slight pricing difference between Scenario 2 and Scenario 3 is generated merely by a matter of timing. In contrast, Tranche B-2 takes a larger hit from the particular foreclosures encountered under Scenario 3 than it did under those foreclosures encountered under Scenario 2, and this is once again reflected in the bond pricing. Finally, although Tranche C is retired before maturity in both Scenarios 2 and 3, the varying interplay between default timing and severity once again combines to alter pricing. Overall, these results clearly illustrate that the location of the collateral is crucial to effective pricing of the security.

Differences Across Contract Terms

By reviewing identical sets of collateral secured under different loan-to-value and debt service coverage parameters, Scenarios 4 and 5 illustrate pricing differences that may occur as a result of differing loan contract terms. Certainly, an increase in loan to value ratio from 70% to 75%, and the decrease of debt service coverage ratio from 1.4 to 1.3 should combine to form a much riskier set of loans.

All tranches do in fact bear out this assertion. Remember that a CDR model would not have considered these differences. Furthermore, while a Monte Carlo approach would illustrate the same conclusion in a general sense, the local market model approach makes the additional contribution of breaking this risk out by geography and property type. This more reflective forecast of property price allows for a more accurate forecast of the borrower's default decision.

The results outlined in Exhibit 5 illustrate that the additional defaults that occur under the riskier set of contract terms affect pricing at all tranche levels. Recall that no advances are considered to have been made by the servicer, and the resultant cash flow shortfall during the default period therefore reduces the value of the senior A-1 tranche.

Furthermore, although the mezzanine B-2 bond does absorb a slight loss of principal in Scenario 4, the far greater foreclosure losses of Scenario 5 take a serious toll on this tranche. Fittingly, the B-2 pricing suffers dramatically from the difference in collateral contract terms.

Finally, it is interesting to note that despite the fact that in both scenarios the C tranche is completely consumed by foreclosure losses, a pricing difference still occurs as a result of the timing of those principal losses. The single default of Scenario 4 occurs much later than any of the defaults in Scenario 5 and the resultant tranche level cash flow differences directly translate into altered pricing.

Exhibit 5: Bond Pricing Across Loan Contract Terms

Tranche	Delta	Scenario	Initial Size	Default Adjusted Value	Default Adjusted Price
A-1	Loan Contract Terms	4	70,000	70,000	100.00
		5	70,000	68,492	97.95
B-2		4	20,000	19,299	96.49
		5	20,000	10,763	53.82
C		4	10,000	4,606	46.06
		5	10,000	3,264	32.64

Exhibit 6: Bond Pricing Across Origination Cohort

Tranche	Delta	Scenario	Initial Size	Default Adjusted Value	Default Adjusted Price
A-1	Origination Cohort	6	70,000	67,827	96.90
		7	70,000	70,000	100.00
B-2		6	20,000	10,245	51.22
		7	20,000	18,656	93.28
C		6	10,000	2,746	27.46
		7	10,000	1,587	15.87

Differences Across Origination Cohort

Scenarios 6 and 7 both encompass pools of loans that would be virtually indistinguishable to many pricing models. Here we have the exact same collateral originated on the exact same contract terms. The key difference, however, is the date of the original underwriting.

The results reported in Exhibit 6 show that this case comparison is in fact similar to the last. Once again, we find effects upon even the most senior tranche as a result of foreclosure period cash flow deficiencies. In addition, the greater number of defaults in Scenario 6 lead to a much higher default loss which in turn overpowers much of the principal of the mezzanine tranche, and Tranche B-2 pricing suffers accordingly.

Most intriguing, however, is the fact that in this set of scenarios, the junior tranche displays a very counterintuitive result. Even though the pool of Scenario 6 has a much greater foreclosure loss than the pool of Scenario 7, Tranche C is worth more in Scenario 6 than it is in Scenario 7.

The backdrop for the explanation lies in the fact that in either scenario, Tranche C does not survive the initial foreclosure. Furthermore, note that the first foreclosure in Scenario 6 occurs 18 quarters into the life of the pool, whereas the opening foreclosure for Scenario 7 occurs only 12 quarters after origination of the pool. As a result, Tranche C receives more cash flow under Scenario 6 simply by staying alive longer.

In other words, this "out of the money" tranche is behaving very similarly to an interest only (IO) piece that receives payments only while it has a notional principal balance outstanding. Such timing factors are crucial and thus it is clear that knowledge of the property market's cycle at the point of origination is critical to proper evaluation of the prospective performance of the bond.

Differences Across Property Type

The final comparison of Scenario 8 versus Scenario 9 deals with underlying performance differences that can occur when the collateral is located in the same urban areas, but is not the same property type. Here we contrast identical contract terms underwritten in identical markets, at an identical point in time, but on two different property types. While both office properties and apartments represent sizable sectors of CMBS issuance, they have not traditionally had the same market cycles. By directly contrasting these two property types, we can analyze the effect of these cycle differences on bond pricing.

In this set of scenarios, although the apartment pool of Scenario 9 performs better than the office pool of Scenario 8 (zero defaults versus one default), we find that in neither of these cases is there enough of an effect from foreclosure loss to affect the senior A-1 tranche. In contrast, the foreclosure loss of the office default that occurs in Scenario 8 affects both the mezzanine and junior tranches, and the obvious result of this increased absorption of losses are the pricing differences reported in Exhibit 7. In this case, the particular market economic conditions during this timeframe strongly favored apartment performance over office performance, and the bond pricing appropriately reflects that distinction. It is therefore apparent that knowledge of the type of collateral is also crucial to proper evaluation of the bond.

CONCLUSIONS

Although mortgage default risk is commonly understood to be a major pricing factor for CMBS, analytical methods for pricing bonds often do not appropriately adjust for the factors that drive default. The analysis we present in this chapter has conclusively outlined substantive pricing differences as a direct result of modest changes in normally overlooked or overgeneralized parameters.

Markets behave differently but naive diversification will not necessarily reduce diversifiable and manageable sources of risk. We have shown that loan pools that appear to be equally well diversified may in fact behave quite differently, and unexpected results may occur if a full range of parameters are not considered. It is therefore far better to have a well-informed opinion of an individual property market's economic cycle, for the consequences will indeed flow through to the security.

Furthermore, our analysis illustrates the need to have an understanding of this specific macroeconomic behavior of markets as it relates to differences in timing, contract terms, and property types. These parameter differences should not be assumed away, or managed with broad scale simulation. Instead, they should be, and can be, appropriately modeled.

Exhibit 7: Bond Pricing Across Property Type

Tranche	Delta	Scenario	Initial Size	Default Adjusted Value	Default Adjusted Price
A-1	Property Type	8	52,500	52,500	100.00
		9	52,500	52,500	100.00
B-2		8	15,000	12,948	86.32
		9	15,000	15,000	100.00
C		8	7,500	3,035	40.46
		9	7,500	7,500	100.00

Index

A

B

D

G

H

I

T

U

V

0W

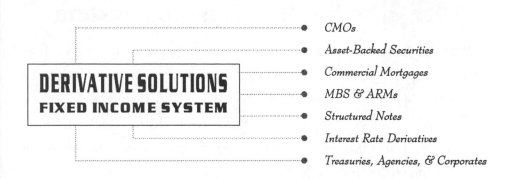

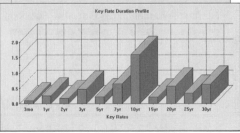

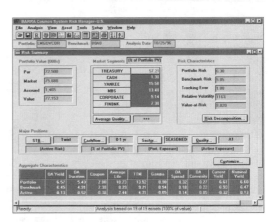

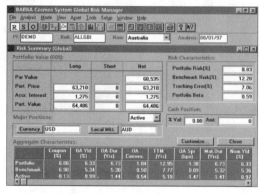

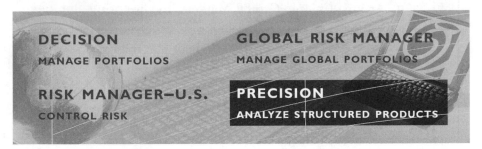

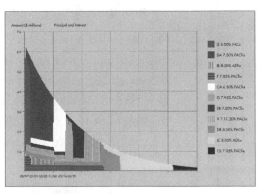

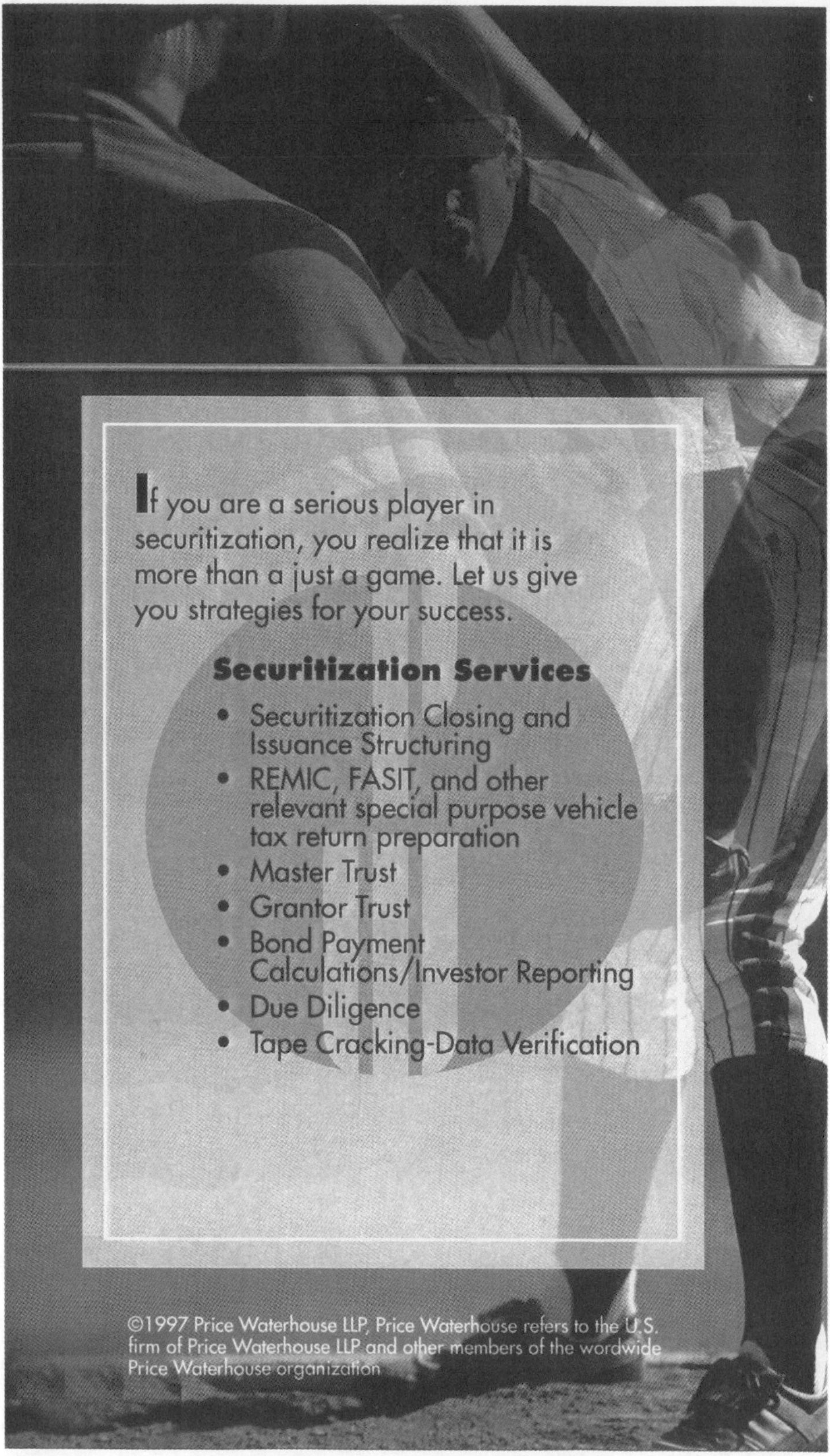
If you are a serious player in securitization, you realize that it is more than a just a game. Let us give you strategies for your success.
Securitization Services
• Securitization Closing and Issuance Structuring
• REMIC, FASIT, and other relevant special purpose vehicle tax return preparation
• Master Trust
• Grantor Trust
• Bond Payment Calculations/Investor Reporting
• Due Diligence
• Tape Cracking-Data Verification
©1997 Price Waterhouse LLP, Price Waterhouse refers to the U.S. firm of Price Waterhouse LLP and other members of the wordwide Price Waterhouse organization

It's a Whole New Ballgame!
Securitization Consulting
• Portfolio Securitization Advisory for First-Time Issuers
• Tax Consulting
• Process Review and "Best Practices" Consulting
• Servicing Consulting
• Strategic Consulting
Securitization Systems and Technology
• Asset Securitization AnalysisPro
• Student Loan AnalysisPro
• Original Issue Discount Market Factor System
• Technology Strategies Consulting
For answers to your questions, contact Shahid Quraishl at 1.703.741.2386.
Price Waterhouse

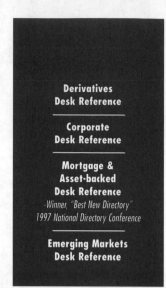

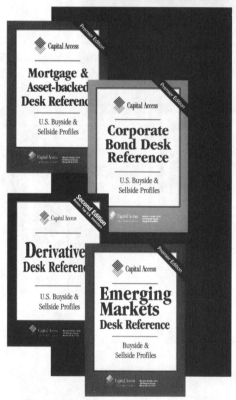

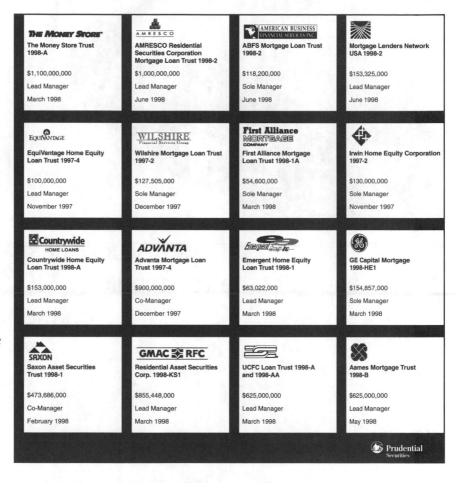

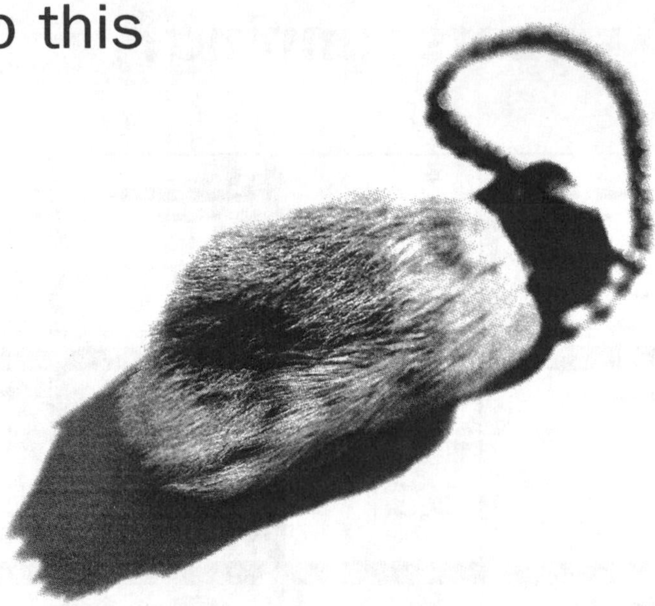

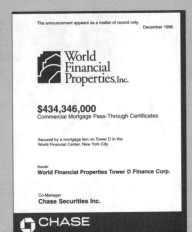

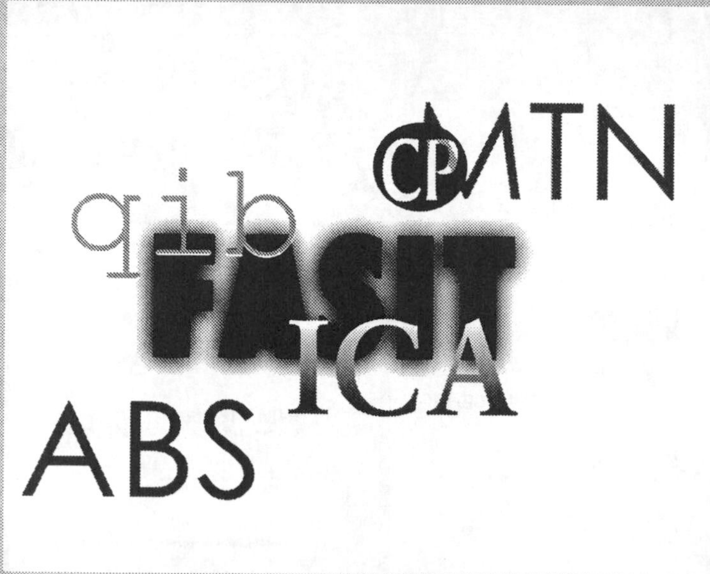
CP
MTN
qib
FASIT
ICA
ABS

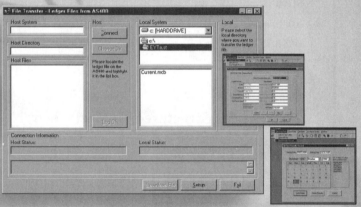

Flexible Format

EYTrust is flexible. The system interfaces with existing servicing structures—without replacing them or interrupting ongoing servicing. Reports and variables can be modified as needed.

Investor Confidence

EYTrust decreases the complexity of trust reporting while increasing its integrity. Issuers can use historical performance analysis to demonstrate the predictive reliability of performance projections to investors.

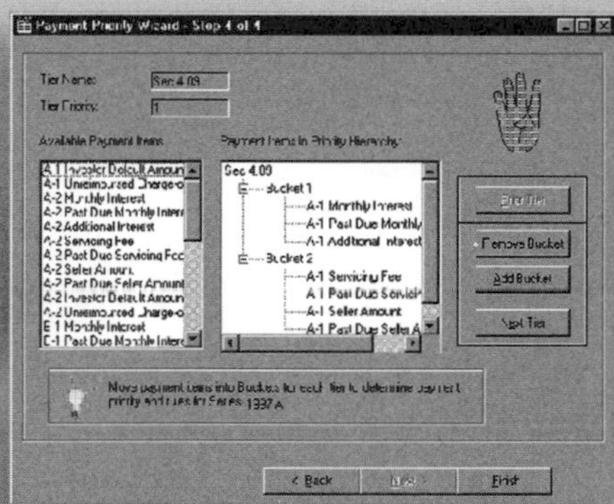

The Answer

EYTrust is automated. With EYTrust, multiple trust calculations can be performed with the click of a mouse.

EYTrust is easy to use. You don't need an engineering degree for EYTrust. The Windows-based format can be operated by any staff member.

EYTrust is fully supported. Ernst & Young provides set-up, training and ongoing support to ensure you get the most from EYTrust.